Diatessarica
PART X, SECTION III

THE FOURFOLD GOSPEL
THE PROCLAMATION
OF THE NEW KINGDOM

THE FOURFOLD GOSPEL

SECTION III

THE PROCLAMATION OF THE NEW KINGDOM

BY

EDWIN A. ABBOTT

Honorary Fellow of St John's College, Cambridge
Fellow of the British Academy

"*The kingdom of God is at hand.*"
St Mark 1. 15

WIPF & STOCK · Eugene, Oregon

Wipf and Stock Publishers
199 W 8th Ave, Suite 3
Eugene, OR 97401

The Fourfold Gospel; Section III
The Proclamation of the New Testament
By Abbott, Edwin A.
Softcover ISBN-13: 978-1-6667-0099-2
Hardcover ISBN-13: 978-1-6667-0100-5
Publication date 2/9/2021
Previously published by Cambridge University Press, 1915

This edition is a scanned facsimile of the original edition published in 1915.

PREFACE

PERHAPS the best Preface to this work might be found in a glance at the Section Headings collected in the Contents. If the title of the book may be said to indicate a high road, the Section Headings may be said to indicate cross roads. The cross roads represent investigations into words. The high road is a continuous investigation into thoughts—the thoughts of the Four Evangelists, severally—and, through these, into the thought of Jesus Himself in proclaiming the Kingdom of God.

Christ's authoritative calling of Simon Peter and the other fishermen; His authoritative acts of exorcism and healing; His authoritative claim to forgive sins; His assumption that He had authority to deal freely with certain precepts of the Law—all these things, related by Mark, are examined along with other things related by the other Evangelists but not by Mark. It is contended that Mark often meant, or assumed, these other things, though he did not express them, and that, when these other things are duly taken into account, they reveal the object of Jesus as being, from the first, not the establishment of what men would commonly call a Kingdom, but the diffusion of what we should rather call the atmosphere of a Family, a spiritual emanation spreading like a widening circle from a source within Himself as its centre, and passing into the hearts of all that were fitted to receive it, so as to give them something of His own power or

PREFACE

"authority"—a term defined in the Prologue of the Fourth Gospel as being "authority to become children of God."

Although thus much may be said in deprecation of the charge that the work has no claim to unity, I do not venture to hope that any but a few specialists will read it consecutively. Pains have been taken to make consecutive reading unnecessary. The Contents at the beginning of the book, and the Indices at the end, will enable readers to ascertain what is said about a special subject, or a special text of Scripture, without a continuous study of the whole.

Let me give here a specimen of the way in which I have found myself, after taking one of the above-mentioned "cross roads" of verbal investigation, brought back again—not without some added knowledge of the surrounding country—into the continuous "high road."

The subject of the investigation (Chap. I. § 27 foll.) is the miraculous Draught of Fishes in Luke compared with the corresponding miracle in John. The verbal portion of it deals with a Greek word, *neuein*. This, in various forms, may mean either (1) "*nod*" or (2) "*swim*." A very ancient Gnostic work, called The Acts of John, describing the Calling of the Fishermen, makes James speak to John about Jesus on the shore as "the child that is *nodding* (*neuein*) to us." Luke, prefixing the preposition *kata*, says that Peter and his friends "*nodded for help*" to James and John because their ship was sinking. But in the whole of Greek literature *kata-neuein* apparently never has that meaning. It has never been proved to include in its meanings a *neutral* "nodding" (*pace* Liddell and Scott "generally, to make a sign by nodding the head") When it means "nod," it appears always to mean, in effect,

PREFACE

"*nod-in-assent*" How then are we to explain Luke's use of it here?

To answer this question, we pass to the miracle in John. A poet of the fifth century (Nonnus) has paraphrased this. A commentator (Chrysostom) has explained it. Both of these writers use *neuein*, but with another prefix. They describe Peter and his friends not as "*nodding for help*," but as "*nodding-in-dissent* (*ana-neuein*)" to Jesus on the shore John himself, it is true, uses no form of *neuein*. But he describes Peter, in effect, as *swimming to the shore*. We have seen that *neuein* may mean "*swim*" Now we have to add that "*swim to the shore*" (no less than "*nod in assent*") is a correct rendering of *kata-neuein*, the word used by Luke.

It will be maintained that this—that is, "*swimming to the shore*" and not "*making signs of assent*"—was the meaning of some early and obscure tradition misinterpreted by Luke, who has also chronologically misplaced it, but who has had the honesty to preserve the difficult word that led him astray. The Preface to Luke's Gospel states that he attempted to "write in [chronological] order," as well as "accurately"; but it also implies that other evangelists had failed in this; and it is not to be expected that Luke would be always successful.

If in this instance Luke has made a mistake, we have at all events compensations We are relieved from the necessity of supposing that Mark and Matthew omitted what (according to Luke) was a turning-point in Peter's career. And in the Johannine substitute we find a narrative that gives us a peculiarly beautiful and (so to speak) natural account of the impression produced on Peter by the sympathetic insight, love, and regenerating power, of the risen Saviour

A similar compensation will be found (I believe) in almost all the numerous instances where John intervenes in the Synoptic tradition. He seems to do this mostly with a view to elucidating Mark where Luke omits, or alters, some Marcan tradition. Take one more instance, the last in this volume—where Jesus, in Mark, defines the family of God as "those that *do the thelēma*, or *will*, of God." Luke substitutes "those that hear the word of God and do it." It will be shewn that, in literary Greek, *thelēma*, if it were used at all, which it hardly ever is, would mean "desire of the flesh." Probably this—but probably other reasons also, including a love of definiteness—induced Luke to alter the word.

What is John's course? First, in his Prologue, he distinguishes the fleshly and the sexual *thelēma*, or "will," from the corresponding act by which "the children of God" are "begotten." Having thereby implied that there is something in God corresponding to the human *thelēma*, he does not hesitate to represent Jesus, later on, as repeatedly saying, in the words of the Psalmist, that He has come to "*do the will* (thelēma)" of the Father who sent Him (Jn i. 13, iv. 34, vi. 38, comp. Ps. xl. 8).

We lose something, it must be confessed, in arriving at the conclusion that Luke's carefully arranged and attractive Gospel—where it attempts to clarify or correct the obscurities and abruptnesses of Mark, and, as in this last case, to extract definiteness out of indefiniteness—cannot always be relied on as bringing us nearer to the words of Christ. But, even here, may we not learn more from Luke and John together—on the supposition that Luke is wrongly correcting Mark, and John rightly explaining Mark—than we should have learned from John alone without the erroneous Luke?

PREFACE

These considerations should bespeak respectful attention for Luke's Gospel even if it should appear, in the course of further investigation, that he is almost always in error where John intervenes to correct him. Luke, as has been shewn in the Introductory Volume (pp. 115—24), is fond of historical and external "proofs," and of a definite "word" followed by definite "doing." And it cannot be denied that this definiteness has tended to immediate and impressive success. Many of the Lucan "proofs" have helped not only to increase the number of those who call themselves Christians, but also to create a genuine Christianity among many of them. But the evidence of the Fourfold Gospel will be found to strengthen the growing conviction that a time must come, for all Christians conversant with the Scriptures, when they will have to dispense with some of these "proofs," and to give up expecting to find any definite "word," prescribing to us what we are to "do," either in the pages of the Bible, or in the interpretations of it by Christendom. The question will then arise as to the best modern substitute for these ancient definite "proofs" and definite "words." Almost all will agree that there must be developments—that the old must be developed into the new. But into what "new"?

Are we to accept, for our new "proof," the conviction that Christ is still with us on our altars, in the Bread consecrated by His appointed priests; and, for our new "word," the prescriptions of these appointed priests, to whom we can make our confession of sins, and from whom, after performing the acts of penitence prescribed by them, we can obtain a definite absolution?

Against this view it may be urged that official "priests" for Christians are not recognised in the New Testament, and that even in Revelation, which does mention Christian "priests," not official priests but ideal priests are contemplated. For the context speaks of all Christians as destined to be "kings and priests." But to this it may be replied that if, in spite of this idealisation, Christians find it expedient, and count it lawful, to have official "kings," they may also find it expedient, and count it lawful, to have official "priests."

This contention is reasonable. Only it must be remembered that it is a question of expediency, not of morality; and that it is a development, not an appointment by Christ. The English word "priest" is simply a shortened form of the Greek for "*elder*"—"*presbuteros*," "*presbyter*," "*prester*," "*prestre*," or "*prêtre*." The Elder, at the confessional, in places where it is deemed expedient that there should be a confessional, must not obscure the One Priest through whom alone our confessions pass to heaven. The same Elder, even when he is celebrating the Eucharist, must still remember that, though he is representing the One Priest in a peculiarly priestly function, he would still be called no "priest" by Peter or Paul or James or John, but only an "Elder."

The Fourth Gospel teaches us, at its outset, that in some sense every human being that has been converted by the Spirit of Christ, the One Priest, begins to partake of the priestly character, and tends to become himself a converter of others—like Andrew, the first convert mentioned by name, bringing his brother to Jesus. And at its close the same Gospel teaches us that Jesus breathed the power of forgiving sins not into the Apostles alone but into all the disciples present. No other Gospel teaches so distinctly that from every genuine Christian there must flow forth to other souls "rivers of living water." No

PREFACE

other Gospel so magnifies at once the dignity and the responsibility of the individual believer, who is to be no solitary anchorite, but to move among his brother men as a natural benefactor, prince and priest in one

But this princedom and this priesthood in every Christian have their source in the One Prince and Priest whom Jesus promised to send as His other Self, the Paraclete, who is in us, and in whom we are. No earthly "elder" or "priest" is to come opaquely between our soul and that Holy Spirit of Christ which speaks in us as well as to us, through all the voices of nature, nature within us and nature without, nature animate and inanimate, testifying to us of the ultimate triumph of the love of the Father, through the revelation of the Son, overcoming and converting to good all powers of evil.

This teaching, if true, is not a merely theoretical truth. Never was there an age when it was more practically needed—an age that has been so far led astray by the impostures of false philosophy and false science as to dream that man's permanent welfare can be brought about by an appeal to enlightened self-interest, through the readjustment of social and political arrangements, with the aid of the marvellous discoveries of modern science.

Against this imposture all the Gospels in various ways protest. But the Fourth Gospel protests most clearly by bringing before us the Incarnation as a part of a Plan from the beginning, the Plan of the Father to conform mankind to His own image and likeness through the assimilating power of the revealed Son. This Gospel uncompromisingly teaches us that there is no hope of any permanent universal good except through a permanent universal change of heart, a regeneration, in all races, nations, and classes of mankind.

PREFACE

Those who reject this hope as a dream will reject the Fourth Gospel. But those who accept the hope will accept the Gospel, also, as that one of the Four which best expresses or suggests it. It is a Gospel, so to speak, of Four Dimensions, incompatible with familiar facts, self-contradictory, sometimes recognising, sometimes ignoring, the existence of evil. Yet it suggests to us a world beyond expression—the length and breadth and depth and height of God's regenerating love, a mystery beyond the experience of the senses and the understanding, yet somehow practical, one that comes home to the business and bosoms of the simplest of mankind. Alone among the Gospels the Fourth goes to the root of the hopefulness of Jesus by taking us to the root of all things, back to the Beginning, in which it calls upon us to discern the Word, the Word that was God, the Word that was at home with God, or in the bosom of God, the Person that was to become flesh as Jesus of Nazareth, in order to reveal the perfect Man.

It is here—in studying the necessarily illogical and inconsistent delineations of the personality of Christ—that the Fourth Evangelist may give us priceless help, if we can but overcome our objections to the indirectness of his method. "Indirect" is indeed too weak an epithet. "Tortuous" would hardly be too strong. Jesus is represented, for example, as saying, not only in effect but in word, "I am the Way and the Truth and the Life," and "I am the Light of the World" and "the Good Shepherd" and "the Resurrection." Nothing can be more unlike the words attributed to Jesus by the Synoptists. Few certainties can be more certain than that Jesus did not utter these exact words. Why then does the Evangelist, thus repeatedly and with obviously deliberate iteration, impute them to Him?

PREFACE

The best explanation is that he *knew* (or, as I should prefer to say, it was revealed to him) *that Jesus meant them*, and he did not know how otherwise to express the knowledge or revelation. He longed to impress upon his readers that this was their meaning; and by this longing he was induced to substitute, throughout his Gospel, the meaning instead of the word, and the spirit instead of the letter, and the Logos instead of Jesus. The Synoptic Gospels had hardly attempted to represent the "rivers of living water" that flowed forth from Jesus in His utterances of the unutterable love of the Father. Yet these utterances were, as Peter says, "words of eternal life." In them the love of the Father streamed forth to mankind, and Jesus was both the channel and the stream. Jesus uses the word "I" in the Fourth Gospel more often than in the Three taken all together. Yet there is no such egotism as some have supposed. It is often a sign of non-egotism, as though He said "I, by myself, could do nothing, and should be nothing. I am wholly dependent on the Father. I am the Father's Love. I am the Way for you to pass into His Love. Take me into your hearts Strive to do as I did. By following in my path, and by loving one another with the love with which I have loved you, you will become the veritable children of God."

The Fourth Gospel represents Christ as saying to His disciples that His words before the Resurrection were but "proverbs" or "dark sayings" as compared with the teaching that He would send to them afterwards, and that "greater works" would be done by them than those done by Himself. These words should lift up our hearts in hopeful readiness for the problems of the future. Paul of Tarsus, Francis of Assisi, and John Wesley—to speak but of a few—shew historically in what varied forms, and

PREFACE

amid what diverse circumstances, the Spirit of Christ will now and then break out into those "greater works" when it finds a preeminently fit recipient of the constraining love of Christ.

But what we need is a recognition on the part of all Christians that this promise includes also those who are not "preeminently" fit. Christendom will not be true Christendom till the most commonplace Christian soul is expected to thank God for having given him a power, to some slight extent at all events, of forgiving sins like a priest, of diffusing the truths of the Gospel like an evangelist, and of reigning over his animal impulses like a king.

The Book of the Universe is full of illusions. Yet God reveals Himself through it. Not one of the heavenly bodies is where it appears to be. We see each in the place that it filled some seconds, minutes, years, or centuries ago. Yet "the heavens declare the glory of God." So does the Fourth Gospel.

Let us turn, then, with fresh hope and faith to its teaching, to the letter as well as to the spirit, but always seeking the spirit through the letter. And let us especially meditate on its reasonable and seasonable doctrine about the Paraclete of Christ, how it has power to "teach" us "all things"—teaching us what to say and what to do in answer to the importunate questionings and clamorous demands thrust upon us by the social, political, and national problems of each generation—and teaching us all this, not through a lesson-book of rules for saving our own souls, but by bringing us into the circle of God's Family, where each soul looks for instruction to the Father's face and finds its weak self strengthened as well as enlightened by Him who gives Himself to His children.

PREFACE

To the friends mentioned in the Prefaces of previous volumes of Diatessarica, Mr W. S. Aldis, Mr H. Candler, and the Rev. J Hunter Smith, my thanks are again due for help in revising the proofs—help that must not be measured by this meagre acknowledgment of their labour and my benefit.

The Indices placed at the end of this volume, and covering the three volumes of *The Fourfold Gospel*, are the work of my daughter, who has also verified all the references in the text and in the notes. If, as I believe, both the references and the Indices are found almost invariably accurate, the merit will be hers.

EDWIN A. ABBOTT.

Wellside, Well Walk
Hampstead, N.W.
29 Jan. 1915.

CONTENTS

		PAGE
REFERENCES AND ABBREVIATIONS		xxiii

CHAPTER I

THE CALLING OF THE FISHERMEN
[Mark 1. 16—20]

§ 1	The Calling, in Mark-Matthew	1
§ 2	The Reminding, in Luke	4
§ 3	The Calling and the Reminding, compared	5
§ 4	Jesus "passing-by," in Mark	8
§ 5	Jesus "walking," in Matthew	13
§ 6	Jesus "walking," in John	15
§ 7	Jesus "standing," and "teaching," in Luke	17
§ 8	"Rabbi," used in all the Gospels but Luke	20
§ 9	"Rabbi," in John	22
§ 10	"Andrew"	26
§ 11	"Casting-about in the sea"	32
§ 12	"Cast the net on the right side of the boat"	35
§ 13	"The right side"	37
§ 14	"For they were fishers"	46
§ 15	"Come (*lit* hither) after me"	47
§ 16	"Following," in John	50
§ 17	"And I will make you to become fishers of men"	57
§ 18	"Fear not, from henceforth thou shalt catch men"	61
§ 19	Complexities in Synoptic metaphor and circumstance	64
§ 20	Greek metaphor, and Luke	66
§ 21	How does John express "fishers of men"?	68
§ 22	The "Ichthus," or Fish, an early Christian emblem	72
§ 23	Influence of this emblem on Johannine doctrine	74
§ 24	"'Have ye anything to eat here?' And they gave him part of a broiled fish," in Luke	77
§ 25	(R.V.) "'Children, have ye aught to eat?' They answered him, 'No'," in John	84
§ 26	Clement of Alexandria on "one fishing"	87
§ 27	Peter swimming to Jesus	91

CONTENTS

		PAGE
§ 28	"Swimming" and "stretching out (*or*, spreading out) the hands"	97
§ 29	Jesus "going on (*or*, forward)"	101
§ 30	"Zebedee"	107
§ 31	"With the hired servants"	110
§ 32	"Sons of Zebedee," in John . .	113
§ 33	"Salome," in Mark	117
§ 34	"Sons of peace"	120
§ 35	"And straightway he called them" . .	124
§ 36	How John expresses "calling" . . .	127
§ 37	The "calling" of the sheep by the shepherd . .	130
§ 38	Effective "calling"	132
§ 39	What did the fishermen "leave"? . . .	135
§ 40	"They left all," in Luke	139
§ 41	"They followed him . . they departed after him" .	144
§ 42	"Departed after" implies a missionary journey . .	146
§ 43	Philip "following"	148
§ 44	Inferences from Mark	150

CHAPTER II

"AUTHORITY" AND "UNCLEAN SPIRITS"
[Mark 1 21—8]

§ 1	"The unclean spirit," in Zechariah	154
§ 2	"An unclean spirit" and "authority," in Mark and Luke . . .	157
§ 3	"Authority" and "law," in Matthew . . .	163
§ 4	"Authority" and Christ's "word," in Luke . .	167
§ 5	"Authority," in Greek writers of the first century .	169
§ 6	"Authority" and the spirit of sonship, in John .	174
§ 7	"Going down to Capernaum" . . .	178
§ 8	"Teaching in synagogue" at Capernaum, in John .	185

CHAPTER III

JESUS HEALING
[Mark 1 29—34]

§ 1	The first miracle of healing	190
§ 2	The details of the healing	192
§ 3	"Fever"	196
§ 4	"Lying down" and "cast [down]" . . .	198
§ 5	The Johannine view of "fever"	202
§ 6	The Johannine view of "thirst"	204

CONTENTS

			PAGE
§ 7	The Johannine view of Messianic "raising"	. .	207
§ 8	Medically "attending," as distinct from "healing," in Greek		208
§ 9	"Divers" or "manifold" diseases	. .	210
§ 10	"At even, when the sun did set"	. . .	213
§ 11	Was Christ's action in any cases tentative?	. .	217
§ 12	The Johannine view, regarded negatively .	. .	220
§ 13	The Johannine view, regarded positively .	. .	223
§ 14	The difference between the Fourth Gospel and the Three		227

CHAPTER IV

JESUS GOES FORTH BEFORE DAWN
[Mark 1. 35—9]

§ 1	Why did Matthew omit this?	232
§ 2	Why did Mark insert this?	235
§ 3	Differences between Mark and Luke, and Johannine illustrations of (1) "pursued," (2) "let us go" .	237
§ 4	"Elsewhere into the next towns" (Mark), "to the other cities also" (Luke)	240
§ 5	"To this [end] came I forth" (Mark), "Toward this [end] was I sent" (Luke)	243

CHAPTER V

THE HEALING OF A LEPER
[Mark 1. 40—45]

§ 1	The prominence of this miracle	. . .	246
§ 2	(R V.) "Strictly (or, sternly) charged," in Mark	.	251
§ 3	God "having compassion" on "Rachel's children," in Jeremiah		252
§ 4	(R.V) "Groaned (or, was moved with indignation)," in John		254

CHAPTER VI

THE FORGIVENESS OF SINS
[Mark II 1—12]

§ 1	The forgiveness and healing of the Paralytic, in the Synoptists	261
§ 2	The healing, without forgiveness, of the man "in infirmity," in John	267

CONTENTS

		PAGE
§ 3	Forgiving sins and retaining sins, in John . . .	272
§ 4	The first mention of "sin," connected with "Cain" in the Bible, and with "retaining" in the Targums	275
§ 5	"Cain," the "man-killer," in the Johannine Epistle .	277
§ 6	Conclusion as to the Johannine view . .	280

CHAPTER VII

CHRIST'S CALL TO "SINNERS"
[Mark ii. 13—17]

§ 1	Technical terms in the Synoptists . . .	284
§ 2	John's use of the words "righteous" and "righteousness"	288
§ 3	What does John say or imply about "sinners"? .	291
§ 4	The "harlots" in Matthew, and the "woman that was a sinner" in Luke	293
§ 5	The woman of Samaria in John	296
§ 6	The Syrophoenician woman in Mark and Matthew	298
§ 7	"Greek" in Mark, and "Greeks" in John . . .	301

CHAPTER VIII

THE OLD AND THE NEW
[Mark ii. 18—22]

§ 1	A complaint of the Baptist's disciples, in the Synoptic Gospels	307
§ 2	Fasting	311
§ 3	The "bridegroom," in the Synoptic reply . . .	314
§ 4	The meaning of "bridegroom," if uttered by Jesus, or if uttered by the Baptist	318
§ 5	Hebrew and Jewish traditions about the Bridegroom	323
§ 6	"In that day," or "in those days" . .	325
§ 7	A complaint of the Baptist's disciples and the reply, in the Fourth Gospel	330
§ 8	The parable of the patched garment . . .	335
§ 9	"This year's wine" and "new wine-skins" . . .	336
§ 10	Luke and John on "good wine"	340
§ 11	The Fourth Gospel on the "old" and the "new" .	343

CONTENTS

CHAPTER IX

JESUS AND THE SABBATH
[Mark ii. 23—iii 6]

			PAGE
§ 1	"When Abiathar was high priest," in Mark	. .	347
§ 2	Does John intervene?	. .	350
§ 3	"The sabbath was made for man," in Mark	. .	352
§ 4	Does John intervene?	. .	354
§ 5	Jesus proceeding to heal on the sabbath	. . .	356
§ 6	Jesus "being grieved" (R V), in Mark	. .	360
§ 7	"At the hardening of their heart," in Mark	. .	362
§ 8	"The Herodians," in Mark	. .	365
§ 9	The absence of technical terms in John	. . .	369

CHAPTER X

THE CONCOURSE TO JESUS
[Mark iii 7—12]

§ 1	Jesus "withdrew"	372
§ 2	"Toward the sea," "Galilee," "beyond Jordan"	379
§ 3	"From Idumaea (*i.e.* Edom)" . . .	380
§ 4	The Johannine view of the concourse to Jesus . .	382

CHAPTER XI

THE APPOINTMENT OF THE TWELVE
[Mark iii 13—19]

§ 1	"Going up into the mountain"	387
§ 2	"Whom he himself would he calleth to himself" .	389
§ 3	"Apostles".	390
§ 4	"That they might be with him, and that he might [from time to time] send them to preach" . .	404
§ 5	"James the [son] of Zebedee and John the brother of James"	408
§ 6	"Sons of thunder" in Mark, "thunder" in John .	410
§ 7	"Thaddaeus" in Mark, "Judas of James" in Luke .	413
§ 8	"The Cananaean" in Mark, "he that was called Zealot" in Luke	416

xxi

CONTENTS

CHAPTER XII

THE KINGDOM OF GOD, A FAMILY
[Mark iii. 20—35]

			PAGE
§ 1	Jesus, in Mark, said by His "friends" to be "beside himself"	.	424
§ 2	"He hath Beelzebub," in Mark	.	428
§ 3	The "brethren" of Jesus, in John	.	431
§ 4	"A devil," in John	.	432
§ 5	Mark's first mention of "parables"	.	435
§ 6	John's mention of "proverbs"	.	438
§ 7	"Parable" implies comparison	.	443
§ 8	"The strong [one]"	.	445
§ 9	The "spoiling" of the Egyptians	.	452
§ 10	The "casting out" of "the ruler of this world"	.	453
§ 11	"All things shall be forgiven to the sons of men," in Mark	.	458
§ 12	(R V) "Guilty of an eternal sin," in Mark	.	460
§ 13	"Guilty," in LXX	.	463
§ 14	"Ye say 'We see' Your sin abideth," in John	.	465
§ 15	"Because they said, 'He hath an unclean spirit'"	.	468
§ 16	"See! My mother, and my brethren"	.	470
§ 17	"Whosoever shall do the will.." in Mark	.	474
§ 18	The difference, as to "the will," between Luke and John	.	478

INDICES

To *Introduction* and *Beginning*. (i) Scriptural Passages, (ii) English, (iii) Greek 487

To *Proclamation*: (i) Scriptural Passages, (ii) English, (iii) Greek 512

REFERENCES AND ABBREVIATIONS

REFERENCES

(1) *a*. References to the first nine Parts of Diatessarica (as to which see pp 545—6) are by paragraphs in black Arabic numbers —

    1— 272 = *Clue*
    273— 552 = *Corrections of Mark*
    553—1149 = *From Letter to Spirit*
    1150—1435 = *Paradosis*.
    1436—1885 = *Johannine Vocabulary*.
    1886—2799 = *Johannine Grammar*.
    2800—2999 = *Notes on New Testament Criticism*.
    3000—3635 = *The Son of Man*.
    3636—3999 = *Light on the Gospel from an ancient Poet*.

(1) *b*. References to the Sections of the Tenth Part of Diatessarica, entitled *The Fourfold Gospel*, are by pages The three Sections now completed are —

    (Section 1) *Introduction*.
    (Section 2) *The Beginning*.
    (Section 3) *The Proclamation of the New Kingdom*

(ii) The Books of Scripture are referred to by the ordinary abbreviations, except where specified below. But when it is said that Samuel, Isaiah, Matthew, or any other writer, wrote this or that, it is to be understood as meaning *the writer, whoever he may be, of the words in question*, and not as meaning that the actual writer was Samuel, Isaiah, or Matthew.

(iii) The principal Greek MSS are denoted by א, A, B, etc., the Latin versions by *a*, *b*, etc., as usual. The Syriac version discovered by Mrs Lewis on Mount Sinai is referred to as SS, *i e.* "Sinaitic Syrian" It is always quoted from Prof. Burkitt's translation. I regret that in the first three vols. of Diatessarica Mrs Lewis's name was omitted in connection with this version.

(iv) The text of the Greek Old Testament adopted is that of B, edited by Prof. Swete, of the New, that of Westcott and Hort.

(v) Modern works are referred to by the name of the work, or author, vol., and page, *e.g.* Levy iii. 343 *a*, *i.e.* vol. iii. p. 343, col. 1

REFERENCES AND ABBREVIATIONS

ABBREVIATIONS

Aq = Aquila's version of O T
Brederek = Brederek's *Konkordanz zum Targum Onkelos*, Giessen, 1906
Burk = Prof F C Burkitt's *Evangelion Da-mepharreshe*, Cambridge University Press, 1904
Chr = *Chronicles*
Clem Alex 42 = Clement of Alexandria in Potter's page 42
Dalman, *Words* = *Words of Jesus*, Eng Transl 1902, Aram G = *Grammatik des Judisch-Palästinischen Aramäisch*, 1894
En = Enoch ed. Charles, Clarendon Press, 1893
Ency. = *Encyclopaedia Biblica*
Ephrem = Ephraemus Syrus, ed Moesinger
Etheridge = Etheridge's translations of the Targums on the Pentateuch.
Euseb = the Ecclesiastical History of Eusebius
Field = Origenis Hexaplorum quae supersunt, Oxford, 1875, also Otium Norvicense, 1881
Gesen = the Oxford edition of Gesenius
Goldschm = *Der Babylonische Talmud*, 1897—1912, ed Goldschmidt
Goodspeed = Goodspeed's *Indices*, (i) *Patristicus*, Leipzig, 1907, (ii) *Apologeticus*, Leipzig, 1912.
Hastings = Dictionary of the Bible, ed Hastings (5 vols)
Hor Heb = *Horae Hebraicae*, by John Lightfoot, 1658—74, ed. Gandell, Oxf 1859
Iren = the treatise of Irenaeus against Heresies
Jer Targ or Targ Jer (abbrev for Jerusalem Targum), or Jon Targ (i e Targum of Jonathan, abbrev for the Targum of Pseudo-Jonathan) = the Targum of Pseudo-Jonathan on the Pentateuch, of which there are two recensions—both quoted (*Notes on N.T Criticism*, Pref p viii) by ancient authorities under the name "Jerusalem Targum " The two recensions are severally denoted by Jer I and Jer II On other books, the Targum is referred to as simply "Targ."
Jon Targ , see Jer Targ.
Justin = Justin Martyr (*Apol* = his First Apology, *Tryph* = the Dialogue with Trypho)
K. = *Kings*
Krauss = Krauss's *Griechische und Lateinische Lehnworter* etc., Part ii, Berlin, 1899
Levy = Levy's *Neuhebräisches und Chaldäisches Worterbuch*, 4 vols , Leipzig, 1889 , Levy Ch = *Chaldäisches Wörterbuch*, 2 vols , 1881.

REFERENCES AND ABBREVIATIONS

L S = Liddell and Scott's Greek Lexicon
Mechilta, see Wu(nsche).
Onk = the Targum of Onkelos on the Pentateuch
Origen is referred to variously, e g *Hom. Exod* 11. 25 = lib 11. ch. 25 of Hom Exod, but Orig. on Exod 11 25 = the commentary *ad loc*; Lomm 111. 24 = vol 111 p 24 of Lommatzsch's edition
Oxf Conc = *The Oxford Concordance to the Septuagint.*
Pec = peculiar to the writer mentioned in the context
Pesikta, see Wu(nsche)
Philo is referred to by Mangey's volume and page, *e g* Philo 11. 234, or, as to Latin treatises, by the Scripture text or Aucher's pages (P A)
Pistis = *Pistis Sophia*, ed. Petermann (marginal pages)
Ps Sol = *Psalms of Solomon*, ed Ryle and James, Cambr. 1891.
R , after Gen , Exod , Lev etc means *Rabboth*, and refers to Wunsche's edition of the Midrash on the Pentateuch, e g. *Gen. r.* (on Gen xii 2, Wu p 177)
Rashi, sometimes quoted from Breithaupt's translation, 1714
S = *Samuel*, s = "see"
Schottg = Schottgen's *Horae Hebraicae*, Dresden and Leipzig, 1733.
Sir = the work of Ben Sira, *i e* the son of Sira It is commonly called Ecclesiasticus (see *Clue* 20 *a*) The original Hebrew used in this work is that which has been edited, in part, by Cowley and Neubauer, Oxf 1897, in part, by Schechter and Taylor, Cambr. 1899, in part, by G Margoliouth, *Jewish Quart Rev*, Oct 1899 (also printed in *About Hebrew Manuscripts* (Frowde, 1905) by Mr E N Adler, who discovered the missing chapters)
SS, see (111) above
Steph Thes = Stephani *Thesaurus Graecae Linguae* (Didot).
Sym = Symmachus's version of O.T
Targ (by itself) is used where only one Targum is extant on the passage quoted
Targ Jer , Targ Jon , and Targ Onk , see Jer Targ., Jon. Targ., and Onk , above
Tehillim = Midrash on Psalms, ed. Wunsche (2 vols).
Test xii Patr = Testaments of the Twelve Patriarchs ed Charles, 1908 (Gk , Clarendon Press, Eng , A & C. Black)
Theod. = Theodotion's version of O T
Thes Syr = Payne Smith's *Thesaurus Syriacus*, Oxf. 1901
Tromm = Trommius' *Concordance to the Septuagint*
Tryph = the Dialogue between Justin Martyr and Trypho the Jew
Walton = *Biblia Sacra Polyglotta*, 1657.
Wetst = Wetstein's *Comm on the New Testament*, Amsterdam, 1751.

REFERENCES AND ABBREVIATIONS

W H. = Westcott and Hort's New Testament.

Wu. = Wunsche's translation of *Rabboth* etc , 1880—1909 (including *Mechilta, Pesikta Rab Kahana, Tehillim* etc)

(*a*) A bracketed Arabic number, following Mk, Mt , etc , indicates the number of instances in which a word occurs in Mark, Matthew, etc., *e.g.* ἀγάπη Mk (0), Mt (1), Lk (1), Jn (7).

(*b*) Where verses in Hebrew, Greek, and Revised Version, are numbered differently, the number of R V is given alone.

(*c*) In transliterating a Hebrew, Aramaic, or Syriac word, preference has often, but not invariably, been given to that form which best reveals the connection between the word in question and forms of it familiar to English readers. Where a word is not transliterated, it is often indicated (for the sake of experts) by a reference to Gesen , *Thes. Syr.*, Levy, or Levy *Ch*

CHAPTER I*

THE CALLING OF THE FISHERMEN[1]
[Mark i. 16—20]

§ 1. *The Calling, in Mark-Matthew*

THE Mark-Matthew account of the Calling of Peter and his companions would not need to be studied with all the detail that will be found in this Chapter if it were not necessary to compare it with what may be called the Lucan Reminding of Peter[2]. The Lucan narrative includes an account of a miraculous draught of fishes. John also describes a miraculous draught of fishes, and connects it with what may be called the Restoration of Peter[3]. But John places it after the Resurrection.

This raises the question how far some of the Evangelists may have been elsewhere chronologically misled so as to place during Christ's life on earth words and acts that should have been placed after the Resurrection while He was still present with His disciples at frequent intervals. It has been

---

* For titles of previous Parts of Diatessarica referred to by abbreviations in this Volume, see pp. 545—6 For other abbreviations see pp. xxiii—xxvi

[1] See Mk i 16—20, Mt iv 18—22, Lk v. 1—2, 9—11, which will be found arranged in parallel columns on pp 5—6

[2] Lk. v 3 foll   See p 4, as to the reasons for so calling it.

[3] Jn xxi 7—19, see pp. 35 foll , 91 foll In this narrative Peter comes to Jesus through the water and receives the charge "Feed my sheep," together with a prediction that he shall die by crucifixion

pointed out in the introductory volume of *The Fourfold Gospel* that "perhaps the Sending of the Seventy—or some of its precepts, such as 'eat those things that are set before you'— may refer to a period after the Resurrection[1]." Matthew masses most of these precepts with the precepts to the Twelve Neither Mark nor Matthew makes mention of any mission of the Seventy. It seems probable that Luke is correct in making the precepts later than those to the Twelve, but incorrect in not making them a great deal later. John leaves no room for us in his Gospel to place appropriately any important and fruitful mission of Apostles, whether twelve or seventy. If he is right in his views, we ought (it would seem) to recognise that some things recorded by the Synoptists may have been recorded out of order, placed too early, and in a setting that makes us unable to understand their spiritual meaning. Such a recognition ought to make us patient to the utmost in investigating the following instance of Lucan divergence from Mark and Matthew, and the apparent Johannine intervention.

In Mark, closely followed by Matthew, the first separate act of Jesus, after He has begun to preach the Gospel, is to call two pairs of brothers—both pairs fishermen. To the first pair, Simon and his brother Andrew, whom Mark describes as "casting-about in the sea[2]," Jesus says, "Come after me, and I will make you fishers of men." Thereupon "they followed him." "Going on a little [further]," says Mark, "he saw James the [son] of Zebedee and John his brother—them, too, in *the* boat, mending[3] *the* nets." Here "*the* boat" means, not the previously mentioned "boat" of Peter, but "*their* boat," and

---

[1] See *Fourfold Gospel, Introduction*, p 110, quoting 1 Cor x. 27 "eat everything that is set before you [to eat]," *i e*, without regard to distinctions of the Mosaic Law. See *Clue* 233 foll, *From Letter to Spirit* 1015 a foll

[2] "Casting-about," ἀμφιβάλλοντας, see p 32

[3] "Mending," καταρτίζοντας (possibly "adjusting"), see p 34.

THE CALLING OF THE FISHERMEN

"*the* nets" means "*their* nets." Matthew says "in *the* boat *with Zebedee their father* mending *their* nets." This implies, not only that "the boat" belonged to the Zebedaean family (and presumably to Zebedee), but also that Zebedee was present. Mark also implies this in his next verse: "And straightway he called them, and leaving their father Zebedee in the boat with the hired-servants, they went after him." Matthew has "And he called them. So they straightway, leaving the boat and their father, followed him"—omitting the clause about "the hired-servants."

Zebedee is never mentioned again in such a way as to imply that he was still alive. There are passages where James and John are called his "sons" And, in Matthew, Zebedee's wife, or his widow, is called "the mother of the sons of Zebedee[1]." This favours the hypothesis that he was dead at the time of the Calling, and that the Mark-Matthew account of his presence is an error. If he was present, several unanswered questions arise. Was not Zebedee included in the Call ("he called *them*")? If he was included, did he disobey, and did his wife leave him and go about with his sons following Jesus? Or did his death happen soon after the Calling and pass unmentioned by Mark and Matthew?

Another question, in connection with the Mark-Matthew narrative, is whether the two pairs of fishermen are to be regarded as called on terms of equality. To the first pair a promise is made, "I will make you fishers of men" No such words are uttered to the second pair Both pairs follow Jesus; but the second pair receives no recorded promise.

To the question "Why did the fishermen follow?" Mark and Matthew give no answer, except what we may infer from their preceding statement that Jesus had begun to preach repentance in public[2]. We have to suppose either—what is

---

[1] Mt. xx. 20, xxvii. 56.
[2] Mk i. 15, Mt. iv. 17 "repent ye"

THE CALLING OF THE FISHERMEN

very improbable—that Jesus here repeated the substance of His preaching, first to one pair, and then to the other, or else that the four fishermen had already heard His preaching, or the report of it, and already knew so much about Jesus that His mere call sufficed to make them follow.

§ 2. *The Reminding, in Luke*

In Luke, there is a somewhat similar narrative about two fishing-boats, one belonging to Simon, and the other to Simon's "sharers [in the work]" or "partners," the sons of Zebedee. Andrew is not mentioned. Nor is Zebedee mentioned, except to say that the owners of the second boat are his sons. Toward the end there is addressed, but only to Simon, an exhortation, "Fear not," followed by a promise, "From henceforth thou shalt take men alive." Finally it is said "And having brought the boats to land, having left all things, they followed him." It will be observed that there is no "calling" here. All "follow" but none are "called"

The reason will be obvious when we compare the three Synoptic narratives, supplementing what is printed below (pp. 5—6) by inserting the Lucan story of a miraculous draught of fishes[1], and also noting that Luke places his narrative *after*, while Mark and Matthew place it *before*, Christ's visit to Peter's house, where He healed Peter's mother-in-law. Mark-Matthew will then be seen to be not really parallel to Luke. Mark-Matthew describes "a calling" Luke appears to have assumed and omitted the Calling[2], and to describe what might be termed "a reminding," which he placed after the Marcan "calling[3]." If that is the case, then, according to Luke, after

---

[1] Lk. v 3—10

[2] Somewhat similarly Luke and John make only a brief and incidental mention of the Baptist's imprisonment, and no mention at all of his death But it must be confessed that the Lucan omission of the Calling is less easily explicable

[3] A friend suggests that Luke may have thought of his narrative

(Mark 1 16—20)

THE CALLING OF THE FISHERMEN

Peter and Andrew had heard the words "I will make you fishers of men," Peter returned to his occupation of fishing. Jesus, finding him thus occupied, works a miracle that brings him to his knees—apparently alarmed, not by the wonder alone, but also by his own conscience, and by the remembrance of his neglected duty to the wonder-worker. Then the Lucan words "fear not," and "from henceforth," imply that the neglect is forgiven but must now come to an end[1]. The "catching," or "taking-alive," of "men" is to begin at once:—"*From henceforth* thou shalt be taking-alive [not fish, but] men."

§ 3. *The Calling and the Reminding, compared*

It might be supposed that we could learn nothing from comparing the Calling with the Reminding, since they do not profess to describe the same events. And indeed a comparison would be misleading if we assumed in them a parallelism of fact. But even a glance at the following columns will probably shew the reader that there is something to be learned from their contrasts or omissions as well as from their similarities or identities:—

Mk 1 16—20 (R.V)[2]	Mt. iv 18—22 (R.V.)[2]	Lk v 1—2, 9—11 (R.V.)[2]
(16) And passing along by the sea of	(18) And walking by the sea of Galilee,	(1) Now it came to pass, while the

as describing a first Calling whereas Mark describes a second. Thus the "rending" of the nets in Luke (v. 6) would precede the "mending" in Mark. But ancient authorities (*e.g.* the *Diatessaron*) do not support this view. And internal evidence appears to be against it.

[1] This is the most obvious explanation of Peter's alarm. But it is not satisfactory. A large draught of fishes, even a stupendous one, is not the kind of phenomenon that is represented in O T. (*e.g.* 1 K xvii 18) as causing similar alarm (or what Alford calls (on Lk v 8) "self-loathing").

[2] Printed here as in the Revised Version. Later on, separate phrases will occasionally be rendered differently, for example, Mk 1 16 "Simon and Andrew...casting-about [a net] in the sea"

THE CALLING OF THE FISHERMEN

Mk 1. 16—20 (R.V.) (*contd.*)	Mt. iv. 18—22 (R.V) (*contd.*)	Lk v. 1—2, 9—11 (R.V.) (*contd*)
Galilee, he saw Simon and Andrew the brother of Simon casting a net in the sea for they were fishers	he saw two brethren, Simon who is called Peter, and Andrew his brother, casting a net into the sea; for they were fishers.	multitude pressed upon him and heard the word of God, that he was standing by the lake of Gennesaret;
(17) And Jesus said unto them, Come ye after me, and I will make you to become fishers of men.	(19) And he saith unto them, Come ye after me, and I will make you fishers of men.	(2) And he saw two boats standing by the lake · but the fishermen had gone out of them, and were washing their nets.
(18) And straightway they left the nets, and followed him.	(20) And they straightway left the nets, and followed him	(3) And he entered into one of the boats, which was Simon's. . ..
(19) And going on a little further, he saw James the [son] of Zebedee, and John his brother, who also were in the boat mending the nets.	(21) And going on from thence he saw other two brethren, James the [son] of Zebedee, and John his brother, in the boat with Zebedee their father, mending their nets, and he called them.	(9) For he was amazed, and all that were with him, at the draught of the fishes which they had taken;
(20) And straightway he called them · and they left their father Zebedee in the boat with the hired servants, and went after him.	(22) And they straightway left the boat and their father, and followed him.	(10) And so were also James and John, sons of Zebedee, which were partners with Simon. And Jesus said unto Simon, Fear not; from henceforth thou shalt catch (*lit* take alive) men.
		(11) And when they had brought their boats to land, they left all, and followed him.

THE CALLING OF THE FISHERMEN

The first question that arises out of these different narratives is "Why does Luke speak of 'the lake of Gennesaret' whereas Mark and Matthew have 'the sea of Galilee'?" A brief answer may be given in the words of an ancient opponent of Christianity, "Those who report the truth of the localities say that there is no sea there, but only a small lake[1]." In LXX, the Greek for "lake" is very rare, and always means "pool[2]." The Hebrew Scripture and the Talmud have but one word for "lakes" and "seas," and the Talmud speaks of "*the sea* of Gennesar," though more often of "*the sea* of Tiberiah" (but not (apparently) "the sea of Galilee"). The prophecy of Isaiah quoted at this stage by Matthew ("toward the *sea*, Galilee of the Gentiles") might naturally induce the authors of the earliest Gospels to call it "*sea of Galilee.*" But Strabo and Josephus speak of "*the lake* of Gennesar" or "the Gennesarite *lake*," and this term would naturally commend itself to Luke, who aims at writing like a Greek historian He never mentions "the sea of Galilee," but only "the lake of Gennesaret."

As regards the name Tiberias, we find Josephus now and then speaking of "the lake of the men of Tiberias" or "the lake near Tiberias." This, as a name of the lake, is also mentioned by Pliny. Tiberias was not founded till A.D. 20—30, and therefore could hardly have given its name to the lake of Gennesar at the time when the Gospel narrative began to be circulated. But after the destruction of Jerusalem it became the principal seat of the learning of the Law. Then Palestinian as well as Roman and Greek influences would favour the introduction of the new name of the lake. John accepts the new name, and (as it were) bridges over the interval between the old name and the new in his first mention of the lake, thus : "Jesus went away to the other side of *the sea of Galilee, which is* [*the sea*] *of Tiberias*[3]."

---

[1] Macarius III. 6 (p. 60).
[2] Ps. cvii. 35, cxiv. 8, Cant. vii 4, comp 1 Macc. xi. 35 "salt pools," 2 Macc. xii. 16.   [3] Jn vi. 1.

THE CALLING OF THE FISHERMEN

These three different ways of describing the scene of some of the most remarkable events in the Gospel are not, in themselves, important. But indirectly the study of the differences throws light on the motives and circumstances of the Evangelists, and on the date of the traditions recorded by them. The study of other differences will be found similarly illuminating. Why, for example, does Luke make no mention of Andrew here? Was Andrew absent from the Reminding though present at the Calling? Or was it merely for brevity? Neither explanation will seem quite satisfactory when we come, a little later on, to Mark's statement that Jesus "came into the house of Simon and Andrew," and find Luke (in this case followed by Matthew) again omitting Andrew's name.

Again, as to Zebedee, was he, too, absent from the Reminding though present at the Calling? That will not suffice to explain why his boat is no longer called his but his sons'. No answer will be satisfactory that does not explain other passages where Mark inserts the name of Zebedee and Luke rejects it. In this and in other cases of narratives that describe similar but not identical events, such as Luke's and John's accounts of a miraculous draught of fishes, the best plan will be to compare them phrase by phrase, in order to ascertain whether one of the two traditions has modified the other.

§ 4. *Jesus "passing-by*[1]*," in Mark*

Instead of "*pass-by*," Matthew has "*walk [about]*," while Luke describes Jesus, first as "*standing*" by the lake, and afterwards as "*teaching*" in Peter's boat. Mark applies "*pass-by*" once more to Jesus thus:—

Mk ii. 13—14	Mt. ix. 9	Lk v. 27
(13) And he went-forth[2] again by the	And *passing-by* thence, Jesus saw a	And after these things he went-forth[2]

[1] In this section, the N T Gk for "pass-by" is παράγω.

[2] "Went forth," ἐξῆλθε, might in certain contexts mean "disembarked," as perhaps in Mk vi 34.

8 (Mark i. 16—20)

THE CALLING OF THE FISHERMEN

Mk ii 13—14 (*contd.*)	Mt ix 9 (*contd.*)	Lk v 27 (*contd*)
sea, and all the multitude resorted unto him, and he taught them. (14) And *passing-by*, he saw Levi the [son] of Alphaeus, sitting at the place of toll	man sitting at the place of toll, called Matthew	and beheld a receiver-of-toll, by name Levi, sitting at the place of toll...

In both the Marcan passages there is a mention of "sea." In the second there is a mention of "place of toll." Now the Greek "*pass-by*" is used by Polybius to mean "come into port," and by Epictetus (apparently) for "touch at a port"; and nouns derived from this verb mean "coming to land," and "dues" payable by a vessel on putting to land or touching at a harbour[1]. Possibly some assumption that Jesus "came by the sea" may explain how the word came to be used by Mark here instead of the ordinary words for "going-by[2]." The thought of Jesus, at this crisis, as "coming by the sea" in some way or other, either "*by the side of the sea*," or "*on the sea*," would be suggested by the prophecy of Isaiah, quoted in the parallel Matthew concerning the "great light" manifested "*by the way of the sea*" in connection with "Galilee of the Gentiles[3]."

But another and quite different allusion to "*passing-by*" might spring from the thought of a parallelism between the calling of the Fishermen by Jesus and the calling of Elisha by Elijah, who is said to have "passed over unto him" or "passed by him." Not that Elijah actually *said* to Elisha "Come after me." Yet that Elisha understood him to *mean*

---

[1] See Steph. *Thes.* vi 235—7.
[2] These would be παρέρχομαι, παραπορεύομαι, etc.
[3] Is ix 1—2.

9 (Mark i 16—20)

THE CALLING OF THE FISHERMEN

it, is certain, though the context is obscure[1]. For Elisha says "*I will* (lit.) *go after thee,*" and it is added that Elisha "*went after*" Elijah and "ministered unto him." In Mark, the Baptist is regarded as "Elijah," and as using about Jesus the words "*there cometh*" and "*after me*[2]" It is therefore antecedently probable that in this narrative, when Mark is about to describe Jesus as saying "[Come] *hither after me,*" and to describe how the fishermen "*went after him,*" he would have in mind the occasion when Elijah virtually said "*Come after me*" and Elisha actually said "*I will* (lit.) *go after thee.*" On that occasion the Hebrew Scripture described Elijah as "*passing-over*" to Elisha, or "*passing-by,*" and Mark might use "*pass-by*" here allusively.

It will be found that this Marcan word for "pass-by," when used of persons absolutely and without qualification[3], is used nowhere in the canonical LXX except in a passage of the Psalms where the Midrash exhibits differences of opinion: "Neither do *they that pass by* say, The blessing of the Lord be upon you[4]." One Rabbi takes it literally. Another refers it to the Gentiles, who "pass-by" like a vapour. Jerome takes it to mean the saints who "have passed away to heaven and to eternity." These variations and other ambiguities of the word both in Hebrew and in Greek may help to explain why Luke never applies this word to Jesus. But they also raise the question, "Does John apply this word to Jesus, and if so, to what effect?"

---

[1] 1 K. xix 19—20, R V, "And Elijah *passed over unto him* (A.V. *passed by him*) and cast his mantle upon him" Gesen. 718 a gives only this instance of "pass-over" with "unto" (foll by person), LXX ἐπῆλθεν (A ἀπῆλθεν) ἐπ' αὐτόν.

1 K. xix 20 (lit.) "Go, return" is interpreted, by some, "Go [home to bid farewell, and then] return [to me]." See Breithaupt's Rashi *ad loc* Contrast Mt. viii 21—2, Lk. ix 59—60

[2] Mk 1. 7

[3] This excludes such an instance as 2 S. xv 18 ἀνὰ χεῖρα αὐτοῦ παρῆγον, R V. "passed on beside him."

[4] Ps cxxix 8

THE CALLING OF THE FISHERMEN

He does apply it once to Jesus, and then (as Matthew uses it in a narrative peculiar to his Gospel) to describe Him as proceeding to heal blindness. "Jesus," he says, "was hidden [from the Jews] and went out of the Temple, and, *passing-by*, he saw a man blind from his birth[1]" The appropriateness of the word here may be illustrated from two phrases in the Johannine Epistle, "the darkness *is-being-made-to-pass-by*," and "the world *is-being-made-to-pass-away.*" Here we have two instances of a passive use of which Stephen's Thesaurus expressly avows inability to find an instance in "received authors[2]."

The explanation of this emphatic reiteration of so rare a word may be that John is playing on it in a new and mystical sense. He regards the Word, the Light of the world, as "*passing into*" the darkness of the world, or perhaps as "*passing by*" the darknesses of the world one by one, in order to "*make-to-pass*," i.e. to banish, the power of that darkness. This is an ancient Hebrew thought. The Scripture says that Jehovah "*passed*," on the night of the first Passover, when He intervened to save Israel[3]. The Targumists there substitute "*revealed Himself*" for "*passed.*" Later on, disliking to speak

---

[1] Jn viii 59, ix 1 (On "was hidden," see *Joh Gr.* **2538—43**) In Mt ix. 27 (pec), xx. 30, παράγω, "pass-by," occurs at the outset of narratives of the healing of blindness

[2] 1 Jn ii 8, 17, quoted in Steph *Thes* vi 235 with the remark "quem passivae vocis usum apud receptos linguae Graecae auctores extare non puto." Wetstein merely quotes this. Westcott takes no notice of this alleged rarity In Clem Alex. 836 the passive is found in its usual sense "The divine nature is not *turned-aside* [*from its purpose*]" Παράγω is not found in the Apostolic Fathers or Apologists in any form (exc 2 Clem Rom x 3 παράγουσιν, see Lightf)

[3] Exod xii 12, 23 "pass," in both cases. The Heb is the root of the name "Hebrew," *Perātes*, "*Passer-over*" (*Light* **3948**) It must not be confused with the root of "Passover" (Pesach) which occurs in the context (xii. 13 "I will *pass* over you," xii. 23 "will *pass* over the door").

THE CALLING OF THE FISHERMEN

of Jehovah as "*passing*"—in their comment on Israel as "*passing*" through the Red Sea and on the Lord as "reigning"—the later Targums speak of "the Redeemer *who maketh-to-pass, but passeth not, who maketh to be changed, but changeth not*[1]"

John would never have dreamed of saying that God "*is-made-to-pass*," but he does not hesitate to speak of God the Word, or God the Light, incarnate in Christ, as "*passing*," in order to "*make-to-pass*" darkness from the blind. For this he prepares the way in his Prologue, saying that "the light shineth in darkness," and that the Word, in whom was the life that is the light of men, "tabernacled among us." This is equivalent to saying, "He 'passed' from 'the bosom of God' into the midst of those who 'sat in darkness,' that He might 'cause to pass' that darkness. He 'came to his own'—the Jews. They 'received him not[2]'" Hence, later on, he describes how Jesus "was hidden [from them] and went out of the temple [of the Jews]. And 'passing by' [to the Gentiles] he saw a man blind from his birth[3]."

The Marcan "pass-by" will come before us again when we discuss the Marcan healing of blind Bartimaeus, where Matthew in two narratives—one parallel and closely similar to that of Mark, but the other less similar—applies the word to Jesus, though Mark and Luke do not[4] This indicates other beside Marcan traditions about the healing influence of "the Passer-by." And it confirms the inference that here we have a case of Johannine intervention. Luke objected to the Marcan word. And we know from Macarius that the Pauline use of

---

[1] On Exod. xv 16—18 (Targ. Jer. I and Jer II).
[2] Jn I. II.
[3] Jn viii. 59—ix I On ἐκρύβη probably implying "was [judicially] hidden," see *Joh Gr.* 2538—43.
[4] Mt ix 27, xx. 30. The former is peculiar to Matthew The latter is parallel to Mk x 46 foll , Lk. xviii. 35 foll (Lk. xviii 37 has παρέρχεται. not παράγει)

12 (Mark I. 16—20)

it in the expression "the fashion of this world *passeth*" was attacked by an early controversialist[1]. John, if he had been writing a first Gospel for Christians, would perhaps hardly have used it. But, finding it in use in Mark and Matthew, though omitted by Luke and perhaps already subject to censure, he adopted it in his Gospel allusively and allegorically, and justified it in his Epistle.

§ 5. *Jesus "walking[2]," in Matthew*

Since Matthew elsewhere uses the Marcan word "pass-by" in describing the call of Matthew the publican, as well as (twice) in describing the healing of the blind[3], we naturally ask why he does not also use it in describing the call of the fishermen, and why he substitutes a word that he never applies to Jesus again except as *"walking on the sea*[4]*."* Matthew has just quoted (and he alone quotes) *"The way of the sea,* beyond Jordan, Galilee of the Gentiles, the people that sat in darkness saw a great light[5]" Now this prophecy describing the Lord as advancing to deliver Israel *"by* the sea" might easily be extended, in Jewish thought, to deliverance *"through* the sea." The Targum actually paraphrases *"the way* of the sea" in the latter sense, as "the mighty-deliverance of the [Red] sea." It also explains "beyond Jordan" as "the miracles [in the passing] of the Jordan[6]." Such an interpretation would bring *"the way of the sea"* into parallelism with the Psalmist's saying *"In the sea* [*is*] *thy way"* (Targ. *"in the Red Sea"*)[7]. The

---

[1] Macarius pp 158, 169 foll., on 1 Cor. vii 31.

[2] "Walk" is περιπατέω in this section, *lit.* "walk about"

[3] Mt ix 9, 27, xx 30

[4] Mt. xiv. 25 foll., also used in Mk vi. 48—9, and Jn vi. 19 about Jesus "walking" on or by the sea (see *Joh. Gr* 2340 foll.) but not used of Jesus in Luke.

[5] Is ix. 1—2, Mt. iv 15—16.

[6] Perhaps the Targumist took "across the Jordan" as "crossing the Jordan"

[7] Ps lxxvii 19

13 (Mark 1 16—20)

THE CALLING OF THE FISHERMEN

Hebrew root of *derek*, "way," occurs also in *dârak*, "make one's way." In Job, where the Hebrew describes God as "making-his-way upon the waves of the sea," the LXX has Matthew's word, "*walking* on the sea as on a pavement[1]."

Job is alluding to the Spirit of God "moving on the waters" at the Creation. The action is typical. Jewish Christians in the first century—or at least those who were imbued with the poetry of the Scriptures—would delight in the thought of the Messiah as coming across the troubled waters to those who are tempest-tossed in the darkness, and as "treading" down the waves while bringing to them at once deliverance and light. But they might differ as to the occasions and ways of the Messianic action. Matthew, although following Mark in deferring Christ's "walking *on* the sea" to a later period, may have been influenced here by Isaiah's prophecy about "*the way* of the sea*," to this extent, that he here substitutes for "passing by" the word used in the LXX of Job to represent "making his way."

Luke, besides omitting the Walking on the Sea, never applies the word "walk" to Jesus. The reason may be, that this particular word, to a Greek ear, sometimes suggested "walking about ostentatiously," or "going about with diffuse discourse." Marcus Antoninus says that he learned "to abstain from rhetorical and poetical and artificial language, and not to *walk in a robe in one's own house*[2]." "*Walk in robes*" is a phrase used by Mark and Luke in a condemnation of the scribes[3]. Epictetus implies contempt for those who "*walk* in purple[4]." Playing on the word *peripatein*, "walk," when applied to the *peripatetic* philosophers, Lucian records a jibe

---

[1] Job ix 8   The LXX use of this word here is unique Περιπατέω, in canon. LXX, occurs nearly thirty times, and the Concordance, where it gives a Heb. equiv., gives always, except here, some form of the Heb "go."

[2] Marc. Ant. I § 7.   [3] Mk xii 38, Lk. xx. 46.
[4] Epict. iii. 22. 10

14 (Mark 1. 16—20)

THE CALLING OF THE FISHERMEN

about a lame philosopher of that sect "There is nothing more shameless than *a halting peripatetic*[1]."

§ 6. *Jesus "walking," in John*

John differs from Luke in often applying to Jesus the word "walk" The first instance is connected with the first mention of Jesus after His baptism: "Looking-stedfastly on Jesus *walking*, he [*i.e* the Baptist] saith, Behold, the lamb of God[2]." The consequence of the utterance is that two of the Baptist's disciples become disciples of Jesus—His first disciples: "They came therefore and saw where he abode; and they abode with him that day. *It was about the tenth hour.*" This was the beginning of the Church, the New Genesis[3].

Bearing in mind the curious and (as it might seem to some) superfluous mention of "*the tenth hour*," let us compare this passage with the first instance of the word "*walk*" in O.T. and with Rashi's comment. The Hebrew has "And they heard the voice of the Lord God *walking* in the garden *in the cool of the day.*" But the LXX has "*in the afternoon*," and Rashi, accepting the view that the phrase describes the evening, says "*they sinned in the tenth hour*[4]."

This indicates, in John, an allusive mention of "the tenth hour," as though the Evangelist said "At the end of the first Genesis, the divine Voice (not the Word[5]) descended to convict

---

[1] Lucian (II. 393) *Demonax* § 54
[2] Jn 1. 36.
[3] Jn 1. 39 For proof that John adapts the context to the form of a "Hexaemeron," see *Joh. Gr.* 2624, *Son* 3583 (ix) *b*, (xii) *c* foll. etc, where however no mention was made of the allusive force of the Johannine περιπατέω.
[4] Gen. III 8. See Breithaupt's note on Rashi's remark *Gen r ad loc.* shews that some considered the "coolness" to be that of the morning But Rashi does not even mention that view In the English Bible, A.V, "the tenth hour" does not occur except in Jn 1 39.
[5] On the inferiority of "voice" to "word," see *Son* 3628 *d*.

THE CALLING OF THE FISHERMEN

man of sin and to sentence him to death. At the beginning of the second Genesis, the divine Word descended to redeem man from that sin and to deliver him from that death. In both cases the hour was that of 'afternoon,' about the time of the evening sacrifice, '*about the tenth hour*[1].' Adam, fallen man, hid himself, and was terrified by the Voice of Him that 'walked' on earth. The men of the new Genesis, on the contrary, 'followed' the Word that 'walked' among them; they also asked Him where He 'abode,' and they 'abode' with Him[2]. Their 'abiding' with Him is dated from 'about the tenth hour,' which is the hour immediately following that of the evening sacrifice — that 'ninth hour' which is connected with the completion of the Sacrifice on the Cross[3], offered up by 'the Lamb of God that taketh away the sin of the world[4].'"

When John comes to the Mark-Matthew description of Jesus "walking on the sea," omitted by Luke, he intervenes to insert it, using their exact phrase. But he suggests, by his context, that he regards Jesus as walking "*on*" the sea in

---

[1] Δειλινόν occurs in Gen iii 8, Exod xxix 39, 41, Lev vi 20, 1 K xviii 29 2 Chr. xxxi 3 (comp. 1 Esdr. v 50, viii 72).

[2] Philo, on Gen iii 8, declares that to hear the Voice of God "walking" is a sign of a disturbed mind It is the mind that "walks," he says, not the divine Being On the symbolical meaning of divine "standing," as distinct from "walking," see *Joh. Gr.* 2307. In Jn 1. 36—9, the new disciples recognise the Word in two aspects, both as "walking" and as "abiding" The latter, by repetition, is emphasized as the higher aspect The two disciples are at first unnamed When one is named it is "Andrew" This, etymologically, is "Man," in a higher sense than "Adam" Adam = ἄνθρωπος, "homo," but Andrew = ἀνήρ, "vir" See below, p 32, n 2

See *Notes* **2998** (xxviii) *f—k* on the Hebrew conception of what may be called, not the "immanence," but the "inambulance," of God (Gesen 236) expressed by LXX περιπατέω and ἐμπεριπατέω Comp Rev. ii 1

[3] Mk xv 34 "*at the ninth hour*," Mt xxvii 46 "*about the ninth hour*" Luke (xxiii 44—6 "darkness *until the ninth hour*...and Jesus cried") leaves the time of the cry undefined.

[4] Jn 1 29, comp 1. 36 (On this, see *Light* **3781** f_1)

THE CALLING OF THE FISHERMEN

the sense in which we speak of a city as being "*on*" a sea or river. That is to say, Jesus was walking on the shore of the sea drawing the disciples towards Himself[1].

Later on, John notes that Jesus "walked in Galilee," and did *not*, for a time, ' walk in Judaea," owing to the hostility of the Jews, but that He did, on a certain occasion, "walk in the Temple," herein, as we shall find, agreeing with Mark against Matthew and Luke[2]. The last mention of the word applied to Jesus says that, owing to further plots, "Jesus walked no longer openly among the Jews[3]." Thus the incarnate Word, who began by "walking" in Israel in such a way as to call forth the Baptist's eulogy, is described as being forced by Israel's rejection gradually to withdraw Himself from them. These Johannine instances of a word rejected by Luke must be considered in the light of the above-quoted LXX use of the word about God in the Fall of Adam, and the vision of Him that "walketh in the midst of the seven golden candlesticks," in Revelation. Adding these to the above-mentioned agreement of John with Mark and Matthew against Luke in describing Jesus as "walking" on the sea, we are justified in saying that John intervenes in favour of a word that Luke rejected. John restores and rehabilitates it by bringing out its Hebrew and mystical associations.

§ 7. *Jesus "standing," and "teaching," in Luke*

The LXX affords instances of confusion between the Hebrew words "*pass-by*" and "*stand*[4]" The latter would be regarded by many as better suited than the former to describe

---

[1] Jn vi 19—21   See *Joh Gr.* 2340—6, 2354.
[2] Jn vii 1, x 23, Mk xi 27 (see p 19)   The Johannine "walking in the Temple" is followed by an attempt to seize Jesus.
[3] Jn xi 54.
[4] See Josh. iii 16, 1 K xxii 36, where LXX reads "*stand*" for Heb. "*pass by*," and 1 S vi 20 where LXX reads "*pass by* (διελθεῖν)" for Heb. "*stand*."

THE CALLING OF THE FISHERMEN

the Saviour here. Philo says "None but the true God *standeth*"; he speaks of "the *standing*, wholesome, and right Logos"; "that which belongs to the world of phenomena," he says, "does not *stand*[1]." The founder of the Simonian sect is said to have claimed to be the Standing One[2]. The Acts of John describes Jesus as simultaneously "*coming*" and "*standing*" when He appears to the two brothers. James sees Him as a "little child." But John replies "Thou (emph) dost not see, my brother James. But [now] seest thou not *the standing* [*one*, yonder]—a [full-grown] man...[3]?" Luke, when collecting the various traditions about the Call of the Fishermen, seems to have found the phrase "*standing by the sea*" in such a context that it might be applied either to Jesus or to vessels drawn up on the beach, so that (as Virgil says) "the sterns *stood* on the shore[4]." The ambiguity may have arisen from a text such as this "It came to pass that the disciples were fishing, having two boats, and that *Jesus saw* [*them*], or, *they*

---

[1] See *Joh Voc* 1725 g quoting Philo and also Origen (on Jn i 26) "There *stands* also His [*i e* the Father's] Logos ever in the act of saving . ."

[2] See Clem Alex 456 and comp Hippol. vi 12

[3] *Acts of John* § 2 οὐ σὺ ὁρᾷς οὐχ ὁρᾷς δὲ τὸν ἑστῶτα—ἄνδρα εὔμορφον, καλόν , Previously it is said ἔρχεται πρός με καὶ τὸν ἀδελφόν μου..

[4] See *Æneid* vi. 902 "Ancora de prora jacitur, *stant litore* puppes," and *ib* 3—5 "Obvertunt pelago proras ; tum dente tenaci Ancora fundabat naves, et *litora curvae Praetexunt puppes*," where "*stant litore*" and "*litora praetexunt*" correspond to Luke's ἑστῶτα παρὰ τὴν λίμνην Wetstein quotes (on Acts xxvii. 30), but without reference, a Greek statement about the suspenders "by which hang the anchors which, when loosed, *bring-to-a-stand* (ἱστῶσι) the ship " Steph *Thes* i 353 quotes, from Pollux, στήσασθαι τὴν ναῦν as a nautical phrase The Index to Polybius gives instances of ἑστώς meaning "stable," "firm," applied to λόγος and λογισμός but not applied to vessels *Acts of John* § 2 εἰς γῆν τὸ πλοῖον ἀγαγόντες ὅπως τὸ πλοῖον ἑδράσωμεν indicates that ἑδράζειν "beach [the boat]" would have been a better word But the context in Luke indicates that he regarded the vessels as already "beached "

18 (Mark 1. 16—20)

THE CALLING OF THE FISHERMEN

saw Jesus, standing by the sea[1]." I have found no instance of the Greek participle "standing," thus applied to vessels. But this may explain why Luke, taking it thus, thinks it necessary to enter into some detail so as to make it clear that the disciples had definitely given up fishing for the time. The fishermen had not only ceased to fish; they had thrown out anchors from the prows, the sterns were by the beach, and the disciples had come ashore and were washing their nets.

This repetition of "standing by the sea," and its use in a rare and apparently forced sense, make it probable that Luke was himself in doubt, and scrupulously retained the words that caused him difficulty, while endeavouring to put upon them the best meaning that he could devise In fact, however, "standing" is not quite appropriate here even when applied to Jesus. It is quite appropriate in the Fourth Gospel, where Jesus "stood on the shore at dawn" and watched the disciples on the sea, continuing the toil of the night and "taking nothing[2]." But it is superfluous in Luke, if all that is meant is, that whereas the fishermen were sitting on the shore, Jesus was "standing" near them.

Turning to Luke's context, we ask whether, besides this apparent attempt to express Mark's "passing by," he has made any attempt to express Matthew's "*walking.*" We have seen above that, according to Greek notions, "*walking,*" when applied to a teacher or philosopher, would often imply lecturing or "*teaching.*" And, later on, we shall find that, where Mark describes Jesus as merely "*walking* in the temple," Luke has "*teaching the people* in the temple *and* preaching the gospel[3]."

---

[1] Ἐγένετο δὲ τοὺς μαθητὰς ἁλιεύειν, ἔχοντας δύο πλοῖα, καὶ ἰδεῖν τὸν Ἰησοῦν ἑστῶτα παρὰ τὴν θάλασσαν

[2] Jn xxi 3—4. This suggests a thought of Lucretius ii. 1 "Suave mari magno. .alterius spectare laborem," but with a difference, since Jesus "standing" on the shore, "stands," not merely to "behold" but also to help.

[3] Mk xi 27, Lk. xx. 1 (the parall. Mt. xxi. 23 has "teaching").

(Mark i. 16—20)

THE CALLING OF THE FISHERMEN

So, here, Luke adds a mention of "teaching" to the mention of "standing." The result is —"He was *standing by the lake* of Gennesaret, and he saw two boats *standing by the lake*... and having gone-on-board one of the boats...he *taught* the multitudes."

§ 8. *"Rabbi," used in all the Gospels but Luke*

When Jesus says to the two disciples of John the Baptist who are following him "What seek ye?" they reply "'*Rabbi*' —which is to say, being interpreted, *Teacher* (*didaskălĕ*)— 'where abidest thou[1]?'" This is the first vocative appellation addressed to Jesus in the Fourth Gospel. The first vocative appellation addressed to Jesus by a disciple in Luke is quite different, "*Master* (epistătă), we toiled all night, and took nothing[2]." No evangelist except Luke uses *epistătă* (and Luke never mentions *Rabbi*). No evangelist except John explains "Rabbi," and none uses it so frequently. What are the differences of thought underlying these differences of word?

In order to answer this question, we proceed to facts. First, the Johannine interpretation of "Rabbi," namely "teacher," is not etymologically correct. It is true that Eusebius interprets it as "*Teacher*" or "*my Teacher*[3]." But Jerome more accurately interprets it "my *Master*," "*Magister* meus." For *rab-bi* meant etymologically "my great one." And *rab*, "*great one*," had come to mean, even as early as some of the later books of the Bible, under Babylonian influence, "*chief*," "*captain*[4]." Hence "*Rabbi*," meaning "*my Master*," began, after the death

---

[1] Jn 1 38 "Teacher (διδάσκαλε)," R V. text follows A.V in using "master" for "teacher," as often elsewhere

[2] Lk v. 5 "Master (ἐπιστάτα)" (Lk 11 48 τέκνον, iv 34 Ἰησοῦ Ναζαρηνέ are not "addressed to Jesus by a disciple")

[3] See *Onomastica Sacra*, Index, 'Ραββί

[4] See Gesen 913 *b* quoting from Jerem. xxxix. 9—10 "chief of guardsmen" ("only as title of Babylonian officer"), Jon 1 6 "*chief* of the sailors," *i e.* captain, etc.

20 (Mark 1. 16—20)

THE CALLING OF THE FISHERMEN

of Hillel, to be applied to a *chief* among teachers, *i.e.* a great and distinguished Jewish Teacher of the Law. But it still retained a notion of "mastership" or "greatness." Matthew represents Jesus as declaring that the Pharisees "loved to be called of men, 'Rabbi,'" and as warning His disciples against it, "Be not ye called 'Rabbi[1].'"

Whenever any Gospel says that Jesus was addressed as "Teacher," it is probable that the word, as uttered, was "Rabbi"; for there is no other Hebrew or Aramaic vocative that would be suitable[2]. Yet "Rabbi" is very rarely retained by any Synoptist. Mark uses it twice as an exclamation of Peter, (1) in the Transfiguration, (2) in the Withering of the Fig-tree, and also (3) as the salutation of Judas[3]. He also uses the form "Rabboni," where blind Bartimaeus exclaims "*Rabboni*, that I may recover my sight[4]!" Matthew—apart from the above-quoted protest against the word—uses "Rabbi" only as the salutation of Judas, and in the preceding question of Judas "Is it I, Rabbi[5]?" Luke never uses either "Rabbi" or "Rabboni."

As for Mark, then, we may say that he adopted "Teacher" as a rule, but made a few exceptions, in two notable instances of Petrine exclamation, or where tradition, as in the "Rabbi" of Judas, had preserved the Aramaic word, or where he wished to express intense feeling, as in the case of Bartimaeus

Matthew, who alone records Christ's warning "Be not ye called 'Rabbi,'" adds "One is your teacher[6]." This suggests

---

[1] Mt xxiii 7—8

[2] In O T (A V) "teacher," used absolutely, occurs only in 1 Chr xxv 8, where it is the participle, "making-to-understand," LXX τελείων (as distinct from μανθανόντων) Dalman (*Words*, p. 336) denies that the passages cited by Levy *Ch* (ii. 42 *b*) prove the use of a noun from *âlaph*, meaning "teacher"

[3] Mk ix 5, xi 21, xiv 45

[4] Mk x 51. The parall. Mt xx. 33, Lk xviii 41 have "Lord!" which Mark never uses except in vii. 28 "Yea, Lord."

[5] Mt. xxvi. 49, 25. [6] Mt. xxiii. 8.

THE CALLING OF THE FISHERMEN

that Jesus permitted His disciples to call Him "Rabbi" But the authorities for the text so vary that we cannot feel sure that this permission was given. If it was not, we may say that Matthew consistently restricts the salutation of Christ as "Rabbi" to Judas, who utters it twice[1].

Luke, who never uses "Rabbi," uses six times—and for the most part in traditions parallel to other Synoptists—the vocative of the classical Greek word *epistătēs*, meaning "prefect," "chief of a department." This is used by canon LXX about eight times to correspond to six different Hebrew words. But it does not express either the etymological meaning ("great") or the derived meaning ("teacher") of the Hebrew "Rabbi" In the Transfiguration, where Peter says, in Mark, "*Rabbi,*" and in Matthew "*Lord,*" Luke has "*Epistătă*, it is good for us to be here[2]." It is not surprising that *epistătēs*, thus applied, took no root in Christian tradition. The word does not occur elsewhere in N.T.—not even in the Acts—nor in any of the early Fathers or Apologists. It must be regarded as a Lucan experiment—scrupulous and well-intended but not successful—to express the Hebrew or Aramaic *Rabbi* with exactness, and to shew that it does not mean "teacher."

§ 9. "*Rabbi,*" in John

John, so to speak, rehabilitates the term "Rabbi," discarded by Luke His treatment of this word illustrates his treatment of something more than mere words. It is an illuminating instance of his method of combining the old with the new, and the rudiment with the development.

First, he tells us that the disciples, from the very beginning, called Jesus "Rabbi" At the same time, he says to us, in effect, "*Rabbi* did not practically mean *Epistătēs*, that is to say, *President* or *Prefect*. It was a respectful term by which

---

[1] Mt xxvi 25, 49
[2] Mk ix 5, Mt. xvii 4, Lk ix. 33.

disciples addressed their teacher, and if it must be expressed in one word, that word is 'Teacher[1].'" Then he shews us how Nathanael, who used this salutation, while adding "Son of God" and "King of Israel," was gently told that he was still comparatively ignorant and he must "see greater things[2]." Later on, Nicodemus calls Jesus "Rabbi" and confesses that He is "come from God [as] teacher," but receives a reply indicating that he too is in ignorance and does not yet know what the true "teacher" is[3]. Afterwards, the disciples collectively say to Jesus "Rabbi, eat," but are told "I have meat to eat that ye know not of[4]."

In subsequent passages "Rabbi" is used by the ignorant multitude, who are rebuked for seeking Jesus from interested motives[5]. But it is also used by the disciples, ignorantly supposing that if a man is born blind, he himself, or his parents, must have sinned ; and again by the disciples, affectionately—but, at the time, causelessly—anxious for their Master's safety[6].

These instances of the word may pass without further comment. But we must note the last of all : "Jesus saith unto her, Mary. She turneth herself, and saith unto him in Hebrew, Rabboni, that is to say, Teacher[7]." Why does John here add that Mary spoke "in Hebrew" ? And why does he repeat—what he told us at the beginning of his Gospel—that the salutation meant "Teacher" ? The moment of utterance is a moment of transition, between the things of earth and the things of heaven, between the Resurrection of Jesus, still on earth, and His Ascension "Touch me not ; for I am not yet ascended unto the Father[8]." Is the utterance intended to

---

[1] Jn i 38 John the Baptist is addressed as "Rabbi" (Jn iii 26) just before his final words are recorded
[2] Jn i 49—50.
[3] Jn iii 2, 10 "Art thou the teacher of Israel and understandest not these things ?"
[4] Jn iv 31—2 [5] Jn vi. 25—6
[6] Jn ix 2, xi 8. [7] Jn xx. 16
[8] Jn xx. 17

THE CALLING OF THE FISHERMEN

convey some hint of such a transition from the thought of "Teacher" to the thought of some one higher, "God"? Can we apply to this salutation a tradition in the Talmud where, in a specially passionate outburst, a Jewish layman, not called a Rabbi, ventures, when pleading the cause of his suffering fellow-countrymen, to call God *Rabbōni*[1]?

That does not seem probable. More probably John is recording a historical utterance, but recording it with an allusive reference to many first-century Christian traditions about "Rabbi" and "Rabban." Some of these may be found—latent under the Greek word "Teacher"—in Matthew and Luke, as well as in John. For example, where John says, "Ye call me '*Teacher*' and 'Lord,'" the Syriac has "Ye call me '*Rabban*' and 'our Lord,'" and Delitzsch also has "*Rabbi*[2]"; and this must be considered along with the Syriac and Hebrew of Matthew "There is no disciple that is more than his *Rabbi*[3]." Both passages must be read along with their contexts, which mention "servant" and "lord" and imply that these terms are severally parallel to "disciple" and "Rabbi[4]." Thus regarded, a "disciple" is a "servant." The Lucan parallel to

---

[1] See *Taanith* iii 9 (8) Mishna, 19 *a*, where Onias "the maker of circles," pleading to God for rain for the people, traces a circle, places himself in it, and says, "*Rabbon of the Universe*, or, *Rabboni*, thy children have placed their trust in me, judging that I am in thy sight as one of the children of the House, I swear by thy great Name that I will not go out hence until thou hast pity on thy children." On the reading "*Rabboni*," see Taylor's note on *Aboth* ii 1

See also Dalman *Words* p 325 "It is a remarkable fact that in the early Jewish literature, apart from the Targums, רבון is scarcely ever used except as referring to God." But he also says (*ib* p 340) that the term "Rabboni" used by Mark and John "cannot have been materially distinguished" from Rabbi, "and therefore John is right in interpreting it as διδάσκαλε." In the Targums, רבוני (Dalman *ib* p 324) represents the Heb *Adonai*, "my lord," applied to persons

[2] Jn xiii 13   [3] Mt x 24

[4] Jn xiii 16, Mt. x 25

THE CALLING OF THE FISHERMEN

Matthew adds "But every one being perfected shall be as his teacher (Syr. Rabbi)[1]." Matthew has "It is enough for the disciple that he should be as his teacher (Syr. Rabbi) and the servant as his lord[2]." These passages obscurely indicate that the terms "servant" and "Rabbi" ought to pass away when the "Rabbi" has "perfected" his "disciple" or "servant," and made him like himself.

John seems to take up this thought in Christ's Last Discourse. After the Washing of Feet, wherein Jesus makes Himself a servant, He bids His servants do the same, saying to them "There is no servant that is greater than his lord." But then He passes on to describe how the Paraclete will come in His name and will "teach" them "all things[3]," and the result will be that the character of servant will be merged in the character of friend · "No longer do I call you servants, for the servant knoweth not what his lord doeth; but I have called you friends, for all things that I heard from my Father I have made known unto you[4]."

Reviewing the facts we shall probably feel diffident about defining John's own feeling about the "Hebrew" appellation "Rabboni!" uttered by Mary for the last time on the morning of the Resurrection, and about its relation to the Greek-Hebrew appellation "Paraclete[5]" mentioned by Jesus for the first time on the night before the Crucifixion. But we can hardly feel doubt that John has *some* feeling of a development and

---

[1] Lk vi 40 SS condenses the whole of the verse into "There is no disciple that is perfect as his Rabbi in teaching," but Walton's Syriac follows the Greek, only rendering "teacher" by "rabbi."

[2] Mt x 25.

[3] Jn xiv 26 "But the Paraclete, the Holy Spirit, whom the Father will send in my name, he shall teach you all things."

[4] Jn xv 15 It is assumed that the teaching of the Paraclete is (xv 9 foll) "abide ye in my love," and from this "love" comes the friendship. What the Son "heard from the Father" is "that a man lay down his life for his friends."

[5] On Paraclete as a Greek-Hebrew word, see *Joh Voc.* 1720 *j—l.*

THE CALLING OF THE FISHERMEN

transition in thus placing "Rabbi" and "Rabboni"—the same word yet uttered with such different feelings—at the opening and at the close of Christ's life on earth. Still less can we doubt that, in retaining this ancient salutation, redolent of "Hebrew," John is tacitly protesting against Luke's Hellenistic substitute. Those who know a word or two of Greek will understand the shock that one would experience if the Evangelist had represented Mary, at the tomb, as saying "*Epistátá*," and even those who know none may feel that they would lose something, if they had to give up "Rabboni," and be content with the Lucan "Master[1]."

§ 10. "*Andrew*"

In Luke, Jesus is said to have entered into one of two boats "which was Simon's," and the other boat is said to have belonged to "James and John...who were partners with Simon"; but Andrew is not mentioned. Mark, on the other hand, mentions "Andrew the brother of Simon" along with the first mention of Simon, and Matthew does the same[2]. Later

---

[1] A full discussion of Jn xx 16—17 would require a discussion of Mt xxviii. 9—10 "And they.. *took hold of his feet* and worshipped him Then Jesus saith unto them, Fear not" (on which see *Notes* **2999** (1) *b* and (11)). John's attitude to such a tradition would seem to be very different from that of Jerome, who (*ad loc*) praises the faith of these women, who "took hold" of the feet of Jesus, as compared with that of "her who sought the living with the dead . and justly heard [the rebuke] 'Touch me not,'" *i e* Mary John seems to say "In what I shall describe, there was no 'taking hold' and no 'fear' Jesus bade Mary *not* to 'take hold' of Him so as to detain Him on earth, since He was on the point of ascending to heaven. But He did not say 'fear not,' for she had no fear And He did not rebuke her for using the old Galilaean appellation 'Rabboni.' He accepted it Yet it was here used for the last time. Henceforth 'Rabboni' was superseded by 'Maran, or 'Marana,' that is, 'our Lord'"

Compare the following verse, "Mary Magdalene cometh and telleth the disciples, *I have seen the Lord*."

[2] Mk 1 16, Mt. iv. 18 See above, p 6.

26 (Mark i. 16—20)

THE CALLING OF THE FISHERMEN

on in the narrative, when Mark says concerning Jesus and those with him, that "they came into the house of Simon *and Andrew, with James and John,*" Matthew and Luke omit the italicised words[1]. In the appointment of the Twelve, Andrew is necessarily named by all the Synoptists[2]. But Mark alone says that, before the Discourse on the Last Days, "As he sat on the Mount of Olives, over against the temple, *Peter and James and John and Andrew* asked him privately" Here Matthew and Luke have severally, instead of the italicised words, "the disciples," and "they[3]"

Matthew, on the above-mentioned two occasions (iv 18, x. 2), and Luke on the one occasion (vi 14), on which they mention Andrew, append him, so to speak, to Simon Peter, as "*Andrew his brother.*" Andrew, in Matthew-Luke, never says or does anything. This, then, is a case where we may expect Johannine intervention

John makes Andrew not only one of the first two converts, but also the first to prepare the way for the conversion of others by bringing to Jesus his brother Simon Peter[4]. He also puts Andrew before Peter again when, after describing how Jesus bade Philip follow Him, he adds "Now Philip was domiciled at Bethsaida, *i e.* the House of Fishing, [*a native*] of [*Capernaum*] *the city of Andrew and Peter*[5]." No fishermen are mentioned. But to a Jew, and especially to a Galilaean, the name Bethsaida ("House of Fishing[6]") would suggest that Philip belonged to that class And the command "follow me," compared with the similar command in Mark-Matthew to the Fishermen, suggests that the Fourth Gospel is here describing an early calling of the whole group of

---

[1] Mk 1 29, Mt viii. 14, Lk. iv 38.
[2] Mk iii 18, Mt x 2, Lk vi 14
[3] Mk xiii. 3, Mt. xxiv 3, Lk xxi 7
[4] Jn 1. 41 [5] Jn 1 43—4
[6] *Enc Bibl* "Place of Fishing, or Hunting," Hastings' *Dict.* "House of Sport," or "Fisher-home."

THE CALLING OF THE FISHERMEN

Fishermen:—first, Andrew and John, secondly, Andrew's brother Peter and John's brother James, and now Philip in addition. The context also suggests that Andrew may have induced the Lord to go forth and save his friend Philip. This would agree with the Marcan juxtaposition of Andrew and Philip in the appointment of the Twelve. There, Matthew-Luke appends Andrew to Simon surnamed Peter. But Mark mentions, first, Simon surnamed Peter, secondly, James and John (with their surname), and thirdly, "*Andrew and Philip.*"

Andrew and Philip are also introduced together by the Fourth Gospel, in the Feeding of the Five Thousand. There Mark, as well as John, records the saying about "bread" and "two hundred pence." But John alone names the speaker (Philip) whom Mark leaves unnamed. In the same context, John also names Andrew as "one of his disciples, Andrew, Simon Peter's brother" in connection with "five barley-loaves and two small fishes" (where the Synoptists name no speaker)[1]. This union of the two disciples in the first Johannine giving of bread ("five barley-loaves") would prepare us for finding them mentioned again together in the Johannine giving of the one "loaf" after the Resurrection. And, though they are not expressly included there, they may be (and probably are) tacitly included in the expression "two other of his disciples[2]" If that is the case, we are to regard them as learning, after the Resurrection, that lesson of the True Bread which (it is implied)

---

[1] Jn vi 7—9

[2] That these unnamed disciples are not the two sons of Zebedee is shewn by the context (xxi 2) "*the* [*sons*] *of Zebedee* and *two other of his disciples.*" The silence as to the names may possibly be explained on the hypothesis that the Evangelist says to the reader "I do not mention their names, for I leave it to you to think who they ought to be. Should I be likely to introduce a pair of disciples hitherto unmentioned? And what other pair of disciples have I previously mentioned except Philip and Andrew?"

28 (Mark i. 16—20)

THE CALLING OF THE FISHERMEN

they failed to understand in the rudimentary sign of the "five barley-loaves[1]."

Papias, when describing his desire to supplement the knowledge he derived from the books about the faith by that which came from a "living and abiding voice," says that he used to cross-examine the Elders of his day, asking them, "*What did Andrew or what did Peter say? Or what did Philip*[2]*? Or what* [said] *Thomas or James? Or what John or Matthew, or any other of the Lord's Disciples,...?*" It is worth noting that Papias here not only puts Andrew first in the list of those of the Lord's Disciples whose traditions he collected from the Elders, but also puts Philip third. This follows the order of the names introduced in the Fourth Gospel. In that Gospel, Philip and Andrew are also introduced as being mediators, so to speak, between the Greeks and Jesus, and as eliciting from Him, in reply to their mediation, the reply about the "grain of wheat" which must "fall into the earth and die" so that it may "bear much fruit[3]."

Viewing the Fourth Gospel in the light of the remarks of Papias, we may fairly infer that the prominence given by both to Andrew represents a protest—such as that uttered by Papias and somewhat similar to that uttered by the Evangelist at the close of his Gospel—against allowing "the books" current among Christians to override oral traditions supplementing and explaining them. Luke's Acts of the Apostles had practically mentioned no "acts" of any "apostles" except Peter and Paul[4]. Yet others, apostles and non-apostles, must have been preaching the gospel and presumably founding churches.

---

[1] On the "barley-loaves," see *Son* 3420, comp. *Joh. Gr* 1985
[2] Euseb. III 39 4.   [3] Jn xii. 20—4
[4] The only exceptions are occasions where John and Peter are said to do or say things jointly (Acts iii. 1—11 "*they* were going up...*Peter* fastening his eyes upon him *with John*...as he held *Peter and John*," iv. 13—19 "the boldness of *Peter and John*... but *Peter and John* answering said," viii 14 "*Peter and John*, who... prayed").

29 (Mark i. 16—20)

THE CALLING OF THE FISHERMEN

Incidentally we learn that the beginnings of a church had been made in Samaria by Philip "the Evangelist" (not "the Apostle")[1].

Paul, in his Epistle to the Church in Rome, not only says nothing as to its indebtedness to any of the Twelve as its founder, but also uses language incompatible with the supposition that it had been founded and established with spiritual gifts by any of them[2]. It is almost certain that Luke regards

---

[1] Acts viii 5, 12, comp ib xxi 8.

[2] Rom i 11—12 "For I long to see you, that I may impart unto you some spiritual gift, to the end ye may be established—*that is, that I with you may be comforted in you*, .. " The italicised words soften, but do not conceal, Paul's assumption that the Romans had not yet received such "spiritual" gifts and such "establishment" as might be derived from him, an "apostle," who had "seen the Lord."

See Lightfoot on the untenableness of the hypothesis that Peter visited Rome before Paul wrote the Epistle to the Romans (*Clem Rom* ii. 491) "S Paul could not have written as he writes to the Romans (i 11 sq , xv. 20—24), if they had received even a short visit from an Apostle, more especially if that Apostle were S Peter."

Rom xv 20 (R V) "that I might not build upon *another man's foundation* (ἀλλότριον θεμέλιον)" affords no grounds for saying "*The other man* must have been Peter" For ἀλλότριον may mean "other *men's*" Thus it is rendered by Fritzsche "*alieno* (ab *aliis* jacto)", and he quotes Theophylact, Ἀλλότριον δὲ θεμέλιον τὴν διδασκαλίαν τῶν ἀποστόλων φησίν, οὐχ ὅτι ἀλλότριοι ἦσαν. Theophylact adds "not because they were *strangers* (or, *aliens*) (ἀλλότριοι) or because they preached other things (ἄλλα) but in respect of the reward. For the reward for the toil performed by *them* (ἐκείνοις) belonged to others (ἀλλότριος ἦν) ..." If Peter afterwards visited Rome, there would be a strong and natural temptation to antedate his visit, and to regard the Church there as founded by the same Apostle that had opened the Church to the Roman Empire in the person of Cornelius (Acts x 1) "a centurion of the cohort called the Italian cohort" Paul might claim to be the founder of almost all the great Churches of Europe That Peter should have founded the Church of Rome would seem so fit and reasonable that in a very few years all would be convinced that it was true.

It should be noted, however, that the *Chronicon* of Eusebius (p 152) describes Peter as having "founded the first (?) church in

THE CALLING OF THE FISHERMEN

Aquila and Priscilla as already Christians, come from the Church in Rome in the early days of the Gospel[1], and long before Peter could have been supposed by anyone to have visited the City. Unnamed disciples seem therefore to have originated and established that Church to which Paul sent his great Epistle. If indeed one of the "acts" of Peter had been to found—or even merely to visit and confirm—the Church in Rome, before Paul was sent there as a prisoner, it is impossible that Luke (or even an early redactor of the Acts) could fail to know it; and if he knew it and failed to mention it, I do not see how he could be acquitted—not only of an astonishing want of sense of proportion, but also of such a suppression of truth as would amount to mendacity[2]

Our conclusion is that Luke, as in the Acts, so in his Gospel, systematically pruned away from Marcan traditions about the Twelve such details as (in his opinion) took off the reader's attention from Peter as their main representative and as the main recipient of Christ's doctrine. John pursues an opposite

---

Antioch (τὴν ἐν 'Αντιοχείᾳ πρώτην (? πρῶτον) θεμελιώσας ἐκκλησίαν) before proceeding to Rome to preach the Gospel" The Acts mentions no such "founding" The only N T mention of a visit of Peter to Antioch is in Gal 11. 11 "But when Cephas came to Antioch, I resisted him to the face." To the statement of Eusebius Jerome adds that Peter preached the Gospel in Rome for *twenty-five years* ("ubi evangelium praedicans *XXV annis* ejusdem urbis episcopus perseverat") Eusebius mentions no definite time "The same [Peter], along with the Church in Antioch, was the first primate of the Church in Rome as well, *until his martyrdom* (ὁ δ' αὐτὸς μετὰ τῆς ἐν 'Αντιοχείᾳ ἐκκλησίας καὶ τῆς ἐν Ῥώμῃ πρῶτος προέστη ἕως τελειώσεως αὐτοῦ)" Eusebius apparently regards Peter's claim to Antioch as being on a level with his claim to Rome

[1] See *Beginning* p 339

[2] It would be futile, against such a charge, to allege that Luke contemplated a sequel to the Acts, in which sequel he might have mentioned the foundation of the Roman Church by Peter For the whole of the narrative of Paul's arrival in Rome, and of what he did there after he arrived, would take a different colour if Peter had arrived before and had founded the Church of Rome.

THE CALLING OF THE FISHERMEN

course. He concentrates his reader's attention on Christ as the Light of the world, by shewing us, dramatically and picturesquely[1], how the Light, while shining now on this disciple, now on that, drew forth from each a responsive beam that helped each to enlighten and evangelize the world. Of these disciples Andrew is the first[2]

§ 11. *"Casting-about in the sea"*

At this stage we have to investigate minute verbal details pointing to the conclusion that Luke's narrative sprang from the same original as Mark's, and that Greek as well as Hebrew ambiguities have caused the Synoptic divergences. Though it is difficult, and perhaps impossible, to restore the original with confidence, it is possible to shew the nature of the early obscurities and the honesty of Luke's attempt to elucidate them

The Greek word for "cast-about," here used absolutely without an object, has not hitherto been found thus used elsewhere (except in Greek borrowed from this Marcan passage) to mean "cast a net" or "fish" Used absolutely, it does not occur

---

[1] "Picturesquely," but with a very different picturesqueness from that of Mark, who spends an appreciable part of his Gospel in describing the feast at which Herodias danced away the life of John the Baptist

[2] Andreas was one of the three fictitious names (Joseph *Ant* xii. 2. 2, see Schurer II iii 306—12) ascribed to those patrons of the Jews who were instrumental in bringing about the translation of the Hebrew Scriptures by the Seventy. The names Aristeas, ("Excellent"), Sosibius ("Save-life"), Andreas ("Manly") are appropriate to their task of introducing the Law of Jehovah to the Gentiles And in the same way there is an appropriateness of names in the Fourth Gospel, when the Greeks are brought to Jesus (Jn xii 22) by Philip and Andrew This does not imply that the narrative itself is fictitious. But it does suggest that in other parts of the Fourth Gospel "Andrew" may represent "man" in a noble sense (Jerome, *Onomast* p 66 "melius autem est...$\dot{a}\pi\dot{o}$ $\tau o\hat{v}$ $\dot{a}\nu\delta\rho\acute{o}s$, hoc est,.. *virilis*") including Jew and Gentile

The Muratorian Tablet says that the Gospel written by John was the result of a vision to Andrew.

32 (Mark 1. 16—20)

THE CALLING OF THE FISHERMEN

in the early Fathers and Apologists in any sense except "*cast-about* [*in one's mind*]," "*be in doubt.*" It is thus used by Justin Martyr and Clement of Alexandria[1]. Macarius, when he repeatedly speaks of Peter "*casting-about*," is referring to him, *not as fishing, but as attempting to come to Jesus on the water,* and "*being-in-doubt,*" *and sinking*[2]

The LXX uses "cast-about" only once, and then with a cognate noun, in Habakkuk, "*cast-about* his casting-net[3]" But the Hebrew is "*empty* his net" This might mean either (1) "*empty*" the net of its contents, fish, weeds, etc., or (2) "*empty*" the net out of the boats so as to encircle a shoal of fish. The latter may be illustrated by the Hebrew phrase "*empty* the sword out of its sheath," and Gesenius favours the proposal to read here "empty the *sword*" (instead of "empty the *net*")[4]. The Vulgate has "*spread,*" the Syriac "*cast*" An edition of Aquila has "*empty-forth,*" with "sword" instead of "net," and with a marginal reading "*make-new.*" These variations in the rendering of Habakkuk may bear on the variations in the Synoptists here. For Mark and Matthew describe the first pair of fishermen as "*casting-about*" (or "casting") · but the second pair they describe as "*adjusting*" (taken by some as "*mending*") their nets, Luke describes the fishermen of the two boats as all "*washing*" their nets[5].

The LXX (in a description of men fishing, angling, and spreading nets) uses the noun "*caster-about*" once, either to paraphrase (in a conflate) "spreader of nets" or, more probably,

---

[1] Clem Alex pp 41, 94, Justin Mart *Tryph* §§ 51, 123 Justin uses it in no other sense.

[2] Macarius p 87

[3] Hab 1 17

[4] See Gesen. 938 *a*, referring to Exod xv 9, Lev. xxvi 33, etc

[5] Lk v 2 "Washing," *i e* purifying, may represent Luke's way of paraphrasing He may mean, "I say 'wash,' because they were not emptying their nets of fish, but discharging weeds and refuse They were not preparing to fish at once, but cleaning with a view to fishing after some interval They had toiled all night and were wearied "

THE CALLING OF THE FISHERMEN

to paraphrase "on the face of the waters[1]." This paraphrase perhaps proceeds from a desire to make it clear that the words indicate the enclosing of a shoal with a net, and not the use of the "angle" (Heb "hook"). The Hebrew of Isaiah "*spread* the net," by itself, is ambiguous It is used in a Mishna where the context justifies Levy in explaining it as "*spread to dry.*" But Schwab ("ne posera pas de pièges") suggests "*setting nets for the purpose of catching*[2]" Variation is all the more excusable because, when Ezekiel speaks of "a place for the *spreading* of nets [to dry]," he uses a different Hebrew word[3]

So far, the evidence bearing on Mark's "*casting-about*" points to an original Hebrew "*spread the nets,*" meaning "*spread them on the water to catch fish,*" erroneously taken by some to mean "*spread the nets out to dry*" Moreover the phrase rendered by R V. "mending their nets," applied by Mark and Matthew to the sons of Zebedee[4], if interpreted according to LXX usage[5], and not as in the Pauline Epistles, would more probably mean "*set in order,*" "*perfect*" (not "*restore*" or "*repair*"). This may be the interpretation of the Mark-Matthew phrase in the Syriac, and certainly is, in a few of the Latin versions.

If this view is correct, then, according to Mark-Matthew, all the four fishermen were trying to catch fish, and, for that purpose, "spreading" or "adjusting" their nets (not "mending" them) when Jesus called them. Luke's notion that they were "washing" them may have sprung, in part at all events, from a different interpretation of Mark, or of Mark's ambiguous original, and from an attempt to explain it by amplification.

---

[1] See Is xix 8 and comp *Oxf Conc* on this text (1) with a query, under ἀμφιβολεύς and (2) under βάλλω
[2] Levy iv 140 b, quoting *Megill* 28 a, Schwab vi 239
[3] Ezek xxvi 5 (on which see Rashi)
[4] Mk 1. 19, Mt iv 21
[5] See καταρτίζω in LXX Concordance

THE CALLING OF THE FISHERMEN

Mark's extraordinary expression "*casting-about*, or, *doubting*, in the sea" may be best explicable as a transposition from some other tradition about Peter the Fisherman, such as Matthew has alone preserved in his account of Peter walking on the waters[1].

§ 12. "*Cast the net on the right side of the boat*[2]"

From the preceding section it appears that "cast-about" could be taken by some literally as meaning "casting [a net]," but by others metaphorically as meaning "cast about [in one's mind]." It might also be regarded as a paraphrase of the ambiguous Hebrew phrase "spread the nets," *i.e* (1) spread them to catch fish, or (2) spread them out to dry. Luke in his narrative of the Reminding of Peter describes the fisher men as having given up fishing and as "washing the nets", and this precedes a miraculous draught of fishes not related by Mark or Matthew.

John supplements all these early narratives by one that relates a miraculous draught of fishes with which Peter has much to do And in John, as in Luke, the fishermen are described as having toiled through the night and taken nothing. But there the resemblance ends. Or rather, we may say, the antithesis begins The Johannine miracle is after the Resurrection; the Lucan one occurs almost at the outset of the Gospel. In John, there is but one boat with seven disciples; in Luke, there are two boats with four. The nets, in Luke, begin to be "*torn*"; John says expressly "the net was *not rent*." In Luke, Peter falls on his knees and begs the Lord to depart from him, in John, Peter girds himself with his

---

[1] Ἀμφιβάλλω, in suitable contexts, also means "Cast [a garment] about [one]" See *Notes* 2999 (xvii) *a—o* on "The Re-clothing of Peter," and see Field on Mk xiv 72 ἐπιβαλὼν, interpreted by eminent scholars "having cast [his garment] over [his head]"

[2] Jn xxi 6 εἰς τὰ δεξιὰ μέρη τοῦ πλοίου, *lit* "to the right-hand parts of the boat"

garment and throws himself into the sea in haste to reach his Master.

There follows, in John, a meal on a loaf and a fish, intended apparently as a *viaticum* for the disciples, who are now to go forth and preach the Gospel. The last words of Jesus in the Johannine narrative are those addressed to Peter "Do thou (emph.) follow me." This supplies what is wanting in Luke —*who nowhere describes Jesus as bidding Peter "follow" Him* Also the Johannine context represents Peter as being drawn toward Jesus by affection, not by the miracle of the draught of fishes.

The symbolical character of John's narrative is recognised by early commentators in many details, such as the one hundred and fifty-three fishes[1], the loaf, the fish, the coal-fire, etc. That being the case, we are led to ask what symbolism, if any, is implied in the wording of the Lord's command to cast the net. Why is the "casting" to be "to the right-hand *parts*," instead of the obvious and frequent phrase "on the right-hand[2]"? Westcott says, "The definiteness of the command (contrast Luke v 4) explains the readiness with which it was obeyed" But was it necessary to insert "*parts*" in order to give this "definiteness"? It is indefinite and perplexing. Blass follows Chrysostom in leaving it out. The omission would be defensible if it were defensible to omit from John every perplexing phrase that has (at present) no precedent in Greek. But Chrysostom is not a safe guide in Johannine interpretation. Thayer explains the phrase as meaning "into the parts (*i.e.* spots *sc.* of the lake) on the right side of the

---

[1] See below, p 42, n 1

[2] Jn xxi 6 βάλετε εἰς τὰ δεξιὰ μέρη τοῦ πλοίου τὸ δίκτυον In N T ἐκ δεξιῶν with genit is frequent, but there is no instance of δεξιὰ μέρη in N.T Nor is there in Steph *Thes*, which omits Josephus' curious saying about the Essenes, that they (*Bell.* ii 8. 9) "avoid spitting toward the middle [of their company] or *the right side* (ἢ τὸ δεξιὸν μέρος)."

THE CALLING OF THE FISHERMEN

ship" "Spots of the lake" opens a wide choice for Peter, and does not favour the above-mentioned hypothesis of "definiteness." Yet Thayer's view is in accordance with the indefinite geographical use of "*parts*" in N T., *e g.* "the *parts*" of Galilee, of Tyre and Sidon, of Caesarea, of Libya, etc.[1]

Turning to Luke we find no mention of "right hand" in the precept given by Jesus "Put out into the deep, and let down your nets for a draught[2]" But it happens that the Hebrew or Aramaic for "*draught*" resembles that for "*part*," and the word for "*sea*" resembles that for "*right hand*"; so that one and the same Hebrew tradition, without much change, might branch into the Lucan or the Johannine version[3]. In deciding, therefore, between Luke and John, those who adopt the view that the two Evangelists are giving two versions of one original "Draught of Fishes" will have to be guided largely by the antecedent probability that such an original would contain some mention of "the right side."

§ 13. *"The right side"*

Here, then, arises for consideration Ezekiel's description of the "fishermen[4]" standing by the side of the life-giving "river" that issues from the Sanctuary This might well be in the mind of any subsequent Jewish prophet speaking about "fishers of men"—as also in the minds of the earliest Christians when describing the acts of the apostolic Fishermen This "river" they would regard as the Holy Spirit, or the Spirit of Jesus, or the Spirit of the Gospel, which, going forth from the Lord, through His disciples, to the world, sweetens all its stagnant or poisoned

---

[1] Mt. 11. 22, xv 21, xvi. 13, etc.

[2] Lk v 4

[3] Heb צד = "side," μέρος, צוד = "catch" Heb. ים = "sea" ימין = "right hand" In Ps cvii 3, Gesen. suggests reading "the south (*lit.* the right hand)" instead of "sea." In Ps. lxxxix 12 "the south (*lit* the right hand)," LXX has "sea"

[4] Ezek. xlvii 10.

THE CALLING OF THE FISHERMEN

streams and gives life to the "fishes" in them. But, by another metaphor—a forced one, but necessitated by Christian thought—it might also be called the Net of the Gospel which draws the "fishes" out of the water into the air, which they are enabled to breathe. Ezekiel's "river" is seldom referred to by the Ante-Nicene Fathers, but Barnabas speaks of it as that river by which grows the Tree of the Cross, thus: "And there was a river drawing-on *from the right*, and there went up from it trees of beauty, and whoso eateth from these shall live for ever[1]" Ezekiel twice describes the river as issuing "*from the right side*" of the Temple[2]. When the metaphor of the Net was substituted for that of the River it would be natural that the auspicious "right-hand," in some form, should be retained.

In the Ezra-Apocalypse, when Ezra asks for a revelation, the Angel says to him "*Stand to the right*"—or perhaps, "*turn thyself toward the right side* and look"—"and I will explain the meaning of a similitude unto thee"; later on, Ezra says "I lifted up my eyes, and saw a woman *upon the right*[3]." In both cases, there may have been a thought of the Psalmist's saying "The Lord is *on my right hand*[4]" This may perhaps have been in the mind of the Essenes, when they forbade "spitting *to the right*[5]." In Mark and Luke an angelic appearance announcing good tidings is described as being "*on the right*[6]."

This however is not quite analogous to the Johannine

---

[1] Barn § 11

[2] Ezek xlvii 1—2   "Side," *lit* "shoulder," Gesen 509

[3] See the Ezra-Apocalypse (ed Box) iv 47 (with Editor's note) and ix. 38

[4] Ps xvi 8   See Rashi   The Targum avoids "right hand" by a paraphrase "Quiescit majestas eius super me." Some paraphrased "the Lord," as meaning "the Law of the Lord."

[5] See p 36, n 2

[6] Mk xvi 5 "on the right," Lk i. 11 "on the right of the altar." (R V in both adds "side," but it is not in the Gk.)

THE CALLING OF THE FISHERMEN

"*casting to the right*" Nor does it explain the addition of "parts," as to which one ancient commentator says that—whereas Moses and the Prophets, "occupying the left-hand position," tried in vain to catch the single nation of Israel—the apostolic net "received as its lot *the right-hand portion*[1]." Apparently he means, by "the right-hand portion," the full result of the Law and the Spirit—that is, Jews and Gentiles together, whom he regarded as being placed "on the right hand" of God. But something is still wanting to explain the plural "*parts*," which, as has been noted above, generally has a geographical meaning in N.T., so that Luke, for example, describes Paul as passing through "the upper *parts*" and coming to Ephesus in the course of his missionary work[2].

If "the right-hand parts," in Hebrew, were used with a geographical meaning in poetry, it would mean "*the south*[3]." Ezekiel describes Samaria as dwelling on "the left hand," *i e* the north, of Judaea; and Rashi, both there and elsewhere, says that Judaea is regarded as being relatively "*on the right hand*[4]" In the Acts, Philip, fresh from evangelizing Samaria, hears an angel saying "Arise, *and go toward the south*." On the road to Gaza he converts the officer of Candace queen of Ethiopia, after which he is "caught away" by the Spirit[5]. This reads like a poetic fulfilment of the prediction that "Ethiopia shall haste to stretch out her hands unto God[6]" The poetic nature of the narrative does not negative the possibility that Philip may thus have passed from Samaria

---

[1] Cramer, on Jn xxi 6 foll

[2] Acts xix 1 τὰ ἀνωτερικὰ μέρη, A V "the upper *coasts*," R V "the upper *country*"

[3] See Gesen 412 a

[4] Ezek xvi 46, iv 6 (Rashi)

[5] Acts viii 26—38.

[6] Ps lxviii 31, quoted by an ancient commentator on Acts viii 27—8 (Cramer) *Hor Heb* (on Acts) quotes Zeph iii 10 See *From Letter* 1015 d, shewing that Luke's narrative seems to borrow expressions from Zephaniah

THE CALLING OF THE FISHERMEN

"*toward the south*" to preach the Gospel in obedience to the Spirit. And (according to the Acts) Peter does the same thing at a little interval. Following on Peter's action in Samaria, his next reported action—after he has "passed through all [parts]"—is toward the South at Lydda, and then in Joppa, where he sees that eventful vision which leads him to receive into the Church Cornelius the Gentile centurion[1]. Meantime the Gospel is being spread by other agencies in the North, partly as a sequel of the conversion of Paul near Damascus, and partly by unnamed missionaries in Antioch, who "spake to the Greeks also," *i.e.* to the uncircumcised, "preaching the Lord Jesus[2]" Apparently this was done in Antioch without definite sanction from Jerusalem, which was not obtained till after Peter in Joppa had been bidden by a vision from heaven not to call "common" what "God hath cleansed."

Peter, even after his enlightenment, seems not to have felt at home in the North—at least on one occasion. "When Cephas came to Antioch," says Paul to the Galatians, "I resisted him to the face." The context, if taken literally and exactly, would seem almost to limit James and Peter and John to the South, or rather to the Jews. The three Apostles agreed—so says the Epistle—"that we should go unto the Gentiles and they unto the circumcision[3]." It would be unreasonable to take expressions of this kind (shewn by the context to be fervid and hyperbolical) as being literally intended in the fullest sense—as though, for example, Peter ought not to have preached to the Gentile Cornelius. Yet in the early days of the Church such Pauline words might have

---

[1] Acts ix 32 "As Peter went throughout all [parts] he came down also to the saints that dwelt at Lydda." Peter's last recorded previous action is the (*ib* viii 14—25) bestowal of the Spirit on those whom Philip had converted in Samaria. It must be admitted, however, that the actual admission of Cornelius takes place in Caesarea (to the North of Joppa).

[2] Acts xi 20.   [3] Gal ii 9—11

THE CALLING OF THE FISHERMEN

been taken at least so far literally as to cause jealousy and disunion; and those evangelists who perceived this danger might shape their narratives of the Calling and Sending of the Fishers of men, the Apostles, so as to shew, symbolically, that they were really united from the first.

Ephrem Syrus interprets Luke's "two vessels" as meaning the vessel of the Circumcision and the vessel of the Gentiles. Luke calls those who were on board the two boats, first "sharers [in the work]¹," and then "partners"—words frequently used literally in contemporary papyri, but also capable of application to participation in the heavenly Calling, or in the preaching of the Gospel². Perhaps Luke had in view some allusion to the Gentiles in mentioning the second vessel, and desired to shew that when the Net of the Gospel was being filled to bursting,

---

¹ "Sharer," μέτοχος, occurs in Berlin Urkunde *passim*, e g 704, 716, 755, 761 etc, but note especially 1123 4 (time of Augustus) τοὺς τρεῖς μετόχους καὶ κοινωνοὺς καὶ κυρίους, ι e "sharers and partners" In LXX it represents Heb *"chaberim"* (i e "fellows," "participators," or "neighbours") In N T it occurs only in Heb 1. 9 (quoting Ps xlv 7 "thy fellows (*chaberim*)"), iii 1 *"partakers* of a heavenly calling," iii 14 *"partakers* of Christ," vi 4 *"partakers* of the Holy Spirit," xii 8 "chastisement of which all have been *partakers*" It is probable that Luke uses the word with some allusion to its Christian sense of "partakers of a heavenly calling"—a sense appropriate to the Calling of the Fishermen

² Lk v 7—10 "They beckoned to the (lit) *sharers* [in the work] (μετόχοις)..the sons of Zebedee who were *partners* (κοινωνοί) with Simon (τῷ Σίμωνι)" Comp Gal ii 9 "they gave to me and Barnabas right hands of *partnership* (κοινωνίας) that we should go unto the Gentiles, and they unto the circumcision" Origen's comment on Lk v 7—10 is lost But on Mt xxi 1 (*Comm Matth* xvi 17) he suggests that the "two disciples" are Peter and Paul "giving one another right hands of partnership"
Ephrem (on Luke, p 59) says "The two boats are the circumcision and the uncircumcision And, whereas they 'beckoned to their companions,' this means the mystery of the Seventy-two [Lk x. 1 (SS)] Disciples, because the Apostles did not suffice for the fishing and the harvesting" This seems to combine two interpretations of the second boat, (1) the Church of the Gentiles, (2) the Seventy-two as the Missionaries to the Gentiles

THE CALLING OF THE FISHERMEN

the Fishermen still acted together as "partners." But a narrative implying duality was liable to the danger of suggesting thoughts derogatory from the unity of the Church.

In the Fourth Gospel there is but one boat. Peter is bidden—but not Peter alone ("cast *ye*")—to cast the net "to the right hand parts of the boat." If this originally contained an allusion to Peter's preaching in the South, it might be adopted by John in a spiritual sense, as indicating work to the glory of the Lord who was always on his "right hand," so that in casting to the right, Peter was casting ultimately and indirectly to the four quarters of the world, yet always to God's glory. That the phrase had *some* mystical significance (beyond that of mere auspiciousness or good luck) is indicated by a number of similar details—non-pertinent if not mystical—such as the exact number of the fish taken by the fishermen[1].

In concluding this comparison of the Lucan and the Johannine accounts of the miraculous Draught of Fishes, and of what followed by the side of the lake, we should note that it is in accordance with Hebrew and Jewish thought that visions of deliverance should be seen, and prayers for deliverance uttered, "by the side of" the waters of some river or sea. Later on, we shall find Matthew quoting Isaiah in full about "the way of the sea." It is by the side of a great river that both Ezekiel

---

[1] St Augustine's mystical view of (Jn xxi 11) "153" accords with a mystical view of Gen vi 3 (LXX) "and the days of men shall be 120 years," taken by Clem Alex 782, "the number is from 1 to 15, *by addition* (κατὰ σύνθεσιν)." That is, 120 = 1 + 2 + 3 .. + 15 Similarly 153 = 1 + 2 + 3.. + 17 Now "17" represents the "ten" Commandments and the "seven" Spirits of God See *Joh Gr* **2283** *c* But it should have been added there that in Plato "*a perfect number*" meant one that is the *sum of its factors* "Six" would be a perfect number in both ways, since it = 1 + 2 + 3 and also 1 × 2 × 3. That there were variations in the way of reckoning the "perfection" of a number is indicated by Philo ii 183 on the perfection of the *Decad*, of which Clem Alex. 782 says "The Decad is agreed to be *all-perfect* (παντέλειος)" (see context)

THE CALLING OF THE FISHERMEN

and Daniel receive their visions[1]. When Ezra proclaims a fast, he adds that it was "at the river Ahavah[2]." Josephus tells us that "by the side of the sea" Jews in Halicarnassus offered up prayers—so frequently (it would seem) that it might be called a "custom of the nation[3]."

Although therefore Luke is (doubtless) recording what he believed to be the fact, and we have no reason to disbelieve the fact, when he writes about Peter as lodging "with one Simon a tanner whose house is *by the sea*[4]," yet that ought not to prevent us from supposing that Luke probably recognised in the place (*"by the sea"*) a symbolical appropriateness to the great vision of that all-enclosing "sheet" which was to descend from heaven, as a type of the all-enclosing Net of the Gospel, to be revealed to the Fisherman, Peter[5]. So, too, as regards the Draught of Fishes There may be at the bottom of Luke's narrative some literal and actual fact that may have occurred at the outset of the Gospel, which Luke may have related as being a Reminding of Peter and as having a literal as well as a symbolical meaning But the evidence, so far as it goes, points to the conclusion that Luke had no such basis. He seems to have interpreted an early version of the Calling of Peter in such a manner that it became a Reminding of Peter, and then to have blended with it a Returning of Peter.

The real and spiritual Returning of Peter is described by John as occurring after Christ's resurrection, first, in the form

---

[1] Ezek 1. 1, Dan x 4   [2] Ezr viii 21.
[3] Joseph *Ant* xiv. 10 23 καὶ τὰς προσευχὰς ποιεῖσθαι πρὸς τῇ θαλάσσῃ κατὰ τὸ πάτριον ἔθος (in a decree of the Halicarnassians). We may perhaps compare Ps cxxxvii. 1 "By the rivers of Babylon, there we sat down, yea, we wept, when we remembered Zion " See also *Notes* 2961.
[4] Acts x 6 An angel says this to Cornelius.
[5] We may also note Acts xvi 13 "*by the side of a river*, where we supposed that there was a place of prayer," no doubt, recording a fact, but still a symbolical fact, the beginning of the Gospel in Europe ("we sat down and spake") in this "place of prayer"

43 (Mark i. 16—20)

THE CALLING OF THE FISHERMEN

of a symbolical miracle, secondly, in the form of a Dialogue between Jesus and Peter—part of which seems to be in a vision—ending with the words "Follow thou me" Even those who cannot feel sure where the fact ends and the vision or symbolism begins, may feel sure that there was such a real and spiritual Return, and that a real and spiritual "following" was the result—a result that has deeply affected the whole of the civilised world.

At this point, without anticipating what cannot be fully discussed till we come to the subject of Christ's resurrection, a word or two on the difference between Luke's and John's attitude towards it may be of use as illustrating the difference between their Gospels as a whole.

Luke writes with a view to scientific or historical proof First, he mentions the evidence of women concerning "a vision of angels" as seeming to all the disciples "idle talk[1]" Then, he mentions an appeal from "all the scriptures," as being addressed to two disciples by their at first unrecognised Master, who presently vanishes[2]. Then, appearing to the Eleven, Jesus appeals to their touch and sight[3]. Lastly, He asks for something to eat, and "did eat before them[4]" As a kind of Appendix, comes the statement that He "opened their mind that they should understand the scriptures," followed by a promise of power "from on high[5]."

John implies that the first revelation of Christ's resurrection was received by Mary through tears and affection, receiving no "proof" except that He called her by name; and a second, by the disciples, after He had said to them "Peace be unto you" and shewn them His hands and His side He also breathed upon them and said "Receive ye the Holy Spirit[6]." Thomas, the affectionate pessimist—who had in former days said "Let us

---

[1] Lk. xxiv. 11, comp. *ib.* 23. [2] *Ib.* 27—31.
[3] *Ib.* 39 "Handle me, and see"
[4] *Ib.* 42—3. [5] *Ib.* 45—9 [6] Jn xx. 16—22

THE CALLING OF THE FISHERMEN

also go that we may die with him[1]," and who was absent from this gathering—refuses to trust the mere "seeing" of the hands and the side and demands to feel them. Accordingly the Saviour appears and bids him plunge himself into His wounds and then believe in His love as a living power[2]. Last of all, Peter, the utterer of the three denials, being now restored to favour and strengthened by the food given him by the Lord, is questioned as to whether he still professes to excel his fellow-disciples in affection for the Master, and thrice professes love, but love without excelling. Placed thus last in order, he is restored to the first place in precedence by receiving a special commission "Feed my sheep" and the precept "Follow thou me[3]."

The difference between Luke and John may be illustrated by a passage in Ignatius describing the conversion of the disciples through the Resurrection "They touched Him and believed, being mingled with His flesh and His blood[4]" The Latin Version gives *"constrained,"* instead of *"mingled."* Similarly Luke regards the disciples as *"constrained"* by external evidence. John regards them as *"mingled"* with the Lord Jesus by internal emotion. Origen says "The Lord 'knew them that were His own' *by being thoroughly blended* with them, and by giving them a share in His divine nature[5]" The *"blending"* might be all the more cogent when it came as a revulsion to Peter the denier, Thomas the pessimist and doubter, and, most of all, to Paul the persecutor.

Paul's first Corinthian Epistle shews that, apart from manifestations to women, the post-resurrectional appearances

---

[1] Jn xi 16   [2] Jn xx 27   [3] Jn xxi 15—22
[4] See Lightfoot on Ign *Smyrn* §3 κραθέντες, but Lat "convicti" pointing to κρατηθέντες, and Westcott on Heb iv 2 (W. H text) συνκεκερασμένους
[5] Origen *Comm Joann* xix 1, Lomm ii 144 "knew (ἔγνω)," *i e.* "took cognizance of" (quoting 2 Tim ii 19), "thoroughly-blended (ἀνακραθείς)," see *Light* **3688** *d*

THE CALLING OF THE FISHERMEN

of Jesus were more numerous than those recorded in our Gospels[1]. Among these, and among the circumstances proving their reality, the test of "eating" might very well suggest itself, in view of Jewish traditions about the Three Visitors to Abraham, about whom the Scripture says "They did eat," but Philo, the Talmud, and the Jerusalem Targum, say, in effect, "They did not eat, but they made as though they ate[2]" But this explanation of Luke's adoption of such a tradition makes it less credible, not more credible, as a fact John's accounts are such as Shakespeare might have invented Those who cannot believe that John was a Shakespeare will prefer to believe that he recorded fact—fact mingled with vision and related with a view to symbolism, but still, like Christ's appearance to Paul in the Acts, substantially fact.

§ 14. "*For they were fishers*[3]"

Mark, with whom Matthew agrees, implies that it was a matter of course that Jesus saw Simon and Andrew fishing, "for they were fishers." It was their business. They were bound to be doing it Luke cannot say this. For, if he consistently adhered to the view that his business was to describe not a Calling of Simon, but a Reminding, then Simon was bound to be doing, not this, but something else, which he had been called by Jesus to do but had not yet done. But Luke does not make any clear distinction between what Peter was doing and what he ought to have been doing

Luke speaks of "two boats"; and then of "one of them" as belonging to Simon—that Simon whose mother-in-law Jesus (according to Luke, *but not Mark and Matthew*[4]) had already healed; and then of "the fishermen" as "gone out

---

[1] *E g* 1 Cor xv 7 "to James"
[2] Gen xviii 8, on which see Jer Targ , Philo *Lat ad loc* and ii 17—18, *Bab Metz* 86 b and *Exod r* on Exod xxxiv 28, Wu p 326
[3] Mk i 16, Mt iv 18   [4] See p 65

THE CALLING OF THE FISHERMEN

of them" and "washing their nets"; and lastly of Peter as avowing that he has "toiled all night and taken nothing." All this amounts to an acknowledgement, or assumption, that Peter still used, as a fisherman, the boat that belonged to him. It might seem then that Luke could have said, with Mark, "for they were fishers." But he does not venture to say this directly. The reason is that he distinguishes the *de facto* from the *de jure* "fisherman." He admits the fact indirectly by speaking of them as "the fishermen." But he will not say that they were reasonably engaged in their labour "for [*the reason that*] they were fishers." For he implies "they ought not to have been any longer fishermen."

John makes the fishing, so to speak, an extemporised affair. Throughout his Gospel he nowhere describes the occupation of any of the Apostles, whether fisherman, or tax-gatherer, or anything else. But in his narrative of the Draught of Fishes, he says that when seven of the disciples "were together," Peter said to them "I am going to fish," and that they replied, "We also come with thee." One of the seven was Nathanael of Cana, who, if domiciled at Cana, could not have been a fisherman by trade. The lesson taught by John appears to be an allegorical one—that Peter, "fisherman" though he was in name, "fished" without success till Jesus had appeared with the dawn and told him how to cast the net. It is conveyed dramatically. Jesus did not *say* as in Mark-Matthew "I *will make* you fishers...." He *made* them "fishers."

§ 15. "*Come* (lit. *hither*) *after me*[1]"

That Luke omits "*Come after me*" when Jesus says to Simon "henceforth thou shalt catch men," cannot cause surprise, on the hypothesis that he is relating a Reminding and not a Calling. But a verbal point is worth noting about the

---

[1] Mk 1 17, Mt. iv 19 δεῦτε ὀπίσω μου, omitted by Luke in v 10 "thou shalt catch men."

THE CALLING OF THE FISHERMEN

rare exclamatory particle "Hither!" here used for "Come!" It is never used by Luke. In Christ's words it is assigned to Jesus once by John, as uttered in the story of the Draught of Fishes ("*Come*, take-breakfast[1]"). It is also assigned by Mark (alone) to Jesus, in the Introduction to the Feeding of the Five Thousand, "*Come*, [by] yourselves apart into a desert place and rest a little"—where "rest" for the purpose of "eating" seems to be implied by the addition "they had no leisure so much as to eat[2]." Matthew represents Jesus as using the particle in His invitation to the "weary" to come unto Him, and also in parables of invitation[3]. And it occurs in his version of what the angels say to the women at Christ's resurrection[4].

Considerations of style may have weighed somewhat with Luke in inducing him to refrain from using this exclamatory or hortatory "Come[5]." But possibly the thought also repelled

---

[1] Jn xxi. 12 δεῦτε ἀριστήσατε. Its rejection by Luke is noteworthy in the Parable of the Heir of the Vineyard, Mk xii 7, Mt xxi 38, Lk xx. 14, "*Come* (δεῦτε), let us kill him," where Luke alone omits δεῦτε.

[2] Mk vi 31 The parallel Mt -Lk omits all this, but mentions the fact that they went "apart," stated in Mk vi 32

[3] Mt xi 28 "*come* unto me," xxii 4 "*come* to the wedding-feast," xxv 34 "*come*, ye blessed of my Father"

[4] Mt xxviii 6 οὐκ ἔστιν ὧδε .. δεῦτε ἴδετε τὸν τόπον. Mk xvi. 6 omits δεῦτε, having οὐκ ἔστιν ὧδε ἴδε ὁ τόπος

[5] Δεῦτε is Homeric and poetic, non-occurrent in Aristotle, Demosthenes, Aristophanes, and the Lexicon to Plato Epictetus iii 23 6 once uses it in a satirical representation of a philosopher inviting folk to come and hear him lecture, δεῦτε καὶ ἀκούσατέ μου It does not occur in Patr Apostol , nor in the early Apologists, except citations and Justin Mart. *Tryph* § 24 (thrice, in a mixture of quotation with personal exhortation) "*come* with me...*come*, let us walk in the light of the Lord,...*come*, all nations, let us gather ourselves" Δεῦτε was regarded as equiv. to a plural imperative, and would therefore be inappropriate in a saying addressed to Peter alone In the Calling of the Rich Man, Lk. xviii 22 follows Mk x 21, Mt. xix. 21 δεῦρο ἀκολούθει μοι.

THE CALLING OF THE FISHERMEN

him, because it suggested invitation rather than command. Command, not invitation, may have seemed to him to be implied whenever Jesus said to anyone "Follow me."

This distinction is an important one. Invitation, rather than command, may perhaps be suggested in the Calling as related in the Acts of John, where James and John hear a voice from a figure on the shore saying "*I have need of you. Come to me*[1]." "Come *to*" is not the same as "come *after*." It is more important to note that in the single instance where "Hither after me" occurs in LXX it is a phrase of invitation. Elisha says to the Syrians, "This is not the way, neither is this the city. *Hither after me*, and I will bring you to the man whom ye seek[2]." In this offer to be a guide there is no assumption of any superiority except in knowledge of the way

If Jesus meant "*Come after me*" in the sense "Let us go together," the question would arise, "Whither were they to go?" It might be to Jerusalem literally—Jerusalem on earth, where the Lord was to die. But it might be to Jerusalem in heaven, the Kingdom of God. In one passage that contains the words "*come after me*," Luke seems to give them a spiritual significance by an addition of his own ("daily[3]") But later on he adds (again an addition of his own) that Jesus "set his face to go *to Jerusalem*[4]." Close on that come precepts about "following," which sound as if Luke took them literally —though, of course, spiritually, too[5].

---

[1] *Acts of John* § 2 Χρῄζω ὑμῶν· ἔλθατε πρός με.

[2] 2 K vi. 19 R V "follow me," Heb *lit* "come after me (LXX δεῦτε ὀπίσω μου)"

[3] Lk ix 23 "If any man would come after me, let him. .take up his cross *daily* and follow me." See *Son* **3432***a*, **3545** on the addition of "daily" etc

[4] Lk ix 51 Just before this, concerning one of those that were "not following," Jesus says (*ib.* ix 50) "Forbid him not"

[5] Lk ix. 57, 59, 61.

THE CALLING OF THE FISHERMEN

§ 16. *"Following," in John*

Let us attempt to place ourselves in the position of John, if he reviewed the Mark-Matthew traditions about "coming after" and "following," in Christ's words, and noted how they were revised by Luke. He would find that the latter had made two omissions. Luke had omitted the command to Peter *"Come after me."* He had also previously omitted the Baptist's words *"after me,"* referring to the "coming" of his successor[1]. Further, though Luke had suggested to his readers that the "following" of Jesus in some cases referred to a literal "following" on the road to Jerusalem but in others to one that was not literal, he had not clearly explained the nature of the latter.

Besides these Lucan defects, there was in the whole Synoptic tradition a stumbling-block for Greeks in the suggestion that "the mightier one" mentioned by John the Baptist called on men to "follow" Him. Plato had said that one must follow God in accordance with Nature—leading his readers to infer "follow God, not men[2]" Philo had declared his allegiance to this maxim, calling it "a chant of all the best philosophers," and basing it on the Deuteronomic edict "Ye shall *walk after the Lord your God*[3]." Epictetus inveighs

---

[1] Mk i 7, Mt iii 11, Lk iii 16 See *Beginning* p 75

[2] See Plato *Legg* iv 716 A The all-including God "goes round unswervingly and completely *according to nature*, Justice ever *follows Him close* (τῷ δὲ ἀεὶ ξυνέπεται Δίκη) ..and *following close*, clinging to Her, comes the man that is destined to blessedness (ἧς ὁ μὲν εὐδαιμονήσειν μέλλων ἐχόμενος ξυνέπεται)" In theory, ξυνέπομαι might mean "follow along with," as though there were something (possibly Nature) that was "followed" by God as well as by Justice. But in practice, ξυνέπομαι appears rarely or never to mean anything (Steph *Thes*) but "follow close" However, both Philo and Clement of Alexandria use ἕπομαι instead of ξυνέπομαι when apparently alluding to the Platonic passage

[3] Philo i 456, apparently alluding to Plato, and subsequently quoting Deut xiii 4 (which is also quoted for the same purpose by Clem Alex 703), comp Clem Alex 893

THE CALLING OF THE FISHERMEN

against the baseness of *"following the mightier one*[1]*."* In the second century, Marcus Antoninus, and Justin Martyr (followed by Clement of Alexandria) take the same line[2]. It was expedient, therefore, for the sake of educated Gentiles, to go to the bottom of these Synoptic traditions about "following," to detach accident and circumstance from essence, and to shew that, whether accompanied or unaccompanied by any bodily change of place, the act of following Christ, the Word of God, implied following on the Way to God, and that to follow the Son was, in fact, to follow the Father.

When we have once taken in this Johannine survey of the antecedent traditions about "following," some in the early Evangelists but some also in the Greek philosophers, we shall receive light on Johannine doctrine as a whole, and, still more, on many Johannine details that appear at first sight petty, or meaningless, or unnecessary suggestions of mystery. "Following," in John, is always the result of the attracting power of the Word, who is the Life and Light of men. Not being a mechanical act, it cannot be mechanically taught. The soul cannot be drilled into it, but must, somehow, grow into it.

"Following" begins, dramatically and literally, when Andrew and his companion, "having heard from [the lips of][3] John" the witness that he bore to Jesus as the Lamb of God, *"followed* Jesus," and Jesus "turned, and saw them *following."* That was the first rudimentary *"following."* But when He asked them what they sought and invited them to see where He "abode," they then heard (so it is implied) from the lips of the Son Himself that which prepared them for a spiritual

---

[1] See *Son* 3603 *a*, quoting Epict. ii 13 22—3.
[2] Marc Ant. vii 31, Justin Mart. *Tryph.* § 80 οὐ γὰρ ἀνθρώποις... αἰροῦμαι ἀκολουθεῖν ἀλλὰ θεῷ
[3] "Hear *from* [the lips of] (παρὰ)" in Jn i 40, vi 45, vii 51, viii 26, 38, 40, xv 15, implies hearing from some one in whose house one sits as a child before parents, or as a pupil before teachers. The "school" of a teacher was called by Jews his "house" (*Son* 3460 *c*).

51 (Mark i. 16—20) 4—2

"following[1]." At all events, Andrew immediately brought Peter, who, it is implied, became a follower of Jesus. Yet, though this is implied concerning Peter, it is not stated either in the context or later on. Nor does Jesus say to any one of these early disciples "Follow me," except to Philip, whom early tradition regards as being surrounded by spiritual dangers of a special kind from which it was needful that he should depart[2].

John teaches us that "the multitude," which at one time literally "followed" Jesus, was not following Him spiritually[3]. To "follow" Jesus required a spiritual sense of seeing and of hearing. The former requisite is implied when He says "I am the light of the world; he that followeth me shall not walk in the darkness[4]." The latter is implied in the Parable of the Good Shepherd, where it is said that only those really follow Jesus who recognise in His words their Shepherd's voice[5]. Later on, a still higher kind of following is hinted at, not that of sheep following the Shepherd, but that of the Shepherd's helpers following in the footsteps of the Shepherd who lays down His life for the sheep[6].

The rest of the Johannine instances of "following[7]" are almost entirely devoted to Peter. They mix the literal and the spiritual in juxtapositions so strange that, in any other work but the Fourth Gospel, the use of the word might be

---

[1] Jn i 37—9

[2] Jn i 43—4. Philip, according to early tradition, was the disciple mentioned in Mt. viii 21—2, comp Lk. ix. 59—60, as being warned "to leave the dead to bury their dead" (see *Beginning* p 213 or *Son* 3377 a).

[3] Jn vi. 2 ἠκολούθει. This same multitude soon afterwards purposed (*ib* 15) to "snatch him away that they might make him a king" Comp Mk i 36 κατεδίωξεν αὐτὸν Σίμων with the more seemly Lk iv 42 οἱ ὄχλοι ἐπεζήτουν αὐτόν, and see below, p 382

[4] Jn viii 12.   [5] Jn x. 4, 5, 27

[6] Jn xii 25—6.

[7] Jn xiii 36 (twice), 37, xviii 15, xx 6, xxi 19, 22 are all applied to Peter, xxi 20 to the beloved disciple (comp xviii 15); xi 31 merely describes Jews as "following" Mary the sister of Lazarus.

THE CALLING OF THE FISHERMEN

confidently pronounced casual and chaotic. The first of these instances is placed after a precept of Jesus about "loving one another." This "loving one another" Peter passes over. He is absorbed in his Master's destiny: "Lord, whither goest thou?" Jesus replies "Whither I go thou canst not follow me now, but thou shalt follow afterwards." Peter has not yet perceived that "love," love in a new sense—love including something more than even his own present affection for Jesus, love and insight combined so as to resemble the Lord's love towards His disciples and apostles—is necessary for those who are to "follow" the Lord. So he protests that he will "follow" to the death, and that at once, "Why cannot I follow thee even now? I will lay down my life for thee."

The next scene opens with Peter keeping his word and "*following Jesus*[1]," who is now a prisoner, on the way to the City Luke omits "*Jesus*" or "*him*" representing "Jesus." Reasoning like a historian Luke would argue that Peter could not be rightly said to "*follow Jesus*" How could he—Jesus being in the middle, or perhaps at the front, of the column of soldiers and officials, while Peter was not even in the rear of it, but behind it?

Nevertheless John says Peter was "*following Jesus.*" Perhaps, having regard to the context, we ought to recognise a thought of this kind · "Jesus said that Peter could not follow Him at once. Peter replied, by implication, that he could[2]. Here you see Peter keeping his promise and literally 'following Jesus' Was Peter then right, and Jesus wrong? That question will be speedily answered by the sequel" And the sequel does answer it. Peter had "followed" in a sense, but

---

[1] Jn xviii 15 "and Simon Peter *was-following Jesus*" Comp Mk xiv. 54 "and Peter from afar-off *followed him*," Mt. xxvi 58 "But Peter *was-following him* afar-off," Lk xxii 54 "But Peter *was-following afar-off*" (omitting "him" or "Jesus")

[2] Jn xiii 36—7 A direct contradiction ("I *can* follow thee") would have been unseemly. But it is implied.

THE CALLING OF THE FISHERMEN

not as yet in the right sense. The scene closes with the Denial, which makes it seem as though the denier had cut himself off from all hope of ever really "following."

In the last scene of all, by the Sea of Tiberias, where the thought of "following" is worked up to a climax, there is a mysterious contrast between the silent "disciple whom Jesus loved," and who *is not* bidden to follow, and Peter, who speaks a great deal, and who *is* bidden to "follow[1]." Of the silent and beloved disciple it is said that, though he was not bidden, "Peter, turning about, seeth the disciple whom Jesus loved, *following.*" This apparently mystical detail leads us to go back to the first manifestation of the Resurrection, in which Peter and John ran together, but John outran his companion and "came first to the tomb....Simon Peter therefore also cometh, *following* him[2]." Is it a mere accident, this mention—unique in the four Gospels—of one disciple "*following*" another? It is of course intended literally[3]. But is it not also allegorical? At all events this "outrunning" of the silent disciple at the tomb, where he is the first to arrive, though Peter is the first to enter, prepares us for the initiative of the former at Tiberias, where John is the first to say "It is the Lord[4]," though Peter is the first to go to Him.

The same double meaning is apparent in the climax of the Dialogue on "following," which is also the climax of the Gospel and the last of the Johannine utterances of Christ. The Dialogue begins with a mention of "loving"—love, taken in that narrow sense in which Peter had taken it, a devotion, a

---

[1] Jn xxi 19, 20, 22   [2] Jn xx 4—6

[3] Comp Lk xxiv 12 (R V txt) "But Peter arose and ran unto the tomb . ," placed in double brackets by W H See *Notes* **2999** (xvii) *g—h,* for parallelisms to "Peter" which might explain variations of this tradition. The existence of it in Luke, even though not in all the texts of Luke, indicates that the corresponding tradition in the Fourth Gospel was not invented by John But he may have selected a form of it adapted to his purpose

[4] Jn xxi 7

THE CALLING OF THE FISHERMEN

zealous and almost jealous devotion to Christ's person, but without sufficient insight, a devotion to the Shepherd apart from the sheep[1]. Jesus proceeds to ask, in effect, for a different kind of love, which may be called two kinds of love combined, love towards Himself as the human Jesus, but love also towards Himself as the Man at once human and divine, who embraced all mankind in His love, and whom Peter could not duly love unless he, too, attempted to love and embrace mankind in the same way. Jesus was the Shepherd of the spiritual Israel, and the proof that Peter loved the Shepherd was to be that he "shepherded" the Shepherd's sheep

When we have taken in this lesson, there is given, as the last lesson of all, the revelation that this "shepherding," this imitation of the Shepherd, is a "following" of the Shepherd in the Shepherd's Way And the Way of the Shepherd is also the Way of the Cross "This he spake, signifying by *what manner of death he should glorify God*. And when he had spoken this, he saith unto him, *Follow me*" Peter, apparently taking this literally, perhaps in a vision, and proceeding to follow Jesus, turns and sees John also "*following*," and asks "What shall this man do?" The question asked by Peter is not answered except with an "if," which leaves the destiny of "this man" unsettled. But the command to Peter is repeated with emphasis "Follow thou (emph) me" These are (in the Fourth Gospel) Christ's last words on earth—a command to Peter to follow. But we are left to feel that the other disciple, too, the silent one, though he has not received the same command, is also "following," and following on the same Way, though in a different manner

Stated barely, the facts seem to put Luke very much in the wrong. "Why," it may be asked, "does Luke rely—if indeed

---

[1] Jn xxi 15 "lovest thou me *more than these* (i e *than these love me*)?" There is probably an allusion to the implied claim of superiority in Peter's words (Mk xiv 29, Mt xxvi 33) "*though all should stumble...*" omitted in Lk xxii 33

THE CALLING OF THE FISHERMEN

he does rely—on the two earlier Evangelists to describe the Calling of Peter, and reserve for himself (apparently as a kind of substitute) a Reminding of Peter? Was it not possible for him to insert both? He has imitated Mark and Matthew in describing the healing of Simon's mother-in-law. Why did he not also imitate them in describing what seems a much more important event, the first call of Simon to follow the Lord?' The facts appear to constitute a striking instance of Johannine intervention. Mark and Matthew say that Jesus said to Peter, while fishing, *Come after me.* Luke nowhere relates this—even though he relates a story about Peter fishing. John relates it—after a story about Peter fishing—as being both said and repeated by Jesus with emphasis.

But we must note that John does not mention the command "follow me" until he has prepared the way for it by his description of the disciples as feeding on the Fish and the Bread—the *viaticum* for the Apostolic Mission—and then by Christ's implied definition of the mission of an Apostle, namely to "feed the sheep." What if both Luke and John perceived that the Mark-Matthew words—placed where they are and expressed as they are—were liable to be misunderstood? What if both Luke and John attempted to prevent misunderstanding, though in different ways?

There is always a danger that the historian, like the dramatist, treating a mass of events as a whole, may adapt the first chapter to the last chapter, without intention to deceive. Much greater would be the danger for a writer like Mark, no historian, but half summarist, half note-collector, many of whose notes would be derived from poetic traditions. If Christian Tradition declared that the Lord Jesus "called H earliest disciples from catching fish to the task of catching men," that would be true But it would by no means follow that this definite "calling" happened at the outset of Christ's public life, or when He first drew disciples around Him Perhaps that definite calling, bidding them cast the net out to

THE CALLING OF THE FISHERMEN

the four corners of the world, did not come till later on, perhaps not till after the Resurrection.

§ 17. *"And I will make you* to-become *fishers of men"*

Part of the subject of this section will be the phrase "fishers of men" But another part, and by far the more important, will be an attempt to answer an apparently quite unimportant question: "Why has Mark—contrary to Greek as well as Hebrew idiom—inserted in his text *'to-become,'* rejected by Matthew, and also by the Syriac versions of Mark itself and by Delitzsch's Hebrew version[1]?"

"Fish," as a verb, occurs only once in Hebrew. It is in Jeremiah, describing the Israelites as destroyed or enslaved by their enemies, who are, in effect, called "fishers and hunters of men[2]." Syriac and Aramaic have no separate verb for "fish" corresponding to the Hebrew one, and the Syriac of Jeremiah renders both "fish" and "hunt" by "catch[3]" Consequently, in Aramaic, "fishers of men" would be *"catchers* of men," where "catchers" would include "hunters" as well as "fishers." The expression takes us back to the legends about Nimrod, described in Genesis as "a mighty-man of *hunting* before the Lord[4]." On that text, Origen says "'Hunt' means evil in the present [passage]," and he asks his readers

---

[1] Mk 1 17 καὶ ποιήσω ὑμᾶς γενέσθαι ἁλιεῖς ἀνθρώπων, Mt iv 19 the same, omitting γενέσθαι

[2] Jerem xvi 16 "...many *fishers*...and they shall *fish* them .. many *hunters* and they shall *hunt* them" The Targ has rendered *"fishers"* and *"fish"* by "killers" and "kill" Rash explains that some are like fish taken out of their element and killed, others (the remnant) are hunted and taken alive The Syr. translates both verbs by *"catch"* (the Heb צוד, Gesen 844 b, which occurs for the first time as a noun ציד in Gen x 9 (*bis*) "a mighty-man of *hunting"*)

[3] Walton renders the Syriac, first by "fishers" and "fish" and then by "hunters" and "hunt," but the exact translation would be "catchers" and "catch" repeated twice

[4] Gen x 9 (*bis*).

THE CALLING OF THE FISHERMEN

to "consider whether it does not mean evil elsewhere"—apparently referring to the only other instance of the correct use of the Greek word, where it is applied to Esau as distinct from Jacob[1]. In Habakkuk, the King of Babylon is virtually described as a fisher of men for evil. "he taketh up all of them with the angle, he catcheth them in his net and gathereth them in his drag[2]" One of the Jerusalem Targums describes Nimrod as "a mighty rebel before the Lord," besides being "mighty in hunting," and the other calls him "mighty in hunting [and] in sin before the Lord, because he was a *hunter* of the sons of men." Another passage, quoted in both Talmuds and in the Midrash, from Proverbs, describes the adulteress as "*hunting* the precious soul[3]"

These passages in O.T., together with several in N.T. that imply the metaphor of Satan hunting for the souls of men, force on us the conclusion that if Jesus really said to His disciples "I will make you become fishers of men," He said something that would be very startling indeed to His hearers[4].

---

[1] Origen on Gen. x. 9 κυνηγός. Comp Gen xxv 27 "Esau was a skilful hunter (κυνηγεῖν)." Origen says Ὁ κυνηγὸς οὐκ ἐπὶ δικαίων κεῖται νῦν καὶ τήρει μήποτε οὐδὲ ἄλλοτε I have rendered νῦν "in the present [passage]" But the meaning is obscure In 1 Chr 1 10 (LXX) κυνηγός, Heb does not insert "hunter"

[2] Hab 1 14—15 So Rashi *ad loc* "Before [i e in the view of] that evil one [Nebuchadnezzar], men are common as the fishes of the sea"

[3] Prov vi 26.

[4] It is remarkable that Philo's Greek text 1 272 quotes (Gen x 8) "began to be a giant on the earth" without here mentioning (Gen x 9) "hunting" Also his Latin text (*Quaest Gen ad loc* "non frustra se habet illud (Gen. x. 9) 'erat gigas contra deum'") omits "hunting" in quotation, though it adds, in comment, "ars eius venatoria" Josephus (*Ant* 1 4 2 τολμηρὸς δὲ καὶ κατὰ χεῖρα γενναῖος) also omits "hunting" So does Onkelos (who renders "hunter" by "powerful") Perhaps some first-century writers, and especially those writing for Greeks, dropped the "hunting" as being obscure to Greek readers To Jews, however, who at an early period (*Gen r* and Jer Targ on Gen xi 27—8) regarded Nimrod as the

THE CALLING OF THE FISHERMEN

On the surface, it would mean, "I will make you like Satan, or like Nimrod, or like the adulteress, secret ensnarers, or open hunters and devourers, of the souls of the sons of men." It can only be explained, if genuine, as a paradoxical use of the metaphor in a good sense, for which no precedent or authority has hitherto been alleged from Hebrew or from Jewish literature[1]

This conclusion leads us to examine every word in the Marcan context and in its parallels in case they may reveal some underlying intention to soften the paradox. How it might be softened we see from the promise to Peter in the quasi-parallel Luke. It is, literally, in Greek, "Men shalt thou be *catching-alive*[2]." But in Syriac it is "men shalt thou be catching [*un*]*to life.*" This alone should suffice to make us ask whether "*to become*" might not be confused with "*to life,*" so that Mark's "fishers of men will I make you *to become*" might have been originally "catchers of men will I make you *to life*" We shall shew that (1) the Marcan insertion of "*to become*" is against Greek as well as Hebrew idiom, that (2) "*to become*" in Hebrew closely resembles "*to life,*" and "becoming" and "living" have been confused in a prominent passage of the LXX. Then it will be reasonable to infer not only that Matthew was justified in omitting "*to become*" as wrong, but also that Luke was justified in substituting what was right, namely, some words implying that the "catching" was, in effect, "life-giving"

---

idolatrous persecutor of Abraham (whom he cast into a furnace) "hunter" would be by no means obscure

[1] On Mk 1 17, Swete refers to no O T. instance except the above-quoted Prov vi 26, Jerem xvi 16 On Mt iv 19, *Hor. Heb* refers only to a saying of Maimonides about "the fishers of the Law" Schottgen is silent, while Wetstein draws all his instances of the word used in a good sense (to which add Epict iii 6. 9) from Greek literature, which uses the metaphor in a good as well as in a bad sense

[2] Lk v 10.

THE CALLING OF THE FISHERMEN

(1) The Hebrew "to become" (with the preposition denoting the infinitive) is frequent in O.T. But in all the instances of it (more than fifty) in the Historical Books, it is very rarely rendered by the Greek "to become[1]." It is never used after "*make*" applied to persons in such phrases as "I will make thee a great people[2]," etc. In such phrases, the Hebrew is "I will make (lit. *appoint* or *give*) thee to [i.e *so that thou mayest become*] a great people." Sometimes "*to*" is omitted, but the Heb. "*to become*" is never inserted. Also in Greek, from Homer downwards, we may speak of Circe as "making" men apes, wolves, etc , or of "making" a person an "example," a "friend," an "enemy," a "partner," but "*to become*" is not alleged in the Thesaurus as being ever inserted. Prof. Swete refers to Winer-Moulton for one instance of it, but Teubner gives a different reading. Even if the word were genuine, that instance would not be a parallel one[3].

(2) The Hebrew "*to life*" is found in Daniel and Proverbs meaning "to life eternal" or "to the life of righteousness," and it is represented in Syriac by the same phrase as that in the

---

[1] See Mandelkern p 315, and *Oxf. Conc* p. 257 foll.

[2] Γενέσθαι occurs about five times in the Historical Books as a rendering of the Heb "to become," *e g* Exod xxiii. 1 "put not thy hand with the wicked [so as] *to become* an unrighteous witness " The Heb frequently means "[so as] to become," but not after "make "

[3] See Mk i 17 (ed Swete) "Mt. omits γενέσθαι (להיות), see WM pp. 757, 760." WM pp 757, 760 quotes only Demosth *Epist* iii 13 (1477) on "education (παιδεία)," thus, ἡ καὶ τοὺς ἀναισθήτους ἀνεκτοὺς ποιεῖν δοκεῖ γίνεσθαι This, if it were correct, would probably emphasize γίνεσθαι, "seems to make them *become* [*that which they are not by nature, namely*] tolerable " But Teubner has δύνασθαι, "seems to *have the power of* making them tolerable " WM. does not render γίνεσθαι in Demosthenes or γενέσθαι in Mark, and illustrates only by Acts iii 3 λαβεῖν, Virg *Æn* 5 262 "donat habere," and Exod xxiii 15 φυλάξασθε ποιεῖν (AF om ποιεῖν), an insertion imitating Deut. v 1 etc (see Gesen 1037 *a*). It should be added that Delitzsch's rendering of Mk i 17 does not contain "to become (להיות) "

THE CALLING OF THE FISHERMEN

Syriac of Luke "thou shalt be catching men [un]to life[1]" The words *"become"* and *"live"* are very similar in Hebrew, and the latter is so much rarer than the former that *"he lived"*—meaning *"he was made to live,* or *restored to life"*—might easily be taken as meaning *"it became"* Then the context would be adapted *"And he revived,"* in the story of the revivification of the widow's child by Elijah, has been rendered by the LXX *"and it became,"* and then *"thus"* has been added[2].

We conclude that the Marcan *"to-become"* is an error for *"unto life,"* which was either part of the actual utterance of Jesus, or was added in the earliest traditions to the verb *"fish"* (i.e. "catch") in order to make the meaning clear Then the question arises, "What connection is there, if any, between the Marcan saying to Peter in the Calling and the Lucan saying to Peter in the Reminding?" This will now be considered.

§ 18. *"Fear not, from henceforth thou shalt catch men*[3]*"*

We have seen above that, in Jeremiah, "fishers" of men was interpreted by the Targum and by Rashi as *"killers"* or *"catchers unto death,"* and "hunters" of men by Rashi as *"catchers" unto life in captivity,* where the Syriac had but one word "catchers" to signify "fishers" and "hunters" It was also shewn that the Marcan *"become* fishers" pointed to an original "fishers *unto life"* But "fish unto life," according to Rashi and the Targum, would seem an absurdity. "The fishes are drawn out of their element and killed; you must say *'hunt unto life'*"—that seems to be Rashi's view A writer like Luke, not without poetic feeling but anxious to distinguish

---

[1] Dan xii 2 "awake *to the life* of eternity," Prov. x 16, xi. 19 "[tendeth] *to life"*

[2] 1 Kings xvii 22 The LXX has contextual omissions and differences, but the *Oxf Conc* takes it, without query, as rendering חיה *"live"* as if it were היה *"become."* Aq has καὶ ἔζησεν, but LXX καὶ ἐγένετο οὕτως

[3] Lk v 10 ἀπὸ τοῦ νῦν ἀνθρώπους ἔσῃ ζωγρῶν. R.V. txt "catch," but marg. "Gr. *take alive"*

THE CALLING OF THE FISHERMEN

poetry from history, adopting this view about "fishing," might naturally substitute for it a Greek word that meant "capture-alive." In classical Greek it meant "spare the life of," "hold to ransom," or "take and enslave." In the LXX, it is not used for "hold to ransom," but means only "spare the lives of"—implying usually (but not always) "keep as slaves"—those taken in war, etc.[1]

In the LXX instances, the Hebrew original is always a causative form of the verb "live." This, besides meaning "spare," "*let-live*," can also mean, and does more naturally mean in Hebrew—"cause-to-live[2]." Perhaps some intention to suggest this Hebraic meaning ("cause to live") may have influenced Luke here. But if so, he cannot be acquitted of obscurity and artificial abstruseness. For the Greek word itself never has this meaning except in a single passage of Homer not imitated in Greek literature[3]. In the only other N T passage where the word occurs, the A.V. and the R.V. are divided as to whether the *"taking captive"* is the act of the devil or of the Lord's servant[4]. Probably it is the act of the Lord Himself. Other Pauline metaphors imply that the Lord "overtakes" us, or "takes us captive," or "leads us in triumph as captives," being rescued by Him from Satan[5], and this

---

[1] Eight times, including 2 Chr xxv. 12 "they carried-away alive," where ἐζώγρησαν represents two Hebrew words, "carry-away" and "alive."

[2] Gesen 311. It is the Pi or Hiph. of חיה.

[3] See Steph. *Thes.* quoting only Aretaeus as imitating *Iliad* v 698 περὶ δὲ πνοιὴ Βορέαο Ζώγρει .. where it is said to be derived from ζωή and ἀγείρω and to mean "restore to life."

[4] 2 Tim ii 26 A V ". out of the snare of the devil, who are *taken captive* (lit *taken alive*) by him. .," R V txt "out of the snare of the devil, having been *taken captive* (lit *taken alive*) by the Lord's servant .." (but see R V marg).

[5] Comp 2 Cor ii 14 θριαμβεύοντι ἡμᾶς, and Phil iii 12 "if perchance I might *catch* (or, *overtake*) (καταλάβω) that for which I was *caught* by Christ." Comp Lk v 10 (in *Diatess* Ed Hogg) "and thus also were James and John. .*overtaken*," and Lk. v 9 (SS) lit "For amazement *took* him .at that catch of fishes which they *took*."

62 (Mark i 16—20)

THE CALLING OF THE FISHERMEN

appears to be the meaning of Luke here. But his phrasing would raise many difficulties for those who were accustomed to the Greek word "take-alive" in the sense of "ransom." It is significant that Luke's word occurs nowhere in the early Fathers and Apologists except in a single passage where Tatian says that demons act like robbers, who *"take [people] alive" and then restore them to their friends for a ransom*[1]. This instance shews the difficulty of applying the Lucan word to Christ's disciples. For, in Luke, as in Mark-Matthew, the meaning required is that the "fishes" are *not to be "restored" to their former element*. They are *not to be "ransomed"* They are to be "for ever with the Lord[2]." This forced and obscure use of the Greek word "take-alive" greatly increases the probability that Luke did not use it as it were spontaneously, but was driven to use it as the best way of including that notion of "life" (or "living") which Mark had omitted in his record of Christ's promise to Peter. If so, it would be worth considering whether other details in Mark and in Luke may not have sprung from one and the same origin[3]. But the full

---

[1] Tatian § 18

[2] Comp. the poem of Clem Alex 312 "O Fisher of men (μερόπων), Of them that are being saved (τῶν σωζομένων), Of the sea of evil-doing (κακίας) Enticing the pure fishes (ἰχθῦς ἀγνούς) Of the hostile wave With [the bait of] sweet life (γλυκερᾷ ζωῇ δελεάζων)"—where the sense would have been quite spoiled, for Greeks, by the use of ζωγρέω applied to the "Fisher" Also the noun ζωγρεῖον means a "stew-pond," and suggests that, when fishes are described as ἐζωγρημένοι, they are not taken out of their old element, but kept in it, only with lessened liberty.

[3] For example, if there were an original "fishers of men *shall ye be for me*," the words "*shall ye be for me*" might be rendered in Mark by "*I will make you*" and in Luke by "*ye shall be*" See 2 S viii 7 "[the shields] *that were*," A οἳ ἦσαν, but LXX οὓς ἐποίησεν, and Is xxxix 7 "*they shall be*," LXX ποιήσουσι, and compare Exod xix 6 "*Ye shall be* unto me a kingdom of priests" with Rev 1 6 (and v 10) "*he hath made us* a kingdom and priests"

The question whether a dative of equivalence, ל (in "*for* fishers") might be confused with a pronominal dative ל ("*to me*"), raises

63 (Mark 1 16—20)

THE CALLING OF THE FISHERMEN

consideration is not adapted for this section, which has confined itself to the *thought* of the Lucan "*catching-alive,*" as compared with the Mark-Matthew "*fishers*" It will be found that the associations with the metaphor of "fish" and "fishing" are very complex and require careful consideration.

§ 19   *Complexities in Synoptic metaphor and circumstance*

Let us review the Synoptic tradition, and the questions that would have to be answered directly or indirectly by John if he wished to present its spiritual essence to his readers. First, what was Christ's spiritual meaning, or meanings, at the bottom of the Mark-Matthew phrase "fishers of men," and the Lucan phrase "taking men alive"?

Fishes, when drawn out of their element, die. Did Jesus base His saying on this, and was it a paradox? In the Talmud, when Alexander the Great asked the wise men of the South "What has a man to do in order to live [long]?" they replied "kill himself[1]." Did Jesus mean this? Did He say, in effect, to the fishermen, "I will cause you to draw men out of the sea of sin so that they shall die unto sin and live unto righteousness"? Luke's phrase "thou shalt be *taking men alive*" implies (at all events on the surface) something quite different and not paradoxical at all   The Marcan tradition implies drawing fish out of the water into the air. The Lucan implies drawing them out of the freedom of their native waters into the captivity of an artificial fish-pond   How was John to deal with these two traditions, in their spiritual aspect?

---

other similar questions, *e g* whether the ו signifying the plural, in "come *ye* (לכו) after me (אחרי)," may have been taken by Luke as a ו ("and") prefixed to the following word, so as to mean "come *thou, and afterwards* (אחר) thou shalt catch men"   "Afterwards" (Gesen 29 *b*) is a frequent meaning of אחר which might be confused with אחרי "after-me"   But of course it is not so appropriate as "from henceforth" (of which the Hebrew would be quite different)

[1] See Levy III 59 *b* quoting *Tamid* 31 *a*, and also *Berach.* 63 *b* "words of Torah are established only for him who *kills himself on* [*the service of*] *it*"

THE CALLING OF THE FISHERMEN

In the next place, how was John to deal with the Synoptic circumstances of time, place, and person? Was there (as the Diatessaron says) first (Mark-Matthew) a Calling of the four fishermen apostles and then (Luke) a Reminding, addressed to Peter alone? If so, was Luke right in connecting the Reminding with a wonderful draught of fishes? According to Luke, Jesus had been to Peter's house and healed his mother-in-law before the Reminding[1]. This would be compatible with Mark if we could place the events thus, 1st, the Calling, 2nd, the Healing 3rd, the Reminding. But the Diatessaron places the Reminding, as well as the Calling, before the Healing. Thus it commits itself, if not to a preference of Mark's chronological arrangement as better than Luke's, at all events to a condemnation of Luke's arrangement[2]

If John intended to avoid a similar preference, or condemnation, he could not venture into detail covering the same ground But he could bring before the reader some new traditions about minor Apostles or Disciples (such as Papias in later days sought after), shewing how Philip of Bethsaida, the House of Fishing, and Nathanael (in some sense, Philip's convert) were led to Jesus soon after Andrew—and all of them led by some kind of attraction which we in modern times might call magnetic. Calling it by no name, the Fourth Evangelist might endeavour to shew its reality and its immediate results, in such a way as to suggest deeper results that were to be revealed later on. Without mentioning the word "fish" or "fishing," he could make the reader feel that Christ had some mysterious attractive power that might be likened to that of a divine Fisherman, disclosed in glimpses at the beginning of the Gospel in a rudimentary form, and to be manifested at the end of the Gospel in a fuller revelation.

---

[1] Lk iv. 38 foll, v 1 foll
[2] Mark places in the following order (1 16 foll) the Calling, (1 21 foll) the Exorcism, (1 29 foll) the Healing.

THE CALLING OF THE FISHERMEN

He could also shew, dramatically, how the first of those attracted thus attracted others to the Fisherman, and thereby proved that He had made them fishermen, in some degree, like Himself, fishers of the souls of men.

§ 20. *Greek metaphor, and Luke*

Greek thought, as well as Jewish tradition, would confront Greek evangelists recording the Galilaean traditions about Christ's fishermen. For example, Plato speaks of the possibility that men might rise out of the dense and misty atmosphere of earth into the pure air of heaven "as fishes peeping up from the sea[1]." This first step toward the metaphor of the fish is natural for all thinkers about reality. After this there might follow particular questions of detail, questions raised by this or that seeker, as to the life of (so to speak) "the new fish." Is it "killed" and replaced by an altogether "new creature"? Or does it remain a "fish," but a fish endowed with new powers of breathing the terrestrial air? Aristotle denied, what Anaxagoras asserted—and others later on—the breathing of fishes[2]. Having presumably such discussions in view, Philo says that fishes are the lowest creatures in the world of living creatures or "Zoogony," and that they are, "after a fashion, living things and not living things, self-moving but soulless[3]." Clement of Alexandria appears to be referring to such discussions when he describes the Egyptians as forbidding their priests to eat fish[4].

The above-quoted passage about the Philonian view of fishes, in relation to the "Zoogony," leads us to ask whether

---

[1] Plato *Phaedo* 109 E   [2] See Mayor on Clem Alex 850
[3] Philo 1 14—15   In the context he says that "the semblance of a soul is scattered about in them" like salt in meat, but yet they are "after a fashion, ..soulless (τρόπον τινα...ἄψυχα)"
[4] Clem Alex 850, where see context and Mayor's note   See also Plutarch *Isis* § 7, as to Egyptian abstinence from some kinds of fish

THE CALLING OF THE FISHERMEN

any form of this word is mentioned in the LXX and in the Gospels. *Zoogonein*, literally, "bring forth alive[1]," is used in the LXX (like *zoopoiein*, "make-living") to represent the Hebrew causative, meaning (1) "cause-to-live," (2) "let-live," "spare," "take-alive[2]." It occurs only once in the Gospels, and then somewhat remarkably, where Luke deviates from the earliest Evangelists after first agreeing with them, as follows.

Before the Transfiguration, Luke, following Mark and Matthew, represents Jesus as saying "Whosoever shall lose (*or*, destroy) his soul (*or*, life) for my sake...shall *save* (so Mk-Lk., but Mt. *find*) it[3]." But later on, "being asked when the kingdom of God cometh," Jesus says, "Remember Lot's wife Whosoever shall seek to preserve his soul (*or*, life) shall lose (*or*, destroy) it, but whosoever shall lose (*or*, destroy) [it] shall (lit.) *bring-it-forth-alive*[4]."

Here we find Luke again, as in the narrative of the Fishing, apparently discontented with the Marcan forms of expression. There, instead of "fishers of men," he preferred "capture men alive"; here, instead of the simple word "*save*," he prefers "preserve" and "bring-forth-alive"—words disagreeably recondite to some readers, but having this advantage, that they do not represent man as doing what—in strictness, and in accordance with the usual language of Christians—only the Saviour can do, i e. "*save*" his own soul. Presumably Luke meant, what John has expressed as follows in one of the very rare passages where he seems to write on Lucan lines, "He that

---

[1] By Aristotle it is used of viviparous, as distinct from oviparous animals.

[2] See above, p. 62

[3] Mk viii 35, Mt. xvi 25, Lk ix 24 ὃς δ' ἂν ἀπολέσῃ τὴν ψυχὴν αὐτοῦ ἕνεκεν ἐμοῦ οὗτος σώσει αὐτήν · Mt, for σώσει, has εὑρήσει. But, in the first part of the antithesis, Mt agrees with Mk and Lk in using σῶσαι, "save," ὃς ..θέλῃ τὴν ψυχὴν αὐτοῦ σῶσαι ἀπολέσει αὐτήν

[4] Lk xvii 33 ὃς ἐὰν ζητήσῃ τὴν ψυχὴν αὐτοῦ περιποιήσασθαι ἀπολέσει αὐτήν, ὃς δ' ἂν ἀπολέσει ζωογονήσει αὐτήν

THE CALLING OF THE FISHERMEN

loveth his soul loseth (*or*, destroyeth) it, and he that hateth his soul in this world, to life eternal shall he guard it If anyone is for ministering unto me let him follow me...[1]"

Yet Luke, in spite of all his pains, did not do all that was needed to be done by an Evangelist writing for Greeks to explain Christ's metaphor of the fish. His application of *zoogonia* to the individual believer reminds us of the only other N T. use of the word in a spiritual sense There it refers to God, who alone, so it is implied, "*quickeneth* (or, *preserveth alive*) all things[2]." And the ambiguity recognised by our Revisers in that passage affords but one of many indications that Luke's use of the word was also ambiguous

§ 21 *How does John express "fishers of men"?*

John deals with all these questionings, variations, and complexities—after his manner—dramatically and indirectly. He implies rather than states. And what he implies is that the "fishing" is a "drawing upward." The Fisherman is the Word, Life, or Light, who became Man in order to draw men to Himself[3]. Becoming Man, He descended into the waters of darkness that He might raise men up into the atmosphere of light. In the waters they could not breathe and had no need of breath. But when they rose up with Him from the waters, they received the Breath or Spirit of a new life, being born again. Those who were thus drawn up by Jesus, and

---

[1] Jn xii 25 φυλάξει "*shall guard*" represents an attitude appropriate for the Christian warrior, and is free from the objections that might be raised against the Lucan ζωογονήσει by those ignorant of its LXX use Also the addition of "*in this world*" softens what Luke says (xiv. 26) εἴ τις...οὐ μισεῖ...ἔτι τε καὶ τὴν ψυχὴν ἑαυτοῦ

[2] 1 Tim. vi. 13. R.V. txt "quickeneth," R.V. marg. "preserveth alive," which does not so well suit the context The only other N T instance is Acts vii 19, R.V. txt "that they should cast out their babes to the end they might not *live*," marg "Gr *be preserved alive*"

[3] Jn xii. 32.

THE CALLING OF THE FISHERMEN

toward Jesus, began by "following" Him on earth in a literal sense, and ended by "following" Him in a spiritual sense, which could not be comprehended till He was "lifted up" on the Cross To speak of the Apostles as fishermen would not accord with the tone and thought of the Fourth Evangelist. Still less could he call Christ Himself the Fisherman. But he goes far beyond that in venturesome implication. Adopting, or originating, a very early mystical image of Christ, as the first to rise out of the waters from which He drew others, he leads us to conceive of Him, not only as the one Bread or Loaf, but also as the one Fish, which we must receive as our spiritual food if we are to follow the Lord indeed into the heavenly life.

The necessity of receiving this spiritual *viaticum* the Evangelist nowhere definitely states. But he suggests it in a picture, at the close of his Gospel, in which the Lord is brought before us inviting His disciples to a "breakfast" where the food is a single loaf and a single fish[1]. The rest, the mystical interpretation, the Evangelist leaves us to supply for ourselves. At the same time, he connects this silent emblem, the mystical food, the fish and the bread, with a spoken doctrine about "following," with which the last words of Jesus conclude.

But all this is told so gradually, line upon line—or rather it is insinuated and suggested so imperceptibly, thought upon thought—that we cannot follow the spiritual development unless we keep our eyes as well as our ears open The mere reading of the words of the Fourth Gospel is sometimes of comparatively little use, especially at its commencement, unless we remember that it is to be read as a play, with the stage-directions left out—to be supplied by the reader. Actions,

---

[1] Jn xxi. 13 This is to be distinguished from the (plural) "fishes" and the "five barley loaves" distributed in the Feeding of the Five Thousand On the meaning of *opsarion*, used in Jn xxi 13 instead of *ichthus*, see below, p. 86

THE CALLING OF THE FISHERMEN

and actors—with their names added, except where one of them is conspicuously left unnamed[1]—these come first in order. Doctrines and discourses come afterwards.

Before discussing the Johannine attitude toward the Synoptic metaphor of "fishing," if we compare the first and the last Johannine instances of "following," we shall see (I think) that the former metaphor is not altogether disconnected from the latter in the Evangelist's mind, even at the beginning, and that the two are closely connected at the end. The first instance of "following" is one of an obviously literal and rudimentary kind based on the testimony of John the Baptist, two of whose disciples, Andrew and another, "heard him speak," and "they followed Jesus[2]." The sequel implies that their "abiding" with Jesus—which came after the "following"—not only made them converts but also made them bring others, their brothers, to become converts in their turn[3]. Thus already Andrew and his companion have become, in fact, "fishers of men," though the phrase has not been uttered.

Next Peter is introduced. But still there is no promise about becoming "fishers of men" nor any command to "follow." But after the introduction of Peter, Jesus "findeth Philip, and Jesus saith unto him, Follow me." Then it is added that "Philip was from Bethsaida[4]" "Bethsaida" means House of Fishing. For those who know this, there is a connection between the call of Philip and "following" and "fishing." Is this intentional? That Philip is made, in some sense, a "fisherman" by Christ's call is at all events implied by the fact that he at once draws into Christ's net Nathanael, who is called "an Israelite indeed[5]." Later on, Philip is again

---

[1] Jn 1 37—40.
[2] Jn 1. 37 It is added (*ib.* 38) that Jesus "turned and beheld them following."
[3] Jn 1. 41. The plural "brothers" is not mentioned but characteristically implied (*Son* 3374 c, 3626 a) in "first" (which implies a "second")
[4] Jn 1 44. See p. 27, n. 6.   [5] Jn 1. 47.

(Mark 1. 16—20)

THE CALLING OF THE FISHERMEN

connected with the place of his domicile. "Greeks," we are told, "came to Philip, *who was from Bethsaida of Galilee*... saying, Sir, we desire to see Jesus[1]." Why is the place repeated? It is because Philip is once more playing "the fisherman." And why is *"of Galilee"* added? It is because the Greeks are "Gentiles," and "Galilee" represents "Galilee of the Gentiles." Isaiah called them "the people that sat in darkness"; but now they are being drawn, through the agency of "Philip of the House of Fishing," toward the Light of Life.

Yet about this same Apostle, so faithful in following, up to his ability, and so powerful to draw Israelite and Greek toward the Lord Jesus, it is implied that he had not really *"known"* the Lord, even after he had brought the Greeks to Him. For Jesus Himself says to Philip, on the night before the Crucifixion, "Have I been *so long time with you [all]*, and *dost thou, Philip, not know me*[2]?" Had he not "followed" the Lord? Yes. He had "followed" Jesus in some sense. He had "been with" Jesus—in some sense—for what Jesus Himself calls "a long time." But Jesus needed something more.

Take, as a contrast, the unnamed disciple, whom Jesus loved, and who, along with Andrew, "followed" Jesus literally at the very beginning, and not only "followed" but also "abode with" Him. We are almost certainly intended[3] to regard him as immediately bringing his brother James to Jesus, as Andrew brings Simon. If so, he too, like Andrew and Philip, was one of the "fishermen" as well as the "followers" from the beginning.

And what as to the end? First, as regards the fishing or drawing of souls toward Christ, we find the beloved disciple saying "It is the Lord" to Peter, so that the latter plunged into the sea to swim to Him. And secondly, as regards the

---

[1] Jn xii. 21. [2] Jn xiv. 9.
[3] See below, p. 114, and *Son* 3374 c.

THE CALLING OF THE FISHERMEN

following, an answer is given in the words "Peter, turning about, seeth *the disciple whom Jesus loved, following*[1]." This, then, is the disciple who both followed at the beginning and also followed at the end. He was not bidden to do so at the beginning, like Philip, nor at the end, like Peter. Yet he followed. The reason seems to be set before us, if we will see it, in the words "whom Jesus loved." It was the attracting love of Jesus in the heart of the beloved disciple that led him to say to Peter "It is the Lord," and to "follow," in his own way, though not bidden to "follow."

§ 22. *The "Ichthus," or Fish, an early Christian emblem*

At this point, the investigation brings before us a question—suggested by a remark of Tertullian, but one that can be shewn to have been brought before Christians long before Tertullian's time—as to the relation between the baptism of Jesus Himself and the baptism of His disciples. "If baptism implies a drawing out of a lower into a higher region, as a fish is drawn out of water into air, and if we, in view of that aspect of baptism, are to call ourselves 'fishes' lifted up in the 'net' of the Spirit, did the Lord Jesus, in view of His own baptism, desire us to regard Him in the same aspect?"—so Christians might ask in the first century. Tertullian uses language that seems to favour an affirmative reply. It is at the outset of his treatise on Baptism: "But we, little fishes, in accordance with our *Ichthus*, Jesus Christ, are born [again, each one of us] (nascimur) in water[2]." Why does Tertullian here use the Greek word *Ichthus*, instead of the Latin "piscis" (which appears only in

---

[1] Jn xxi. 7, 20

[2] Tertull *De Bapt* § 1 He does not say "nati sumus" but "nascimur," meaning apparently "born day by day," as each is brought to the font He adds "Nor are we safe otherwise than by remaining in the water." It would be interesting to ascertain how he would reconcile this with Mt xiii 47 foll He regards the water (*De Bapt*. § 3) as ordained (1) "animas proferre," (2) "in baptismo animare"

THE CALLING OF THE FISHERMEN

the context as "little-fishes (pisciculi)")? It is because the Greek *Ichthus* was used, certainly in the second century, and almost certainly in the first, to denote "Jesus Christ the Son of God, the Saviour."

This answer is supported by many facts which point back to a time, not realised by us without some difficulty—a time later than Nero's days and therefore not traceable in the Pauline Epistles—when Christians, under stress of systematic persecution, began to use the Ichthus, the Fish, as the secret sign of their religion[1]. It was natural for some to regard it as the sign of their baptism, which sealed them as the baptized followers of the Protobaptized, their Lord. They were, as Tertullian says, His "little fishes," following Him the Great One. How naturally this must have tended to increase the belief in the efficacy of baptism in water, as distinct from baptism with the Spirit, may be easily imagined, and we know that many, including Constantine, delayed to be baptized, owing to their belief that all the sins they might commit before baptism were assuredly washed away, while as to post-baptismal sins they could never feel a similar assurance.

---

[1] *Dict Christ. Ant* 1. 674 a "There can be little doubt that... till Constantine's time, no public use of the cross was made, as a sign of the person of the Lord Till then, the fish-anagram was perhaps in special and prevailing use, and it may have yielded its place from that time to the cross, the sign of full confession of Jesus Christ" See *Orac Sibyll* viii 217 foll. and Lightfoot on Ignatius Vol 1 480 containing an ancient poem by Abercius, also *Dict Christ Ant* 1 713 a King's *Antique Gems and Rings* ii pp 27, 37 prints a "signet" with HΛEIC above ꟽX HI and adds "*El*, the Kabbalistic title of the Sephira, *Mercy*, was often applied to Christ, as may be read on the Bâsle altar frontal (Cluny Museum)—

'Quis sicut Hel fortis, medicus, soter, benedictus?'"

He accounts for HI—*i e* the inverted IH instead of the inverted IHC, the usual form—by reference to "the Hebrew *Jod* and *He*" But IH occurs where there is no suspicion of Hebrew, in Bœckh 9082 where IH is above ꟽX I have been unable to find from books, or from experts whom I have consulted, a single ancient instance of this "often applied" *El*

THE CALLING OF THE FISHERMEN

§ 23. *Influence of this emblem on Johannine doctrine*

Against such an attitude of mind (that of Tertullian) the Fourth Gospel sets itself from the beginning. It does not narrate the baptism of Jesus in the water, and therefore does not mention the simultaneous "opening of the heaven" above Him. But it does represent Jesus, in His first promise to the disciples, as apparently referring to this opening of the heaven, and as promising that they shall "see" it and shall "see" "the angels of God ascending and descending on the Son of Man[1]." That is to say, baptism must be more than a washing. It must bring with it a "seeing." And this "seeing" is to be connected with "the Son of Man" as the mediator between earth and heaven. In the next stage of doctrine, Nicodemus is warned that the baptized cannot "*see*" those super-terrestrial realities which constitute "the kingdom of God," unless they are "born from above[2]." The baptism of John—a baptism

---

[1] Jn i. 51.
[2] Jn iii. 3. (For the rendering of ἄνωθεν "from above" (as R V marg.) see *Joh. Gr.* 1904—5, 2573.) We must remember that, about the middle of the first century, if not before, the question would arise concerning little children born of Christian parents who were prepared for the Coming of the Lord from heaven at any time, "If these little ones are not baptized as soon as born, will they be regarded by the Lord as outside His Church?" Paul indirectly answers the question by saying to parents of whom one alone is a believer, that the belief of even one parent sanctifies the child (1 Cor. vii. 14) "Else were your children unclean, *but now are they holy.*"

Connecting this verse with Jn iii 6, Clement of Alexandria (549) says "That which is begotten (γεννώμενον) of the flesh is flesh, so that which is from the spirit [is] spirit (οὕτω τὸ ἐκ πνεύματος πνεῦμα) not only as to the [act of] childbearing *but also as to the [act of] learning* (οὐ μόνον κατὰ τὴν ἀποκύησιν ἀλλὰ καὶ κατὰ τὴν μάθησιν). αὐτίκα (1 Cor vii 14) ἅγια τὰ τέκνα αἱ εὐαρεστήσεις τῷ θεῷ τῶν κυριακῶν λόγων νυμφευσάντων τὴν ψυχήν." The meaning of this is obscure to me. But comp. Tertull. *De Anim.* § 39 "Hinc enim et Apostolus ex sanctificato alterutro sexu sanctos procreari ait, tam ex seminis praerogativa *quam ex institutionis disciplina.*" Tertullian's context implies that

THE CALLING OF THE FISHERMEN

with water alone—will not suffice. "Except a man be born from water and wind (*or*, spirit, *or* breath) he cannot enter into the kingdom of God[1]." The context appears to play on the different meanings of one and the same word—"wind," "spirit," "breath"—very much as in the vision of Ezekiel where the prophet declares concerning the "dry bones" of Israel that "there was no *breath* in them" and then is bidden to appeal to "the breath"·—"Come from the four Breaths, O *Breath*, and breathe upon these slain that they may live[2]." And it is probable that the "water" here mentioned, as well as the "wind (*or*, breath)," is celestial not terrestrial, being the "fountain of the Holy Spirit," in which an ancient Hebrew Gospel declares that Jesus Himself was baptized[3].

If this is the meaning of the "water" and the "breath (*or*, spirit)" in the Dialogue with Nicodemus, it answers the question, raised elsewhere, as to what is to become of the human "fishes" when taken out of the water, the answer being, "They are endued with a power of breathing the celestial air, the very breath of God, concerning which Ezekiel said, 'Breathe upon

---

from birth and onwards the child of heathen parents is polluted by worship of false gods, but he does not attempt to shew how the child of *one* heathen parent and *one* Christian parent must necessarily be free from such pollution and must be called "holy." Paul indicates that the influence of even one Christian parent would prevail over unholy influences so as to make the child "holy." Baptism he does not mention, but his remark seems to assume that the child could be "holy" before baptism. The logic of the argument is not clear. But he seems to see, and to try to make us see, the Holy Spirit breathing and quickening and conquering in ways past understanding.

[1] Jn iii 5   [2] Ezek xxxvii 9 foll
[3] For the baptism of Jesus with the "whole fountain of the Holy Spirit descending," as described in a Hebrew Gospel quoted by Jerome on Is xi. 2, see *From Letter* **1042**. The second-century poem of Abercius (Lightf on Ignatius Vol. 1 480) speaks of Christ as "the fish from the *fountain.*" *Dict Christ. Ant* ("Fisherman") gives a print of an early representation of the "fisherman" drawing the fish from "waters which flow from the rock in Horeb."

THE CALLING OF THE FISHERMEN

these slain that they may live.'" And the rest of the Johannine chapter goes on to shew how the "lifting up" of "the Son of Man" is to help those who believe in Him to receive "eternal life," and to "come to the light" and be "saved[1]."

No further mention is made in the Gospel of the effect of baptism. But the Evangelist represents Jesus as emphasizing the need of the internal and "living water" as compared with that of "Jacob's well[2]." He also suggests, by a typical sign at the pool of Bethesda, the ineffectuality of the purifications of the Jews as compared with the power of "making-alive" given by the Father to the Son and exerted by the Spirit[3]. This imparting of life is described as the result of the Son's act in giving His own flesh and blood to men, as their "living bread." And, in various scenes, the "drawing" power of the Father or of the Son is mentioned or implied[4]. But it is reserved for the last scene of all—after the Lord has breathed upon the disciples and bestowed on them the Holy Spirit—to represent Jesus as, in effect, the Fisherman directing the 'fishing" of the Seven Missionaries, and also, immediately afterwards, as the Bread (or Loaf) and Fish that is to be their morning food preparing them to go forth to preach His Gospel.

In Jerome's letters the only reference that I have found to this Johannine "breakfast" appears to be a phrase included in a confused reference to quite a different event, related by

---

[1] Jn iii 14 foll.   [2] Jn iv 5 foll.

[3] Jn v. 1—21 "quickeneth," $\zeta\omega\pi o\iota\epsilon\hat{\iota}$, comp vi 63 "it is the spirit that quickeneth" "Water" is not there mentioned in Christ's words Christ's only other mention of water is in vii 38 "rivers of living water" But the Evangelist mentions it in (xiii 5) the Washing of Feet, and (xix 34) the "blood and water" from Jesus on the Cross

[4] Jn vi 44, xii. 32 both mention "drawing ($\dot{\epsilon}\lambda\kappa\dot{\upsilon}\omega$)", but Jn vi 68 "Lord, to whom shall we go? Thou hast words of eternal life," and other passages, suggest it perhaps even more forcibly by implication

THE CALLING OF THE FISHERMEN

Luke: "*He asked for a fish broiled on the coals* that He might confirm the doubting Apostles [i e by His eating], who did not dare approach Him because they thought they saw not a body but a spirit[1]." This is neither Lucan nor Johannine. In Luke, the question asked by Jesus is "Have ye anything to eat here?" and there is no mention of "coals" In John, the question asked by Jesus may be interpreted as asking about "fish" ("Have ye any fish [taken by your nets]?") and there is a mention of "a fire of coals" and "a fish laid thereon", but this fish is regarded as provided by Jesus, not by the disciples. The disciples eat. Jesus gives the food.

Chrysostom, in his comment on John, remarks, with a careful negative, "It is *not said here* that He ate with them." But the language of Jerome indicates that he took a different view. It also suggests that he may have confused the Johannine "Have ye [caught] any fish?" with the Lucan "Have ye anything for me to eat [that I may shew you that I am not a disembodied spirit]?" We shall now compare the two.

§ 24. "'*Have ye anything to-eat here?*' *And they gave him part of a broiled fish*," *in Luke*[2]

The Lucan word meaning "to-eat," or "eatable," occurs nowhere in the Old and New Greek Testament except here, and in rendering the extremely rare O T. phrase "every tree-of

---

[1] *Letters and Select Works of St Jerome* (Oxford, 1893) p. 442 referring to Jn xxi. 9. [The Index gives Jn xxi. 9 as referred to on p. 376, but it should be Acts xxi 9. The Index also gives Jn xxi. 13 as referred to on p. 401, but the reference appears to be chiefly to Luke ("part of a broiled fish and of a honeycomb").] On p 442, the preceding words are "Why did our Lord eat a honeycomb? To prove the resurrection...," and then "He asked for a fish broiled on the coals.."

[2] Lk. xxiv. 41—2 ἔχετέ τι βρώσιμον ἐνθάδε, perhaps a better rendering would be "*Ye have* [*of course*] *something to-eat here?*" Comp. ἔχετε in Aristoph. *Eccles* 68.

THE CALLING OF THE FISHERMEN

food (lit. *tree-of eating*)[1]." This phrase—apart from the Pentateuch and Nehemiah, where it means literally "fruit-tree"—occurs only in Ezekiel's description of "*every tree of food*" that grows by the river of life that proceeds out of the Temple: "It shall bring forth new fruit every month, because the waters thereof issue out of the sanctuary, and the fruit thereof shall be for food, and the leaf thereof for healing[2]." This apparently refers to the fuller form "*tree good for food*" which occurs in Genesis, "every tree that is pleasant to the sight and *good for food*[3]." In Revelation, though "food" is merged in "fruit," the imagery of Ezekiel is retained, thus, "On this side of the river and on that, the tree of life, bearing twelve [manner of] fruits, yielding its fruit every month; and the leaves of the tree were for the healing of the nations[4]"

Thus it happens that, to readers familiar with the language of the LXX and with the imagery of the Scripture, Luke's rare word "[*fit*] *to eat*" would suggest the thought of the "fruit" of the Tree of Life, or, in other words, "spiritual fruit." This thought pervades the Hebrew prophecies. The cry of the last of their prophets was "Bring forth therefore fruits worthy of repentance[5]." We all know how prominent the thought is (even where the word "fruit" is not mentioned) in Christ's parables and doctrines, and we might fairly anticipate that it would find a place in any precepts, traditions, or revelations, recorded by the disciples in closest sympathy with Him as having proceeded from the risen Saviour. It is therefore reasonable to ask (1) whether Luke intended his readers here to assume some allusion to this doctrine, (2) whether

---

[1] In O T., βρώσιμος, i e "fit-to-eat," occurs only in πᾶν ξύλον βρώσιμον (three times), Heb "tree-of *eating*" occurs (Gesen. 38 a) four times. In Lev. xix 23, Nehem ix 25, Ezek. xlvii. 12, LXX has βρώσιμον In Deut xx 20, with neg, it has οὐ καρπόβρωτον

[2] Ezek xlvii. 12   "For food" is εἰς βρῶσιν

[3] Gen ii 9, rep iii 6   [4] Rev xxii 2.

[5] Mt iii 8, Lk. iii. 8

78 (Mark 1 16—20)

THE CALLING OF THE FISHERMEN

the original tradition implied some such allusion (although Luke has not drawn it out but has contented himself with faithfully setting down the expressions that point to it).

The first of these two questions must be answered in the negative. There is no indication whatever that Luke regarded the question as having any spiritual meaning or as being anything more than an introduction to a "proof" of the Lord's bodily resurrection. The Lucan tendency to give undue prominence to "proofs" has been discussed already[1]. But this tendency makes it all the more necessary for us to ascertain whether his own language does not reveal something deeper than his own thought It may of course be the historical fact that Jesus, instead of saying "Bring me a morsel of bread," used an extremely rare epithet, which, by a mere coincidence, suggested what Ezekiel calls "tree of food," and what Revelation calls the "fruit" of "the tree of life." But such a coincidence ought not to be accepted as casual except after close investigation.

A parable in Luke represents the Lord of the Vineyard as coming to the Gardener and seeking fruit[2] from a fig-tree. A Mark-Matthew narrative represents Jesus as coming to a fig-tree for the same purpose[3]. These traditions shew that the question "Have ye aught fit for eating?" might mean "fit for *me* to eat " Jesus had appointed the Apostles to bring forth fruit. He desired that "fruit" *from them*—that is to say, the fruit due from Apostles, the salvation of the souls of men. In that sense the Saviour might say to them after His resurrection, in order to stimulate them to their apostolic toil, "Have ye any food—food for me and food for yourselves, because it is your food and mine to do the will of the Father by saving the souls of men?" But of course this meaning would be lost by those who took the words to mean simply

---

[1] *Introduction* p 122 foll.   [2] Lk. xiii. 6
[3] Mk xi. 13, Mt. xxi. 19.

THE CALLING OF THE FISHERMEN

"Have ye anything here that I might eat in your presence, so as to prove to you that I have a body capable of eating?"

Here we must point out that in the passage of Ezekiel mentioning "every tree of *food*" there is a preceding mention of "fishers" and of "fish" that are to be "exceeding many[1]." All the Synoptic Gospels assume that Jesus, at the outset of the Gospel, used the metaphor of "catching fish" as a symbol of fruitful apostolic action. We are now invited to believe that He used, at its close, language blending the two thoughts. It will presently appear that the Johannine "*Have ye any food?*" actually blends the two thoughts, since, in vernacular Greek, it may mean, in effect, "Have ye [*caught*] any fish?"

But before passing to that, we must touch on a very small point, the epithet "broiled," applied by Luke to the fish. Admitting readily that Luke's reason for recording it was simply, or at all events mainly, that he found it, or thought he found it, recorded by predecessors, we still have to ask why they took the trouble to register so small a detail as this—which did not strengthen the proof—namely, that the food by eating which the Lord proved that He was not an apparition was not only a "fish" but also a "broiled fish."

Clement of Alexandria adduces Luke's phrase and context in support of simple diet, probably having in view the saying in Plato's *Republic*, that Homer favoured the use of meat "broiled rather than boiled[2]." It is also interesting to note

---

[1] Ezek. xlvii. 9—10.

[2] Clem. Alex. in a discourse against (171) "gluttony (ὀψοφαγία)" speaks of the Lord as (172) "having blessed the loaves and the *broiled* (ὀπτοὺς) fishes with which He feasted the disciples." Then (173—4) after praising a diet of vegetables, he says "And if there be need of *broiled* meat, or boiled, it must be shared [with others] (κἂν ὀπτοῦ δέῃ κρέως ἢ ἑφθοῦ, μεταδοτέον)." Then he quotes Luke. "*Have ye aught to eat here?* said the Lord to the disciples after the Resurrection. And they, as having been taught by Him to practise frugality, presented (ἐπέδωκαν) to Him a portion of a *broiled* fish. And having eaten before them, He said to them (says Luke) what

THE CALLING OF THE FISHERMEN

that, although Clement agrees with Luke's correct text in omitting—what our A.V. inserts, and our R.V. places in the margin—"and (of) an honeycomb[1]," Clement adds, as a consecutive remark of his own, that feasters according to the Logos ought not to be deprived of "[honey]-combs[1]" Clement's application of the passage will, of course, strike us as a far-fetched explanation. But it ought also to strike us as indicating that he perceived something that needed to be explained.

The true explanation, however, seems to have been hidden from Clement by Plato, who overshadowed Moses in his mind. For in fact this apparently superfluous Lucan epithet "broiled" points back to the institution of the Passover. The only passage in LXX that uses Luke's word is that which enjoins—repeating the word twice—that, in the first Passover meal, the lamb is to be *"broiled with fire,"* adding "not boiled at all with water but *broiled with fire,"* and to be eaten "with loins girded, shoes on feet, staff in hand[2]." And why? The reason is obvious. It is a military order. The army of the Lord is to march forth at short notice from Egypt to the Promised Land. This Passover is their *viaticum.* No doubt Plato used similar language about "broiled food, not boiled," being best for soldiers, and Plutarch repeated it from Plato. But the original of the Lucan tradition is much more likely

---

He did say. In addition to these things it is not to be suffered that those who dine in accordance with the Word should be deprived of sweetmeats and honeycombs (πρὸς τούτοις οὐδὲ τραγημάτων καὶ κηρίων ἀμοίρους περιορατέον τοὺς δειπνοῦντας κατὰ Λόγον)." I have given the Greek of passages where my translation differs from that of T and T Clark, which has "If flesh is wanted, let roast rather than boiled be set down...it is not to be overlooked that those who feed according to the Word are not debarred from dainties in the shape of honey-combs"

[1] Lk xxiv 42 μέρος [καὶ ἀπὸ μελισσίου κηρίον]. Clem. has κηρίων W H has the bracketed words in the list of "rejected readings."
[2] Exod. xii. 8—11.

THE CALLING OF THE FISHERMEN

to have been derived from allusion to the Passover in Exodus than from Plato or copies of Plato—even though Luke failed to perceive the allusion[1]

From a very different point of view there presents itself a second-century literary jest about "broiled fish," which has no signs of being a jibe derived from the Lucan tradition, and which, if it is not derived from Luke, points back to an early recognition of a play on the words "broiled" and "visible." It is preserved by Athenaeus, who wrote about the end of the second century, quoting from an anonymous poet who must have been some years earlier.

It happens that the Lucan word *optos* is identical with another *optos* (connected with our "optic" in its various forms) meaning "visible." Hence this ancient poet undertook to prove that a raw fish was *"broiled"* by pointing out that it was *"visible*[2]*."* Now Luke is the only writer of N.T. to use the verb akin to *optos* expressing visibility. It is mostly used of divine things divinely seen in visions. Luke uses it but once, and that at the beginning of the Acts, to describe Jesus as *"divinely-appearing"* unto the disciples[3] Could Luke have been influenced by some obscure

---

[1] Plat. *Pol* iii 13, 404 c notes that Homer "feasts his heroes neither with fish, nor with boiled flesh, but only with broiled, which would be most convenient for soldiers", Plutarch—speaking about Scipio's regulations as to "breakfast," to be taken by the men "standing" and with "fireless food"—probably has Plato in view *Moral.* 201 c ἀριστᾶν μὲν ἑστῶτας ἄπυρον ὄψον, δειπνεῖν δὲ κατακειμένους ἄρτον ἢ πολτὸν ἁπλῶς καὶ κρέας ὀπτὸν ἢ ἑφθόν

[2] See Steph. *Thes.* v 2121, which also quotes Hesychius as saying "*Opticon* and *opton* have the same meaning—'visible,' manifest, foresighted," and "'Οπτὸς, φαινόμενος" Thomas deprecates this use of the word Κάτοπτα λεγε, καὶ μὴ ὀπτά, ἤτοι θεατά. Neither grammarian mentions the extreme rarity of the word in this sense Steph *Thes* alleges only one instance of it, and that from Lucian *Lexiph* § 9 where it occurs amidst a group of pedantical misuses of words

[3] Acts 1 3 foll ὀπτανόμενος αὐτοῖς. See *Notes* **2892—907** on this difficult passage.

THE CALLING OF THE FISHERMEN

Greek traditions in which this verb might mean either "*broiled*" or "*made visible*"? It is true that no instance is alleged of the verb as meaning "*broil*" till quite late times[1]; but it is not unreasonable to suspect—in view of the jest above mentioned—that some confusion may have existed in first-century Greek traditions about the divine Fish as being *optos* in two senses, first as "made-visible" after the Resurrection, secondly, as "broiled" like the flesh of the Paschal Lamb. Avoiding such a confusion, or such a play on words, the Fourth Evangelist, instead of "broiled," substitutes "a fire of charcoal," and "a fish lying thereon[2]"

It will be obvious that if "broiled," in Luke, refers to the Passover meal, it will not be appropriate to food given by the disciples to Jesus. It would be appropriate only to food given by "Christ, our Passover," giving Himself to the disciples. There is probably some error in Luke. The alteration of a single letter would turn "they gave" into "he gave[3]." The Curetonian Syriac of Luke adds that Jesus also gave some of the fish to the disciples[4]. Origen, laying stress on "portion," appears to regard the "*portion* of broiled fish" presented by the Apostles to Jesus as representing the very inadequate return which was all that they could make at present for the Word that had

---

[1] Steph *Thes* alleges only one from Nicetas Chon. in Andronicus Comnenus But it gives an instance where ὀπτανία, "an oven," was erroneously explained as "looking-at," ἀπόβλεψις, in Suidas.

[2] Jn xxi. 9.

[3] See Prof Burkitt's *Evang. Da-Mepharreshe* ii. 305 "Clement of Alexandria (p. 174) definitely quotes the passage," *i.e.* Lk xxiv. 42—4 "thus ἐπέδωκεν...." This would mean "*he* gave." But in fact Clement quotes it correctly, ἐπέδωκαν, *i.e.* "they gave." Prof. Burkitt's volumes are conspicuously accurate as a rule, and therefore I have selected this misprint of ε for α to shew how easily "*he* gave" and "*they* gave" might be confused.

[4] Lk xxiv. 43 Curet. Syr (Burkitt, vol. ii. p. 305) "And while he took [and] ate before their eyes and took up that which was over [and] gave to them...."

THE CALLING OF THE FISHERMEN

been imparted to them[1]. Luke (as has been admitted above) seems to have had no such allegorical meaning. But if we presently find John combining a presentation of fishes by the disciples to Jesus with a presentation of fish, in return, from Jesus to the disciples, we shall then have to ask whether this double act, this action and reaction, is not in spiritual accord with Christ's doctrine as a whole, and with the manifestations of Christ's resurrection in particular[2].

In concluding these remarks about the Lucan presentation of "broiled fish," we must not overlook the cumulative evidence derived from Luke's contextual[3] use of unique or rare expressions. Luke appears to be feeling his way through ancient and obscure traditions, which he sets down as he found them even though he is doubtful about their exact meaning.

§ 25 (R.V.) *"'Children, have ye aught to eat?' They answered him, 'No,'"*[4] *in John*

The Johannine question is couched in Greek that may be described as at once vernacular and technical. The first part

---

[1] Origen *Comm Matth* xi 2 (Lomm iii 69) "He ate of a broiled fish...taking 'a part' from the disciples and receiving from [them] such divine-teaching as they were able, [but only] 'in part,' to report to Him about the Father."

[2] On ἐπιδίδωμι "give" or "present" (Lk xxiv 42 ἐπέδωκαν, used also in *ib* 30 ἐπεδίδου) see Hermas *Sim* viii 1—2 foll where the branches that Michael "presents" to men for fruitful use are "presented" again by them to Michael that he may inspect their fruitfulness

[3] "Contextual" should include the beginning of the Acts, *e g.* i 3—4 δι' ἡμερῶν (see *Notes* 2892 *a*, 2904) ὀπτανόμενος, and συναλιζόμενος

[4] Jn xxi 5 Παιδία, μή τι προσφάγιον ἔχετε, ἀπεκρίθησαν αὐτῷ Οὔ. Blass adds "ὄψον attice Clem Al" Perhaps "You have caught no fish, have you?" would be a more faithful rendering (see *Joh. Gr.* 2235 *d*, 2307 *a*, 2703 (3)) Clem Alex 104 has σταθείς (φησίν) ὁ κύριος ἐπὶ τῷ (Jn εἰς, or ἐπὶ, τὸν) αἰγιαλῷ (Jn—ὄν) πρὸς τοὺς μαθητὰς—ἁλιεύοντες δὲ ἔτυχον—ἐνεφώνησέν τε, Παιδία, μή τι ὄψον ἔχετε, Steph. *Thes*, which gives no other instance of ἐμφωνεῖν, suggests ἀνεφώνησεν, *i.e.* "shouted." But there remains the difficulty of the superfluous

84 (Mark 1. 16—20)

of it is what Greeks used to say when asking a fisherman or bird-catcher whether he had "got anything[1]" The other part, "*anything-to-eat*"—literally meaning "anything to be eaten with [bread]," a "relish," including fruit, vegetables, and fish —is not alleged to be connected with fishing or hunting. It is regularly used in contracts about the daily food forming part of a workman's wages. Those who are questioned here are fishermen at their work Hence, not only must the "relish" mean "fish," but also the whole question must mean "Have you [caught] any fish to eat with your bread [as the fruit, or wages, of your labour in fishing]?" This tends to bring the Johannine question into harmony with the interpretation assigned above to the corresponding Lucan question "Have ye anything to eat?"

We traced back the latter to Ezekiel. And Luke's Greek word "eatable" was shewn to be identical with the very rare word applied in LXX to the fruit of the trees described by the prophet as growing near the mystical river that flowed from the Sanctuary. "In John," it may be objected, "Tiberias, not Jerusalem, is the scene" The reply is, 1st, that the prophet himself speaks of the mystical river as extending to various regions, 2nd, that the first of these is called by the LXX Galilee, 3rd, *that Rashi explains this as referring to Tiberias*[2].

Now against the hypothesis of a mystical or emblematic

τε For προσφάγιον, "fish," see *Joh Gr* 2235 d, and add that the Indices of Berlin Urkunde (1—1209) give π in 916 (time of Vespasian) in an agreement as to wages and food of workmen, placed after "oil," but with no distinct intimation of its meaning

[1] See Field on Jn xxi 5, quoting the Scholiast on Aristoph *Nub* 733 ἔχεις τι, where the words are said to contain "a witty allusion to the question commonly put to fishermen or bird-catchers" Field adds a quotation from Nonnus, ἦ ῥ' ἔχομέν τι, where the Scholiast has ἆρα ἐθηράσαμέν τι,

[2] See Rashi on Ezek xlvii 8 (LXX) "This water that goeth forth to Galilee that is to the east (εἰς τὴν Γαλιλαίαν τὴν πρὸς ἀνατολάς)."

THE CALLING OF THE FISHERMEN

purpose in the Johannine narrative, it may be objected, that the word *ichthus*—which has been shewn to have had an emblematic meaning toward the end of the first or beginning of the second century—is not used here at all to represent the Lord Jesus, or to represent His gift to the disciples. This is true. We may almost say that *ichthus*, in this high sense, is conspicuously put aside to make way for another word, a humble one, *opsarion*, which has no pretensions to an emblematic meaning[1].

But is not this consistent with a mystical purpose that deprecates some emblems and substitutes others? The *Ichthus* was an emblem of Greek not Jewish origin. In the minds of some, connecting "Jesus Christ the Son of God[2]" with the thought of Him as the Fish in the Waters of Baptism, it tended to a disproportionate estimate of the external purification with water. As an antidote for such an error, the word *opsarion* came appropriately as meaning "*something that was to be eaten with bread.*" That implied combination with the Bread, the Living Bread—a metaphor emphasized in the Fourth Gospel. John, and John alone, uses the word *opsarion* when speaking of the "two *fishes*" in the Feeding of the Five Thousand. Now he repeats it in the Feeding of the Seven Disciples. In both cases the choice of the word appears to be deliberate.

As regards John's preference of other words ("a fire of charcoal, and a fish laid thereon") to Luke's word "broiled" (which appeared to allude to the Passover) it has been pointed out above that the Lucan word was liable to jibes from those

---

[1] This does not appear in our English Versions. But in Jn xxi. 6, 8, 11, "fishes"= $ἰχθύων$ (in narrative), *ib* xxi 10 "fishes" (R V "fish," but the word is plural) = $ὀψαρίων$ (in Christ's words) In Jn xxi. 9, 13, "fish" = $ὀψάριον$ (in narrative) In the Miracle of the Five Thousand, John alone uses the word (vi 9, 11) $δύο\ ὀψάρια,\ ἐκ\ τῶν\ ὀψαρίων.$ On $ὀψάριον$ meaning "sauce," "flavour," "fish," see *Joh Gr.* 2235 d

[2] See above, p. 73, on *Ichthus*, as an abbreviation of this title

THE CALLING OF THE FISHERMEN

who did not understand its allusion And the description in John, besides being more vivid, and more like what would be seen in a vision, has perhaps a significance in view of the previous mention—the only other one in N T —of "a fire of charcoal[1]." It is an ancient observation that Peter thrice denied his Master near "a fire of charcoal"; and now the time has come when, near another "fire of charcoal," he is thrice to affirm his faithful devotion to that same Master, who, while accepting it, will predict that he will be faithful unto death[2].

§ 26. *Clement of Alexandria on "one fishing"*

Clement of Alexandria, in his *Instructor*, says, "Let our seals be either a dove, or a fish, or a ship running before the wind, or a musical lyre (used by Polycrates) or a ship's anchor (which Seleucus used as his engraved device); and, if it be *one fishing*, he [*i e* the wearer] will thereby remember *an apostle and the 'children' caught-up [like fish] out of water*....[3]"

"One fishing" is probably Jesus; and "children" may be explained by an earlier reference in the *Instructor* to "children[4]"

---

[1] Jn xviii 18 "the servants and the officers. .having made a fire of charcoal " Ἀνθρακιά, "fire of charcoal," does not occur in N T except in Jn xviii 18, xxi 9

[2] See Ephrem Syrus quoted in *Joh Voc* 1711 *f* foll , and *Son of Man* 3369 *a* foll

[3] Clem Alex 289 κἂν ἁλιεύων τις ᾖ, ἀποστόλου μεμνήσεται καὶ τῶν ἐξ ὕδατος ἀνασπωμένων παιδίων The next words are οὐ γὰρ εἰδώλων πρόσωπα ἐναποτυπωτέον, "for we must not engrave on them the faces of idols"—a caution necessary for Greeks, who would not worship the Dove or the Fish, but might worship the Fisherman

For ἀνασπάω, used of an angler "hoisting up" or "jerking up" a fish out of water, see Steph *Thes* quoting Ælian and Lucian (e g *Pisc* § 48, 1. 615) "It [*i e* the fish] nears the hook! It is caught (εἴληπται)! Let us *hoist up* (ἀνασπάσωμεν)!" Luke xiv 5 "*hoist* (ἀνασπάσει)" out of a "well (φρέαρ)" is parall. to Mt xii 11 "*lift* (ἐγερεῖ)" out of a "pit (βόθυνος)," where ἀνασπάσει implies more haste than ἐγερεῖ The word might also be applied to a quick "drawing up" of "nets," etc Comp Acts xi 10

[4] The title of the treatise, Παιδαγωγός, naturally leads to the thought of παῖδες and hence to Christ's παιδία

THE CALLING OF THE FISHERMEN

There, in a discourse on Children of God, Clement gives the first place (in a long list of quotations) to the utterance of Christ on the shore to the disciples fishing on the sea of Tiberias, "*Children*[1]!" That "one fishing" means Jesus is indicated by the hymn at the end of the *Instructor* where Christ is called "Fisher" as well as Shepherd "*Fisher* of articulate-speaking [men], of those who are being saved, enticing the pure fishes of the sea of evil, the hostile surge, with the sweet [bait of] life[2]." Greeks were accustomed to worship Artemis as "the Huntress." Becoming Christians, they might be tempted to worship Christ as "the Fisherman," especially if they saw His figure engraved on Christian seals in that character. Clement warns them that they are not to worship Him thus. The figure is to arouse, not worship, but remembrance—"remembrance of *an apostle and of the* [*other*] '*children*'...," that is, those whom the Lord hailed as "children" on the sea of Tiberias, where they had been fishing in vain, and He, the Fisherman, taught them how to fish to good purpose.

Elsewhere, "fishing" is attributed to Peter, practising the art that he had learned from Jesus: "But better is this kind of catching [of fish] which the Lord granted to the disciple, teaching him to fish for men, even as [we fish] for fishes, *through* water[3]." But where "*an apostle and the children*" are

---

[1] See above, p 84, n 4.

[2] Clem Alex 312. "Enticing (δελεάζων)" suggests fishing with a hook rather than with a net "Articulate-speaking (μερόπων)" is used for "men," because "fishes," both in Greek and Latin, are proverbially "dumb" See also *Notes* 2999 (vii)*a* quoting Clem Alex 172 τῶν ἐξ ὕδατος ἀνιόντων ἐπὶ τὸ τῆς δικαιοσύνης δέλεαρ

[3] Clem. Alex. 284 αὕτη δὲ βελτίων ἡ ἄγρα ἦν ἐχαρίσατο ὁ κύριος τῷ μαθητῇ, καθάπερ ἰχθῦς διὰ ὕδατος ἀνθρώπους ἁλιεύειν διδάξας Comp. Acts ii. 38—41 where Peter, after his preaching, says "repent and be baptized," and "*they that had received his word* were baptized," to the number of three thousand. See *Notes* 2999 (vii)*b* quoting Origen on Mt xvii 24—7 (Lomm. iii 232—3) παρακαλῶν τὸν μαθητὴν [i e Peter] ..δίδωσιν αὐτῷ δύναμιν τοῦ ἁλιεῦσαι ἰχθὺν πρῶτον, ἵνα ἀναβάντος αὐτοῦ παρακληθῇ...where the meaning seems to be that

THE CALLING OF THE FISHERMEN

mentioned, it is implied that Peter, and those who are called "children" along with him, are caught up out of the water by the Fisherman previously mentioned as "one fishing" In other words, *before Peter "catches fish," he is regarded as being "caught" himself*

Clement's obscure allusion to the Johannine fishing on Tiberias, where he lays such emphasis on "children"—when supplemented by his mention of "children" in his interpretation of "one fishing" engraved on Christian gems, and then by his hymnal appeal to Christ as "Fisherman"—leads us to see that the Johannine picture may have been regarded by Clement—perhaps in accordance with John's intention—as suggesting, first, Baptism, and secondly, Eucharist The penitent Peter, as the representative of the Seven Disciples, plunges into the lake and is drawn to Himself by the Saviour. Thus he is taught to be "a fisher of men through water" by being himself drawn "through water" to the Fisherman. That is Baptism. Peter and the Apostles have nowhere before been described as having been baptized Now they are baptized. The next thing is to receive the Eucharistic "breakfast," the one loaf and the one fish.

Obscure though they are, these allusions of Clement to the Johannine story are of greater value than the clear-cut statements of Jerome · "How do you explain," says the latter to a heretic, "the fact that Peter *saw the Lord standing on the shore and eating a piece of a roasted fish and a honey-comb? If He stood, He must certainly have had feet*[1] " Both here and elsewhere Jerome, besides making serious mistakes in quoting the

---

Peter is "comforted" by being allowed to be the first to catch a fish, or to catch the first fish. On ἀναβαίνω here and Jn xxi 11, and on "comforting," see *Notes* **2999** (vii).

[1] *Letters* cviii 24   Comp *To Pammachius* § 34 (*Letters* p 442) "*He asked for a fish broiled on the coals* that He might confirm the doubting Apostles, who did not dare approach Him because they thought they saw, not a body, but a spirit "

THE CALLING OF THE FISHERMEN

text, introduces materialistic conjectures of his own that appear far more distant from the truth than are the symbolistic imaginations of Clement[1]. Jerome represents the beloved disciple as being the first to recognise the Lord because he was "a virgin" and therefore "recognised a virgin body." But he ignores the fact that there was no recognition, even by the beloved disciple, till the Seven had obeyed the Lord's command to "cast the net," and had proved themselves "fishers." Then, and not till then, did the Chief Fisherman begin to draw His "children" towards Himself, using the spiritual insight of the beloved disciple as His instrument, and thus drawing first Peter, "through water," and then the rest, "in the little boat."

It will be noted that in Clement's list of Christian seals one was a "fish" and another was an "anchor." The anchor is found on Jewish coins as early as Seleucus. The Cross, by itself, somewhat resembles an anchor, but wants something at its foot to express the anchor's prong. When a gem contains the Christian *ichthus* placed transversely at the foot of the Cross so as to represent the prong, the two make up a close resemblance to an anchor[2]. The Gospel of Peter represents the Cross as following Jesus in His ascension to heaven. The Cross is questioned "Hast thou preached to them that are asleep

---

[1] E g *Against Jovinianus* i 26 (*Letters* p 365) "*The virgin alone* [i e John] recognised a virgin, and said to Peter 'It is the Lord' Our Lord said to him [i e to Peter] 'What is that to thee *if I wish him so to be* [i e to remain a virgin] ?'.. Here we have a proof that *virginity does not die*, and that the defilement of marriage [in the case of Peter] is not washed away by the blood of martyrdom... " Comp *To Pammachius* § 35 (*Letters* p 443) "Virginity is the first to recognise a virgin body." These passages reveal the extent to which materialistic prepossessions may weaken a commentator's sense of spiritual fitness, and his power of accurate interpretation

[2] See *Dict of Christ Ant* 1 713 *b* for this combination on a gem apparently much more ancient than one that represents (*ib.* 1 714 *b*) a perfect anchor with a dolphin twisted round it

THE CALLING OF THE FISHERMEN

[*i e.* in Hades][1]?" It replies "Yea" In other words, the Cross and the Ichthus have already gone down like the Anchor of Hope into the waters of Sheol to carry the Gospel of Hope Now they are going up in triumph to be "an anchor of the soul, [a hope] both sure and stedfast, and one that entereth into that which is within the veil[2]." There seems some mixture of metaphor in an "anchor," likened to a hope that "entereth" into a heavenly region, that is to say, *goes up* But the objection to it disappears when we regard it as a phase of Christian thought arising out of an earlier phase in which Christ descending into Sheol was regarded as "the anchor" *going down.*

All this is Greek thought, not Hebrew But it is also from Greek thought and Greek vocabulary that the mystical ICHTHUS came into the Church This consideration should warn us against ignoring the possibility that Greek vocabulary may have influenced Luke—that one of the Evangelists who writes most in the style of a Greek historian—in describing the Reminding of Peter

§ 27. *Peter swimming to Jesus*[3]

Is there anything in Luke's narrative about Peter in the Draught of Fishes corresponding to the most striking of the Johannine details—namely, that Peter swam to Jesus[4]?

---

[1] *Evang Petr* § 10
[2] Heb vi. 19 It is a Greek thought The word "anchor" does not occur in O.T
[3] On the subject of this section see Preface, pp vi—vii.
[4] Jn xxi 7—8 The others did not swim They came "in *the little boat*" This seems curiously distinguished from "*the boat*" mentioned just before Τὸ πλοῖον occurs in xxi 3, 6, but τὸ πλοιάριον in xxi 8 Luke's narrative mentions two πλοῖα See below, pp 96—7, as to the Talmudic distinction between "a little boat" and "a big vessel" in crossing the "waters of swimming" in Ezekiel Westcott says "The change of word may point to the use of some smaller vessel which was attached to the 'ship,' as the words are distinguished in vi. 22, or it may be a more exact description of the vessel."

THE CALLING OF THE FISHERMEN

"Swimming," it is true, is not mentioned, but only "he threw himself into the sea." Yet, as the distance from the shore is said to be "two hundred cubits," swimming may fairly be said to be implied. We shall proceed to investigate whether—not only in Luke but also in ancient traditions or expositions connected with Luke or with John—there is anything that points to the conclusion that what John took to mean "swimming," Luke had previously taken to mean something else[1].

An affirmative reply is indicated by the following considerations. As we have seen above, both the Lucan and the Johannine narratives appear to allude to the River of Life in Ezekiel with its "trees of food" on the bank. Now concerning that River, after it has been measured out four times in spaces of "a thousand cubits," it is said that its waters became "waters of *swimming*[2]." The regular Greek word for "*swimming*," *neusis*, might also, in theory, mean "*making signs*[3]." The learned author of the Greek Thesaurus himself has confused the present tense of "swim" with the

---

[1] In Jn xxi 7, SS includes in its paraphrase "and was swimming," Nonnus χεῖρας ἐρετμώσας, Chrys νηχόμενος

[2] Ezek xlvii 5. The Heb noun there used for "swimming" (Gesen 965 b) occurs only there in the Bible (though existent in New Hebrew, Aramaic, and Syriac) and it is omitted by LXX.

[3] Νεῦσις (from νέω, νεύσομαι, "I swim") is regularly used for (1) "swimming." Νεῦσις (from νεύω, νεύσω, "I incline," "bow," "nod") often means (2) "inclination," "tendency." It might, in theory, mean (3) "nodding," but it never does.

The Lexicons are somewhat confusing. L S says "νέω...aor ἔνευσα, cf. Eur. *Hipp* 470, Thuc ii 90." But these passages do not contain ἔνευσα but ἐκνεῦσαι and ἐξένευσαν. And a reference to προσνέω, ἐννέω, ἐπινέω in Steph *Thes* shews that, although *compound verbs* in -ευσα mean "swam," no instance is given where the uncompounded ἔνευσα means "swam." Yet in view of νευστέον in Plato 453 D "*one must swim*," and ἐξένευσα (as L S) in Thuc and Eurip., no Greek author could be blamed for similarly using κατένευσα, "*I swam to shore*" (or other compounds, if the context made the meaning clear.

THE CALLING OF THE FISHERMEN

present tense of "make-signs[1]." If therefore we discover in Luke's Draught of Fishes a statement that Peter and his crew "*made-signs*," that will, in itself, suggest that the Lucan expression "*made-signs*" corresponds to the Johannine implication "*swam*" If we also discover other authorities independently mentioning the "*making of signs*," either about Jesus or about the fishermen in connection with the Lucan or the Johannine narrative, the two discoveries will go far toward demonstrating that there has been a confusion of the two words

But before shewing that this is the case we must point out that in Luke's "they *beckoned* unto their partners[2]," the verb is, as the Thesaurus indicates, unusually if not inaccurately employed. Its usual meaning is "*nodded assent*" No instance has ever been alleged where it really means "beckoned for help[3]" On the other hand although it might, analogously to Attic usage, mean "swim to shore," yet no instance is alleged of that either[4]. Luke, therefore, choosing between two interpretations (1) "Peter *swam to shore*" and (2) "Peter *made signs of assent*," and believing the former to be out of the question, might adopt the latter, faithfully adhering to the exact form of the difficult word, but using it quite exceptionally to mean "*beckoned for help*." The substitution of Peter's

---

[1] See Steph *Thes* v. 1470 where the Editor—concerning the dictum of Steph. "Νεύω,. nato"—says "HSt non recte finxit praesens"

[2] Lk v 7

[3] See Steph *Thes* shewing that κατανεύω regularly means "nutu confirmo" In *Odyss*. xv 463 the meaning is "nodded that all was arranged," in accordance with preconcerted agreement In Polyb xxxix 1 3 it is ironically said that Hasdrubal, described as κενόδοξος καὶ ἀλαζών, instead of advancing to pay his respects to a prince, "[graciously] nodded to him [permission] to advance (κατένευεν αὐτῷ προιέναι)"

[4] That is to say, if ἐξένευσα in Thuc and Eurip means "I swam out," κατένευσα might analogously mean "I swam *to shore*," κατά being the regular prefix to denote "return *to port*" etc

THE CALLING OF THE FISHERMEN

companions ("those round Peter") for "Peter" would present no difficulty, since such Greek expressions are constantly interchanged[1] Luke might easily come to the conclusion that it was not Peter *by himself* who made these signs, but the immediate companions, or crew of Peter, who made signs to his more distant companions or partners. This Luke took to mean that "Peter and his companions *made-signs* to James and John, to come and help them[2]"

Let us suppose, then, that there was an early oral Greek metaphorical tradition connected with Peter, to the effect that he "swam to the shore" to Jesus, and that "swam" was erroneously taken by some to mean "made signs." Since, in this sense, the compound verb often implied signs of assent, or consent, as coming from a superior, interpreters adopting this sense would have either to alter the context as Luke alters it according to our hypothesis ("made-signs" [not to Jesus, but] *"to their partners*[3]*"*), or else to alter the word Nonnus

---

[1] For οἱ περὶ Πέτρον "those round Peter" interchangeable with Πέτρος, see *Notes* **2999** (xvii) *g*—*h*

[2] The only instance where John uses νεύω is in xiii 24 The context there is entirely different from that of Luke, except in this single respect, that the person to whom Peter "makes signs" is the beloved disciple, presumably John the son of Zebedee But it must be added that Luke uses ἐννεύω (only here in N.T.) about the friends of the father of John the Baptist, who (i 62) "beckoned to his father [asking] what he would wish him to be called " Such a tradition might be expressed in Greek thus "*Those about [the infant] John* beckoned [to his father] saying 'Say what is [to be] his name'" This, if it referred to *John the son of Zebedee*, might have quite a different meaning Placed on the night of the Last Supper it might mean (as in Jn xiii 24) "[The companions of John the son of Zebedee, and especially] Peter, made signs [to John] saying, 'Say [to Jesus], What is his name [*i e* the name of the traitor] ? '" It will be seen below that the *Acts of John* describes a companion of John—not however Peter, but his brother James—as saying to John that Jesus is "the little-child that is beckoning to us "

[3] If Luke combined this with a paraphrase of κατένευσε as ἐξένευσε—in the sense of Eurip. *Iph Taur* 1330 "made signs

THE CALLING OF THE FISHERMEN

and Chrysostom (according to our hypothesis) alter the word. In their paraphrase or comment on the Johannine narrative, they both say that Peter and his companions *"made signs negatively"* to Jesus in answer to the question "Have ye aught to eat[1]?" The Acts of John alters both the word and the agent. In describing the Call of the Fishermen, it attributes the "making-of-signs" (using the uncompounded *neuein*) to Jesus Himself. Also, it mentions Him, not as using the word "children" to the fishermen, but as appearing to James, the brother of John, in the form of a "child".—"For when He had chosen Peter and Andrew, who were brethren, He cometh unto me and my brother James, saying, 'I have need of you. Come unto me' And my brother said this, 'John, this *child*, that called to us on the shore—what does it want?' And I said, 'What *child*?' And he [said] to me again, 'The one that is *making-signs* to us[2].'"

It may be said, in explanation of this last passage, that the word "make-signs" has been derived by the Acts of John not from the Fourth Gospel but from the Third: "The author has

---

that we should go away (ἐξένευσ' ἀποστῆναι)"—the paraphrase might be developed into a tradition saying that Peter exclaimed (Lk. v 8) "Depart from me, O Lord."

Comp Justin Martyr *Tryph* §9 "It seemed good to Trypho also that we should do so [*i e.* that we should retire to a quiet place from noisy companions], *and accordingly, slipping-away* (καὶ δὴ ἐκνεύσαντες) we came to the middle stadium of the Xystus" The sense seems to demand this meaning But the Latin renders ἐκνεύσαντες *"quumque inter nos innuissemus"* And the English has (T and T Clark) *"and accordingly having agreed upon it"*

[1] It might be objected that Nonnus was constrained by the necessities of metre, which obliged him to use ἀνανεύω in order to reproduce in hexameters the prosaic Jn xxi. 5 ἀπεκρίθησαν αὐτῷ Οὔ which he paraphrases by ἀμειβόμενοι δὲ μαθηταὶ Οὐδὲν ἔχειν ἀνένευον But the futility of such an objection would be shewn by Nonnus' paraphrase of the very same expression in Jn i. 21 καὶ ἀπεκρίθη Οὔ where he does not use ἀνανεύω It does not occur again in Nonnus Chrys. says ‛Ως δὲ ἀνένευσαν μηδὲν ἔχειν

[2] *Acts of John* § 2 "child," παιδίον, "making-signs," νεῦον

THE CALLING OF THE FISHERMEN

borrowed *'child'* from John, and *'making signs'* from Luke, and has transferred both words from the disciples to Jesus[1]." But this would not explain the "making signs" attributed to the fishermen in John by Chrysostom and Nonnus. They can hardly be supposed to be borrowing it from Luke. Still less could they have borrowed it from the Acts of John. The combined evidence points back to some very early tradition, earlier even than Luke and John, in which a Semitic original was interpreted by an ambiguous Greek word.

If this is the case, and if the Lucan *"making-signs"* and the Johannine description of *swimming* are two interpretations of one Hebrew original, there can be little doubt that the latter is the correct one. For we have seen that the form of Luke's question ("aught-to-eat") pointed to the poetic description of the River—including the "waters of swimming"—in Ezekiel. It is more likely that Luke, in his desire to emphasize historical "proofs," has reduced poetry to prose, than that John has sublimated prose to poetry. Moreover the Johannine implication of swimming, taken along with the curious distinction between "the boat" and "the little boat," seems to correspond to Talmudic distinctions which are connected with Ezekiel's

---

[1] The transposition of παιδία might be explained from a tradition that Jesus "called to them *as [to] children* (ὡς παιδίοις)." This, if ωc παιΔιοιc were taken as ωc παιΔιοῖc, would mean "*As a child, Jesus* called to them." See Clem Alex 104—12, a section on spiritual "children." It begins with a loose quotation of the passage we are considering (Jn xxi. 4—5 "*children*") and ends with a declaration that Jesus is *the "Child"*, "O the great God! O the perfect (*or*, full-grown) *Child* (παιδίου)...the Son of God, the Infant (τὸν νήπιον) of the Father." In quoting Jn, he says σταθεὶς...ὁ κύριος ἐπὶ τῷ αἰγιαλῷ πρὸς τοὺς μαθητὰς...(?) ἐνεφώνησέν τε, Παιδία, μή τι ὄψον ἔχετε, τοὺς ἤδη ἐν ἕξει τῶν γνωρίμων παῖδας προσειπών. That is to say, he describes Jesus as "calling aloud 'children'" and then "accosting [as] children (παῖδας προσειπών)" those that were already in the position of disciples. His reason for passing from παιδία, lit "little children," to παῖδας, "children" or "boys," is perhaps that he is beginning a treatise about παῖδες to be entitled Παιδαγωγός.

THE CALLING OF THE FISHERMEN

River, and which distinguish between (1) "swimming," (2) passing in a "small boat," (3) passing in a "large boat[1]."

In the preceding paragraphs the possibility of confusing the two meanings of *kat-eneusa* "*I made signs of assent*" should have been illustrated by the various meanings of *di-eneusa*, namely (1) "*swam through,*" (2) "*winked*" or "*made signs,*" (3) "*avoided*"; and of *an-eneusa* (1) "*made signs of dissent,*" (2) "*lifted up the head,*" (3) "*swam up*[2]." Also *kat-ĕneusa* might easily be confused with *kat-ēnusa* "*I accomplished [my course]*[3]."

§ 28. "*Swimming*" and "*stretching out* (or, *spreading out*) *the hands*"

Each correspondence of detail between the story of the Fishermen in John and the vision of the Fishermen in Ezekiel strengthens the inference that other apparent correspondences, which, if taken singly, would not have a claim to be regarded as more than casual coincidences, are something more than casual. Such is the Johannine "right hand parts of the boat," mentioned above as possibly alluding to "the right hand of the

---

[1] See Jer *Shekalim* vi. 2 (3) (Schwab v. 304) which quotes Ezek. xlvii. 2—5 (including "waters of swimming") and Is xxxiii 21 *b* (mentioning vessels of two kinds, see Rashi) and goes on to speak of "swimming" in Is xxv. 11 Rashi, on Is. xxv 11 "he shall *spread out his hands*...for swimming," takes the first clause as implying sorrow, and illustrates the second from Ezek. xlvii 5. On "*stretching out the hands,*" applied to Peter in Jn xxi. 18, see the next section.

[2] See Steph. *Thes* on διανεύω and ἀνανεύω, quoting Clem Alex 83 ἀνανεύσατε τῆς γῆς εἰς αἰθέρα "lift up your heads from earth to heaven" and Ael. *N A* v 22 ἀνανεῦσαι (fr ἀνανέω) "swim up," "emerge"

[3] See Clem Rom § 25 διανύει, v r διανεύει, Syr *migrat volans,* where Lightf says "Several instances of the confusion of διανύειν and διανεύειν by transcribers are given by Jahn *Methodius* II. p 110" In Berlin Urkunde 1119 24, 1120 30, κατανεύων must be corrupt, and may be meant for κατανύων "finishing in a workmanlike manner," but the context makes the inference doubtful

THE CALLING OF THE FISHERMEN

altar" in Ezekiel[1]. Such, too, might be the measurements by "cubits" introduced by both into their descriptions of the waters of fishing. The contexts, and the purpose of these symbolic measurements in the two writings are, of course, very different. In Ezekiel, the mentions of a "thousand cubits" symbolize the development of the River of Life In John, the "two hundred cubits," through which Peter and his companions have to pass in order to reach Jesus, perhaps suggests "repentance[2]"

But we have now to ask whether in correspondence to Ezekiel's "waters of swimming," we find in John, later on, something that corresponds more closely to Jewish thought about "swimming" than does the bare phrase "cast himself into the sea" which describes Peter's actual plunge. The only passage in which human "swimming" is mentioned in the Bible[3]—the swimming of the dragon of Egypt being set aside—connects the action with "*spreading out [the hands].*" And "*spreading out*" is frequently represented in the LXX by "*stretching out*" Thus Peter's swimming—"he cast himself into the sea"—which is, in effect, "swam"—prepares the way for the prophecy that he shall die his Master's death : "When thou shalt be old, thou *shalt stretch out thy hands*"—that is to say, upon the Cross. If this is allusive, we may go on to say that Peter's other previous action, "he *girt* his coat about

---

[1] See above, p. 37 foll.

[2] Jn xxi. 8 "But the other disciples came in the little boat (for they were not far from the land, but about *two hundred cubits* off) dragging the net [full] of fishes " On this, see *Notes* **2999** (xvii) *o* "They are 'not far' from Him It is only 'about *two hundred cubits* ' This number of years (according to Philo on Gen v 21—4 (LXX) represents the length of the penitence of Enoch " The numbers in Gen v 21—4 (LXX) differ from those in the Hebrew text "Two" is freq used in connection with probation, or waiting, see *Paradosis*, Index, "Two "

[3] Is xxv 11 "as he that swimmeth spreadeth out [his hands] to swim " R V has "spread forth" in Isaiah, but Gesen. 831 gives "spread out."

THE CALLING OF THE FISHERMEN

him," is allusive also. It prepares the way for the other part of the prediction, "Another shall *gird* thee" That it is predictive of crucifixion is indicated by the following words, "Now this he spake signifying *by what manner of death he should glorify God*[1]."

If the thought of Peter "swimming" was really at the bottom of the tradition from which Luke as well as John derived the tradition of the Draught of Fishes, we are led to important inferences bearing on future investigation. One is, that Greek as well as Hebrew corruption must be reckoned with as a factor in the origination of divergencies. But a still more important one is, that sometimes, where we may have been disposed to regard John as simply writing poetry of his own imagination, he may be drawing out the meaning of early Christian poetic tradition, that recorded, under picturesque symbols, a history of spiritual fact.

Not that we are to discard motive also as a factor. Motive is apparent all through this Johannine Appendix. In it the Evangelist appears to reveal his unwillingness to close his Gospel with a mere external "proof"—such as convinced Thomas—that the Saviour is living. The only real proof (he feels and makes us feel) is that of an inward energizing "love" This it is that saves the swimming Apostle, drawing him—penitent, humbled, and purified—to his Master on the shore This it is that gives food and strength to him, when saved, that he may go forth and bring salvation to others. And this it is also that prepares Peter's special companion, the

---

[1] Jn xxi. 18—19. The Heb. of Is. xxv. 11 "*spread*" is rendered seven times by LXX ἐκτείνω, *e g.* in Is. 1 15 ὅταν ἐκτείνητε τὰς χεῖρας, which is the Johannine phrase here See *Notes* **2929** on the double meaning (1) "*stretch out the hands*" *in prayer to God*, (2) "*stretch out the hands,*" *literally, at the bidding of the executioner* But it should have been added that the Evangelist prepares the way for this play on words by first presenting Peter to us "stretching out the hands" as a swimmer, passing through the deep waters to the Saviour who is drawing him and his companions safe to the shore.

THE CALLING OF THE FISHERMEN

unnamed disciple, to work for his Lord. The two work for the Shepherd by working for His sheep in various ways, one of them "following," the other "tarrying."

All this manifest motive, and the dramatic beauty of its expression, must not induce us to do the author the injustice of supposing that the whole story is a fiction. On the contrary, whereas the Three Synoptists are incomplete or misleading, the Fourth Gospel, though perhaps mixing vision with fact, or substituting metaphor for fact, appears at all events to set before us the spiritual reality—what may be described as the real Calling—in closer accordance with history and in its correct chronological position, the Johannine view being to this effect.—"The original tradition taught that Peter, who had been called to be a fisher of men and had abandoned his task for a time, returned to it after the Resurrection. This 'returning' was called, in Christian poetry, '*swimming*'—a *swimming back* through the deep waters of repentance. Coming after the Resurrection, it has been omitted in the extant Gospel of Mark Matthew placed a version of it in the story of a storm, during which Christ walked on the waters. Matthew described Peter as attempting to come to Jesus over the water[1], and as in danger of sinking, if Jesus had not taken hold of him. But Mark, though describing the storm and the walking of Jesus on the water, omits all mention of Peter's attempt.

"Luke omits the whole narrative, even the walking of Jesus on the water. But he places what seems to be a version of it shortly after the Call of Peter in a story of the Reminding of Peter. Here Peter and Jesus are described as being together in a boat. But the context is quite different. The boat is filled and in danger of sinking; but it is filled with fishes, not with water. Luke also appears to have confused '*Peter swimming*' with '*Peter making signs*' Neither Mark nor Matthew has any such story as Luke's in any part of the

---

[1] Mt. xiv. 31.

THE CALLING OF THE FISHERMEN

Gospel. The right course seems to be to relate the 'swimming,' as 'swimming,' perhaps accepting it as a literal fact (though it was more probably in part or whole a vision) but at all events describing it in its right place, after the Resurrection, and giving to it a spiritual as well as a literal significance."

§ 29 *Jesus "going on* (or, *forward)"*

Evidence has been adduced to shew that, in the Synoptic accounts of the Calling (or Reminding) of Peter, there have probably been errors of chronology as well as Greek verbal confusions. Luke seems to have confused the Greek for "swim to the shore" with the Greek for "make signs of assent," and in Mark or Matthew there seems some confusion between "cast about [a net]" and "cast about [in one's mind]"; but Luke seems also to have placed much too early an account of a miraculous Draught of Fishes which John places much later[1].

These probabilities, if accepted as such, should induce us not only to investigate thoroughly and patiently other verbal differences between Mark-Matthew and the quasi-parallel Luke, especially if the language used by any of the three is rare, but also to bear in mind that we may have to look much further on, to the close of the Gospel, in order to find those differences explained.

Here we have to deal with:—

Mk i. 19 (R.V.)	Mt. iv. 21 (R.V)	Lk. v. 3 (R.V.)
And going-on a little further[2].	And going-on from thence[3].	to put-out[4] a little from the land.

---

[1] See above § 11 and § 28

[2] Καὶ προβὰς ὀλίγον, SS "and when he walked-on again a little," where "walk-on" = הלך, the word used by Delitzsch in Lk v 3 Syr. Walton has "passed." R.V. "further" should have been omitted here, or else inserted also in Mt. iv. 21, the Greek προβάς being identical. Codex D has προcβΑc, but with the first c cancelled (*d* "progressus").

For notes 3 and 4 see next page.

THE CALLING OF THE FISHERMEN

The phrase "went-forward a little" is applied by Mark-Matthew to Jesus again—though the Greek words differ—in the narrative of Gethsemane.

Mk xiv. 35 (R.V.)	Mt. xxvi. 39 (R.V)	Lk xxii. 41 (R V.)
And he went-forward a little[1].	And he went-forward a little[2]	And he was parted from them about a stone's cast[3].

In the latter narrative, the Lucan "about a stone's cast" as a substitute for "a little" may be illustrated by

---

[3] Καὶ προβὰς ἐκεῖθεν, Curet. "and when he removed thence," SS "and he drew-near again and..." (which would partly agree with Mk (D*)), Syr. Walton "passed thence," b "praecedens inde "
'Εκεῖθεν might represent an original Heb "from them," i e from the people mentioned in the context, see note on Mt xii. 15 below, p 105, n 2

[4] SS and Walton "put-it-out," using (see Brederek's *Concordance* p. 145) an Aramaic equiv of the Heb hif of הלך "go," which Delitzsch has here, lit "cause-to-go " The Lat codd. vary —a "producerent terra," b "inducerent ad terram," Brix. "a terra reducere," Corb "ut duceret a terra," Gat "ducere", e has "ut exaltaretur a terra "

[1] Καὶ προελθὼν μικρὸν..., several MSS, including D, have προσελθὼν μικρὸν (d "processisset paululum"), SS "and he (lit) separated [himself] a little," the Syr means "take-away" and hence "withdraw" in various senses (Burk "departed a little"), but Syr Walton has "accessit paululum" (perhaps meaning "drew near [to God]" in prayer for help), a "et progressus paulum," Brix "et cum processisset paululum " Προέρχομαι in LXX, as a rendering of Heb , occurs only twice, and then with various readings It = Heb "pass "

[2] Καὶ προελθὼν μικρὸν..., several MSS, including D, have προσελθὼν μικρὸν, d "accedens pusillum", but SS has "and he removed from them a little," Syr Pesh has "and he separated [himself] a little" (Walton, "recessit paululum "), the Lat codd. have "progressus modicum, or, pusillum."

[3] Καὶ αὐτὸς ἀπεσπάσθη ἀπ' αὐτῶν ὡσεὶ λίθου βολήν, SS "and he (Curet +himself) separated [himself] from them about a stone's cast," Latin codd. "avolsus" etc except Brix. "discessit."

THE CALLING OF THE FISHERMEN

Mk xiv. 70 (R.V.)	Mt. xxvi 73 (R.V.)	Lk xxii. 59 (R V.)
And after a little while again[1].	And after a little while[2]	And after the space of about one hour[3]

Luke, writing as a historian, tries to define what Mark-Matthew describes vaguely as "a little" in these two passages. The Hebrew for "a very little," "just a little" etc., is very often "as-it-were a little[4]." Perhaps this partly explains Luke's use of "as-if" (*i e* "about") in both cases. In Peter's Denial, he decides, partly perhaps from the Mark-Matthew context, and partly from other information, that the interval, which is clearly one of time, is "about one hour[5]." In the narrative of Gethsemane, he first decides that the interval is not one of time (a quite possible meaning, "he separated himself from them *for a little* [*time*]") but one of space. Then he has to consider that the interval of space must be such that the disciples were able to see Jesus though it was night. Homer says that in a night favourable to thieves "one sees *as far as*

---

[1] Καὶ μετὰ μικρὸν πάλιν, Cod *a* "et post pusillum iterum "

[2] Μετὰ μικρὸν δέ, SS and Syr Walton *lit* "and from after a little," Lat codd "post pusillum "
Lk xxii 58 has μετὰ βραχύ, but that is parallel to Mk xiv. 69 πάλιν (Mt xxvi. 71 om)

[3] Lk xxii 58—9 combines two expressions of time, Καὶ μετὰ βραχύ . καὶ διαστάσης ὡσεὶ ὥρας μιᾶς, Curet "and after a little ..and after one hour," but SS "and after a little.. and it came to pass [in] about one hour," Codex *a* omits "little" and "hour," and inserts "door," perh from Mk-Mt , "et egressum illum ad januam vidit alia et...quem paulo post cum vidisset quidam", *b* "et iterum post pusillum...et intervallo facto horae unius" (and sim Brix , Corb and *e*). See *Clue* 127 for confusion arising from Heb "hour" in Dan iv 19 (A V) "one hour," (R V) "a while."

[4] See Gesen. 590, comp Cant. iii. 4 "I had *as-it-were a little* passed from them and I found," ὡς μικρὸν ὅτε παρῆλθον ἀπ' αὐτῶν

[5] Note Luke's deviation from Mark-Matthew, as to the hour ; he inserts (xxii. 66) "as soon as it was day" where Mk xiv 55, Mt xxvi. 59 have no such detail, and, later on (Lk. xxiii 1) he omits the reference to "morning" in Mk xv 1, Mt xxvii 1.

THE CALLING OF THE FISHERMEN

one can cast a stone," and Eustathius, using Luke's expression, says that this is "*a stone's cast*[1]."

If Luke's expression is suggested by Homer—and in the Thesaurus no other instance has been alleged of the "stone's cast" as a recognised distance—that is an indication that we are in a part of his narrative likely to be influenced by Greek expression and poetic paraphrase. It happens that the change of a single letter might convert "casting [of a stone]" into "a-draught-of-fishes[2]." Adapting to Greek phrases the Jewish habit of "paronomasia," a Christian poet of the first century might say, "Read not that Jesus went before the Fishermen disciples as if for 'the [space of the] casting of a stone'; but read rather that He, the Fisherman, went before them 'for the casting of the Net of the Gospel,' which was to enclose the fishes of this world."

It must be observed that the object has been, throughout this section, not to explain the origin of Luke's narrative of the Draught of Fishes, but to explain its position. Its origin might well be some metaphorical account of Peter's repentance followed by his converting the "three thousand" and the "five thousand" in Jerusalem[3] But its position would still require to be explained, coming as a Lucan insertion in the Reminding of the Fishermen which is a quasi-parallel to the Mark-Matthew Calling of the Fishermen. This Lucan insertion about Christ as sitting in a boat with Peter needs

---

[1] See Wetstein, on Lk. xxii. 41, quoting Eustathius on *Iliad* iii. 12, τόσσον τίς τ' ἐπιλεύσσει ὅσον τ' ἐπὶ λᾶαν ἵησιν, where the Scholiast says, "Ὅσον ἐπὶ λίθου βολήν.

[2] That is to say, ΒοληΝ, "casting," would become ΒολοΝ (see Steph. *Thes.* ii. 319) which might mean (1) "net," (2) "a-cast-of-the-net," (3) "[the result of] a cast of the net," *i.e.* "a draught of fishes." In Aramaic the phrase would be (as it is in SS) "the casting of *cephas*," which might lend itself to poetic developments taking *cephas* as Cephas the Apostle

[3] Acts ii 41, iv. 4.

(Mark i. 16—20)

THE CALLING OF THE FISHERMEN

to be considered along with Lucan omissions of similar incidents :—

Mk iii. 7—9	Mt. xii. 15 [iv. 24—25]	Lk. vi 17—19
(7) And Jesus with his disciples withdrew to the sea[1].... (9) And he spake to his disciples that a little boat should wait on him because of the crowd, lest they should throng him.	And Jesus perceiving [it] withdrew from thence[2].	Omits.

Still more remarkable is the Lucan omission before the Parable of the Sower :—

Mk iv 1—2	Mt. xiii. 1—3	Lk. viii 4
(1) And again he began to teach by the sea side. And there is gathered unto him a very great multitude, so that he entered into a boat, and sat in the sea; and all the multitude were by the sea on the land. (2) And he taught them many things in parables ..	(1) On that day went Jesus out of the house, and sat by the sea side. (2) And there were gathered unto him great multitudes, so that he entered into a boat, and sat, and all the multitude stood on the beach. (3) And he spake to them many things in parables ...	And when a great multitude came together, and they of every city resorted unto him, he spake by a parable

---

[1] Mk iii. 7 b—8 is parall. to Mt. iv 24—5, Lk. vi. 17 b.
[2] In Judg xiv. 19 (A), Is xxx. 6 (LXX) ἐκεῖθεν, the Heb. is "*from them,*" so that Matthew's ἐκεῖθεν might imply "*from those [mentioned in the context],*" i e, as Mark says, "*from the crowd,*" or "*because of the crowd.*"

105 (Mark i 16—20)

THE CALLING OF THE FISHERMEN

The impression left by the Lucan insertion and omissions, taken together, is that Luke regarded Mark as having misunderstood the tradition connecting Jesus with Peter, James, and John, the three leading Apostles, in the Reminding of the Fishermen on the Lake of Gennesaret. Mark's narrative (he might think) had destroyed the prominence that should have been given to Peter and to the promise made specially to him ("thou shalt catch men") in response to the cry of his alarmed conscience ("fear not"). Mark seemed to Luke (in the narrative of Gennesaret) to have broken the story in two by taking Christ's *"going forward a little" in the boat, with Peter, from the land*, as though it meant *"passing onward" from calling Peter to call the sons of Zebedee*. But that (according to Luke's view) was not the case. The three fishermen were practically together, "partners and sharers" in the work of fishing. But they had failed. Jesus came to their aid. First, He "went forward a little" in the boat with Peter in order that He might Himself teach the Gospel, which was, in effect, the casting of the net. Then, and not till then, He bade Peter go still further forward into the deep water, that Peter, too, might cast the net after the example of his Master[1]

How John's narrative of the Draught of Fishes deviates from, and at the same time supplements, that of Luke—and

---

[1] It should be added that Luke, as a stylist, may have had a special objection to the phrasing of Mk i. 19, Mt iv. 21 προβάς "going forward." It does not occur elsewhere in N T., except in Lk i 7, 18, ii 36, and there it always means "advanced in years" This is also its meaning in LXX, seven times out of ten where it represents a Hebrew word It occurs twice in Hermas *Vis* iv 1 5, *Sim* vi 2 5, and both times with μικρόν meaning simply "went on a little [further]." But this, like other peculiarities of Hermas, may be borrowed from the vernacular Greek of Mark. The only instance in canon LXX where προβαίνω, applied to persons, does not mean "advanced in years," is Gen. xxvi. 13 (*lit.*) "and he went-on going-on" (Field "et procedebat procedendo"), LXX καὶ προβαίνων, al exempl καὶ ἐπορεύετο προβαίνων, where the meaning is "and he prospered exceedingly."

perhaps other Lucan traditions—has been in part described above. Here we may add that if it should be ascertained that Luke's "about a stone's cast" meant in the first century a distance of "about a hundred yards" (that is, about two hundred cubits)—which is antecedently a very probable estimate—we should then find one more detail in which John agreed, and at the same time disagreed, with Luke. Luke took the "stone's cast" as a material distance not too great to prevent the disciples from seeing their Master who had separated Himself from them in order to pray. John took the "stone's cast" as "two hundred cubits," a spiritual distance, arising from the fact that the disciples had for a time separated themselves from their Master, and even now needed some further repentant experience to teach them to depend on Him, as their sustenance and food, in their attempts to do His work. "They were not far off from the land," says John, meaning, the land where Jesus was waiting for them, "but [only] as it were a distance of two hundred cubits[1]." The *"as-it-were"* reproduces the *"as-if"* of Luke, and the *"not far...but [only]"* reproduces the *"little"* of Mark and Matthew. The *"two hundred cubits"* reproduces the Lucan *"stone's cast,"* but adds (as has been shewn above) a symbolical suggestion of returning through repentance[2].

§ 30. *"Zebedee"*

We have now come to the first of several Marcan passages relating, directly or indirectly, to Zebedee or his family. Some

---

[1] Jn xxi 8

[2] Since these hypotheses about such phrases as "going on" and "a stone's cast"—phrases far removed from one another and belonging to different narratives—lead at present to no definite conclusion, it might have seemed well to defer them till they could be more fully considered in their order But the facts here collected will be of use later on when the time comes for their fuller consideration.

THE CALLING OF THE FISHERMEN

of these appear to contradict the rule of Johannine Intervention. For example, "Zebedee," apart from "son(s) of," is here mentioned by Mark-Matthew, but not by Luke in his parallel :—

Mk i. 19—20 (R.V)	Mt. iv. 21—2 (R.V)	Lk. v. 10—11 (R.V.)
(19) He saw James the [son] of Zebedee, and John his brother, who also were in the boat . (20) and they left their father Zebedee in the boat with the hired servants.	(21) He saw other two brethren, James the [son] of Zebedee, and John his brother, in the boat with Zebedee their father, (22) And they straightway left the boat and their father..	(10) And so were also James and John, sons of Zebedee, which were partners with Simon .. (11) And.. they left all.

Here Mark (followed by Matthew) describes Zebedee as still living. But, later on, he is not mentioned in any Gospel except in special phrases (*e g.* "the sons of Zebedee" and "the mother of Zebedee's sons") such as would either imply, or accord with, the supposition that he was dead.

Mark, and Mark alone, here describes Zebedee as being left "with the hired servants." Also, later on, Mark alone describes the two sons of Zebedee as being called by Jesus "Boanerges" or "sons of thunder." And immediately after the Crucifixion, Mark alone twice mentions—among the women near, or coming to, Christ's tomb—"Salome," whom modern writers identify, as Origen did, with "the mother of the sons of Zebedee[1]."

The most remarkable of Luke's deviations from Mark-Matthew on this point relates to the petition of the sons of Zebedee (or their mother) to sit on Christ's right and left hand in His kingdom. Christ's answer, mentioning His "cup" and "baptism," might naturally be taken to predict martyrdom

---

[1] Mk xv. 40, xvi i See Origen on Mt xxvii 56 (Lomm. v 76—8), where he refers to Mk xv. 40

THE CALLING OF THE FISHERMEN

for the questioners[1]. Yet only James actually suffered death. Luke, possibly for this reason, omits both the petition and the answer[2].

On the other hand, Luke alone relates that "a village of the Samaritans" rejected Jesus, and "when his disciples, James and John, saw [it]," they said, "Lord, wilt thou that we bid fire to come down from heaven and consume them[3]?" Somewhat similar to this in tone is a passage peculiar to Mark and Luke—the only passage in the Gospels[4] where "John," used absolutely and without a contextual "James," means anything but "John the Baptist." It says that, while the doctrine of "receiving" a "little child" was being taught by Jesus, "John said unto him, Master, we saw one casting out devils in thy name, and we forbade him, because he followeth not with us[5]."

The impression that would be left by these Marcan passages on Greeks—and probably the impression left on most modern readers—is that the sons of Zebedee were called "sons of thunder" because of a certain masterful or tempestuous element in their characters. They seem to resemble Elijah, who was rebuked by the vision that culminated in the still small voice[6]. This impression is confirmed by the Lucan tradition above quoted concerning Samaria. It will be shewn that the Fourth Gospel apparently differs from this. But before considering the Johannine view, we must discuss the words, peculiar to Mark in the present passage, saying that Zebedee was left by his sons "with the hired servants." Unimportant in themselves, the words acquire importance from

---

[1] Mk x 35—40, Mt xx. 20—3.
[2] See *Notes* 2935 foll. controverting "The modern hypothesis of the early death of John the son of Zebedee"
[3] Lk ix 54
[4] Jn i. 42, xxi 15—17 "Simon son of John" ought perhaps to be mentioned as exceptions
[5] Mk ix. 38, Lk. ix. 49.   [6] 1 K. xix 12.

THE CALLING OF THE FISHERMEN

the fact that they must affect our views of the origin of Marcan traditions in general, as well as our views of the motives of Matthew and Luke in rejecting this particular tradition

§ 31 *"With the hired servants*[1]*"*

If the sons of Zebedee "left him in the boat," in the midst of his work, alone, they might be blamed by some as undutiful. If they left him *"with the hired servants"* the blame is avoided, or softened. Why then should Matthew omit this detail? That he does omit it indicates either that he was ignorant of its existence, or that he rejected it[2].

If Matthew rejected it, we may suppose that he rejected it as an early gloss, and if it was a gloss based on prophecy, the prophecy to which we should look as a source would be the one alleged in the parallel Matthew to have been fulfilled by Jesus about this time. "He came and dwelt in Capernaum which is by the sea, in the borders of Zebulon and Naphtali...that it might be fulfilled...'*The land of Zebulon and the land of Naphtali,* Galilee of the Gentiles...[3].'" This is Matthew's preface to the Call of the Fishermen. Two of them, namely, Peter and Andrew, lived in Capernaum, which is in "the land of Naphtali." This fulfils "Naphtali," but what fulfils "Zebulon"? Jerome's reply—in commenting on this prophecy

---

[1] Mk i. 20 "And they left their father Zebedee in the boat *with the hired servants* (μετὰ τῶν μισθωτῶν), and went after him," Mt. iv. 22 "And they straightway left the boat and their father, and followed him."

For other explanations of the clause see pp. 138—40. The one given in this section appears to me improbable, taken by itself, but not improbable if taken with other traditions which (p. 140, n 1) shew "navy" and "servants" in parallel passages of O T.

[2] Pseudo-Jerome implies that the "hired-servants (mercenarii)" as well as the "net" and the "boat," and the "father" himself, are all evil ("navem pristinae conversationis," "Adam, qui genitor est noster secundum carnem" etc). Μισθωτός is mostly used in a bad sense

[3] Mt iv. 13—15

THE CALLING OF THE FISHERMEN

of Isaiah—is derived from the Psalms : "The princes of Zebulon and the princes of Naphtali, their leaders." He adds "Because in these tribes were the villages [coming] from which our 'leaders,' the Apostles, became-believers[1]." That Jerome followed a much earlier tradition is shewn by a fragment of Irenaeus, which—after saying that Christ was prefigured in Joseph, descended from Levi and Judah, and acknowledged by Simeon in the Temple—adds "*Through Zebulon* He was believed on among the Gentiles, as says the prophet, '*the land of Zebulon*'; and through Benjamin, [that is] Paul, His glory was proclaimed and carried into all the world[2]."

In the early Galilaean Church we may reasonably suppose that there would be a tendency to emphasize any circumstances that seemed to bring out a coincidence between the Galilaean Calling and the prophecy of Isaiah about Galilee. In particular, there would be a desire to indicate a connection with "Zebulon," since it was not in itself obvious, Zebulon not being known to be the residence of any of the Apostles. Now James and John are not introduced as Peter is, simply by their names[3]. They are called "sons of Zebedee" "Zebedee" is an O T. name derived from *zâbad* "endow," *zebed* "endowment" The noun and the verb occur only once in the Bible, "God hath endowed (*zâbad*) me with a good endowment; now will my husband dwell (*zâbal*) with me...and she called his name *Zebulun*[4]." The reader will perceive here the play on the roots of the words "Zebedee" and "Zebulon." But, further, the preceding context in Genesis describes the birth and naming of "Issachar," which

---

[1] Jerome on Is ix 1, quoting Ps lxviii 27.
[2] Iren *Fragm*. Grabe pp 469—70, Clark vol ii p 168, No 17. Irenaeus might have included (Lk ii 36) "the tribe of Asher"
[3] One reason for this would be that "John," by itself, at this stage, would naturally mean "John the Baptist"
[4] Gen xxx 20. Jer Targ retains *zâbad* and *zebed* See Gesen. 256*a* which quotes 2 Chr xxiv 26 "Zabad" (elsewhere *Jozacar* 2 K xii 21), LXX *Zabel, Zabeth, Zabath*.

THE CALLING OF THE FISHERMEN

name means either "*a man of hire*," or "*there is hire.*" Jewish traditions recognise a very close connection between Zebulon and Issachar. The Song of Moses says "Rejoice, Zebulon, in thy going out, and Issachar, in thy tents," and the Midrash on Genesis, alluding to this juxtaposition, says "*There is hire* in the tents of Zebulon[1]."

Thus we find, in the first Biblical mention of "Zebulon," a connection between that name and other names or words that suggest the name of "Zebedee" and the thought of "hire," and this in a context describing the origin of the tribes of Galilee[2]. When these facts are combined with Matthew's emphatic statement that the action of Jesus fulfilled a prophecy about "Zebulon," "Naphtali," and "Galilee," it becomes more easy for us to realise that an early Jewish tradition may have added to "*Zebulon*" some such phrase as "*along with Issachar*," and that this was taken to mean "along with *the men-of-hire*, or *hirelings.*"

If we accept this as a working hypothesis, it is creditable to Matthew that he rejected it because he knew it did not belong to the original Tradition of Mark. It is also less discreditable to the Marcan editor to suppose that he inserted it because he found it in existence, and because it seemed a probable extraneous explanation, than to suppose that he invented it for the purpose of shewing that the sons of Zebedee were not so undutiful as at first sight appeared[3].

---

[1] Midr on Gen. xxx. 18—20, quoting Deut xxxiii. 18.
[2] Gen xxx. 8—20 Naphtali, Gad, Asher, Issachar, Zebulun.
[3] Comp 1 Chr. xii. 32 "And of the sons of Issachar, *men that had understanding of the times, to know what Israel ought to do*..." and note Rashi's application of this to Judg. v. 14—15 "Out of Zebulun they that handle the marshal's staff; and the princes of Issachar were with Deborah; as was Issachar, so was Barak...." Rashi says that the princes of Issachar "*were continually with Deborah* to teach statutes and judgment in Israel." Thus apparently he would explain the silence about Issachar previously, when Barak is bidden by Deborah to summon Naphtali and Zebulon to the

THE CALLING OF THE FISHERMEN

§ 32. *"Sons of Zebedee," in John*

Zebedee, by himself, is nowhere mentioned in the Fourth Gospel. The sons of Zebedee are mentioned once, at its conclusion "There were together Simon Peter, and Thomas (called Didymus), and Nathanael (from Cana of Galilee), and the [sons] of Zebedee, and others of his disciples, two [in number][1]." At first sight, therefore, it seems hardly worth while to say anything about "'*sons* of Zebedee' in John" except to call attention to this single mention, this unemphatic abbreviation[2] (as it were, "the Zebedaeans," not "the sons of

---

war (Judg iv 6, 10) Someone might ask why this tribe had not been mentioned before and might infer that it did not actively help Barak Rashi replies by quoting "and [as] Issachar so Barak," which he renders "and the rest of the tribe of Issachar was also with Barak, ready to fulfil all his behests " So here, an early Galilaean tradition applying to the rise of the Church the prophecy of Isaiah concerning Galilee, Zebulon, and Naphtali, may have added that these were "*also with Issachar*" And this might suggest, later on, Mark's clause about "hired servants "

The passage in Chronicles above quoted gives to the tribe of Issachar a special and non-military character, and indicates that in any traditions of Galilaean Christians about the rise of the Gospel among the northern tribes of Galilee some reference to Issachar would seem appropriate In some sense it was "a gathering of the clans," like that under Deborah and Barak, and a Galilaean might say, "Where Zebulun finds mention, Issachar should be mentioned as well "

It might be supposed that, in view of the permanent captivity of the ten tribes, Jews could no longer regard themselves in Galilee as representing Zebulon and Naphtali and the rest But comp *Test XII Patr Joseph* xix 4 (Arm) "there gathered to them"— *i e* to the "three harts" previously mentioned—"the nine harts, and they became as twelve sheep," and the Editor's comment "As our author addresses the Twelve Tribes in his twelve Testaments, it is to be presumed that he regarded them as all actually present in Palestine." And comp Lk ii. 36 "of the tribe of Asher."

[1] Jn xxi 2

[2] The abbreviated phrase "the [son] of" is not used by the Synoptists with "Zebedee," without "James," or "John," or both. In Mk x. 35, Mt. xx 20, xxvi. 37, xxvii. 56, Lk v. 10, υἱοί is inserted

THE CALLING OF THE FISHERMEN

Zebedee") and to add, "The Synoptists give great prominence to the sons of Zebedee, John gives them but one unobtrusive mention"

But it will be found, on close examination, that, without this unobtrusive phrase, we should miss much of the Evangelist's meaning. We should not even know that he wrote in the name of John the son of Zebedee[1]

It will also be found that this unobtrusiveness—which we may call Zebedaean self-suppression if we suppose the writer to be identifying himself with a son of Zebedee—begins from the moment when Jesus is described as attracting followers. The same passage that relates how two disciples of the Baptist "followed Jesus," adds that "one of the two...was Andrew, Simon Peter's brother," but suppresses the name of the other. The writer proceeds "He [i e Andrew] findeth first his own brother Simon[2]." What does "*first*" mean? Does it mean that "*first*"—that is, in the first place—Andrew found *his own* brother, Peter, and *secondly* the unnamed disciple found *his own* brother? We are not told this, either here or anywhere; but, if we look onward, we shall see that it cannot well mean anything else. It is gradually revealed to us that there is, among the disciples, one, unnamed, whom "Jesus loved." He is mentioned as present on various occasions with other disciples From these, one by one, as they come before us and are mentioned by name, we gradually learn to distinguish him.

The last mention of this specially loved disciple shews that he was in the above-mentioned group of seven. "Peter, turning

---

[1] For the stages of evidence through which this conclusion is reached, and for its dependence on Jn xxi 2, see *Son* **3374** *c*, **3460** *a—i*.

[2] Jn 1 40—41 It has been suggested that for πρῶτον "first" (א πρῶτος) we should read πρωΐ "in the morning," comp codd *b* and *e* But the temptation to alter πρῶτον (or πρῶτος) to πρωΐ would be so great that the slight evidence for the latter may be fairly put aside as insufficient

114 (Mark 1 16—20)

THE CALLING OF THE FISHERMEN

about, seeth *the disciple whom Jesus loved,* following[1]." Hence he must have been either (1) one of "the [sons] of Zebedee" or else (2) one of "others of the disciples two [in number]." Logically, we have no definite reason for rejecting the latter alternative, but we are made to feel that the Evangelist intends us to reject it[2] It follows that he was either James or John the son of Zebedee. But he could not have been James because the context goes on to imply that his life would be prolonged, whereas James is described in the Acts as having been executed by Herod Agrippa in the days of Claudius. Thus by a series of exclusions, and silences, and ambiguous utterances, we are led to infer that this disciple whom Jesus loved was John the son of Zebedee. Peter, when bidden by Jesus to "follow" Him, saw this disciple also "following," and, when he asked "What shall this man do?" received the reply "If I will that he tarry till I come, what is that to thee?" Then the Gospel adds "This is the disciple that beareth witness of these things and wrote these things and we know that his witness is true[3]"

Comparing the Synoptic with the Johannine aspect—taken as a whole, omissions as well as insertions—we perceive that while the former, in a Calling, or Reminding, names the sons of Zebedee, James and John, at the beginning, when Jesus, their

---

[1] Jn xxi 20
[2] See *Son* 3460 *g—h* "No sufficient *data* are given...till the end of the gospel (see xxi 2, 7, 20, 23) Even then, the problem needs patience To this day, some critics doubt as to the solution "

In *theory*, the beloved disciple might be any one of the Twelve not named by John, such as Matthew the Publican But in *fact* we are made to feel that, with the addition of Thomas the Doubter, the six disciples who are united at the beginning are here united at the end—Andrew, Peter, Philip, Nathanael, the sons of Zebedee Then they were called Now they are confirmed. To suppose that any one of these first six disciples could be here left out is—we are made to feel—to suppose what was not spiritually possible Comp p 28, n 2.

[3] Jn xxi 20—24.

THE CALLING OF THE FISHERMEN

Lord, first came preaching the Gospel by the shore of Gennesaret, and preparing them to preach it, the latter mentions the Zebedaean pair nowhere but at the end (though implying their presence at the beginning) They are by the same shore indeed, and they are being prepared to preach the same Gospel, and to follow the same Lord; but there is this difference, that they are now to receive from the Lord that food which is to give them a vital knowledge of what they had not known before, the nature of the way on which they are to "follow"—that is, the Way of the Cross

The Marcan tradition, rejected by Matthew and Luke, that the pair were called "sons of thunder," whatever may have been its origin and meaning, was almost certain to be misinterpreted in the West[1]. And the Mark-Matthew tradition, that the two brothers asked to sit next to Jesus in the Kingdom, not only represented the pair as coveting supremacy, but also assigned to Jesus words implying that both the brothers would drink the same "cup" of martyrdom as Jesus Himself was to drink Luke rejects this John, in the narrative containing his only mention of "the sons of Zebedee," seems to say, or to imply, that, whatever may have been their errors before Christ's death, they had learned their lesson now, and that in different aspects, yet treading the same path, the two brothers unobtrusively "followed" Jesus on the way of the Cross. The one, James, he does not mention All Christians knew that he was the first of the Apostles to die for the Lord. The other, John, was the last of all the Apostles to die, and did not die technically as a "martyr," *i e* as a "witness [through violent death]" Yet he was, in the spiritual sense, a martyr, being a "witness" to the Lord —"This is the disciple that *beareth-witness* of these things[2]"

In consistency with this Zebedaean self-suppression, James

---

[1] See *Notes* **2969—77**
[2] Jn xxi 24

THE CALLING OF THE FISHERMEN

the son of Zebedee is absolutely mute throughout the Gospel[1]. And the only words that John the son of Zebedee utters by himself, and of himself, are "It is the Lord," whom he is the first to perceive on the shore of Tiberias[2]. This cannot be said to contradict, though it contrasts with, the Synoptic aspect of the two brothers. Nor is there anything manifestly incompatible with the earlier Gospels in the frequently conveyed suggestion that John was "the disciple whom Jesus loved."

§ 33. "Salome," in Mark

We cannot conveniently pass from the discussion of "the sons of Zebedee" without some notice of their mother, whose name appears to have been Salome, if we may trust the parallelism in .—

Mk xv. 40—1	Mt xxvii 55—6	Lk. xxiii 49
(40) And there were also women beholding from afar. among whom [were] both Mary Magdalene, and Mary the mother of James the less, and of Joses, and Salome, (41) Who, when he was in Galilee, followed him, and ministered unto him, and many other women which came up with him unto Jerusalem.	(55) And many women were there beholding from afar, which had followed Jesus from Galilee, ministering unto him (56) Among whom was Mary Magdalene, and Mary the mother of James and Joses, and the mother of the sons of Zebedee	And all his acquaintance, and the women that followed with him from Galilee, stood afar off, seeing these things

---

[1] So, it may be said, are Matthew, Bartholomew, etc But they are not brought on the stage, or mentioned in the Fourth Gospel "James," being included in "the sons of Zebedee," is consequently brought on the stage

[2] Jn xxi. 7. Previously he says (i 38) "Rabbi, where abidest

(Mark i. 16—20)

THE CALLING OF THE FISHERMEN

In John, a corresponding passage, but not mentioning "far off," says "But there were standing by the cross of Jesus his mother, and his mother's sister, Mary the [wife] of Clopas, and Mary Magdalene[1]." John adds "When Jesus therefore saw his mother, and the disciple standing by, whom he loved, he saith unto his mother, Woman, see, thy son[2]!" This, with the following context, is absent in the Synoptists. And the question seems to arise, "Were all the Synoptists ignorant of this historical utterance of Jesus and of its historical consequence, or has John derived it from some non-historical source?"

The full discussion of the Marcan "Salome" must be deferred till it claims our attention in its proper place. But here the following reasons may be given for thinking that Mark has preserved an ancient and obscure Galilaean tradition which John has attempted to explain. In the Talmuds and Midrash, "Salom(e)" occurs as the name of the wife of R. Eliezer. But there is attached to it "Imma" or "Emma." This, as a rule, means "the mother," or "mother" (corresponding to Abba "father" or "the father"). But when added to "Salome" it is treated by modern Hebraists, though by some doubtfully, as part of her name· "*Mother* (or *Imma, Emma*) *Salome*, wife of R Eliezer, sister of Rabban Gamaliel[3]" It occurs several times in the Talmuds thus. But the Midrash, instead of "R. Eliezer said to *Imma Salome* his wife," takes "Imma" as "*the mother*" and "Salome" as "*peace*," thus: "said to *the mother, Peace*[4]" Although these are much later traditions

---

thou?" but this is with Andrew, of whom he is the unnamed companion He also says (Jn xiii. 25) "Lord, who is it?" but this is but a repetition of words suggested to him by Peter (*ib* 24).

[1] Jn xix 25 [2] Jn xix. 26.
[3] So Levy i 92 *b*, referring to *j Git* i 43 *b*, *Sabb.* 116 *a—b*, *j Shebi* vi 36. But Goldschmidt and Schwab (vol ii 378) give "Imma' without query as a proper name
[4] So Wunsche p. 134 in *Lev. r* (on Lev xvi. 1) It connects "wife" with what follows

THE CALLING OF THE FISHERMEN

than our Gospels, yet they shew possibilities of confusion connected with this particular name, when used with the word "mother" Moreover, both for Jews and for Greeks (especially if they happened to know something of the history of the Herods) there were associations that might induce the later Evangelists to omit the name used by Mark. One Salome was a sister of Herod. Another was a daughter of Herodias. A name thus associated with the Herodian family might be offensive to Christians We also know that in very early times startling utterances of Jesus were connected by heretics with Salome. These things may have contributed to bring the use of the name into disrepute[1].

This being the case, it would be natural for Matthew and Luke to avoid the name. One way of doing this was obvious. It was agreed that the Marcan Salome was the mother of the sons of Zebedee. Then why not say "the mother of the sons of Zebedee"? Matthew at all events uses this appellation both here and on a previous occasion[2] Or again, if, as was said by many, she was also the sister of the Mother of the Lord, she might be called "His Mother's sister." John uses this appellation, and apparently, as quoted above, applies it to Salome This would explain the three variations in the nomenclature of one of the women mentioned as beholding the crucifixion — (1) "Salome" (in Mark), (2) "mother of the sons of Zebedee" (in Matthew), (3) "his (*i.e.* Christ's) mother's sister" (in John).

But further, the name "Salome," in Hebrew, might be regarded, either literally or allusively, as *shel-imma*, i e.

---

[1] Comp *Anc Hom. Clem. Rom* § 12 "The Lord being questioned by *some-one* (τινος)," where Lightfoot adds "By *Salome*," and shews that Salome's question was reported in the Gospel of the Egyptians

[2] See Mk x 35 "And there come near unto him James and John, the sons of Zebedee," parall to Mt xx 20 "Then came to him *the mother of the sons of Zebedee* with her sons."

THE CALLING OF THE FISHERMEN

"belonging to the Mother¹" It would be noted that it did not occur in any Gospel till the Crucifixion, but that it was there used by Mark where "mother of the sons of Zebedee" was used by Matthew. The inference would follow that "*a son of Zebedee*" was also "*a son of Salome*," which meant, in effect "*a son of one belonging to the Mother of the Lord*" But this, in Hebrew, might be practically indistinguishable from "*a son belonging to the Mother of the Lord.*" From a statement that this name was for the first time given in the Gospels when Jesus was described as hanging on the Cross, there might be no very violent transition to a statement that the name, in effect, was actually given by Jesus Himself at that moment to "a son of Zebedee" to whom He entrusted His Mother²

Amid much that appears doubtful and obscure in connection with this Marcan name, this at least appears to be fairly clear—that John adds something to what Matthew tells us indirectly about the Marcan Salome, about whom, whether directly or indirectly, Luke tells us nothing.

§ 34. "*Sons of peace*"

The suggested tradition about a "son of *Salome*" as being also appointed to be "*son belonging to my mother (Shelimme)*" leads us to think of a much more obvious play on the name. "Shalôm" means "peace," and "Salome" would mean "my peace." That Jesus, teaching in the midst of the Twelve, and speaking of the Gospel of *Peace*, would sometimes play on the appropriateness of "the sons of *Salome*" for "the Gospel of *Shalôm*," would be all the more probable if He had "sons of Salome" in that small circle Luke says that Jesus bade His missionaries, when preaching that Gospel, to say, on entering a house, "*Peace* [Shalôm] be unto this house !" According

---

¹ See above, p 118, for the connection of *Shalom*, i e Salome, with *Imma* or *Emma*, i e Mother

² Jn vii 5 "even his brethren did not believe on him" accords with the Johannine tradition about Mary's adopted son

THE CALLING OF THE FISHERMEN

to Matthew's parallel, Jesus added "And if *the house be worthy*, your peace shall light upon it" But Luke almost certainly approaches more closely to the original thus, "And if *a son of peace* [Shalôm] *be there*[1]."

In the Johannine account of the Last Supper Jesus is represented as applying to Judas the quotation "he that eateth my bread[2]", but Origen adds the context, which is, both in Greek and in Hebrew, "the man of *my peace* (Shalômē)" And the context in the Gospel suggests an antithesis, between Christ's false and pretended "son of peace" who was to betray Him, and Christ's true "son of peace" who was "at the table, reclining in Jesus' bosom, one of his disciples, whom Jesus loved[3]." The first Johannine actual mention of "peace" does not occur till a little later, but this Eucharistic scene indicates what it is that Judas rejects and the son of Salome receives It is the inexpressible influence of the Love of Christ It cannot make its way into the heart of one given over to self But it comes freely, as to its home, into the heart of one whose love for Jesus is such that it may be described rather as the Lord's gift or grace given to the disciple, than as the offering given by the disciple to the Lord.

The Johannine tradition that Jesus commended His own mother to the son of Salome in the words "See, thy mother," is not likely to have been based on a mere misinterpretation of any passage of Mark[4]. The Gospel adds "And from that hour the disciple took her unto his own [home]" This would

---

[1] Lk x 5—6, Mt x 12—13 Comp Deut xxv 2 (Heb lit) "*a son* of stripes," and 1 S xxvi 16, 2 S xii 5 (Heb lit) "*a son* of death," where either the LXX, or Sym , has "worthy" This suggests that in Mt v 9 "Blessed are the peacemakers," the original was "*sons* of Shalôm," and not, as SS, "workers," Delitzsch "pursuers," of Shalôm

[2] Jn xiii 18, quoting Ps. xli. 9 See Origen, *Comm Joann.* xxxii 8 (Lomm ii 419—21)

[3] Jn xiii 23

[4] See below, p 470 foll , on Mk iii 34.

THE CALLING OF THE FISHERMEN

hardly have been stated if it were not the fact that John did henceforth regard Mary the Lord's mother as his own. And it is conceivable—some might say natural—that while the crucifixion was going on, the penitent and remorseful disciple, who, with the rest of the Twelve, had fled from his Master for the time, received some vision, or some germs of a vision, in which this adoption of the Lord's Mother was enjoined on him by the Lord Himself[1]

Summing up, we may say that although the Fourth Evangelist nowhere intervenes verbally to tell us that "Boanerges" was not in the Western sense, "sons of thunder," or that "Salome" meant "peace," or to vindicate the character of "the sons of Zebedee," as meaning sons of "dowry," yet he does succeed in conveying to us, from the beginning of the book of his Gospel, that the book was written by, or in the name of, a genuine "son of Salome," a genuine "son of peace"—one who feels a deep ultimate peace and concord between the visible and the invisible, feeling at home in heaven with the Eternal Son, but at home also on earth with the

---

[1] It must of course be admitted that the Fourth Gospel does not relate any abandonment of Jesus by the disciples at the moment of the arrest. But compare the vision in the *Acts of John* § 12 "The Lord went forth [to trial and death] and we, like people led astray, or like people that have snatched a moment's slumber [and then awakened], fled each his own way. Then I for my part, having seen Him [on the Cross] did not even abide by the place of His passion (ἐγὼ μὲν οὖν αὐτὸν ἰδών, οὐδὲ προσέμεινα αὐτοῦ τῷ πάθει) but fled to the Mount of Olives, weeping over that which had come to pass. And when He was hanged on the Bush of the Cross, at the sixth hour of the day, there came darkness over all the earth. And our Lord stood in the midst of the cave and lighted it up and said, 'John, unto the multitude down below in Jerusalem I am being crucified and pierced with lances and reeds, and gall and vinegar is given me to drink but unto thee I am speaking, and that which I am speaking do thou hear. It was I that put it into thy heart to come up into this mountain, that thou mightest hear matters needful to be learned by disciple from teacher and by man from God'" See p. 473.

THE CALLING OF THE FISHERMEN

incarnate Son whose mother, Mary, had been commended to him as his own. A homely and domestic scene—a home dependent on "love"—seems to be his view of the life to come "If a man love me he will keep my word and my Father will love him; and we will come unto him and make our abiding with him[1]."

Somewhat similarly, in a primitive way, Leah says in Genesis about the "dower"—which she calls *Zebed* and which she connects with Zebulon—"God hath *dowered* me with a good *dowry*, now will my husband *dwell with me*[2]" The "dwelling," "abiding," or "tabernacling," of the Lord with Man—this, and nothing else, is the Gospel of Peace. "Where *abidest* thou?" is the first question put to Jesus by the unnamed Evangelist It is "abiding"—not "teaching"—that makes him and Andrew converts. "They came, therefore, and they saw where he *abode*, and they *abode* with him[3]." That is all that the son of Salome tells us expressly about the nature of his conversion.

This sense of unity between the home in heaven and the home on earth pervades the Fourth Gospel It is manifest through the whole of the introductory Prologue, which closes with a mention of the invisible God in heaven as being declared on earth by the Only-begotten, who is "in the bosom of the Father[4]." It is manifest in Christ's introductory calling of apostles or disciples, which concludes with a promise that they shall see the heaven opened, and "the angels of God ascending" —"ascending" from earth before they "descend" from heaven —"upon the Son of man[5]." It is manifest in Christ's introductory miracle, or "sign," wrought in a homely circle at Cana, where Christ's mother is one of the guests, and where, through her friendly intercession, the host is spared the shame of saying what she says to her Son, quietly between themselves, "They have no wine[6]."

---

[1] Jn xiv 23 [2] Gen. xxx 20. [3] Jn i 38—9
[4] Jn i 18   [5] Jn i 51   [6] Jn ii 3

(Mark i 16—20)

THE CALLING OF THE FISHERMEN

From the water and the wine that are Christ's sign at Cana the transition is great indeed to the water and the blood that are Christ's sign on the Cross. But it may be taken as certain that we are intended by the Evangelist to connect the two. The water becoming wine, at the feast or "joy[1]" at Cana, represents a prediction of the "joy" that is in heaven over one sinner that repenteth and is redeemed. The water and the blood, the Passion at Golgotha, represent the fulfilment of that prediction, and the bringing into the world of the new Love—the Love that redeems. Thus Jesus died, says the Epistle to the Colossians, "*having made-peace through the blood of his cross,*" and again "Ye that once were far off are made nigh *in the blood of Christ; for* he is our *peace....*[2]" To see this vision of the redemptive stream of Peace was not given to all. No Gospel but the Fourth records it. And the Fourth records the "seeing" of it as if it were a vision, and the "witnessing" of it as if it were the duty of the seer :—"And he that hath *seen* hath *borne witness,* and his witness is true ; and he knoweth that he saith true that ye also may believe[3]." To see it was appropriate for the son of Salome—by birth "a son of Peace," and by adoption the son of that Mary who had long ago called forth from Jesus the response about His "hour"—regarded as coming, though "not yet"—in answer to her indirect petition "They have no wine[4]"

§ 35. "*And straightway he called them*[5]"

Returning to our immediate subject, the Calling of the Fishermen, we note a slight contextual difference between

---

[1] For "joy" meaning "feast," see *Son* 3492 *c*, 3583 (viii)
[2] Col 1 20, Eph ii 13—14
[3] Jn xix 35   See *Joh Gr* 2383—4
[4] Jn ii 3—4
[5] Mk 1 20 "And straightway he called them, and they left. .," Mt iv 21—2 "And he called them, and they straightway left... " "Call" is καλέω, here and throughout this section

THE CALLING OF THE FISHERMEN

Mark and Matthew. The latter, by transposing "straightway" ("and they straightway left") seems to say: "I do not feel sure that *the act itself, the calling of James and John, followed* '*straightway*' that of Simon and Andrew It is safer to say that '*they themselves followed straightway*' i e without delaying. For the same reason, instead of saying, with Mark, that Jesus 'went on *a little,*' I have said that He 'went on *from thence.*' There may have been some interval between the two events, an interval both of place and of time "

Antecedently, there is something to be said, either for Matthew's view that there was perhaps a considerable interval, or for the view (which might be called the Lucan view but for the fact that Luke is probably describing a Reminding and not the Calling) that there was no interval at all. Mark's view is intermediate, and presents some difficulty if it obliges us to suppose that, when Jesus had uttered those impressive words to Peter and Andrew, He walked on, for a hundred yards or so, and then, after a few minutes' interval, repeated them to the sons of Zebedee.

John describes no Calling or Reminding by the sea of Galilee or Tiberias till he comes to the period after the Resurrection. But he mentions what amounts to a first Calling of the four fishermen, as occurring earlier even than the Synoptic Calling This was not by the sea, but in the place where Jesus was abiding, beyond Jordan, where the Baptist was baptizing According to John—though he veils the facts in enigmatic expression, not made clear till the reader reaches the end of the Gospel—Andrew and his unnamed companion, John, were not so much "called" by Jesus as rather callers to Jesus, callers for guidance, addressing Him as "Rabbi," and asking "Where abidest thou ?" Then it is said that Andrew—who was introduced as "Simon Peter's brother"—"findeth first his own brother Simon" and "brought him unto Jesus." It is at this point that John introduces the first of the only two Johannine instances of the word "call." "Jesus looked upon

THE CALLING OF THE FISHERMEN

him [*i.e.* Simon] and said, Thou art Simon, son of John; *thou shalt be called* Cephas (which is by interpretation Stone (*Petros*))[1]"

In this immediate explanation of the surname in "Simon Peter" there is a superiority to Luke's unexplained introduction of the surname for the first time thus: "But Simon *Peter*, when he saw it [*i e* the draught of fishes], fell down at Jesus' knees, saying, Depart from me; for I am a sinful man, O Lord[2]." In preceding verses, as well as in the preceding chapter, Luke repeatedly called the fisherman "Simon[3]." Yet now, in the very sentence that describes him as falling down in alarm at his sins, Luke calls him "Simon *Peter*," that is, "Simon [*strong as*] stone"! Then "Peter" is dropped till the Naming of the Apostles[4]. The Lucan narrative goes on to tell us who were "*Simon's* partners" and what Jesus "said unto *Simon*."

John might naturally be expected to correct what might appear to him a dislocation in Luke. But there is reason to suppose that he found also in Matthew a deviation from Mark that seemed to him to demand correction. For Matthew not only describes Simon here as "Simon who is [now] called

---

[1] Jn 1 42.   [2] Lk v. 8.
[3] Lk iv 38 (*bis*) "into the house of *Simon*," rep v 3, 4, 5, 10 (*bis*) Mark's first mention of "Peter" is in the Naming of the Apostles (Mk iii 16) ἐπέθηκεν ὄνομα τῷ Σίμωνι Πέτρον Matthew calls him Peter at the moment when Jesus first sees him, by the sea of Galilee, but tells the reader that he is anticipating, (iv 18) Σίμωνα τὸν λεγόμενον Πέτρον, "Simon *who is* [*now*] *called* Peter " But even in the parallel to the Marcan Naming of the Apostles, Matthew omits the act of naming, and repeats "Simon who is [now] called Peter" (x. 2) πρῶτος Σίμων ὁ λεγόμενος Πέτρος This might give the impression that Simon was not called Peter for the first time by Jesus until the Confession followed by the blessing in Mt. xvi 18 "and I say unto thee that thou art Peter ." But, if Mark is right, the meaning of "thou art Peter," in Matthew, would seem to be "thou art Peter *indeed*," i e. "*true to the name of Peter which I formerly bestowed on thee*"
[4] Lk. vi 14 Σίμωνα ὃν καὶ ὠνόμασεν Πέτρον

THE CALLING OF THE FISHERMEN

Peter," but also later on, where Mark says that Jesus "gave Simon the name of Peter," Matthew still has "First, Simon, who is [now] called Peter"—making no mention of the act of naming. Indeed there is no mention of the act at all in Matthew, unless we can suppose that he dramatizes it in a passage peculiar to his Gospel recording the blessing that follows Peter's Confession, "Blessed art thou, Simon Bar Jona...and I say unto thee that *thou art Peter.*" This certainly gives the impression that now, for the first time, was this name given to Simon, that is to say, on an occasion when the other two Synoptists describe the Confession but make no mention of a name-giving.

§ 36. *How John expresses "calling"*

The Johannine account of the first interview between the fishermen and Jesus supplements the Lucan and Matthaean traditions in some points (or corrects the interpretations likely to be put on them) while accepting them in others.

In the first place, John agrees with Matthew in dramatically representing Jesus as calling Simon "*stone*," that is, in Aramaic, *Cephas*, or in Greek, *Petros*. Also, except that he corrects "Jonah" into "John," he admits that Matthew is approximately right—in word at all events, though not in thought—in saying that Jesus addressed Simon as "son of Jonah (or John)." In the second place, agreeing (in some sense) with Luke, he implies that Simon's name of "*stone*" is rightly connected with the first interview between the Master and the Disciple.

But he puts all these things in a new light. Matthew, beside substituting "Jonah" for John, might seem to have regarded "son of Jonah" as an honorific part of Christ's blessing. But, in accordance with Semitic usage[1], it is—if not depreciative—

---

[1] Comp. Numb. xxiii. 18—19 "Rise up, Balak, and hear, hearken unto me, *thou son of Zippor*. God is not a man...neither the son of man," where there is a manifest intention (see Rashi and Origen *ad loc.*) to shew that Balak is below the level of the prophet who is

THE CALLING OF THE FISHERMEN

at all events suggestive of a lower spiritual level from which the Apostle has now emerged to a higher one. And the Fourth Evangelist uses it thus, only with reference to a future, not a present, emergence.

"Son of John," in the Fourth Gospel, means that Simon was at present *only* "son of John," but that he was hereafter to be transmuted into the nature of "the living stone." "Christ's words"—so the Fourth Evangelist appears to maintain—"were predictive[1], not descriptive; He did not say *Thou art even now 'stone'* (or, to be exact, *Cephas*, which is somewhat different from the Greek word[2]). He said *Thou art to be*, or, *Thou shalt be called by God, 'stone.'* That meant, 'Thou art destined for the building of the Temple of God, thyself to be both stone and builder—but not yet.'" What the Lord meant here in saying 'son of John' I shall shew more clearly later on when He repeats it after the Resurrection. Simon had thrice denied Him. The Lord, after the Resurrection, while preparing him to receive the full assurance of forgiveness, thrice called him '*Simon, [son] of John*[3].' That was not a title of honour but an appellation of

---

rebuking him. Somewhat akin to this is (Gesen. 120 b) son of "without personal name (often with implication of contempt)," e.g. 1 S. xx. 27 "wherefore cometh not *the son of Jesse* to meat?" (rep. *ib.* 30). To be called "son of" an obscure person such as "Kish," "Remaliah," "Tabeel," often implied that the "son" was an upstart. Jerome (on Mt. xvi. 17 where *e* has *variana*) gives the two interpretations, "Jonah" *dove*, and "John" *grace of God*, but makes no comment on "*son of*." Gesenius gives no instance of "*son of [an obscure person]*" used honorifically.

[1] Some may say, "Yes, predictive after the event—an unjustifiable invention." John is frequently found to have been *adapting* something that he appeared at first sight to be *inventing*. It is probably rash to charge him with "inventing" here. It is certainly ungrateful to ignore the debt due to him for elucidating the full meaning of the appellation "son of John."

[2] In Greek, "stone," applied to a person, would mostly imply callousness or stupidity.

[3] Jn. xxi. 15—17.

THE CALLING OF THE FISHERMEN

rebuke It was thrice accompanied by the question 'Lovest thou me?'—a gentle reproach, but still a reproach, intended to prepare the disciple to rise above the weakness of 'Simon, son of John' into the strength denoted by the honourable title of '*Cephas*'"

Passing to the consideration of the Johannine method of expressing "calling" in general, we find that John, in "thou shalt be *called* [i e. named] Cephas," uses the same Greek word as the one in Mark-Matthew here, "he *called* [i.e. summoned, or invited] them[1]" In the latter sense, John says, a little later, that "Jesus also was *called* [. e. invited], and his disciples, to the marriage" at Cana[2]. He never uses the word again in any sense[3] Yet we might suppose he could hardly avoid a word that is not only frequent in Matthew and Luke, but also found in the threefold tradition · "I came not to *call* [the] righteous, but sinners[4]"

But here we must stop to modify the phrase "in the threefold tradition" For though Matthew is identical with Mark, Luke is not Luke adds "*to repentance*" "*Call to repentance*" is not the same thing as "*call*" The addition is really an alteration—though not technically so—indicating that Luke deemed Mark too indefinite. It is therefore a case where John might naturally intervene ; and we are led to ask, "What, according to John, is the essence of the divine 'calling' introduced by Jesus, and how does John express it ?"

In the first place, to answer this question negatively, he does not accept the Lucan modification, "to *repentance*." This is a word that John never uses. Nor does he substitute "choose"—a word that Matthew distinguishes from "call," in the saying which he alone assigns to Jesus, "Many are

---

[1] Mk 1 20, Mt ɪv 21 ἐκάλεσεν, Jn 1. 42 κληθήσῃ
[2] Jn ɪɪ 2 (R V) "was bidden"
[3] In Jn x. 3 txt rec has καλεῖ κατ' ὄνομα, but it is an error for φωνεῖ κατ' ὄνομα
[4] Mk ɪɪ 17, Mt ɪx 13, comp Lk v. 32.

called, but few are *chosen*[1] " Negatively, therefore, it must be said that John does not use any of the Synoptic terms to express the effectual "calling" of Jesus. But positively, he expresses it in part by dramatic representation of concrete instances, and in part by metaphor

The metaphors are varied There is the metaphor of attraction or "drawing," when Jesus says, "I, if I be lifted up..., will *draw* all men unto me[2]" There is the metaphor of a "voice," like that of thunder, addressed to the dead by the Son, so that all those who are in the tombs, and who hear, will awake, and come to Him and live[3]. There is also the metaphor of light, falling on those who are in darkness, and causing those who come to it to reach the salvation of the Truth But the particular metaphor that is most appropriate for our purpose of comparing the Fourth Gospel with the Three is that of the shepherd "calling (or, 'calling to') his own sheep by name[4]"

§ 37 *The "calling" of the sheep by the shepherd*

The Greek word for the shepherd's "calling (*phōnein*)"—latent in the English "phon-etic" and "*tele-phone*"—is quite distinct from the word we have been hitherto discussing (*kălein*). In LXX, both these Greek words represent one

---

[1] Mt xxii 14 John describes Jesus as mysteriously recognising that even His own "choosing" might include one that had a devil—so far at least as concerned His initial choosing of the Twelve See Jn vi 70 "Did not I [myself] choose you, the Twelve, and one of you is a devil?" In Jn xiii 18 "I know whom ($\tau\acute{\iota}\nu\alpha\varsigma$) I chose," $\tau\acute{\iota}\nu\alpha\varsigma$ is not $\pi o\acute{\iota}o\upsilon\varsigma$, but it includes $\pi o\acute{\iota}o\upsilon\varsigma$. "I know who they are [and of what kind they are] whom I chose" Jesus "chose" all the Twelve, and "washed the feet" of all But neither the "choosing" nor the "washing" could avail for Judas Jn xv 16, 19, "I *chose* you out of the world" does not exclude the Son's prayer to the Father (Jn xvii 15) "that thou keep them from the evil [one]"

[2] Jn xii 32 [3] Jn v. 25—8

[4] Jn x 3 "he calleth ($\phi\omega\nu\epsilon\hat{\iota}$) his own sheep by name ($\kappa\alpha\tau$' $\check{o}\nu o\mu\alpha$)"

THE CALLING OF THE FISHERMEN

Hebrew word (*kârâ*) which means "call" in a great number of senses Among these are (1) "call to a meeting, interview, feast etc.," (2) "call by name," (3) "call to, by name." *Kălein* may be used in all three senses, but would not be used in the third sense if oral "calling" needed to be emphasized[1]. In Luke, Jesus seems to say, in effect, to those who are preparing a feast, "Do not merely *call orally and familiarly (phōnein)* your neighbours and relations to your feast, but *send-and-invite (kălein)* strangers, the poor, the maimed, and the blind[2]." Here *phōnein* is used by Luke to imply antecedent personal relations between the "caller" and the "called "

That is also what is implied by John when he uses *phōnein* in the Parable of the Good Shepherd. The language of the Johannine Parable is quite different from that of the Synoptists, but its thought may be found in an interpretation of Mark's phrase about "calling." Rejecting the Lucan addition "to repentance," John seems to say, in effect : "The Good Shepherd did not 'come to call sinners *to this or that condition of mind or soul*—for example, *to repentance.*' It would have been truer perhaps to say that John the Baptist came to do this. John indeed 'came to call sinners *to repentance,*' or, at all events, to the Son through repentance But this was before the coming of the Son. When the Son came, His call was not 'to repentance,' but through repentance, to Himself That is what Mark's tradition, though it is brief and obscure, most naturally means When a man 'calls' another, to whom does he 'call' him if not to himself ? "

---

[1] In Gen xii 18, xx. 9 where Pharaoh and Abimelech "*called* (ἐκάλεσεν) Abraham and said...," the meaning is, "called by messenger."

[2] Lk. xiv. 12—13 For καλεῖ σε meaning "invites you," or "requests the pleasure of your company," see *Oxy. Pap.* 747, 926, 927. Of course it is not to be understood that letters of invitation are sent to "the poor," but it is understood that they are to be courteously "invited."

THE CALLING OF THE FISHERMEN

§ 38. *Effective "calling"*

But how, in fact, did Jesus, in the Johannine Gospel, call His earliest disciples, or perhaps we should say make His earliest converts—six in number? To Andrew and Andrew's unnamed companion (John, the son of Zebedee) who asked Him where He abode, He said "Come, and ye shall see [1]" The third, Peter, was brought to Jesus by Andrew On him Jesus looked stedfastly and said "Thou art Simon, the son of John, thou shalt be called Cephas[2]." It is implied, but not stated, that he at once became a convert The fourth, James the son of Zebedee, is assumed to have been brought to Jesus by the unnamed disciple, his brother, but neither the bringing nor the conversion is described[3]. To the fifth, Philip—and to Philip alone—is given a calling direct and unmistakeable, "Follow me[4]." The sixth, Nathanael, is not called at all Jesus says of him that he is "truly an Israelite," and adds "I saw thee," and the circumstances in which He "saw[5]." And that is enough. Though not called in word, he is called in fact, if the essence of being called by Christ consists in being drawn into Christ.

The impression left upon us by this rapid succession of "callings" is that they are acts rather than phrases. In different spiritual shapes, adapted to the different characters and circumstances of the several converts, the regenerating or leavening seed of the Word has been invisibly passing into the heart of each. Nothing has been audible except a brief phrase or two. But under these phrases the Spirit has been breathing And the breathing has resulted in words and acts of spiritual life.

Of the four thus called, three[6] shew the effect of the seed

---

[1] Jn 1 39.   [2] Jn 1 42
[3] See pp. 71, 114, 133, n. 2
[4] Jn 1 43   [5] Jn 1 47—8
[6] "Three," namely, (1) Andrew, (2) the unnamed (presumably), and (3) Philip.

(Mark 1. 16—20)

THE CALLING OF THE FISHERMEN

at once by bringing converts to Jesus. Peter does not. He is the only one that is "called" by a new name. But it is prospective. He brings no converts now But the readers of the Gospel are made to feel that he is as it were kept in reserve, to bring converts on a vast scale hereafter

Nathanael is the only one of the six that receives a title of honour, yet he is not included in the Synoptic Twelve[1]. Andrew and the unnamed are together in going to Jesus. But Andrew remains Andrew to the last The unnamed receives the greatest name of all—greater even, we must needs think, than that of Simon. For he becomes "the disciple whom Jesus loved" and about whom He said to His mother, "See, thy son[2]."

What are we to say about the anticipatory use of the name "Simon *Peter*" ("Andrew, brother of Simon *Peter*")—where "Peter" need not have been inserted? It is closely followed by a statement that at present the disciple's name was merely "Simon" ("Thou art Simon the son of John, thou shalt be called (kălein) Cephas (which is, by interpretation, Peter)[3]"). Are we to suppose that although "shalt be called"

---

[1] See Hastings' *Dict* iii 489 *a*, "The now widely accepted identification of Nathanael with Bartholomew is not known to have been adopted until the 9th century"

[2] What are we to say about James the son of Zebedee, the brother of the unnamed? No words of Jesus to him are recorded. Even the fact that he was brought to Jesus by John is not stated as a fact but left as an inference Perhaps the Evangelist felt that the unique glory of James consisted in his being the protomartyr of the Twelve In this respect James, the first to die, surpassed John, who was the last to "tarry" (Jn xxi 22) John, suppressing himself in this Gospel, suppresses his brother still more absolutely, with the feeling that his brother's name is of a kind to be "written in heaven" and not in that most inadequate of records of personality, "a book" (comp Jn xxi 25)

[3] Jn i 40, 42 In Mark, "Peter" does not occur till Mk iii 16. In Matthew (iv 18), the first mention of "Peter" is with Σίμων ὁ λεγόμενος As to Luke, see above, p 126 foll John perhaps takes a pleasure in introducing Andrew as "the brother of [him whom all

THE CALLING OF THE FISHERMEN

means, on the surface, merely "thou shalt be called *by name*," yet it implies also "thou shalt be called *to become*," so that it predicts a summons to fulfil a newly revealed destiny, a purpose of God ? This is in accordance with Hebrew precedent and doctrine When God calls Abram Abraham, or calls Jacob Israel, not only does He call both by new names, but He also calls both into new characters, so that Abraham becomes, in the very act of being newly named, "a father of many nations," and Jacob becomes at once consecrated by a connection with "God[1]."

Isaiah describes the Lord as "calling the generations from the beginning," and as saying to Jacob "I have called thee by thy name, thou art mine[2]" Ibn Ezra, on the former passage, says that God "knows all future generations and *cites each of them to appear in its right time*" This thought is probably at the bottom of John's unique mention of "calling" applied to Cephas. Whenever God, so to speak, mentions a new name—such as "light"—the mysticism of Hebrew thought assumes that the thing springs into existence, because God has, as it were, taken the thought by His Hand or by His Word, and brought it into the region of reality.

And so it was with Simon. When Jesus looked stedfastly on him[3], and said "Thou shalt be called [by name] Cephas," the "look," and the prospect of the "calling [by name]," must be regarded (if we accept the Johannine view of things) as acting together immediately, and with a force that was to increase during a long future. They constituted

---

the Church knows as] Simon Peter," as much as to say. "Andrew *was first in point of time*, and I assert this, though well knowing that he *was not first in point of fame*"

[1] The precise meaning of "Israel" (Gen xxxii 28) is disputed. But all agree that the word includes "God"

[2] Is xli 4, xliii 1.

[3] See *Joh Gr* 2649 *a* quoting Judg. vi 14 "And the Lord *looked on* him [Gideon]"

THE CALLING OF THE FISHERMEN

(so it would seem) an immediate "calling" in the sense of "summons"—a calling to the work of a disciple. And yet, later on, we are to find Simon thrice denying discipleship and thrice hearing from Jesus his old earthly designation, without his title of honour, "Simon, son of John, lovest thou me?"

Here is a paradox, that Simon, in the Fourth Gospel, is the only disciple whose name is connected with "calling," the only disciple who denies discipleship, and the only disciple to whom the Lord thrice gives the precept to feed His sheep, accompanied with the prediction that he shall be honoured by dying the death of his Master. Taken all together, this exalting promise to "Simon" that he shall be "called Peter," and the momentary casting down to the degenerate condition of "Simon," and then the permanent re-exaltation to a level with his Master's Cross, seem to be the acts of a drama of warning and comfort—warning, not to trust in man's dreams or dogmas about God's "calling," in any technical outward sense apart from inward reception of the Son, comfort, from the thought that God's "calling," in spite of all appearance to the contrary, will never be found in the end to have been ineffectual

§ 39 *What did the fishermen "leave"?*

Mark and Matthew say that the first pair of fishermen "left *the nets*," and that the second (Mark) "left *their father Zebedee in the boat with the hired servants*," or (Matthew) "left *the boat and their father*[1]" Luke says, that all the (three) fishermen "brought the boats (R V their boats) to the land and left *all*[2]."

---

[1] Mk i 18, 20, Mt iv 20, 22

[2] Lk v 11 καὶ καταγαγόντες τὰ πλοῖα ἐπὶ τὴν γῆν, ἀφέντες πάντα... Luke gives only three names He does not mention Andrew See above, p 26 On ἐπί, lit "toward," or "on-to," see below, p 140 foll. The same verb for "leaving," ἀφίημι, is used throughout this narrative by the three Synoptists

THE CALLING OF THE FISHERMEN

Luke's "left *all*" is repeated later on by Mark-Matthew, but not by Luke, thus —

Mk x 28 (R.V.)	Mt xix 27 (R V)	Lk xviii. 28 (R V)
Peter began to say unto him, Lo, we have *left all*, and have followed thee.	Then answered Peter and said unto him, Lo, we have *left all*, and followed thee What then shall we have?	And Peter said, Lo, we have left *our own* [marg. or, *our own (homes)*] and followed thee.

This last variation may be explained from an original Hebrew "We have left our home (lit. *house*) and followed thee." The Hebrew "*house*" is expressed in LXX, and could be expressed in N T., both by "*own*" and by "*all [things]*[1]." There are noteworthy variations in Christ's reply enumerating the things "left" —

Mk x 29	Mt xix 29	Lk xviii 29
There is no man that hath left *house*, or brethren, or sisters, or mother, or father, or children, or lands (*lit* fields)	And every one that hath left *houses*, or brethren, or sisters, or father, or mother, or children, or lands (*lit.* fields)	There is no man that hath left *house*, or wife, or brethren, or parents, or children

This invites comparison with the Call to Abraham (LXX) "Go forth from thy land and from thy kindred and from *the house of thy father*[2]." In O T "*house of thy father*," that is, home, comes last and crowns the list In N T it comes first. This would naturally be the case if it were the only word actually used by Jesus—the other words being merely

---

[1] See *Corrections* **447** (iv) quoting Esth viii 2 "over *the house of* Haman," LXX ἐπὶ πάντων τῶν ’Α , and Esth v 10, vi. 12 "to his *house* (εἰς τὰ ἴδια) " On Lev xvi 17 "for himself and for *his* (lit) *house*," the Mishna in *Joma* 2 a says "that means *his wife* "

[2] Gen xii 1, on which see Philo 1 436, as to the spiritual meaning of Abraham's threefold leaving

THE CALLING OF THE FISHERMEN

evangelistic interpretations, shewing that "house[1]" included household, and kindred, and everything that we have on earth. Luke inserts "*wife*." This may be because Peter, the questioner, was married, and because (*according to Luke*) *Peter, after he had been reminded of his duty by Jesus, left his wife,* "and followed him," that is, followed Jesus to the various "cities" mentioned immediately afterwards[2].

It was not quite so in Mark. There, after the Calling of Peter and the rest, they "go into Capernaum," and into the synagogue, and, from the synagogue, they "came into *the house of Simon and Andrew*," where Jesus heals "*Simon's wife's mother*[3]." The presence of the "wife" in the house would make it seem inconsistent to say that Peter left his "wife" immediately after he was called. Indeed it might be objected that Peter did not leave his "house" either; for he went back to his "house" from the synagogue. Perhaps for that reason Matthew altered "house" into "houses." But the real meaning was "house" in the sense of "home." In the case of some of Christ's disciples, and at certain times, the "leaving," and the "home," were literal and local. In the case of others, and in later times, it might be recognised as possible to "leave all that they had" in a spiritual sense, if, remaining where they were, they devoted themselves and all that they had to the service of the Father in heaven[4].

Why does Mark (followed by Matthew) insert "fields"

---

[1] Matthew alters the sense by adopting the plural, "houses"—which makes the word mean "house-property."

[2] Lk v 11—12 "left all and followed him. And it came to pass, while he was *in one of the cities* ..." See below, pp 143—4, on Peter and Peter's wife.

[3] Mk 1 21, 29

[4] According to Mark 1 38 "Let us go elsewhere into the next towns," Jesus went forth on a missionary journey on the morning after He had healed Peter's mother-in-law, and Mark assumes that Peter accompanied Him. Philo, while not denying that Abraham's threefold leaving is literal and local, maintains that it is also spiritual

THE CALLING OF THE FISHERMEN

(among the things "left"), which Luke omits? Perhaps because Mark confusedly follows the threefold classification in Genesis, only reversing the order so as to make it (1) "house of his father"; (2) "kindred"; (3) "land." Only, as Matthew altered "house" into "houses," so Mark altered "land" into "lands." Luke puts Genesis aside, as being inapplicable to the Apostles, since Abraham took his wife and all his belongings with him, when he obeyed God's call

In Mark and Matthew (but not in Luke) this question, and the reply to it about "leaving one's house and home" for Christ's sake, are followed almost immediately by the petition of the sons of Zebedee (or their mother) for places near Christ's throne. The juxtaposition suggests that they *thought*—though they did not say—"We, too, have 'left all and followed thee,' as Peter did." According to Mark and Matthew, they might say "We have done more, in one respect. For we left our father[1]." This leads us back to a question that previously came before us, as to the origin of the Marcan tradition that the sons of Zebedee "left their father in the boat with the hired-servants," supposing Luke to be right in omitting it as erroneous.

It has been maintained above that Zebedee was probably dead at the time of the Calling. This view may be illustrated from Genesis where the death of Abraham's father, Terah, is described first, and yet the command follows afterwards "Get thee out of *thy father's house*[2]." One of Rashi's explanations is, that Terah's death was related before its chronological order so as to avoid the inference that Abraham neglected his father. The other is, that Terah, being an idolater, was

---

[1] Mk x 29 "mother or father," Mt xix 29 "father or mother" becomes in Lk xviii 29 "parents." The change is perhaps not merely for brevity. The sons of Zebedee could not say that they had left their "parents," since their mother was with them. But they could say (according to Mk-Mt) that they had left their "father." D omits "father" both in Mk and in Mt

[2] Gen xi 32, xii 1, comp Josh xxiv 2

THE CALLING OF THE FISHERMEN

called "dead" before the time of his literal death. This would suggest a parallelism between the Call of Abraham as described in Jewish tradition, and the Call of Philip of Bethsaida as described in the early Christian tradition of Clement of Alexandria, who represents Philip as being the disciple to whom Jesus said, "Follow me" and "Let the dead bury their dead[1]." Philip is the only one of the disciples, in the Fourth Gospel, whom Jesus calls with the words "Follow me," and the only one whose place of residence is mentioned   Jesus called him "from Bethsaida," that is, "from *the House of Fishing*" This might be explained, in accordance with the Synoptic narrative, "Jesus called him from the house of earthly occupation, and from the service of the flesh, to the house of heavenly occupation, and to the service of the Gospel, from catching fish in the sea, to catching souls for heaven"

§ 40. *"They left all," in Luke*

Let us consider the bearing of all these facts on the parallelism in :—

Mk	Mt.	Lk
left *their father* Zebedee *in the boat with the hired servants.*	left *the boat and their father*	left *all*

Does it not appear probable—in the light of the later Gospel parallels between the Greek "*all*" and the Greek "*own*," indicated as pointing to an original "*house*" or "*father's house*"—that, here too, the original was "left *their father's home*" and that this was paraphrased very fully by Mark and less fully by Matthew and rendered "*all*" by Luke[2] ? "*The*

---

[1] Mt. viii 22, Lk ix 59—60, comp Jn 1 43—4 See *Son* 3377 *a*

[2] As regards fulness of paraphrase, it should be noted that Mk x. 29—30 is much fuller than the parallel Mt xix 29, Lk xviii. 29—30.

(Mark 1 16—20)

THE CALLING OF THE FISHERMEN

house of their father" might be interpreted as meaning "the household and their father," or "their belongings and their father" in the abstract, or "their boat and their father[1]" in the concrete

Here we must note something unusual in the Lucan use of "bring (*lit* bring down)[2]" Elsewhere Luke uses it with the preposition "to," but not with "on" And the Thesaurus gives no instance of its use (in its naval sense) with "*on*" or "on [*to*]" instead of "*into*[3]." The Acts of John implies that there was first a bringing of the ship *to* the land, and then a "settling" of it *on* the land[4]. Something of this kind may be Luke's intention. But, if he found "*on*" the land in his original, the question arises whether he may not have mistaken

---

[1] If "their father [together] *with the boat*" were altered to "their father *with the hired-servants*," we might illustrate from 1 K x 11 "the *navy* also of Hiram" = 2 Chr ix 10 "the *servants* also of Huram", 1 K x 22 "with the *navy* of Hiram" = 2 Chr ix 21 "with the *servants* of Huram" It may be added that the Greek πατριά "*father's-house*" freq represents Heb "*father*" (e g Exod vi 14, 25 etc) And note the Greek corruption in 1 Chr xvi 28 "Give unto the Lord, *the Father* (πατρὶ) of the nations," where A has, correctly, "*the families* (αἱ πατριαὶ) of the nations" In Mark, "with the *boat*" might be explained as meaning "with the [*boat's*] *crew*, or *servants*," and then the two might be combined. Such a paraphrase, combined with a tradition connecting the sons of Zebulon, or Zebedee, with the sons of Issachar implying *sons of hire* (s above, pp 111—12) might combine to form the Marcan text now extant

[2] Lk v 11 καταγαγόντες τὰ πλοῖα ἐπὶ τὴν γῆν, lit "having brought down the vessels on-to the land"

[3] See κατάγω εἰς in Steph *Thes* Comp Acts ix 30 etc (many of which instances are naval)

[4] *Acts of John* § 2 καὶ οὕτως εἰς γῆν τὸ πλοῖον ἀγαγόντες εἴδομεν καὶ αὐτὸν ἅμα ἡμῖν βοηθοῦντα ὅπως τὸ πλοῖον ἑδράσωμεν, *i e* "to settle it" on its "rollers" (Steph *Thes* ἑδράζω) or "on the land" We should expect ἐπὶ τῆς γῆς not τὴν γῆν, but see Mt xiii 2 ἐπὶ τὸν αἰγιαλὸν ἱστήκει, and Jn xxi 4 ἔστη εἰς (marg ἐπὶ) τὸν αἰγιαλόν SS in Lk v 11 has "*brought the ships near* to the land," not explaining how the disciples came ashore (comp Jn xxi 8 "in the little boat") Perhaps it means "made the ships touch the land."

THE CALLING OF THE FISHERMEN

"*on the earth*" for "*on the land*," and then have transposed the phrase to make sense. If so, the original would have been "Having left...*everything* [*that they had*] *on the earth*, they followed him."

Whatever may be the most probable conclusion about the origin of the Lucan narrative as a whole, it is certain that this particular Lucan phrase, "bring-down on-to the earth," when used in LXX, means, not "bring-back to the land" from the sea, but "bring-down to the ground" in humiliation or destruction[1]. There are also the possibilities of minute Greek verbal corruption, as well as those of paraphrastic error, latent in the Lucan context[2]. Taken as a whole, the Lucan narrative, touching on one of its sides the Mark-Matthew Call of the Fishermen, and on the other the Johannine Draught of Fishes—which might perhaps be called the Return of the Fishermen—appears to indicate a mixture of Hebrew and Greek, of prose and poetry, of metaphor and literalism, that points back to a very early stage of tradition—much earlier than Luke's work—when this part of the Gospel story consisted largely of Songs—"Songs," perhaps, "of the Fisherman," or "of Cephas," or (in Greek) "Songs of the Ichthus"—out of which a scrupulous and painstaking historian, such as Luke was, would have great difficulty in framing a narrative that should be at once consistent with itself and yet not inconsistent with the Gospels of Mark and Matthew[3].

---

[1] Ob 3 Τίς με κατάξει ἐπὶ τὴν γῆν, The Heb phrase "They that *go down to the sea*" suggests that the idiomatic Greek "*bring-down* (κατάγω) *into port*," i.e. "*bring back from the sea*," would be alien from Jewish idiom.

[2] E.g. "they left their father *with the servants*," if expressed by σὺν τοῖς παισίν, might be confused with σὺν τοῖς πᾶσι, which, though not very good Greek, might be taken to mean "together with everything." Comp 2 S viii 14 (rep 1 Chr xviii. 13) ἐν πᾶσιν, "in all things," Lk xxiv 21 σὺν πᾶσι τούτοις, "together with all these things." For παισίν v r πᾶσιν, see 1 Chr xx. 3, comp xxii 17. Less probably πάντα might be confused with πατέρα.

[3] Take, for example, the following comment on Jn xxi 7 "[Peter]

THE CALLING OF THE FISHERMEN

How does John deal with these manifold traditions about the fishermen's "leaving all things" and subsequently asking "What shall we have[1]?" He puts them all aside. Not that he denies them. But he calls the reader's attention away from what the apostles "*left*" to what they "*found*." "We have *found* the Messiah," says Andrew to Peter, and, still more fully, Philip to Nathanael, "We have *found* him of whom Moses (in the law) and the prophets did write, Jesus of Nazareth, the son of Joseph[2]"

This indeed is startling. What "law" and "prophets" did Philip refer to? Philip, above all, who did not even know enough about the "prophets" to be aware that the Messiah must be born in Bethlehem! We cannot answer this question logically. But we can answer it illogically thus. Philip had been "walking in darkness," and in Jerusalem there had flashed on him "a great light." In a moment of ecstasy, he thought of the Bringer of this Light as summing up in Himself all that was good and blessed in the Deliverer of Israel promised by the Scriptures. Isaiah had connected the "great light" in "Galilee" with a manifestation of a "Prince of Peace." Here

---

...cast himself into the sea," made by so late a writer as Chrysostom, "He *cast-away* (ἔρριψε) everything (πάντα), both the fishes and the nets." Also, at the same point, Nonnus, taking five lines to describe the "coat" which Peter "girt about him," calls it ἀμφίβλημα. We have seen above what a large part ἀμφιβάλλω, in the sense of "cast-about," plays in Petrine stories and in early comments on them. And it does not seem fanciful to suppose that Nonnus, here, is giving us one more allusion to the word. If so, we may suppose that Chrysostom's strained introduction of πάντα ἔρριψε arises from a desire to repeat, even in a Johannine comment, something like the Marcan phrase (Mk i 18, Mt. iv 20) "having left the nets," or the Lucan phrase (v. 11) "*having left all things.*"

[1] These *words* are only in Mt xix 27 (not in the parall. Mk-Lk.) But the *thought* is in the parall. Mk x 28, Lk xviii 28. Comp. Gen. xv 2 "And Abram said...What wilt thou give me?"

[2] Jn i. 41, 45.

THE CALLING OF THE FISHERMEN

was the Deliverer, this Jesus of Nazareth, who had brought eternal peace to Philip's soul[1]

Later on, in a time of defection, when Jesus says to Peter, "Do ye also desire to go-back?" Peter implies that he, too, has "found" the greatest of treasures, when he exclaims in answer, "Lord, to whom shall we go? Thou hast the words of eternal life[2]" And similarly as regards the first two converts, Andrew and his unnamed companion—who "abode with" Jesus from "the tenth hour" onward—what they "found" is not indeed described, but the result is that Andrew *"finds"* his own brother Simon and says, We have *found* the Messiah." The inference is obvious—and rises in our minds much more clearly than if the fact had been stated—"These first converts also found in Jesus words of eternal life" Combining the Synoptic with the Johannine language we may say that those who "left houses" for the sake of Christ "abode with him" and were received into His Father's house.

So far John could proceed without contradicting any of the Synoptists. But what as to the doctrine of renouncing home and wife and kinsfolk in detail? We have seen above that Luke, and Luke alone, mentioned a *"wife"* in the list of the personal renunciations of Christ's disciples; and he placed the mention of Peter's "house" and *"wife"* before, not after, Christ's words to Peter, "Thou shalt be catching men," so as to leave it open to suppose that Peter left his wife from the time when he heard these words. About Peter's wife no mention is made in the Fourth Gospel. Probably Peter did leave her when he accompanied Jesus on His missionary journeying, but we know from the Epistle to the Corinthians

---

[1] Is ix 1—6, mentioning "Galilee," "the people that walked in darkness," "a great light," and "unto us a child is born...Prince of Peace"

[2] Jn vi 68.

THE CALLING OF THE FISHERMEN

that this leaving was only temporary[1]. About such a renunciation, temporary or otherwise, the Fourth Gospel has nothing to say. But indirectly it conveys two lessons bearing on the subject By placing, at its outset, Christ's presence at a wedding, and by making His first "sign" the production of wine for the wedding-feast, it suggests that Jesus was not one who would bid a disciple "leave his wife," as one might "leave houses or fields," for the mere sake of self-training and spiritual development And yet, at the close, when Jesus places before Peter the Way of the Cross, and predicts to him "by what manner of death he should glorify God," we are manifestly taught that a disciple might sometimes be called to "leave all"—including wife and life itself—in fulfilment of the command that is the last utterance of Jesus in this Gospel—"follow thou me."

§ 41. *"They followed him...they departed after him*[2]*"*

The best explanation of these different Marcan phrases is, that they mean different things. The former means that Peter and Andrew "came after Jesus" in the sense of "became the followers of Jesus", the latter means that James and John (perhaps accompanied by Peter and Andrew) "followed Jesus away from the place where they were to another place." The thought of "another place" may be illustrated by what the Acts of John says concerning James and John, immediately after they had "settled their boat" on the beach. "We *removed from the place* having gladly made-up-our-minds to

---

[1] 1 Cor ix 5 (R V) "to lead about a wife that is a believer (ἀδελφὴν γυναῖκα περιάγειν) even as . Cephas" Chrysostom does not even mention the notion that γυναῖκα, in such a context, could mean "a woman" But Jerome says (*Letters* cxviii 4) "Peter was married, too, but when he forsook his ship and his nets he forsook his wife also"

[2] Mk 1 18—20 ἠκολούθησαν αὐτῷ. .ἀπῆλθον ὀπίσω αὐτοῦ, Mt iv 20—22 ἠκολούθησαν αὐτῷ (*bis*), Lk v. 11 ἠκολούθησαν αὐτῷ.

THE CALLING OF THE FISHERMEN

follow Him[1]." According to Mark, it could hardly have been said that Peter and Andrew "removed from the place," if Jesus, whom they "followed," merely moved on a little way along the shore to call James and John But it might be said about James and John For the next words in Mark are "And they go into Capernaum." This involves at all events a change of scene, from the shore to the city. And further, Mark, and Mark alone, after thus making his first mention of Capernaum, and of the synagogue there, differs as follows from Matthew and Luke.—

Mk i. 29	Mt viii 14	Lk. iv. 38
And straightway, when they were come out of the synagogue, they came into the house of Simon and Andrew *with James and John*.	And when Jesus was come into Peter's house.	And he rose up from the synagogue and entered into the house of Simon.

This seems to differentiate (in Mark's view) the two pairs of converts. Peter and Andrew return from the synagogue to *their own house.* James and John, instead of returning to their own house, "went after Jesus" to a house that was not their own. Perhaps however Mark, or Mark's original tradition, intended to distinguish, not one pair of disciples from another, but one stage of "following" from another. Jesus said, in the first stage, "Hither! Come ye after me on the Way of Salvation." The disciples responded by "following," that is, by ranking themselves among His followers in the Way[2]. But in the

---

[1] *Acts of John* § 2 ὡς δὲ ἀπέστημεν τοῦ τόπου αὐτῷ βουληθέντες ἕπεσθαι. Both in Jas 1 18 βουληθείς (on which see Mayor, quoting Clem Alex 114, 855 as to God's θέλημα and βούλημα) and in Mt. 1. 19 ἐβουλήθη ("had made-up-his-mind") the past tense adds to the weight of the verb. Αὐτῷ is emphasized by its position "to follow Him [and no other]."

[2] See *Light* 3755 *c—j* on "The Way of the Lord" and "The Way."

THE CALLING OF THE FISHERMEN

second stage it became necessary that they should "follow" Jesus, literally as well as spiritually, "going after" Him in His missionary journeys and finally "up to Jerusalem."

§ 42. *"Departed after" implies a missionary journey*

The failure to recognise this apparently unimportant distinction between the Marcan "followed him" and the Marcan "departed after him" might hinder us from recognising three important facts. The first and most important of these is, for our purpose, fundamental :—that Mark, though he has many faults, has not that fault of artificiality which leads some writers to vary words for variety's sake. This the reader of these pages has probably perceived already, and it will be made still clearer as we advance The second is, that "following" had a kind of technical significance in popular Stoical philosophy so far affecting some very early Christian writers that they agreed in saying that men ought not to "follow" anyone or anything except God[1] The third is, that *"went after him,"* if interpreted according to Hebrew and Jewish tradition, is free from the objection that might be raised by Greeks against the sacrifice of freedom implied in *"followed him"*

The third is the only point that need detain us here. The illustration of it is complicated by the fact that "follow" is in Hebrew most naturally represented by *"go* (or *walk*) after"; and the past tense of the Hebrew "go" is expressed in English sometimes by "went" and sometimes by "came." There may be a great difference between *"go* after" and *"come* after[2]." Take the first instance of "follow" in A V. The speaker is the servant whom Abraham is sending to Mesopotamia to bring back a wife for Isaac, "Perhaps the woman will not be willing

---

[1] See above, p 50
[2] The Heb "walk," "go" (used in "go after strange gods" etc) is rendered πορεύομαι some hundreds of times, ἔρχομαι comparatively seldom, less than thirty times.

THE CALLING OF THE FISHERMEN

to *follow me*...[1]." The Hebrew is "*go after me*" The LXX has "*go with me*...," but one MS has "*come with me.*" The rendering of the LXX is explained by the conclusion of the Hebrew sentence "to go after me *to this land*" That is, in effect, "to *come with me back* from the house of her father to this [Abraham's] house" Hence the LXX takes "*after*" as "*back*" (which is often the meaning of the Hebrew) and paraphrases thus "*go* (v r *come*) *with me back to this land*"

In this instance, then, "go after" means "go after" *iterally*, as one following the *indications of a guide* Elsewhere in the Bible it means "go after" *literally*, as one following the *commands of a military leader*. But in the Bible it does not mean "go after" a person *metaphorically*, that is, in the sense of following imitatively or morally[2]. From the Talmud, too, no instance has been alleged where it has that meaning[3] "Sit before," rather than "walk after," would appear to be (at all events in some Jewish traditions) the designation of a pupil[4].

It is therefore in accordance with Jewish tradition to suppose that the Marcan phrase at the conclusion of the Call of the Fishermen originally denoted (even though Mark may

---

[1] Gen xxiv 5, LXX πορευθῆναι (D, ἐλθεῖν) μετ' ἐμοῦ .

[2] In the Bible, the nearest approach to the meaning of moral imitation is in 2 K xiii 2 "walked after the sins of Jeroboam" But "sins" makes all the difference Without it "walked (*or*, went) after Jeroboam" would mean "seceded to him"

[3] In the Talmud there are several anecdotes about disciples "walking (*or*, going) after a Rabbi" But they all imply (so far as I have seen) a *literal* "walking" Sometimes the Rabbi is riding on an ass and the disciple "going after him" See Schlatter on Jn i 7, 43 Paul never uses the word "*follow*" in a moral sense Where A V (as freq) has "followers" in this sense, the Greek and R V have "imitators," or "zealous for," *e g* 1 Cor iv 16, xi. 1, Eph v 1 (comp Philipp iii 17 etc)

[4] For instances where a pupil is designated as "sitting *before*" his instructor, see Wetstein on Acts xxii 3, and *Gen r* on Gen xlix 14 (Wu pp 486, 499)

THE CALLING OF THE FISHERMEN

not have understood the special denotation) that those thus called quitted their occupation and went forth following Jesus henceforth literally on some missionary journey or journeys. But at the same time the act, and the language in which the act was expressed, prepared the way for later words of Christ in which He appeared to speak mysteriously of His last journey to Jerusalem in connection with the words "to-day" and "to-morrow" and being "perfected" on "the third day[1]"—alluding to similar words in which Hosea exhorted his countrymen: "After two days will he revive us, on the third day he will raise us up, and we shall live before him. And let us know, *let us follow on to know the Lord*[2]." Thus it is easy to see how Jewish phrases about literal following might pass into Christian phrases about spiritual following.

§ 43. *Philip "following"*

How John expressed the doctrine of spiritual following in various metaphors and scenes—culminating in the dialogue of Jesus with Peter, and the precept "Follow thou me"—has been detailed above. But something remains to be said about the calling of Philip for this reason, that this Apostle is connected by John with the coming of "Greeks" to Jesus, and what we read about him may perhaps bear on the Greek objection mentioned above, "We must follow God, in accordance with Nature, not Man."

Remembering, then, that Philip is the only Apostle to whom Jesus said "Follow me"—until we come to the very

---

[1] Lk. xiii 32—3.

[2] Hos. vi 2—3. Here "follow-on" = Heb "pursue," "chase," "press-hard," almost always used in a hostile sense. It is once used in Heb and Targ. concerning a leader saying to his troops (Judg. iii. 28) "*Follow-on*, or *press-hard*, or *chase, after me*," but the LXX (perhaps correctly) reads "*go down after me*" (Gesen 922 b). Delitzsch has Heb. "*chase after*" to express Mk i. 36 κατεδίωξεν αὐτόν, lit "chased him down," where R.V. "followed-after him" does not express the Greek.

THE CALLING OF THE FISHERMEN

end of the Gospel—we ought to ask in what sense and with what success he obeyed this command. That he "followed" Jesus literally and locally from the place where Jesus "found" him we may assume as certain. But to what extent did he, in the above-quoted words of Hosea, "*follow on to know the Lord*"? The answer is contained in the words of Jesus, "Have I been so long time with you [all], and *dost thou not know me, Philip*[1]?" He had "followed," but he had not "known" whom he followed. There is no reproach in this that does not apply to all the Apostles—including Peter to whom Jesus said, "Thou canst not follow me now." But the context, and the dialogue as a whole, seem to shew what would have been the Evangelist's answer to the above-mentioned objection of the Greeks. Jesus has previously described Himself as the Way, the Truth, and the Life, adding "No one cometh unto the Father, save through me." It is Jesus as the utterer of these words, and as the avenue to the Father, whom Philip has "not known." Philip asks for a material manifestation ("Shew us the Father") and thereby brings on himself his Master's reproach.

By this, the Evangelist seems to say to us, "The Philosophers tell us that 'we ought not to follow men, but only Nature or God.' This is true. But how can we know God except through knowing that which is most like God? And has not Plato said, '*God is righteous in the highest degree, and there is nothing more like God than whosoever of us is righteous in the highest degree*[2]'? We Christians follow *the Man whom we believe to have been* '*righteous in the highest degree.*' But we follow Him, not merely because of what we believe Him to have been in the past, but also because of what He is to us still—only more manifestly than before—namely the perfection of Love.

---

[1] Jn xiv 9 "with *you* [*all*] (ὑμῶν)" pl., followed by the sing "thou"

[2] Plato 176 C, *Theaet.* § 25.

THE CALLING OF THE FISHERMEN

In following Him we follow God and Nature. For He, the Son, was proclaimed to be at one with the Father, and His voice to be in accord with the voice of spiritual Nature, when it became manifested that His love could not be conquered or silenced by death. In the hearts of His disciples death made Him stronger, not weaker, drawing us on still to follow Him on the Way of the Cross, the Way of Love and Truth and Life, that we might pass through the love of the Son on earth to the love of the Father in heaven. There is no servitude in such 'following' as this. This 'following-on to know the Lord' is a 'following' that leads us—if we really and truly follow—out of the servile squalour of the fear of death into 'the liberty of the glory of the children of God[1].'"

§ 44 *Inferences from Mark*

If this distinction between "following" and "departing after" is to hold good as to the original tradition of Mark, so that the latter is to suggest "departed after Jesus [on a missionary journey, or on a journey up to Jerusalem]," the question will arise, "How far does this agree with John?" It is also natural to ask, "Does John take the view that henceforth the disciples constantly followed Jesus?"

These questions we cannot discuss fully till we come to the Naming of the Twelve and the Precepts to the Twelve in the Three Gospels, along with the Precepts to the Seventy peculiar to Luke. Here we must merely add that John nowhere represents Jesus as sending away the Twelve to preach the Gospel apart from Himself. From the moment when the first converts are made in the Fourth Gospel, they are represented as being with their Master, and we receive the impression that they never leave Him. When He is "invited" to Cana they are "invited" too, though His own brethren are not

---

[1] Rom. viii. 21.

THE CALLING OF THE FISHERMEN

said to be invited[1]. They are then mentioned as accompanying Him to Capernaum[2]. After that, though they are not mentioned as accompanying Him to Jerusalem, their presence is implied[3], and they are mentioned as going with Him (apparently from Jerusalem) into the land of Judaea[4]. Henceforth they appear to be practically inseparable from Him[5].

This is important as a positive aspect. But there is also a still more important negative aspect. John does not seem to leave in his Gospel—though it covers three visits to Jerusalem—any place whatever into which we might fit in a narrative of the Sending Forth of the Twelve, or of the Seventy. Can it be that he believed the Precepts to the Twelve—like the Lucan Precepts to the Seventy and the Lucan Draught of Fishes—to have been antedated, and to refer (if rightly placed) to a period after the Resurrection? Stated barely, that is improbable. But there may have been a mixture of precepts given before the Resurrection, with those given after it.

Without aiming at a premature conclusion on this difficult question, we may strengthen ourselves in keeping a mind open to evidence on both sides by the following considerations. (1) The Fourth Gospel openly proclaims itself, as it were, a Gospel of incompleteness, by omitting all mention of the death of John the Baptist while stating that, at a certain date, he had "not yet" been cast into prison. (2) The imprisonment should probably be placed about, or shortly after, the Dialogue

---

[1] Jn. ii. 1—2. This is the more striking because His "mother" as well as His "disciples" are said to be "invited," and because His "brethren" are mentioned a little later along with His "mother" and disciples (*ib.* ii 12) as going down to Capernaum.

[2] Jn ii 12   [3] Jn ii 22

[4] Jn iii 22

[5] They are absent from Him for a brief interval during the dialogue with the Samaritan woman, and for a few hours during the storm on the sea of Tiberias. That is all.

THE CALLING OF THE FISHERMEN

with the Samaritan woman[1]. (3) At the close of this Dialogue, Jesus addresses the disciples—who had left Him for a brief interval that they might purchase provisions—on the Harvest of the Gospel and on the wages of the reapers[2] (4) Similar language is placed by Matthew and Luke, severally, just before Matthew's Precepts to the Twelve, and at the outset of Luke's Precepts to the Seventy[3]. (5) The death of John the Baptist was antecedently likely to induce Jesus to appoint successors to carry on His work in case He also should be put to death. (6) The Fourth Evangelist may have omitted the Precepts to the Twelve for nearly the same reasons that induced him to omit the death of John the Baptist—because he considered that the Precepts had been detailed at some length by Matthew and (if we include the Precepts to the Seventy) by Luke; and the Baptist's death had been narrated at great length by Mark and Matthew. (7) The Evangelist tells us that Jesus, in the neighbourhood of John the Baptist, "baptized[4]"; then he adds "Howbeit Jesus himself baptized not, but his disciples[5]"; then, later on, "The Spirit was not yet [given][6]"—thus leaving us under the impression that what the disciples did in the way of proselytizing was done, not at a distance from their Master, but round Him as their centre, and that it was of a rudimentary nature, repeating the baptism of John, with perhaps some additions—so that nothing in their action or in their doctrine could afford an exact precedent to the Church, the Holy Spirit being not yet present.

There is much to be said for the historical correctness of this view. It is noteworthy that none of the Synoptists says that the Twelve (or the Seventy) received a precept to

---

[1] The Baptist's last words in the Fourth Gospel are (Jn iii 30) "He must increase but I must decrease." The Dialogue with the Samaritan woman begins at iv 7

[2] Jn iv 35—8   [3] Mt. ix. 37, Lk x. 2.
[4] Jn iii. 22.   [5] Jn iv. 1—2.
[6] Jn vii. 39.

THE CALLING OF THE FISHERMEN

"baptize[1]" But there can be little doubt that they *did* "baptize." The admission of this fact raised an awkward question, like that in the Acts "Unto what then were ye baptized[2]?" John alone helps us to understand the state of things. It was altogether rudimentary—"baptism," with the Holy Spirit left out.

---

[1] Mk vi. 8—13, Mt x. 1—15, Lk ix 1—5, comp. Lk x. 1—12
[2] Acts xix. 3 foll.

Addendum on ἐν τῷ with temporal infinitive

In *Introduction* pp 112—13 (comp. pp. 121, 126) and *Beginning* p. 111, attention was called to the Lucan use of ἐν τῷ as a sign of translation from, or imitation of, Hebrew. It was my intention to include in the present volume all the Lucan instances of this idiom, illustrating them from LXX. But the results proved too bulky. I must therefore refer the reader to *Son* 3333 *e—g*, making two additional remarks. (1) Aquila uses ἐν τῷ as a literal rendering of Heb. in O T (2) Of the relatively very rare passages (seven at the utmost) that may claim to exemplify this idiom in the Acts (in some of which the infinitive can hardly be called temporal) three are either in Petrine speeches or in an apostolic Hymn of Praise, and two have in their context the Lucan ἐγένετο "it came to pass that," which is a sign of Hebraic style (though not necessarily of translation)

CHAPTER II*

AUTHORITY" AND "UNCLEAN SPIRITS[1]"
[Mark 1 21—8]

§ 1. *"The unclean spirit," in Zechariah*

MARK, after relating the Call of the Fishermen, represents Christ's first act to have been what the multitude described as "a new teaching! with authority he commandeth even the unclean spirits, and they obey him[2]."

What was Mark's motive in selecting this to stand first in his narrative of the acts of Jesus? No other Evangelist does this. It is hardly enough to say that Mark believed it to be the first We may be sure that he would not have related it so fully—giving to it as much space as he gives to the Lord's Supper—if he had not regarded it as a fit beginning for the

---

* For titles of previous Parts of Diatessarica referred to by abbreviations in this Volume, see pp 545—6 For other abbreviations see pp xxiii—xxvi

[1] This section covers Mk 1 21—8 "And they go into Capernaum ..all the region of Galilee round about," Lk iv 31—7 "And he came down to Capernaum a city of Galilee ..every place of the region round about" Matthew (vii 28—9 "astonished at his teaching . having authority") inserts a parallel to the statement of Mk-Lk about the "astonishment" at the "authority" of Christ, but places it long after Mt iv 13 "leaving Nazareth he came and dwelt in Capernaum" Matthew wholly omits the casting out of the unclean spirit For the parallel texts see pp. 158—9

[2] Mk 1 27 "What is this? A new teaching!" Comp Lk iv 36 "What is this word?"

"AUTHORITY" AND "UNCLEAN SPIRITS"

Messiah's Gospel   Now what could seem "a fit beginning," in the eyes of the Christians of the first century, if it did not point back to prophecy, or rest on prophecy? It is true that Mark seldom quotes prophecy. But he habitually rests on it and frequently alludes to it[1]. Our first task, therefore, must be to inquire whether any prophet has written about the casting out of an "unclean spirit" as an act to be accomplished in the days of the Messiah.

There is but one such prophecy. But it comes from one of the most Messianic of prophets, to whom Christians most frequently appealed from the earliest times, Zechariah. He, after the mysterious prediction "They shall look unto me (*or*, unto him) whom they pierced," and the description of the mourning that will follow, says   "In that day there shall be a fountain opened to the house of David and to the inhabitants of Jerusalem for sin and for defilement[2],...and I will cut off the names of the idols out of the land...and also I will cause the prophets and *the unclean spirit* to pass out of the land[3]." This is Targumized as follows : "At that time there shall be the teaching of the Law, opened like a fountain of waters for the house of David and for the inhabitants of Jerusalem, and I will remit their sins even as they are cleansed with the water of sprinkling and with the ashes of the heifer[4] that is [offered] for sin...And I will cut off the name of the idols of the peoples from the land...and also I will cause the false prophets and the unclean spirit to cease from the land "

The word "unclean" occurs in our Version of O T about one hundred and sixty times, but "unclean spirit" only here.

---

[1] See *Son* 3518 *d*

[2] A V (followed by R V) has "uncleanness" But the Heb. *niddah* (often meaning "separation," "that from which one must separate oneself") is different from the word rendered below (and regularly) "unclean"

[3] Zech xii 10—14, xiii 1—2.

[4] See Numb xix 2

"AUTHORITY" AND "UNCLEAN SPIRITS"

The juxtaposition of "[false] prophets" and "unclean" recalls the Levitical prohibition against resorting to "*necromancers*" (R.V. "those that have familiar spirits") "to be *made-unclean* by them[1]." But Kimchi (on Zechariah) separates the "prophets" from the "unclean spirit," making three stages of evil :—1st, idolatry, before the First Temple ; 2nd, false prophecy, during the First Temple ; 3rd, "evil desire," after the First Temple. R. Jochanan, like the Targumist, connected the prophecy of Zechariah with the purification by means of the Red Heifer. A Gentile—confronting the Rabbi in the midst of his pupils—had objected to it as being a kind of sorcery. Jochanan asked the Gentile what his own people did when an evil spirit entered into anyone : "We burn roots under his nose," said the man, "and dash water over him, and the evil spirit flees." Jochanan explained that the Jews achieved just the same result with "the water of defilement (*lit.* separation[2])" that had received the ashes of the Red Heifer, in accordance with the words of Zechariah.

The Gentile, who then departed, was apparently satisfied. But the Jewish pupils were not. "You have put this man off," they said, "with a straw. What do you say to *us*?" Jochanan replied, "By your life! it is not the slaughtered

---

[1] Lev. xix. 31. See Gesen. 15*a* on the Heb. '*owb* "skin-bottle, necromancer," always meaning "necromancer" except in Job xxxii. 18—19 (Elihu) "I am full of words. The spirit of my belly constraineth me, behold, my belly is as wine that hath no vent, like new wine-skins that are ready to burst." The Heb. '*owb* is mostly (Tromm. 10) rendered by LXX ἐγγαστρίμυθος, i.e. "speaker through the belly," or ventriloquist. This suggests a new and Jewish aspect of Philipp. iii. 19 and Rom. xvi. 18, illustrated by Ezek. xiv. 3. A man serving idols may serve (as one of them) his own egotistic and artificial verbosity.

The Heb. is rendered θελητής (Hesych. = προαιρετικός) twice by LXX and five times by other translators (perhaps meaning "one that does as he likes," "serves his own will").

[2] Numb. xix. 9 (R.V.) "water of separation," marg. "impurity."

"AUTHORITY" AND "UNCLEAN SPIRITS"

animal that takes away uncleanness, nor does the water cleanse. But it is the decree of the King of Kings. God has said 'A statute have I given, a decree have I made binding. No man shall transgress my decree,' as it is written, *This is the statute of the law*[1]." The passage is remarkable as indicating that in R. Jochanan's time it was customary to attempt (and the Rabbi implies, with success) to cast out devils with "the water of defilement[2]." To some such practice Jesus may be referring when He says to the Pharisees "By whom do your children cast them out[3]?" But if the attempts had been to any great extent successful we should have heard more about them in the Gospels, the Talmuds, and Josephus[4].

§ 2. *"An unclean spirit" and "authority," in Mark and Luke*[5]

From "the unclean spirit" in Zechariah, unique in O.T., we pass to the first mention of "unclean spirit" in Mark. It is in a narrative of exorcism, wholly omitted by Matthew, who

---

[1] See *Numb r.* on Numb xix. 2, and also *Pesikt* iv, Wu. p 47

[2] *Hor. Heb*, on Mt. xii 27, referring to *Joma* 57 a, says "In the Gloss, mention is made of a devil cast out by a Jew at Rome" The text mentions "sprinkling," but not the casting out of a devil.

[3] Mt xii 27, Lk. xi. 19   Jerome admits this as one explanation but prefers to explain "your children" as the "apostles"

[4] The only mention of "Exorcism" in Schwab's Index to Jer. Talmud is to *Sanhedr*. x. 1, where the Mishna forbids the "muttering" of the words in Exod. xv 26 as a charm, to avert some plague. Josephus (*Ant* viii. 2 5) indicates that a Jewish exorcist sometimes used "incantations" and "roots" supposed to have been discovered by Solomon (which apparently Jochanan would have altogether disowned).

[5] Luke, in iv 6 "I will give unto thee all this authority," has mentioned "authority" before. Mark has not   In both, "unclean" occurs here for the first time

157   (Mark 1. 21—8)

"AUTHORITY" AND "UNCLEAN SPIRITS"

however has (in various parts of his Gospel) one or two phrases of agreement printed in black below:—

Mk i. 21—8 (R V)	Mt. iv 12—3, vii. 28—9 (R.V.)	Lk. iv. 31—7 (R.V.)
(21) And they go into Capernaum, and straightway on the sabbath day he entered into the synagogue and taught.	(12) Now when he heard that John was delivered up, he withdrew into Galilee,	(31) And he came down to Capernaum, a city of Galilee. And he was teaching them on the sabbath day
(22) And they were astonished at his teaching, for he taught them as having authority, and not as the scribes.	(13) And leaving Nazareth, he came and dwelt **in Capernaum**, which is by the sea, in the borders of Zebulon and Naphtali.	(32) And they were astonished at his teaching; for his word was with authority.
(23) And straightway there was in their synagogue a man with an unclean spirit, and he cried out,		(33) And in the synagogue there was a man, which had a spirit of an unclean devil, and he cried out with a loud voice,
(24) Saying, What have we to do with thee, thou Jesus of Nazareth? art thou come to destroy us? I know thee who thou art, the Holy One of God	(28) **And** it came to pass, when Jesus ended these words, the multitudes **were astonished at his teaching**. (29) For he **taught them** as [one] having **authority**, and not as their scribes	(34) Ah! (*or*, Let alone!) what have we to do with thee, thou Jesus of Nazareth? art thou come to destroy us? I know thee who thou art, the Holy One of God
(25) And Jesus rebuked him (*or*, it), saying, Hold thy peace, and come out of him		(35) And Jesus rebuked him, saying, Hold thy peace, and come out of him. And when the devil had thrown him down[1] in the midst, he came out of him,
(26) And the unclean spirit, tearing (*or*, convulsing) him[1]		

---

[1] "*Tearing* (σπαράξαν)," parall to "*thrown down* (ῥίψαν)," may

(Mark 1. 21—8)

"AUTHORITY" AND "UNCLEAN SPIRITS"

Mk i. 21—8 (R V.) (*contd.*)	Mt iv. 12—3, vii. 28—9 (R V) (*contd.*)	Lk iv. 31—7 (R.V.) (*contd*)
and crying with a loud voice, came out of him		having done him no hurt.
(27) And they were all amazed, insomuch that they questioned among themselves, saying, What is this? a new teaching! with authority he commandeth even the unclean spirits, and they obey him		(36) And amazement came upon all, and they spake together, one with another, saying, What is this word? for (*or*, this word, that) with authority and power he commandeth the unclean spirits, and they come out
(28) And the report of him went out straightway everywhere into all the region of Galilee round about.		(37) And there went forth a rumour concerning him into every place of the region round about

It will be observed that Luke alters "*he taught them* as having authority" into "*his word* was with authority." Later on, he again alters "a new *teaching*!" into "what is this *word*?" and, instead of "with *authority*," he has "with *authority and power*" (before "he commandeth the unclean spirits"). He also cancels Mark's addition "*not as the scribes*" (after "having authority") One object of all these changes seems to be to shew that the "authority" had nothing to do with "teaching" "No 'teaching,'" Luke seems to say, "can expel an evil spirit.

---

be illustrated by Dan viii 7 "*cast down*," LXX ἐσπάραξεν, Theod ἔριψεν Σπαράσσω may mean "*tear [a thing] up and down*" (as a dog "worries" anything) In Daniel (and probably in Mark) it is more picturesque but less accurate than ῥίπτω

"AUTHORITY" AND "UNCLEAN SPIRITS"

Nothing but a *fiat* can do this, a '*word*' from the Master who has 'authority' over every evil spirit, and who can say to it, 'Go,' and it goeth."

Mark's view appears to have been that the "teaching," of itself—by reason of something in it that Mark called "authority"—had power to rouse in one of Christ's hearers a sense of hostility. The man uneasily perceived that an unclean spirit within himself, one that he at that moment felt to be part of himself, was being threatened with expulsion as it listened—or as he listened, or as both together listened—to the Gospel of the Kingdom of God which made war against all the power of Satan. The listener was possessed with more wills than one. The "I" had become "we." And first the "we" cried out "Hast thou come to destroy *us*?" Then, in the same moment the "I" confessed "*I* know thee who thou art, the Holy One of God!" Then and not till then came the "rebuke" to the unclean spirit, even as, in Zechariah, "The Lord said unto Satan, The Lord *rebuke* thee, O Satan; yea, the Lord that hath chosen Jerusalem *rebuke* thee! Is not this a brand plucked out of the fire[1]?"

Perhaps if Mark had been writing in his own person, he would have distinguished between the authority of the teaching and the authority of the exorcism; but he seems to set before us in a very natural way the confusion of the two notions that might have actually occurred in the mind of the multitude, and just what the multitude might have said. At the same time it must be added that this typical act of Messianic power, redeeming a soul from bondage to Satan, might naturally be

---

[1] Zech. iii. 2. See Gesen. 172 *a* on Heb "rebuke," LXX ἐπιτιμάω. It is applied to the sea in Ps. cvi 9 etc., as it is to the "wind(s)" in Mk iv. 39, Mt viii 26, Lk viii. 24 It is applied to "evil spirits" again in Mk iii. 12, and to a "fever" and "devils" in Lk. iv. 39, 41. All the Synoptists represent Jesus as healing the "fever" of Peter's wife's mother, but Luke alone describes Him as "rebuking" it. See below, pp 192—5.

regarded by the early Jewish evangelists as a kind of firstfruits of a second Redemption, a second Exodus and a second Passover.

Is there anything in this Marcan narrative—even a mere word or phrase—that might recall to Jews (though not to us) some feature in the institution of the first Passover? It will be found that there is, if we have patience to consider the ancient Biblical associations with the words "What is this?"

First, we must distinguish "this," here used absolutely, from the very frequent use of "this," not used absolutely (in such phrases as "what is this that thou hast done?" etc.). Secondly, we must distinguish it from the saying "What is it (*or*, that)?" about the first appearance of "manna[1]," although that, too, was mystically interpreted in the first century by Philo and probably by others. Thirdly, we must recognise the frequency of the Jewish mystical use of "this" (to which attention was called in the *Johannine Grammar*) as referring to the Messiah[2]. Lastly, we must ask whether the phrase

---

[1] Exod. xvi. 15 "They said, one to another, What is it?" lit "What [is] that?" R V marg "It is *manna*. Heb *Man hu*." Mechilt gives as the explanation of the allegorizers ("die Erklärer nach Andeutungen") "The Israelites named it *Man*, i e '*prepared*.'" On this, see Philo i 121 "They question one another—these souls that have already experienced the Word (Logos), but have it not in them to say '*What it is*' (πεπονθυῖαι μὲν ἤδη τὸν λόγον, οὐκ ἔχουσαι δὲ εἰπεῖν τὸ 'τί ἐστι')." He then quotes "This is the bread that the Lord hath given you to eat This is the thing (LXX ῥῆμα) that the Lord hath commanded, Gather of it...." first paraphrasing it so as to distinguish between ῥῆμα and λόγος, and then quoting it so as to suit his distinction, thus —Οὗτός ἐστιν ὁ ἄρτος, ἡ τροφὴ ἣν ἔδωκεν ὁ θεὸς τῇ ψυχῇ, προσενέγκασθαι τὸ ἑαυτοῦ ῥῆμα, καὶ τὸν ἑαυτοῦ λόγον· οὗτος γὰρ ὁ ἄρτος ὃν δέδωκεν ἡμῖν φαγεῖν, τοῦτο τὸ ῥῆμα. Comp. *ib*. 566 "Οὗτός ἐστιν ὁ ἄρτος ὃν ἔδωκε κύριος αὐτοῖς φαγεῖν." Τίς οὖν ὁ ἄρτος; Εἰπέ. "Τοῦτο," φησί, "τὸ ῥῆμα ὃ συνέταξε κύριος"

[2] *Joh Gr*. 2396 "Schottgen (ii 45) gives a multitude of instances in which 'this thing,' represented by the Hebrew feminine '*this*' (mostly altered as to gender in LXX) is mystically interpreted as referring to the Messiah." This Heb. fem. is not used in Exod. xvi 15.

"AUTHORITY" AND "UNCLEAN SPIRITS"

"What is this?" so familiar and commonplace to us both in written and in spoken English, would seem equally commonplace to Jewish readers of the Hebrew Bible.

The answer to this last question may be as surprising to many of my readers as it was to me. "*What is this* (Heb. fem)?" occurs nowhere in the Bible (so far as can be ascertained from the English Concordance) except in the question to be put by the son to the father concerning the redemption of the firstborn instituted in connection with the Passover, "And it shall be when thy son asketh thee in time to come, saying, *What is this*[1]?"

The Jerusalem Talmud, commenting on this question, describes four classes of questioners, the infant, the simple-minded, the bad, the wise. The wise questioner would ask in detail concerning the laws, precepts, and ordinances of the Lord. But the simple-minded one, just above an infant, would merely ask "What is this[2]?" All Jewish boys, as a rule, in Christ's time, had asked "What is this?" and had heard it asked, at the Passover. Peter would be no exception to the rule. There is nothing surprising if the multitude in the synagogue of Capernaum, amazed at the first exposition of Christ's exorcistic power, startling them in the midst of His interrupted preaching, exclaimed some words equivalent to "What is this?" And if they did, nothing could be more natural or justifiable than that the Petrine Gospel, describing the exclamations of the multitude, should include this one in particular, endeared as it was by its redemptive associations[3].

In Deut xxxii 29 "*this* (fem)" LXX has ταῦτα but Aq. αὐτήν. Schottgen's instances are from the Cabbala. Levy i. 513 *a* includes one fem. instance.   [1] Exod xiii 14

[2] See Rashi, *Mechilta*, and *J Pesach* x (4) (Schwab v 151) on Exod xiii 14

[3] In that case a Hebrew Gospel would give the words of Exod. xiii 14 as Delitzsch does in Mk i 27 "*what this* (Heb. fem)?" In LXX Greek, this would be Τί τοῦτο, or τί ἐστι τοῦτο; but in literal Greek it would be αὕτη, not τοῦτο. Alteration of the literal Greek

"AUTHORITY" AND "UNCLEAN SPIRITS"

§ 3. *"Authority" and "law," in Matthew*

Matthew, after the Call of the Fishermen, ending with "followed him," instead of describing the exorcism of a particular "unclean spirit," gives a general description of acts of "healing" (not of "casting out") as follows: "And Jesus went about in all Galilee, teaching in their synagogues, and preaching the gospel of the kingdom, and healing all manner of disease and all manner of sickness among the people. And the report of him went forth into all Syria · and they brought unto him all that were sick, holden with divers diseases and torments, possessed with devils, and epileptic, and palsied; and he healed them. And there followed him great multitudes from...and [from] beyond Jordan. And seeing the multitudes, he went up into the mountain...[1]." Then follows the whole of the Sermon on the Mount, with the appended comment, "He taught them as [one] having *authority*..."—Matthew's first mention of "*authority*[2]."

Not till after this does Matthew mention particular acts of healing:—(1) the cleansing of a leper, (2) the healing of the centurion's "boy" at a distance, (3) the healing of Peter's wife's mother[3]. Then follows a second general description in which "casting out" is included: "And when even was come, they brought unto him many possessed with devils, and he cast out the spirits with a word, and healed all that were sick: that it might be fulfilled which was spoken by Isaiah the prophet, saying, Himself took our infirmities and bare our diseases[4]."

It will be observed that Matthew not only mentions

---

feminine might cause other alterations, and, *inter alia*, the introduction of διδαχὴ καινή in Mark. In Exod xiii 14, "*what is this?*" is expanded by Jer. Targ. into "*What is this precept as to the first-born?*"

[1] Mt. iv 23—v 1 (R.V.).   [2] Mt v 2—vii 29
[3] Mt. viii. 1—15.
[4] Mt viii 16—17, quoting from Is liii 4.

"healing" without "casting out" in his first description, but also crowns his second description with a quotation from Isaiah about the Messianic "bearing" of "diseases." He does not mention "*authority*" in connection with healing of any kind except so far as it is indirectly suggested in the words of the centurion to Jesus "Only say [it] with a word[1], and my boy will be healed. For I also am a man under *authority*, having under myself soldiers...," that is to say, "Thou hast *authority* over diseases as I have *authority* over soldiers, and canst say to the disease 'Go,' and it goeth[2]."

Even here, it is not shewn that Matthew, speaking in his own person, would have used—or would have regarded as anything but a popular usage—this language about "authority." Matthew himself seems to say "The Messiah's authority was revealed in its highest form, not when He cast out spirits with a word, but when He ascended the mountain and gave the New Law, *teaching with authority and not as the scribes*, and saying to His disciples, 'This or that was said in old days, but *I* say unto you something that is better and higher.'"

One disadvantage of Matthew's arrangement is that he does not give us the historical facts in their historical order. Indeed he hardly professes to do so. He throws into one Law, or Discourse, doctrines that Luke assigns to several distinct times and occasions. Perhaps Matthew did not recognise any fitness—and indeed perceived some unfitness—in the Marcan arrangement, which brought Christ for the first time before our eyes as the Healer, casually, so to speak, and in consequence of a madman's outburst, in a synagogue where He happened to be preaching.

---

[1] Comp Mt viii. 16 "cast out the spirits *with a word*," where the parall Mk i 34 has simply "cast out many devils," and Lk iv. 41 "there went out devils from many"

[2] Mt viii 8—9 parall to Lk vii 7—8 Comp Lk iv. 36 "What is this word?" The words of the centurion are practically identical in Mt. and Lk.

"AUTHORITY" AND "UNCLEAN SPIRITS"

We must be thankful to Mark for doing this. It helps us to realise how strangely prolonged—for a Messiah—was that period of waiting during which the power of Jesus lay unrevealed, and through what unexpected occasions it revealed and developed itself. But Matthew's view also deserves sympathetic consideration. He depicts Jesus, not as the unexpected Exorcist of "the unclean spirit" from Israel, but as the Servant of the Lord, foreordained to heal And the healing is to be, not by casting out but by "bearing" and suffering. According to the LXX version of Isaiah, the Messiah was to be one who "is under the stroke [of affliction] and knoweth how to bear *sickness*," or (with Symmachus) "born-to-distress and known to *disease*[1]." The word used here by the LXX for "sickness" occurs but thrice in N.T The three instances are all in Matthew, and all in the phrase "heal(ing) every disease and every sickness." There can be little doubt that Matthew uses this as a kind of Messianic refrain, first, to describe the beginning of the Messiah's unassisted work, immediately after He had called the fishermen[2]; secondly, at a considerable interval, to describe the conclusion of that stage, when Jesus repeated a round of teaching, preaching, and healing, but felt that there was need of more "labourers[3]"; thirdly, and that immediately afterwards, when He "called his twelve disciples" and gave them "authority" to continue the work that He had been doing[4].

---

[1] Is liii 3 (Field) *Vir dolorum et notus* (familiaris) *morbo* LXX ἄνθρωπος ἐν πληγῇ ὤν, καὶ εἰδὼς φέρειν μαλακίαν. Aq. (ἄνδρα) ἀλγηδόνων καὶ γνωστὸν ἀρρωστίᾳ. Sym. ἀνὴρ ἐπίπονος, καὶ γνωστὸς νόσῳ. Theod (ἀνὴρ) ἀλγηδόνων καὶ γνωστὸς μαλακίᾳ.

[2] Mt iv. 23

[3] Mt ix. 35—8

[4] Mt. x 1 "And he called unto him his twelve disciples, and gave them authority over unclean spirits, to cast them out, and to heal *every disease and every sickness* " This is the only instance where Matthew mentions "unclean spirits (pl)," and here he agrees with Mk vi 7 "the unclean spirits." In the only instance where

165 (Mark 1. 21—8)

"AUTHORITY" AND "UNCLEAN SPIRITS"

Thus, by his arrangement, by his choice of words, and by his use of refrains, Matthew warns us as it were that we are in a region of poetic history, describing fulfilments of prophecies. The fulfilments are actual and historical, but couched in language borrowed from the past and not always exactly and literally applicable to the present—as, for example, the statement that Jesus healed "*every* disease and *every* sickness." This must not be taken as if it meant "*every*" disease, or even "*every kind of*" disease in Palestine.

Such statements may be illustrated by the Odes of Solomon, where the first mention of God's Kingdom is connected with sickness, "Sicknesses have removed far from my body, and it stood up to [serve] the Lord in His good-pleasure, because His Kingdom is true[1]." The author of the Odes was thinking mainly of the promises made in the Law, and especially the promise concerning the banishment of "*every sickness*" from Israel[2]. Our Evangelist, too, is thinking of that. But he is thinking also of the promise made in the Prophets concerning the Messiah who was to be "known to *disease*[3]." Elsewhere Matthew, also, if he does not disparage exorcism, at all events warns readers against supposing that this, or the claim to it, was a test of spiritual goodness. His Gospel (and no other) contains, as an ineffectual appeal from "workers of iniquity," the words "Lord, did we not cast out devils in thy

---

Matthew has (xii. 43) "the unclean spirit (sing.)" he is followed by Luke (xi. 24) "the unclean spirit."

[1] *Odes* xviii. 3, on which see *Light* 3940 *a*.

[2] See *Light* 3940 *a* "In Hebraic Greek—which does not use the word παντοῖος, but only πᾶν γένος where παντοῖος is urgently needed—'*every sickness*' may mean '*all sickness*.' The ambiguous phrase is rare. It occurs nowhere in LXX except Deut. vii. 15 'The Lord will take away from thee *every* (R.V. *all*) *sickness*, and he will put none of the evil diseases of Egypt...upon thee,' *ib.* xxviii. 60—61 'He will bring upon thee all the diseases of Egypt...also *every* (so R.V.) *sickness* and every plague...'"

[3] Is. liii. 3 according to Symmachus, see above, p. 165.

166 (Mark i. 21—8)

"AUTHORITY" AND "UNCLEAN SPIRITS"

name[1]?" He also rejects the Marcan tradition (accepted by Luke) that Jesus forbade John to hinder certain exorcists who used His name without following Him[2]. Other peculiarities of his Gospel will come before us later on, not important in themselves, but tending to shew that the subject of exorcism was much discussed in the first century and that he believed the Marcan account of it to be inadequate[3]. Everyone will now admit that Matthew's picture of the Messiah as bearing sins appeals to the whole world more powerfully and deeply in these days than Mark's picture of the Messiah as casting out devils; but that must not prevent us from recognising that Mark is in this matter historically and chronologically right, and Matthew wrong.

§ 4. *"Authority" and Christ's "word," in Luke*

In Luke, "authority" is the power possessed by a ruler to accomplish his will as he utters it to those over whom he rules. In O.T the highest form of this authority is that of the Creator, who "spake and it was done[4]." But Luke's first mention of "authority" is assigned to Satan, who claims "all the kingdoms of the world," saying to Jesus, "To thee will I give all this *authority* and the glory of them; for it hath been delivered

---

[1] Mt. vii 22. They add "And in thy name we did many mighty-works." And perhaps both claims are to be regarded as false. In the parallel Lk. xiii 26, the claim is "We have eaten and drunk in thy presence..." Celsus attacks Mt. vii. 22, as a confession on Christ's part that exorcism was an imposture. Origen (*Cels.* i. 6, ii. 49) admits that *sometimes* the name of "Jesus," uttered by "unworthy (φαύλων)" exorcists, has had power to exorcise.

[2] Mk ix. 38—9, Lk. ix 49—50

[3] Among several minute details is Mt.'s use (peculiar to him) of "lunatic" in Mt. iv. 24 (pec) δαιμονιζομένους καὶ σεληνιαζομένους, and, still more remarkably, in Mt xvii. 15 σεληνιάζεται καὶ κακῶς ἔχει (where the parall Mk-Lk, though very full, does not contain "lunatic") The word is discussed by Origen (on Mt. xvii 15). It is not in LXX, and Steph. *Thes.* gives no early authority for it

[4] Ps. xxxiii 9

"AUTHORITY" AND "UNCLEAN SPIRITS"

unto me, and to whomsoever I will I give it[1]." Jesus, in a scriptural quotation, puts the claim aside. But the whole of Luke's Gospel indicates that, in some sense, *de facto* though not *de jure*, Satan at present possesses an "authority"—a false authority, from which he is to be dispossessed by the true authority of the Messiah[2]

The nature of the false authority, and the nature of the true authority, are indicated immediately afterwards by Christ's first public words in the synagogue of Nazareth: "The Spirit of the Lord is upon me, because he anointed me to preach good tidings to the poor; he hath sent me to proclaim *release to the captives*...[3]." Who is the captor of these "*captives*"? According to the Acts, it is Satan. For Peter tells us there, about the "good tidings" of Jesus, how "God anointed him with the Holy Spirit and with power, who went about doing good, and healing *all that were oppressed by the devil*[4]." The first mention of "*captive*" in the Bible is where Abraham, hearing that "his brother, Lot, was *taken captive*," arms "Eliezer" (as Jewish tradition interprets the passage) —the symbol of the Help of God—and brings back the captives rescued[5] In Luke's Gospel, Jesus is regarded as the seed of Abraham, similarly rescuing those who are "taken captive" by the devil. Luke also is the only Evangelist that has put on record Christ's words about a woman

---

[1] Lk. iv 6 For this, Mt iv 9 has simply "I will give thee all these things."

[2] Comp Acts xxvi 18 "that they may turn from darkness unto light, and from the [*false*] *authority* of Satan unto God," with Rom. xiii 1 "there is no [*true*] *authority* save [ordained] by ($\dot{\upsilon}\pi\dot{o}$) God " On two occasions, where Mark (i. 27, vi 7) has only "authority," Luke (iv. 36, ix 1) combines "power" with "authority" in order to shew that it is, from his point of view, *true* "authority."

[3] Lk iv. 18 quoting Is. lxi. 1—2.   [4] Acts x. 38.

[5] Gen xiv. 14 The text mentions "318"; for the interpretation "Eliezer" see *Notes* **2994** quoting Philo i 481, *Gen r* ad loc , and Barn ix 8, also *Light* **3730** c.

"AUTHORITY" AND "UNCLEAN SPIRITS"

whom Luke himself describes as one that "had a spirit of infirmity eighteen years," but Jesus as "a daughter of Abraham, whom *Satan had bound*, lo, [these] eighteen years[1]."

Consistently with this view, Luke dwells, more than any other Synoptist, on that Messianic act of "rebuking," referred to above in the words of Zechariah "the Lord *rebuke thee, O Satan!*" Where Mark says simply "He suffered not the devils to speak," Luke prefixes "*rebuking them*[2]." Where Mark (and similarly Matthew) says of Peter's mother-in-law, that Jesus "took her by the hand and raised her up and the fever left her," Luke says that Jesus "stood over her and *rebuked the fever* and it left her[3]." Apparently Luke sees no connection between the authority expressed by this effectual "rebuking," and the authority expressed by Christ's "teaching." At all events, as has been shewn above, besides making these Lucan additions, he substitutes a mention of the "*word with authority*" for the Marcan "*taught them as having authority*," and has, later on, "What is this *word?*" where Mark has "What is this? a new *teaching*[4]!"

§ 5   "*Authority*," *in Greek writers of the first century*

A glance at the Indices or Concordances to Plato, Aristotle, LXX, Epictetus, Early Fathers and Apologists, will shew that the Greek *exousia* has different meanings varying with their contexts. It is a term savouring of law and not used by Aristophanes. The Definitions of Plato call it the "*permission*

---

[1] Lk xiii 11—16 [2] Mk i 34, Lk iv 41
[3] Mk i 31, Mt viii 15, Lk iv 39
[4] Mk i 22, 27, Lk iv 32, 36   See above, pp 158—60. Lk iv 32 "for his *word* was with authority," may be taken as meaning "He cast out the spirits by a direct 'word,' or *fiat*, and not, in part, indirectly and preparatively, by His 'teaching'" Origen instructively recognises that the power of Christian exorcists in his day was exercised (*Cels* 1. 6) "by the name of 'Jesus' *along with the narration of His acts and words* (μετὰ τῆς ἀπαγγελίας τῶν περὶ αὐτὸν ἱστοριῶν)"

"AUTHORITY" AND "UNCLEAN SPIRITS"

(or, *commission*) of Law[1]." Etymologically, perhaps, it means "that which is [permitted in a special province removed] from [interference][2]." Hence, dropping one of the two qualifications, it branches out into two opposite meanings.—(1) power in a special province, (2) power that is free from interference, *i.e* absolute In the LXX, outside Daniel, it is rare and mostly implies limitation[3]. But in Daniel, besides being used of earthly rulers of places, and especially of the authority given to Nebuchadnezzar, it is also used of God's power, and especially of the power of the Messianic kingdom, which is to be for ever[4]. "Permission," applied to the power of the Supreme, would seem a misnomer. Yet Philo applies *exousia* thus, saying "In the one and only true God the highest and first powers[5] are two—goodness and *authority* (*exousia*). By means of goodness God begot all that is By *authority* (*exousia*) He rules the begotten." This suggests no basis—such as Wisdom or Love—for Authority. It leaves us still in the dark as to how God can be said to "rule" by anything that is,

---

[1] See Plato *Defin* 415 B Ἐξουσία, ἐπιτροπὴ νόμου. The only N T. instance of ἐπιτροπή coupled with ἐξουσία is Acts xxvi 12 μετ' ἐξουσίας καὶ ἐπιτροπῆς τῆς τῶν ἀρχιερέων, closely followed by a contrast in *ib* 18 ἀπὸ...τῆς ἐξουσίας τοῦ Σατανᾶ ἐπὶ τὸν θεόν

[2] Lucian's Index gives it mostly as referring to πατρικὴ ἐξουσία.

[3] In Ps. cxxxvi 8—9, 2 K xx 13, Is xxxix 2 it describes the sun's power by day and the moon's by night, and Hezekiah's power (R V. "dominion") boastfully exhibited to the Babylonians. But see also Ps cxiv. 2 (R V) "Israel his dominion," *i.e* the Lord's peculiar and favoured dominion

[4] See Dan iv. 17 foll (LXX), vii. 12 foll R V "and as for the rest of the beasts, their *dominion* (ἐξουσία) was taken away...there came one like unto a son of man...and there was given him *dominion* ...his *dominion* is an everlasting *dominion*..."

[5] Philo i 143—4 "Powers," δυνάμεις. Having thus used δύναμις generically Philo was precluded from using it again specially. The context indicates that Philo believed this conception to have come to him by some kind of inspiration He adds that "Third[ly], uniting both together, midmost, is Logos (τρίτον δὲ συναγωγὸν ἀμφοῖν μέσον εἶναι λόγον)."

"AUTHORITY" AND "UNCLEAN SPIRITS"

according to the Platonic Definitions, of the nature of "permission."

Much more definite and satisfying is the language of Epictetus, who recognises two kinds of authority, one fleshly, the other spiritual, following a treatise attributed to Aristotle, which says, "It is the sign of greatness of soul to bear aright both good fortune and ill fortune...and not to admire [blindly] [a position that commands] luxury, and obsequious service, and *authority*[1]" The context shews that this does not condemn respect or admiration for wise and just and good "authority." But it does condemn admiration for a great deal of "authority"—pompous, unjust, self-seeking—which the world admires. This condemnation Epictetus repeatedly and pointedly expresses, representing the young and rising philosophers as saying to their Teacher: "Here on earth, Master, these robbers and thieves, these courts of justice and kings, have the upper hand. These creatures fancy that they have some sort of authority over us, simply because they have a hold on our paltry flesh and its possessions! Suffer us, Master, to shew them that they have authority over nothing[2]."

What then is the basis of true authority and whither must we look for it? No one can have it, says Epictetus, who has not knowledge Unless the judge knows what the truth is, his "authority" is no authority But he recognises that "God has bestowed on all men, if they will but accept and use it, *authority* over their own wills, so that we may conform our wills to His, as children do with a Father[3]" And, in a special

---

[1] *De Virtut.* §5 Μεγαλοψυχίας δέ ἐστι...καὶ τὸ θαυμάζειν μήτε τρυφὴν μήτε θεραπείαν μήτε ἐξουσίαν... This is condensed by Bonitz into μεγαλοψυχίας μὴ θαυμάζειν ἐξουσίαν—which might mislead.

[2] Quoted from *Silanus the Christian* p 17. See *Notes* **2801** for a full list of the Epictetian references to ἐξουσία contained in the context, 1 9 15, 1. 30 6—7, 11 13 21—7, etc

[3] *Silanus* p 19 Comp Gen iv 7 Jer Targ where God says to Cain "Into thy hand have I given *authority over evil desire itself*

171 (Mark 1 21—8)

and higher form, "authority" has been bestowed by God on a few mortal natures akin to Himself, whereby they receive a spiritual kingship. "Kings and tyrants receive from their armed guards the power of rebuking and punishing wrong-doing, though they may be rascals themselves. But on the Cynic"—that is the term he uses—"this power is bestowed by the conscience." By "conscience" he means "the consciousness of a life of wise, watchful, and unwearied toil for man, in co-operation with God[1]."

Before passing to the Fourth Gospel, we may note some instances of *exousia* in the earliest of the Fathers and Apologists. Clement of Rome, in the only passage where he uses the word, says, "Thou, Lord-and-Master, hast given to them [*i.e.* to our rulers and governors upon the earth] *the authority* of the kingdom...thou...givest to the sons of men glory and honour and *authority* over those things that are upon the earth[2]." This means deputed power. Barnabas tells us that we ought to take heed, "times being evil and [the evil one] himself—he that is inwardly-working [the evil]—having *the authority*[3]." He also warns us not to slacken our energies "lest the evil ruler

---

(potestatem ipsius concupiscentiae malae)." It is added "et ad te erit appetitus ejus, et tu dominaberis illi, sive ad justitiam sive ad peccatum." The Aramaic (which is also Hebrew) here used for "authority" occurs repeatedly in Midrash quoted by Schlatter on Jn 1. 12 "he gave them *authority* to become children of God" (Schlatter, "Vollmacht").

[1] *Silanus* p 20.
[2] Clem. Rom § 61 ἔδωκας τὴν ἐξουσίαν τῆς βασιλείας should be taken with the following appellation βασιλεῦ τῶν αἰώνων. God is the King, but deputes "the authority of the kingdom."
[3] Barn. 11. 1 ἡμερῶν οὖν οὐσῶν πονηρῶν καὶ αὐτοῦ τοῦ ἐνεργοῦντος ἔχοντος τὴν ἐξουσίαν. Either τοῦ πονηροῦ, or τὸ πονηρόν, or both, must be supplied from the preceding πονηρῶν. The evil days proceed from an evil worker. Later on, vi 18 (on Gen 1 26) τὸ ἄρχειν ἐξουσίας ἐστίν means that "ruling" over beasts implies "authority" over beasts, "so that one should exercise-lordship by mere command (ἐπιτάξας κυριεύσῃ)"—to which men have "not yet" attained

172 (Mark 1. 21—8)

"AUTHORITY" AND "UNCLEAN SPIRITS"

receiving *the authority over us* [that would be permitted by reason of our slackness] should thrust us away from the kingdom of the Lord[1]." On the other hand he speaks of those to whom the Lord has given "*the authority* of the Gospel, twelve in number for a testimony to the tribes[2]" Finally he says "There are two ways (?)—*of teaching and of authority*, the [way] of light and the [way] of darkness[3]." We might be disposed to assume that "teaching and authority" is here loosely used for the Synoptic "*teaching with authority.*" But the context gives no support to this view. The *Didaché* also favours a different interpretation, namely, that Christ's "teaching" and Satan's "authority" are here contrasted as "light" and "darkness" or as "life" and "death." Barnabas goes on to say "Over the former Way are set light-proclaiming angels of God, over the latter, angels of Satan. And the former [namely, God] is Lord from [the] ages and to the ages, but the latter [namely, Satan] is ruler of the season that now is, [the season] of lawlessness." We should therefore probably adopt the rendering : "There are two ways—[one] of [heaven's] teaching and [one] of [this world's] authority." But the fact that a Christian writer could write thus, either late in the first century or early in the second, adds to the proof that if the author of the Fourth Gospel desired to bring home to the hearts of his readers the real nature and the real basis of that

---

[1] Barn. iv. 13 ἵνα μήποτε...καὶ ὁ πονηρὸς ἄρχων λαβὼν τὴν καθ' ἡμῶν ἐξουσίαν ἀπώσηται ἡμᾶς ἀπὸ τῆς βασιλείας τοῦ κυρίου.

[2] Barn. viii 3.

[3] Barn. xviii. 1 Ὁδοὶ δύο εἰσίν—διδαχῆς καὶ ἐξουσίας—ἥ τε τοῦ φωτὸς καὶ ἡ τοῦ σκότους Comp *Didach* 1. 1 Ὁδοὶ δύο εἰσί—μία τῆς ζωῆς καὶ μία τοῦ θανάτου The Latin fragment of the latter (p. 102) has "Viae duae sunt *in saeculo*, vitae et mortis, lucis et tenebrarum."

It may be added that ἐξουσία does not occur in the *Didaché*. In *Canon Eccles* 14 ἐξουσίαν ἐὰν ἔχητε should perhaps be ἐξ οὗ ἐάν (with V). But *ib.* 30 represents Peter as saying ταῦτα, ἀδελφοί, οὐχ ὡς ἐξουσίαν τινὸς ἔχοντες πρὸς ἀνάγκην, ἀλλ' ἐπιταγὴν ἔχοντες παρὰ κυρίου, ἐρωτῶμεν ὑμᾶς φυλάξαι τὰς ἐντολάς....

"AUTHORITY" AND "UNCLEAN SPIRITS"

authority which Christ actually claimed and exercised, he had many difficulties to surmount—difficulties arising not only from the earliest written Gospels, but also from later Christian traditions, and from comments that might be made on Christian views by educated Greeks.

§ 6. *"Authority" and the spirit of sonship, in John*

The Johannine view of authority is, briefly, this, that it consists in a conscious unity with God. It has not to do primarily with driving out but with letting in. It is not a power to cast out Satan from the souls of others; it is a letting in of the Spirit of the Son into our souls—the Son, who, when we let Him in, not only keeps Satan cast out from ourselves but also helps us to cast out Satan from others.

"But was not this," we may ask, "the hypothesis of Epictetus? Did not he teach that the 'authority' of the Philosopher, who went about benefiting mankind, wearing the true and invisible crown and wielding the sceptre of true royalty, arose from the consciousness of a unity with God?" Yes, but from "a unity" with what kind of God? The God of Epictetus is not a God of love, much less of sympathy; and the Philosopher whom Epictetus regards as God's representative is also accordingly unsympathetic. For Jesus, there is trouble of heart or spirit because of the death of Lazarus and the tears of his sister Mary and the treachery of Judas[1]. For the Epictetian Philosopher there is no such trouble. At all events, there ought not to be. Epictetus warns us against it: "Let not what is contrary to Nature in another be an Evil to you; for you were not born to be depressed and unhappy, along with others, but to be happy along with them. And, if anyone is unhappy, remember that he is so for himself; for God made all men to enjoy Felicity and a settled good Condition. He hath furnished all with Means for this Purpose, having

---

[1] Jn xi. 33, xiii. 21.

174 (Mark i. 21—8)

given them some Things for their own, others not for their own[1]." If John, in composing his Gospel, learned anything from Epictetian doctrine as to the needs of the Greeks and the best means of meeting them, this certainly was one lesson, that the hard facts of life presented a knot that could not be loosed by any exercise whatever of mere reason, nor even be severed by any fervour of faith in a Supreme God, unless that God was recognised as a Father capable of that kind of love for His children which we call sympathy. By this we mean, not a condescending appearance of fatherly sorrow over infantile and imaginary evils, but a real fatherly sorrow over real filial evils. In particular, the Fourth Gospel means by it such a sympathy as might lead a father to die for his sons, or, if that were not possible, to send one son to die for the rest.

The keynote of this theory of authority is struck in words of the Prologue:—"As many as received him [*i.e.* the Logos, or Son] to them gave he *authority to become children of God*[2]." This means children of Him, and like in nature to Him, who is the Giver of all Good, continually giving forth Himself to men in various gifts, but above all, in His beloved Son. It is not everyone that can thus "give." A man, as Paul says, may "give his body to be burned," and yet it "profiteth nothing" if he gives for fame, or for immortality, or for self in any form. He lays down his life, but he does not lay it down in such a way that he can say as the Son does, "I have *authority* to lay it down and I have *authority* to take it again; this commandment received I from my Father[3]." The primary object of

---

[1] Epictet. III. 24. 1 (Mrs Carter's transl.). I have not found in the Dissertations any repetition of Plato *Theaet* 176 c θεὸς...ὡς οἷόν τε δικαιότατος. The nearest approach is Epictet. 1 29. 13 ὁ τοῦ θεοῦ νόμος κράτιστός ἐστι καὶ δικαιότατος. But this is very far below the passionate and loving trust and reverence expressed in the unusual combination Jn xvii 25 πατὴρ δίκαιε On the priority of the circulation of Epictetian doctrine to the publication of it by Arrian, see *Introduction*, p. 154

[2] Jn i 12   [3] Jn x. 18.

"AUTHORITY" AND "UNCLEAN SPIRITS"

this "authority" is not to drive out, or to take away, but to give. "Thou [i e. the Father] gavest him *authority* over all flesh, that—all that thou hast given him—to them he may give eternal life[1]."

"Authority to judge" is not excluded. But it is subordinated "I came not to judge the world," says Jesus, "but to save the world[2]." To those that refuse to be saved, and to accept life from the Son, there must come judgment This judgment the Son has "authority" to execute, but it is as it were on a lower plane, not as Son of God but as Son of man: "As the Father hath life in himself, even so gave he to the Son also to have life in himself, and he gave him *authority* to do judgment because he is Son of man[3]" It is interesting to note, by contrast, how the Roman Governor, later on, boasts of that very "authority" which is here (we may almost say) depreciated, that of condemning or acquitting: "Speakest thou not unto me? Knowest thou not that I have *authority* to release thee and have *authority* to crucify thee?" The reply is "Thou wouldest have no *authority* against me except it were given thee from above"—implying (among other things) that Pilate was ignorant of the responsibility that rested on him as representative of the Roman Empire which was, in some sense, ordained by God, and that he did not know what real "authority" meant[4].

So much for the direct Johannine doctrine about "authority." Indirectly the Fourth Gospel appears to set itself to shew that the power exercised by the Son was expressed by Him rather in "drawing" men towards Himself than by "casting out" evil from them, rather by sowing the corn than by rooting up the tares. Once and once only does He use the word "cast out" in any exorcistic sense, and that is not till He has proclaimed the necessity that the "grain of corn"

---

[1] Jn xvii. 2
[2] Jn xii. 47.
[3] Jn v. 26—7
[4] Jn xix. 10—11, see *Joh Voc.* **1577**.

(Mark i. 21—8)

"AUTHORITY" AND "UNCLEAN SPIRITS"

shall die, in accordance with God's glorious Law of self-sacrifice, which leads Him to cry "Father, glorify thy name," and to receive from heaven the answer that God has glorified it and will glorify it again. Then and not till then comes the moment of the great exorcism. "Now is the judgment of this world; now shall the ruler of this world be cast out. And I, if I be lifted up from the earth, will draw all men unto myself[1]"

We ought not to conclude without some notice of the Johannine frankness in representing what we should call—if speaking about an ordinary ruler—the "failures" of "authority." No other Evangelist describes the desertion of Christ by "many" of His disciples, and His sad expostulation with the Twelve who still remain ("Will ye also depart[2]?"); and the retrogression of others who had begun to believe[3]. Above all in intensity of gloom is the record of what appears to be Christ's attempt—unless it is to be regarded as an implied confession that all attempt was useless—to drive out Satan from Judas at the Last Supper[4]. Matthew describes Jesus as saying "All *authority* has been given to me in heaven and on earth[5]," but in John the corresponding saying of the Son to the Father is (as we have seen) "*authority* over all flesh, that—*all that thou hast given him*—to them he may give eternal life." It appears to be implied that "all flesh" is not to be "given" at present to the Son. God Himself will not, and cannot, constrain men by bribes, or fears—or in any way that does not allow some free response on their part—to receive the love and the life that He offers. It is assumed that the Kingdom of God—which we can never hope in this life to comprehend—is better apprehended as a Family, with something at present

---

[1] Jn xii. 24—32   It is added "But this he said signifying by what manner of death he should die"
[2] Jn vi. 66—7   [3] Jn viii. 31 foll.
[4] Jn xiii 18—26.   [5] Mt. xxviii. 18.

"AUTHORITY" AND "UNCLEAN SPIRITS"

outside it which we cannot understand, and which is not yet conformed to the Father's will, than as a Despotism, which includes all that is, and which has God as its centre and Despot.

§ 7. *"Going down to Capernaum"*

John only thrice describes Jesus as "teaching," and only once as "teaching in synagogue[1]" Comparing this with the frequency of the Synoptic traditions about Christ's teaching, we ought to be prepared to suppose that John attached special importance to this particular "teaching in synagogue" and some importance to the fact that it was at "Capernaum" This supposition is confirmed by the fact that John agrees with Luke in using the phrase *"went down* (or, *came down) to Capernaum"* to introduce (apparently) a new stage in the proclamation of the Gospel[2]. It is also confirmed (not weakened) by the fact that the compiler of the Diatessaron omits the phrase in Luke[3],

---

[1] Jn vi 59 ταῦτα εἶπεν ἐν συναγωγῇ διδάσκων ἐν Καφαρναούμ. The other two passages mentioning Jesus as "teaching" are vii 14—28, viii 20 ἐν τῷ ἱερῷ But comp Christ's own words in xviii. 20 πάντοτε ἐδίδαξα ἐν συναγωγῇ καὶ ἐν τῷ ἱερῷ This implies that Jesus habitually *"taught in synagogue,"* and that John chooses out one of many instances to shew how He taught there and how He was misunderstood

[2] Lk iv 31 καὶ κατῆλθεν εἰς Καφαρναούμ..., Jn ii 12 μετὰ τοῦτο κατέβη εἰς Καφαρναοὺμ αὐτὸς καὶ ἡ μήτηρ αὐτοῦ καὶ..

[3] The omission of Lk iv 31 *a* in the *Diatessaron* may be explained by the context in the *Diatessaron* The compiler had just before included a statement from Matthew about Jesus as coming and dwelling in Capernaum (*Diatess* vi 36 foll) "(Mt iv 13—16) And *he left Nazareth and came and dwelt in Capernaum by the sea shore* .. in the shadow of death, there appeared unto them a light (Lk iv 31*a* om) [*And he came down to Capernaum, a city of Galilee*]. (Lk iv 31*b* foll) And he taught them on the sabbaths And they wondered " The preceding words in Luke describe the attempt on Christ's life in Nazareth, Lk iv. 30 "But he, passing through the midst of them [*i e.* the Nazarenes], went his way " The *Diatessaron* places this attempt much later on, and appends to it words indicating that Jesus did *not* "come down to Capernaum" after that attempt

"AUTHORITY" AND "UNCLEAN SPIRITS"

and not only the phrase, but also the context in John. That indicates—for those at least who have studied the Diatessaron and its ways—that in early times discussion was probably frequent about this "going down to Capernaum" and about the questions "Whence did He come down?" and "What did He do when He had come down?"

According to Tertullian, Marcion so mutilated the Gospel of Luke as to make it appear that Jesus came down *"from heaven,* straight to the synagogue" in Capernaum[1]. Heracleon, dealing with the Johannine "going down to Capernaum," said that "the beginning of another dispensation was indicated, since 'went down' is not without significance." He added that Capernaum signifies "the uttermost parts of the Cosmos, the regions of matter into which He 'came-down[2].'"

So far, Origen, who quotes Heracleon as above, might agree with Heracleon as to the inferior and negative character of the revelation at Capernaum. But he demurs to what Heracleon says concerning the following words—"and there [*i.e.* at Capernaum] they abode not many days. And the passover of the Jews was at hand, and Jesus went up..."—on which Heracleon says "By reason of the strange and alien

---

(*Diatess* xvii. 52 foll.) (Lk. iv. 30) "But he passed through among them and went away. (Mk vi 6*b*) And he went about in the villages which [were] around Nazareth, and taught in their synagogues."

[1] Tertull *adv Marc* on Lk iii 1, iv 31 "'In the fifteenth year of the reign of Tiberius'—for such is Marcion's proposition—'He came down to the Galilaean city Capernaum'.. *From heaven straight to the synagogue*"

[2] See Origen on Jn ii 12 (Lomm 1 291) quoting Heracleon to this effect. Origen himself says (Lomm 1 288) that Capernaum means "*field* (ἀγρὸς) of Consolation." Jerome calls it (*Onomast* p 64) "*ager* vel *villa* consolationis." In his comment on Mt iv 13, viii 5, Jerome is silent as to its meaning. Pseudo-Jerome, on Mk i 21, calls it "*villa* consolationis." Euseb has (*Onomast* p 176) "consolation of the village," (*ib* p 203) "field, or house, of consolation."

"AUTHORITY" AND "UNCLEAN SPIRITS"

nature of the place, He is not even said to have done or spoken anything in it [*i.e.* in Capernaum]¹."

Yet Origen's only ground for demurring is that Mark and Luke relate, as occurring during this visit, the exorcism in the Capernaum Synagogue. To this Heracleon would have an obvious reply: "The Marcan exorcism could not have occurred during the Johannine visit to Capernaum; for Mark says clearly that what he relates about Capernaum took place *after the Baptist's arrest*, John makes it no less clear that what he relates here about Capernaum took place *before the Baptist's arrest*²" It is hardly possible to doubt that Heracleon is right at all events in calling attention to the fact that Jesus "is not even said to have done or spoken anything" in the first brief (Johannine) visit to Capernaum. But about the Evangelist's motive in thus recording an apparently resultless action of Christ there may very well be doubt—or, at least, doubt at the first view of the subject.

At the second view, we shall probably come to the conclusion that John did not regard this action, or any action of Jesus, as being resultless. He identified the visit with the Marcan visit to Capernaum. But he thought that Mark had placed it wrongly after the Baptist's arrest and had made it unduly prominent. "Other Jews," he might say, "some impostors but some not, could exorcize with more or less success. But other Jews could not work such a sign as that of Cana. By an error of judgment Mark and Luke have combined to make the exorcism of an unclean spirit, and the demoniac's confession of Christ, the threshold, so to speak, of the Gospel, the very beginning of the 'signs,' or 'mighty works,' of the Messiah Is this right? Is it well that readers of the Gospels should believe this to have been the beginning?"

---

¹ "Strange and alien (ἀνοίκειον)"
² Mk i 14 "after John was delivered up", Jn iii 24 "John was not yet cast into prison," which comes at a considerable interval after the visit to Capernaum (ii 12)

"AUTHORITY" AND "UNCLEAN SPIRITS"

Matthew, perhaps, like John, thought it was not well. At all events, as we have seen, Matthew goes the way to remove the impression. He omits the detailed description of the single act of exorcism—inserting in its place a mention of the healing of a multitude of diseases and cases of demoniacal possession[1]—and then passes to the Sermon on the Mount, the New Law, the Law of Love, a love that might be called superhuman, summed up in the precept "Love your enemies...that ye may be sons of your Father who is in heaven." Might not this have satisfied the Fourth Evangelist?

No doubt he welcomed it, but could he be "satisfied" with it? "Love your enemies" was an admirable precept to hear; but *how* were the hearers to acquire this most difficult art? And further, Matthew mentioned "his disciples[2]," but who were they? The word has not been mentioned by him before. All that we have heard has been that four fishermen "followed" Jesus when He called them and said that He would make them fishers of men. Did that suffice to make them "disciples?" And were others made with the same ease? These questions force themselves on those who read Matthew's Gospel, at this stage, consecutively. Luke gives us a partial answer by shewing us how some of the sayings in the Sermon were uttered on such different occasions and in such different circumstances as to reveal something of the personality of Him who uttered them and of the power of His Spirit to penetrate the souls of others. But more of that kind remained to be done to shew—or rather to indicate by brief suggestions—how Jesus first drew towards Himself, and then bound closer to Himself, His earlier disciples.

According to John, this was not done by "teaching." The "teaching" of Jesus is expressly said by Jesus Himself to have been "always in synagogue and in the Temple[3]," and it

---

[1] Mt iv 23—4 This resembles Mk i 39 and iii 10
[2] Mt v 1 "His disciples came unto him."
[3] Jn xviii 20

"AUTHORITY" AND "UNCLEAN SPIRITS"

was not there that He found His first followers. They were found in private. "They said, Rabbi...where abidest thou? He saith unto them, Come, and ye shall see. They came therefore and saw where he abode; and they abode with him that day[1]." We are left to imagine what this thrice-mentioned "*abiding*" implied, and to infer that the "seeing" it must have included a partial "beholding" of the glory of the Son, who is "in the bosom of the Father[2]." Then, after a number of utterances severally addressed and adapted to Simon, Philip, and Nathanael, Jesus is introduced to us in the guest-chamber in Cana, where the "sign" of the new wine is performed so quietly that it is not even known to the ruler of the feast who tastes it. Yet it "manifested his glory, and his disciples believed on him[3]."

It is at this point that John introduces that "going down to Capernaum" which Luke also mentions as one of Christ's earliest acts. But Luke regards the descent as being from Nazareth, where Jesus had been rejected and violently handled; John regards it as being from Cana, the scene of Christ's first sign and manifestation of glory. There are indications in

---

[1] Jn i 38—9 See *Beginning* pp 247—8
[2] Comp Jn i 14 "we beheld his glory," and Jn i 18
[3] Jn ii. 11 On this "sign," see *Joh Gr* **2281**—3 and *Son* **3390** (iv), **3426** *k*, **3583** (xii) *c*—*d* "Cana" (*Son* **3555** *a*) is generally recognised as meaning "acquisition" or "purchase" (comp Ruth iv 10 "purchased to be my wife") *Exod r* (on Exod xvi 4, Wu p 192) represents God as saying (Prov ix 5) "eat of my bread and drink of my wine, which I have mingled"—in connection with Exod. xv. 25 "he gave them a statute and an ordinance"—and as adding, "For the sake of my bread [*i e* because ye have received my statute] *ye have received the bread of the manna*, and for the sake of my wine which I have mingled [*i e* because ye have received my ordinance] ye have drunk the water of the stream [that flowed from the rock]" This indicates how John may have regarded the sign at Cana as an anticipatory indication of a divine law, set forth in "teaching" afterwards in the synagogue of Capernaum, and fulfilled upon the Cross.

"AUTHORITY" AND "UNCLEAN SPIRITS"

Luke's Gospel itself that he found inconsistent traditions and perhaps set them down as he found them. For he implies that the people of Nazareth had already heard of wonders wrought by Jesus at Capernaum[1], and yet he mentions no visit to Capernaum till afterwards. Origen's comment is "In Capernaum, so far as Luke's history is concerned, Jesus has not yet abode, nor is he described as having worked any sign there... Hence I infer that there is some mystery latent in the text before us, and that Nazareth [was] typical of the Jews while Capernaum preceded as typical of Gentiles[2]." This is not very clear or satisfactory even from an allegorical point of view, but it is worth noting as one of many indications that "Capernaum" would be allegorized even in the first century—by some perhaps favourably as the Village of the Comforter, and "his own city" (as Matthew appears to call it), but by others as the type of Christ's unbelieving fellow countrymen, those in whom familiarity with the Messiah bred not reverence but contempt, so that it brought on itself the curse "And thou, Capernaum, shalt thou be exalted to heaven? Thou shalt be cast down to Hades[3]."

In the *"going down to Capernaum"* some Jews might find an allusion to the first city that sought to "exalt" itself. That

---

[1] Lk iv 23 "Doubtless ye will say unto me ..*Whatsoever we have heard done at Capernaum*, do also here in thine own country."

[2] Origen on Lk iv 23. Lomm (v 209) reads "In Capharnaum, quantum *ad lucem historiae* pertinet, necdum moratus est Jesus. Unde puto aliquid in sermone praesenti latitare mysterii, et Nazareth in typo Jadaeorum, Capharnaum in typo praecessisse gentilium." But I have ventured to read "*ad Lucae historiam*." For it is only Luke, not Mark, who puts the teaching in the synagogue of Capernaum after the visit to Nazareth. And even Luke's order appears to have been shifted by Marcion so as to put Capernaum before Nazareth. See Tertull *adv Marc* ad loc where he refers to Lk iv 24, 29, 30 after referring to Lk iv 34, 35. Origen's comment seems obscure. Does "in typo praecessisse" mean "went before, as a type of"?

[3] Mt xi 23, Lk. x 15.

was Babel whose "top" was to reach "unto heaven." But the Lord "*came down* to see the city" and the prospective citizens were scattered through the world[1]. That is the first instance in which the Lord is described as "coming down" in the Bible. In Matthew, however, the context does not mention Babel but only Sodom. Yet there, too, when the cry of it came up to heaven, the Lord said "*I will go down* and see[2]" That is the second instance in the Bible of the Lord's "going down." These two are instances of chastisement. In the third instance, deliverance of the oppressed predominates over chastisement of the oppressor. The Lord "comes down" now "to deliver," not "to see," for He *has* "*seen*," and He "*knows*," because His heart is with His oppressed people — "And the Lord said, Surely I have seen the affliction of my people who are in Egypt, and have heard their cry by reason of their taskmasters; for I know their sorrows and am *come down* to deliver them out of the hand of the Egyptians[3]"

All these facts prepare us to believe that when such a writer as John, toward the end of the first century, found himself called on to deal with a much discussed tradition about Christ's "*going down to Capernaum*," he could hardly have regarded it as a mere geographical expression. They confirm Heracleon's view, that John regarded any wonderful works that might have been done in Christ's first visit to Capernaum as not worthy of mention—or at all events not worthy of repetition, since Mark had already described them—in comparison with the "sign" in Cana. And later on, the typical inferiority of Capernaum to Cana is suggested in the passage where the "nobleman" in Capernaum has to come up to Cana for the sake of his son's life, and needs to have his faith strengthened by

---

[1] Gen xi 5, 7   [2] Gen xviii 21
[3] Exod iii 7—8 (see Gesen 433 *a* which gives this and the two preceding instances of the absolute use of the verb when meaning divine "descending")

"AUTHORITY" AND "UNCLEAN SPIRITS"

the reproof "Except ye [*i e* ye unbelievers in Capernaum] see signs and wonders, ye will in no wise believe[1]"

§ 8. *"Teaching in synagogue" at Capernaum, in John*[2]

We pass now to John's account of Christ's second visit to Capernaum when He taught in the synagogue there It was after the Feeding of the Five Thousand, when Jesus proclaimed in that synagogue the doctrine of the living Bread And here we may note that in a very striking sevenfold repetition of the phrase *"come down out of heaven*[3]*"*—a phrase used by no other Evangelist except the Fourth—John brings before us something very much like the recently quoted[4] epigram of Tertullian. Marcion had said *"came down to the Galilaean city*

---

[1] Jn iv 48 *Diatess* omits Jn ii 12—13 "After this he went down to Capernaum ..and Jesus went up to Jerusalem" The healing of the Paralytic is thus introduced by the Synoptists —

Mk ii. 1—2	Mt ix 1	Lk. v 17 *a*
And when he entered again into Capernaum after some days he spake the word unto them	And he entered into a boat and crossed over and came into his own city	And it came to pass on one of those days that he was teaching Lk. v. 17 *b* And there were Pharisees.. to heal

Diatess omits Lk v 17 *a* Jerome, on Mt ix 1, says "We understand '*his own city (civitatem ejus)*' to be no other than Nazareth," but does not explain how he reconciles this with Mk ii 1. These and many other facts point to early discrepancies in traditions about Capernaum Some of these might arise from various interpretations of "his own city"

[2] Jn vi 59 Ταῦτα εἶπεν ἐν συναγωγῇ διδάσκων ἐν Καφαρναούμ The punctuation is not certain But R V. marg. "in a synagogue" is probably incorrect in view of Jn xviii 20 "I always taught *in synagogue*" (as we should say "in church") Lk vii 5 τὴν συναγωγὴν αὐτὸς ᾠκοδόμησεν ἡμῖν, "He himself [at his own cost] built *the synagogue* for us" appears to imply that there was only one synagogue at Capernaum

[3] Jn vi 33—58   [4] See above, p 179, n. 1

185 (Mark 1 21—8)

"AUTHORITY" AND "UNCLEAN SPIRITS"

of Capernaum." Tertullian's comment had been, *"from heaven straight to the synagogue"* Tertullian is referring to the Marcan scene in which the demoniac in the synagogue exclaimed "I know thee who *thou art, the Holy One of God."* John places outside the synagogue of Capernaum, but at a short interval after the teaching in it, a scene where Peter uses precisely the same appellation, "We believe and know that *thou art the Holy One of God*[1]"

"*The Holy One of God*" occurs nowhere else in the Bible, exactly thus, except in these two passages The coincidence can hardly be casual It seems scarcely credible that John, in recording Peter's confession of "*the Holy One of God*," did not say to himself, "A demoniac had previously uttered a confession similar in words, but different in spirit The demoniac said he '*knew*' it Peter said 'we *believe and know* it' '*Knowledge*' of a person is nothing without belief, trust, or faith Peter clung to Jesus as his beloved and only Saviour, saying, 'Lord, to whom [else] shall we go?' Very different was the demoniac's cry, 'Art thou come to destroy us?' Different also were the words put by Luke into the mouth of Peter himself when the latter exclaimed to Jesus, 'Depart from me, for I am a sinful man, O Lord'"

Following out this line of thought, let us attempt to imagine how John, recognising the historical accuracy of Mark's account, might attempt to draw out from it something of the deep spiritual mystery underlying Christ's action and inherent in Christ's nature "Mark," he might say, "mentions Christ's 'authority,' and also His 'new teaching' (as the crowd called it) But he did not bring out for his readers what was implied in these familiar terms. Without contradicting anything that he has recorded as said or done by Jesus in the Capernaum synagogue, I will set before them a second scene in the same synagogue, where 'authority,' though

---

[1] Jn vi 69.

186 (Mark 1 21—8)

not mentioned, shall be implied, and where its 'newness' and its twofold influence—repelling for the moment as well as attracting—shall be made apparent in the characters of Peter and Judas Iscariot, as well as in the murmurings of the multitude and the backsliding of many of the disciples.

"In Mark, the multitude exclaims 'What is this? A new teaching!' with amazed admiration, but here they exclaim 'This is a hard saying' In Mark, they are like children at the Old Passover, welcoming an intelligible Feast. But now they are confronted with a new doctrine of bread from heaven—the mystery of the flesh and blood of the Son, given by Him to mankind that He may pass into them and possess them for good, casting out all evil This disappoints or repels them It means nothing for them, or it means too much—more than they care to try to understand In Mark, the visible and startling submission of the unclean spirit exclaiming 'I know thee who thou art, the Holy One of God,' satisfies the multitude that Jesus has indeed 'authority' Here Peter exclaims almost the same thing Yet no one mentions 'authority' The disappointed multitude has gone away, leaving Jesus with the Twelve. Peter himself does not think of Christ as having 'authority,' but rather as having 'words of eternal life' which draw him and his fellow-disciples toward the Lord as their only hope and help

"In the eyes of the world, this was a great failure And the worst was yet to come Not all the Twelve were faithful. Peter said, '*We* know' and '*we* believe,' and he probably intended to include all the Twelve But, if so, he was in error One of the Twelve did not believe. Teaching in the synagogue of Capernaum on the first occasion Jesus cast out a devil Teaching in the same synagogue on the second occasion, Jesus recognises that there is a devil, present, and that, too, in one of the Twelve, a devil that He Himself cannot cast out:—'Was it not I that chose you, the Twelve, and one of you is a devil?'

"AUTHORITY" AND "UNCLEAN SPIRITS"

"Thus the history of Israel in the Church of the Wilderness repeated itself in the two scenes of the synagogue in Capernaum. In the first scene, there was nothing but admiration and fervour of belief, 'What is this? A new teaching!' That corresponds to the night of the Passover. In the second scene, the mystery of the living bread from heaven corresponds to the gift of the manna, as to which they began by asking 'What is that?' but soon degenerated into murmuring: 'There is nothing at all, we have naught save this manna to look to[1].'

"So it was with the signs and words of Jesus and His influence on the men of His generation. They did not understand that all His doctrine was based on the axioms 'God is the Great Giver, He is the Blessed One; it is more blessed to give than to receive.' When He fed the Five Thousand, He did not make bread out of stones. He assumed that He and His disciples must provide bread for the multitude ('Whence must we buy bread?') Yet it could not be 'bought'; for it was 'without price.' Here was a paradox. Again, according to the ancient Gospels, He said to His disciples '*Give ye them to eat*'. Here was another paradox. The *giving* was a necessary part of the sign[2]. Only those who can '*give*' as God gives become like God, the Giver of all Good.

"Neither Peter nor the rest of the faithful disciples could fully comprehend this truth at the time, nor till after the Resurrection. But they apprehended it, even before the Resurrection, through the vitalising power of those 'words of eternal life,' to which Peter testifies as having already made

---

[1] Exod. xvi 15 foll., Numb. xi 6

[2] That is to say, the "sign" would have been no sign at all—except such a one as Satan desired (Mt iv 3, Lk iv 3)—if Jesus had commanded stones to become bread, and if He had not said to the Twelve "*Give ye* them to eat" All the Synoptists say this (Mk vi 37, Mt xiv 16, Lk ix 13) John does not therefore intervene, except in the suggestive irony of the words (Jn vi. 5) "Whence are we to *buy bread* that these may eat?"—which must be considered later on

"AUTHORITY" AND "UNCLEAN SPIRITS"

some entrance into his heart and the hearts of his companions. All the more powerful and cogent was this entrance into the souls of the faithful few when they saw their Master abandoned by almost all His followers.

"Thus it came to pass that even in this second scene in the synagogue of Capernaum, though there was no visible 'casting out' of an evil spirit, there was an invisible preparation for that later time when Jesus exclaimed 'Now shall the prince of this world be *cast out*[1]' And, though no mention is made of 'authority,' yet there was real 'authority,' since already the Son had begun to exercise the highest authority of all—that of the Supreme God, who does not drive men as slaves to fulfil a despot's commands, but draws them as His children to love His Fatherly nature, and to delight in doing His Fatherly will."

---

[1] Jn xii 31

CHAPTER III*

JESUS HEALING
[Mark 1. 29—34]

§ 1. *The first miracle of healing*

MARK, followed by Luke, represents Christ's first miracle of healing as being the healing of Simon's wife's mother, which they both place immediately after Christ's first act of exorcism. Matthew, omitting all mention of the act of exorcism, and confining himself to a general mention of the healing of a number of diseases[1], does not particularise Christ's miracles of healing till later on, 1st, the healing of a leper, 2nd, the healing of the centurion's servant, 3rd, the healing of Simon's wife's mother[2]

We may reasonably explain Matthew's arrangement as follows, in accordance with his well-known habit of grouping things according to their nature and not their chronological order The healing of a leper—especially by "touching" the unclean man, as to which "touching[3]" all the Synoptists are

---

* For titles of previous Parts of Diatessarica referred to by abbreviations in this Volume, see pp 545—6 For other abbreviations see pp xxiii—xxvi

[1] Mt iv 23—4

[2] Mt viii 1—4 (the leper) parall to Mk 1 40—44, Lk v 12—14, Mt. viii 5—13 (the centurion's servant) parall to Lk vii. 1—10, Mt viii 14—15 (Simon's wife's mother) parall to Mk 1 29—31, Lk iv 38—39

[3] Mk 1. 41, Mt. viii. 3, Lk v 13

JESUS HEALING

agreed—was a particularly marvellous instance of the "marvellous lovingkindnesses" of Jesus[1]. Hereby, in a special way, He typically took uncleanness as well as disease upon Himself, fulfilling the prophecy of Isaiah "He hath borne our griefs (*or*, sicknesses) and carried our sorrows." Matthew himself, after describing these three acts of healing, quotes these words in a version of his own, shewing that he applied them to "diseases[2]." No other Evangelist quotes these words. There is something very impressive in the position of this (literally and superficially) unlawful miracle, coming immediately after the proclamation of the New Law, and breaking the letter of the Old Law. We cannot be surprised that Matthew regards this positive infusion of purity and healthful "cleanness" as symbolically superior to the negative ejection of "an unclean spirit," and as entitled to stand first in his Gospel among the miracles of healing—if the first place was due to that miracle which was first in the scale of "marvellous lovingkindness."

Nor is there any difficulty in explaining, from Matthew's point of view, why the second place was given by him to the cure of the centurion's servant. For that was a special instance of the power of faith—faith so great that Jesus Himself "marvelled" at it[3]. It was also an act of healing at a distance, of which Mark affords no instance. But that Matthew should give the third place to the healing of Peter's wife's mother, sick of a fever, is not so easy to explain. Was it because of the prominence given to it by Mark? That is hardly a sufficient

---

[1] Ps xvii 7 "*Shew* thy *marvellous* lovingkindnesses," lit "*make-separate*" or "*make-unique* (LXX θαυμάστωσον) thy lovingkindnesses," on which Origen says that the healing of the leper and the healing of Simon's mother-in-law were both "made-marvellous" by "*touching* (ἀφῇ)," which distinguished them from ordinary acts of healing.

[2] Mt viii 17 "That it might be fulfilled which was spoken by Isaiah the prophet, saying, Himself took our infirmities, and bare our diseases," quoting Is liii 4, where "stricken" (in the context) is rendered by Aq and Sym "leprous" (see below, pp 194, 250).

[3] Mt viii 10 parall to Lk vii 9

reason For if Matthew omitted the Marcan exorcism, why might he not omit the Marcan cure of fever? Had fever, like leprosy, any typical meaning in Matthew's estimation? And are there any traces of a similar view in Luke? If we are to attempt to answer these questions, we must examine the Synoptic texts in detail.

§ 2. *The details of the healing*

The healing is briefly introduced as follows after the statement that they came into Simon Peter's house :—

Mk i. 30 (R.V.)	Mt. viii 14 (R V)	Lk. iv. 38 (R.V.)
Now Simon's wife's mother lay sick of a fever; and straightway they tell him of her.	And when Jesus was come into Peter's house, he saw his wife's mother lying sick of a fever.	And Simon's wife's mother was holden with a great fever, and they besought him for her.

Mark appears to represent the simple and homely fact. When Jesus passed from the synagogue into Simon's house, the women folk were in confusion because his mother-in-law had been taken with fever; and they had to explain their apparent unreadiness to receive Him by "*telling him about her.*" Matthew omits the "*telling about her,*" supposing that Jesus "saw" the state of things for Himself, and perhaps interpreting an original "*behold,* Peter's mother-in-law lying sick" as "*beheld*[1]."

Luke assumes that they must have known the mighty work of exorcism that had just been accomplished in the synagogue, and infers that "*telling* about her" meant "*requesting* about her[2]," *i e.* requested that He would do for her what He had

---

[1] There is probably some corruption in Mk i 30 ἡ δὲ πενθερὰ Σίμωνος (Lk iv 38 b πενθερὰ δὲ τοῦ Σ), where ἡ δε may point back to a confusion of ιδε or ειδε "behold" or "he saw " Ὅδε represents Heb "behold" in Gen xxv 24, xxxviii. 27, Lev x. 16, Numb. xxiii 6 etc

[2] Mk λέγουσιν αὐτῷ περὶ αὐτῆς, Lk ἠρώτησαν αὐτὸν περὶ αὐτῆς.

JESUS HEALING

done for the demoniac, and drive out the fever as He had driven out the unclean spirit.

So far, there is no difference that cannot be explained as being a slightly different interpretation of one and the same original But now come differences that seem, at first sight, to require to be explained as resulting from difference of motive —

Mk i. 31	Mt. viii. 15	Lk. iv. 39
And having come-near he raised her, having taken hold of [her] hand..	And he touched her hand and she rose (*lit* was raised) ..	And having stood over-above her he rebuked the fever and immediately she rose up...

Here we may well suppose that Mark describes what actually happened, using very nearly the same language as later on about the "raising" of a demoniac child whom Jesus heals[1]. In the Acts, Peter is twice described as "raising up" with his "hand," or "taking by the right hand," a lame person or a lifeless one[2] If the Marcan or Petrine Gospel is here right, we may say that Peter in the Acts is described as imitating what he saw Jesus do for the first time in his own house in the healing of his mother-in-law There is no difficulty in this supposition But, if this was the actual fact (and very natural fact), how can we explain the deviations of the later Evangelists?

For example, Matthew has "touched her hand" instead of "came-near. .and took her by the hand " One cause of this—but we must remember that there may be more causes than one—may be that Matthew desires to emphasize that

---

[1] Mk 1 31 ἤγειρεν αὐτὴν κρατήσας τῆς χειρός, and ix 27 κρατήσας τῆς χειρὸς αὐτοῦ ἤγειρεν αὐτόν. In both passages the parallel Mt and Lk omit the active "raising"

[2] Acts iii 7 καὶ πιάσας αὐτὸν τῆς δεξιᾶς χειρὸς ἤγειρεν αὐτόν, comp ib ix 41 δοὺς δὲ αὐτῇ χεῖρα ἀνέστησεν αὐτήν

"touching" to which attention was called above. He also takes off the emphasis from the "raising" or "lifting," by substituting "was raised" for "he raised her." And here we may remark, as to "*touching*," that the Greek noun "*touching*" is often used by the LXX to mean "*stroke*" or "*plague*" referring to a preceding mention of "*leprosy*" In Isaiah's description of the Suffering Servant as "*stricken*," Symmachus uses this noun and Aquila the corresponding verb, so as to convey the notion of "leprosy[1]." Must we infer that Matthew has deliberately substituted "*touched*" for the Marcan "*drew near*," in order to heighten the fulfilment of the prediction of the Messiah as one taking on Himself the infection of disease? There may be some influence of this kind at work But it would probably not have been effectual but for the Semitic similarity between "touching" and "drawing near" In Hebrew (both old and new) and in Aramaic, the same word may mean "*touch*" and "*draw near to*" And the same ambiguity exists in the Syriac versions of the Gospels[2] Here, then, if Matthew interpreted "*having come near*" as "*having touched*," he naturally combined it with "*having taken hold of her hand*" and condensed the two into "*having touched her hand*" But then, as a mere "touch" of the hand was not sufficient physically to "raise" the sufferer, he interpreted "raised her" as meaning "caused her to rise up [by the power of a mere touch]" expressing it by the passive "*she was raised*"

We have now to consider Luke's deviation from the Marcan text in introducing the word "rebuked." This is not so easy to explain as Matthew's deviation, but it may fairly be explained, like Matthew's, from our hypothesis of an original Hebrew

---

[1] Is liii 4 "stricken" ἐν πόνῳ, where Jerome has "And we did esteem him *unclean*, or as the LXX, *in sorrow*, for which Aquila and Symmachus have *leprous*" Aq has ἀφημένον, Sym ἐν ἀφῇ ὄντα

[2] See *Notes* **2999** (1) *a—b* quoting Dan ix 21, LXX προσήγγισέ μοι parall to Theod ἥψατό μου, and many other instances.

JESUS HEALING

word "drew near" or "touched." That word occurs in connection with king Uzziah, the leper, in the sense of "touched" or "smitten [with leprosy]" as follows.—

2 K. xv. 5 (Heb.)	2 Chr. xxvi 20 (Heb)
And the Lord (lit) *touched* the king so that he was a leper.	And behold, he was leprous .. yea, himself hasted to go out because the Lord had (lit) *touched* him

Here the LXX has in Kings "*touched*," but in Chronicles "*reproved*" —

ib. LXX	*ib* LXX
And the Lord *touched* the king.	Because the Lord *reproved* him[1].

No doubt "*reproved*" is not the same as "*rebuked*" But the two words frequently occur as equivalents in A V. and R.V [2] Luke, if he regarded the "*rebuking*" of "an unclean spirit" as being a "*reproving*" of "the hidden things of darkness[3]," may quite pardonably have substituted the former for the latter

In accordance with this aspect of Jesus as an authoritative "rebuker," Luke may have taken the causative "made her to stand" as "stood[4]." Or perhaps he followed traditions that applied "stood up" to Jesus as well as to the woman : "he stood up" to rebuke the fever and "she stood up" to

---

[1] "Touched," ἥψατο, "reproved," ἤλεγξε. "Rebuked" would be ἐπετίμησε

[2] Comp (1) Prov ix 8, Is ii. 4 etc A V. "*rebuke*," R V "*reprove*," (2) 2 K xix 4, Job xxvi 11 etc A V. "*reprove*" or "*reproof*," R V "*rebuke*."

[3] Eph v 11

[4] For ἵστημι corresponding to ἐγείρω, comp Dan viii. 18 "He touched me and *made-me-to-stand* (LXX ἤγειρε, Theod. ἔστησεν) " For causative forms confused with non-causative, see *Clue* and *Corrections*, **8, 19, 140, 142, 244, 381, 505, 510** foll

JESUS HEALING

minister to the guests[1]. These Lucan modifications shew a prepossession, as also do those of Matthew. Luke desires to represent Jesus as an expeller, Matthew as a bearer, of disease. But the prepossession appears to manifest itself only in interpretations of an obscure original, not in alterations of it.

§ 3. *"Fever"*

Assuming—what few will doubt—that Peter's mother-in-law was actually cured of fever by Jesus, we have to ascertain the aspect in which the healing of this particular disease by a Messiah would present itself to Jews, and the manner in which this aspect might affect our Evangelists.

The Greek word here used for fever occurs only once in LXX, in a list of diseases with which God will punish the sins of Israel, and the Hebrew word, differently translated, occurs once previously in a similar list[2]. In Aramaic, the same word means both "fire" and "fever." To quench the fire [of fever] (says the Talmud) which only God can quench, is greater than to quench the fire of Nebuchadnezzar which man kindled and man could quench[3]. Such a saying lends itself to a spiritual application—quenching the fire of passion. We cannot therefore be surprised if some of our Evangelists gave this miracle a prominent place in Christ's acts of healing.

The Fourth Gospel does this. It represents Christ's first separate act of healing as having been a cure of "fever," an act of faith-healing at a distance, performed on a boy in

---

[1] Lk iv 39 applies ἐπιστάς to Jesus, ἀναστᾶσα to Peter's mother-in-law.

[2] Deut xxviii 22 "fever (πυρετός)," Lev xxvi 16 "fever (ἴκτερος or (?) ἴκτηρ)" on which Rashi explains the noun "fever" or "kindling," from the verb in Deut xxxii. 22 "a fire is *kindled* in mine anger."

[3] *Ned* 41 *a*, quoted by Wetstein on Mt viii 14, and by Levy iii 403 *b*. On Gen. xxi 15, the Targum says that Ishmael drank up all the water because he was seized with a fever, having wandered, with his mother, after strange worship.

Capernaum. It is parallel in some respects to the act of faith-healing performed on a boy in Capernaum, related by Matthew and Luke. In both cases, the faith is not that of the patient, but that of his master or father. Matthew does not call the disease "fever"—not at least if his text is correct. Luke leaves the nature of the disease an open question. They say severally :—

Mt. viii. 6 (lit.)	Lk. vii 2
My *boy* is cast [down] in the house, paralytic, terribly tortured [every moment][1].	The *servant* of a certain centurion, in grievous condition, was on the point of ending [his life][2].

John introduces a "king's officer" whose "*son* was sick" in Capernaum and "on the point of dying." To him Jesus, in Cana, says "thy *son* liveth." The father, returning from Cana to Capernaum, is "met" by his "servants," who say that his "*boy*" lives, and they add, "Yesterday about the seventh hour *the fever* left him[3]." Not till the last line of the narrative is the name of the disease, as it were, casually disclosed and shewn to be similar to that which is placed first by Mark and Luke —"*the fever* left him."

Returning from the Johannine to the Matthew-Luke faith-healing we are led to ask —"Why does not Luke mention the name of the disease? Why does Matthew call it '*paralytic*,' and add 'terribly tortured'—which is not appropriate to ordinary paralysis—but not add 'on the point of ending [his life]'? Is any difference of meaning intended between

---

[1] Mt viii 6 Ὁ παῖς μου βέβληται ἐν τῇ οἰκίᾳ παραλυτικός, δεινῶς βασανιζόμενος.

[2] Lk vii 2 Ἑκατοντάρχου δέ τινος δοῦλος κακῶς ἔχων ἤμελλεν τελευτᾶν.

[3] Jn iv 46 foll. βασιλικὸς οὗ ὁ υἱὸς ἠσθένει...ἤμελλεν γὰρ ἀποθνῄσκειν (so Lk ἤμελλεν τελευτᾶν)...ὁ υἱός σου ζῇ...οἱ δοῦλοι αὐτοῦ ὑπήντησαν αὐτῷ λέγοντες ὅτι ὁ παῖς αὐτοῦ (so Mt. ὁ παῖς μου) ζῇ...ἀφῆκεν αὐτὸν ὁ πυρετός (so Mk-Mt. ἀφῆκεν αὐτὴν ὁ πυρετός, and sim Lk, in the healing of Peter's mother-in-law).

JESUS HEALING

Matthew and Luke, where '*boy*' in the former is parallel to *servant* in the latter?" Light is perhaps thrown on these questions by the fact that, in John, the word "*boy*"—attributed to the "servants" ("that his *boy* lives")—follows the previous reiterations of "son" ("whose *son* was sick," "to come down and heal his *son*," "come down ere my child ($\pi\alpha\iota\delta\iota\sigma\nu$) die," "thy *son* liveth"). John appears to have deliberately shaped his narrative so as to supplement and illuminate the corresponding narrative in Matthew-Luke, and it becomes reasonable to suppose that John agreed with Luke in regarding Matthew's *paralytic* as an error

If it was an error, we ought to look for the cause in some Greek corruption (not Hebrew) since the interchange of "boy" and "servant" points to an early Greek source[1]. I should venture to suggest that Matthew's "*paralytic*" is an error for *purectic* (or, *puretic*), i.e. attacked with fever. Or, still more probably, *puretos*, "fever," may have been confused with *paretos*, "paralysed," which Matthew accepted in the form regularly used by Mark, namely, "*paralytic*[2]."

§ 4. "*Lying down*" *and* "*cast* [*down*]"

Another question arises as to the precise meaning attached by Matthew to the word "*smitten*" or "*cast-*[*down*]" used by him thrice where the other Synoptists do not use it[3]. In the

---

[1] On the ambiguous παῖς, see *Joh Voc* 1862 b, *Joh. Gr* 2584 b, *Son* 3335 c.

[2] For πυρε(κ)τικός and πάρετος see Steph *Thes* (and Sophocl Lex) quoting Diodor. iii. 26, and (*inter alia*) Jo Malal p 262 νόσῳ βληθεὶς καὶ πάρετος (cod πάραιτος) γενόμενος ἐτελεύτα Sophocl refers also to Orig III 1101 A.

Παραλυτικός, lit "given to paralysis," is not quoted by Steph *Thes*. from any author earlier than Mark. "Paralyticus" is used by Pliny Artemidorus uses παράλυτος Luke never uses παραλυτικός, and in v. 24 conspicuously substitutes παραλελυμένος, "paralysed" (but marg. παραλυτικός) Steph *Thes*, under παράλυσις, indicates that the word was frequently corrupted, or corruptly introduced.

[3] Mt viii. 6, 14, ix. 2

JESUS HEALING

healing of Peter's wife's mother-in-law, R.V. "lying" does not open our eyes to the difference which may be expressed thus[1]:—

Mk 1. 30	Mt. viii. 14	Lk iv 38
Lying-down feverish.	Smitten (*or*, cast-[down]) and feverish.	Racked by a great fever.

Mark, who uses a word that elsewhere he twice applies to "lying-down" at a meal[2], is corrected by Matthew and Luke But are they simply trying to express "prostrated" clearly and at the same time in such a way as to suggest the thought of Messianic healing ? Or are they trying to translate some original that Mark has not adequately translated ?

Against applying the latter view to Matthew, there appears (at first sight) the fact that Matthew seems elsewhere to insert (not substitute) "smitten (*or*, cast-[down])" in the cure of the palsied man, thus —

Mk ii. 3	Mt. ix. 2	Lk v 18
And they come bringing to him a paralytic, lifted by four	And behold, they were bringing-near to him a paralytic on a couch *smitten* (or, *cast* [*down*])	And behold, men bringing on a couch a man who was paralysed

But when Mark's context is examined (Mk ii. 4 "they let down the bed (*lit*) where the paralytic was *lying-down*") it will be seen that he inserts "*lying-down*" here too, as above (Mk 1. 30), so that Matthew, here too, is perhaps not adding, but substituting what he deems an adequate rendering ("cast [down]") for an inadequate one.

In *Clue*, it was suggested that Mark's "lifted" (in "lifted by

---

[1] Mk κατέκειτο πυρέσσουσα, Mt. βεβλημένην καὶ πυρέσσουσαν, Lk ἦν συνεχομένη πυρετῷ μεγάλῳ.

[2] See Mk ii 15, xiv 3, comp 1 Cor viii. 10. But it is applied to the sick in Jn v. 3, 6, Acts ix 33, xxviii 8 (comp Lk v 25)

four") was taken by Matthew as meaning "stretched [helplessly on a sick bed]," the two Hebrew words "lift (*nâtal*)" and "stretch" being interchanged in Samuel and Chronicles[1]. But it should have been added that *Horae Hebraicae* explains, by a reference to this word *nâtal* (in a peculiar sense), Matthew's use of "smitten" in the two places where it is used absolutely It is said to mean "*laid forth for death*," in a kind of hyperbole —— "*A dead man laid forth*, in order to his being carried out. The power and dominion of the disease is so expressed. The weak person lieth so, that he is moved only by others; he cannot move himself, but is, as it were, next door to carrying out. So ver 14, of Peter's mother-in-law, ἦν βεβλημένη καὶ πυρέσσουσα, *was laid, and sick of a fever*[2]." This phrase, "*a dead man laid forth*," occurs in the Mishna of Berachoth and elsewhere and is translated by Levy as above[3]

It may be objected that Matthew's Greek word "cast-[down]," far from expressing "laid out [for burial]," would naturally signify to a Greek reader "cast-on-the-ground" or "cast-aside," and this can hardly be denied[4]. But if the Hebrew

---

[1] *Clue* 196 (1) footn points out that נטל "lift," which = (2) αἴρω, "is interchanged with the much more common נטה 'stretch' in 2 S xxiv 12, 1 Chr xxi 10 The latter = (2) αἴρω, (1) βάλλω, (1) ἐπιβάλλω "

[2] *Hor Heb* on Mt viii 6 "Βέβληται, lieth מוטל, *laid forth* Thus מת מוטל, *a dead man laid forth*, in order to his being carried out etc "

[3] Levy iii 379 *a* quotes Mishna "Ber 17 *b* Jem , dessen Todter vor ihm (לפניו) liegt (מוטל)," and also "trop das 18 *a*, so lange Jemdm die Pflicht obliegt, seinen Todten zu begraben, so ist das ebenso, als ob letzterer vor ihm läge " This "metaphorical" use ("as if the dead man were *laid-out* before his eyes") is of importance as supporting the metaphorical interpretation asserted by *Hor Heb* above The phrase occurs also in *Moed Kat.* 23 *b* and (Levy says) frequently

[4] Steph *Thes* (βάλλω, ii 95) quotes *Fab Æsop* 257 Λύκος ὑπὸ κυνῶν δηχθεὶς καὶ κακῶς πάσχων ἐβέβλητο, as to which, note that Matthew alone perhaps uses (xvii 15) κακῶς πάσχω (W H marg) and alone applies βέβληται to disease In Lk xvi 20, ἐβέβλητο must be taken

original was capable (1) of meaning "lift up" and (2) of being confused with "cast-aside," and (3) of being technically used in the sense of "laid out for burial," it becomes quite intelligible that Matthew should paraphrase it from a Greek point of view as if it meant "cast-aside-as-helpless," though it really had the technical meaning of "laid-out-for-burial as though dead[1]" We may illustrate the ambiguity of the Hebrew from the versions of Isaiah (R.V) "He *taketh-up* the isles" where Aquila has "*being cast-down*," and Ibn Ezra adopts the rendering "*throweth*," while admitting that it may mean "*taketh up*[2]" All agree that the word conveys a notion of weakness and insignificance, but as to how it is conveyed there is much disagreement.

Returning, then, to the Synoptic narrative of the healing of "fever," we may reasonably say that Matthew's phrase may be explained as a rendering of a Hebrew word implying "helplessness" and "next door to carrying out to death," and, in any case, not as a substitution of a new tradition for an original Marcan one, but as a more adequate rendering of an original that Mark had inadequately expressed. At the same time we may admit that Matthew was also influenced in his language as well as in his arrangement by a sense of Messianic appropriateness. We have seen that, in accordance with a very ancient interpretation of a prophecy in Isaiah[3], it would be appropriate that the Messiah should identify Himself with the

---

with πρὸς τὸν πυλῶνα "laid [by friends] at the gate" Mk vii 30 βεβλημένον ἐπὶ (L ὑπὸ) τὴν κλίνην means "*lying [where she had been] cast-down* on the bed" (Swete "the exhaustion had not yet spent itself, though the foul spirit was gone")

[1] In Jn iv 47, ἤμελλεν ἀποθνήσκειν resembles Lk vii 2 ἤμελλεν τελευτᾶν.

[2] Is xl 15 Aq βαλλόμενον, other renderings are "decidit" or ἀποπίπτω The Editor (Friedlander) points out that יטול can be passive of טול "*cast*" as well as active of נטל "*lift*" Rashi takes the meaning to be "lifted up" like dust that vanishes into the air

[3] See above, p 191, n. 2, and p. 194.

JESUS HEALING

sufferings of a leper, and Matthew has given the first place in the miracles to the healing of a leper. Somewhat similarly, it would be in accordance with the tone of the Psalms that the Messiah, in His two following miracles, should reveal Himself, by typical action, as the representative of Him who "*upholdeth all them that fall*," and who watches over the sufferer so that "Even if he *fall* he shall *not be utterly cast down*, for *the Lord upholdeth his hand*[1]."

§ 5. *The Johannine view of "fever"*

In John, the "fever" is not (as it is in Luke) "rebuked." Nor is the patient (as in Mark) "raised" or (as in Matthew) "touched." The fever is regarded as being cured by the word of Jesus. In Matthew-Luke, the centurion bids Jesus, not to come to him, "but merely speak in word (*logos*)[2]." In John, Jesus *does* "merely speak in word." That is to say, He refuses to "go down" to the patient, but says to the father "Thy son liveth". and it is added that "the man believed *the word* (logos) that Jesus had spoken," and that the man's servants speedily met him saying "Thy boy liveth." As the Prologue of the Gospel says "Whatsoever was in Him, *i e* in the complete Logos, was life," so here the uttered *logos* of Jesus is "Thy son liveth," and it produces faith in the hearer and life in the sufferer.

In view of the general Johannine avoidance of Synoptic details about healing, and even of Synoptic names of diseases and demonic troubles, the prominence that John gives to fever seems to require some comment from a Greek point of view, in addition to the illustration given above from Jewish tradition. It may be explained perhaps in part by the fact that the fiery fits and fancies of fever somewhat resemble the attacks of demoniacal possession which are prominent in the Synoptists

---

[1] See the Midrash on Ps cxix 116 "Uphold me according to thy word that I may live," which quotes Ps cxlv 14, and xxxvii 24

[2] Mt viii 8 ἀλλὰ μόνον εἰπὲ λόγῳ, Lk vii 7 omits μόνον

but not mentioned by John[1]. We note that Christ's acts of exorcism occur apparently all in Galilee, or, at all events, not in Jerusalem ; and Galilee is emphasized by John as the scene of the cure of fever : "This is again a second sign that Jesus did, having come *out of Judaea into Galilee*[2]."

Another reason may be that "fever" is (really, though not obviously) a good metaphor to describe the greedy thirst of an uncontrolled selfishness. For utter selfishness, whether it be that of a cold and calculating villain or that of a fervid headstrong villain, is, in the eyes of the Allseeing, of the nature of a feverish delirium Regarded in that way, "fever," and the "thirst" that accompanies fever, might well stand first in the list of diseases cured by the Healer of mankind[3]

Epictetus, however, selects this special disease for a discussion that seems to borrow some phrases from Christian writers[4], in order to hold them up to ridicule His doctrine is that, if we have fever, we ought not to ask to be cured of it but rather to make it our object—he almost implies, our sole object —to be virtuously feverish, or, "to have the fever rightly[5]."

---

[1] Comp Origen on Jn iv 46 foll (Lomm ii 118—19), quoting Eph vi. 16, and describing the nobleman's son as "the race of Israel, ailing in the worship of God and in the observance of God's laws, and on the point of dying to God through the fire of (πεπυρωμένον) 'the fiery (πεπυρωμένων) darts of the enemy,' and, on this account, said to 'be in a fever (πυρέσσειν) '"

[2] Jn iv 54, see p 221 below

[3] It is placed by Philo (ii˙ 432 πυρετοί) first in the list of diseases with which God chastens His people See Lewis and Short for passages shewing that there were temples erected to Fever in Rome

[4] See Epictet iii 10. 5 foll, and comp ib. 8 νομίμως ἤθλησας with 2 Tim. ii 5 ἐὰν μὴ νομίμως ἀθλήσῃ, also ib 13 κομψῶς ἔχεις with Jn iv 52 κομψότερον ἔσχεν, and ib 14 κακῶς ἔχεις and κακῶς ἔχειν with Lk. vii 2 κακῶς ἔχων All these phrases are vernacular Greek, but their co-occurrence in a lecture on "fever" seems to point to N T. Mrs Carter also illustrates ib 15 ἐὰν σὺ θέλῃς, κύριε, καλῶς ἔξω from Mt viii 2 κύριε, ἐὰν θέλῃς δύνασαί με καθαρίσαι

[5] Epict iii 10. 12—13 ἂν καλῶς πυρέξῃς...τί ἐστι καλῶς πυρέσσειν ; Μὴ θεὸν μέμψασθαι, μὴ ἄνθρωπον....

"Provided that I am still a philosopher," he says, "let what will happen," and again "What prevents you, in a fever, from keeping your ruling faculty according to nature[1]?"

But how can a man whose "ruling faculty," in accordance with nature, is giving way under the influence of fever, be expected still to "keep" it in a condition to rule over his life? Possibly Epictetus would reply that, in such a case, the Master is opening the door for us to depart out of life. For in his philosophy God is represented as (so to speak) our Master in athletics; He has watched our performance of the philosophic exercises in the gymnasium, the preparatory combats that were to prepare us for our duties and trials and combats, and presently He calls us to the arena, for the actual conflict. "Now is your time for a fever. Bear it well.—For thirst. Bear it well.—For hunger. Bear it well[2]." Epictetus does not represent the Master as adding "For brainlessness. Bear that well."

§ 6. *The Johannine view of "thirst"*

How, if at all, does John deal with the deep questions arising out of the conception of spiritual "fever" and the means of healing it? He never mentions the word again, after the "sign" in Galilee. But if we accept the view that "fever" may be a metaphor for the greedy thirst of uncontrolled selfishness, we are led back to ask how "thirst" is used in ancient Hebrew literature and in the earlier Gospels. And then it may occur to us that in the Pentateuch there are several instances where Israel sins through thirst, and in the Psalms instances where the soul "thirsts" righteously for God's presence[3]. But the Synoptic Gospels are comparatively deficient in any expression of the wrong and the right kind of

---

[1] Epict. iii. 10. 5 and 11.
[2] Epictet. iii. 10. 8.
[3] See Ps. xlii. 2 "My soul thirsteth for God..," lxiii. 1 "My soul thirsteth for thee," comp. Is. xli. 17, lv. 1.

thirst. Philo speaks of "those who thirst and hunger for goodness and virtue[1]." But in the Synoptists, only one passage of Matthew in the Double Tradition says anything about such thirst—nor indeed is the word ever used by Mark and Luke—and, where Matthew represents Jesus as saying, "Blessed are they that hunger and thirst after righteousness," Luke has "Blessed [are ye] that hunger now[2]"—which might include, or even be restricted to, literal hunger Is not this a defect that might naturally induce John to intervene—we cannot say, "in favour of Mark," but "in favour of the fundamental truth on which all the Synoptic Gospels were based?

At all events, whatever may be his motive, John does intervene —as if to shew that the evil thirst that underlies all the sins and miseries of men cannot be extinguished except by calling forth and satisfying a good thirst, the thirst for God. That is the lesson of the first of the Johannine signs at Cana. That also is the lesson of the doctrine in Jerusalem concerning the Brazen Serpent, signifying, as the Evangelist suggests, the conflict between the thirst for evil and the thirst for good, the fiery serpent and the seraph[3]. This lesson is carried on in Samaria by the Dialogue about the living water between Jesus and the woman with the "five husbands," who has no real "husband[4]" Again, in the synagogue at Capernaum, and afterwards in the Temple, the right thirst is appealed to in the words "He that believeth on me shall never thirst," and "If any man thirst let him come unto me and drink[5]." Last of all, on the Cross, Jesus Himself, "knowing that all things are now finished," exclaims "I thirst[6]" These words call forth an

---

[1] Philo i. 566 τοὺς διψῶντας καὶ πεινῶντας καλοκἀγαθίας Philo also has i. 626 τὸ πάντα διψῆν θεοῦ.

[2] Mt v. 6, Lk vi 21

[3] See *Son* 3391—3407, and esp 3397 (where however the remark about Jerome as "probably following Origen" should be cancelled)

[4] Jn iv 13—18   [5] Jn vi 35, vii 37.

[6] Jn xix 28 foll

act—an offering of vinegar—variously reported by Mark and Matthew, and placed earlier and in a different context by Luke[1].

Then, while the reader is reflecting on the strange paradox of "I thirst," and on the apparent breaking of the implied promise in "let him come unto me and drink," there come the mystical words, "One of the soldiers pierced his side, and straightway there came out blood and water...and another scripture saith, They shall look on him whom they pierced[2]." Thus Jesus might be said, in reply to Epictetus, to hear indeed the Voice that says "Now is the time for you to thirst; bear it well," and to "bear it well" beyond all Epictetian dreams of philosophic perfection The Son, in "bearing" thirst, bears it for others, calling forth faith from the woman of Samaria, and kindness from the soldiers round the Cross. In the former case there follows the gift of the living water to Samaria , in the latter, the vision of the mingled blood and water that are to satisfy the thirst of all mankind[3]

---

[1] Mk xv 36, Mt xxvii 48 (following the cry "Eloi" or "Eli"), Lk xxiii 36 ἐνέπαιξαν . ὄξος προσφέροντες, parall to Mk xv. 31, Mt. xxvii. 41

[2] Jn xix 34—7

[3] John's view of Christ's mystical thirst may be illustrated by the following considerations   (1) In Jn iv 6 foll , the words "Give me to drink" are preceded by the statement that Jesus was "wearied (κεκοπιακώς)," and followed by a repetition of κοπιάω (ib iv 38) "I sent you to reap that [over] which you have not wearied [-yourselves-with-toil], others have wearied [-themselves-with-toil] and ye have entered into their toil " The word occurs nowhere else in the Fourth Gospel , and in the first six books of O T it occurs only in Deut xxv. 18 (bis) of the rearguard of Israel ("when thou wast faint (LXX ἐπείνας) and weary") and in the words of the first Jesus (Josh xxiv 13 about the Land of Promise) "a land whereon thou hadst not wearied [thyself with toil] " It seems probable that John sees a likeness between Israel in the wilderness under the first Jesus, and the Church (so to speak) in Samaria under the second Jesus , whom His disciples have left for the moment, and who,

JESUS HEALING

§ 7. *The Johannine view of Messianic "raising"*

It was noted above that Matthew and Luke omitted Mark's statement that Jesus "raised up" the sufferer. They omit also several Marcan words, including "raised up," in their account of the cure of an epileptic boy[1]. There they are so obviously abridging Mark's very lengthy narrative that no other explanation of their motive is necessary. Nor can it be expected that John should intervene in a detail of this kind. Yet the description of Jehovah as the Father (Deut. i. 31) "carrying" the Child Israel would commend itself to such an Evangelist. And this "carrying" or "lifting" is suggested by Mark in two passages where he describes Jesus as "taking in his arms" a little child, or "children." To both of these passages, as well as to the healing of the epileptic child, there

---

though thirsty and faint, resists both thirst and faintness, and gains the victory over Samaria.

(2) But John will not accept the view, suggested by ἐπείνας, that Jesus was "hungry." In the Fourth Gospel, Jesus, in reply to His disciples bidding Him "eat"—says (iv 32) "I have meat to eat that ye know not of." In the Temptation, Matthew and Luke say that Jesus "hungered", and "hunger" may seem so essential a part of the story that no Evangelist, however brief, could omit it. Yet Mark omits it. He nowhere represents Jesus as "hungering" except for fruit from the barren fig tree of Israel (Mk xi 12, Mt xxi 18). That kind of "hunger" is different (comp. Philipp iv 17 "not that I seek for the gift, but I seek for the fruit that increaseth to your account").

(3) Epictetus would perhaps have quoted against John Is. xl 28 "The Lord...fainteth not, neither is weary." But John's view is that the incarnate Son takes upon Himself the human weaknesses of faintness or weariness and thirst, and triumphs, not only over them, but through them, over the weaknesses of His brethren. John's avoidance of the metaphor of hunger may be explained by the fact that Israel is supposed to have had manna regularly in the wilderness, even when they needed water.

[1] Mk ix 25—7 "Thou dumb and deaf spirit...But Jesus, having taken him by the hand, *raised him up*, and he stood up."

JESUS HEALING

are parallels in the other Synoptists, but they omit this gesture of tenderness[1].

This being the case, the rule of Johannine Intervention would lead us to expect, not only that John would emphasize passages describing Christ's personal affection for this or that friend or disciple, but also that he would lay stress on His character of the Restorer or Uplifter of the fallen, or of the lifeless. This he does repeatedly. The keynote to a succession of thoughts of this kind is to be found in the first Johannine use of the Marcan word: "Destroy ye this temple and in three days *I will raise it*[2]." It is implied that the purification of the temple by the mere expulsion of the evil will be of no avail. If that were all, the evil would return. The old must be destroyed and the new raised up, for (says the Evangelist) "as the Father *raiseth* the dead and causeth them to live, so also the Son causeth to live whom he will[3]." Jesus Himself never again uses the Marcan word "raise" transitively to express His own action, but He implies it in various ways and especially in the saying "I, if I be lifted up from the earth, will *draw* all men unto me[4]."

§ 8. *Medically "attending," as distinct from "healing," in Greek*

In the Gospels, "heal" stands for two words, quite distinct in meaning. One of these, anglicised in the rare English word "*iatric*," really means "heal," but is seldom used except by Luke[5]. The other, anglicised in the English "*therapeutic*,"

---

[1] See *Son* 3518a quoting the Marcan passages with ἐγείρειν, describing Christ's gestures, and their Matthew-Luke parallels.

[2] Jn ii. 19 ἐγερῶ αὐτόν.

[3] Jn v. 21 (perhaps not the words of Jesus, see *Joh Gr.* 2066 b).

[4] Jn xii 32 Jn v 8 has ἔγειρε, and xiv 31 ἐγείρεσθε.

[5] It is significant that Luke, the Evangelist that most frequently uses ἰᾶσθαι, is himself called (Col iv 14) ἰατρός. Mk uses ἰᾶσθαι but once (v. 29), Mt. thrice, and once in quotation; Jn once certainly

is freely used by all the Synoptists; but its exact meaning is "attend." It is only in certain contexts that it means "attend medically." More rarely it means "attend medically with the result of healing." In LXX, the "iatric" word is the only one used in the sense of healing; the "therapeutic," when it represents a Hebrew word (which it rarely does) means six times "attending as a worshipper, or as a courtier," and once "attending to," or "dressing," the feet of a lame man[1]. Obviously "attending" is different from "healing." A democracy, says Plato, expects its statesmen "both to *attend* and to *heal*" its diseases with "pleasant remedies." In a second-century papyrus, a physician says to a judge "I *attended* so-and-so," and receives the reply "Perhaps you *attended* un-satisfactorily[2]."

To the question why Mark prefers the *therapeutic* to the *iatric* word, two answers may be given, one derived from the nature of the words, and the other from the nature of Christ's acts. It happens that the Greek *therapeia*, "[medical] attendance," is also Hebraized. In that form, it is connected by Jewish tradition with a similar word in the Hebrew of Ezekiel, concerning the mystical trees (on the banks of the stream from the Temple) of which "the fruit shall be for meat and the leaf for *healing* (*therapeia*)[3]." Here the LXX has "soundness" instead of "healing," but Revelation, differing from LXX, says "the leaves of the tree were for the *healing* of the nations[4]."

(iv 47), once doubtfully (v 13, see Blass), once in quotation, Lk. 11 times

[1] Esther ii. 19, vi 10, Prov xix 6, xxix 26, Is liv 17, Dan vii 10 (LXX), 2 S. xix. 24 (R V.) "*dressed* his feet."

[2] Plato *Legg* 684 C θεραπεύειν τε καὶ ἰᾶσθαι, *Oxy Pap* No 40 (early 2nd cent) ἐθεράπευσα...τάχα κακῶς αὐτοὺς ἐθεράπευσας.

[3] Ezek xlvii. 12 "the leaf for *healing* (LXX ἀνάβασις αὐτῶν εἰς ὑγίειαν)" On the Hebrew *therapeia* see Krauss p. 594 and Levy iv 674 b The Heb , of which the consonants are identical with those in *therapeia*, does not occur elsewhere (Gesen. 930 a)

[4] Rev xxii 2 εἰς θεραπείαν τῶν ἐθνῶν.

Barnabas, though he does not quote these words, refers to Ezekiel's picture of the trees, applying it to the Christian doctrines of the Cross and Baptism, and indirectly confirming the inference from Revelation that Jewish Christians would connect Ezekiel's "healing" with the thought of Christ's acts of *therapeia*.

It remains to add that Philo, in his treatise on the Contemplative Life, says that those whom he calls *therapeutai* are truly so called either because they practise a *therapeusis*, i.e. healing, of souls, or because they have been trained to the *therapeusis*, i.e service, of the IS (i e that God who is Supreme Truth)[1]. All Philo's treatises are permeated with the thought that man, when he thus "*serves*," or "*attends on*," God, is also "*serving*" or "*attending on*" himself, in the highest sense[2]. These facts suffice to shew that the Marcan word *therapeuein* had a history, and various meanings, before Mark used it for the first time in his Gospel, applying it to acts of Christ And the question now arises, In what precise sense did Mark use it? But before we deal with this we must examine what he says of the diseases.

§ 9. "*Divers*" *or* "*manifold*" *diseases*[3]

The word here translated "divers" or "manifold" means literally "various, or variable," in nature, form, colour,

---

[1] Philo ii 471—2.
[2] See Philo i 201—2. We are to "honour" our "father" and our "mother" The "Father" is the Generator of the Cosmos. The "Mother" is Wisdom "Neither the All-including God (ὁ πλήρης θεὸς), nor the Supreme and All-accomplishing Knowledge, needs anything" It follows that "the man that *attends-on* (θεραπευτικὸν) these is profiting, not those whom he *attends-on*—since they need nothing—but, above all, himself (ἀλλ' ἑαυτὸν μάλιστα ὠφελεῖν) "
[3] Mk i 34, Mt iv 24, Lk iv 40 These three passages severally contain the first mention of pl νόσοι in the three Synoptists All have ποικίλαις with νόσοις, but Mt adds καὶ βασάνοις συνεχομένους For the texts in full, and for Mt viii 16—17, which is the parall to Mk i 34, Lk iv 40 (since the three describe the healing of disease outside Peter's house), see p 217.

behaviour, etc. It often conveys a notion of art, and sometimes of too much art, as when Plato ironically describes the luxurious people who "humorously" contrive to make their diseases *"more artistically varied* and more severe than before[1]." But such a Platonic phrase would not suffice to explain the fact that Mark, Matthew, and Luke, who never use this epithet again, agree in using it in the passages in which they severally describe Jesus as for the first time healing not one disease—as in the case of Peter's mother-in-law—but many.

The Petrine Epistle appears to give us a clue to the meaning when it applies the epithet to two opposite things. First, it is applied to the "*manifold* temptations (*or,* trials)" that "put men to grief" (with an apparent allusion to the "fiery trial" of persecution that comes on men "with a view to temptation (*or,* trial)[2]." Then it is applied to "the *manifold* grace of God[3]," which enables us to pass through temptations. In the Epistle of James the phrase "*manifold* temptations" recurs[4]; and though the context mentions man's own nature ("his own lust") and not the devil, as the tempting agent, yet the use of the epithet in other epistles ("*manifold* lusts," "*manifold* lusts and pleasures," "*manifold* and strange teachings") shews that the source of temptation might be traced, through "the flesh" and "the world," to "the ruler of this world," or Satan[5].

---

[1] Plato *Pol.* IV (426 A) χαριέντως διατελοῦσιν ἰατρευόμενοι γὰρ οὐδὲν περαίνουσι, πλήν γε ποικιλώτερα καὶ μείζω ποιοῦσι τὰ νοσήματα. In LXX it is applied to "speckled" or "ringstraked" sheep, and to Joseph's coat "of many colours" etc.

[2] 1 Pet 1. 6—7, where ἐν ποικίλοις πειρασμοῖς..διὰ πυρὸς δὲ δοκιμαζομένου prepares for *ib.* IV 12 τῇ ἐν ὑμῖν πυρώσει πρὸς πειρασμὸν ὑμῖν γινομένῃ

[3] 1 Pet IV 10 ποικίλης χάριτος θεοῦ   [4] Jas 1 2

[5] 2 Tim III 6, Tit III 3, Heb XIII 9. Hermas *Sim.* VI. 3 4 repeats ποικίλος four times while describing the ποικίλαι τιμωρίαι, or βάσανοι, or ἀσθένειαι, which proceed from the ἄγγελος τιμωρίας. Comp 2 S XXIV 1 "*the anger of the Lord* was kindled against Israel, and he moved David ..saying Go, number Israel" with 1 Chr XXI 1 "*Satan* stood up against Israel, and moved David to number Israel."

JESUS HEALING

Now in the Acts of the Apostles a Petrine speech, which shews signs of very early origin, describes the Gospel as "beginning from Galilee" where Jesus "went through [the land], benefiting and healing all that were *oppressed by the devil*[1]." If therefore we can find in any Greek document of the first century or thereabouts some instance of the word under consideration, applied to "*tortures*" *inflicted by an oppressor*—not merely as being "*manifold*" but also as being "*artistically*" calculated to break down resistance—we should be on safe ground in attributing to Mark a similar metaphor. "*Manifold*" is so applied no less than four times in the Jewish story of the Seven Martyrs[2], and the traditional word is carried on in the Christian accounts of the martyrdoms of Polycarp and the Christians at Lyons[3]. Other associations may have contributed to the first-century prevalence, among Christians, of this language about "*manifold* diseases and torments[4]"; but one of the most powerful (in the days of persecution and martyrdom) would be that of the *many-sidedness* of the shapes assumed by oppression and temptation, proceeding from Satan. The view of Mark's original, then, seems to have been

---

[1] Acts x 38 ὃς διῆλθεν εὐεργετῶν καὶ ἰώμενος πάντας τοὺς καταδυναστευομένους ὑπὸ τοῦ διαβόλου

[2] 4 Macc xv. 24 τὴν τῶν στρεβλῶν ποικιλίαν, xvii 7, xviii. 21 ποικίλαι with βάσανοι, xvi 3 (some MSS) ποικίλως βασανιζομένους But note 3 Macc ii 6 where (somewhat as in Hermas) the epithet is applied to the "punishments" with which God "tried" (δοκιμάσας) Pharaoh

[3] *Mart Polyc* § 2 ποικίλων βασάνων, Euseb *H E* v 1 40 ἀντὶ πάσης τῆς ἐν τοῖς μονομαχίοις ποικιλίας αὐτοὶ (1 Cor iv 9) "θέαμα γενόμενοι τῷ κόσμῳ," *ib* 61 τοιαύτην εἶχε τὴν ποικιλίαν

[4] Comp Justin *Tryph* § 134 "Jacob served for the sake of the speckled and spotted sheep," and "Christ...served . for the *manifold* and many-formed men from every race (τῶν ἐκ παντὸς γένους ποικίλων καὶ πολυειδῶν ἀνθρώπων)" Philo's phrase 1 192 ποικίλῳ καὶ πολυπλόκῳ connects "*manifold*" with "*many-folded*"—an epithet of the Serpent (Eurip *Medea* 481) and of Typhon (Plato, *Phaedr*. 230 A θηρίον Τυφῶνος πολυπλοκώτερον)

JESUS HEALING

this, that simultaneously with the descent of the Son of God to reclaim fallen men for Himself, there was an uprising of the Serpent to maintain his hold upon them as his lawful captives, so that Satan, the Demon, compelled his victims the demoniacs to bid Jesus go back to His own kingdom.

Matthew is the only Synoptist that inserts a mention of "torment," along with "manifold," in his description of Christ's first appearance as the Healer; but the insertion is very appropriate if we are to regard "manifold" as referring (like the instances in Maccabees) to the machinations of the tormenting Adversary called in the Acts "the oppressor" and "the devil." Matthew's list is worded as follows · "All [the class of] those that were in grievous condition, [through] being holden with *manifold* diseases and torments—[namely,] demoniacs and lunatics and paralytics[1]." His intention seems to be to shew that he is referring to that kind of disease which he described in the previous verse as "all disease and all sickness," and which Deuteronomy describes as punishment for sin[2]. He is not referring to dumbness, lameness, and blindness, but only, or mostly, to diseases affecting the body through the mind and the will[3].

§ 10. *"At even, when the sun did set"*

The Synoptists vary, as follows :—

Mk i. 32 (lit.)	Mt viii. 16 (lit.)	Lk. iv 40 (lit.)
But, it having become late, when the sun [had] set	But, it having become late	But, the sun setting...[4]

---

[1] Mt. iv 24 πάντας τοὺς κακῶς ἔχοντας ποικίλαις νόσοις καὶ βασάνοις συνεχομένους, δαιμονιζομένους καὶ σεληνιαζομένους καὶ παραλυτικούς.

[2] Deut vii 15, xxviii 61 πᾶσαν μαλακίαν, on which see above, p 166, and *Light* **3940** a.

[3] As in Mt viii 16, ix. 12, xiv. 35, οἱ κακῶς ἔχοντες is a general term. Then the cause is expressed by the clause ποικίλαις νόσοις καὶ βασάνοις συνεχομένους Then the νόσοι and βάσανοι are particularised in three classes

[4] Mk 1 32 ὀψίας δὲ γενομένης ὅτε ἔδυσεν ὁ ἥλιος, Mt viii 16 ὀψίας δὲ γενομένης, Lk iv 40 δύνοντος (D δύσαντος) δὲ τοῦ ἡλίου..

JESUS HEALING

In *Clue* it was argued that Mark had combined two Greek translations of some non-Greek original, and that the original mentioned only the setting of the sun. This would be probable *a priori* since Mark is given to such combinations[1]. And we might support the hypothesis by shewing that Codex D, in Luke, has "when the sun *had* set[2]." There may have been an early hesitation between "*setting*" and "*having set*." A scribe or editor might suggest—as a safe and neutral paraphrase—"*late*." This Mark might combine with his literal rendering. Matthew might substitute it for a literal rendering.

But before accepting this explanation as complete, we ought to ask whether O.T. contains any instance of a reduplication of time-phrases of this kind—any special instance that might possibly influence Mark. And this is all the more necessary because the Jews were accurate to a nicety in distinguishing the exact time of the coming on of the sabbath in the evening. It is true that Mark's noun for "late," *opsiā*, does not occur in O.T.[3] But the kindred adverb, "late," *opse*, in one of its four LXX instances, represents the Hebrew "*between the two evenings*[4]." This is a phrase of peculiar religious significance and noteworthy associations for Jews. It occurs for the first time in Exodus in connection with the killing of the passover lamb: "Ye shall kill it *between the two evenings*[5]." This phrase, very obscure for modern readers, is explained to Jews in a Deuteronomic phrase which contains the duplication that we

---

[1] See *Clue* 128—55, especially 130.

[2] Comp. Deut xxiii 11 (R V) "when the sun is down," δεδυκότος ἡλίου with *ib*. xxiv. 13 (R V) "when the sun goeth down," πρὸς δυσμαῖς (AF περὶ δυσμὰς) ἡλίου, where the Heb is the same, in both cases, "like [*i.e.* about] the going down of the sun."

[3] Ὀψία, in LXX, occurs only in Judith xiii 1.

[4] Exod xxx 8 (R V) "When Aaron lighteth the lamps *at even*," where R V marg has "Heb., *between the two evenings*."

[5] Exod xii 6. The second instance is *ib* xvi 12 "*Between the two evenings* ye shall eat flesh, and in the morning ye shall be filled with bread."

are attempting to illustrate, only that, instead of "late," the Hebrew has "in the evening," thus · "Thou shalt sacrifice the passover *in the evening, about the going-down of the sun*, the appointed-time [for] thy going-forth from Egypt[1]." These words are quoted in Mechilta to explain "between the two evenings" in Exodus[2] They are also quoted in both Talmuds ; and all the Rabbis agree (amid some differences of opinion as to the rest of the text) that a distinction is intended between "in the evening" and "about the going-down of the sun[3]."

Of course it cannot be contended that Mark, or Mark's authority, supposed the evening that he is describing to be the evening of the Passover. But it can be contended, and that confidently, that this particular evening—the evening when

---

[1] Deut xvi 6 ἑσπέρας, πρὸς δυσμὰς ἡλίου Gesen. 787b quotes for this combination 1 K xxii 35—6 But this is not quite parallel, as two actions are described, "The king died . *in [the] evening*...and there went out a cry *about the going down of the sun*" This has a quasi-parallel in 2 Chr xviii 34 "Stayed-himself-up until *the evening*, and he died *toward* (lit *to*) *the time of the going down of the sun*" (where LXX has δύναντος, but A δύνοντος, illustrating the v r in Lk iv. 40 quoted on p 213) I have not found anything of interest in the Talmuds bearing on 1 K xxii 35—6, except a suggestion in *j* Sanhedr iv 13 *ad fin*, that the Heb "cry" stood for Gk. εἰρήνη, and, in *b* Sanhedr 39 b, that it meant (as it usually does) a song of joy, and especially praise to Jehovah (Gesen 943 b)

[2] *Mechilt* on Exod xii 6 (Wu pp 17—18)

[3] See *b Berach* 9a quoting R Eliezer and R Jehoshua, and *j Pesach* v(1) (Schwab v 62), etc, also *Gen r* on Gen xxi 2 The first of "the two evenings" began from the sixth hour (*i e* noon)

Note Luke's deviation from Mark-Matthew as to the "carrying" or "leading" of the sick to Jesus —

Mk i 32	Mt viii 16	Lk iv 40
ἔφερον	προσήνεγκαν	ἤγαγον

If it was the sabbath, and if the sun, as Luke says, was still "setting," the sick ought not (according to the views of strict Jews) to be "carried" to Jesus Luke may have considered that Mark used φέρειν loosely, as in Mk xi 2 φέρετε (Mt -Lk ἀγάγετε) about the ass They were not allowed before sunset to "*carry*" the sick, they were only allowed to "*lead*" them

JESUS HEALING

Jesus was for the first time publicly proclaimed to be the Holy One of God, the Destroyer of the spirits of evil—would be regarded by all Jewish Christians in the early Church of Galilee as introducing a night of special solemnity. It was indeed "a night to be much observed unto the Lord for bringing them out of the land of Egypt"—out of the spiritual Egypt, the land of darkness and of the shadow of death, overshadowed by Satan and "oppressed by the devil[1]." Matthew helps us to feel this when he describes the healing of the crowds at even as a fulfilment of "that which was spoken by Isaiah the prophet, saying, *Himself took our infirmities and bare our diseases*[2]." Mark quotes nothing—neither Isaiah on "bearing diseases," nor Exodus on "the two evenings," nor Deuteronomy on "the evening" and the "going down of the sun." But his non-quotation cannot reasonably be alleged to prove non-allusion in view of the fact that elsewhere he frequently alludes and hardly ever quotes[3].

If the Marcan reduplication is allusive, it may reasonably be regarded as containing a trace—cancelled in Matthew and Luke—of a Petrine reminiscence. Peter could never forget that first night of marvel upon marvel when, after the miracle of healing within his own house, pandemonium seemed to collect round his doors—the Prince of darkness and death breaking out, as it were, into rebellion, only to be suppressed by the Healer endowed with the power of light and life. Coming "between the two evenings," this outpouring of deliverance might well remind him of the deliverance of the Passover. He could not indeed at that early date have said—in the words assigned to John the Baptist in the Fourth Gospel—"Behold, the Lamb of God which taketh away the sin of the world"; but in after days, recalling that eventful night, and the Great Deliverance that it introduced, he might

---

[1] Exod. xii 42, Acts x 38
[2] Mt. viii 17, quoting Is liii 4.
[3] See *Son* 3518 *d*

JESUS HEALING

naturally regard it as a recurrence, or rather as a fulfilment, of that first night of the Passover of Israel, the night of the Lamb of God :—slain between "the evening" and "the going down of the sun." It is a reasonable and even probable supposition, that Peter imprinted this thought on his oral Gospel, and that Mark has preserved a touch of it in his written record.

§ 11   Was Christ's action in any cases tentative ?

The Revised Version gives the details of the healing as follows :—

Mk 1 32—34 (R V.)	Mt. viii. 16—17 (R.V.)	Lk. iv. 40—41 (R.V.)
(32) And at even, when the sun did set, they brought unto him all that were sick, and them that were possessed with devils. (33) And all the city was gathered together at the door (34) And he healed[1] many that were sick with divers diseases, and cast out many devils, and he suffered not the devils to speak, because they knew him [*many anc. auth add* to be Christ].	(16) And when even was come, they brought unto him many possessed with devils: and he cast out the spirits with a word, and healed[1] all that were sick: (17) That it might be fulfilled which was spoken by Isaiah the prophet, saying, Himself took our infirmities, and bare our diseases.	(40) And when the sun was setting, all they that had any sick with divers diseases brought them unto him, and he laid his hands on every one of them, and healed[1] them. (41) And devils also came out from many, crying out, and saying, Thou art the Son of God. And rebuking them, he suffered them not to speak, because they knew that he was the Christ.

But this does not express one textually slight difference of Luke from Mark-Matthew which might make a great difference

---

[1] "Healed ($\theta\epsilon\rho\alpha\pi\epsilon\acute{u}\omega$)," *lit* "medically attended" (s above, p 208).

in the meaning. It is that, whereas Mark-Matthew has the aorist, "he healed," Luke has the imperfect[1], which, whatever may be its meaning, does at all events *not* mean "he healed."

It might conceivably have a tentative meaning "*attempted to heal.*" Take for example Luke's use of the imperfect of the verb "persuade" in the Acts, where A V has "*persuaded* them to continue in the grace of God[2]." Here R V has "*urged* them to continue," and this, or something like it, is a necessary correction. For the imperfect must mean "began to" or "attempted to," and only the latter seems to make sense. Again, where the sons of Zebedee say to Jesus that they "*attempted to prevent*" a stranger from exorcizing in the name of Jesus, the MSS vary greatly, many of them having "*we prevented*[3]."

So here, it is conceivable that Luke, writing like a very scrupulous historian, felt that Mark and Matthew had exaggerated, reasoning as follows:—"It was hyperbole in Mark to say that 'all the city gathered at the door.' It was only 'all those who had any sick with manifold diseases.' And it would convey a wrong impression to say, as Matthew is supposed to say, 'he healed all that were sick.' Matthew says in fact 'he attended to all that were sick.' I shall therefore by a very slight change, the mere dropping of one letter, express that the Lord's action was in each case tentative. People take the Synoptic verb as meaning 'heal.' Well then I shall say what people will understand as meaning 'He attempted to heal.' Where faith was present, healing was effected. Where it was absent there was no healing."

---

[1] W H marg gives the aorist, but (1) the consensus of the best authorities is decidedly for the imperf., (2) Luke has the imperf in the context (iv 41 W H txt ἐξήρχετο, marg ἐξήρχοντο), (3) the inferior MSS would probably be influenced by the desire of scribes to conform Luke to the text of Mark-Matthew.

[2] Acts xiii 43

[3] Mk ix 38 ἐκωλύομεν, with the best MSS, Lk ix 49, W. H ἐκωλύομεν, Tisch ἐκωλύσαμεν. R V "we forbade."

JESUS HEALING

But this, though conceivable, is not probable. Why should Luke use Mark's *therapeutic* word in the *iatric* sense and alter its meaning by a mere tense-change? Why should he not have used the *iatric* word, for which, as has been shewn above, he has a predilection[1]? It is better to suppose that Luke used the imperfect to imply deliberate continuousness. That is to say, the multitude was not healed as a whole by the mere sight of the Healer. Nor did Jesus say to the multitude as a whole "Be ye healed" and they were healed. He moved from this sufferer to that, offering His tendance to each. This will explain not only the Lucan addition of the phrase that Jesus "laid his hands" on "each" sufferer, but also the Lucan use, unique in N.T., of the present participle in this phrase, "[continuously] laying his hands" on sufferer after sufferer[2].

Thus we are still left in some doubt as to the precise results of Christ's action, because we do not know the precise meaning attached by any of the Synoptists except Mark to the therapeutic word. Mark, it would seem, must mean that Jesus "*healed* many." For we cannot suppose his words to mean that Jesus merely "*offered attendance to* many," passing by and neglecting some. But how is the Marcan "*healed many*" to be reconciled with Matthew's statement that Jesus "*healed all that were sick*"? Only if we suppose that Matthew gives to the Marcan word a non-Marcan significance and means "he *attended to all*." Luke, at all events, would seem to have done this—that is, to have used the therapeutic word in a non-Marcan sense, "attended to"—and to have added the phrase about "laying the hands" in order to explain the nature of the

---

[1] See above, p. 208 foll., on ἰάομαι "heal," as distinct from θεραπεύω "attend [medically]", also p. 229, n. 1.

[2] Lk. iv. 40 ἐπιτιθείς. The aorist ἐπιθείς is very frequent. It occurs in Mk. vi. 5, viii. 23, Mt. xix. 15, Acts ix. 12, 17, xiii. 3, xix. 6, xxviii. 8. Note the rare imperf. followed by another imperf. in Acts viii. 17 τότε ἐπετίθεσαν καὶ ἐλάμβανον, "they [duly and solemnly] laid their hands...and they [duly] received the Holy Spirit."

therapeusis If this is Luke's meaning, we may suppose that in some cases the "healing," the *iatric* result, was believed by him not to have taken place till afterwards, as he relates to have happened to a leper, who was not "healed" till some time had elapsed after Jesus had bidden him shew himself to the priests[1]. In that case Jesus said to the man, "Thy faith hath saved thee." That being so, it is conceivable that in other instances, where "faith" was not present or was very imperfect, the *therapeusis* offered by Jesus was not followed by permanent "healing" Matthew records a conditional act of healing, when Jesus said to two blind men, "According to your faith be it done unto you[2]." No other Synoptist states a condition so definitely. But it is reasonable to suppose that the condition, even when not stated, always existed, and that, without faith on the part of the sufferer or the sufferer's representative, no cure was effected.

§ 12. *The Johannine view, regarded negatively*

The Fourth Gospel does not verbally recognise a conditional character—the existence of an "if," or "according to your faith" —in the *performance* of any of Christ's signs. But it does recognise a conditional character in the *permanence* of the results of a sign The Evangelist represents Jesus as saying to a man that had been healed of an "infirmity" apparently resembling paralysis, "Sin no longer [*i.e.* continue no longer in sin] lest a worse thing befall thee[3]."

There is also a negative character in John's attitude toward collective healing generally. He does not deny the historical

---

[1] Lk. xvii 14—15

[2] Mt ix 27—30 This is peculiar to Matthew. In the healing of blindness near Jericho, Matthew xx 34 omits all mention of "faith," whereas the parallel Mk x 52, Lk xviii 42 have "Thy faith hath saved thee"

[3] Jn v 14, s *Joh Gr* 2437 foll , *Son* 3148, 3154*c* Comp Mt xii. 44—5, Lk xi 25—6, which, though only a parable, may very well be based on facts

JESUS HEALING

accuracy of Mark's account of the manifestation of the Gospel at Capernaum in what may be called an outbreak of exorcisms and faith-healings. He assumes it and passes it over as being a brief episode sufficiently described by all the Synoptists. "After this, he went down to Capernaum...and *there abode not many days*[1]." The first working of "signs," collectively, is located at Jerusalem. There "many" are said to have "believed" in Jesus on account of "the signs that he was [continually] doing", but it is added, in what seems irony, that Jesus did not reciprocate this "believing[2]". Nicodemus says indeed that "no man" can do such signs "except God be with him"; but instead of commending the Rabbi's faith, Jesus directs his attention to realities, to mysteries of heaven, to the new birth, and to higher signs, typified by the uplifting of the brazen serpent in the wilderness[3].

A subsequent reference to collective signs is implied in the statement that "the Galilaeans received" Jesus because they had "seen all the things that he did in Jerusalem", and disparagement of this kind of proof seems to be implied in Christ's saying to the nobleman "Except ye [in Capernaum] see signs and wonders ye will not believe[4]" The nobleman however does believe, and an act of healing is recorded thus: "This again is a second sign that Jesus performed, having come from Judaea into Galilee[5]."

"*A second*" must, it would seem, not be confused with "*the second*," so as to mean "*the second* of the signs wrought by Jesus in Galilee." If it were so taken, it would exclude the possibility of signs previously wrought in Capernaum. The Diatessaron,

---

[1] Jn ii 12. "Abiding" is thrice connected with the first converts (Jn i 38—9) and twice with the Samaritan converts (Jn iv 40). Here its use in a negative phrase probably implies, as Heracleon said (see above, p 179), that no great spiritual result was effected

[2] Jn ii 23—4 πολλοὶ ἐπίστευσαν τὰ σημεῖα ἃ ἐποίει αὐτὸς δὲ Ἰησοῦς οὐκ ἐπίστευεν αὐτὸν αὐτοῖς (*Joh Gr* **2644**)

[3] Jn iii. 2—14   [4] Jn iv 45, 48   [5] Jn iv. 54

221 (Mark i 29—34)

JESUS HEALING

it is true, appears to take it thus. But, in order to do so, it (1) omits the Johannine account of Christ's going down to Capernaum[1], and (2) places the healing of the nobleman's son before the Synoptic miracles in Capernaum at the beginning of the Gospel, thus. "And when Jesus heard that John was delivered up he went away into Galilee (Mt. iv 12) and he entered again into Cana, where he had made the water wine (Jn iv 46)." The truth seems to be that "*a second*" means a sign that the Evangelist selects to *record in detail, and to place second* in his small list of detailed "signs." He has told us above that Jesus was "[continually] doing signs" in Jerusalem, but he has described none of them in detail.

We can imagine the Evangelist explaining his silence thus: "I did not mention the fact that Jesus had also been working signs during His short stay in Capernaum. All know that. Mark and Luke have described them fully. But they were only of rudimentary importance. They were such signs as Jesus had in His mind when He said to the nobleman, 'Except ye [in Capernaum] see *signs and wonders*, ye will not believe.' They did not produce the higher kind of faith. The 'first' sign at Cana was 'first,' and the 'second' sign at Cana was 'second'—*in spiritual order*[2]. There is a tendency in some to

---

[1] Jn ii 12—13

[2] Comp Chrysostom on Jn iv 54, "He has not simply (οὐδὲ ἁπλῶς) added the epithet '*second*,' but still [further] (ἔτι) he extols (ἐπαίρει) the wonder [of the faith] (τὸ θαῦμα) of the Samaritans, shewing that, even when a '*second*' sign was wrought, these [people in Capernaum] who beheld [signs] did not attain to the height of those others (ἐκείνων)—those who had seen nothing [of the nature of a 'sign']." Cramer omits ἐπαίρει. Ἁπλῶς might mean "simply" in the sense of "superficially," "with popular inexactness."

Origen *Comm Joann* xiii 60 *ad fin* enumerates seven scenes of Christ's early visitations (ἐπιδημίαι)—Bethany (MS Bathara), Cana, Capernaum, Jerusalem, Judaea, Samaria, and Cana again. He concludes thus "*In-the-sixth-place* (ἕκτον) He taught in Samaria...and *in-the-seventh-place* (ἕβδομον) He (lit) *becomes in Cana of Galilee for-the-second-time* (ἐν Κ τῆς Γαλ δεύτερον γίνεται)." At the beginning of

magnify all the signs of the Lord Jesus without distinction, because they were very many, and because He seemed to some most marvellous when He worked many signs simultaneously. They were sometimes, in fact, healings of a multitude rather than of individuals. I do not deny that there were such healings. But they were not signs of the highest kind. They might be (sometimes) such as those that may have happened after the Lord's Resurrection, when people in Jerusalem placed their sick folk in the street, so that the shadow of Peter, passing by, might benefit some of them[1] Such signs there were in Capernaum at the beginning of the Gospel, but I pass over them in order to relate others in which Jesus healed this or that individual, and taught this or that new truth in each act of healing. I shall also give the readers the Lord's own thought— not the words, but the *thought*, the meaning of the words— concerning the reasons why He sometimes healed one and not another."

§ 13. *The Johannine view, regarded positively*

Some thought of this kind appears to throw light on the narrative that immediately follows It represents Jesus as selecting one out of a multitude of sick folk near a pool, and healing him alone The narrative will come before us again when we compare it with the Synoptic healing of the "paralytic[2]," with which it has some points of similarity (though more of contrast), but we must note here the exceptional circumstance that the man did not know who had healed him, even after he had been healed. The man's faith, therefore,

---

the chapter he says (in a passage where MSS vary) that Jn iv 54 is "ambiguous" (ἀμφίβολον) But his own view is manifest, that between the first visit to Cana and the second a hexaemeron (see *Joh Gr* 2624, *Son* 3583 (ix) *b*, (xii) *d*)—not literal, but mystical— must be supposed to have elapsed.

[1] Acts v 15.
[2] Origen *Comm Joann.* xiii. 39 calls the man παραλυτικόν.

(Mark i. 29—34)

JESUS HEALING

if any, was not faith in Jesus as a well-known Healer. It must have been faith called up in a moment by the power of the unknown Person who said to him with an apparent suggestion of reproach for his sluggish inertness "Hast thou a desire to be made whole[1]?"

Such a question as this has no parallel in the Gospels. And, at first sight, it appears to have no parallel in the Hebrew Scriptures. But when we ask what Hebrew corresponds to the Greek "whole" or "sound," and find that it is "life" or "living[2]," we are led back to several passages which exhibit Israel as having, in effect, *no "desire"* for the ways of life, which are the ways of the Lord. Israel needs the Deuteronomic warning "*Choose life*[3]." And the Psalmist asks, "What man is he that *desireth life?*" before prescribing the means of attaining to it[4]. The Petrine Epistle, perhaps blending these words with their context, has "he *that desireth to love life*[5]," an extraordinary phrase which at all events emphasizes the *"desire"* or *"will"* that is required from him that is to walk in the Lord's way. In the Fourth Gospel, it seems probable that the man that lay "thirty-eight years" by the pool, is the type of Israel in the wilderness, for whom a period of "thirty-eight years" is mentioned as being terminated by the passage "over the brook Zered[6]." The man is made "sound" or "living," but he is warned not to "continue in sin" lest a worse

---

[1] Jn v 6 θέλεις ὑγιὴς γενέσθαι Delitzsch gives for θέλεις the same Heb (Gesen 342 b) as that in Ps xxxiv 12 ὁ θέλων ζωήν This is different from the LXX use of θέλω in negative phrases, where LXX *"not willing"* corresponds to Heb *"refusing"*

[2] Ὑγιής is rare in LXX But it represents Heb. adj "living" in Sir xxx 14, as well as in Lev xiii 15—16, and Heb verb "live" in Is xxxviii 21

[3] Deut xxx 19

[4] Ps xxxiv 12 (LXX) Τίς ἐστιν ἄνθρωπος ὁ θέλων ζωήν, followed by ἀγαπῶν ἰδεῖν ἡμέρας ἀγαθάς

[5] I Pet iii 10 ὁ γὰρ "θέλων ζωὴν ἀγαπᾶν καὶ ἰδεῖν ἡμέρας ἀγαθάς."

[6] Deut. ii. 14.

thing befall him. He does not thank Jesus, even when he knows who Jesus is. He gives information about Jesus to His enemies, the Jews, who persecute Him for healing on the sabbath[1]. The outcome of this sign, the giving of "soundness," is by no means a giving of "soundness" to those who witness it. On the contrary, Jesus exclaims to the Jews, "*Ye desire not to come to me that ye may have life*[2]." Far from coming to Him for life, they have begun to seek His death[3].

It may be asked why Jesus selected for healing, out of a multitude of sufferers, this particular man, who apparently proved ungrateful. We are perhaps invited to suppose that Jesus did it in part because He "knew that he had been now a long time" in that pitiable condition[4]. That we can understand—the motive of a special pity. But further, another and a different cause is stated, and more than once, by Jesus Himself. He implies that every such action of the Son corresponds to some vision, received by the Son, of an action of the Father: "The Son is not able to do anything from himself—unless he seeth the Father doing something[5]." This also is the reason given for working the sign on the sabbath.

This explanation of the "inability" of the Son, in certain circumstances, to perform acts of healing, will come before us again when we discuss passages where this inability is asserted by Mark but passed over by one or both of the other Synoptists[6]. Here we shall merely say a word in answer to the obvious objection that this explains nothing, but merely admits that the motives of Jesus are inexplicable as human motives, because they are superhuman. Christ's answer does not of course

---

[1] Jn v. 15—16.   [2] Jn v. 40.   [3] Jn v. 18.
[4] Jn v 6. Not only the duration of the suffering, but the hopeless torpor of the sufferer, a defect of will, may have given cause for special pity.
[5] Jn v 19, comp. *ib.* 30 "I am not able, from myself, to do anything."
[6] See *Introduction* p. 4 foll.

"explain" everything; for who can "explain" the exact relation between even a good man and God, not to speak of the relation between the incarnate Son and the Father? But John's view does explain something. His support of Mark, on this point of inability, is of historical as well as of spiritual importance. It answers a question that might otherwise have perplexed us: "How was it that Jesus is nowhere recorded in the Gospels to have been accused by His enemies of failing in an attempt at exorcism or healing?"

The reply of the Fourth Gospel appears to be: "Although occasionally multitudes at a time received from Jesus healing or assuagement of suffering through His mere presence and their faith, yet those whom He specially chose to heal were few. When He chose this person or that, it was through revelation, or vision, from the Father. He was always giving to the Father His filial *therapeusis, service,* or *attendance,* in all His acts. But sometimes the Father said to the Son '*Serve* me by *serving* this or that sufferer. Give him your *therapeusis,* and, by giving it to him, give it to me' Such are the signs of healing recorded in this Gospel. They were the signs of Him whom Isaiah described as the Suffering Servant. But the multitude did not recognise Him as the Servant. When they followed Jesus 'because they were continually beholding the signs that He was doing on the sick[1],' they did not recognise that all His signs were signs of *service*. To be kings, not to be servants, was their ideal. They sought to 'snatch Him away to make Him a king[2].'"

The conclusion concerning this particular sign is, that it typified what Paul calls the *election* of Israel. On no other occasion did Jesus so conspicuously choose out, or "*elect,*" one

---

[1] Jn vi 2.
[2] Jn vi 15 The preceding words "This is of a truth the prophet that cometh into the world" are to be regarded as a proof, not of spiritual insight, but of spiritual blindness—subjection to conventional terms such as (Jn i. 21) "the prophet," and "he that cometh"

JESUS HEALING

out of many. The man had not besought Jesus. No one had besought in the man's behalf. It was election pure and simple, with no definite reason alleged for it. And the result may be described in Paul's words, "A hardening in part hath befallen Israel[1]." Paul adds "until the fulness of the Gentiles be come in," and "the fulness of the Gentiles" is probably typified in the Fourth Gospel by the healing of the man born blind, for which this sign is at once a preparation and a contrast.

§ 14. *The difference between the Fourth Gospel and the Three*

Summing up the differences between the Synoptic and the Johannine views of Christ's acts of healing, we may say that the Three lay more stress than the Fourth on small details as to the "many" or the "all[2]," and on the number and nature of the diseases healed, and on the consequent glorification of God by the multitude. The Fourth, while not denying all these things, regards them as largely superficial It keeps in view the ideal Shepherd of Ezekiel who does all that the evil shepherds fail to do—who feeds and protects as well as "heals" and "strengthens" the sheep[3]. At the same time it recognises that the sheep, too, have their part to perform. They must "know" the Shepherd's voice and follow where He calls[4]. It is the absence of this knowledge or insight in the flock of Israel that Isaiah deplores. The prophet speaks bitterly as if his own message was destined to "make fat" the heart of the people, "lest they see with their eyes, and hear with their ears, *and understand with their hearts, and turn again, and be healed*[5]." The Three represent Jesus as quoting or

---

[1] Rom xi. 25

[2] "*Many*" would be appropriate to Is. liii. 12 "bare the sins of *many*"; "*all*," to Is liii 6 "*all* we like sheep" and "laid upon him the iniquity of us *all*."

[3] Ezek. xxxiv 4—16.   [4] Jn x 4.

[5] Is vi 9—10 "Go and tell this people...'see ye indeed but perceive not.' Make the heart of this people fat.. ."

alluding to a portion of this prophecy[1]. But Luke omits "*turn again and be healed.*" Mark has "*turn again and be forgiven.*" Matthew, with whom Luke largely agrees so far as concerns the words of Jesus, proceeds to add a quotation of his own from Isaiah (attributing this also to Jesus) in which he gives the prophet's words fully as the LXX gives them, ending with "*lest they should turn again and I should heal them.*" John does a somewhat similar thing in his account of the close of Christ's public teaching, when he states the reasons for the unbelief of the nation as a whole. There he puts forth the startling statement, but not attributing it to Jesus, that "they were not able to believe *because Isaiah said...He hath blinded their eyes...that they might not turn and I should heal them*[2]." But John's preceding and following context indicates that, in his belief, the Jews had prepared the blinding of their own eyes. They had "loved the glory of men rather than the glory of God[3]," and when the greater glory fell upon the eyes that they had habituated only to receive the lesser, they were blinded by the excess of light.

This quotation from Isaiah attributed by Matthew to Jesus, is the only passage in the Gospels where Jesus is represented as using the LXX "heal"; and it is used in the national sense, which is frequent in the prophets but occurs rarely in the Law: "I will put none of the diseases upon thee, which I have put upon the Egyptians; *for I am the Lord that healeth thee*[4]." Jewish tradition takes this primarily as referring to

---

[1] Mk iv 12, Mt xiii 13—15, Lk viii. 10.
[2] Jn xii. 39—40.   [3] Jn xii 43
[4] Exod xv 26 "that healeth thee," ὁ ἰώμενός σε. Jewish tradition regards this as referring to the health that comes (Prov. iii. 8, iv. 22) from the Law, see *Mechilt.* and Rashi *ad loc* In Deut xxx. 3 ἰάσηται Κύριος τὰς ἁμαρτίας σου, the Heb has "turn, or, return to, thy captivity," Jer Targ "accept your repentance," Aq ἐπιστρέψει . τὴν ἐπιστροφήν σου Mk iv 12 ἀφεθῇ αὐτοῖς is a paraphrastic parall. to Mt xiii. 15 ἰάσομαι αὐτούς. This passage of Isaiah is also quoted in Acts xxviii. 27.

the health that comes from the Law. Luke, conspicuously among the writers in the New Testament, uses the word in a literal sense[1]. But in the Acts he takes it in its national and spiritual sense in one important passage where Paul, in his final utterance to the unbelieving Jews, includes the same quotation from Isaiah as that attributed by Matthew to Jesus Himself. There Paul repeats, without paraphrase, the words "*lest I should heal them*[2]."

As regards the order of the quotation, Matthew places it early in his Gospel, in Christ's commentary on the first of His parables, somewhat as Isaiah places it—early in the book of his prophecies, when he is first sent forth on his mission. John in his Gospel, like Luke in the Acts, places it late, as summing up the results of the preaching of the Gospel to the Jews, and as recognising the deplorable and paradoxical result—the rejection of the Chosen People.

For this paradox the Fourth Gospel prepares us in a way in which the Three do not. It represents the faith generated by Christ's signs of healing as being, from the first, superficial. It omits that refrain about "glorifying God" which is' so prominent in Luke's conclusions of stories about miracles[3].

---

[1] Luke uses ἰάομαι in his Gospel 11 times, and always literally. In Acts ix 34, xxviii 8 it is literal In *ib* x 38 ἰώμενος πάντας τοὺς καταδυναστευομένους ὑπὸ τοῦ διαβόλου, it is perhaps spiritual, besides referring to exorcisms and acts of healing In *ib* xxviii 27 Paul quotes Is. vi 10 It occurs only once in Mark (lit), four times in Matthew (3 lit + 1 (quoting Is vi 10) metaph), thrice in John (2 lit.+ 1 (quoting Is vi 10) metaph.). In the rest of N T. it occurs thrice, Heb xii. 3, 1 Pet. ii. 24 (metaph), Jas. v 16 (doubtful)

[2] Acts xxviii 27.

[3] Δοξάζειν τὸν θεόν occurs only once in Mark (ii. 12), twice in Matthew, eight times in Luke (ii 20, v 25, 26, vii 16, xiii 13 etc), once in John (of Peter's death, xxi 19) In connection with a "sign," the phrase "give glory to God" occurs in Jn ix 24 But it means, in effect, "Glorify God by saying that Jesus is an impostor."

It warns us, in the Prologue, that the Light of the World shines in darkness, and teaches, at an early stage, that only those who love the Light can be drawn to the Light. It suggests in narrative after narrative, sentence after sentence, and phrase after phrase, that "health" and "healing" are not externalities to be wrought by amulets or charms, but that they must come to us, if they come at all, from the reception of this Light into our inmost being. Then it shews us how the clouds of darkness and death gather round the Light to suppress His attempts at healing; how they gather strength and power to drive Him out of the world that He came to heal; how all His healing proves, and must prove, a failure for Israel after the flesh, because Israel clings to the bondage of Egypt; and lastly, how nothing is left but that the Light must be hidden for a time, and the Healer Himself must die, so that He may rise again—"the Sun of righteousness, with healing in his wings[1]"

The attitude of the Fourth Gospel toward collective faith-healing may be illustrated from the Appendix to Mark and the First Epistle to the Corinthians. The Appendix gives, as Christ's promise, "These *signs* shall follow them that believe," and then—after enumerating victories over sickness, "devils," "serpents," and "any deadly thing"—it adds that the Eleven "went forth and preached everywhere, the Lord working with them, confirming the word by the signs that followed[2]." The Epistle speaks of "healing" thrice as a "gift," and implies that it was not extended to all believers, asking "Have all gifts of healings[3]?" All admit that the early Christian power of faith-healing rapidly diminished. At the end of the first century it would become a pressing need for Christians to

---

[1] Mal. iv 2.   [2] Mk xvi. 17—20.
[3] 1 Cor. xii. 9, 28, 29.

JESUS HEALING

realise that they must no longer count upon such "signs" as the Mark Appendix mentions, but must depend on that permanent Spirit of which those "signs" had been only a particular and transitory manifestation[1].

---

[1] 1 Cor. xii. 1 foll insists on the unity of the Spirit as compared with "diversities of gifts," e g "to another, gifts of healings, in the one Spirit"

CHAPTER IV*

JESUS GOES FORTH BEFORE DAWN[1]
[Mark i. 35—9]

§ 1. *Why did Matthew omit this?*

IN Mark-Luke, there are only, at the most, five narratives[2] (and those very brief) omitted by Matthew: (1) the exorcism above discussed; (2) the "going forth," now to be considered; (3) the command given to John the son of Zebedee not to "forbid" some who exorcised in Christ's name; (4) the narrative of the widow's mite; (5) the guidance of the disciples by "a man bearing a pitcher of water" on the night of the Last Supper[3].

The first of these (the exorcism) Matthew may well have omitted as being but one of many exorcisms, which he mentions in general terms as occurring about this time[4]; and similarly the second (the "going forth") he may have omitted as not being important enough to come at the outset of the Gospel, or Good Tidings, which, in his view, began more suitably with the Sermon on the Mount. The third ("forbid them not") might be used by "vagabond exorcists[5]" to justify themselves. This is indicated by a tradition peculiar to Matthew, where

---

* For titles of previous Parts of Diatessarica referred to by abbreviations in this volume, see pp 545—6 For other abbreviations see pp. xxiii—xxvi

For notes 1—5, see p 233

JESUS GOES FORTH BEFORE DAWN

exorcists receive a rebuke after appealing to the Lord, saying "In thy name have we not cast out devils[6]?" The fourth ("the widow's mite") may be illustrated by the fact that, where Luke has "Blessed are *ye, the poor*," the parallel Matthew

---

[1] Matthew omits all the Marcan narrative except the last verse —

Mk i. 35—9	Mt iv 23	Lk iv 42—4
(35) And in the morning, a great while before day, he rose up and went out, and departed into a desert place, and there prayed (36) And Simon and they that were with him followed after him, (37) And they found him, and say unto him, All are seeking thee (38) And he saith unto them, Let us go elsewhere into the next towns, that I may preach there also, for to this end came I forth (39) And he went into their synagogues throughout all Galilee, preaching and casting out devils	And Jesus went about in all Galilee, teaching in their synagogues, and preaching the gospel of the kingdom, and healing all manner of disease and all manner of sickness among the people.	(42) And when it was day, he came out and went into a desert place and the multitudes sought after him, and came unto him, and would have stayed him, that he should not go from them (43) But he said unto them, I must preach the good tidings of the kingdom of God to the other cities also for therefore was I sent. (44) And he was preaching in the synagogues of Judaea

In Lk iv 44, R V instead of "Judaea," has "Galilee," but marg "very many ancient authorities read '*Judaea*'" W H has "Judaea" without alternative (s *Beginning* p 209 foll)

[2] "Narratives" There are several instances of Mark-Luke picturesque "*details in a narrative*" (e g Mk v 18—20, 30—33, 35—37) omitted by Matthew, but not of separate "narratives"

[3] See Mk i 23—8, 35—8, ix 38—40, xii 41—4, xiv 13 and parallels in Luke

[4] Mt iv 24

[5] Acts xix 13

[6] Mt vii 22, where contrast the parall. Lk. xiii. 26 "we ate and drank in thy presence."

JESUS GOES FORTH BEFORE DAWN

has "Blessed are *the poor in spirit*[1]." Luke is probably giving the exact words—which happen to suit his own views about literal poverty—while Matthew is deviating from the exact words in order to give their meaning. If so, the same fear of being misunderstood which led Matthew there to add something to "the exact words"—in order to guard against an interpretation of them as praising poverty in itself, and for itself—may have led him here to omit the Marcan story of the Widow. In the fifth instance ("a man bearing a pitcher of water") it is hardly possible to conceive that Matthew can have discerned anything that could cause believers to go wrong. More probably he thought that it was a detail that he might well omit on an occasion so eventful as that of the Last Supper, in order to make room for other traditions of his own, which Mark had not inserted[2].

Returning to the Marcan tradition about Jesus "going forth before dawn" and "departing into a desert place," we may say that Matthew omits it partly because it ended in no definite and important result, and partly because it distracted attention from Jesus as fulfilling a prediction of Isaiah about "*the gospel*" in connection with the words "beautiful *upon the mountains*[3]." It is in accordance with his principle of grouping events that after the first mention of "*the gospel*," and its attraction for the multitude, he should add "and seeing the multitudes, he went up *into the mountain*[4]." These words

---

[1] Lk. vi. 20, Mt. v. 3.

[2] Origen (on Mt. xxvi. 17—18, Lomm iv. 408) interprets this last Marcan narrative allegorically as well as literally The "pitcher" of water prepares the way for the "cup" of the New Covenant; or the Law prepares the way for the Gospel. He doubts whether the water is (1) "mundatoria" or (2) "potabilis."

[3] Is. lii. 7 "How *beautiful upon the mountains* are the feet of him that *bringeth good tidings* (i e. the *gospel*)."

[4] Mt. iv. 23—v. 1 "And Jesus went about...preaching *the gospel*....(25) And there followed him great multitudes from Galilee... and [from] beyond Jordan. (v. 1) And seeing the multitudes, he *went up into the mountain*." The parallel Luke (vi 20) makes no

JESUS GOES FORTH BEFORE DAWN

introduce what we call "the Sermon *on the Mount*"—and rightly, for Matthew intended an emphasis on *"mountain."* After the Sermon, Matthew relates acts of healing, separate and collective And here he expressly quotes Isaiah as having predicted them: "Himself took our infirmities and bare our diseases[1]." He did not quote Isaiah before about "the mountains"; but the two verses in Isaiah are divided by only a short interval, and Matthew probably had both in view. Having before him such an aspect of the beginning of the Gospel of Christ, Matthew might put aside—and reasonably, from his point of view—a Marcan tradition about the exact hour in the very early morning when Jesus went forth on His missionary work from Capernaum.

Besides seeming unimportant in fact, it might seem a little harsh in expression. For when Mark says that "Simon and they that were with him *followed after*" Jesus, he uses a word that mostly means "pursued" in a hostile sense, or "persecuted" On the whole, the question seems to be, not so much why Matthew omitted such a narrative as rather why Mark inserted it. This question we shall now attempt to answer.

§ 2. *Why did Mark insert this?*

It is not enough to say that Mark probably inserted the "going forth before dawn" because it came to him from Petrine sources as a historical Petrine reminiscence of actual fact. That would apply to a multitude of reminiscences. The question is, Why did he, when selecting a very small group out of the multitude, include this in the selected group? Is it because some early poetic traditions recorded it at first as

---

mention of *"mountain."* Luke has (vi. 12) "he went out into the mountain to pray...(vi. 17) he came down with them and stood on a level place"

[1] Mt viii. 1—17, quoting finally Is liii 4, which follows not long after Is lii. 7.

JESUS GOES FORTH BEFORE DAWN

symbolic, and did the record remain when the symbolism was forgotten?

The Bible thrice records concerning Abraham that he "*rose early in the morning.*" On the third of these occasions he was going forth on a journey to sacrifice his son on Mount Moriah[1]. Jewish traditions have preserved the Jewish belief that whatever the hospitable Abraham did for God, when the Three appeared to him, God did in return for Abraham's descendants[2]. Much more might it be expected that what Abraham did for God in sacrificing his own son Isaac, God would, in some way, do again in recompense. Accordingly, when God sent forth His own Son on a journey that was to end in the sacrifice of Himself on Mount Moriah, it was fit (so Christian Jews would think) that He, too, should "rise early in the morning," or even "very early," while, as Mark says, "there was still much of the night."

The Hebrew word *shâcam*, "rise-early," denotes eager readiness, and Mark's paraphrase emphasizes it. But further the "*going forth*" of the Messiah is predicted by Hosea in connection, not only with the "morning" but also with the above-mentioned word "*pursue*" Generally, as we have seen, it implies hostile pursuit, but it does not in Hosea. Both of these expressions occur in a passage that is at the root of Christ's predictions about being "raised up on the third day," reiterated in the Synoptists. "Come, and let us return unto the Lord...

---

[1] Gen xix 27, xxi 14, xxii 3 On שכם "rise-early," see Gesen 1014 *b* In Gen xix 27 "Abraham *rose-early* (R V. gat up early) in the morning to the place where *he had stood* before the Lord," Jewish tradition interpreted "stood" as referring to "prayer" See *From Letter* 944 Mark also represents Jesus as "praying" Abraham's "prayer" had been on the preceding day, but we are perhaps to assume that he repeated it.

[2] See Schottgen ii. 61 quoting *Gen r* and *Numb r* e g. "Dixit R. Eleasar...Quodcunque Abrahamus Angelis ministerialibus praestitit Deus retribuit filiis ejus in exitu ex Ægypto, et dabit quoque temporibus Messiae. Sic de Abrahamo invenitur (Gen. xviii 4)...."

JESUS GOES FORTH BEFORE DAWN

After two days will he revive us, *on the third day he will raise us up*...And let us know, let us *pursue* (R.V *follow on*) to know the Lord *His going forth is sure as the morning*[1]."

If there was an allusion to Hosea, in "pursued him," Luke seems not to have understood it, or else to have perceived that it would not be understood by others At all events he paraphrases it at such length as to shew that it has no hostile meaning. Also there appears to have been some early doubt as to *who* "pursued." Perhaps the original was simply "*those with him*," that is, "with Jesus in Peter's house", but others took it as "the multitude that had previously gathered round Peter's door," or "the household of Peter," or both[2]. Mark appears to have preserved the tradition in its earliest form. It implies that Christ's success as a Faith-healer was felt by Him to be in danger of interfering with the work set before Him, which Mark here calls briefly "preaching," having above called it, more fully, "preaching the gospel of God."

§ 3. *Differences between Mark and Luke, and Johannine illustrations of* (1) "*pursued*," (2) "*let us go*[3]"

(1) Mark's bold statement that Jesus was "pursued" or "chased," softened by Luke, may be illustrated by the words

---

[1] Hos vi 1—3 See *Introduction* p 43 quoting *Paradosis* 1218, 1297, 1306 Delitzsch, in Mk 1 36 "pursued," uses the same Heb word that is in Hos vi 3 It is mostly used (Gesen. 922—3) to mean "pursue as an enemy," "persecute" etc.

[2] For instances where "Peter," or "Simon," is parallel to some different expression, see *Notes* 2999 (xvii) *g*—*h*, comp 2875. Hippolytus, according to a commentary of Bar-Salibi, said (see *Hermas in Arcadia*, Rendel Harris, p. 48) "Christus, postquam baptizatus fuerat, abiit in desertum, et quando inquisitio facta erat de illo per *discipulos Johannis* et per populum, quaerebant eum et non inveniebant eum, quia in deserto erat" This contains perhaps a trace of Jn 1. 37 where Jesus is "followed" by two *disciples of John*—another interpretation of "*they that were with him*"

[3] Mk 1 36, 38 Luke's omission of Mk 1 35 "*and was praying*" can hardly be called a disagreement, in view of Lk. v. 16 "*and praying*" It seems to be rather a transposition than a disagreement.

JESUS GOES FORTH BEFORE DAWN

inserted by John alone, after the Feeding of the Five Thousand, "Jesus, perceiving that they were about to come *and snatch him away*, to make him a king[1]." Mark does not say that here. But, no doubt, some of those Galilaeans who "chased after Jesus" would have liked to "make him a king." In the Fourth Gospel, Nathanael, after a sentence or two had passed between him and Jesus, exclaims "Thou art Israel's King[2]." John may well have felt that Mark's strong word conveyed a historical fact that was not to be ignored —from the beginning, Jesus was "pursued," blindly "followed," by multitudes, with the result that He was soon "pursued," in a different sense, blindly "persecuted," by the Pharisees.

(2) In connection with "let us go," the Greek *agōmen*, meaning "*Let us go [forward]*," has been fully discussed elsewhere. It is used by Epictetus to mean "*Let us go* to the proconsul [that he may judge between us]"; also, being a Hebraized word, it is used in a Jewish fable about the inferior beasts who say "*Let us go* [on a deputation, to his Majesty, the lion][3]" Luke avoids it here Luke also omits it and its context in the narrative of Gethsemane, where Mark and Matthew have "arise, *let us go [forward]* (*agōmen*)[4]." John uses it on the night of the Last Supper, "Arise, *let us go* hence[5]." There it is ambiguous for it might mean "Let us retire from danger." But he has previously used it, just before the raising of Lazarus, where Jesus says "*Let us go* into Judaea again" Judaea was the place where His life had been attempted, and accordingly the disciples remonstrate Jesus repeats "Nevertheless *let us*

---

[1] Jn vi 15 Comp. also Jn 11. 23—4 where the repetition of πιστεύω indicates that Jesus did not reciprocate the "belief" of those who "believed on his name, beholding his signs which he did " He "did not trust himself to them "

[2] Jn 1. 49.
[3] *Paradosis* 1372—7
[4] Mk xiv 42, Mt xxvi 46, om. by Lk xxii. 46 foll.
[5] Jn xiv. 31.

JESUS GOES FORTH BEFORE DAWN

go unto him." Thomas then exclaims: *"Let us go*—us also, that we may die with him[1]."

John's threefold repetition of *agōmen* before the raising of Lazarus throws light on his single ambiguous use of it before the Passion. It shews that on both occasions he means by it *"go forth to meet danger,"* and, at the same time, *"go forth to the performance of an appointed duty."* Perhaps Luke omitted it because he thought that *"Go ye,"* rather than *"Let us go,"* suited the dignity of the Messiah. But Hosea combines the two in saying *"Come ye, and let us* return unto the Lord," and Micah declares that this shall be the cry of many nations, *"Come ye and let us go up* to the mountain of the Lord[2]." According to Mark, Jesus had previously uttered the *"Come ye!"* to Peter and Andrew[3]. Now He adds, what might mean in effect, "Let us go up to the mountain of the Lord," that is to say, "Let us go up to the establishment of the New Temple of the Lord, not made with hands." The context in Hosea contains the words "On the third day he will raise us up." Rashi paraphrases this as meaning "By the building of a third temple He will revive us" Thus the drift of Mark—both here, and above, in the Call of the Fishermen—leads us to think that Jesus is already contemplating probably a literal, but certainly a spiritual, "going up"—not a mere circuit of missionary journeyings and synagogue-discourses diversified with instances of faith-healing, but some kind of active appeal to the Father, some intention to bring matters to a crisis by staking life on the issue of a journey to Jerusalem, knowing it to be the Father's will that His Kingdom should speedily come, and His spiritual Temple rise anew in Israel.

---

[1] Jn xi. 7, 15, 16.
[2] Hos vi. 1, Mic. iv 2
[3] See above, p 47 foll., on δεῦτε. In Mic iv. 2 "come ye" is δεῦτε

JESUS GOES FORTH BEFORE DAWN

§ 4. *"Elsewhere into the next towns" (Mark), "to the other cities also" (Luke)*[1]

Mark's word for "towns" is unique here in the Greek Bible, and hardly occurrent elsewhere except in Strabo[2]. There the word means towns not worthy to be called cities; but the meaning in Mark is not so simple. Even if it could be explained here as meaning "towns superior to villages in that they possessed synagogues" (as *Horae Hebraicae* suggests) the question arises, "How are we to explain Mark's non-use of the term later on among the many instances where he speaks of 'villages,' 'cities,' etc.[3]?" Codex D and several Latin and

---

[1] Mk 1. 38 ἀλλαχοῦ εἰς τὰς ἐχομένας κωμοπόλεις, Lk. iv. 43 καὶ ταῖς ἑτέραις πόλεσιν. In Mark, ἀλλαχοῦ is omitted by most versions and MSS but inserted by the best Greek MSS. It occurs nowhere else in N T or LXX. In the early Apologists and Fathers it occurs only in Justin Martyr, once with ἄλλοι (*Apol* § 24) and thrice with a quotation ("[he says] *in another place*," *Apol* § 37 (bis), *Tryph* § 122). Delitzsch renders it by the Heb "*from this [place]*" (=LXX ἐντεῦθεν), as also he renders ἐντεῦθεν in Jn xiv. 31 ἄγωμεν ἐντεῦθεν, "let us go *hence*."

[2] See Strabo 537, 557, 568, 594. Swete (on Mk 1. 38) refers to Joseph *Ant* xi. 86, but it is not in Niese's xi. 86, and Niese gives πόλεις without v. r. in *Ant.* xi. 8. 6 ταῦτα διοικησάμενος ἐν τοῖς Ἱεροσολύμοις ἐξεστράτευσεν ἐπὶ τὰς ἐχομένας πόλεις. *Hor Heb* (on Mk 1. 38) recognises (1) cities girt with walls, places of trade, and populous (*kerach*), (2) villages, or country towns, without walls and without a synagogue (*caphar*), (3) "cities" in an inclusive sense, including places fortified and not fortified, with synagogues and without (*îr*). By κωμοπόλεις *Hor Heb.* understands here cities belonging to the third class, i e "towns where there were synagogues, which nevertheless were not either fortified or towns of trade."

[3] See (1) Mk vi. 6 περιῆγεν τὰς κώμας κύκλῳ (sim Mt. ix. 35 τὰς πόλεις πάσας καὶ τὰς κώμας), Lk. xiii. 22 κατὰ πόλεις κ. κώμας κ. πορείαν ποιούμενος εἰς Ἱεροσ , where Mark describes a *circuit*, but Luke a *journey to Jerusalem*; (2) Mk vi. 36 τοὺς κύκλῳ ἀγροὺς κ. κώμας (Mt xiv. 15 τὰς κώμας), Lk. ix. 12 τὰς κύκλῳ κώμας κ. ἀγρούς; (3) in Mk vi. 56 (Mt om , Lk om.) ὅπου. εἰς κώμας ἢ εἰς πόλεις ἢ εἰς ἀγρούς, ἐν ταῖς ἀγοραῖς ἐτίθεσαν, SS has "cities, or villages, or farmsteads, in the streets," D ἀγρούς before πόλεις and πλατείαις for ἀγοραῖς;

JESUS GOES FORTH BEFORE DAWN

Syriac versions have "villages" and "cities" separately; but that is so natural as a correction that it cannot be accepted as likely to be the original text. We are led therefore to ask whether the word may have had in the first or second century some technical sense in this particular passage which it has not elsewhere. Aquila and Theodotion are said on good authority to have used the word in connection with *towns near Jerusalem*[1]. Now if Mark's original meant "the towns and villages *near* [*the Great*] *City*," i e. *Jerusalem*, or at least was thus interpreted by Luke, this would accord with the following words in the correct text of Luke, "And he was preaching in the synagogues of *Judaea*," that is to say, *in those towns, round about the Metropolis, which were large enough to have synagogues*[2].

---

(4) Mk viii 23—6 sing ἡ κωμή (pec), (5) viii 27 τὰς κώμας Καισαρείας, Mt xvi 13 τὰ μέρη Καισαρείας (Lk ix 18 προσευχόμενον κατὰ μόνας) Luke mentions Jerusalem or Judaea in connection with κώμη or πόλις in iv 43—4 (where Mk i. 38 does not) (see *Beginning* p 209 foll), and xiii 22 (where Mk vi 6 does not) He also has, in describing a journey to Jerusalem, ix 51—2 (pec) τοῦ πορεύεσθαι εἰς Ἱερ ...εἰς κώμην Σαμαρειτῶν, ib ix 56 (pec.) εἰς ἑτέραν κώμην In Lk v. 17, ἐκ πάσης κώμης τῆς Γαλιλαίας καὶ Ἰουδαίας καὶ Ἱερουσαλήμ appears to mean "out of every village of Galilee and [every village of] Judaea and [out of] Jerusalem," the Great City being contrasted with every other place (called relatively "village")

[1] Josh xviii 28 "Zelah, Eleph, and the Jebusite (the same is Jerusalem), Gibeath [and] Kiriath—cities fourteen with their villages " Field attributes to Aq and Theod. κωμόπολις in this passage, and he refers to "Mk i 38 in versione Philox " The Syr. of Aq and Theod is literally "villages of the City." The LXX (B) has certainly transliterated "cities" as Jarim It has also probably taken *Kiriath* (out of place) as being another word for "cities" and has transposed it—the result being "and cities and Gabaoth, Jarim, cities thirteen and their villages " A has "and Gabaath (*sic*) and city Jarim cities thirteen and their villages "

[2] Lk iv 44 καὶ ἦν κηρύσσων εἰς τὰς συναγωγὰς τῆς Ἰουδαίας. It is worth noting that Mark's epithet ἐχομένας is applied to the cities near Jerusalem in Joseph. *Ant* xi 8 6 τὰς ἐχομένας πόλεις "the adjacent cities" (after a mention of "Jerusalem").

It would also enable us to give a literal sense to the words "O Jerusalem, Jerusalem,...*how often have I desired to gather thy children*...and ye would not[1]!"

If on the other hand Jesus meant, by "the next village-towns," the towns adjacent to Capernaum, then the following words, "to this [end] came I forth," would seem to mean "To this [end] I came forth out of Peter's house in Capernaum in order to preach to the village-towns near Capernaum." But is this likely to have been a saying of the Messiah that would be selected for permanent record? Instead of "*I came forth*," Luke has "*I was sent*," apparently taking "I came forth" to mean "I came forth from the Father." The "coming-forth" will be discussed in the next section. Meantime, however, we may say that Luke's view of it appears to suit the context. And if the verb is to be interpreted, as Luke interprets it, with this weighty significance, then the contextual noun, "village-cities," would also seem to require more weight than could attach to "the towns round about Capernaum." And it would receive this weight if it meant "the villages, or towns, round the City," that is, round Jerusalem.

It was natural for Jews, even for Christian Jews, to regard Jerusalem, and the "circle" round it, as being the centre of the spiritual world, the starting-place of the Gospel[2]. Christian Jews would also exult in traditions about the measuring of the

---

[1] Mt. xxiii. 37, Lk. xiii. 34. Origen and Jerome (*ad loc.* Matth.) explain this as referring to the pre-incarnate Christ preaching through "omnes prophetas." This is a difficult hypothesis. It would be easier to suppose that Jesus uttered these words as the saying of the Wisdom of God. But if Luke and John are right in saying that Jesus preached often near Jerusalem the words may also refer to His preaching in a literal sense

[2] See *Beginning* p. 208 foll. It is probable that this thought is latent in Rom. xv. 19 punctuated thus, "*from* Jerusalem and round about—even unto Illyricum." Paul did not preach *in* Jerusalem and its circle. But he would regard it as the centre and source *from* which was to issue the Gospel which (Lk xxiv 47) was to be preached "to all nations beginning *from* Jerusalem."

new and enlarged Jerusalem, concerning which Zechariah had predicted that by reason of the influx of citizens it would be "inhabited as villages without walls[1]." It is a mistake to suppose that all the countrymen of Ezekiel lost, after Ezekiel's time, every vestige of the vision of a spiritual and personified Temple. A tradition taught in the name of R. Jochanan says "There are three that are named after the Name of the Holy One (blessed be He!)—the Saints, the Messiah, and Jerusalem[2]." To accomplish Ezekiel's vision was assuredly Christ's purpose—whether expressed, or not, in words—from the beginning of His Gospel. No doubt some Jews of Essene tendencies, and perhaps John the Baptist, held aloof from the material Temple. But Jesus did not. There is very much to be said for Luke's tradition here, that at an early period Jesus paid a visit to Judaea which Mark has erroneously taken to be a visit to Galilee. And, if Jesus did this, we are led on to a further inference that He may have paid an early visit to Jerusalem, recorded neither by Mark nor by Luke, but by John alone.

§ 5. *"To this [end] came I forth" (Mark), "Toward this [end] was I sent" (Luke)*[3]

Luke makes it clear that the "coming forth" was not merely a coming forth from Peter's house. It was Christ's coming forth out of private life to public work, the preaching of the Gospel, to which He had been sent by God. "Sent," then, is the term preferred here by Luke to the Marcan "came." All the Synoptists elsewhere describe Jesus as saying "He that sent me[4]." John does this more frequently than any of

---

[1] Zech 11 4.
[2] *Baba Bathra* 75 b. And see *The Yalkut of Zechariah* by E. G. King, Cambridge, 1882, p. 6 foll.
[3] Mk 1 38, Lk iv. 43.
[4] Mk ix. 37, Mt x. 40, Lk. ix. 48, x. 16 ($\dot{a}\pi o\sigma\tau\epsilon\lambda\lambda\omega$).

them¹. We might therefore argue that "John would see no reason to take up this Marcan phrase 'came forth,' since it is better expressed by 'sent.'"

But is that the case? Is there not something better in "going forth," if rightly qualified, as it is in Hosea, who says "His *going forth* is sure as the morning, and he shall come unto us as the rain²"? Micah also speaks, in a double sense, of the "*going forth*" of the "ruler in Israel," who shall be Israel's "peace"; who is to "*go forth*" unto God from "Bethlehem Ephrathah," and "whose *goings forth* are from of old from everlasting³." The Hebrew "*going forth*," or "*coming forth*," is applied to the blessings that God, through Nature, is regarded as giving with a special spontaneousness, as well as to what we call more particularly "offspring." This spontaneousness is better expressed by "*I came forth* from God" than by "I was *sent* from God." Accordingly John uses the former as well as the latter He introduces John the Baptist as "a man *sent* from God⁴." But he represents Jesus as saying concerning Himself—when claiming to be loved as God's offspring and therefore like God—"If God were your Father ye would love me, for I *came forth* [as offspring] and am come [to you] from God⁵."

---

¹ Jn iv 34, v 24 etc John uses both πέμπω and ἀποστέλλω (*Joh Voc* 1723 *d—g*)

² Hos vi. 3.

³ Mic. v 2, 5 There is perhaps irony in Jn vii. 42, where the writer puts into the mouth of the Pharisees the question "Hath not the scripture said that the Christ *cometh* (Delitzsch *goeth forth*) of the seed of David and from Bethlehem, the village where David was?" The speakers take one half of the prophecy, "Bethlehem"; but not the other, "from everlasting."

⁴ Jn i 6.

⁵ Jn viii 42. On ἐξέρχομαι with ἐκ, παρά, and ἀπό before πατρός in Jn xvi 27, 28, 30 see *Joh Gr* 2326—7. But perhaps ἀπό should be explained as denoting inadequate understanding in the disciples, as in Nicodemus, who says (Jn iii 2) οἴδαμεν ὅτι ἀπὸ θεοῦ ἐλήλυθας διδάσκαλος

JESUS GOES FORTH BEFORE DAWN

A glance at the word "go forth" in a Hebrew Lexicon will shew that the verb and noun together denote the "going forth," or "utterance," from the mouth, as well as the "dayspring" of dawn, and "springs" of water, and the "coming forth" of the prisoner to freedom, and of that which is hidden to the light[1]. This accords with the tone of the Fourth Gospel, which, while it regards the Word as a Person, yet never ceases to regard its influence as being, in a certain sense, impersonal, that is to say, working as the forces of Nature work, in many forms and through various channels, a "going forth" of goodness from the Father through the Son[2].

---

[1] Gesen. 422—5.
[2] See *Beginning* p. 211 n "The first O.T 'coming forth' describes (Gen. 11. 10) the River, which (Philo 1 250, 690) waters the world 'with four virtues'"

CHAPTER V*

THE HEALING OF A LEPER[1]
[Mark i. 40—45]

§ 1. *The prominence of this miracle*

This miracle is placed by Matthew first in the list of separate miracles and immediately after the Sermon on the Mount.

---

* For titles of previous Parts of Diatessarica referred to by abbreviations in this Volume, see pp. 545—6. For other abbreviations see pp. xxiii—xxvi.

[1] Mk i. 40—45 (R.V.)

(40) And there cometh to him a leper, beseeching him, and kneeling down to him, and saying unto him, If thou wilt, thou canst make me clean.
(41) And being moved with compassion, he stretched forth his hand, and touched him, and saith unto him, I will, be thou made clean
(42) And straightway the leprosy departed from him, and he was made clean
(43) And he strictly (*or*, sternly) charged him, and straightway sent him

Mt viii 1—4 (R V.)

(1) And when he was come down from the mountain, great multitudes followed him.
(2) And behold, there came to him a leper and worshipped him, saying, Lord, if thou wilt, thou canst make me clean
(3) And he stretched forth his hand, and touched him, saying, I will; be thou made clean And straightway his leprosy was cleansed
(4) And Jesus saith unto him, See thou tell no man; but go thy way, shew thyself to the priest, and offer the

Lk. v 12—16 (R V)

(12) And it came to pass, while he was in one of the cities, behold, a man full of leprosy. and when he saw Jesus, he fell on his face, and besought him, saying, Lord, if thou wilt, thou canst make me clean
(13) And he stretched forth his hand, and touched him, saying, I will; be thou made clean. And straightway the leprosy departed from him.
(14) And he charged him to tell no man: but go thy way, and shew thyself to the priest,

THE HEALING OF A LEPER

Epictetus seems to allude sarcastically to a phrase in it, "[*My*] *lord, if thou wilt,*" when he bids his pupils not to "fawn on" their physician, not to be frightened as to what he may pronounce about them, and not to be delighted to excess if he says "*You are getting on nicely.*" In particular, they are not to say to him "*If thou wilt,* [*my*] *lord, I shall do well*[1]." It is perhaps not a casual coincidence that, in the Healing of the Nobleman's Son—the only narrative where John introduces a petition for healing—he has a form of the phrase "*get on nicely,*" as well as the respectful appellation "*my lord*[2]." The narrative of John differentiates Jesus from the ordinary physician, while at the same time not attributing to the petitioner the phrase "*if thou wilt.*" The Johannine view of the Son's acts of

Mk 1 40—45 (R V) (*contd*)	Mt viii 1—4 (R V) (*contd*)	Lk v 12—16 (R V) (*contd*)
out, and saith unto him, (44) See thou say nothing to any man but go thy way, shew thyself to the priest, and offer for thy cleansing the things which Moses commanded, for a testimony unto them. (45) But he went out, and began to publish it much, and to spread abroad the matter (*lit* word), insomuch that Jesus could no more openly enter into a (*or,* the) city, but was without in desert places and they came to him from every quarter	gift that Moses commanded, for a testimony unto them.	and offer for thy cleansing, according as Moses commanded, for a testimony unto them (15) But so much the more went abroad the report concerning him · and great multitudes came together to hear, and to be healed of their infirmities. (16) But he withdrew himself in the deserts, and prayed

[1] Epict iii 10. 13—14 "Thou" is emphatic, ἐὰν σὺ θέλῃς, κύριε, καλῶς ἕξω

[2] Jn iv 52 "he inquired of them the hour at which he (*lit*) got on more nicely (κομψότερον ἔσχεν)," comp Epict iii. 10. 13 κομψῶς ἔχεις. No form of κομψός occurs elsewhere in the whole of the Greek Testament.

THE HEALING OF A LEPER

healing is that they depend rather on the insight, than on the will, of the Son : "The Son is able to do nothing of himself but what he seeth the Father doing." When He "sees" a work of this kind, He wills it. But the will depends on the "seeing[1]."

Epictetus, too, lays stress on insight in the business of moral healing. The moral Healer, he would say—meaning the Philosopher, God's servant—would go about, like a physician on his rounds feeling men's pulses and telling this man and that "You have this disease and you that, you must do this or that[2]." But in all this there is little or no mention made of sympathy, compassion, or love. If the patient passionately appeals for deliverance from the memories of unalterable evildoing, and from the haunting consciousness of sin, Epictetus replies, in effect, "Therein the patient must minister to himself[3]." The insight of Jesus is a sympathetic insight. It sees into, and lovingly sympathizes with, the sins and sorrows of men, and it sees into, and lovingly accords with, the desire of God, in this case and in that, to intervene in a special way so that the disease may be healed by the love and compassion of the Father passing through the Son.

Now in the Marcan narrative of the Healing of the Leper the reader will notice that Mark alone says that Jesus "strictly charged," or, according to the margin, "sternly charged," the man whom he had healed. Matthew and Luke omit this. And it is not surprising, since Greeks would naturally take the meaning of the phrase to be "He bellowed at him, or, roared at him[4]." There are few parallel passages in the Synoptists as to which we can be quite so certain as here that Mark has preserved a very early and difficult tradition, softened down by the later Evangelists, and consequently constituting a good test of the rule of Johannine Intervention.

---

[1] See *Introduction* p 5 quoting Jn v. 19, comp above, p 225
[2] Epictet. iii 22. 72—3.   [3] *Macbeth* v. 3 45.
[4] *Joh. Voc.* 1811 a—c

THE HEALING OF A LEPER

John, though he nowhere mentions "leper" or "leprosy," does use this particular word to describe an utterance of Jesus, and that twice, in the Raising of Lazarus. We shall presently consider the meaning of it both in Mark and in John, and John's motive in using it. But first let us note those special and pathetic circumstances in the disease which might naturally draw forth from Jesus some special manifestation of His feelings in the act of touching the leper "The leper," said the Law, "shall dwell alone" He was to cry "unclean, unclean," to warn people from approaching him.

Marcion, condemning the whole of the Law as alien from the will of the Good God, the Father of love and pity, would condemn especially this Law of Leprosy It is in connection with the healing of the leper that Tertullian first mentions what seems to have been an habitual phrase of Marcion's to describe the fate that in this world awaits Christ's faithful follower; he is to be Christ's "partner in suffering," Christ's "partner in being hated[1]." Is not the leper the type of such a character?

---

[1] Tertull. *Adv Marc* iv 9 "Sed quoniam attentius argumentatur apud illum suum nescio quem συνταλαίπωρον (id est, *commiseronem*) et συμμισούμενον (id est, *coodibilem*) in leprosi purgationem...." Comp iv 36 "Age, Marcion, omnesque jam *commiserones et coodibiles* ejus haeretici, quid audebitis dicere?"
By ὁ συμμισούμενος Marcion meant the typical Christian, who, if faithful, must be "*hated in partnership* [*with his Lord*]" Comp. Jn xv. 18 foll. "if the world *hateth* (μισεῖ) *you*...it hath *hated me* before you" This is expressed by Luke, but not (verbally at least) by the parall Matthew in —

Mt v 11	Lk. vi 22
Blessed are ye when they shall revile you and persecute [you]...for my sake.	Blessed are ye when men shall *hate* you, and separate you from [themselves], and revile [you]...for the Son of man's sake

Marcion, however, really combines Luke's word, "*hate*," with the sense of Matthew's "*persecute*" For ταλαιπωρέω in LXX is used (thrice) transitively, meaning "oppress," "despoil" (as well as intransitively). Perhaps also the saying of Oedipus at Colonus

THE HEALING OF A LEPER

Aquila and Symmachus give "leprous," for "stricken," in Isaiah's description of the Suffering Servant[1]. The Talmud also gives "leper" as one of the Messiah's names[2]. The leper, more than any other diseased person, might call forth from Jesus not only compassion for the sufferer but also some kind of protest that this particular disease was more than a mere physical evil—an evil that had power to break the bonds of brotherhood and to convert a living and loveable being into a semi-living unloved one. Such a sufferer, shut up in the tomb of his solitude, might be described, with no great hyperbole, as "dead." The Messiah, when releasing him, might be regarded as feeling something like a personal denunciation of such an evil, as being an enemy of mankind[3]. Ephrem Syrus concludes one of several comments on the healing of the leper with the words "But note that Christ was *angry, not with him, but with the leprosy*[4]." Correct or not, this is an intelligible view. But the discussion of it will come more appropriately in the next section.

(1 1136) was in Marcion's mind, "Of mortal men, those only who have had experience are able to *be partners in these sufferings* (συνταλαιπωρεῖν τάδε)" Marcion regards the Son of Man as the Hated, the Persecuted, and his readers as sufferers with Him (comp. Rom. viii 17 "*joint-heirs* with Christ, that is, if we *are-partners-in-suffering* with [him] (εἴπερ συνπάσχομεν) that we may be also *partners-in-glory* with [him] (ἵνα καὶ συνδοξασθῶμεν) "

[1] See *Notes* 2995, and Is liii 4 (Field), also above, p 191, n 2
[2] See *Sanhedr.* 98 b
[3] Comp. 1 Cor. xv 55 "O death, where is thy victory?" quoting freely from Hos xiii 14 (LXX), where the Hebrew, too, as interpreted by R.V, contains a similar denunciation Hosea, according to this interpretation, describes first (xiii 1) how Ephraim "*died*," and then how the Lord said, concerning Ephraim's children, (*ib* 14) "I will ransom them from the hand of Sheol. *O death, where are thy plagues?*" There are objections to this in the following context; but, if *ib* 15—16 can be regarded as an abrupt insertion, the interpretation (though not like the rabbinical one) appears at all events consistent.
[4] Ephrem Syrus, p. 145.

THE HEALING OF A LEPER

§ 2. (R.V.) "*Strictly* (or, *sternly*) *charged*," in *Mark*[1]

A collection of instances of the Greek word rendered "strictly charged" shews that its regular meaning was "roar," "bellow," "murmur," etc.[2] In Matthew's two accounts of the healing of blindness, of which the first is peculiar to Matthew while the second corresponds to the Marcan healing of Bartimaeus, Matthew has "roared" in the first, but "had compassion" in the second[3]. This is note-worthy because, in the Marcan Healing of the Leper, "*had compassion*" precedes "*strictly-charged*," and Matthew and Luke omit both words In Mark, instead of "*had compassion*," several authorities have "*was angered*[4]." The same Syriac verb, in different forms, has both meanings[5]. This deserves all the more attention because Mark, besides using the rare word "strictly-charge[6]," is also introducing us to a new verb in the Greek language, namely, "have-bowels" in the sense of "have-compassion." It is not alleged to occur

---

[1] Mk 1 43 [2] *Joh Voc* 1811 a—c

[3] Mt ix 30 καὶ ἐνεβριμήθη αὐτοῖς Matthew's parall (xx 34) to the story of Bartimaeus (Mk x. 52, Lk. xviii. 42), has σπαγχνισθείς, which does not occur in Mk-Lk's narrative

[4] *Son* 3163 a. In Mk 1 41, D has ὀργισθείς, a and Corb "iratus" (b om)

[5] See Nestle referring to *Thes Syr* 3953 Ephrem Syrus (p 144) mentions "anger" repeatedly in his comment, and compassion only once "Dominus duo ..ostendit, reprehensionem cum ei irasceretur, et misericordiam cum eum sanaret," which seems to mean that compassion was only *implied in the act, not mentioned by Mark* (according to Ephrem's interpretation)

[6] It occurs but once in the LXX, namely Dan xi 30, R V "he shall be *grieved*" (Gesen 456b "shall be *cowed* (כאה)"), LXX ἐξώσουσιν αὐτὸν καὶ ἐμβριμήσονται αὐτῷ, Theod ταπεινωθήσεται The meaning "shall be *cowed*," is paraphrased by LXX as "they [i e. the Romans] shall *drive out* the invader and shall *threaten* (lit *bully*) *him*" It will be noted that Mk 1 43 (lit.) "having *roared against him* he *drove him out*" contains a similar combination The Heb כאה occurs thrice and is not so common as the word זעם rendered by Theod. ἐμβρίμησις in Is. xxx. 27

before Mark's Gospel. Lightfoot speaks of it as perhaps invented by "the Greek dispersion[1]" We are therefore led to ask what Hebrew or Jewish traditions were likely to be in the mind of Peter, or Mark's other authorities, concerning the "bowels" or "compassion" of God, of such a nature that they might be interpreted in the two senses above mentioned :— (1) "roaring" etc., (2) "having compassion"

§ 3 God "having-compassion" on "Rachel's children," in Jeremiah

The "bowels of God" is a conception implied by Jeremiah in a passage where he describes the Lord as unable to restrain His compassion for Ephraim the grandson of Rachel—in spite of his frequent rebellions. When Ephraim once more repents and when Rachel appears, "weeping for her children," God exclaims "As often as I speak against him, I do earnestly remember him still ; therefore *my bowels do sound for him ; pitying will I pity him*[2]." The Hebrew verb here rendered "*sound*" is rendered by Gesenius "*murmur*," "*growl*," "*roar*," "*be boisterous*," and "*groan*[3]." When it has "*bowels*" as subject, it is said to express "the *thrill* of deep-felt compassion or sympathy," followed by the dative of the "person pitied." The LXX has completely missed the meaning. Aquila has "my belly *sounded*" or "my entrails *were shaken*." Symmachus has "my inner parts *were troubled*." It is easy to understand that these expressions would repel many educated Greeks. If Jeremiah's phrase was in Mark's original, Mark's "had compassion" would very fairly express it. But it might be

---

[1] Lightf. on Phil 1 8 Σπλαγχνίζομαι does not occur in the early Apologists and Fathers except Hermas (8 times), 2 Clem (1).

[2] Jerem. xxxi. 20. LXX, for "my bowels do sound," has simply ἔσπευσα, "I hastened," Aq. ἤχησεν ἡ κοιλία μου, aliter ἐσείσθη τὰ ἔντερά μου, Sym. ἐταράχθη τὰ ἐντός μου

[3] Gesen. 242 *a*, המה.

THE HEALING OF A LEPER

interpreted as meaning "*was angry*." We know from Matthew how prominent among Christians was the thought of Rachel weeping for her children. It would be especially prominent among Jewish Christians. It is true that this passage of Jeremiah is seldom if ever quoted by the Talmud. But it is abundantly quoted in the Midrash, which appears to regard God as being (like Joseph in the presence of his brethren) hardly able to restrain His own yearnings of compassion for the sorrows of Rachel weeping for her offspring[1].

A similar thought is expressed by Isaiah where, after saying, concerning God and the affliction of Israel, that in old times, "in all their affliction, he was afflicted[2]," the prophet introduces Israel as expostulating with God on His change of feeling: "*The sounding of thy bowels* and thy compassions are restrained toward me[3]." Here Rashi illustrates the "*restraining*" from Genesis, where it is said about Joseph that "his bowels did yearn upon his brother, and he sought where to weep," and, after weeping, he "restrained himself[4]." The scene, and the thought to which we are introduced by these traditions about the weeping of Rachel and the weeping of Joseph, somewhat resemble the scene of the Raising of Lazarus in the Fourth Gospel where Jesus "wept" in response to the weeping of Mary. It will now be shewn that in that narrative there occurs this rare word above rendered "strictly-charge." It is used by John to mean some very deep emotion such as would accompany "weeping."

---

[1] See Rashi *ad loc*., who gives an imaginary dialogue between Rachel and God. Rashi does not here comment on the "sounding" of the "bowels." But Is. lxiii. 15 "the sounding of thy bowels" is illustrated by him from Jerem. xxxi. 20.

[2] Is. lxiii. 9.

[3] Is. lxiii. 15. The LXX has πλῆθος, taking the word in its sense of "noisy throng," "boisterous multitude."

[4] Gen. xliii. 30—31.

THE HEALING OF A LEPER

§ 4 (R.V.) *"Groaned* (or, *was moved with indignation)," in John*[1]

In earlier volumes of Diatessarica the reader will find some notice of the textual variations in this passage, of the renderings of the word under consideration by the different versions, and of the uses of the word (or of forms of it) by the Greek translators of O.T (as distinguished from LXX)[2]. Here we shall assume that John could not but know that Mark (and also a passage in Matthew) had applied the word to Jesus; and that its ordinary meaning suggested "roaring against," "bullying," "angry denunciation," "violent excitement."

Opponents of Christianity, and especially those who favoured a popularised form of Stoicism like that of Epictetus, would naturally attack the Christian ideal of a Healer who (they might say) "roared at those whom he healed." In answer to such objections John says here, in effect, "I do not deny the *action*—what may be called the 'roaring.' But I do deny the object or motive. I will take Mark's very word, though it is not one that I should have chosen, and I will shew by the context that what the Psalmist calls 'roaring by reason of disquietness of heart[3],' was, in the case of the Saviour, not a 'disquietness' for Himself, but for others, whom He came to

---

[1] Jn xi 33 (R.V.) "*he groaned* (marg *was moved with indignation*) in the spirit (ἐνεβριμήσατο τῷ πνεύματι) and was troubled (*marg. Gr.* troubled himself) (ἐτάραξεν ἑαυτόν)," *ib.* 38 (R V.) "Jesus therefore again *groaning* (marg. *being moved with indignation*) in himself (ἐμβριμώμενος ἐν ἑαυτῷ)." Ἐτάραξεν ἑαυτόν, differing altogether from the middle ἐταράξατο, necessitates, as the literal rendering, "troubled himself." It seems deliberately intended to be distinguished from "suffered trouble."

[2] Ἐμβριμάομαι. It is differently rendered by SS (see Burkitt), Palest., Walton (Syr) and Delitzsch. The Latin versions agree in "fremuit" or "infremuit." The LXX, besides the above-quoted Dan xi 30 ἐμβριμήσονται αὐτῷ, has a noun-form in Lam. ii. 6 ἐμβρίμημα See *Joh Voc.* 1713 *e*, 1811 *a—c*, and Index, also *Son* 3163 *a*, 3545—7.

[3] Ps. xxxviii. 8.

THE HEALING OF A LEPER

save. In the Raising of Lazarus it will be perceived that the inarticulate sound that issued from Jesus on that occasion was not directed against men, nor caused by anger against men. I do not venture to explain it wholly. But I know that it was caused in part by sorrow, a sorrow that constrained even the Lord Jesus to weep."

Chrysostom, in his comment on these Johannine phrases, declares that John has supplied here—"by the mourning [of Jesus]"—something like what the Synoptists have inserted (but John himself has omitted) in the scene of the Agony in Gethsemane[1]. Probably this is true. But that explanation is inadequate. Something is needed to explain why John, when "supplying" a detail corresponding to the Agony in Gethsemane, introduced such a word as "roaring"—a word confessedly most difficult and (so to speak) scandal-causing. And a good explanation is furnished by the hypothesis that here, as elsewhere, John deliberately uses a word employed by Mark, but rejected by Luke, to express some very strong emotion occasionally manifested by Christ when healing disease.

There appears also something deliberate in the Johannine use of "the spirit" in connection with the first mention of the "roaring." Does it mean "roared *in the spirit*" or "roared *against the spirit*"? "Against" would naturally be the meaning of any ordinary dative after "roared against," as elsewhere[2]. But, with such a word as "spirit," the dative may mean "in," as in the Marcan tradition that Jesus "sighed (or, groaned) deeply *in* his spirit[3]." In Chrysostom's comment,

---

[1] (Migne *ad loc.*) οὐδὲν γοῦν περὶ τοῦ θανάτου τοιοῦτον εἶπεν οἷον οἱ λοιποὶ ὅτι (Mk xiv. 34, Mt. xxvi. 38) περίλυπος γέγονεν, ὅτι (Lk. xxii. 44) ἐναγώνιος. He adds τὸ γοῦν ἐλλειφθὲν ἐκεῖ ἀνεπλήρωσεν ἐνταῦθα διὰ τοῦ πένθους

[2] Mk i. 43, xiv. 5, Mt. ix 30, Is. xvii 13 (Sym.).

[3] Mk viii 12 ἀναστενάξας τῷ πνεύματι αὐτοῦ, comp Lk. x. 21 ἠγαλλιάσατο τῷ πνεύματι τῷ ἁγίῳ, R V. txt "*in* the Holy Spirit," where however Tisch. inserts ἐν, and R.V. marg. has "*by* the Holy Spirit."

255 (Mark i. 40—45)

THE HEALING OF A LEPER

"*in* the spirit" does not occur here or in the context. He says that the phrase means "*He rebuked the passion* [*of sorrow*]"— and this, as to both verses, making no distinction between the phrase that contains "*spirit*" and the phrase that contains "*in himself*[1]" Chrysostom seems to mean, by "spirit," the human spirit of Jesus roused to an extremity of sorrow by passionate affection and sympathy with the sorrow of those around Him; this "spirit" he paraphrases as "passion" and describes as "rebuked"

On the other hand Nonnus, with whom Chrysostom often agrees, drops altogether the notion of "rebuking" in one or both of the passages: (1) "He, *being-shaken by the Spirit* of the Father, cried out, Shew me, where have ye laid him?" (2) "Drawing up a cry-of-sorrow *with a roar* from His grieving mind[2]." Neither Chrysostom nor Nonnus helps us to understand what difference is intended, if any, between the phrase that contains "*spirit*" and the phrase that contains "*within himself.*" But the remark of Chrysostom that John is filling up his "deficiency" in the narrative of Gethsemane may be of use in guiding us to a helpful passage in the Psalms, "Why art thou bowed down, O my soul, and why art thou disquieted within me[3]?"

---

[1] Chrys *ad loc* "He shews what there was of human nature [in Him] For He weeps and is confused [as it were] (συγχεῖται).... Then, *having rebuked the passion* (πάθει)—for the phrase ἐνεβριμήσατο τῷ πνεύματι has this meaning—He restrained the confusion (ἐπέσχε τὴν σύγχυσιν)...." Afterwards he says "He comes therefore to the tomb and again He *rebukes the passion*" See context Cramer has (1) "rebuked the *mourning* (πένθει)," (2) "rebuked the *passion* (πάθει)"

[2] Nonn (1) πνεύματι πατρῴῳ δεδονημένος ἴαχε φωνήν.... (2) ἀχνυμένης βριμηδὸν ἀπὸ φρενὸς οἶκτον ἀνέλκων It does not appear that βριμηδόν expresses or implies rebuke.

[3] Ps. xlii 5, 11, xliii 5 ἵνα τί περίλυπος εἶ, ἡ ψυχή, καὶ ἵνα τί συνταράσσεις με, Except in these Psalms, the vocative in Heb "O my soul" is mostly dropped by LXX as in Jerem iv 19 (LXX) ἤκουσεν ἡ ψυχή μου

THE HEALING OF A LEPER

The LXX there renders "bowed-down" by "*exceeding-sorrowful*"—a word extremely rare in LXX and N T, but used by Mark-Matthew in the phrase "*exceeding-sorrowful* even unto death[1]" The Hebrew for "disquieted" is the word "sound," "murmur," or "roar," which we have been so long considering; and, instead of "*disquieted within me*," LXX has "*altogether-troublest me*," while Aquila (and similarly Symmachus) has "*makest-uproar against me*[2]" In the Psalm, the conflict, or rebellion, is between the "soul" and the speaker represented by "I." In the Agony of Gethsemane, the "spirit" is described as "willing," the "flesh" as merely "weak," the "soul" as "exceeding-sorrowful" No definite enemy or rebel is mentioned We are made to feel that the Tempter, who, as Luke says, left Jesus in the wilderness only "until a season," is now present again in Gethsemane. But the presence is only to be inferred from Christ's warning to the disciples "Pray that ye enter not into temptation" Luke, perhaps in part because of its indefiniteness, omits both the confession of "exceeding sorrowfulness" and its context[3].

Returning to the scene near the grave of Lazarus we must confess that there too, as in Gethsemane, much is left undefined. Negation about it is far easier than affirmation We feel that no word in the passage is accidental—that, for example, the phrase "He *troubled himself*" must be read along with "Now is

---

[1] Περίλυπος occurs, in Heb LXX elsewhere, only in Gen iv 6 and Dan ii 12 In N T, it occurs only in Mk xiv 34, Mt. xxvi 38 (Gethsemane), and in Mk vi 26, Lk xviii 23

[2] LXX συνταράσσεις με, Aq ὀχλάζεις ἐπ᾽ ἐμέ, Sym θορυβῇ κατ᾽ ἐμοῦ or θορυβεῖς ἐπ᾽ ἐμέ The Heb is המה, see p 252, n 3

[3] That is to say, Lk. xxii 40 foll. has no parall to Mk xiv 33—4, Mt xxvi 37—8 Luke has also no parallel to the other passage in which Mk-Mt speaks of Christ's "soul" (Mk x 45, Mt xx 28), whereas Jn represents Jesus as saying "my *soul* (or *life*)" thrice (*Son* 3434).

If Lk. xxii 43—4, placed in double brackets by W.H., is accepted as genuine, it expresses, in the form of fact, what Mk-Mt expresses in words of Christ

my soul troubled," later on, and with "He was *troubled in spirit*," latest of all, at the Last Supper; and yet what is implied in "*He troubled himself*" we cannot precisely say[1].

This, however, we can say with confidence, that John wrote in part with a view to meeting such a doctrine as that of Epictetus, that no man has a right to be troubled, for "*men are troubled not by facts but by their notions about facts*[2]," and such talk as that in the Encheiridion, that when you see anyone weeping in mourning because a child is going on a journey, or is dead, you are to remember that it is only the man's notion that is really paining him; you may indeed allow yourself to be carried away with him up to a reasonable limit, "Nay, you may even perhaps go so far *as to groan with him*; but be careful not to groan *from within*[3]."

There is a sense in which every Christian must admit, at least in theory, that he "ought not *to groan from within*," because there is in him, or ought to be, beneath the deepest and most heart-rending sorrows, a still deeper peace—a "within" that is "too deep for tears." But the manner in which the Epictetian doctrine is put forth, with its claim for philosophic superiority to the "women" and the "simple folk," shews a tendency to Pharisaism. John at all events in his narrative of the Raising of Lazarus protests, directly or indirectly, against such a claim. And that perhaps induced him—in a kind of desperate attempt

---

[1] Jn xi. 33, xii. 27, xiii 21 (see *Joh Gr* 2614 c, *Son* 3476, 3548 f).

[2] See *Joh. Voc.* 1727 c quoting Epict. *Ench.* § 5.

[3] *Ench.* § 16 ending thus μέχρι μέντοι λόγου μὴ ὄκνει συμπεριφέρεσθαι αὐτῷ, κἂν οὕτω τύχῃ, καὶ συνεπιστενάξαι πρόσεχε μέντοι μὴ καὶ ἔσωθεν στενάξῃς. Comp. Epict. ii. 13 17 "No good man mourns or groans."

The philosophic superiority to women, and to "simple folk (ἰδιώταις)," who shed genuine tears, is illustrated by Epictetus (i. 29. 65—6) from the *Phaedo* (p. 116 D), where Socrates says about his jailer Ὡς γενναίως με ἀποδακρύει Socrates, he says, does not tell the man "I sent the women away to avoid a scene of this kind", to his disciples he tells the truth, "the jailer he humours (συμπεριφέρεται) as if he were a little child."

THE HEALING OF A LEPER

to express what he could not express—to say that Jesus, on this occasion, "troubled himself." John may mean to say to the Stoics, "Not only did the Messiah put aside that craving for untroubledness which you Stoics feel and encourage, but He did more. As He took our sins and infirmities upon Himself, so He took 'trouble' into Himself. He did it, because He felt—and in order that He might feel—at its keenest, that kind of trouble which is felt by the 'women' and the 'simple folk' whom you philosophers despise."

And perhaps something of the same indefinite kind may be said about the inarticulate sounds recorded by John to have been twice uttered by the Messiah along with His "weeping" and His act of "self-troubling." Logically, the Evangelist ought to have told us whether he used this ancient Marcan word to mean "groan" or "rebuke", and, if in the latter sense, what was the person or thing rebuked; and what was the precise meaning of "in himself" following after a mention of "the spirit." But is it not possible that the Evangelist himself did not know the exact shades of distinctive meaning to be attached to all these words? May he not have received them, or some of them, as part of a tradition—of which the interpretation may have been not uninfluenced by visions as well as remembrances—visions of the Messiah weeping over Jerusalem, visions of the weeping of Rachel comforted by the sounds of the compassion of Jehovah groaning for Ephraim? When the Evangelist wrote of the Raising of Lazarus, attempting to convey all that it meant to him as a "sign," he may have written as he wrote about the water and the blood that flowed from Jesus, not as a mere chronicler, but as a Seer, a Prophet under inspiration. The difficulty of supposing this would, from some points of view, be less than the difficulty of supposing that John deliberately wrote with an obscurity that has defied all attempts at confident interpretation. My own conviction is that John used this difficult word to imply not only "rebuke" and "sorrowful complaint," but also that indescribable intercession which Paul has attempted to describe as being "with *groanings that cannot be uttered*[1]."

---

[1] Rom. viii. 26. See *Joh Voc* 1752 *a—f*, which contrasts Mt xii 19 οὐδὲ κραυγάσει with Jn xi 43 ἐκραύγασεν Comp Heb v 7 μετὰ κραυγῆς ἰσχυρᾶς καὶ δακρύων, of which Westcott says "There can be little doubt that the writer refers to the scene at Gethsemane" The verbal similarity illustrates what Chrysostom says about John, as "supplying" in the narrative of Lazarus what was "left out" by him in the narrative of Gethsemane. Κραυγάζω and κραυγή are nowhere applied to Jesus except in Jn xi. 43 and Heb. v. 7 But in Heb., the *"crying"* of Jesus is for Himself, in Jn, it is for Lazarus

CHAPTER VI*

THE FORGIVENESS OF SINS
[Mark ii. 1—12]

§ 1 *The forgiveness and healing of the Paralytic, in the Synoptists*

IN this narrative, Luke follows Mark in many details where Matthew deviates from Mark, as will be seen below[1]. This

---

* For titles of previous Parts of Diatessarica referred to by abbreviations in this Volume, see pp 545—6. For other abbreviations see pp xxiii—xxvi.

[1]

Mk ii 1—12 (R V)	Mt. ix. 1—8 (R.V.)	Lk. v 17—26 (R V)
(1) And when he entered again into Capernaum after some days, it was noised that he was in the house (*or*, at home)	(1) And he entered into a boat, and crossed over, and came into his own city	(17) And it came to pass on one of those days, that he was teaching, and there were Pharisees and doctors of the law sitting by, which were come out of every village of Galilee and Judaea and Jerusalem and the power of the Lord was with him to heal (*lit* that [he] should heal *many anc auth* that [he] should heal them)
(2) And many were gathered together, so that there was no longer room [for them], no, not even about the door. and he spake the word unto them	(2) And behold, they brought to him a man sick of the palsy, lying on a bed and Jesus seeing their faith said unto the sick of the palsy, Son (*lit* Child), be of good cheer; thy sins are forgiven	
(3) And they come, bringing unto him a man sick of the palsy, borne of four	(3) And behold, certain of the scribes said within themselves, This man blasphemeth.	(18) And behold, men bring on a bed a man that was palsied and they sought to bring him in, and to lay him before him.
(4) And when they could not come nigh (*many anc auth.* bring him) unto him for the crowd, they uncovered the roof where he was and when they had broken it up, they let down the bed whereon the sick of the palsy lay.	(4) And Jesus knowing (*many anc auth* seeing) their thoughts said, Wherefore think ye evil in your hearts?	(19) And not finding by what [way] they might bring him in because of the multitude, they went up to the housetop, and let him down through
(5) And Jesus	(5) For whether is easier, to say, Thy sins are forgiven, or to say, Arise, and walk?	
	(6) But that ye	

261 (Mark ii 1—12)

THE FORGIVENESS OF SINS

Mk ii. 1—12 (R V) (*contd*)	Mt ix 1—8 (R V.) (*contd*)	Lk v 17—26 (R V) (*contd*)
seeing their faith saith unto the sick of the palsy, Son, (*lit* Child) thy sins are forgiven. (6) But there were certain of the scribes sitting there, and reasoning in their hearts, (7) Why doth this man thus speak? he blasphemeth who can forgive sins but one, [even] God? (8) And straightway Jesus, perceiving in his spirit that they so reasoned within themselves, saith unto them, Why reason ye these things in your hearts? (9) Whether is easier, to say to the sick of the palsy, Thy sins are forgiven; or to say, Arise, and take up thy bed, and walk? (10) But that ye may know that the Son of man hath power (*or*, authority) on earth to forgive sins (he saith to the sick of the palsy), (11) I say unto thee, Arise, take up thy bed, and go unto thy house (12) And he arose, and straightway took up the bed, and went forth before them all, insomuch that they were all amazed, and glorified God, saying, We never saw it on this fashion.	may know that the Son of man hath power (*or*, authority) on earth to forgive sins (then saith he to the sick of the palsy), Arise, and take up thy bed, and go unto thy house (7) And he arose, and departed to his house (8) But when the multitudes saw it, they were afraid, and glorified God, which had given such power (*or*, authority) unto men.	the tiles with his couch into the midst before Jesus (20) And seeing their faith, he said, Man, thy sins are forgiven thee (21) And the scribes and the Pharisees began to reason, saying, Who is this that speaketh blasphemies? Who can forgive sins, but God alone? (22) But Jesus perceiving their reasonings, answered and said unto them, What (*or*, Why) reason ye in your hearts? (23) Whether is easier, to say, Thy sins are forgiven thee, or to say, Arise and walk? (24) But that ye may know that the Son of man hath power (*or*, authority) on earth to forgive sins (he said unto him that was palsied), I say unto thee, Arise, and take up thy couch, and go unto thy house. (25) And immediately he rose up before them, and took up that whereon he lay, and departed to his house, glorifying God. (26) And amazement took hold on all, and they glorified God, and they were filled with fear, saying, We have seen strange things to-day.

262 (Mark ii. 1—12)

THE FORGIVENESS OF SINS

therefore is not a place where we may expect John to intervene as to Marcan words or phrases not used by the parallel Synoptists. There happens to be, however, one such word here, namely, "pallet" (instead of "bed") used by Mark here four times "Pallet" is also used by John four times in the narrative of the healing of the "man in infirmity" near the pool of Bethesda[1]. It is never used by Matthew or Luke Its use is expressly forbidden by the grammarian Phrynichus, and it was perhaps distasteful to educated Greeks That John agrees with Mark in using it, is an instance, though only one of many unimportant instances, of Johannine intervention.

But besides what has been said about this word in *Johannine Vocabulary*, it should be added that the Greek *krabattos* is used as a Hebrew word, and Rabbis appear to have distinguished between a "*krabattos*" and a "bed," in questions as to what might, and what might not, be carried on the sabbath[2]. This is a point of more than verbal importance in John's narrative of the healing at the pool of Bethesda, because the charge of sabbath-breaking is there introduced But even this point—though well worth noting—is of little importance as compared with the Synoptic doctrine of "*authority to forgive sins on earth*" and the Johannine attitude to that doctrine[3].

"What is meant here by authority?" is the first question that presents itself. "To whom does this authority belong?" is the second The two questions cannot perhaps be completely answered separately. But, in answer to the first, we

---

[1] Jn v 8 "take up thy *pallet* and walk," rep v 9, 10, 11
[2] See *Joh Voc* **1736** *a* But reference should also have been made to Krauss on κράβατος, and especially to p 545 on κλιντήριον and κραββατάριον. See also Levy iii 568 *b* on the Rabbinical dislike of certain words of this kind Levy quotes *Sabb* 29 *b* "A Rabbi took out a stool *on the sabbath*" (comp. Levy i 365 *a*)
[3] For Mk ii. 2 "and *he spake unto them the word*"—om. in Mt ix. 1—2, and parall. to Lk v 17 "and *the power of the Lord was [with him] to heal*"—see (later on) the comment on Mk iv 14 (also comp. *Son* **3162** *a*).

may say at once that "authority" does not mean "power to do as one likes" It may be described as "lawful power," "power held on trust," "power based on righteousness"—power, at all events, with something more behind it than mere force backing arbitrary "will" good or bad. There is a danger, however, of failing to discern in the Synoptic narrative any indication that the "authority" is of this higher kind. Readers of it may argue, as perhaps some of the spectators at the time argued : "The circumstances indicate that 'authority' here meant the power of Jesus to do what He liked, with a mere word. He proved it by doing, not by talking He first said, in effect, '*Be forgiven !*' No one could see the forgiveness. But He proved its existence by saying '*Walk !*'—and everyone could see the 'walking' The seen proved the unseen It shewed that we had before us a man able to do whatever he liked to do, a man above Nature."

Such a view seems to be suggested by Matthew—at least as being the view of "the multitudes"—when he closes his narrative with the words, "But when the multitudes saw it, they were afraid, and glorified God in that he had given *such authority to men*[1] " These words are not in Mark and Luke, who say nothing here about "the multitudes " Chrysostom says "The multitudes are still trailing on the ground ... For the flesh blocked their view," and Theodorus says about them, "They recognise the thing done to be divine, yet they see the Doer [only as] a human being[2] " According to them, Matthew meant, in effect, "The scribes remained silent but keeping their evil thoughts , the 'multitudes' saw a man that could do

---

[1] Mt ix 8 τὸν θεὸν τὸν δοντα ... R V "God *which* " The Greek seems to include two thoughts, (1) "*the* God *that* had given. ," (2) "God, *in that* he had given.. "

[2] See Cramer *ad loc* , Chrys ὅμως οὖν καὶ οἱ ὄχλοι ἔτι χαμαὶ σύρονται προίστατο γαρ αὐτοῖς ἡ σάρξ, Theod θεῖον τὸ πρᾶγμα γινώσκουσιν, τὸν δὲ ποιήσαντα ὁρῶσιν ἄνθρωπον

as he pleased, but still only one among many '*men.*'" Is this correct?

Mark and Luke do not help us to answer this question. They both say that "all" were "*amazed*" at what they had "*seen*[1]" But "all" had only "*seen*" the cure of paralysis. What about that which they had not "seen"—the forgiveness of sins? Is it implied by Mark and Luke that what the multitude had "*seen*" was to be regarded, in a large sense, as including what they had *heard*, too—the whole transaction, the twofold "word-healing," so to speak, the visible word-healing of the body following the invisible word-healing of the soul? And is it for this great and unheard of combination of deliverance that they "glorified God"?

Even if we accept this explanation as reasonable, we still have to ask what moral reason there was why Jesus should forgive the sins of the paralytic borne by his four bearers. It is said that He pronounced the words of forgiveness "seeing their faith." Was this the sole reason? If so, was it "faith" simply in His power to heal, that is to say, "faith" that might be expressed in the words, "Jesus cured my neighbour so-and-so, and others besides and I am sure he *can* cure me, if he likes"? Or was it some higher kind of faith? Or was there some other reason beside "faith"—some knowledge of the man's past life in Capernaum, and of the four friends that were taking all this trouble in his behalf?

Educated Gentiles would have all the more reason for asking questions of this kind because the Old Testament vocabulary of forgiveness uses various metaphors, some of which—unless allowance is made for anthropomorphic expression and poetic hyperbole—might give an impression that God is unjust and partial. "Blessed is he," says the Psalmist, "whose transgression is forgiven, whose sin is *covered*, blessed is the man unto whom the Lord imputeth not iniquity, and in whose

---

[1] Mk 11. 12 οὕτως οὐδέποτε εἴδαμεν, Lk. v 26 εἴδαμεν παράδοξα σήμερον

265 (Mark 11 1—12)

spirit there is no guile[1]." We can dimly understand a "forgiveness," which is in Hebrew a "taking away," or "lifting up," of the burden of sin; but is "*covering*" our sins the sort of thing one should ask God to do, even in metaphor? Apparently the passionate imagination of Hebrew poetry would not shrink from it. For one of the finest of the Psalms represents David, in the anguish of a heartfelt repentance, as exclaiming to God "*Hide thy face* from my sins[2]" There is no hypocrisy here, no desire that God should do anything that is unjust. The petitioner has already said, "Thou desirest truth in the inward parts," and goes on to say, "Create in me a clean heart, O God, and renew a right spirit within me." Yet still he does not cancel his petition uttered to the God of truth, "*Hide thy face* from my sins."

The need of a solution of the problems that gather round any theory of forgiveness, or else the need of a straightforward acknowledgment that the problems are insoluble, becomes all the stronger if we admit, as Matthew seems to say, that the "authority" to forgive, exerted by Jesus on this occasion for the first time, was intended to be "given unto *men*." What "men" are to exercise this "authority"? Towards whom are they to exercise it? If not towards all, how are they to distinguish the sinner that is fit, from the unfit, to receive forgiveness? Such are the questions that must have presented themselves to the Fourth Evangelist concerning the authority to forgive, and we shall now try to find out how, if at all, he answers them.

---

[1] Ps. xxxii 1—2, cited in Rom iv 7—8. The word for "*cover*" here is not *câphar*, one of the three words regularly used to mean "forgive" or "pardon" (Hastings *Dict* ii. 56).

[2] Ps li 9 foll.

THE FORGIVENESS OF SINS

§ 2. *The healing, without forgiveness, of the man "in infirmity," in John*[1]

The heading of this section, "healing without forgiveness," must not be taken as precluding the possibility of learning

---

[1] This miracle is described as that of "the paralytic man" by Irenaeus ii. 22. 3, and *Acta Pilati* (A) § 6 blends details from it with details from the Synoptic Healing of the Paralytic. See also *Son.* 3414 *d* for a passage from Clem. Alex. indicating an early tendency to use general terms so as to include both the Synoptic and the Johannine narratives. We cannot dispassionately criticize the latter, if we disregard this external evidence indicating that very early Christian writers regarded it as supplementing the former. We must not imagine John as saying "I will create an entirely new narrative of my own." On the other hand, we must not regard John as limited to the Three Gospels in his choice of materials, and as supplementing them merely by his own interpretations and visions. There were probably many such accounts of Jesus healing helpless sick folk, some of them on the sabbath, and John selected such details as symbolized Israel (as distinct from the Gentiles, symbolized later on in "the man born blind"). Thus Jn v. 5 "thirty-eight years" may allude to Deut. ii. 14 "thirty-eight years"—both being periods of chastisement. But that does not exclude the possibility that the Johannine "thirty-eight" may represent what John believed to be fact. Compare the story in the Acts of the healing of a man (iii. 2) "lame *from his mother's womb*," whose age we subsequently find to be (iv. 22) "more than *forty years*"—that is, more than the period of the wandering of Israel in the wilderness.

See *Notes* 2961 (1) *c*—*d* on Lk. xiv. 2 "*dropsical*," quoting (1) Syr. Pesh. "*who had gathered waters*," (2) *Thes. Syr.* 1774 "Hadrian died *in a gathering of waters*" (which does not mean "*in a pool*," but "*in dropsy*"), (3) the Heb. phrase "by the hand of" (a river, waters, etc.) meaning "by the side of" the water. "A house of gathering (*or* congregation)" is regularly used for "synagogue." These facts—especially when considered along with Jn v. 4 ("an angel...troubled the water"), an interpolation (no doubt), but one that supplies something almost necessary for the understanding of the text—all shew how large a field of old tradition was probably open to the Fourth Evangelist from which, without inventing new traditions, he might illustrate the moral and spiritual doctrine latent in corresponding Synoptic accounts.

267 (Mark ii. 1—12)

THE FORGIVENESS OF SINS

from the Johannine narrative anything about "authority to forgive sin." True, it contains no mention of "forgiving"; but it contains a warning of Jesus about "sinning," couched in such terms as to imply, either that the man warned has not yet been forgiven, or else that, although he has been, in some sense, forgiven, he is in danger of falling back into a worse state than before "Afterward Jesus findeth him in the temple and said unto him, Behold, thou art made whole; no longer continue in sin lest a worse thing befall thee[1]."

Also, the context of the narrative indirectly meets the above-mentioned objection of arbitrariness, and exposes the fallacy that "authority" consists in "power to do as one likes." This is effected, somewhat paradoxically, in two ways. First, the narrative accumulates outward signs of arbitrariness. Then it represents Jesus as expressly disclaiming arbitrariness, and as claiming to be (so to speak) the most dependent of all men, being absolutely dependent on the will of the Father in heaven ("The Son can do nothing of himself, but what he seeth the Father doing[2]")

First, as to outward circumstances, no single sufferer is here (as in the Synoptists) brought before the eyes of Jesus by faithful friends There is a mixed crowd of sufferers[3]. Out of these one alone is chosen No reason for the choice is stated. Is it pity for the long duration of the man's sufferings? That may be implied in the words, "Jesus having seen him lying, and having understood that he had been [thus] now for a long time[4]" But we are left uncertain Nor are we informed of

---

[1] Jn v 14 "No longer *continue-in-sin* (μηκέτι ἁμάρτανε)," see *Son* 3148, 3154 c, 3408 foll

[2] Jn v. 19

[3] Jn v 3 "a multitude of them that were sick, blind, halt, withered"

[4] Jn v 6 R V "knew," γνούς Γνούς is applied to Jesus by Mk viii 17 (parall Mt. xvi 8) A V "knew," R V "perceiving," and by Mt xii 15, xxii 18, xxvi 10 In all these passages the meaning seems to be "perceived" When Mark desires to suggest

268 (Mark ii. 1—12)

THE FORGIVENESS OF SINS

the source whence Jesus "understood" the long duration of the suffering. The use of the word in the other Gospels rather favours the conclusion that Jesus was informed of it by those around Him; and this sufferer of "thirty-eight" years' standing could hardly fail to be widely known, like the man in the Acts, lame from his birth, about whose healing (by Peter) it is said that "all men glorified God for that which was done, *for the man was more than forty years old on whom this miracle of healing was done*[1]."

But this and other details are left in a provoking obscurity. For example, do the words "No longer continue in sin" imply that the disease was the penalty of sin? And is the man's complaint, "I have no man to put me into the pool," intended to convey the impression that it was the man's own fault that he had "no man" to help him—whereas the paralytic had four? From the beginning to the end of this narrative there is no indication that "the multitude," or anyone soever, "glorified God," even after it had been noised abroad that Jesus had performed this miracle. The sufferer himself, if he did not turn against his benefactor, at all events acted in such a way as to seem ungrateful: "The man went away and told the Jews that it was Jesus that had made him whole, and for this cause did the Jews persecute Jesus[2]." And how are we to explain the question, at the outset, "Hast thou a desire to be made whole?" Does it not seem that the man was destitute of will? Destitute of faith in Jesus, before Jesus addressed him,

---

preternatural perception he adds "in his spirit" in Mk ii 8 ἐπιγνοὺς τῷ πνεύματι Γνούς is never applied to Jesus by Luke In Mk xv 45 γνούς means "[Pilate] *having-been-informed* [by the centurion]" In Jn vi 15, it means "perceiving [that there was a project to make him king by force]."

On the single occasion when Luke uses γνούς thus—not ὁ γνούς as in xii 47, 48—it is (ix 11) in the plural and applied to the multitudes In the Acts it occurs once, applied to Paul (xxiii 6) "perceiving" the division of opinion in the Council of the Jews.

[1] Acts iv. 22. [2] Jn v. 15—16.

269 (Mark ii 1—12)

THE FORGIVENESS OF SINS

he certainly must have been—since he did not, even afterwards, know who Jesus was. He was apparently destitute of gratitude after Jesus had healed him. Can it then be denied that the act of Jesus, taken by itself without His subsequent comment ("the Son can do nothing of himself"), does suggest arbitrariness, an exercise of authority not based on reason or right, but simply on the will of the worker—"*sit pro ratione voluntas*"?

The answer is that we have no right to take the act without the comment. And the comment, although it will not spiritually satisfy anyone that has not a deep faith in Christ, will intellectually satisfy even a disbeliever, who says "I do not and shall not believe, but I want to understand." For even the purest rationalist understands that there are such things as the "mystics" whom he despises. The comment is altogether mystical. It amounts to this, that Jesus healed this man because He saw this particular act of healing performed by the Father in heaven and therefore appointed to be performed by the Son on earth. Perhaps the Evangelist, in his own mind, adds "Yes, and it was also foreordained to be a type of the Calling of Israel as distinct from the Gentiles, Israel the Chosen, chosen without merit, sluggish in responding to the Call, and not grateful after being called." But he does not venture to impute to Jesus any statement of this kind, or anything more than a general avowal of His dependence on the Father: "The Son is able to do nothing from himself, except only that which he seeth the Father do," and again "I can from myself do nothing[1]."

It will be remembered that all the Synoptic narratives of the healing of the paralytic contain the words, "But that ye may know that *the Son of man hath authority*," in connection

---

[1] Jn v 19 (*Joh Gr* 2516 lit "nothing from himself—[nothing] unless he be [at the moment] seeing the Father doing something"), *ib* 30.

THE FORGIVENESS OF SINS

with "*on the earth*" and "*to forgive sins.*" In the Johannine comment there is no mention of "forgiving sins," but there is a mention of "quickening," or "giving life[1]." And, soon after that, there comes a statement that connects "*authority*" with "*the Son of Man,*" thus. "As the Father hath life in himself, even so gave he to the Son also to have life in himself. And he gave him *authority to execute judgment because he is the Son of man*[2]."

This is one of several passages where the Fourth Gospel insinuates into its readers a perception of the versatile character of the word "authority." It means one thing in the mouth of Pilate ("I have *authority* to acquit thee and I have *authority* to crucify thee[3]") and another thing in the Prologue ("to them he gave *authority* to become children of God[4]") and another thing here. Here it signifies, as it did in Pilate's lips, the authority to "judge"—only with a very great difference as to the conditions of "judgment." Pilate implied—with a characteristic recklessness unworthy and unusual in a Roman Governor—that he could "judge" as he liked. The Son avows that He *cannot* "judge as he likes," saying "*As I hear, I judge, and my judgment is righteous, because I seek not mine own will, but the will of him that sent me*[5]." "As I *hear*" means "As I *hear from the Father*[6]." The passage perhaps contains an allusion to Messianic intuition into the Father's will predicted by Isaiah, who prophesied that the Messiah would *not* judge "according to the hearing of the ears[7]." The Evangelist says,

---

[1] Jn v 21. This is a Johannine equivalent of "forgiving sins," which is not mentioned till toward the close of the Gospel (xx. 23). "Heal" is another—but (in this sense) only as a quotation, Jn xii. 40, quoting Is vi 10.
[2] Jn v. 26—7.   [3] Jn xix. 10.
[4] Jn i 12.   [5] Jn v. 30.
[6] Comp. Jn viii. 26 "*The things that I heard from him* [i e God], these speak I unto the world," *ib.* 40 "Ye seek to kill me, a man that hath told you the truth *which I heard from God*"
[7] Is. xi 3 "And he shall *not judge after the sight of his eyes, neither*

THE FORGIVENESS OF SINS

"Yes, He will thus judge, but according to the 'hearing' of the spiritual 'ears.' The Son, though on earth, was constantly hearing the voice of the Father in heaven. And, *as He heard, so He judged*. The Father said, about one man, 'I give thee authority to forgive,' and the Son forgave; about another, 'I give thee authority to judge,' and the Son judged."

These considerations may help us to perceive that, although, strictly speaking, the healing at the pool of Bethesda is (according to the title of this section) "Healing without Forgiveness," yet it is closely connected with the *thought of forgiveness*. Perhaps it would be truer to say "with the *thought of non-forgiveness*." "Forgiveness" is expressed by "giving life." "Non-forgiveness" is expressed by "judging." "Judging"— not "forgiving," as in the Synoptists—is connected, in John, with the "authority" received by the Son of God because He is "Son of man." All this makes it natural to ask, "When and where does the Fourth Evangelist begin to use the plain intelligible Synoptic word—'*forgive*'? When he does use it, how does he define it? And does the context—there, too, as here—say anything about 'judging'?"

§ 3. *Forgiving sins and retaining sins, in John*

The first use of the word "forgive," in John, occurs after the Resurrection, when Jesus fulfils His promise to "leave"

---

reprove after the hearing of his ears, but with righteousness shall he judge the poor ..." There is no contradiction spiritually. For in the preceding words (as interpreted by the Rabbis and Ibn Ezra) Isaiah has attributed to the Messiah a preternatural "smell" or "scent," saying "And his *scent* shall be in the fear of the Lord." Ibn Ezra calls this "investigation," and says "The sense of *smell* alone is not deceived . he will *investigate*.. by his piety." The Rabbis said that, in Hadrian's time, Bar Cochba, whom R Akiba had accepted as Messiah, was killed because he could not (Is xi 3) "*smell*." That is, he was deceived into falsely "judging," and killing, his own uncle (see *Sanhedr* 93 b and Derenbourg p. 433, quoting *Gittin* 57 a).

272 (Mark ii. 1—12)

THE FORGIVENESS OF SINS

His peace behind Him for His disciples. The promise was "Peace I leave unto you, the peace that is my own I give unto you[1]." He fulfils it when He says "Peace [be] unto you · as the Father hath sent me, even so send I you[2]." Then the Evangelist adds, with an apparent allusion to God's "breathing into man's nostrils the breath of life" in Genesis, that Jesus—as it were in a second Genesis—regenerated the disciples: "He breathed in [them] and saith unto them, Receive ye the Holy Spirit[3]." Then Jesus says—using the same word "*leave*" as before, but in a quite different sense—"Of whomsoever ye *leave* [i.e. *let go*, or, *forgive*] the sins, they are *left* [i.e. *let go*, or, *forgiven*] unto them."

So far, there is no difficulty at all in the mere words. The Greek word for "leave" may mean "leave hold of," "let go," or "remit," applied to a debt. The metaphor of "remitting debts" may be applied to remitting the due punishment for sins. This may also sometimes be used for a higher kind of remission where the person offended not only "lets go" any debt that the Law might have permitted him to exact, but also "lets go" the very thought of the offence out of his mind, and treats the offender as though he had never offended. There is a danger lest the lower kind of remission should be sometimes confused with the higher, and we may complain that the Greek phrase "let go sins" is inadequate. "Letting go sins,"

---

[1] Jn xiv. 27 Εἰρήνην ἀφίημι ὑμῖν, εἰρήνην τὴν ἐμὴν δίδωμι ὑμῖν, R V "Peace I leave with you, my peace I give unto you" "My" (*Joh Gr* 1993, 2609 b) is emphatic, and the meaning seems to be "*I leave it to you as a legacy*, nay, I am [on the point of] giving it to you already."

[2] Jn xx. 21. The first O T mention of peace is connected with the close of Abraham's work on earth (Gen xv 15) "And thou shalt go to thy fathers *in peace*." The first Johannine mention of peace is connected with the beginning and preparation of the work of the Apostles, who are to preach to the world the Gospel of the fulfilment of the Promise to Abraham.

[3] Jn xx. 22. On the "in-breathing," see *Son* 3086 *e*, 3623 *g—j*.

we may say, "is a very much narrower thing than "regenerating," or "giving life." This is true, and the Fourth Evangelist, up to this time, represents Jesus as repeatedly speaking of His mission to give "life[1]," but never of a mission to "forgive." But is it not possible that he intends here to perplex us a little in order that we may make an attempt to get down to the truth latent beneath popular language—very often unintelligent and sometimes immoral—about "the letting-go of sins"?

At all events we shall be on a right track of investigation if we refuse to go further afield for explanation till we have examined the following words, apparently intended to be antithetical to those that precede: "Whose soever [sins] ye retain, they are retained." At first, they seem to increase the darkness. For whereas "the forgiving of sins" is one of the most common of phrases, "the retaining of sins" is—so we are told on high authority—"without parallel" in Jewish literature[2]. If this is so, it is surely unwise to assume that "retaining" must be intended to express something old and familiar—such as exclusion from the community—in a new phrase "without Jewish parallel." It is reasonable to ask first whether the Evangelist is not here, as often, writing like a poet, and with a view to some poetic metaphor, different from the "binding" and the "loosing," which were commonplaces with the Jews. We have found above that, in the context, the "in-breathing" takes us back to the first mention of such "breathing" in the Creation of Adam. We shall now ask whether there are

---

[1] Jn iii 15, v 24 etc
[2] Dalman *Words* p 216 "Exclusion from the community on account of some offence includes the 'retaining' of the sins ..The only remark to be made here is that the term κρατεῖν in John has no Jewish parallel" Dr Dalman dismisses the rendering of it by Salkinson ("impute"), and regards that of Delitzsch as "merely a make-shift" Schlatter gives copious illustrations of Jn xx 23 "forgive," but none of *ib.* "retain" This confirms Dalman's "without parallel."

274 (Mark ii. 1—12)

THE FORGIVENESS OF SINS

reasons for thinking that the "retaining" of "sins" takes us back to the first mention of "sin" in the Bible, and, if so, whether there is anything there that implies "retaining."

§ 4. *The first mention of "sin," connected with "Cain" in the Bible, and with "retaining" in the Targums*

The first Biblical mention of "sin" occurs in God's rejection of Cain's sacrifice: "If thou doest well, shalt thou not be accepted (*or*, shall it not be lifted up)? And if thou doest not well, *sin coucheth at the door*[1]." The LXX completely alters the sense of this[2]. Jewish interpretation takes "*sin coucheth at the door*" to mean the evil "Yetzer" or "tendency" in man, that is, man's tendency to sin. Symmachus and Theodotion render the Hebrew "coucheth" here by the same word as the LXX uses in Ezekiel's description of "the great dragon that *coucheth* in the midst of his rivers", and the Greek word is also applied by the LXX to a serpent "*couching*" on the road and ready to spring[3]. Here it may perhaps be best conceived as a hound, chained at the door of a prison-house, and preventing the guilty soul from going forth to the world out of the darkness that it has created for itself[4]. The thought of the hound, or wild beast, as being always kept chained at the door, is perhaps expressed in the Targums on the Cain-passage in Genesis by the word "*retained*" or "*reserved*": "If thou doest thy work well, will not thy guilt be forgiven thee? But if

---

[1] Gen. iv. 7 "coucheth" (A V "lieth"). The Heb. is applied to a lion in Gen xlix. 9, Ps civ 22, Ezek xix 2 (Gesen 918)

[2] Οὐκ ἐὰν ὀρθῶς προσενέγκῃς, ὀρθῶς δὲ μὴ διέλῃς, ἥμαρτες, ἡσύχασον "Is it not true that, if thou offerest aright but dost not divide aright, thou hast sinned? Be quiet" Jerome comments on this error and its cause Philo and Origen follow the LXX.

[3] Ezek xxix 3 ἐγκαθήμενον, Gen. xlix 17

[4] Jerome says *ad loc* "If thou do evil, there will thy sin sit before thy porch, and by such a door-keeper (janitore) wilt thou be accompanied"

THE FORGIVENESS OF SINS

thou doest not thy work well in this world, *thy sin is retained unto the day of the great judgment, and at the doors of thy heart lieth thy sin*[1]."

This juxtaposition of "forgiveness" and "retention [for the day of judgment]" resembles a tradition, not in Mark, but placed by Matthew in the Precepts to the Twelve (while Luke places a similar one in the Precepts to the Seventy) about any city that rejects the Gospel of Peace "It shall be more tolerable for the land of Sodom and Gomorrah *in the day of judgment* than for that city*[2]*" The preceding context in Matthew, and in Luke (to the Seventy), has repeatedly mentioned "peace" as being first offered by the preachers of the Gospel, but as "coming back again" to them, if it is rejected[3]. In effect, therefore, *this Gospel of "peace" brings, not forgiveness, but retention of sins unto "the day of judgment," for those that reject it.* This doctrine appears throughout the Pauline Epistles in many various expressions, and John appears to imply that

---

[1] So Jer I (Etheridge), and simil Jer II. They combine (1) the literal "*lieth at the door*" with (2) the paraphrastic "*is retained*" Onkelos drops the literal phrase (Etheridge) "If thou doest thy work well, is it not remitted"—*i e*, is there not remission—"to thee? And if thou doest not thy work well, *thy sin unto the day of judgment is reserved*...." Etheridge has rendered the same Aram "*reserved*" in Onk., but "*retained*" in Jer I and Jer. II The Syr represents κρατεῖν in Mk vii. 4 ("*keep*" in the sense of "*observe*") but also "watch," "guard," as in Acts xvi 23, 27 "*keeper* of the prison," Jn x. 3 "*keeper* of the door" (see *Thes Syr.* 2353—4).

After "lieth thy sin," Jer I (and sim. Jer. II) has (Etheridge) "And into thy hand have I delivered the power over evil passion, and unto thee shall be the inclination thereof, that thou mayest have *authority over it*, to become righteous, or to sin" Onk concludes thus, "*Thy sin is reserved unto the day of judgment*, when it will be exacted of thee if thou convert not; but, if thou convert, it is remitted unto thee."

[2] Mt x 15, comp Lk x 12 "I say unto you that in that day it shall be more tolerable for Sodom than for that city." This is not in Luke's Precepts to the Twelve (ix 3 foll).

[3] Mt x. 12—13, Lk x. 5—6.

THE FORGIVENESS OF SINS

a doctrine of the same kind was taught by Jesus after the Resurrection. First, there was to be the Gospel of "peace" and "forgiveness," and, in order that the disciples might preach this Gospel and impart this peace and forgiveness, He breathed into them His Spirit of peace. But at the same time He said that whenever they found it rejected and pronounced a sentence of "retention unto judgment," such "retention" would take effect.

§ 5. *"Cain," the "man-killer," in the Johannine Epistle*

The Fourth Evangelist, if he connects this doctrine with the warning to Cain concerning the "retention of sin," is acting consistently with his habit of lifting his readers out of the region of technical and controversial terms and legalities, into the region of personifications and types and scriptural precedents[1]. But further, he is writing in his Gospel consistently with what he writes in his first Epistle, where Cain is a personified principle, an "antichrist[2]."

The Epistle does not mention the name of Cain till it has brought the thought of Cain before the reader by the words "Whosoever doeth not righteousness is not of God, neither he that loveth not his brother[3]." This phrase, "*loveth not,*" seems, at first sight, weak. "Why," we ask, does the writer not say 'hateth'"? The reason is this, that he uses "*loveth not*" to mean "breaks the commandment of God who bids us love." This we perceive from the following words: "This is the message that ye heard from the beginning—that we should love one another[4]." For from these we see that the character, the

---

[1] Comp Mk x. 5—6 (sim. Mt, om Lk) "For your hardness of heart he [Moses] wrote you this commandment. But from the beginning of the creation (Gen 1. 27) '*Male and female created he them*'" So Mk ii. 25 (sim. Mt -Lk) "Have ye never read what David did...?"

[2] 'Ἀντίχριστος occurs in N.T. nowhere except 1 Jn ii. 18, 22, iv. 3, 2 Jn 7.

[3] 1 Jn iii. 10.   [4] 1 Jn iii. 11.

antichrist, who is being brought before us, is violating two divine precepts—the precept of "righteousness" and the precept of "love" The violation of the second means more than that he is "unloving" in the sense of indifferent. It means that, whereas God, through Christ, says "I bid you love," the antichrist replies "I refuse to love." That implies antagonism to God, the Father, and to men, His children. Thus we are prepared for the mention of Cain as the type of the character that humanity is to avoid : "Not as Cain was of the evil one, and slew his brother. And wherefore slew he him ? Because his works were evil and his brother's righteous[1]."

The Epistle passes on to shew that this attitude of "not-loving," toward such an object as the image of God, must end in "hating"; and "man-hating," when carried into effect, is "man-killing." "Man-killing," in Greek, is quite different from "murder." It means, in Euripides and later, "*killing men [instead of beasts, as sacrifices]*[2]" Some thought of this kind, this peculiarly unholy "killing," some suggestion of Cain, first offering a rejected sacrifice, and then, a moment afterwards, "*killing a human being*," his own brother, out of

---

[1] 1 Jn iii 12 Comp the above-quoted Targ on Gen where God says to Cain, "If thou doest thy work well will not thy guilt be forgiven thee ?"

[2] The word seems to have come into use, in this special sense, from Euripides. Comp Eurip *Iph Taur* 389 ἀνθρωποκτόνους. Clem. Alex. 36 says that the gods "enjoy man-killing (ἀνθρωποκτονίας)" (1) in the arena, (2) in war, (3) in pestilence, when human sacrifices are offered up, (4) *among the Taurians, systematically sacrificing strangers to Artemis in Tauris, "as Euripides represents on the stage"* Steph. *Thes* also quotes Porphyr *De abst.* 2, 56, p 203 for a statement that all the Greeks "*kill-men* (ἀνθρωποκτονεῖν, i e *offer up human sacrifices*) before going out to war" It is used of food made out of men killed by the Cyclopes in Eurip *Cycl* 127 βορᾷ χαίρουσιν ἀνθρωποκτόνῳ Steph. *Thes* quotes no other ancient passages (except Eur *Hec* 260 v r), but adds "apud Greg Naz. ἁ τοῖς δαίμοσιν, homines sacrificare." It occurs only once in Goodspeed's Concordances, viz Tatian § 8, where Æsculapius, who saves life, is contrasted with Athene "*killer of men*"

envy, appears to be present in the following words. "Marvel not, brethren, if the world hateth you We know that we have passed out of death into life, because we love the brethren. He that loveth not abideth in death. Whosoever hateth his brother is a man-killer, and ye know that no *man-killer* hath eternal life abiding in him[1]"

Here the word "man-killer" seems clearly to refer to Cain. In the only other passage where it occurs in the whole of the Greek Testament it refers to the devil, of whom it is said "He was a *man-killer* from the beginning[2]" This, no doubt, means "The devil, in the beginning, brought about man's fall, and consequently man's death." But it seems also to mean· "There was in the beginning an antagonism of darkness against light, of envy against love, of death against life" The Wisdom of Solomon says, "*Through the envy of the devil* came death into the world[3]" As it came invisibly through the devil, so it came visibly through Cain. The one is the invisible, the other is the visible, representative of death, darkness, and hatred[4].

Since the "killing" by Cain takes place in connection with an act of external religion, we may perhaps be disposed to say that Cain was destroyed by his own sacrifice to God: "If he had not sacrificed, he would not have envied; and if he had not envied his brother, he would not have killed him." But the truth is quite otherwise if Cain is to be regarded as essentially envious. For then we see that his envy, which manifested itself in "man-killing," was merely revealed, not caused, by his act of religion. The Fourth Evangelist seems to desire us to see, in those whom he calls "the Jews," a re-incarnation of Cain. Cain looked on at Abel, sacrificing with an

---

[1] 1 Jn iii 13—15.   [2] Jn viii. 44.
[3] Wisd ii 24.
[4] The name "Cain" is explained by the Heb and LXX of Gen. iv 1 as from "*acquire*" And Jerome always explains it so. Eusebius regularly gives the alternative "*envy*," and once (*Onomast.* p. 193) ζηλοτυπία, without alternative.

THE FORGIVENESS OF SINS

offering to which "the Lord had respect[1]" "The Jews" looked on at Jesus, offering to God acts of kindness for sufferers, to which acts also—if inference might be drawn from their success—"the Lord had respect." Cain envied. "The Jews," too, envied. Not that they are expressly said by John to have "envied," as they are said by Mark and Matthew[2]. But John dramatizes them as envying "Behold how ye prevail nothing" —they say to one another—"lo, the world is gone after him[3]." They did not despise "the world." They loved its glory, and their rulers envied Jesus His success with the world, that is, with the multitudes: "They loved the glory of men more than the glory of God[4]." Thus the effect of the Light of the World on the rulers of the nation was to "blind their eyes[5]"; and the effect of the blood of "the Lamb of God that taketh away the sin of the world" was, as regards the sins of "the Jews," not to "forgive," but to "retain[6]."

§ 6. *Conclusion as to the Johannine view*

This, it may be objected, is a gloomy "gospel" It is at all events an honest gospel. It is not a gospel of charms, or incantations, or professional magicians or priests. It throws on each man a man's responsibility—which no priest can take

---

[1] Gen iv 4. Theodotion renders "had respect" by ἐνεπύρισεν, implying "answered with fire" Jerome approves

[2] Mk xv 10, Mt xxvii. 18 "He [Pilate] knew that through *envy* they had delivered him up" Pilate's sense of their "envy" is latent, but perceptible, in Jn xviii 38 foll

[3] Jn xii 19.

[4] Jn xii 43   [5] Jn xii 40

[6] Comp Wisd ii 12 foll "Let us lie in wait for the righteous [one] because he is not for our turn, and he is clean contrary to our doings ... He professeth to have the knowledge of God, and he calleth himself the child of the Lord He was made to reprove our thoughts" Here the sins, or sinful thoughts, of the unrighteous are, in effect, "retained," and called out into action, by "the child of the Lord"

THE FORGIVENESS OF SINS

off his shoulders. It gives to all the true disciples of Jesus, to all the recipients of His Spirit of peace, the power of imparting that peace, through forgiveness of sins, to every man that will receive it. But it warns them that, along with that power of imparting a remission of sins to those who accept that peace, there comes also a necessary power of "retaining sins" in the case of those who reject that peace. The Evangelist does not attempt for a moment to persuade us that the gospel has already triumphed over the world. It is true that he represents Jesus as saying "Be of good cheer, I have overcome the world"; but in the same sentence Jesus says "In the world ye have tribulation[1]." Before the eyes of the Allseeing, the world is already "overcome." But before the eyes of Christ's disciples—who "walk by faith, not by sight[2]"—many centuries of tribulation and spiritual conflict were to pass away before they could hope to say honestly, as from their own sight, not *de jure* but *de facto*, "the world is overcome."

It is perhaps this feeling in the Fourth Evangelist that prevents him from ending his Gospel with a note of triumph, as Matthew and Luke do[3]. He knows indeed that Jesus, in the sphere of reality, in the heaven of heavens, "has overcome" already that spiritual enemy which by a convenient metaphor is called "the world." But he knows also that it is not overcome visibly or perceptibly at present, nor destined to be overcome in the immediate future.

In his Epistle, he even ventures to say "*the world wholly lies in the evil one*[4]." It may be objected "This is because his

---

[1] Jn xvi 33 [2] 2 Cor v 7
[3] So also does the Mark-Appendix, but not the genuine Mark, which ends with (xvi. 8) "they were afraid"—being possibly incomplete.
[4] 1 Jn v 19 "the world wholly (ὁ κόσμος ὅλος)" This is not inconsistent with *ib* ii 2 "He is the propitiation ..for *the whole world* (περὶ ὅλου τοῦ κόσμου)" "The world [of the flesh]," in the technical sense of the term, "lies *wholly* in the evil one" But, in

THE FORGIVENESS OF SINS

view is narrow and false." But may it not be replied "This is because his view is high and true"? He sees where "the world" *is*, and he sees where it *ought to be*, and he sees that it is not in the same position now as before the Incarnation. If the Light had not come there would have been a lower standard of judgment. The Light has come and has been, in large measure, rejected. Hence comes condemnation. "If I had not come and spoken unto them," says Jesus, "they had not had sin, but now they have no excuse for their sin[1]."

But is this pessimism? Is it not merely a frank recognition that with every new gift from God to man there comes a new responsibility of man to God?

Recognising consistently, to the last, the antagonism of the World to the Spirit, and the necessity of a permanent warfare between the servants of selfishness and the servants of the Crucified, the Fourth Evangelist places at the very end of his Gospel, as the last words of Jesus, a precept embodying the stumbling-block of the crucifixion, "Follow thou me," that is, "Follow me on the Way of the Cross[2]." In the same honest candid spirit, looking at things as a whole, he recognises how everything in this multiform universe works according to different circumstances, so as to produce infinitely differing results, some good, some evil, yet all to be regarded as, in some sense, issuing from One God, and all as tending toward One God. Writing in this spirit, he gave us in the Prologue of his Gospel both sides of the truth, by saying that "the light shineth in darkness[3]." Now, toward the close of his Gospel, he gives us both sides of

---

its non-technical sense, "the world," meaning "mankind as a whole," is wholly included in God's redemptive purpose. John would not have denied that in myriads of non-Christian human souls, within and without the limits of the Roman Empire, the Light of the World was shining (Jn 1 9) "coming into the world," and enlightening those who had never heard the name of Jesus.

[1] Jn xv 22
[2] Jn xxi 22.
[3] Jn 1 5

282 (Mark 11 1—12)

THE FORGIVENESS OF SINS

the truth again, by warning us that "sins forgiven" must be thought of in connection with "sins retained[1]"

---

[1] See *Son* 3532 on the "authority" of the Son of Man, as being "the authority of the Man over the Beast". "The Beast" includes the Serpent and "all the power of the enemy". Whether sins are "forgiven" or "retained," this "authority" is exercised. The Beast is regarded as being made to subserve ultimately, in some inscrutable way, the righteous purposes of God. Some feeling of a twofold authority is apparent in the Targum quoted above (p. 276, n. 1) on the "sin lying at the door", but the similarity is rather verbal than spiritual. "Into thy hand have I delivered the power over evil passion, and unto thee shall be the inclination thereof, that thou mayest have *authority over it, to become righteous, or to sin*." The Targumist protests that man has "authority" over his own will; the Evangelist, that righteousness has "authority" over sin.

CHAPTER VII*

CHRIST'S CALL TO "SINNERS"
[Mark ii. 13—17]

§ 1. *Technical terms in the Synoptists*

AFTER forgiving the sins of the paralytic whom He heals, Jesus proceeds to call a tax-gatherer (named Levi or Matthew) as described below[1]. There follows a discussion, ending with

---

* For titles of previous Parts of Diatessarica referred to by abbreviations in this Volume, see pp 545—6 For other abbreviations see pp xxiii—xxvi.

[1]
Mk ii 13—17 (R.V txt)	Mt ix 9—13 (R V txt)	Lk v 27—32 (R V txt)
(13) And he went forth again by the sea side, and all the multitude resorted unto him, and he taught them. (14) And as he passed by, he saw Levi the [son] of Alphaeus sitting at the place of toll, and he saith unto him, Follow me And he arose and followed him. (15) And it came to pass, that he was sitting at meat in his house, and many publicans and sinners sat down with Jesus	(9) And as Jesus passed by from thence, he saw a man, called Matthew, sitting at the place of toll and he saith unto him, Follow me And he arose, and followed him. (10) And it came to pass, as he sat at meat in the house, behold, many publicans and sinners came and sat down with Jesus and his disciples (11) And when the Pharisees saw it, they said unto his	(27) And after these things he went forth, and beheld a publican, named Levi, sitting at the place of toll, and said unto him, Follow me (28) And he forsook all, and rose up and followed him. (29) And Levi made him a great feast in his house· and there was a great multitude of publicans and of others that were sitting at meat with them. (30) And the Pharisees and their

284 (Mark ii. 13—17)

CHRIST'S CALL TO "SINNERS"

the words, "I came not to call the righteous, but sinners," where Luke adds "to repentance."

This Synoptic tradition was probably in the mind of Celsus, when he asserted that Christians say "It was to sinners that God has been sent." On this, his comment is, "Why was He not sent to those that were without sin? What evil is it not to have committed sin?" and again, "What is this preference of sinners over others[1]?" Origen meets this by explaining that Christ was sent to all, because all have sinned, and, even if some have passed out of sin, they still need the Redeemer's help. But would educated Greeks regard this as a satisfactory explanation? Luke, at all events, by adding "to repentance," seems to indicate his belief that Mark's text is either obscure or incomplete

The difficulty of deciding what was Mark's exact meaning is greatly increased by the fact that "righteous," in the New

Mk 11 13—17 (R V txt) (contd)	Mt ix 9—13 (R V txt) (contd)	Lk v 27—32 (R V txt) (contd)
and his disciples for there were many, and they followed him (see p 383, n) (16) And the scribes of the Pharisees, when they saw that he was eating with the sinners and publicans, said unto his disciples, He eateth and drinketh with publicans and sinners. (17) And when Jesus heard it, he saith unto them, They that are whole have no need of a physician, but they that are sick I came not to call the righteous, but sinners	disciples, Why eateth your Master with the publicans and sinners? (12) But when he heard it, he said, They that are whole have no need of a physician, but they that are sick (13) But go ye and learn what [this] meaneth, I desire mercy, and not sacrifice for I came not to call the righteous, but sinners	scribes murmured against his disciples, saying, Why do ye eat and drink with the publicans and sinners? (31) And Jesus answering said unto them, They that are whole have no need of a physician, but they that are sick (32) I am not come to call the righteous but sinners to repentance.

[1] Origen *Cels.* iii. 62, 64.

Testament, often has a technical sense, being applied to those who fulfilled the commandments of the Law externally, without an internal fulfilment of those two great commandments ("love God," "love thy neighbour") which Jesus described as constituting, in reality, the whole of the Law[1]. "Except your righteousness shall exceed [the righteousness of] the scribes and Pharisees[2]," said Jesus. But He did not mean that the righteousness of His disciples was to be *more in amount* than that of the Pharisees. He meant that it was to be *different in kind*. It is possible that Jesus was here using the word in the technical sense in which it was used by those who "trusted in themselves that they were *righteous*, and despised all others[3]." If so, although it would be true to say that Christ "*was sent to all*," yet it would be misleading in Christ to say "*I came to call all*," without adding that the "*call*" would make no appeal to those who were perfectly satisfied with their own "righteousness."

Akin to the technical sense of "righteous" is that of "sinners." As the former sometimes implied "those who observe the Law of Moses," so the latter sometimes implied "those who do not observe the Law of Moses," that is, Gentiles[4]. In the present narrative, along with "sinners" are mentioned "publicans," *i e* "tax-gatherers"—as though they, too, were necessarily an immoral class. But the two words are on a different footing. The technicality of "sinners" is purely Jewish. The technicality, if it can be so called, of "tax-gathering" and "tax-gatherers" is to be found in the Greek language from Aristophanes downwards[5], and the meaning of dishonesty attached to it arises necessarily in every country where taxes, or customs, are so collected as to encourage (or not discourage) over-collection and fraudulent extortion.

---

[1] Mt xxii 37—40. [2] Mt v. 20.
[3] Lk xviii 9. R V txt "all others," *lit* "the rest [of the world]."
[4] Comp Gal ii 15 "We being Jews by nature and not *sinners* of the Gentiles."
[5] See Wetstein on Mt. v. 46.

CHRIST'S CALL TO "SINNERS"

In the use of the word "tax-gatherer," Mark differs from Matthew and Luke by never placing it in an utterance of Jesus. Matthew ventures to represent Jesus on several occasions as using it in an opprobrious sense One of these instances is in a tradition peculiar to Matthew[1] But in the Double Tradition also—in the Sermon on the Mount—Matthew has "tax-gatherers" where Luke has "sinners[2]" Other words of Jesus recorded by Matthew say that "the tax-gatherers *and the harlots*" believed John the Baptist, and had precedence over the Pharisees , but the parallel Luke omits "*and the harlots*[3]."

Luke nowhere represents Jesus as countenancing the opprobrious use of the word "tax-gatherer." On the contrary, according to him, when the tax-gatherers said to John the Baptist "What shall we do ? " instead of replying "Cease to be tax-gatherers," he merely said "Exact no more than that which is appointed you[4]." Luke also records a story told by Jesus, contrasting the prayer of a complacent Pharisee with that of a penitent tax-gatherer[5]. Lastly, Luke represents Jesus as saying about Zacchaeus, "a chief tax-gatherer," and "rich," who made restitution for wrongful exaction and gave half of his goods to the poor, "To-day is salvation come unto this house, forasmuch as he also is a child of Abraham[6]"

---

[1] Mt xviii. 17 "Let him be unto thee as the Gentile (ὁ ἐθνικὸς) and the *tax-gatherer* " In Mt. xi 19, Lk vii 34 "a friend of *tax-gatherers* and sinners," Jesus is simply repeating the charge brought against Him by others

[2] Mt v 46, Lk vi 32 In Mt v. 47, ἐθνικοί is parall to Lk. vi 33 ἁμαρτωλοί Possibly the original had "Gentiles" in all four texts. The Heb for "Gentile" closely resembles one Heb. word used for "exactors of dues" or "bailiffs" (Levy 1. 293 *a*, *Aboth* iii. 25 (16)).

[3] Mt xxi 31—2, Lk vii 29—30.

[4] Lk iii 12—13

[5] Lk xviii 10—14.

[6] Lk xix. 1—9 Clem. Alex. 942 remarks that Jesus "does not command Zacchaeus and Matthew to part with their property "

§ 2. *John's use of the words "righteous" and "righteousness"*

Reviewing the technical terms above mentioned, we perceive that the Rule of Johannine Intervention does not bind John here to intervene as to any of them. For not one of them is used by Mark and omitted or corrected by Luke. But it would be absurd to suppose that John never intervenes except when the Synoptists disagree. He might also intervene, even where all the Synoptists agree, if he had reason to think that the threefold agreement still left something obscure that might be made clear, or something inadequate that might be more fully and satisfactorily expressed, or something clear and full in appearance, but not so in spirit and in truth

As regards "tax-gatherers," there was no need that John should add a word. For Mark had been silent, so far as concerns any words of Jesus; and Luke had corrected and supplemented Matthew's tradition in such a way as to make it impossible to suppose that Jesus shared in the general unfairness to them as a class. This class, then, John never mentions.

As to "righteousness" and "righteous," John says indeed very little, but what he does say appeals to the common sense of all right-minded people, and yet goes down deep to a divine foundation. "Righteousness" may be described roughly as the faculty of judging fairly and rightly between this and that claim—"judge" and "claim" being used in their fullest senses. When the claim was put into words before the judges of Israel, they had the following precept of Moses for their guidance:—
"Hear [the causes] between your brethren, and judge righteously between a man and his brother, and the stranger that is with him. Ye shall not respect persons in judgment; ye shall hear the small and the great alike; ye shall not be afraid of the face of man; for the judgment is God's[1]." The

---

[1] Deut 1 16—17.

Jerusalem Targum explains "Hear between" thus. "So hear your brethren that one may not [be permitted to] speak all his words, while another is compelled to cut his words short; and so hearken to their words, as that it may be impossible for you not to judge them and deliver judgment in truth .." It is in this spirit of fairness that Nicodemus says to the Sanhedrin "Doth our law judge a man, except it first hear from himself and know what he doeth?" To this their only reply is "Art thou also of Galilee? Search, and see that out of Galilee ariseth no prophet[1]"

These "judges" are hopelessly unfair—hopelessly, because they are self-blinded, shutting their eyes to the beauty and justice of the Law. Of its essential meaning they know nothing. And yet they have just pronounced something like a curse on the multitude for knowing nothing of it. "Hath any of the rulers believed on him? Or any of the Pharisees? But [as for] this multitude that knoweth not the law—they are [all] under-a-curse[2]." This is one of many instances of Johannine irony The judges of the Jews are here self-judged, while, in effect, judging "the multitude" They take in their mouths the very word of Moses "*Cursed* be he that confirmeth not the words of this law to do them," and while applying the curse to the despised rabble they bring it down on themselves[3]

In order to emphasize the importance of this common-sense virtue of fairness, or justice, or righteousness, John, who uses the adjective but thrice, applies it twice to "judgment," and once to the word "Father" in prayer proceeding from the

---

[1] Jn vii 51—2 (R.V) Probably the right rendering is "ariseth not the prophet" (see *Joh Gr* 2492)

[2] Jn vii 48—9 ἐπάρατοι. This is the equivalent, in classical Greek, of Deut. xxvii 26 (quoted in Gal iii 10) ἐπικατάρατος, which is not given by Steph *Thes* as occurring anywhere in classical Greek. Ἐπικατάρατος occurs once in the Index of Boeckh (No 2664 "barbarus titulus") whereas ἐπάρατος occurs ten times

[3] Compare Cramer (p. 271, *ad loc*) τὸν ὄχλον δὲ. ἐπάρατον εἰπόντες εἶναι μᾶλλον αὐτοὶ κατάρας ὑπεύθυνοι γεγόνασιν...

Son ("O righteous Father!"). In the first instance, Jesus says "The judgment that I give is *righteous*," and adds the reason, namely, that it is based on the will of God ("the will of him that sent me")—somewhat as the judges in Israel are told by Moses "the judgment is God's[1]" In the second instance, Jesus appeals to a common-sense view of what God would judge to be right to do on the sabbath, "If a man receive circumcision on the sabbath...are ye wroth with me, because I made a man every whit whole on the sabbath ? Judge not according to appearance, but judge *righteous* judgment[2]."

Here arises the question "How can a human being judge except (in some sense) according to 'appearance'—the things that appear to the senses, the documents, the utterances, and the demeanour, of witnesses and of the parties to the suit ?" The answer is that the Lord's "judge" must be as far as possible like the Lord, "who seeth not as man seeth, for man looketh on the outward appearance, but the Lord looketh on the heart[3]." That is to say, "Heart-knowledge, as well as eye-knowledge and mind-knowledge, is needed to make up, in its completeness, righteous judgment" The Fourth Gospel teaches that the Father in heaven, and He alone, is "righteous" in this highest sense of all ; and reserves this as the highest of the divine attributes, above the attribute of "holiness[4]," for the climax of the last prayer of the Son to the Father, as though this divinest kind of righteousness were the sphere in which we are to conceive the knowledge of the Father by the Son · "O *righteous* Father, the world knew thee not, but I knew thee....[5]" "Righteousness" John mentions only in

---

[1] Jn v 30 ἡ κρίσις ἡ ἐμή (emph). . (see *Joh Gr.* **2559**), Deut.1 17.
[2] Jn vii 23—4. [3] 1 S xvi 7
[4] Jn xvii 11 "O holy Father (ἅγιε)" precedes *ib* 25 "O righteous Father (δίκαιε)"
[5] Comp Plato *Theaet* 176 c θεὸς ὡς οἷόν τε δικαιότατος Δίκαιος, in the fullest sense, applied to the ideal Judge, implies (1) will, (2) knowledge, (3) power to pronounce a self-executing judgment

CHRIST'S CALL TO "SINNERS"

one passage as one of the three things in respect of which Jesus declares that the Paraclete will "convict the world," namely "sin," "righteousness," and "judgment[1]" It is added, "of *righteousness*, because I go to the Father and ye see me no more," where the meaning seems to be that to be driven out of an unrighteous world is a proof of "righteousness." The thought is akin to that in Wisdom, where "the ungodly" say, about him whom they persecute and kill, "Let us lie in wait for the *righteous*...he is *clean contrary to our doings*[2]." Thus, in effect, they "convict" themselves of "sin," and of hostility to "righteousness," and they pass "judgment" on themselves. The "righteousness" here spoken of is manifestly divine, not human, in its origin. It consists in a right relationship typified by fatherhood, sonship, and brotherhood, and is very far removed from the conception, condemned by Paul, of "the righteousness that is from the Law[3]," that is, from the Law of Moses[4]

§ 3 *What does John say or imply about "sinners"?*

In the Fourth Gospel, Jesus never mentions the word "sinner." It occurs only in one passage—a discussion between "the Jews" and a man born blind, but recently healed by Jesus on the sabbath[5] There it brings into sharp contrast

---

that shall do that which is best for all collectively and for each individually

[1] Jn xvi 8—11 (*Joh Gr* 2182)
[2] Wisd ii 12 (p. 280, n 6)   [3] Rom x 5
[4] The Johannine Epistle uses δίκαιος and δικαιοσύνη as follows Beginning from δίκαιος as applied to the Redeemer 1 Jn 1 9, ii. 1, 29, it passes to man's δικαιοσύνη (ii. 29) ἐὰν εἰδῆτε ὅτι δίκαιός ἐστιν, γινώσκετε ὅτι πᾶς ὁ ποιῶν τὴν δικαιοσύνην ἐξ αὐτοῦ γεγέννηται That is to say, there is no "righteousness" for man except in regeneration from God But this "righteousness" is not a mere theory (*ib* iii. 7), "*he that doeth righteousness* is righteous even as he [the Lord] is righteous," *ib* 10 "*everyone that doeth not righteousness* is not from God " Abel's works are (*ib* 12) "righteous "
[5] Jn ix 16—34

the Pharisaic view, and the common-sense view, of the meaning of the word. The Jews, it is said, "called a second time the man that was blind, and said unto him, Give glory to God, we know that this man is *a sinner*[1]."

"Give glory to God" means (as is shewn by some of the passages referred to in the margin)[2], "Confess that you have sinned." The man, when previously asked "What sayest thou of him?" had replied "He is a prophet." He is now required to confess that he has sinned in saying this. But the context seems also to shew that the Jews meant more than this —meant (as Chrysostom says) "Confess that this man did nothing," i.e. nothing miraculous, nothing at all worth mentioning[3]. How the man is to say this with any appearance of truthfulness, they do not explain. That is the man's affair, not theirs. For them, "the rulers," the conclusion was as certain as a demonstration of Euclid. The healer had "worked" on the sabbath. Whoever worked on the sabbath "broke the Law." Whoever "broke the Law" was "a sinner." Therefore Jesus, the healer, was a sinner. "*We know*," they say, "that this man is a sinner." And from their point of view, they were quite right. If "sinner" meant what they thought it meant, Jesus *was* "a sinner."

The dialogue continues with technical legality on the side of the Pharisees, with common-sense on the side of the man born blind, and with Johannine irony (as it were) looking on. "We know," said the Jews, "that God hath spoken unto Moses; but as for this man we know not whence he is." They were quite right on this point. The "whence" was "from the Father." Him the Jews did not "know." Well might they say "*We know not whence he is.*" As for the blind man, he, taking the common-sense view of things, does not at first attempt to deny that Jesus may be a "sinner" from the

---
[1] Jn ix 24
[2] Josh vii 19, Jer xiii 16, 1 S vi 5.
[3] Chrys on Jn ix 24

Pharisaic point of view. They say they *"know"* it. He implies that such confident *"knowing"* belongs to professional theologians, not to plain men like himself. "Whether he be a sinner I know not, one thing I *know*, that whereas I was blind, now I see." And from that he passes to the conclusion that since "God heareth not sinners," this man cannot be so called · "If this man were not from God, he could do nothing."

The sequel ends with an instructive contrast between an unreal, external, and (so to speak) artificial or official "binding of sins," "retention of sins," or "excommunication," and the real, internal, and natural act of which the former is (in this particular instance) a parody. The blind man, for refusing to "give God glory" by denying that he owes his sight to Jesus, is "cast out of the synagogue." The Pharisees say that they "see," in the very moment when they are going to commit an act of blind injustice. They are therefore allowed to blind themselves. Nay, they are *made to "become blind"* It is the *"judgment"* of God on them. "For *judgment* came I into this world," says Jesus, "that they that see not may *become blind*", and then—to the Pharisees, who scoffingly asked whether they, too, were blind—"If ye were blind, ye would have no sin, but now ye say, We see. Your sin *abideth*[1]." That is to say, it is *"retained."* They are excommunicated, cast out. The blind man is cast out of the synagogue, the Pharisees out of the Light—into "the outer darkness[2]"

§ 4   The "harlots" in Matthew, and the "woman that was a sinner" in Luke

Luke's narrative, which will be discussed later on in a comment on the Anointing at Bethany, is merely mentioned

---

[1] Jn ix 39—41

[2] Mt viii 11—12 (comp Lk. xiii 28) on the "casting out" of "the sons of the kingdom," and the admission of the Gentile world. The blind man in John is generally regarded as the type of the Gentile world

here as containing his only representation of those whom Matthew calls *"the harlots"* Matthew, who alone attributes this word to Jesus[1]—and that, in only one passage—represents them, along with the tax-gatherers, as having "believed" John the Baptist. But the parallel Luke differs, as follows —

Mt. xxi 31—2	Lk. vii. 29—30
Verily I say unto you, that *the tax-gatherers and the harlots* go before you into the kingdom of God. For John came to you in the way of righteousness, and ye believed him not, but *the tax-gatherers and the harlots* believed him, but ye, having seen [it], did not even repent afterwards that ye might believe him.	And *all the people, having heard, and the tax-gatherers,* justified God, having been baptized [with] the baptism of John, but the Pharisees and the lawyers rejected the counsel of God [with regard] to themselves, not having been baptized by him

There is difficulty in Luke, but much more in Matthew For neither Mark nor Matthew has made any previous mention of "harlots" as coming to John ; nor has Luke, though mentioning "multitudes," and "tax-gatherers," and "soldiers[2]." Moreover, as John's baptisms seem to have been public and on a large scale, it does not seem likely that women of this class could have come and been baptized by him, without exciting censure, or at all events attracting notice from such writers as Luke and Josephus[3] The most probable explanation is that Matthew has been deceived by the practical identity of the Hebrew *"proselytes"* with the Aramaic *"adulterers*[4]*"* The baptism of John was a baptism for *"proselytism,"* not for

---

[1] In the Gospels, πόρνη occurs only in Mt xxi 31—2 and Lk xv. 30 (the words of the elder brother of the prodigal son) "having devoured thy substance with harlots "

[2] Lk iii 7, 12, 14   [3] Josephus *Ant* xviii 5 2

[4] See Levy *Ch* i 131 *b* shewing that the Heb *gûr* "to be a sojourner," means, in Palestinian Aramaic, "to commit adultery " The Heb verbal noun *gêr* is regularly rendered προσήλυτος by Aquila

CHRIST'S CALL TO "SINNERS"

Levitical purification[1] The Hebrew for "proselyte" is twice transliterated by the LXX as *geiōras*[2] Matthew seems to have taken it in its Aramaic sense of "adulterer[3]" Luke's expression "all the people *having heard*" is not without suspicion, partly because "all the people" is a phrase practically peculiar to him among the Evangelists[4], and partly because it may easily be a confused version of "all the people *that were hearing*, i e. *hearkening-to*, or, *disciples of*, John[5]", and this may have been Luke's way of representing an original *geiōrai*, i e. proselytes There are other possibilities of explaining Matthew's text as an error, but none (as far as I see) of explaining it as literally and historically correct[6]

After rejecting Matthew's tradition concerning the "harlots" that came to John the Baptist, Luke goes on to give, in Christ's words, a brief contrast drawn by "this generation" between John the Baptist and Jesus Of the former it is said "he hath

---

[1] See *Hor Heb* ii 54

[2] Exod xii 19, Is xiv 1 γειώρας

[3] See Jerem iii 6—8 where "played the harlot" and "committed adultery" are interchanged, and comp Ps lxxiii 27 πάντα τὸν πορνεύοντα ἀπὸ σοῦ (Targ "aberrarunt a timore tui") with Clem Hom iii 28, which describes such a ψυχή as πορνεύσασα ἢ μοιχευσαμένη

[4] It occurs several times in Luke, but elsewhere in the Gospels only in Mt xxvii 25 (pec , a solemn execration of Israel on itself), Jn viii 2 (an interpolation in Lucan style)

[5] SS has "all the people and the toll-gatherers that heard "

[6] *Baba Kama* 94 b "For herdsmen (Hirten) and *tax-collectors* (Zolleinnehmer) and *tax-farmers* (Zollpachter) repentance (die Busse) is difficult" is worth noting, but in Hebrew neither of the two italicised words could well be confused with πόρναι

Jas iv 4 "*ye adulteresses* (μοιχαλίδες)," *addressed to all sinful souls*, might suggest an explanation of Matthew's text, if "*tax-gatherers*" did not occur in Matthew's context, and Jas iv 4 may help us to understand how an original GEIŌRAS, meaning "proselyte," but having been taken to mean "*adulterer*," was adopted in the latter sense, first metaphorically as meaning γενεὰ μοιχαλίς "*an adulterous generation*," and then literally as πόρναι.

295 (Mark ii 13—17)

CHRIST'S CALL TO "SINNERS"

a devil", of the latter, "a friend of publicans *and sinners*[1]"
In this brief contrast Luke agrees verbatim with Matthew. But
then follows, in Luke, a long narrative, peculiar to his Gospel,
about a meal in a Pharisee's house, where Jesus "sat down to
meat, and behold, a woman that was in the city, *a sinner*...[2]"
If Luke reflected that he had taken on himself some responsibility in rejecting Matthew's tradition about the "harlots,"
who "believed," or "had faith," in John the Baptist, he might
naturally place here a narrative about a woman of this class,
who had faith, *not in John the Baptist (as Matthew erroneously
supposed) but in Jesus* It comes most appropriately, from
Luke's point of view, directly after the contrast between John
and Jesus ; and it exhibits Jesus as doing what John would not
have attempted to do, in consequence of the woman's "faith"
and "love" · "Her sins, which are many, are forgiven, for she
loved much," "Thy faith hath saved thee ; go in peace"

§ 5 *The woman of Samaria in John*

In Mark and Matthew, there is a narrative of the Anointing
of Jesus by a woman in Bethany, shortly before the Crucifixion,
resembling, in some respects, Luke's narrative above mentioned,
but differing in others and especially in that Mark and Matthew
neither state nor suggest that the woman was "a sinner" Luke
omits the anointing in Bethany. John inserts it and adds
that the woman was that Mary (the sister of Martha) whom
Luke himself describes (in the words of Jesus) as having
"chosen the good part[3]," and whom, therefore, he could not
reasonably be supposed to identify with the "sinner[4]." Yet

---

[1] Lk vii 31—5   [2] Lk vii 36—50
[3] Lk x 42 Yet Origen (on Mt xxvi 6—8) says that "many" identified the two women The interpolation in John (viii 1—11) about the woman taken in adultery is in a palpably Lucan style
[4] It may be replied that there may have been two periods in her life, but, if Luke had known of them, would he not have mentioned them (comp Lk viii 2 "seven devils")?

(Mark ii 13—17)

"many" Christians, before Origen's time, identified the two women. And if this identification prevailed even after John had supported Mark and Matthew, it would naturally be much more prevalent before John had written.

If it was so, and if John believed it to be an error, and if he also desired to correct what seems to be Matthew's error about the "harlots" that "believed" in John the Baptist, it would be natural that he should put on record some tradition about Christ's attitude toward such women. This he does in a dialogue between Jesus and a woman of Samaria, who says to Jesus "I have no husband," and to whom Jesus replies, "Thou saidst well, 'I have no husband'; for thou hast had five husbands, and he whom thou now hast is not thy husband[1]."

In this dialogue, and the sequel, John illustrates Christ's attitude, first, towards a woman that was a sinner, and secondly, to Samaritans. The woman's hostile prejudice is disarmed by Christ's condemnatory intuition blended with kindness. Then hostility is changed into sympathetic faith by the revelation to her of a new aspect of a Jewish Messiah. Here is a Jew who will welcome all worshippers of God, whether from Jerusalem or Gerizim, if they come to Him "in spirit and in truth." She does not understand all of it, but she understands and feels enough to give her a wholesome moral shock. We are led to suppose that it might permanently alter her character. At all events it is described as, for the time, making her an evangelist among her own people.

So much for the woman herself. Secondly, as to the Samaritans, John appears to imply a contradiction of the

---

[1] Jn iv 17—18. Comp. Philo i 131 on the "seducer ($\phi\theta o\rho\epsilon\nu\varsigma$)" who acts through the five senses, and i 532 (on Gen xiv 9) about the conflict between the four passions and the five senses. The Samaritans are said to have made (2 K xvii 30—1) five idols corresponding to their five nations. But the number "five," in this connection, does not seem to have been much commented on in the Talmuds and Midrash.

CHRIST'S CALL TO "SINNERS"

tradition—recorded by Matthew alone—that Jesus forbade His apostles to "enter into any city of the Samaritans", for here Jesus is said to have "abode with" the Samaritans "two days," and the disciples apparently along with Him[1]. Luke, too, though he mentions no such precept of Jesus as given either to the Twelve or to the Seventy, and though he has several traditions, peculiar to his Gospel, that favour the Samaritans, yet relates that Jesus was refused reception in one Samaritan village with the result that James and John requested to be allowed to call down fire on the inhospitable villagers[2] John does not deny this But, as in several other instances, he seems to say "*Audi alteram partem*; there was another aspect of Samaritans, in which they appeared not only hospitable but also believers, convinced that Jesus was 'The Saviour of the world[3].'"

§ 6 *The Syrophoenician woman in Mark and Matthew*[4]

This narrative must be discussed later on, in its order. Meantime it must be noted that Luke omits it, so that it is a case where John should intervene. There is all the more reason for intervening since Mark and Matthew apparently represent Jesus as classing the woman with "the dogs" Probably this is an error. There are many reasons for thinking that it was not Jesus, but the disciples, who wished to repel the sorrowful mother in this contumelious way—somewhat as

---

[1] Origen on Jn iv 40—1 has a curious explanation "It is not the same thing to '*abide with*' the believer and to '*enter into his city*,'" while Jerome, on Mt x 5, does not attempt to reconcile it with Jn. Origen—who admits the plausibility of those who find a contradiction (οὐκ ἀπιθάνως τις συγκρούσει)—does not venture to assert that the journey contemplated in Matthew is different from that contemplated in the parallel Synoptists, who make no mention of such a prohibition He explains the prohibition spiritually
[2] Lk ix 51—5 [3] Jn iv 42
[4] Mk vii 24—30, Mt xv 21—8. See *Son* 3353 (iv) *a—j* from which are borrowed the few facts that will be stated here

CHRIST'S CALL TO "SINNERS"

Gehazi wished to repel another sorrowful mother from Elisha. Elisha said to Gehazi "Let her alone[1]" Similarly it is probable that Jesus said to the disciples, in the uncorrupted original, "*Let her alone*," perhaps using the Aramaicized Greek word *aphès* ("do thou let alone") as an ejaculation addressed to the disciples[2] This, in Greek, being an ungrammatical use of the singular for the plural, would lead to substitution of the plural, and to other corruptions arising from the various meanings of the word in Greek[3]

The narratives in Mark and Matthew appear to be based on a brief and obscure original Its obscurities Mark and Matthew severally try to remove by additions, which were not in the original. Mark says that Jesus "desired that no man should know" of His presence[4] But the parallel Matthew omits this[5]. If it is omitted, we are free to believe that Christ's journey to the parts of Tyre and Sidon was not purposeless or for the mere purpose of escape from danger. It may have been to preach the Gospel as Jonah preached it to Nineveh

---

[1] 2 K iv 27 "*Let her alone*" (ἄφες αὐτήν)

[2] Comp Jn xii 7 ἄφες αὐτήν, in the Anointing at Bethany, with the parall Mk xiv 6 ἄφετε αὐτήν, and also Mk xv 36 ἄφετε with the parall Mt xxvii 49 ἄφες

[3] Ἄφετε αὐτήν, if written αφεται αυτη, might easily be confused with ἀφίεται αὐτῇ or ἀφεῖται αὐτῇ "she is forgiven," comp Lk vii 47—8 (where however the form used is different) on the forgiveness of the sins of the woman that was a sinner

See *Son* 3353 (iv) *h* "The drama, according to the hypothesis stated above, would read thus —

1 The woman throws herself at Christ's feet The disciples attempt to prevent her

2 Jesus says '*Let her alone*,' using the Aramaic *aphès* as an exclamation addressed to all the disciples

3 The disciples say, 'It is not fit to take the bread of the children and cast it to the dogs'

4 The woman, appealing to the Lord against His disciples, says, 'Nay, Lord, even the dogs....'"

[4] Mk vii 24   [5] Mt xv. 21

CHRIST'S CALL TO "SINNERS"

It is true that Jesus is reported by Matthew to have said "I was not sent but unto the lost sheep of the house of Israel." But Mark does not report this. And how could Jesus say it consistently with what He had said before, when He performed one of His earliest miracles, the healing of the centurion's servant? The centurion was rich and popular, but he was a Gentile. Jesus lauded his faith above the faith of Israel and healed his servant. After doing that, how could Jesus excuse Himself from healing the poor Syrophoenician's daughter on the ground that He was sent only to Israel[1]?

If Jesus followed a precedent of the prophet Jonah, that ought not to surprise us, since we find both Matthew and Luke representing Him as predicting that no "sign" will be given by the Son of Man except "the sign of Jonah[2]." It is true that they interpret this "sign" differently. But that does not destroy the importance of their agreement in this point, that out of all the prophets, Jesus selected Jonah, the Missionary to Nineveh, as the one in whose footsteps He, *in some sense,* followed.

That Luke felt compelled to omit the story of the Syrophoenician mother may be all the more easily understood from the mention of the widow of Zarephath and Naaman in his version of Christ's first public discourse. There were many widows in Israel, it says, but Elijah was sent to none of them, but only to that one in the land of Sidon; there were many

---

[1] See *Son* **3353** (iv) *a* foll. which suggests, as one explanation, that Mt xv. 24 "the lost sheep of the house of Israel" may be a paraphrase for "sinners" generally, "Israel" being the spiritual Israel, not "Israel after the flesh." It should have been added that Origen takes this view (*ad loc.*, and *Comm. Joann* xx. 5) "The simpler folk," he says, take "Israel" literally. If "Israel" is to be taken spiritually, one version of the story may have been as follows "The disciples said to Jesus 'Send her away.' But Jesus answered 'Nay, I was not sent except to *lost sinners and sufferers such as this,*'" comp. Lk xv. 4—32, xix. 10 "*that which was lost.*"

[2] Mt xii. 39 foll., Lk xi. 29 foll., comp. Mt xvi. 4

300 (Mark ii. 13—17)

lepers in Israel, but none of them was cleansed by Elisha, but only Naaman the Syrian[1]. Naaman was an idolater at the time when he was healed. Even after he was healed, he still "bowed in the house of Rimmon" on state occasions. Yet Jesus speaks of the healing almost as if it might be a precedent for acts of His own, and certainly not with reprehension. How then was it possible for Luke to describe Jesus as treating the poor Syrophoenician woman with a contumely none the less bitter because it was indirect, by classing her with "the dogs[2]"?

§ 7. *"Greek" in Mark, and "Greeks" in John*

We have now to ask how John intervenes. If there were any evidence that in the first century the Syrophoenician woman was regarded as "a sinner," and hence supposed to be classed with "dogs," we might say that John intervenes indirectly in the Dialogue with the Samaritan woman. But in the Clementine Homilies the name of the Syrophoenician is given as Justa, without any suggestion that she was of dissolute life. Not improbably, in publishing the Dialogue, John may have had in view discussions about Christ's apparently harsh and austere treatment of a foreign woman, which he meets by saying "See how He treated the woman of Samaria, and ask yourselves whether He could have thus treated the woman of Syro-Phoenicia." More than this we cannot say, so far as concerns the Dialogue.

---

[1] Lk iv 25—7
[2] *Clem. Hom.* ii 19 (See *Son* 3353 (iv) *j*) "Jesus said, It is not lawful to heal the *Gentiles*—who are *like dogs*, because they have different food and habits, the table that is according to the Kingdom having been given-as-due (ἀποδεδομένης) to the sons of Israel."

In Acts xi 3, after Peter had baptized Cornelius, "they of the circumcision" condemned him, not for giving the converts baptism, but for eating with them. "Thou wentest in to men uncircumcised, and didst eat with them." The institution of the Eucharist, with its One Loaf, brought to the front the question. "May a Christian Jew eat with a Christian Greek?"

CHRIST'S CALL TO "SINNERS"

But more may be said in favour of the hypothesis that John noted the difference between Mark, who calls the woman "*a Greek [woman], a Syrophoenician by race*," and Matthew, who calls her "*a Canaanitish woman.*" John often lays stress on typical or generic words, capable of symbolic meaning. And there is a great difference, even in the minds of Jews, between a "*Greek*" and a "*Canaanite.*" The Canaanite is regarded, throughout the Bible, as defiled and defiling, and the prophecy of Zechariah closes with a prediction that there shall be "no more the Canaanite in the house of the Lord[1]." The Greeks, the sons of Javan, though hostile[2], are not thus regarded. Philo ventures to say that "Hellas is the only land that veritably *produces-men*, scion of heaven and offspring of divine nature," meaning the philosophic mind[3]. No doubt, Philo is not a typical Jew. But he is typical of the philosophic Jew. And the author of the Fourth Gospel appears to have had a tincture of his philosophy. We may therefore reasonably suppose that John would do something to destroy the painful impression produced on Greek readers by the fact that the only instance of the word "*Hellene*" in the early Gospels mentioned a *Hellenis*, *i.e.* Greek woman, to whose petition for help for a suffering daughter Jesus replied at first by saying that it was not fit to take the children's bread and to cast it unto dogs[4]. At all events it is worth inquiring whether John ever mentions "Hellenes," and, if so, in what light he represents them.

---

[1] Zech. xiv. 21. This is the only instance of "Canaanite" (sing.) in the prophets (A.V.). Ezek. xvi. 3 (R.V.) "the land of the *Canaanite*" implies defilement.

[2] Comp. Zech. ix. 13 "I will stir up thy sons, O Zion, against thy sons, O Greece (*Heb.* Javan)."

[3] Philo ii. 646—7 Μόνη γὰρ ἡ Ἑλλὰς ἀψευδῶς ἀνθρωπογονεῖ φυτὸν οὐράνιον καὶ βλάστημα θεῖον....

[4] That pain would not be diminished when the reader met with the phrase in the Jewish Law (Exod. xxii. 31) "Ye shall be holy men unto me, therefore ye shall not eat any flesh that is torn by beasts in the field, ye shall *cast it to the dogs.*" Rashi's note indicates that "dogs" might be interpreted as "Gentiles."

He mentions them in two passages The first is an utterance of the Jews, after Jesus has said to them "I go unto him that sent me, ye shall seek me, and not find me, and, where I am, ye cannot come" The Jews ask "Will he go unto the Dispersion of (*i e* among) *the Greeks*, and teach *the Greeks*?" Here they "unconsciously predict the manner in which the Spirit of the risen Saviour, travelling abroad in His disciples, would teach, first, the Dispersion [*i e* the scattered Jews] among the Greeks, and then the Greeks themselves[1]" By "the Greeks" are meant the civilised nations of the Roman empire—those whom Paul calls "Greeks" as distinct from "Jews" and "Scythians"

The second passage mentioning "Hellenes" is in narrative, not speech "Now there were certain *Greeks* among those that went up to worship at the feast. These therefore came to Philip...saying, *Sir, we would see Jesus*[2]" When Jesus is told this, He exclaims "The hour is come that the Son of man shall be glorified," and sets forth the law of the dying "grain of wheat," of life through death. A voice from heaven follows, and Christ predicts "judgment" for "the prince of this world," and "lifting up" for Himself. The "lifting up" is to be on the Cross —"I, if I be lifted up from the earth, will draw all men unto myself But this he said signifying *by what manner of death he should die.*" The discourse closes with the warning to the multitude around Him, "While ye have the light, believe on the light, that ye may become sons of light," after which Jesus "departed and was hidden from them[3]."

What is the connection, if any, between this coming of the "Greeks," and the warning to "the multitude" to become "sons of light"? It is this. Jesus was "the light of the world," as well as the Son of God. The Greeks come saying "We

---

[1] Quoted from *Joh Gr* 2046 (on Jn vii 35) Comp the unique mention of "Romans" in the Gospels, which is also an unconscious prophecy (Jn xi. 48).

[2] Jn xii 20—21.   [3] Jn xii 32—3, 36—7.

would see Jesus." This means that they, "the nations," come to see the light of the world Thus they fulfil the prophecy of Isaiah, "Arise, shine, for thy light is come...The Lord shall arise upon thee, and *his glory shall be seen upon thee*, and *nations shall come to thy light*[1]." Isaiah's next words describe the submission of "the nations" to Israel, a willing submission, the result of a spiritual conquest. Zechariah describes what Christian interpreters would call the same conquest, but he describes it in different terms. He speaks of it first as the result of words of "peace[2]." But immediately afterwards he speaks of it as won by the "sword"; and here comes one of the very few mentions of "Greece" in prophecy "I will stir up thy sons, O Zion, against thy sons, *O Greece*, and will make thee as the sword of a mighty man[3]."

This is one of the very rare instances where the word "Hellene" occurs in the Canonical LXX[4], and the rarity of the name makes it probable that John, who has just quoted the preceding words in Zechariah about the Messiah "riding upon an ass[5]," is now alluding to the same prophet's prediction about "Greece" and the "sword" of Zion Only he takes the sword to be the "sword of the Spirit," which was to descend after Jesus had been "lifted up" Wielding this "sword," Jesus, on the throne of the Cross, would conquer "the nations" in a spiritual conquest, drawing them out of the darkness into light, that is to say, into Himself For the author of the Fourth Gospel, it is probable that "Israel" meant "*seeing God*[6]." "The Greeks," therefore, who came to "*see Jesus*,"

---

[1] Is lx 1—3.
[2] Zech ix 10 "he shall speak *peace* unto the nations"
[3] *Oxf Conc* gives Joel iii (iv) 6, Zech ix 13, Is ix 12, Dan viii 21, x 20, xi 2
[4] Zech ix 13
[5] Zech ix 9 quoted in Jn xii 15
[6] That is assumed to be the meaning by Philo and Origen (see *Son* 3140 *a—b*, and add Origen in *Cant Prolog* Lomm xiv 313) To these add Clement of Alexandria (334) διορατικός

304 (Mark ii 13—17)

being thus drawn into Him, would be drawn into the ranks of the spiritual Israel, and at the same time become "sons of light."

If we were non-Christians in the first or second century, reading the Gospels for the first time, we should probably feel a shock—much greater than the uneasiness that a few thoughtful Christians may now feel—at Christ's alleged treatment of the Syrophoenician woman. If we were Greek-speaking readers at the same period, we should certainly feel an additional repulsion in the fact that this woman, in the Synoptic Gospels, was the sole representative of the Greek world in the life of Christ. The Johannine description of the Greeks "wishing to see" Jesus, and of the welcome that Jesus gave to their desire, would go far to assure us either that the Mark-Matthew narrative was erroneous, or that there was something else, unrecorded, beneath or beyond it, which would bring the picture of Christ as drawn by the first two Evangelists into harmony with the picture of Christ as drawn by the fourth. To produce such an assurance was an object well worthy of the writer of the Fourth Gospel, and the facts alleged above make it reasonable to believe that he had this object in view.

Returning to the Marcan tradition "I have come to call *sinners*," we perceive that it was a brief and fervid way of saying "I have come to call *those who feel themselves to be unrighteous*." To those who felt themselves to be righteous enough already, Jesus addressed no call, or rather the call that He addressed to them (as to all the world) was as if not uttered, because their hearts were closed against it by their self-righteousness. It was a call to enter into the family of the One God, worshipped by Israel as Jehovah, and now revealed in the Son as the Father of all mankind.

Logically and spiritually this call would seem to include Gentiles as well as Jews. It is difficult to believe that Jesus would have rejected the centurion of Capernaum if he had presented himself as a candidate for baptism; yet in the Acts

CHRIST'S CALL TO "SINNERS"

Peter is described as requiring a special revelation before he admitted the centurion Cornelius Is it not reasonable to suppose that Jesus contemplated such inclusion from the first?

According to Luke, Jesus quoted—as, in some sense, precedents for His own conduct—the beneficent actions of Elijah and Elisha toward non-Israelites. Circumstances restricted His action almost entirely to His own countrymen, but we are not justified in believing that He definitely imposed this restriction either on Himself or on His disciples Possibly Matthew may have misunderstood some temporary post-resurrectional precept to the Twelve as applying to Christ's own conduct. The permanent and essential message of Christ seems to have been unrestricted by national limitations. "I have come to call sinners," "Come unto me, all ye that are weary," "If any man thirst, let him come unto me," "Blessed are they that hunger and thirst after righteousness," "I, if I be lifted up from the earth, will draw all men unto me[1]." Only the first of these five traditions belongs to Mark and the Synoptic Tradition. But the other four spring out of the first—the historical utterance that Jesus "came to call sinners." The accusation that He also "ate with" them Jesus does not condescend to meet.

---

[1] Mk 11 17 and parall Mt and Lk, Mt xi. 28, Jn vii 37, Mt v. 6, Jn xii. 32

CHAPTER VIII*

THE OLD AND THE NEW
[Mark ii. 18—22]

§ 1. *A complaint of the Baptist's disciples, in the Synoptic Gospels*

THIS Chapter will deal with two contrasts between the old and the new. The first is of a particular kind—between fasting, an old practice, and non-fasting, a new one. The second is general—insisting that old practice must not go with new doctrine, but that both must be old, or both must be new.

To this second contrast Luke, alone among the Synoptists, prefixes the words "and he spake also a parable unto them"—thus separating it from the first. On the other hand, Mark and Matthew take the two contrasts as one continuous discourse. We shall follow Luke in this matter. Reasons for this course will be given later on, indicating that the particular saying about "fasting" is to be kept distinct from the general saying about the old and the new, the former being perhaps uttered by John the Baptist, the latter by Jesus.

These reasons are derived, in part from the texts, in part from the thoughts. First as to the texts, it will be observed that Mark's opening words—if taken by themselves, apart from

---

* For titles of previous Parts of Diatessarica referred to by abbreviations in this Volume, see pp 545—6. For other abbreviations see pp xxiii—xxvi.

THE OLD AND THE NEW

the parallel Matthew-Luke, and apart from what follows in Mark—might be interpreted as follows —"The disciples of the Baptist and the Pharisees happened to be at that time fasting. And they came and said to *him*"—that is, to *John*—what follows[1]. It is true that Mark's next words, "Why do *John's disciples* fast?" remove this impression; for we naturally say "If that had been the meaning, they would have said, not '*John's disciples*' but '*we*.'" But Matthew *does* substitute "*we*," and the substitution of "*we*" in Mark (interpreted as above) would not destroy sense It would only produce a different sense   "The Baptist's disciples and the Pharisees came to John saying Why do *we* and the disciples of the Pharisees fast?"

So far, the remodelled Marcan narrative has gone on consistently in the form of a complaint made to John by his own disciples on the subject of fasting But now comes a check. If it is still to be consistent, it ought to proceed thus. "But the disciples *of Jesus* fast not." Instead of this, the three Synoptists have "but *thy* disciples (fast not)" Here, then, we have to pause and ask whether there is evidence to shew that "*Jesus*" and "*thy*" could be easily interchanged.

There is such evidence. The repetition of one vowel and the insertion of another would change "*thy*" into "*of Jesus*[2]" Conversely, "the disciples *of Jesus*" might easily become "*thy*

---

[1] Mk ii 18 (R V)

And John's disciples and the Pharisees were fasting and they come and say unto him, Why do John's disciples and the disciples of the Pharisees fast, but thy disciples fast not?

Mt ix 14 (R V)

Then come to him the disciples of John, saying, Why do we and the Pharisees fast oft (*some anc auth omit* oft), but thy disciples fast not?

Lk v 33 (R V)

And they said unto him, The disciples of John fast often, and make supplications, likewise also the [disciples] of the Pharisees, but thine eat and drink

[2] That is to say, Mt ix 14 οἱ δὲ μαθηταὶ σοῦ, would become οἱ δὲ μαθηταὶ Ἰησοῦ, by a corruption of AICOY into AIIHCOY (or into AIIOY, see *Corrections* **504** *a*)

308 (Mark ii 18—22)

THE OLD AND THE NEW

disciples[1]." Above all, there is the well-known contrast in Matthew between "*Jesus* Barabbas" and "*Jesus* Christ." This was so offensive to Origen that he protested against it on the ground that it was "not fit" that anyone called "*Jesus*" in the Bible should be a sinner; but all that he can say for cancelling it, on textual grounds, is that "*in many copies it is not contained* that Barabbas also was called Jesus[2]." "*Jesus Barabbas*" is the reading of the recently-discovered Syro-Sinaitic Version; and we may now regard it as highly probable that this was in Matthew's original Greek text[3] If it was, the cancelling of the name "Jesus" may be explained as being the result, not of prejudice alone, but of prejudice combined with obscurities arising from Greek abbreviations of the name[4].

Applying these facts to the next verse in Mark and Matthew "and Jesus said unto them," we see that "Jesus" is preceded, in both, by the Greek letters that constitute the abbreviation of the name[5]. We also note that this particular phrase for introducing words of Jesus is not characteristically Synoptic but Johannine[6]. These are all small points in themselves;

---

[1] See *Joh Gr* **2661** *c* quoting Jn xviii 5 (B) "I am *Jesus* (IC̅)," where IC̅ is probably a repetition of the first syllable of the following word ICTHKEI Comp Sir xliii 23 (LXX) Ἰησοῦς where the Heb. has "islands," *i e* νήσους, which, after a preceding ν, has been corrupted into Ἰησοῦς

[2] Origen on Mt xxvii 17 (Lomm v 35) He suggests that "in haeresibus tale aliquid superadditum est"

[3] See SS ed Burkitt, vol ii pp 277—8

[4] *E g* in Mt xxvii 16, D inserts τόν in connection with "Barabbas" In *ib* 17, B does the same This may be a corruption of IN̅, *i e* Ἰησοῦν Also, between IN̅ and BAP, in *ib*. 17 ἀπολύσω ὑμῖν Βαραββᾶν, an intervening IN̅, meaning "Jesus," might be cancelled without dishonesty, as a scribal repetition of the preceding IN̅

[5] Mk ii 19 (Mt ix 15) καὶ εἶπεν αὐτοῖς followed by ὁ Ἰησοῦς, *i e*. OIC followed by OIC̅ Luke has v 34 ὁ δὲ Ἰησοῦς εἶπεν πρὸς αὐτούς

[6] This is the only passage in Mt where εἶπεν αὐτοῖς ὁ Ἰησ occurs (apart from xvii 22 συστρ δὲ . εἶπεν αὐτοῖς ὁ Ἰησ) In Mk it occurs here and i 17 Lk has it in xx 34 (but with var readings) It is characteristic of John vi 35, viii 25, 42 etc and very frequently with οὖν (vi 32, 53 etc).

THE OLD AND THE NEW

but in view of the fact that the Fourth Gospel describes a complaint made by John's disciples *not to Jesus, but to John, and a reply from John mentioning "the bridegroom,"* we are justified in suspending our judgment about the person to whom the complaint was made until we have studied what that Gospel says about the complaint and about the answer made to it. We may fairly use the word *"complaint"* because the language is shewn by the context in all the Gospels to be that of *complaint*, not of merely dispassionate inquiry.

In the first place it should be noted that, whereas Mark and Matthew both describe the complainants as "coming" to some one, whether to Jesus or to the Baptist, Luke omits all mention of such "coming." In his Gospel, the complaint is part of the "murmuring" just mentioned, in the house of Levi, at the feast where Christ's disciples were eating and drinking with tax-gatherers and sinners. Jesus has replied that He came "to call, not righteous folk, but sinners *to repentance.*" There Luke alone has *"to repentance."* The retort that follows, in Luke, perhaps implies a jibe at *"repentance,"* having, in effect, this meaning. "There is not much 'repentance' in your disciples. The disciples of John fast often[1] and make supplications, likewise also do '*those of the Pharisees*,' but yours eat and drink[2]." According to the rule of Johannine Intervention, we should expect the Fourth Gospel to correct Luke,

---

[1] By inserting "often" here, Luke makes it clear that the meaning is *not* (in his view) as one might infer from Mark, "the disciples of John *happened to be fasting at that time.*"

[2] Lk v 30—33 "And the Pharisees and their scribes were murmuring...And Jesus answering said unto them ...And they said unto him, The disciples of John fast often,...likewise also *the [disciples] of the Pharisees*, but thine eat and drink." This is consistent with itself except for the words italicised, where "*we*," or "*our disciples*," would have been a more natural expression, the speakers being themselves Pharisees. But Luke is influenced by Mark-Matthew, which represents the complainants as mentioning "the Pharisees" or "the disciples of the Pharisees."

310 (Mark ii 18—22)

THE OLD AND THE NEW

and to say "There was a 'coming' that preceded this complaint. The complaint was not a sudden retort such as Luke supposes. And those who 'came' were the disciples of John Only, they 'came,' not to Jesus, but to their own Master, to John " We must not here anticipate the discussion of such a passage in the Fourth Gospel, but will simply remind the reader of its existence[1].

§ 2. *Fasting*

Fasting is nowhere mentioned in the Law of Moses as binding on Israel But it is implied in the commandment "ye shall afflict your souls " To do this was binding on one and only one day in the year, the Day of Atonement "In the seventh month, on the tenth day of the month, *ye shall afflict your souls* and shall do no manner of work... for on this day shall atonement be made for you to purify you from all your sins shall ye be pure before the Lord It is a sabbath of sabbathizing unto you and *ye shall afflict your souls*[2] " Later on it is said concerning this day: "*Ye shall afflict your souls*...ye shall do no manner of work in that same day. ..For whatsoever *soul it be that shall not be afflicted* in that same day, he shall be cut off from his people[3] " The second passage makes it obvious that death would be inflicted on any Israelite who did not manifest in some external way that he "afflicted his soul"; and Jewish tradition assumed that one necessary self-affliction on this day was "fasting[4]."

We must note the emphasis laid on this unique day On most sabbaths it would be wrong to fast, but this day was

---

[1] Jn iii 26 "They [i e John's disciples] came unto John and said to him, Rabbi, he that was with thee...the same baptizeth ..."

[2] Lev xvi 29—31

[3] Lev. xxiii 27—9 "Be afflicted," LXX ταπεινωθήσεται, but "Ἄλλος" νηστεύσῃ

[4] See *Jôma* 76 a

THE OLD AND THE NEW

to be both "a sabbath of sabbathizing" and a fast-day[1]. The solemn repetition of "*afflict your souls*" is heightened by a repetition of what our Revised Version calls "*that same day*" The literal Hebrew is "*the bone, or substance, of the day*" It is a phrase applied only to epoch-making events, such as Noah's entrance into the Ark, the Covenant of Circumcision with Abraham, the Exodus from Egypt etc.[2] To many Israelites this single yearly "self-affliction" would doubtless be a genuine spiritual act, in which they would not only fast but also review and amend their lives But Isaiah bitterly censures the formal "self-affliction" of the selfish hypocritical oppressor, who bowed his head down "as a rush," in "sackcloth and ashes," but continued his oppression and did not "let the oppressed go free[3]" He apparently connects the fast with the remission of debts and restoration of lands enjoined on the jubilee But he also passes beyond the injunctions of the Levitical Law into a high region of spiritual morality, when he says "If thou *draw out thy soul to the hungry*, and satisfy the afflicted soul, then shall thy light rise in darkness[4]"

This introduces a new kind of "afflicting the soul." It is not a "self-affliction," like that practised by the priests of Baal,

---

[1] See Gesen 992 b on the application of "sabbath of sabbathizing"

[2] See Gesen 783 a referring to Gen vii 13, xvii 23, 26, Exod xii 17 etc It means "the *bone, substance,* or *essence,* of the day" It occurs three times in Lev xxiii 28—30

[3] Is lviii 1—6 "Cry aloud...lift up thy voice like a trumpet .. let the oppressed go free and break every yoke" Comp Lev xxv 9—10 "In the day of atonement shall ye send abroad the trumpet . and proclaim liberty ..."

[4] Is lviii 10 The phrase "*draw out* (or *produce*) thy soul" was variously interpreted in early times, but Resch Lakisch (*Lev r* Wu p 245), Jerome, Aquila, Symmachus, and Theodotion substantially agree in the rendering "effuderis animam tuam" It is the opposite of (1 Jn iii 17) "shut up the bowels [of compassion]" It is not to exclude, but to accompany, material giving The LXX δῷς πεινῶντι τὸν ἄρτον ἐκ ψυχῆς σου means, perhaps, "not only give, but give from thy soul, that is, heartily, cheerfully"

THE OLD AND THE NEW

who "lanced themselves" to propitiate their god Nor is it directed against one's own animal nature, an "affliction," or "mortification," of the flesh That is an action, often wise and useful, but undertaken for one's own sake But Isaiah's "self-afflicting" is of a different nature, being that which arises in the kind-hearted, who will not shrink from sympathizing with sorrow while attempting to relieve it

Passing to the fasting of Esther, Daniel, Ezra, and Nehemiah, we perceive that it was for the nation, not for themselves. It was a genuine affliction of soul brought on them by some national crisis which led them naturally to abstain from food while they turned to God for help and guidance. In later days—even when there was no such crisis, but only subjection to Gentiles, and sorrow that the sceptre had departed from Jacob—many pious Jews might fast, like Anna, or Simeon, looking for "the consolation of Israel[1]" They fasted twice in the week. But so (in Luke) does the Pharisee, who makes a merit of it and shews no sign of looking for "the consolation of Israel[2]." In Matthew's Sermon on the Mount Jesus says to His disciples "Whenever ye are fasting, be not as the hypocrites[3]" This assumes that those whom He was addressing were in the habit of fasting—if not twice a week, at all events more often than on the one Day of Atonement. Jesus does not forbid the act, but on the contrary urges those who do it not to destroy its efficacy by doing it ostentatiously. Luke, however, omits this passage, and it may reasonably be supposed that he omitted it because he regarded it as negative, partial, and temporary, not intended for Gentiles who were not in the habit of fasting. The fact seems to be that the great mass of Christ's disciples were not in the habit of fasting and were not bidden

---

[1] Lk ii 37 (of Anna) "worshipping with fastings and supplications," *ib* 25 (of Simeon) "looking for the consolation of Israel"

[2] Lk xviii 11—12 "God, I thank thee that I am not as the rest of men ..I fast twice in the week"

[3] Mt vi 16—18

by Him to fast, but those who came to Him, confirmed in the habit of fasting, were warned by Him to see that they did not lose the moral benefit of it by fasting like the Pharisees.

According to Maimonides, Jewish congregations fasted for certain calamities, and an individual fasted for corresponding calamities "If any that belong to him be sick, or lost in the wilderness, or kept in prison, he is bound to *fast* in his behalf[1]." John the Baptist was at this time "in prison" (according to the Synoptists) His disciples, therefore, would have a special reason for "fasting oftentimes" And they might—not unnaturally from their point of view—find fault with Jesus for abrogating the practice of fasting among His disciples Perhaps it was not positively abrogated by Him, but only negatively allowed to drop. Perhaps "*do not fast*" should have been modified by "*as a rule*," or, "*for the most part*" But we may feel sure that the complaint was actually made, and was actually true—that the disciples of Jesus did not observe, and were not taught by Jesus to observe, the practice, prevalent among the Pharisees, of weekly "fasting."

§ 3. *The "bridegroom," in the Synoptic reply*

We pass now to the reply made to the complaint. It is almost identical in the Three Gospels, being to this effect, that fasting is impossible for "the sons of the bride-chamber" while the bridegroom is with them, but that a time will come when the bridegroom shall be taken away from them and then they will fast[2]

---

[1] *Hor Heb* (on Lk xviii 12) quoting Maimonides on *Taanith* chap. 1

[2] Mk ii 19—20 (R.V.)

(19) And Jesus said unto them, Can the sons of the bride-chamber fast, while the bridegroom is with them? as long

Mt ix 15 (R V)

And Jesus said unto them, Can the sons of the bride-chamber mourn, as long as the bridegroom is with them?

Lk v. 34—5 (R V)

(34) And Jesus said unto them, Can ye make the sons of the bride-chamber fast, while the bridegroom is with them?

We naturally ask what the Synoptists have elsewhere to say about "the bridegroom," thus for the first time mentioned by them. Matthew mentions "the bridegroom" in one of the last of his parables inculcating expectancy of the day of the Lord[1] But Mark and Luke never mention the word again. As for "the children of the bride-chamber," *Horae Hebraicae* tells us that the exact phrase is "*children of the [bridal] canopy*," that is, of the "*canopy*" under which the wedded pair were united[2] But Jerome and almost all the Latin Versions render it "children of the *bridegroom* (*sponsi*)" This misses the meaning[3] It is not "children of the bridegroom," but "the invited guests," many of whom accompany "the bridegroom."

Still we are left in doubt as to the precise meaning of the metaphor. Is "the bridegroom" loosely used for the central person in any joyful feast? Or does it contain any allusion to the Jewish mystical Bridegroom, that is, the Lord? If so, are we to think of the Messiah, the Son of David, as being a greater and more spiritual Solomon, a Builder of the perfect Temple, in which the Bridegroom and the Bride, the Lord and

Mk ii 19—20 (R V) (*contd*)	Mt ix 15 (R V) (*contd*)	Lk v. 34—5 (R V) (*contd*)
as they have the bridegroom with them, they cannot fast (20) But the days will come, when the bridegroom shall be taken away from them, and then will they fast in that day.	but the days will come, when the bridegroom shall be taken away from them, and then will they fast	(35) But the days will come, and when the bridegroom shall be taken away from them, then will they fast in those days

[1] Mt xxv 1—13

[2] *Hor Heb* on Mt ix. 15 calls it *bride-chamber* "The days of the bride-chamber, to *the sons of the bride-chamber*, that is, to the friends and acquaintance, were seven" The Heb (which is also in Delitzsch) means "canopy" in Is iv. 5, but "chamber" of bride or bridegroom in Joel ii 16, Ps xix 5 (Gesen 342 *b*)

[3] Mt ix 15 In Mk ii 19, Codex *b* and Pseudo-Jerome have "filii nuptiarum," but "filii sponsi" is the usual rendering

THE OLD AND THE NEW

the Nation, were to be united? The answer would depend to some extent on the personality of the speaker; John the Baptist might use the term in one sense, Jesus in a sense somewhat different. It would also depend on the extent to which, if at all, the term had been *previously used by the Baptist, or by Jesus, or by both*. According to the Fourth Gospel, the Baptist, even before he was cast into prison, called Jesus "the Bridegroom." What if Jesus, at this later period, is referring to that fact? In that case, He is saying to the disciples of John, in effect, "The bridegroom [as your Master called me]." Or, if John is speaking, then it is, "The bridegroom [as I have called Jesus, before now, in your presence]."

These uncertainties greatly complicate our investigation. But it is antecedently probable that the utterance, although Christians at a very early period regarded it as a prediction of Christ concerning His Passion, was originally not of this character, but had some vernacular and homely meaning. Against this view it may be urged that the word "taken-away" ("the bridegroom shall be *taken away*") implies the Passion and was so interpreted in early times[1]. That it was so interpreted is true. But what if the interpretation sprang from some very simple and natural misunderstanding of the customs of a Palestinian wedding not understood by Christians in the West? Let us look into the word.

The Greek for "taken-away" means literally "lifted-away," and the Syro-Sinaitic has "taken-up." In the active, it is frequently used by LXX to mean "journey," "break up [camp]," "remove." But the passive is not known to be thus used[2]. If we are to render it faithfully we seem driven to interpret

---

[1] See *Apostolic Constitutions* v 18 "Do you therefore fast on the days of the Passover. [v r adds *six days*, in agreement with v 15 he commanded us to fast *these six days*].," followed by a quotation of the Synoptic saying about "the bridegroom" as being "taken away." The fasting on some of the days was not to be complete. See below, p 325

[2] Ἀπαίρομαι in Hesych = ἀποδημέω, but is probably middle.

THE OLD AND THE NEW

it as meaning "lifted-away" in some such circumstances as would resemble those of Elijah, concerning whom the sons of the prophets say to Elisha, "Knowest thou that the Lord will *take thy master from-above thy head* to-day[1]?" The Hebrew of "*from-above thy head*" conveys the thought "*from his headship over thee*" So the question arises, "Could it be said about a bridegroom in Galilee that he was in any sense 'head' over 'the sons of the canopy' during the seven days of the wedding feast, and that, when this 'headship' terminated, the feast terminated at the same time?"

There are reasons for thinking that this was the case. In the first place, there is the custom of the Palestinian fellaheen in marriage feasts · "During the seven days... the young couple are treated by the villagers as *king* and queen....The proceedings end with a supper, and *the degradation of the king to his proper rank*[2]" Marriage-customs often point back to very ancient times, and, in the present instance, there are curious indications in the Fourth Gospel that the writer was aware of Jewish or Galilaean distinctions between "the sons of the canopy or bride-chamber," who were many, and "the friend of the bridegroom," whom he regards as being but one[3]. The

---

[1] 2 K ii 3, 5

[2] Hastings *Dict* iii 272—3 quoting J G Wetzstein from *Zeitschrift fur Ethnologie*, vol v p 287 foll (1873) The feast goes out somewhat sordidly "The festal regulations are annulled ..and scarcely is the meal over when a pair of hands smear the king's face from a dung-heap (*ib* p 293)"

[3] Jn iii 29 "*the friend of the bridegroom*" On "the friends of the bridegroom," "*shoshbenin,*" or "*paranymphs,*" Wetstein quotes Kethub. 12 a "Formerly *in Judaea* they used to appoint two paranymphs, one for the bridegroom, the other for the bride, to minister to them when they enter the canopy (chuppam) but in Galilee there was no such observance" He also quotes a tradition from *Gen r.* (on Gen ii 22) that Michael and Gabriel were "paranymphs" of Adam, and another (*Aboth Nathan* iv) that God Himself was Adam's paranymph (which is confirmed by *Erubin* 18 b) *Hor Heb* on Jn ii 1 quoting *Kethub.* 12 a omits "in Judaea," but it is inserted also in *j Kethub.* 1 1 (Schwab vol. viii p 6) *Hor. Heb* (*ib*) also omits

THE OLD AND THE NEW

Evangelist also introduces, in his account of the wedding at Cana, a "governor of the triclinium," a term that in Greek or Latin would mean a "king" of the feast elected by the guests to regulate the toasts and songs[1]. Ben Sira mentions such a "master" of a feast and gives him advice: "Have they made thee *Master*? Be not puffed up.... And when thou hast done all thine office take thy place[2]." What were the precise objects of the Evangelist in recording the details at Cana it is impossible to say with confidence. But it is reasonable to suppose that among them was the object of illustrating the Hebrew and Jewish conception of the Bridegroom, and the form in which it presented itself to the last of the Prophets, John the Baptist, and the form—perhaps a different form—in which it was fulfilled by the Messiah to whom the Prophet bore witness. Along with this object, or as part of this object, would be the desire to correct erroneous impressions about the Bridegroom derivable from various interpretations of the Synoptic Gospels. Returning, then, to the Synoptic version of the reply, we ask what it could mean, first, if Jesus uttered it, and then if John uttered it.

§ 4. *The meaning of "bridegroom," if uttered by Jesus, or if uttered by the Baptist*

If Jesus uttered the words "when the bridegroom shall be taken away," their context must be taken as a prediction implying a command, apparently meaning "My disciples will fast

---

"*and*" before "*the children*" in translating (though not in quoting) Maimonides "The bridegroom and all the *paranymphs and the children of the canopy*." The omission might give the impression that the two terms meant the same thing

[1] Jn ii 8—9 τῷ ἀρχιτρικλίνῳ...φωνεῖ τὸν νυμφίον ὁ ἀρχιτρίκλινος. The word τρικλίνιον is freq in Hebrew (Krauss), but Levy (ii 191—2) does not give an instance of the word along with "king," "governor," or "head."

[2] Sir. xxxii (xxxv.) 1 foll. "Master," ἡγούμενον, Syr. "*rab*," Vulg "rectorem"

out of sorrow and longing for me in my absence." The writer of the *Apostolic Constitutions*, however, takes it as a command to bewail during the week of the Passion, *not because of Christian sorrow—for Christians are "blessed"—but because of the impiety and perdition of the Jews who crucified Him*. "Ye ought therefore to *bewail over them*....*Ye therefore are blessed*....But unto unbelieving Israel He says....[1]" And it cannot be denied that this view of Christian "blessedness" accords with the words of Jesus in the Gospels which say "I am with you alway even unto the end of the world," and "I will see you again, and your heart shall rejoice, and your joy no one taketh away from you[2]"

No doubt, to us, it is a matter of great difficulty to realise that the Apostles, after Christ had been taken up from them to heaven, could feel as "blessed" as when He moved among them in Galilee[3]. But both Paul and the Fourth Evangelist compel

---

[1] Only as to the fasting on the Saturday before the Resurrection is there any indication that we are to fast out of sympathy with Jesus, and even there the impiety of the Jews in "apprehending the Lord on their very feast-day" is perhaps the prominent thought *Const Apost* v 15 "But He commanded us to fast on the fourth and sixth days of the week, the former on account of His being betrayed, and the latter on account of His passion. But He appointed us to break our fast on the seventh day at the cock-crowing" [*i e*, as in v 18, the cock-crowing *of the night*], "but to fast on the Sabbath-day Not that the Sabbath-day is a day of fasting, being the rest from the creation, but because we ought to fast on this one Sabbath only, while on this day the Creator was under the earth For on their very feast-day they apprehended the Lord..."

[2] Mt xxviii 20, Jn xvi. 22 The interval of sorrow is to be "a little while" After that, there is to be permanent "joy." There is no indication in the Acts of the Apostles that fasting was practised except before the laying on of hands in appointing elders or special missionaries

[3] Possibly we overrate the joy of that life of personal intercourse with Jesus, because we underrate the extent to which the disciples misunderstood His words and doubts about His future (not to speak of their anxieties for His safety) Certainly we underrate

THE OLD AND THE NEW

us to believe that it was so. And indeed, if it was not so, would not the Gospel have been a failure—a "no-gospel," being "tidings," not of "great joy," but of great joy becoming sadly less? This being the case, it is hard to believe that Jesus, almost at the outset of His Gospel, said concerning His disciples, "The days will come when my disciples will fast, not for one day only as under the Law, but for a whole week, mourning that I have been taken away from them[1]."

If Jesus had given any precept at all about fasting we might naturally expect that it would have been on the lines of Isaiah who bids us "draw out the soul to the hungry[2]." Something of this kind may be implied in the original form of a tradition where Jesus bade us, according to Matthew, "cleanse the inside" of the vessel, but, according to Luke, "give as alms that which is inside" the vessel[3]. The *Testaments of the Twelve Patriarchs* describes Joseph as fasting that he might give to the needy[4]. Hermas also holds up such fasting for imitation, and gently ridicules the unintelligent observance of fasting technically known as a "station[5]." But the tendency of Christians to do some definite religious act of asceticism, such as fasting, for Christ's sake, would be greatly strengthened by

---

(most of us) the joy of that life of personal intercourse with the Spirit of Jesus (after His resurrection) which may be traced in the Acts, the Fourth Gospel, and the Epistles

[1] Tertullian (*De Jejun* § 2) far from being contented with the view that "those days in which the Bridegroom was taken away were definitely appointed for fasts," condemns this as a heresy of the Psychics. The *Didaché* uses "fast" as parallel to "pray" in a precept where the Sermon on the Mount does not use it (1 3) "Pray for your enemies and *fast* (νηστεύετε δέ) for them that persecute you." It also words the warning against "fasting with the hypocrites" thus (viii 1) "But let not your fasts be with the hypocrites, for they fast on the second day of the week and the fifth, but *do ye fast during the fourth and Preparation* (i.e. *the sixth*)"

[2] See above, p. 312, n 4   [3] Mt xxiii 26, Lk. xi 41
[4] *Test XII Patr Joseph* iii 5
[5] Hermas *Sim.* v 1. 1—2

THE OLD AND THE NEW

periods of persecution when Christians waited for the Consolation of the Church, as Jews for the Consolation of Israel. We cannot be surprised to find the Didaché recognising that the pious Christian was expected to say, no less than the pious Pharisee, "I fast twice in the week." When allowance is made for these tendencies we shall perceive that, although Jesus was unlikely to enjoin fasting on His disciples, yet, when they began actually to practise fasting, they might naturally transfer to their own Master a logion in favour of it actually uttered by John the Baptist[1]

This brings us to the question what the reply would mean if uttered by the Baptist to his own disciples. In that case, it would seem to bespeak indulgence for the disciples of Jesus, on the ground that they are like "the sons of the bride-chamber"

---

[1] It would be interesting to ascertain the first instance of the Greek word στατίων See Hermas *Sim* v 1 1—2 "'Why have you come hither [so] early in the morning?' 'Because, sir,' I answered, 'I have a *station*' 'What is a *station*?' he asked 'I am *fasting*, sir,' I replied 'What is this fasting,' he continued, 'which you are observing?' '*As I have been accustomed*, sir,' I reply, 'so *I fast*' 'You do not know,' he says, 'how to *fast unto the Lord*, nor is it [real] fasting—this useless [fasting] which you observe to Him'" The Shepherd proceeds to inculcate fasting from evil, and, later on, fasting literally in order to give food to the needy

Steph *Thes* and *L S* do not recognise the existence of στατίων, and Goodspeed's Concordances give only Hermas *Sim* v 1 (see *Light* **3996** *g*) Perhaps it came to Hermas from Roman Jews The Latin "stationarius" was adopted into Hebrew See Levy 1 119 *a* "Soldaten, die auf Posten aufgestellt sind," referring to *Cant r* (on Cant vii 1) and also to *Gen r* (on Gen xxvii 28, Wu p 319) where it is said that Israelites are God's "outposts" or "guards" (*lit* "stationarii") in this world and the next The word would suit the tone of the military metaphors in the Epistles

The notion of the Christian life as an unmixed "joy," or "feast," though right in a certain sense, might lead in practice to excesses at the Christian *Agapae* Comp Eph v 18 "Be not drunken with wine, wherein is excess," 1 Cor xi 21 "One is hungry and another is drunken" "Be sober, be vigilant" would be good antidotes But these would prepare the way for "Be abstinent, fast, be like *stationarii*" surrounding the Bridegroom, the king of the feast, in the height of their week of joy. When that week is ended, though the union between Bridegroom and Bride will remain as a permanent result, the feast will be over, and the king of the feast, the Bridegroom, will be "taken away" from his headship over the circle of the feasters. Then the regular course of married life will begin, and the regular habits of holiness will be resumed. John the Baptist might naturally have said something of this kind, in prison, or out of prison. But it would perhaps be most natural in prison, when he himself had not only seen himself superseded in the minds of the multitude by Jesus, but had also been literally "taken away" by violence from the headship of those who still adhered to him as their teacher.

In either case it would be of the nature of an apology, the utterance of a man believing in regular fasting as a necessary part of a holy life, and not able to conceive that Jesus Himself could ultimately fail to act on the same belief. Tertullian expresses this view of the necessity of fasting when he says (but of course attributing the apology to Jesus) "He did not defend the disciples—but rather excused them, as if they had not been blamed without some reason—and He did not reject the discipline of John but rather conceded it [to be right], referring it [for the present] to the time of John, although destining it [in the future] for His own time[1]." In fact, however, Jesus does appear to have implied a rejection of "the discipline of John" when He spoke of him as "coming in the way of righteousness[2]," that is, the righteousness of the Law, whereas He Himself came in a new way, the way of the Gospel, that is, the way of Grace. And accordingly here, *what the sense seems to demand is a phrase expressing this contrast between the teaching of John and the teaching of Jesus*—after the words "then will they fast in that day"—something like

---

[1] Tertull *Adv Marc* on Lk. v 34—5
[2] Mt xxi 32

what Luke has inserted. "*But Jesus spake a parable*, No man rendeth a piece from a new garment....¹"

§ 5. *Hebrew and Jewish traditions about the Bridegroom*

In attempting to look at facts as they actually occurred, and to understand John the Baptist's words as they were understood at the moment of utterance, we must not forget that a great prophet, like a great poet, in moments of ecstasy, may say somewhat more than he himself fully understands. Permeated with a belief that such prophecies as those of Isaiah were on the point of fulfilment, John, the last of the prophets, could hardly speak of the bridegroom at a marriage feast without some thought of the prophetic traditions concerning the wedlock uniting Israel with Jehovah. The giving of the Old Law on Mount Sinai was regarded as a wedding in which Jehovah was the Bridegroom meeting the Bride in the Tabernacle[2]. The building of the Temple by Solomon, the Temple on which the Shechinah descended, was regarded as a ratification of that wedding; and the Song of Solomon repeatedly assumes that the King, in his ideal character, was the Bridegroom's representative[3] The Targum on that Song also represents Israel as begging the Messiah to go up with them to Jerusalem and to teach them the Law of the Lord that they may drink "the old wine" together, the wine made from the time of the creation of the world[4]

---

[1] Lk v 36 "And he spake also a parable unto them, 'No man rendeth .. '" Of course it is not contended that Luke believed that the preceding words were uttered by John the Baptist But he probably perceived that there was a break of some kind between the two utterances, and he may have had before him some tradition in which the second utterance was recognised as a separate "parable"

[2] See *Son* 3583 (ix) *a—c*

[3] See *Light* 3649. Codex ℵ repeatedly inserts ὁ νυμφίος, e g Cant 1. 8, 15 etc. in order to shew that the bridegroom is speaking.

[4] Targ on Cant. viii 1 foll

THE OLD AND THE NEW

The Pauline doctrine of the wedlock between Christ and the Church, and the imagery of the Bride in Revelation, testify to the influence of Hebrew and Jewish traditions about the Bride and the Bridegroom from the beginning of the Gospel The recently discovered Odes of Solomon contain, in its Aramaic form, the very word that we discussed above ("canopy")— and this, with a manifest reference to the union between Christ and the Church[1]. The Midrash tells us that of the ten instances in which Israel is called "Bride," six are in Solomon's Song, three in Isaiah, one in Jeremiah[2]. To this we may add that although the thought is frequent in prophecy, Isaiah alone uses the word Bridegroom in connection with Jehovah Himself[3]. The prophecies of Isaiah, whether quoted or not, underlie almost all the utterances of John the Baptist and the earliest utterances of Jesus, and make it all the more probable here that "sons of the bridal chamber" contains an allusion to the guests gathering round the Messiah, as the representative of the Supreme Bridegroom[4].

It is also possible that John, when in prison, was visited by thoughts that a destiny or chastisement similar to that which

---

[1] Odes xlii 11 "as the *canopy* that is spread out [in] the house of the wedded-pair" See Levy *Ch* i 149 *a*. For "spread out" applied to "the heavens" (as a tent) see Is xl 22 "Canopy" seems a better rendering than "couch" The Aram represents Heb "canopy" or "chamber" in Joel ii 16, Ps xix 5 (p 315, n 2)

[2] *Pesikt* Wu. p 209, rep *Deut r* Wu p. 40.

[3] Gesen 368 *b*, Is. lxi 10, lxii 5

[4] See Is lxi. 10, lxii. 5. According to Luke, our Lord's first public discourse was based on a reading of Is lxi 1 foll "The Spirit of the Lord God is upon me...." Isaiah's first mention of a "bridegroom" is in the same chapter (*ib* 10 foll) "I will greatly rejoice in the Lord. .he hath covered me with the robe of righteousness, as a bridegroom decketh himself...."

The text of the Scripture might lead some readers to suppose that "I" means the same speaker in both cases To make it clear that this is not the fact, Targ inserts (lxi 1) "*The Prophet says*," and (*ib*. 10) "*Jerusalem says*" In lxii 5 the metaphor is applied not only to Jehovah but also to Israel "So shall thy sons marry thee"

THE OLD AND THE NEW

had fallen on himself, might await even Jesus, the present source of light and joy to all around Him, so that the nation might be forced to say for a time "The breath of our nostrils, the Anointed of the Lord, was taken in their pits, of whom we said, Under his shadow we shall live among the nations[1]."

§ 6. *"In that day," or "in those days"*

We have seen above that, according to the *Apostolic Constitutions*, Jesus was regarded as charging His disciples to fast during the six days of the Passion-week. Later on, the writer says that if anyone cannot fast continuously through the Friday and the Saturday (the sabbath), he should at least observe [*i.e* fast during] the sabbath· "For the Lord saith somewhere, Himself speaking about Himself, 'When the Bridegroom shall be taken away from them, they shall fast in those days[2]'" Here he distinctly quotes from the Synoptists Also Tertullian says that those whom he calls Psychics alleged the Synoptic authority They pointed, he says, to definite days for fasting ordained by God For fasting under the Law, limited to the Day of Atonement, they quoted Leviticus. For fasting under the Gospel, also limited (as they believed), they quoted the Synoptists, "They think those days were definitely appointed for fasts in which '*the Bridegroom was taken away*,' and that these are now the only legitimate days for Christian fasts....[3]" Tertullian vigorously dissents

---

[1] Lam iv 20 See also King's *Yalkut of Zechariah* p 69, n 5 And comp Is liii 8 (LXX) αἴρεται ἀπὸ τῆς γῆς ἡ ζωὴ αὐτοῦ, Heb. "He was cut off out of the land of the living"

[2] *Const Apost* v 18

[3] *De Jejun* § 2 "Certe in Evangelio illos dies jejunus determinatos putant in quibus 'ablatus est sponsus,' et hos esse jam solos legitimos jejuniorum Christianorum...." Tertullian gives the name of Psychics to those, for example, who allowed second marriages (see *De Monogamia* § 1).

325   (Mark ii 18—22)

from this view. These differences of opinion call attention to a difference in the Synoptic texts as to the "days":—

Mk ii. 20 (lit.)	Mt. ix 15 (lit.)	Lk v 35 (lit.)
But days will come when and then will they fast *in that day*	But days will come when ... and then will they fast.	But days will come, and when then will they fast *in those days.*

Why does Mark say, first, "*days* will come," and then, not "in those days," but "*in that day*"? Matthew presents no difficulty. Although it may be presumed that he would not deviate from the Marcan tradition of Christ's own words without what seemed to him good reason, yet here he may well have supposed that he had good reason. Mark has many repetitions and "conflations," and Matthew may have regarded Mark's "in that day" as a mere repetition of "then" for emphasis, and as a repetition that might cause difficulty since it was liable to more than one interpretation. Luke seems to be giving a literal rendering to a form of the Hebraic idiom "lo, days are coming *and*" (meaning "days are coming *when*")[1]. But in Greek—where "and" is not used for "when"—"and" has the effect of detaching the second part of the sentence from the first: "But *days [of trial]* will come. And, *when* the bridegroom shall be taken away, then will they fast *in those days.*" Thus Luke leaves it doubtful whether the fasting is to be practised at intervals during "those days [of trial]," or during "those days [in which the bridegroom shall be taken away][2]"

---

[1] See Gesen. 400 *a*, who renders it "lo! days are coming, when." It is very frequent in Jeremiah, *e.g.* Jerem. xxx. 3 "Behold, days are coming *and* (R.V. and A.V. *that*) I will turn again the captivity..." This is followed by a description of the particular day of trouble and deliverance (*ib.* 7 foll.) "Alas, for *that day* is great, so that none is like it... it is even the time of Jacob's trouble, but he shall be saved out of it... And it shall come to pass *in that day*... I will break his yoke..."

[2] Contrast Lk. xxi. 6 ἐλεύσονται ἡμέραι ἐν αἷς, which expresses the Hebrew idiom, not literally, but in correct Greek.

THE OLD AND THE NEW

Luke's course, like Matthew's, is intelligible. But it is difficult to understand why Mark should have, as it were, gone out of his way to raise a difficulty, by writing first "days" and then "day"

There are two ways of explaining Mark's text. One is that, as in the passage quoted above from Jeremiah, a prediction about "days" in general ("days are coming") is followed by a mention of the particular day ("*that day* is great," "in *that day*")[1] It must be admitted, however, that in Mark, the two phrases come much closer together than in Jeremiah, and that, although "*in that day*" is very common in prophecy, it rarely (if ever) comes as a repetition of a preceding "then[2]." The repetition of "*in that day*," as a final refrain in Isaiah, is quite exceptional[3] Still it is conceivable that the phrase was here used for emphasis, not perhaps by the original speaker (whether John or Jesus), but by the original Evangelist, who used it with allusion to the Fasting Saturday that preceded the early Christian Easter Sunday About this, as we have seen, the *Apostolic Constitutions* says "Not that the Sabbath-day is a day of fasting, being the Rest from the Creation, but because *we ought to fast on this one Sabbath alone*, the Creator, during it, being still under the earth," and afterwards, "At least let him observe [by fasting] *the Sabbath-day*[4]"

---

[1] Jerem xxx 3, 7, 8

[2] In the only other passage where Mark uses "in that day," it is with "Jesus saith," as follows —

Mk iv 35	Mt viii 18	Lk viii 22
And *in that day*, when even was come, he saith unto them, Let us go over unto the other side	Now when Jesus saw great multitudes about him, he gave commandment to depart unto the other side	Now it came to pass *in one of those days*, that he entered into a boat, himself and his disciples, and he said unto them, Let us go over unto the other side of the lake and they launched forth

[3] Is ii 11 "The lofty looks of man...*in that day*," ib. 17 "The loftiness of man...*in that day*"

[4] *Const. Apost.* v. 15, and 18 See above, pp. 319, n 1, 325

THE OLD AND THE NEW

If this view is correct, the Marcan tradition represents a very early Christian doctrine about Fasting, namely, that as the Day of Atonement was appointed to be the only Fast-day for Jews, so the day between the Crucifixion and the Resurrection was to be the only Fast-day for Christians It was the only day during the whole of which Christ's disciples had been constrained to "afflict their souls" because they believed that He was dead And yet it was their Sabbath, their literal Jewish Sabbath, on which they were bound to "rest" Later on we shall find Luke alone calling attention to the fact that the women at all events did "rest on the sabbath[1]" John says that "the day of that sabbath was a great one[2]" The context indicates that it was "great" from the point of view of the Jews, who feared lest it should be desecrated. But it can hardly be doubted that John writes also from the point of view of the redeemed Church for whom that "sabbath" was to be henceforth uniquely "great" Not merely did it conclude an old Creation, but it introduced a new one.

A combination of "fasting" with "sabbathizing" is mentioned in the recently discovered Oxyrhynchus Papyri: "Jesus saith, If ye fast not [as to] the world, ye shall assuredly not find the kingdom of God, and, if ye sabbathize not the sabbath, ye shall not see the Father[3]." Whatever may be the detailed

---

[1] Lk xxiii 55—6 "And having followed [to the tomb] the women...beheld the tomb. and having turned back they prepared ointments and myrrh *And during the sabbath they rested according to the commandment....*" Mk xvi 1 has "And when the sabbath was past (διαγενομένου) Mary. bought ointments ..," Mt xxviii 1 "Late on the sabbath day, as it began to dawn toward the first [day] of the week, came Mary.. ."

[2] Jn xix 31

[3] *Oxy Pap* No 1 On a sabbath, at the pool of Bethesda, Jesus sabbathized or rested, not by resting from, but by finding rest in, an act of goodness (Jn v 16—17) On another sabbath, concerning which John says "the day of that sabbath was a great one," Jesus—according to the Petrine Epistle (1 Pet iii 19)—"went and preached to the spirits in prison."

THE OLD AND THE NEW

explanation of these words, there appears nothing in the Bible to which they can point in a literal sense, except the fasting on the Jewish Day of Atonement, fulfilled in the fasting on the first Christian Saturday before the first Easter Sunday

The other way of explaining Mark's text is to suppose that, in the original, a separate Logion terminated, as Matthew makes it terminate, with the words "and then will they fast," and a separate Logion began, "*In that day Jesus said.*" The ambiguity may be illustrated from the Hebrew and the Greek accounts of the entrance of the Israelites into the Promised Land. The Hebrew, using the above-mentioned[1] emphatic phrase, "on that self-same day," says "They did eat...unleavened cakes and parched corn *in the self-same day* And the manna ceased on the morrow." But the LXX says "*In the self-same day* the manna ceased[2]"

We may also illustrate the ambiguity from the Oxyrhynchus Logia. Each one of them begins, or ends, with "*saith Jesus*[3]." An editor, combining Logia that he supposed to have been uttered about the same time, might justifiably omit "*saith Jesus*" (as Matthew appears to have done in the Sermon on the Mount) Mark may have done this in the present instance. But the original may have meant · "*In that day, or thereabouts, Jesus said* [making a reply to the preceding words of John the Baptist] No man seweth... "

This would explain Luke's deviation from Mark as being a compromise. Luke believed that the original made no distinction between "days" in general and one great "day" in particular He therefore substituted "in those days" for

---

[1] See above, p 312, n. 2   [2] Josh v 11—12

[3] It is translated by the editors as coming *at the beginning of each Logion, e g* " .the mote that is in thy brother's eye   *Jesus saith* (ΛΕΓΕΙ ΙC), Except ye fast ..ye shall not see the Father *Jesus saith* (ΛΕΓΕΙ ΙC) .." Probably this is correct   But the fragmentary condition of the Logia, and the absence of the beginning and the end of the MS, make it impossible to deny that "saith Jesus" might be intended to come *at the end of each Logion*

THE OLD AND THE NEW

"in that day." At the same time he believed that "in that day" might be intended to have a transitional force suggesting doctrine uttered about that time, though not at that very time. Accordingly he implies transition by saying that Jesus proceeded to speak a "parable[1]"

In concluding this discussion of the Synoptic reply to the complaint of the Baptist's disciples, we have to admit that the data are not sufficient to prove that the reply was uttered by the Baptist himself, and therefore not sufficient to demonstrate its exact meaning in the mind of the speaker. But we shall have learned from an examination of the ancient interpretations of the passage to recognise two truths. First, there was a very strong tendency among pious and practical Christians, in the days of early persecutions, to read into the Gospels an inculcation of fasting, on the part of Christ, for which no basis can be found in their uncorrupted texts[2]. Secondly, there is abundant evidence to shew that Jesus, while not forbidding fasting as means to a moral end to be used at the discretion of His disciples, discouraged formal fasting both by example and by precept, and regarded the Jewish "affliction of soul" prescribed by Law on the Day of Atonement as swallowed up in the "joy" of that "victory" over Death and Sheol which was promised by His Gospel.

§ 7. *A complaint of the Baptist's disciples and the reply, in the Fourth Gospel*

The Fourth Gospel does not contradict the tradition that the Baptist's disciples, after their Master's imprisonment, complained to Jesus about the non-ascetic life of His disciples,

---

[1] This is the first occasion where Luke uses "parable" in his own words to describe what Jesus proceeds to say. "Parable" occurs before (but not in Luke's own words) in Lk iv 23, "Doubtless ye will say unto me this *parable*, 'Physician, heal thyself'"

[2] On "hungering," attributed to Jesus in the Temptation by Matthew and Luke, but not by Mark, and never attributed to Jesus by John, see p 207, footnote

THE OLD AND THE NEW

and that Jesus called Himself "the bridegroom" in His reply. But it sets before us a statement, of an opposite character, concerning something that happened before the imprisonment At that earlier date (it says) the Baptist's disciples complained to their own Master about Jesus, and their Master, in his reply, called Jesus "the bridegroom." The complaint does not mention "fasting" but only "purifying"—and this, in the introductory context, which speaks of a "questioning" on the part of the disciples of John, "together with a Jew (*or*, Jews)," about purifying Then the complaint mentions "baptizing" thus: "Rabbi, he that was with thee beyond Jordan, to whom thou hast borne witness, behold, this [man] baptizeth and all men come to him[1]"

At first sight there may seem nothing here that is connected, even remotely, with fasting. But let us put ourselves in the position of the complainants. We are Jews. We believe in the efficacy of the Day of Atonement As to this it is written "On this day shall atonement be made for you *to purify you from all your sins before the Lord ye shall be pure*[2]." Now this is the only passage in the Law where "*purification from sins*" is mentioned[3]. And the following words are "It is a sabbath of sabbathizing unto you, and *ye shall afflict your souls*" But "*afflict the soul*" meant, as we have seen, "*fast*" Thus all Jews, even the most illiterate, if they practised the Law at all, would recognise that there was a close connection between "purification from sins" and "fasting."

---

[1] Jn iii 25—6 See *Joh Gr* **2350** *c* on the variations in the text and on its probable meaning—"that the Jews and some of the Baptist's disciples wished to incite him to jealousy of Jesus"— ζήτησις, "questioning," meaning here "a quarrelsome discussion"

[2] Lev xvi 30. The punctuation is doubtful, LXX "to purify you from all your sins before the Lord, and ye shall be purified," Vulg "In hac die expiatio erit vestri, atque mundatio ab omnibus peccatis vestris, coram Domino mundabimini"

[3] Gesen 372 *a* R V. marg refers to Ps li 2, Jer xxxiii. 8, Heb x 1, 2, 1 Jn i 7, 9

THE OLD AND THE NEW

Now John the Baptist had come, avowedly, to prepare the way for *some special purification from sins*, and his message had been "*repent and be baptized.*" Those who were baptized by him "confessed their sins" (as Mark and Matthew say). Luke probably assumes this, and adds that many said "What shall we do?"—that is, "What shall we do to amend our sinful lives?" All this is characteristic of the Jewish confession of sins on the Day of Atonement[1]. No mention is made of the fasting of the applicants for baptism. But we may be quite sure that they did fast before being baptized. This fact gives point to the complaint of the Baptist's disciples as being, in effect, part of a general complaint about the heterodoxy of Jesus on the subject of purifying. "Master, you taught us to prepare ourselves *by baptism as for a great day of Atonement. We fasted. We confessed our sins.* This man, Jesus, to whom you testified, he, too, baptizes. But he baptizes on his own account, independently of you and differently from you. He does not insist, as you did, upon fasting. He eats and drinks with publicans and sinners. And he is leading the multitudes after him."

The Baptist's reply is directed, not to any question about baptism that may be implied in the word "baptizeth," but to the personal question implied in "this man": "Ye yourselves bear me witness that I said, 'I am not the Christ,' but [that] 'I am sent before him [*i.e.* the Christ].'" This second statement has not been recorded before in this Gospel, though it has been implied[2]. It is equivalent to a statement—made for the first time here—that Jesus, "before" whom the Baptist has been "sent," is the Christ. The Baptist adds, at once,

---

[1] See *Jôma* 36 *a*, 41 *b*, 86 *a*, also *j Jôma* iii 6 (Schwab v 194 and foll.)

[2] In the Fourth Gospel the *word* "Christ" or "Messiah" is never uttered by the Baptist except in negation. But the Baptist is represented as implying that his successor is the *person*, Christ, —whom he dramatically shews to be expected by everyone, *e.g.* Andrew, Philip, and the Woman of Samaria.

THE OLD AND THE NEW

"He that hath the bride is the bridegroom " Here again he utters none but a general statement—a truism to the ear—but he clearly implies that Jesus, besides being the Christ, is also "the bridegroom " As for the "questioning" about "purifying" and "baptizing," the Baptist is silent Perhaps he is to be supposed to regard it as a "questioning" that will answer itself when the disciples once accept the "Christ" who is also the "Bridegroom "

"Fasting"—we said above—is not mentioned in the Johannine narrative. Yet indirectly, if fasting implies self-affliction or anything alien from joy, the Baptist implies that fasting would be out of place for Christ's disciples, because the presence of the bridegroom and the sound of His voice must needs bring joy. "The friend of the bridegroom, he that standeth and heareth him, rejoiceth with [exceeding] joy because of the bridegroom's voice[1] " The Baptist calls his "joy" emphatically "the joy that is mine," meaning "the joy of the duty assigned to me[2]." He it is that has been sent before the Bridegroom's face to prepare His way That duty has now been discharged, and the joy of the Friend passes into the background, having prepared the way for the joy of the Bridegroom and the Bride, "This therefore *the joy that is my own* hath been fulfilled. He must increase, but I must decrease."

It is instructive to turn to the next mention of "joy" in this Gospel. It is a long way on, in Christ's final utterance to His disciples, when He is on the point of leaving them: "*These things I have spoken* unto you that *the joy that is my own* may be in you, and that your joy may be fulfilled[3]." If we ask what are the "things" that He has "spoken," which are to have the effect of making Christ's own "joy" abide in the disciples, the context tells us: He has said "Even as the Father hath loved

---

[1] Jn iii 29
[2] Jn iii 29 See *Joh. Gr.* 1987—8, 2581 on the emphasis implied by ὁ ἐμός
[3] Jn xv 11

THE OLD AND THE NEW

me, I also have loved you. abide ye in *the love that is my own*[1]."
It is implied that a new kind of love has been brought down from heaven to earth, and that this new love results in a new joy.

Comparing together these two kinds of "joy," the rudimentary one peculiar to the Bridegroom's Friend, and the perfect one peculiar to the Bridegroom, now called the Son of the Father in heaven, we see that the one prepares for the other, and that neither of them seems to leave room for that kind of "self-affliction," "self-humbling," or "fasting," which would be appropriate before the Bridegroom, or the Son, had arrived and been recognised. We ought not to be surprised if the Baptist's teaching, on this and other points, varied toward the end of his career, during the interval between Christ's baptism and his own execution in prison There may have been moments when John thought that the new Messiah would carry all before Him at once as the victorious Redeemer of Israel There may have been others when he thought that the end was not to come yet

Returning to the order of the Fourth Gospel and to its attitude toward "joy," we should note two more passages where it is mentioned One of these does expressly mention an interval or break in which there shall be weeping, lamenting, and sorrow But this appears to refer to the brief interval ("a little while") between Christ's death and resurrection· "A little while and ye behold me not, and again *a little while* and ye shall see me.... Ye shall weep and lament, but the world shall rejoice; ye shall be sorrowful, but your sorrow shall be turned into joy." After this second "*little while*," there is to be no repetition of such sorrow, but "joy" like that of "the woman delivered of the child," unbroken joy.—"I will see you again, and your heart shall rejoice, and *your joy no one taketh away from you*.... Ask and receive, that *your joy* may be

---

[1] Jn xv 9

(Mark ii 18—22)

THE OLD AND THE NEW

fulfilled[1]." To the same effect is the final mention of the Messiah's joy in the Son's prayer to the Father for the disciples left in the world· "These things I speak in the world that *they may have the joy that is my own fulfilled in themselves*[2]."

These passages favour the view that, for some years after Christ's death, before any formal rules for fasting were laid down by the Church, many Christians spontaneously fasted on that saddest of all days for the first generation, the most intimate circle, of His disciples—that Sabbath which they had to pass through in the belief that their Lord's life had ended in failure, so that they had to say to themselves "We used [once] to hope that it was he that was destined to redeem Israel[3]"

§ 8 *The parable of the patched garment*

The lesson taught by this parable resembles that which Philo deduces from a Levitical precept He tells us "not to weave together the heterogeneous substances wool and flax," because, "in the case of these, not only is the difference a dissociation, but also the predominance of [the one or] the other, and the predominant one will cause a rending instead of a uniting when need comes to use [the garment][4]."

It will be seen below that Luke does not quite agree with

---

[1] Jn xvi 19—24

[2] Jn xvii 13 We must beware of confusing this "joy" with immunity from "tribulation" The disciples are to have "tribulation," but at the same time a confidence in the Messiah's victory over the world (*ib* xvi 33) "These things have I spoken unto you that in me ye may have peace In the world ye have tribulation, but be of good cheer, I have conquered the world"

[3] Lk xxiv 21 These words were uttered on the Sunday after the Crucifixion by the two disciples walking to Emmaus Words like them must have been uttered by all the disciples on the preceding Saturday or Sabbath

[4] Philo ii 370 on Lev xix 19 (Deut xxii. 11) καὶ γὰρ ἐπὶ τούτων οὐ μόνον ἡ διαφορότης ἀκοινώνητον, ἀλλὰ καὶ ἡ ἐπικράτεια θατέρου ῥῆξιν ἀπεργασομένου μᾶλλον ἢ ἕνωσιν, ὅταν δέῃ χρῆσθαι

THE OLD AND THE NEW

Mark and Matthew in his version of the parable[1]. They describe the patching of an old garment with a piece of new heavy stuff which pulls the old threadbare cloak to pieces. Luke describes the patching of an old garment with a piece out of a new garment, with the result of disfiguring the old one and rending the new It is told about the Cynic philosopher, Crates, that he "stitched a fleece on to his philosopher's cloak," and some recollection of this old popular story may have influenced Mark's tradition[2] Mark's text contains one word ("sew-on") not known to occur elsewhere in Greek, and both the text and its interpretation are doubtful Nor is it necessary to discuss here in detail Luke's deviations, since Luke does not contradict Mark but only adds something more Consequently the Fourth Gospel ought not to be expected to intervene.

§ 9. *"This year's wine" and "new wine-skins"*[3]

What the Revised Version calls "new wine" is paraphrased above as "this year's wine" in order to call attention to the

---

[1] Mk ii 21 (R V)	Mt ix 16 (R V)	Lk v 36 (R V)
No man seweth a piece of undressed cloth on an old garment else that which should fill it up taketh from it, the new from the old, and a worse rent is made	And no man putteth a piece of undressed cloth upon an old garment, for that which should fill it up taketh from the garment, and a worse rent is made	And he spake also a parable unto them, No man rendeth a piece from a new garment and putteth it upon an old garment, else he will rend the new, and also the piece from the new will not agree with the old

[2] Diog Laert vi 91 κῴδιον αὐτόν φησί ποτε προσράψαι τῷ τρίβωνι See Steph *Thes* on προσράπτω, ἐπιρράπτω, ἐπίβλημα, and ῥάκος Ἐπιρράπτω (as far as I can find) is not alleged to occur (as a correct reading) anywhere else in Greek except in this passage of Mark Also ἐπίβλημα (which means a "shawl," as in Is iii. 22 (LXX)) is not alleged to mean "patch" except in Josh ix 5 (11) (Sym). Ῥάκος sometimes means a "napkin "

[3] R V *"new"* wine" does not distinguish νέος, used here, from καινός in Mk xiv. 25, Mt xxvi 29 "when I drink it *new*" (Lk xxii 18

fact that the Hebrew Bible has two separate words to represent (1) "wine" and (2) "new-wine," or "must[1]." This paraphrase also helps us to connect the metaphor with such passages in Isaiah as speak of "the acceptable year of the Lord"—the year of the "trees of righteousness, the planting of the Lord," when "the Lord God will cause righteousness and praise to spring forth" as "the earth bringeth forth her bud"—and also of "the new wine (lit. *the must*, or *this year's wine*) that is found in the cluster[2]." The prophet says elsewhere "Ho, every one that thirsteth, come ye to the waters, and he that hath no money; come ye, buy, and eat, yea, come, buy wine and milk without money and without price[3]," clearly meaning that kind of moral "wisdom" which man was to attain through the Law by "loving God" and "loving" his "neighbour" In the threefold Synoptic tradition printed below, "wine of this year," commonly called the "new-wine," appears to be the wine of "the acceptable year of the Lord" which Jesus said He came to proclaim[4],

---

differs) Νέος means "young," "new-born," "new by nature" Καινός means "newly made," "unused" Νέος might be applied to wine regarded as a product of nature, the juice of the grape, καινός to wine as made by man, or, metaphorically, in connection with the thought of a New Covenant Καινός, here applied to "wine-skins," means "unused," or "newly tanned," so as to endure the expansive pressure of "this year's wine" In Hebrew, separate names are given to (Gesen 406 a) "wine," and (Gesen 440 b) "must, fresh or new wine" But the LXX does not observe the distinction For it renders the latter 36 times by οἶνος, and only once by μέθυσμα, and once by ῥώξ "This-year's wine" is given above as a paraphrase, intended to call attention to the difference between natural newness and artificial newness

[1] Onkelos represents both (1) יין "wine," and (2) תירש "new-wine," by חמר

[2] Is lxi 2—11, lxv 8 LXX ῥώξ The Targ has "As Noah was found in the generation of the deluge"

[3] Is lv 1 Comp *Gen r* on Gen xxvii 28 "the dew of heaven.. the fatness of the earth.. corn *new-wine*" This is the first mention of "new-wine" One comment in *Gen. r* explains "*new-wine*" as meaning "the Haggada"

[4] Lk iv 19, quoting Is. lxi 2

THE OLD AND THE NEW

the wine of the "good tidings," in other words, the new wine of the Gospel.

But what are the "new wine-skins" and the "old wine-skins" corresponding to "this year's wine" and the "old wine"? They are mentioned by all the Synoptists as follows.—

Mk ii. 22	Mt. ix 17	Lk v. 37—8
And no one putteth this year's wine into old wine-skins Else, the wine will burst the wine-skins, and [so] the wine perisheth and the wine-skins [with it]. [But [men put] this year's wine into new wine-skins][1]	Nor do [men] put this year's wine into old wine-skins Else, the wine-skins are burst, and the wine is spilled, and the wine-skins perish. But [men] put this year's wine into new wine-skins, and both are kept-safe-together	And no one putteth this year's wine into old wine-skins. Else, this year's wine will burst the wine-skins, and will itself be spilled, and [besides] the wine-skins will perish. But one must put this year's wine into new wine-skins

Origen's explanation is, in effect, that what Paul calls "the old man"—meaning the man not yet made young by regeneration—is not fit to drink "the new wine[2]" The metaphor of the leathern bottle or wine-skin is repellent to Greek ears Paul adapts it to them when he writes "We have this treasure [i e. the Spirit] in [fragile] earthen vessels[3]" But in

---

[1] W H bracket the last sentence in Mark Βάλλωσιν is omitted The parallel Luke supplies βλητέον, "one must put "

[2] Origen Lev Hom vii 2 "Vides ergo quia impossibile est de nova vite novum poculum bibi ab eo qui adhuc indutus est veterem hominem cum actibus suis 'Nemo enim,' inquit, 'mittit vinum novum in utres veteres ' Si vis ergo et tu bibere de hoc novo vino, innovare, et dic quia 'et si exterior homo noster corrumpitur sed quia intus est renovatur de die in diem '"

Comp Acts ii 13 "Others, mocking, said, They are *filled with new-wine* (γλεύκους)" Origen (*Lev. Hom* ii 2) takes this as true, though uttered in mockery "Et vere haec fuerunt recentia, quia erat novum, unde et '*musto repleti*' dicebantur "

[3] 2 Cor iv 7

Job it is unconcealed "The spirit within me (*lit.* of my belly) constraineth me. Behold, my belly is as wine that hath no vent, *like new wine-skins that are ready to burst*[1]." The wine-skin was prepared to bear the expansive pressure of the must by tanning and "seasoning in smoke[2]," and this is the way in which the Targumist explains the utterance of the Psalmist: "My soul fainteth for thy salvation...mine eyes fail for thy word, saying, When wilt thou comfort me? for I am become *like a bottle in the smoke*", that is, as the Targum interprets it, "*like a wine-skin hung up [to be seasoned]* in the smoke[3]." The thought is somewhat the same, though the metaphor is not, as in the Psalm beginning, "As the hart panteth after the water brooks[4]." In both, there is a thirst that longs to be satisfied But if the thirst for the new wine is to be satisfied, an important condition has to be fulfilled which does not exist with regard to the thirst for the water. There must be a "making new," a "seasoning."

We may illustrate the need of this "seasoning" from an interpolation that follows, in Codex D, almost immediately, where Jesus defends His disciples against the charge of sabbath-breaking because they picked and rubbed some ears of corn on the sabbath "On the same day, having beheld one working on the sabbath, He said unto him, 'Man, if thou knowest what thou art doing, blessed art thou But if thou knowest not, thou art liable to a curse, and a transgressor of the Law[5].'" In other words, all depended on the spiritual state of the man.

---

[1] Job xxxii 19 ὥσπερ ἀσκὸς γλεύκους ζέων (A γέμων), comp Acts xviii 25 (of Apollos) and Rom xii 11 τῷ πνεύματι ζέοντες. Job refers to (Hastings 1 311 *b*) "the distension that the leather underwent once, and once only, during fermentation," not "bursting" but "ready to burst"

[2] Hastings 1 311 *b*

[3] Ps cxix 83 Walton renders the Heb "sicut uter *in fumario*," Targ "*qui pendet ad fumum*" The Syr and the Vulg follow LXX which renders "smoke" by πάχνη, "frost"

[4] Ps xlii 1   [5] Lk vi 5 (D)

If he had been "seasoned," or "made new," to such an extent that he felt in his heart the whole of the Law to be summed up in the love of the Father and the brethren, so that henceforth he needed not to observe "days and months and years," then he was blessed, rejoicing in the wine of the Spirit. But if he, being a Jew, was working on the sabbath without this spiritual conviction, but acting against his conscience and in self-will—saying (and trying to believe it) "The New Law means that one can do as one likes"—then he was accursed. Such a man's moral nature—what there had been of it—was shattered by the new doctrine, the "bottle" was "burst" by "this year's wine," and "the wine," so far as he was concerned, had "perished."

§ 10 *Luke and John on "good wine"*

Returning to the three Synoptic parallels we observe that, so far, they are in verbal as well as substantial agreement, and there is no reason for expecting Johannine intervention. But now Luke adds a brief appendix: "And no one, having drunk old [wine], desireth this year's [wine] (*lit.* new). For he saith, 'the old is good[1].'" There is nothing in the parallel Mark or Matthew corresponding to this. It seems an attempt to explain why some reject the New Wine of the Gospel. But by its way of explaining, it appears to defend, the rejection. Ben Sira says, and doubtless it was a familiar proverb in Christ's days, "Forsake not an old friend, for the new is not comparable to him; *a new friend is as new wine;* when it is old thou shalt drink it with pleasure[2]." Such a proverb commends itself. Luke, therefore, seems to represent Jesus as putting into the mouths of His adversaries, when He offered them the new wine of the Gospel, an effective retort: "You yourself have taught us what to reply. We will have none of your 'new wine.' For us 'the old is good.'"

---

[1] Lk. v 39   [2] Sir ix. 10

THE OLD AND THE NEW

Possibly there were early doubts about the genuineness of this Lucan tradition. Some good authorities omit it[1]. Mark's tradition ends perhaps ungrammatically and certainly abruptly; and Luke, in amending it, may have inserted here, in a wrong place, a truncated tradition about "the good wine" as being "old," which, if stated fully, and in its right place, would have explained that the "good wine" was indeed "old," being prepared by God from the beginning, and yet it was "new," having been kept during the lapse of many generations, so that it should not be manifested till the coming of the Son of Man, the Bridegroom of humanity. But as it is, Luke's text (we may reasonably suppose) must have presented a stumbling-block to readers of the Gospels in the first century. We naturally ask whether John, though silent about "fasting," and about the "garment," has anything to the point about "good wine."

Many will at once think of the saying of the "ruler of the feast" at Cana to the bridegroom, "Thou hast kept *the good wine* until now[2]." But probably not so many will realise that "*the good wine*" is a phrase that occurs only once elsewhere in Scripture, and then in connection with the Bridegroom described in the Song of Songs "Thy mouth is like *the good wine*," *i.e.* the wine pre-eminently and uniquely good[3]. Jewish tradition gives a mystical meaning to the context, which speaks of the wine as "gliding through the lips of them that are asleep." "The *good wine*" is regarded as the love of God expressed in the Covenant with Abraham, which constrains the "lips," even of those "sleeping" in their graves, to repeat His praises[4].

---

[1] It is omitted by D and the best Latin MSS, and bracketed by W.H.

[2] Jn ii 10

[3] Cant vii 9 (Rashi vii 12, in Midrash sometimes vii 10). Gesen 373 b, 406 b renders it (like R V) "wine of the best sort," or "the best wine." But the literal Heb is "*the good wine*," and it occurs nowhere else in the Bible

[4] So R V. text (Gesen 179 a), but R V marg "causing the lips...to move *or* speak." See the Targum, Rashi, *Sanhedr* 90 b

THE OLD AND THE NEW

The epithet "*good*," here attached to the wine of the Bridegroom, appears in another tradition with reference to the wine drunk at the feast of the Child at Circumcision. While the father offers it to the guests, he says, "Drink from *this good wine*. From it I will give you to drink at his wedding-feast[1]."

In the story of Cana, the visible "ruler of the feast" is, so to speak, a mere marionette, not being the real Ruler of the Feast, but a mere mortal unconsciously uttering a celestial mystery. And the bridegroom of Cana, too, the visible bridegroom, is not the real Bridegroom. It is said to him "*Thou* hast kept the good wine." But *he* has not kept it. Jesus, in the background, is the true Bridegroom, and Jesus has provided the good wine. We, the readers, who are admitted to the secret, know that literally He could not be said to have "kept" it. He made it a few moments ago. But a Jew, a Christian Philo, taking it allegorically, might say that the Father provided it at the feast of the Promised Son, Isaac, the feast of the Circumcision, and is now bringing it forth at the feast of the Son's Wedding. Or, going back still further, he might say that "the good wine" was provided in the moment of the Creation, when God said, "Let us make man *in our image*," and that it was "kept" till the Incarnation, when the sentence was completed and the purpose fulfilled—"*after our likeness*[2]" The complete (but not completed) purpose (implied in "our likeness") preceded the partial practice ("our image"). The former lay deep down in what St Paul

---

and *J Berach* ii 1 The Midrash varies in detail, but agrees in referring to the belief that the departed, though dead, still speak

[1] See *Eccles r* on Eccles iii 2, Wu p 41 I have followed Schlatter (on Jn ii 10) who gives the Hebrew, and who differs somewhat from Wunsche

[2] See Origen on Rom iv 16—17 (Lomm vi. 266) "Et hoc est fortassis quod in initiis homo, cum propositum fuisset (Gen 1 26) ut '*ad imaginem et similitudinem*' Dei fieret, (*ib* 1 27) '*ad imaginem*' quidem factus est, '*similitudo*' autem dilata est, ob hoc, ut priu confideret in Deum et ita fieret similis ei ..."

THE OLD AND THE NEW

calls "the depth" of "God's wisdom and knowledge[1]." It came later to view. It fulfilled that Law of spiritual Nature which is at the root of spiritual patience and spiritual victory, "Nothing is hidden except that it may be manifested[2]."

§ 11. *The Fourth Gospel on the "old" and the "new"*

The Fourth Gospel nowhere mentions the "old." But it implies the "old" in the (almost) single passage[3] in which it mentions the "new": "*A new commandment* give I unto you, that *ye love one another, even as I loved you,* that ye (emph.) also love one another." The Law of Moses commanded "love" —love both of God and of man. But these words imply the Evangelist's belief that a new kind of love, love like that of Christ, has been brought into the world by Him, bringing, along with itself, the constraining force of "a new commandment." And John's Epistle, beginning from the results of the Gospel, after describing how "the blood of Jesus...cleanseth us from all sin," and after speedily passing to the mention of the practical Christian life in "the love of God," adds "Beloved, *no new commandment* I write unto you, but *an old commandment*....Again, *a new commandment* write I unto you, which [thing] is true in him and in you....[4]." That is to say, "I have called the commandment 'old,' I now call it 'new'; and truly the newness is manifest. It is manifest in Him, who gave His blood for us; it is manifest in you, who are purified and incorporated in Him by His blood[5]."

The pervasive thought of the contrast between the old and the new may explain why the Evangelist lays stress on what (apart from allegory) may seem to us quaint and insignificant details in the miracle of Cana. Take, for example, the preliminary precept to "fill to the brim" the six stone waterpots

---

[1] Rom xi 33 [2] Mk iv 22
[3] Jn xiii 34 There is also (Jn xix 41) "a *new* tomb"
[4] 1 Jn ii 7—8 [5] See *Joh Gr* **2412**

THE OLD AND THE NEW

that were set "in accordance with the purification of the Jews." Not till this was done did Jesus say "Draw *now* [fresh water from the well]¹, and carry to the ruler of the feast " In itself, all this is bewildering rather than edifying. But what if the Evangelist desires to draw a line of demarcation between the water of the Law, used only for external purification, and the water of the Gospel, a type of the blood of Christ, used for internal as well as external purifying ² ?

Later on, as if to constrain us to keep our minds free from bondage to any single metaphor, the Dialogue with Nicodemus teaches the doctrine of regeneration from above through Water and Spirit Later still, the Dialogue with the Samaritan woman brings us back to water, not wine, which is to quench the thirst of the soul and to bestow spiritual life With manifest irony, the Evangelist describes the woman with the five husbands near Jacob's well as informing the Saviour that "the well is deep" and that He has "nothing to draw with." What she calls "the well" the Evangelist calls "the *fountain*," saying

---

¹ Or possibly "Draw now [*from the waterpots*]" (see *Joh Gr*. 2281—3 on Jn ii 6—8) But in the light of Joseph *Ant* iii 1. 2 quoted below, I prefer to supply "*from the well*," as in *Indices* p xxviii n 3

² There may be latent in this detail some allusion to mystical Jewish traditions about the water of Marah, which was (Exod xv 25) "made sweet for" the Israelites, so that they could drink it Josephus, *Ant* iii 1. 2 (quoted and discussed in *Indices* p xxi foll), says that Moses "ordered those [men] that were in their prime to take their stand round [the water] and to draw off ($\dot{\epsilon}\xi\alpha\nu\tau\lambda\epsilon\hat{\imath}\nu$) [water] What remained, he said, would be drinkable for them, when the greater portion had been first emptied out " The two acts of "drawing" water in Cana, one of which is implied ("fill to the brim"), the other of which is mentioned ("*draw* now") may be contrasted with those at Marah (according to Josephus) At Marah the water is all for drinking, some bad, some good, but all for one purpose At Cana the water is *all* good, but for two purposes. The first supply of water is for "purifying," the second supply is for internal joy of heart, such as comes from "the wine that maketh glad the heart of man."

THE OLD AND THE NEW

that it was "near the parcel of ground that Jacob gave to his son Joseph, and Jacob's *fountain* was there[1]." Joseph is the only one of Jacob's sons whom Jacob's Song of Blessing connects with a "fountain" ("a fruitful bough by a fountain[2]"); and the song goes on to speak of "blessings of heaven above, blessings of *the deep* that coucheth beneath." This "fountain" therefore might well be taken as representing the depth, or literally the "abyss," of the protecting Love, concerning which Israel is told in the Song of Moses "The eternal God is thy dwelling place, and underneath are the everlasting arms[3]."

From another point of view, the Johannine "fountain" corresponds to Synoptic doctrine expressed by quite different metaphors. One and the same Hebrew word, *En* (or *Ain*), represents both *"fountain"* and *"eye."* The first mention of *"fountain"* in Scripture is where "the angel of the Lord found Hagar by a *fountain*[4]." It is said that Hagar "called the name of the Lord that spake unto her, 'Thou art a God of *seeing*[5]'" Then she adds "Can it be that I have here *seen*...him that *seeth* me[6]?" Therefore "the well was called 'The well of the living one that *seeth* me'"

The Midrash on this passage comments on the condescension of "the Lord" in speaking to a woman on this occasion, and its

---

[1] Jn iv 5—6 "fountain (πηγή)" (comp *ib.* 14), but the woman calls it a "well (φρέαρ)"

[2] Gen xlix 22, 25 The LXX completely misses the meaning The Heb for "deep" is rendered by Aquila ἄβυσσος in Gen i 2 etc

[3] Deut xxxiii 27 Deut xxxiii 13 repeats the phrase of Gen "the *deep* that coucheth beneath," LXX ἀβύσσων

[4] Gen xvi 7 has πηγή, Heb *Ain*, *ib* xvi 14 has φρέαρ, Heb. *Beer*, "well" ("the *well* was called *Beer*-lahai-roi")

[5] See Gesen 909 *a* The meaning appears to be, a God that sees all things and sees my misery

[6] Gen xvi 13, R V "have *looked* after him that seeth me" This fails to shew the repetition of the same verb "*see*" Vulg has "Profecto hic *vidi* posteriora *videntis* me" Does this take the meaning to be as in Exod xxxiii 23 "videbis *posteriora* mea," implying the inferior attributes of God?

345 (Mark ii 18—22)

THE OLD AND THE NEW

remarks remind us of the Johannine saying that the disciples of Jesus "marvelled that he spake with a woman[1]." But far more important is the connection between God's "seeing" the human soul, and the soul's being consequently "made to see." To say that the eye of the Lord is like the sun in seeing all things, is merely to say what Greek, Roman and Egyptian theology would say. But the story of Hagar by the fountain teaches us that the eye of the Lord *not only "saw" but "caused to see."* And the Fourth Gospel goes even beyond this. For it teaches us that those who are thus caused to see cause others to see. God, the Father and Fountain of Light and Life, is regarded as sending into each soul that receives Him through the Son, a separate fountain of his own, from which each can refresh himself and prepare others to receive what he has received[2]. This subject will come before us again when we consider the Synoptic metaphor of the good eye and the evil eye, which has much in common with the implied metaphor of that good fountain or evil fountain which may be described as "the abundance of the heart[3]."

---

[1] Jn iv 27, see *Gen r* on Gen xvi 13 and also *ib* Wu pp 229, 298

[2] See Jn vii 38. In *Test XII Patr Judah* § 24, Dr Charles brackets "this Fountain giving life unto all" (as possibly a Christian interpolation) but with hesitation, noting Prov xiii 14, xiv 27, and Jer ii 13, xvii 13. It may be added that Philo i 575 quotes Jer ii 13 as proving that God "is the most ancient of all fountains," just before commenting on the story of Hagar at the fountain

[3] Comp Mt xii 34, Lk vi 45

CHAPTER IX*

JESUS AND THE SABBATH

[Mark ii. 23—iii 6]

§ 1. *"When Abiathar was high priest," in Mark*[1]

THE parallel texts given below agree in all important points[2] except that Mark inserts a date for the precedent, "when

---

* For titles of previous Parts of Diatessarica referred to by abbreviations in this Volume, see pp 545—6. For other abbreviations see pp xxiii—xxvi

[1] Mk ii 23—6 (R.V.)

(23) And it came to pass, that he was going on the sabbath day through the cornfields, and his disciples began, as they went, to pluck (*lit* began to make [their] way plucking) the ears of corn

(24) And the Pharisees said unto him, Behold, why do they on the sabbath day that which is not lawful?

(25) And he said unto them, Did ye never read what David did, when he had need, and was an hungred, he, and they that were with him?

(26) How he entered into the

Mt xii 1—4 (R V)

(1) At that season Jesus went on the sabbath day through the cornfields, and his disciples were an hungred, and began to pluck ears of corn, and to eat

(2) But the Pharisees, when they saw it, said unto him, Behold, thy disciples do that which it is not lawful to do upon the sabbath

(3) But he said unto them, Have ye not read what David did, when he was an hungred, and they that were with him,

(4) How he entered into the house of God, and did (*some anc auth* and

Lk vi 1—4 (R V)

(1) Now it came to pass on a (*many anc auth insert* second-first) sabbath, that he was going through the cornfields, and his disciples plucked the ears of corn, and did eat, rubbing them in their hands

(2) But certain of the Pharisees said, Why do ye that which it is not lawful to do on the sabbath day?

(3) And Jesus answering them said, Have ye not read even this, what David did, when he was an hungred, he, and they that were with him;

(4) How he entered into the house

[2] For note see page 348.

Abiathar was high priest." Jerome calls attention to the fact that the high priest at the time was "not Abiathar but Ahimelech, the same that was afterwards put to death with the rest of the priests by Doeg at the command of Saul[3]"; and he regards Mark as having made an error here like the error in the opening of his Gospel, where he has attributed words of Malachi to Isaiah

These facts explain why Matthew and Luke omitted the phrase, but they do not explain why Mark inserted it The error is not like that of briefly attributing to Isaiah two prophecies combined together of which the second alone is Isaiah's[4]. And the hypothesis of error does not explain why any high priest's name should be inserted at all, since the event would be known without such insertion to everyone whom Jesus was addressing. A better explanation is, first, that Abiathar became high priest after the eating of the shewbread, secondly, that he is frequently connected in Scripture with

Mk ii 23—6 (R V) (*contd*)	Mt xii. 1—4 (R V) (*contd*)	Lk vi 1—4 (R V) (*contd*)
house of God when Abiathar was high priest (*some anc auth* in the days of Abiathar the high priest), and did eat the shewbread, which it is not lawful to eat save for the priests, and gave also to them that were with him?	they did) eat the shewbread, which it was not lawful for him to eat, neither for them that were with him, but only for the priests?	of God, and did take and eat the shewbread, and gave also to them that were with him, which it is not lawful to eat save for the priests alone?

[2] On Lk. vi 1 "rubbing them in their hands," see *Hor. Heb* On *ib* R V marg "second-first," see Jerome *Epist* lii 8 "My teacher, Gregory of Nazianzus, when I once asked him to explain Luke's phrase σάββατον δευτερόπρωτον, that is 'the second-first Sabbath,' playfully evaded my request saying 'I will tell you about it in church, and there, when all the people applaud me, you will be forced against your will to know what you do not know at all For, if you alone remain silent, every one will put you down for a fool'"

[3] Jerome *Epist* lvii 9, referring to 1 S xxi 1, xxii 16—18
[4] Mk 1 1—3.

the "ephod," or divine oracle, consulted by David. *Horae Hebraicae* says, "it was common to the Jews, under '*Abiathar*,' to understand '*the Urim and Thummim*.'" Adopting this explanation, *Horae Hebraicae* paraphrases Mark as follows: "David ate the shewbread given him by the high priest, who had the oracle by Urim and Thummim present with him, and who acted by the divine direction[1]." This view—identifying the traditional "ephod-wearer" with "divine direction"—may be illustrated from Hosea, who prophesied that a time would come when Israel should be "without king and without prince...and without *ephod*", and Ezra and Nehemiah speak of referring a knotty question about pedigree to a time when it could be oracularly solved by "*a priest with Urim and Thummim*[2]."

If this explanation is correct, we are to suppose that the original Gospel described Jesus as alleging an argument that would appeal to the "scribes," who declared that Christ must be "the son of David[3]", and as defending His followers against the charge of violating the sanctity of God's holy day by pleading the precedent of David himself, who violated the sanctity of God's holy bread. It was to be eaten by none but priests. Yet David took it for his followers, and it is implied that he did this with the sanction of Abiathar, who was not only his friend and counsellor, but also afterwards high priest, and who, more than any other character in scripture, was connected with the oracular "ephod," or "Urim and

---

[1] *Hor Heb* quotes *Sanhedr* 16 b "Benaiah, the son of Jehoiada, that is, the Sanhedrim, *Abiathar, that is, Urim and Thummim*" This is repeated in *Berach* 3 b *Sanhedr* 95 b says that, if Abiathar had not been saved from destruction, David's descendants, too, would have been destroyed. After Abiathar, there is scarcely any mention of the oracular ephod. R V marg explains Exod xxviii. 30 "the Urim and the Thummim" as "The Lights and the Perfections"

[2] Hos iii 4, Ezr ii 63, Nehem vii. 65.

[3] Mk xii 35, Mt xxii 42, Lk. xx 41.

JESUS AND THE SABBATH

Thummim." Accepting this explanation, we easily understand that—beside the anachronism in calling Abiathar "high priest"—the allusion to what may be called his oracular character would be too technical and too indirect to be understood by the generality of Gentiles. Matthew and Luke therefore would naturally omit it. But then, in accordance with our rule, we are bound to ask, "Does John insert anything corresponding to it?"

§ 2. *Does John intervene?*

John omits the whole story about the disciples picking wheat on the sabbath. His narratives of Christ's two alleged infractions of the sabbath are both connected with acts of healing. Neither of these gives occasion for any mention of the irregular feeding on the shewbread But both of them give us occasion for asking whether John recognised the existence of some special divine revelation to the Son in this or that instance of healing. Did John find in the Marcan mention of "Abiathar" as representing "Urim and Thummim," some suggestion of a principle underlying those exceptional cases where Jesus was alleged to have broken the sabbath? Not many of these are recorded in any Gospel. On very many sabbaths, and in very many synagogues, there must have been sufferers in Christ's presence whom (we may presume) He made no attempt to heal What dictated His exceptional action? Did Jesus know beforehand from His own knowledge, or did He perceive at the moment from His own perception, the necessity that He should work this or that sign of healing, with the certainty that He should offend the Jews? Or did He perceive it from a special perception—a perception that He recognised to be, in some sense, not His own, but of the nature of an "oracle"?

The answer in the Fourth Gospel given by Jesus, after performing His first sabbath-work of healing, is "The Son can do nothing of himself, but what he seeth the Father do....For the Father loveth the Son and sheweth him all things that

JESUS AND THE SABBATH

himself doeth[1]." In other words, the Son has no need of an "oracle," or of an Abiathar with Urim and Thummim, that is to say, "Lights" and "Perfections." The Father Himself is His "Abiathar." And here we may note that a Jew would find an allusion to "Father" in the name "*Abiathar*," which Jerome renders "*Father overflowing*[2]." Also, in the preface to the second sabbath-work of healing, the healing of the man born blind, a Jew might find a thought of the ancient oracle. For Jesus says that the man must needs be healed "that the works of God should be made manifest in him....I am *the light of the world*[3]." In the mouth of a Jewish Messiah, the words "I am *the Ur*," that is, the Light, suggest that in Him the ancient "oracle" of the "*Urim*," or Lights, was fulfilled or superseded.

This discussion does not assume that the name "Abiathar" was actually uttered by Jesus, or even that it was part of the tradition that Mark, Matthew, and Luke had, in common. Mark may have introduced it by error. All that is here assumed is that John found the name established in Mark—and probably used against Christians as a proof of the Evangelist's inaccuracy. Starting from these assumptions, and working on the hypothesis of Johannine intervention, we have endeavoured to shew how, even here, where John has not a single word peculiar to him and Mark, the Marcan tradition may have left its trace on the Johannine thought and expression

---

[1] Jn v 19—20. See above, pp 225, 248, 268, 270

[2] *Onomast* p 34 "pater superfluus." Eusebius has (*ib* p 186) κενόν (v r. ην) which I cannot explain (even if it is meant for καινόν). For "Abiezrite" rendered by LXX "*father of* Ezri," see Judg vi 11, 24 and comp viii 32 (A)

[3] Jn ix 3—5 It is interesting to compare the Johannine "*I am* the light of the world" with the Matthaean (v. 14) "*Ye are* the light of the world" (omitted in the parallel Lk xiv 34 foll) Jesus certainly did not say the former Possibly He did not say the latter But He meant both He felt that the Spirit within Him, the Spirit of Sonship and Brotherhood, was "the light of the world," and, if His disciples were not this light, they were not His.

JESUS AND THE SABBATH

§ 3. *"The sabbath was made for man," in Mark*

The Synoptists all agree that Jesus said "The Son of man is lord of the sabbath[1]." But they differ as to what precedes the saying Mark and Matthew regard it as a conclusion arising out of previous words of Jesus. Luke regards it as a separate saying

Mark inserts *"so that"* in such a way as to prepare us to expect, in what precedes, some statement about the Son of Man, such as *"The Son of Man* was in God's thought when He appointed the first sabbath." But, instead of that, we find a statement about *"man"*: "The sabbath was made for *man*, and not man for the sabbath *so that the Son of man...*"

Matthew inserts something different, perhaps feeling that not *"man"* pure and simple, but *man representing God, man as a "priest," was intended* · "the *priests* in the temple profane the sabbath and are guiltless." Then he adds—as if to shew that the Son of Man is a very much greater person than a "man" or even than a "priest"—"I say unto you that one

---

[1] Mk ii 27—8

(27) And he said unto them, The sabbath was made for man, and not man for the sabbath
(28) So that the Son of man is lord even of the sabbath

Mt xii 5—8

(5) Or have ye not read in the law, how that on the sabbath day the priests in the temple profane the sabbath, and are guiltless?
(6) But I say unto you, that one greater (*lit* a greater thing) than the temple is here
(7) But if ye had known what this meaneth, I desire mercy, and not sacrifice, ye would not have condemned the guiltless
(8) For the Son of man is lord of the sabbath

Lk vi 5

(5) And he said unto them, The Son of man is lord of the sabbath [This follows "not lawful to eat save for the priests alone "]

352 (Mark ii 23—iii 6)

JESUS AND THE SABBATH

greater than the temple is here." But further, he seems to feel that the character of this Person—"one greater than the temple," who can override even the sabbath—ought to be suggested by something more than the official "priest." So he adds a warning about the God who presides over the Temple and who says "I desire kindness and not sacrifice[1]."

In reality, however, the tradition peculiar to Mark needs no alteration It is in accordance with the nobler type of Jewish tradition which said to Israel, "The sabbath is delivered to you and not you to the sabbath," where the context indicates that the sabbath may be broken for the saving of life[2]. And if we find a want of sequence in Mark's argument from "man" to "the Son of man," that is perhaps our fault, because we have read into the latter appellation a technical and official signification that it did not have in Christ's lips. Later on, His disciples took Son of Man to mean a Person *raised far above* humanity But Jesus used it to mean a Person *representing* humanity. We may call it "the character of the Son of Adam," if we remember that the appellation,

---

[1] Hos vi 6 ἔλεος, "kindness," see *Son* **3495** *c*, **3566** *a*, comp. *Notes* **2840*** *a* foll These words of Hosea are said to have been quoted by R Jochanan ben Zakkai to console a disciple of his who mourned over the fall of Jerusalem as if the Temple were the only means of making propitiation for sins (*Aboth R N* iv, referred to by Taylor on *Aboth* i 2) Jochanan said "We still have *the bestowal of kindnesses* (Hos vi 6)" *Aboth R N* iv also quotes Ps lxxxix 2, which the Targum renders "The world *will be built up with kindness*" (Walton "aedificatus est," by error)

[2] See *Mechilt* on Exod xxxi 13 quoted in *Son* **3171** It is also found in *Jôma* 85 *b* The word for "deliver" is *mâsar*, παραδίδωμι, used (Levy iii 177—8) to mean (*inter alia*) "delivering-up" fugitives to their enemies, or to the government, and hence applied to "informers" or "betrayers ' Hence "ye are not delivered up to the sabbath" might very well be a maxim in the mouth of Mattathias (1 Macc ii 39—42) urging his countrymen, when contending against their oppressors, not to sacrifice their lives to a literal observance of the rule against bearing any burden (*e g* weapons) on the sabbath (see I Abrahams, M A , *Cambridge Biblical Essays*, p 186)

JESUS AND THE SABBATH

besides including every human being, may also be typically and mystically used of that particular Son of Adam (that second or last Adam, as Paul says) whom subsequently Christians recognised as remedying, in the Redemption, the evil inflicted in the Fall.

The ninety-second Psalm, entitled in the Bible "A Psalm, a Song for the Sabbath Day," is entitled in the Targum "The psalm and song that was spoken *by Adam of old* (i.e the first Adam, or the first Man) concerning the sabbath day " This leads us to see how Jews of spiritual minds might regard the sabbath as not made for Israel alone, nor as introduced to mankind for the first time through the Law of Moses It was God's gift to Adam, for him and for the Sons of Adam after him Adam fell. But it would be reserved for a Son of Adam in later days to reverse the Fall and to re-institute a sabbath, or sabbatical *aeon*, of spiritual rest. Such a doctrine as this is certainly found in Paul. It is also certainly not found in any passages hitherto alleged from the Talmuds We may therefore infer that Paul derived it from mystical Christian tradition, such as Christ Himself might teach, but such as would not be taught, in His days, by any prosaic Rabbi, and would be discouraged, after His days, by all Rabbis, as belonging to "the doctrine of the Nazarenes[1]."

§ 4. *Does John intervene?*

If the rule of Johannine Intervention required that John should represent Jesus as somewhere saying, "the sabbath was made for man," then we should have to confess that the rule is broken Jesus does not say this either in the first Johannine sabbath-healing, the one at Bethesda, or in the second, that of the man born blind. In the former we are told that, when the Jews "persecuted Jesus" because He did these things on the sabbath, Jesus answered them, "My Father is working

---

[1] See *Son* 3021, 3478

JESUS AND THE SABBATH

[every moment] until this-moment. And [so] I, too, work[1]." In the latter Jesus says, "We must work the works of him that sent me while it is day; the night cometh when no man can work. When I am in the world I am the light of the world[2]."

In neither case does Jesus mention the sabbath[3] In the former, He speaks as if He were the Son, or the Word, through whom all things were made by the Father, and through whom also all things are being continually sustained and vitalised, so that He, too, the Son, must be continually working. In the latter, if the text is correct[4], He associates Himself with fellow-workers ("*we* (emph.) must work") and speaks as one "sent" into the world for a limited time soon to be broken off by "night," when "no man can work" The great difference between the two passages makes it all the more remarkable that in both there is the same ignoring of sabbath-obstacles to an act of healing. But as regards Johannine intervention in favour of Mark, we cannot say more than this, that the two passages together represent Jesus as indirectly teaching that about the sabbath, as about any other six days of the week, a disciple of His was bound to act on the rule "We must work the works of him that sent me while it is day[5]."

---

[1] Jn v 17   [2] Jn ix 4—5

[3] He mentions it, however, between the two narratives, in vii 22—3

[4] See *Joh Gr* 2428 *b—e*

[5] Comp Jn xi 9—10 "Are there not twelve hours in the day? If a man walk in the day he stumbleth not...but if a man walk in the night he stumbleth" The context (*ib* 7—11) raises the question whether Jesus shall go to Lazarus in Judaea—where the Jews were lately "seeking to stone" Him—that He may "awake him out of sleep," *i e* restore him to life Jesus seems to imply that a man cannot "stumble" when he acts in the daylight of the consciousness that he is doing the Father's beneficent will towards a brother man The word here meaning "stumble," *lit* "dash [the foot] against," προσκόπτω (apart from Mt vii 27 of the "dashing" of rain and floods and wind) occurs in the Gospels only here and in

JESUS AND THE SABBATH

§ 5. *Jesus proceeding to heal on the sabbath*

The texts given below describe Christ's first Synoptic sabbath-healing[1]. All agree that it is in the synagogue. Mark

Mt iv 6, Lk iv 11—quoted by Satan from Ps xci 12 "lest thou *dash* thy foot against a stone," where Origen *ad loc* says "The '*foot*' is the soul, the '*stone*' is sin." Comp. *Pesikt* sect. 16 (Wu p. 173) on brotherhood. There Joseph says to his brothers—trembling because they had persecuted him—"*The day has twelve hours*, the night has twelve hours, the year has twelve months. ," as though "twelve" were a part of God's beneficent order, illustrating the Law of Brotherhood. Brotherhood, the context says, is expressed, not in Cain, Ishmael, and Esau, but in Joseph. Wunsche adds, from *Debarim r* sect. 4, "How can I become the enemy of my father? Did he give you life and shall I give you death?"

John differs from *Pesikta* in making "night" not parallel, but antithetical, to "day." He suggests a thought similar to that in Ps civ 23 "Man goeth forth unto his work.. until the evening." There "man," the Worker, is contrasted with (*ib* 20) "the beasts of the forest" "creeping forth" to seek their prey. Comp. Lk xxii 53 "this is your hour" and Jn xiii 30 "it was night." Chrysostom's two explanations of Jn xi 9—10 will be discussed when the doctrine about "offence," σκάνδαλον, and "stumbling," πρόσκομμα, comes before us in its order. Having regard to the rare use of προσκόπτω in the LXX, we may reasonably suppose that John is alluding to Ps xci 12 as if Jesus said "There is no need of Gabriel or Michael to prevent you from 'stumbling.' 'Go forth' to your 'work until the evening,' like Man, the child of God, working for God's other children. Employ the daylight of God's 'twelve hours.' Walk in the light of the Light of the World. Then you will not 'stumble.'" Concerning the man that "walks" thus the Johannine Epistle says (1 Jn ii 10) "He that loveth his brother abideth in the light, and in him offence has no existence (σκάνδαλον ἐν αὐτῷ οὐκ ἔστιν)."

[1]

Mk iii 1—6 (R V)	Mt xii 9—14 (R V)	Lk vi. 6—11 (R V)
(1) And he entered again into the synagogue, and there was a man there which had his hand withered. (2) And they watched him, whether he would heal	(9) And he departed thence, and went into their synagogue. (10) And behold, a man having a withered hand. And they asked him, saying, Is it lawful	(6) And it came to pass on another sabbath, that he entered into the synagogue and taught and there was a man there, and his right hand was withered

(Mark ii. 23—iii. 6)

JESUS AND THE SABBATH

(followed by Matthew) says that *"they"* watched Jesus, or questioned Him, to see whether He would heal on the sabbath—without telling us exactly who *"they"* are Matthew, having previously mentioned *"their* synagogue" (Mk [*"the"*]¹, Lk. *"the"*) may claim to have indicated that "they" means "the rulers of the synagogue." But in Mark, we cannot tell at once whether "they" means "people"—a sense in which Mark

Mk iii 1—6 (R V) (*contd*)	Mt xii 9—14 (R V) (*contd*)	Lk vi 6—11 (R V) (*contd*)
him on the sabbath day, that they might accuse him (3) And he saith unto the man that had his hand withered, Stand forth (*lit* Arise into the midst) (4) And he saith unto them, Is it lawful on the sabbath day to do good, or to do harm? to save a life, or to kill? But they held their peace (5) And when he had looked round about on them with anger, being grieved at the hardening of their heart, he saith unto the man, Stretch forth thy hand And he stretched it forth and his hand was restored (6) And the Pharisees went out, and straightway with the Herodians took counsel against him, how they might destroy him	to heal on the sabbath day? that they might accuse him (11) And he said unto them, What man shall there be of you, that shall have one sheep, and if this fall into a pit on the sabbath day, will he not lay hold on it and lift it out? (12) How much then is a man of more value than a sheep! Wherefore it is lawful to do good on the sabbath day (13) Then saith he to the man, Stretch forth thy hand And he stretched it forth, and it was restored whole, as the other (14) But the Pharisees went out, and took counsel against him, how they might destroy him	(7) And the scribes and the Pharisees watched him, whether he would heal on the sabbath, that they might find how to accuse him (8) But he knew their thoughts, and he said to the man that had his hand withered, Rise up, and stand forth in the midst And he arose and stood forth (9) And Jesus said unto them, I ask you, Is it lawful on the sabbath to do good, or to do harm? to save a life, or to destroy it? (10) And he looked round about on them all, and said unto him, Stretch forth thy hand And he did [so] and his hand was restored (11) But they were filled with madness (*or*, foolishness); and communed one with another what they might do to Jesus

¹ In Mk iii 1, W.H. om "the" before "synagogue," see below, p 373.

frequently uses "they"—or whether it means the small group of officials of the synagogue. Luke says it was "the scribes and the Pharisees," that is to say, the official group (which would include any visitors of official position)

We are helped to understand why these men "watched" Jesus by a preceding passage in Luke, just before the healing of the paralytic: "He was teaching, and there were Pharisees and doctors of the law sitting by...and the power of the Lord was that he should heal[1]." That day happened not to be a sabbath, so that no charge of sabbath-breaking could be on that occasion brought against Jesus. But Luke gives us the impression that at certain times, more than at others, "the power of the Lord" might be felt by Jesus impelling Him to acts of healing. Thus Luke prepares us for inferring that whenever Jesus saw a sick man before Him, and felt this special "power of the Lord" upon Him, He would in that same hour heal the man, sabbath or no sabbath. "The scribes and Pharisees" might also perceive this, from the signs of compassion in His countenance, and from other indications that He was preparing to act. If so, we can understand that they "watched" Jesus, and even that they prearranged the presence, and perhaps the prominent presence, of the suffering man for the purpose of convicting Him of sabbath-breaking

Jesus, when He saw the sick man thus placed before Him, and when, at the same instant, He recognised the presence of "the power of the Lord that he should heal," perceived that He was in what the world would call "a trap." Heal the man He must; and, in healing him, He would probably have on His side not only all His disciples but also a large number of the congregation. But that would not avail Him against the enmity of the whole body of the scribes and Pharisees. Though He knew that He could do in an instant for this sufferer what

---

[1] Lk. v 17 (*lit*) "and the power of the Lord was [tending] to his healing"

JESUS AND THE SABBATH

He had previously done for the paralytic, He determines first to make a direct appeal to the common sense of humanity in these officials, asking them (as it were) to let Him do this good deed with their good will, and to open their hearts to it as a revelation of God's kindness

The situation appears to have been somewhat like another, described by Luke alone, where "the ruler of the synagogue" and the "adversaries" of Jesus are on one side and "the multitude" on another There, Jesus heals "a daughter of Abraham" on the sabbath. The ruler "had indignation and said to the multitude, There are six days on which men ought to work" Jesus felt that the attack proceeded from the "adversaries" as a whole and replied not to the "ruler" alone but to them, "Ye hypocrites," alleging the common-sense inference of humanity from the kind treatment of beasts to the kind treatment of men The result was, Luke says, "All his adversaries were put to shame; and all the multitude rejoiced for all the glorious things that were done by him[1]"

In the present instance, the first instance of sabbath-healing, there is this important difference that Jesus, standing as it were at the parting of the ways, asks the Pharisees whether they will not go with Him, on the way of kindness And He waits for their answer To have in His hands, as He has, the power of giving life, and yet to give no life, might seem to Him like giving death—like "killing." It is hyperbole, but Mark ventures on it—"Is it lawful. .to save a life or to *kill*[2]?" Matthew shrinks from it. Luke follows Mark. Luke does not, however, add Mark's next words "But they held their peace"

Perhaps Luke thought that they were unnecessary since Christ's question was rhetorical and not intended to have an answer. But if it was not rhetorical and was intended to have an answer, then we can realise that Mark's addition has a bearing on what follows For if Jesus gave the scribes and

---

[1] Lk xiii. 14—17   [2] Mk iii 4

Pharisees time to answer, and if they remained silent, we may infer that they did so because they wished to render Him open to future accusations on some convenient occasion, and yet to avoid committing themselves to immediate unpopularity with the multitude—expectant of a miracle—by saying definitely "It is not lawful to heal on the sabbath." Yet even to the multitude, and assuredly to the right-minded among them, as well as to Christ's avowed disciples, such a silence must have caused indignation mingled with regret that a rupture seemed imminent between the new Teacher and the recognised teachers of the Law This will have to be borne in mind when we attempt to explain Mark's next words, rendered by R V.—but not quite satisfactorily—"And when he had looked round about on them with anger, being grieved at the hardness of their heart[1]."

§ 6. *Jesus "being grieved" (R.V), in Mark*

The Greek word translated by R V. "*being grieved*" occurs nowhere in N.T. except here. In Greek literature, so far as hitherto alleged, it means "*share in grief*," "*grieve out of sympathy*," as when Plutarch says that we ought to seek the society of manly natures, "not such as *grieve out of sympathy* and stir up lamentations for flattery's sake, but such as take away griefs by noble and solemn consolation[2]." If it has that meaning here, it would seem to mean that Jesus felt mingled grief and indignation—grief in sympathy with His followers, but indignation because of His failure to touch the hearts of

---

[1] Mk iii 5

[2] Plut *Mor* ii. 117 F ἀνδράσι μὴ τοῖς συλλυπουμένοις καὶ διεγείρουσι τὰ πένθη διὰ κολακείαν. It occurs twice in LXX, Ps lxix 20 "I awaited *a sympathizer* (συλλυπούμενον)," Is li 19 "who will *sympathize with thee* (τίς σοι συλλυπηθήσεται,)?" Aristotle says (*Eth Nic* ix 11 med) "manly natures avoid making their friends *grieve* with them (εὐλαβοῦνται συλλυπεῖν τοὺς φίλους αὐτοῖς) " So Steph *Thes* , but ed Weise συλλυπεῖσθαι αὐτοῖς).

the Pharisees The congregation, and some of His own disciples, were likely to be grieved by the refusal of the Pharisees to respond to His appeal, and He was "grieved along with them " Both He and they were also grieved *at* the hardness of heart of the official class, but it cannot be said that they shared *in* the feelings of the officials (much less, in any "grief" of theirs).

The distinction however is not clear in Mark between the officials and the congregation. Luke suggests the distinction by two insertions First, he says that it was only "*the scribes and Pharisees*" that "watched" Jesus; secondly, he says that Jesus "looked round about on them *all*" before He pronounced the words of healing These insertions hardly suffice for perfect clearness But, taken along with the healing of the "daughter of Abraham" above described, they indicate that we must make a distinction, not made by Mark, between two classes in the synagogue, namely, the rulers and the multitude. The hearts of the former were hardened; the latter were indignant and distressed Jesus sympathized with the distress and was indignant at the hardening.

In accordance with this view we shall be able to interpret "them" in Mark's looked round about on "*them*" as not referring to the officials but to the sympathetic congregation called by Luke "all" And this will accord with the Marcan use in other instances where Jesus "looks round on those about him," or "looks round" in the presence of His disciples, after something has happened of a nature to disturb and shake their faith, before He proceeds to reassure them[1].

There is nothing in the Fourth Gospel that directly and verbally illustrates Mark's use of this special word expressing "sympathetic grief" But in thought John dramatically expresses the Marcan "sympathy" when he describes Jesus

---

[1] Mk iii 34 περιβλεψάμενος τοὺς περὶ αὐτὸν κύκλῳ καθημένους, x 23 περιβλεψάμενος ὁ Ἰησοῦς λέγει τοῖς μαθηταῖς αὐτοῦ Περιβλέπομαι does not occur in N T except in Mark (and in Lk vi 10 following Mark).

in the presence of Mary the sister of Lazarus, and tells us that when He saw her weeping and the Jews weeping, He Himself "wept[1]."

§ 7. *"At the hardening of their heart," in Mark*

Mark and John are the only Evangelists that use this peculiar word for "hardening," applied (either as a noun or as a verb) to the "heart." It has nothing to do with "hardening" in the sense of obstinacy or stubbornness (as in the "hardening" of the "heart" of Pharaoh). Literally, and medically, it means "callousness," or "stony nature"—in Greek, *pōrōsis*—such as attacks the human frame. The *Thesaurus* quotes Aristotle as saying that "blood, when corrupted, becomes matter, and, from matter, *pōros*, i e. *callous* or *chalky* substance." The *Thesaurus* also quotes Isaiah as saying "He hath blinded their eyes and *made-callous their heart*[2]." But these words are not in Isaiah (whether Greek or Hebrew). They are only in John's paraphrase of Isaiah, where the Evangelist sums up the reasons why "they [*i e* Israel as a whole] were not able to believe." The words in Isaiah are "*Make fat the heart* of this people" What led John to paraphrase them thus?

The LXX does not elsewhere use *pōrōsis*, "hardening," either as a noun or as a verb, except as a doubtful rendering of "dim-sighted" (*lit.* "faint" or "dim" applied to the eye)[3].

---

[1] Jn xi 33—5 κλαίουσαν κλαίοντας ἐδάκρυσεν Jesus (Rom xii 15) "weeps with them that weep" In Luke (xix 41) Jesus "weeps," not "with," but "over," Jerusalem Jerusalem does not weep

[2] See Steph *Thes*, on πῶρος, 2302, quoting Aristot *H A* iii. 19, and 2303, quoting "Esai. 6, [10] τετύφλωκεν αὐτῶν τοὺς ὀφθαλμοὺς καὶ πεπώρωκεν (sic) αὐτῶν τὴν καρδίαν ." But the words occur only in Jn xii 40 Isaiah has "make fat," LXX ἐπαχύνθη "was made fat" Comp. above, pp 227—8

[3] Job xvii 7 "mine eye is dim," πεπώρωνται, but Aא[2] πεπήρωνται and Aq, Theod, Sym ἠμαυρώθησαν [It occurs as an error in Prov x 20, πεπωρωμένος for πεπυρωμένος] In the Apostolic Fathers and early Apologists the only instances of πωρόω etc. are Herm *Mand*

But a saying is preserved by Athenaeus that, in certain circumstances, an incision does not cause sensation, "by reason of the flesh, which was *made-callous owing to its fat*[1]." Now the Targum on Isaiah ("*make-fat* the heart") paraphrases "*make-fat*" by "*make-gross*"—using a word that in Hebrew occurs only once, as follows: "The proud have forged a lie against me...their heart is as *gross* as grease, but I delight in thy law. It is good for me that I have been afflicted, that I might learn thy statutes[2]."

This helps us to understand not only Isaiah's meaning but also its radical connection with the doctrine of Christ, and also, at the same time, the verbal obstacles in the way of teachers from the East endeavouring to expound the doctrine to learners in the West. To a Greek, Isaiah's "fattening the heart" was an unintelligible metaphor. All the Synoptists omit it in connection with the Parable of the Sower when they represent Jesus as using language based on Isaiah's utterance, and John paraphrases it[3]. But the thought of Israel as Dives, faring sumptuously at the Table of the Law and "fattening" his heart, while the Gentile Lazarus waits for the crumbs outside the door, pervades the close of the argumentative portion of the Epistle to the Romans[4]. Later

---

IV 2 ἡ καρδία μου πεπώρωται, Lat "excaecatum," XII 4 τὴν καρδίαν αὐτῶν πεπωρωμένην, Lat "obtusum". The Lat transl perhaps took the Gk as implying "a cataract," so to speak, of "the heart". There was also a natural tendency to substitute πηρόω, a word implying general disablement, for the difficult πωρόω implying particular disablement.

[1] See Steph *Thes* VI 2303 quoting Athenaeus XII 549 B, quoted more fully by Wetstein (on Mk VI 52) ὑπὸ τῆς πεπωρωμένης ἐκ τοῦ στέατος σαρκός

[2] Ps CXIX 69—71

[3] Mk IV 12, Mt XIII 14, Lk VIII 10, Jn XII 40 uses ἐπώρωσεν. Mt XIII. 15 appends a correct quotation of Isaiah (LXX) with ἐπαχύνθη Comp above, pp 227—8

[4] Rom XI 7—25 "The rest [of Israel] were *made-callous* [*in heart*].. *a spirit of stupor* . Let *their table be made a snare* the *fatness* (πιότητος) of the olive tree . a *callousness* [*of heart*] in part

JESUS AND THE SABBATH

on Mark uses it twice, once in his own person, but once in words of Jesus Himself, implying that even Christ's own disciples were not free from this fault, and, in both instances, connecting the word with the Feeding of the Five Thousand[1].

We may conclude from these facts that in this deliberate antagonism of the scribes and the Pharisees to sabbath-healing Jesus recognised that same antagonism of Israel to the Spirit of Jehovah which had been predicted to Isaiah during his vision of the Lord in the Temple. The word "callousness" is to be taken as a key-word. By it Mark says, as it were, to his readers, "Note this word. For at this moment Jesus began to recognise that 'a *callousness* in part' had befallen Israel, and that, as Paul said afterwards, 'That which Israel seeketh for...the election obtained it and the rest *were made callous*[2]'"

---

hath befallen Israel" Such "callousness" may be the insolent callousness of the oppressor whose eyes (Ps lxxiii. 7) "stand out with fatness," or of sensual Gentiles (Eph iv 18—19) "alienated from the life of God because of the *callousness* of their heart" so that they "work all uncleanness with greediness" But it may be also the callousness of Israel, selfishly exulting as God's favourites, and hence regarding Him as a God that favours unjustly, a Respecter of Persons, whence (2 Cor iii 14—15) "their minds *were made callous* . a veil lieth upon their heart"

[1] (1) Mk vi 52 "for they had not understood (συνῆκαν) in the matter of (ἐπὶ) the loaves, but their heart was in-a-state-of-callousness (ἀλλ' ἦν αὐτῶν ἡ καρδία πεπωρωμένη)" om in parall Mt xiv 33 Luke omits the whole narrative (2) Mk viii 17 πεπωρωμένην ἔχετε τὴν καρδίαν ὑμῶν, (om in parall Mt xvi 9)

[2] May we infer from this narrative, and from Mark's subsequent non-mention of "synagogue"—except in vi 2 (of Nazareth) and in words of Christ—that Jesus henceforth gave up teaching "in synagogue"? Probably not. When Mark says (vi 6) περιῆγεν τὰς κώμας κύκλῳ διδάσκων, Matthew (ix. 35) adds πόλεις and ἐν ταῖς συναγωγαῖς αὐτῶν, and Luke (xiii. 22) adds πόλεις It seems probable that the "teaching," mentioned by them all, was often in synagogues Comp also Jn vi 59, xviii 20

JESUS AND THE SABBATH

§ 8 *"The Herodians," in Mark*

Mark mentions "the Herodians" or "leaven of Herod' thrice (1) here (where Matthew and Luke omit the term); (2) "the leaven of the Pharisees and the leaven of *Herod*," Matthew "the leaven of the Pharisees and *Sadducees*," Luke "the leaven, *which is hypocrisy*, of the Pharisees[1]"; (3) "they send some of the Pharisees and of *the Herodians*," Matthew "they [i e the Pharisees] send to him their disciples with *the Herodians*," Luke "they sent *spies, hypocritically-pretending that they were righteous*[2]" These facts point to an original name for "*Herodians*," such as "men of *the Hypocrite*," or men of some type that might include both Sadducees and Herodians, e g. "men of *the Lawless*" If that was the origin, Mark has consistently rendered it "Herodians" Matthew has first omitted it (perhaps in perplexity), then rendered it "Sadducees," and then "Herodians" Luke has first omitted it, then rendered it "hypocrisy," then rendered it "spies hypocritically pretending." (1) What Hebrew word, if any, could have two such different meanings as "*hypocrite*" and "*lawless*"? (2) Could such a word be naturally applied to Herod Antipas? (3) Is there any evidence that it was so applied? These three questions we shall now attempt to answer.

The word "hypocrite" is used twice by LXX, and four times elsewhere by Aquila and Theodotion[3]. In all these passages the Hebrew is one word, *chânêph*. It is rendered by R.V. "*godless*" But in LXX it is rendered (*inter alia*) "*lawless*," "*impious*," "*law-breaking*," "*hypocrite*" and "*pollute-by-murder*[4]." Levy says that the radical meaning of *chânêph* is

---

[1] Mk viii 15, Mt xvi 6, Lk xii 1
[2] Mk xii 13, Mt xxii 16, Lk xx 20 ἀπέστειλαν ἐνκαθέτους ὑποκρινομένους ἑαυτοὺς δικαίους εἶναι.
[3] Job xxxiv 30, xxxvi 13, in LXX, Job xv 34, xx 5, Prov xi 9, Is. xxxiii 14 in Aquila and Theodotion
[4] Trommius gives ἄνομος (3), ἀσεβής (5), παράνομος (2), ὑποκριτής (2), φονοκτονεῖν (3)

to "change" or "shift," and hence (1) "change one's attitude by flattering," (2) "change one's religion[1]." But the only instance of *chânêph* in the Pentateuch is connected with bloodshed· "Ye shall not *pollute* the land wherein ye are; for blood, it *polluteth* the land[2]" It is for the most part national pollution—pollution of the "land," or "priests," or "prophets"—to which this word refers. A passage in Josephus declares that the defeat of the army of Herod Antipas by king Aretas was regarded by many Jews as a judgment for the murder of John the Baptist[3]. Hence Antipas might receive a nickname from *chânêph* as being both "*polluter*" and "*polluted*[4]." Such a nickname, even though not given till after the execution of the Baptist, would naturally colour the vocabulary of the earliest Evangelists, and even the language of Christ Himself. There was also another way in which Herod Antipas might be known as "the *chânêph*." Daniel, in a prediction interpreted by Jerome as referring to the times of the Maccabees under Antiochus Epiphanes, says "Such as do wickedly against the covenant shall he *pollute* (*chânêph*) by flatteries," meaning "*He shall cause them to adopt the worship and customs of the Greeks*[5]." Antiochus Epiphanes "*polluted*" rather more by persecution than by "flatteries";

---

[1] Levy ii 83—4 Gesen 337 b connects it with "inclining"
[2] Numb xxxv 33 (LXX) φονοκτονεῖν τὴν γῆν (*bis*) Φονοκτονεῖν is not alleged by Steph *Thes* as occurring earlier
[3] Joseph *Ant* xviii 5 1—2 The genuineness of the passage has been assailed But the omission of Herod's oath indicates that it is not written by a Christian (as also does the tone of the whole).
[4] It may be said that Antipas laid the blame for the execution of John the Baptist on his "oath" Josephus does not mention the "oath" Those who called Antipas a "fox" (Lk xiii 32) would not attach much weight to the excuse of the "oath" In 2 K vi 32 ("this son of a *murderer*") Elisha assumes that Ahab was Naboth's "murderer" though it was his wife who, leaving him in nominal ignorance, actually brought about the murder (1 K xxi 7—13)
[5] Dan xi 32 R V. "pervert," marg Heb "make profane," comp 1 Macc 1 43—61.

JESUS AND THE SABBATH

but Daniel's prophetic *chânêph* would apply well to Herod Antipas so far as he induced his countrymen to adopt Greek habits.

The Talmuds apparently make no mention either of Antipas or of John the Baptist. But in the recently discovered *Fragments of a Zadokite Work* there is a contrast between "a teacher of righteousness" and a "man of mocking," called also "the commanding one," who is vaguely connected with the charge of "taking two wives," and who "dropped to Israel waters of lying." In that work, the Pharisees are called "they that builded the wall and daubed it with untempered mortar," and it is said that these (Hos v 11) "followed after the commanding one"

I have endeavoured to shew[1] that this "commanding one" is an appellation of Herod Antipas But how could "dropping" (a word applicable rather to prophets) be applied to Antipas? It seemed to me explicable from a passage in Proverbs saying "The lips of the strange woman *drop* honey," which Rashi regards as the seducing doctrine of "*Epicureismus*[2]." Herod Antipas, as favouring Hellenism, might be said to "drop" *Epicureismus*. But now a better, or perhaps a supplementary explanation suggests itself from the Jerusalem Targum, which appears to use this word, "*drop*," concerning the contaminating influence of blood-pollution connected with the unique mention of *chânêph* in the Law:—"Nor contaminate (*tânaph*) ye the land in which ye are, because innocent blood that hath not been avenged will *drop-on* (*nâtaph*) the land[3]." The passage at all events illustrates the probabilities of a play on the words *chânêph*, "pollute," and *nâtaph*, "drop."

It should be noted that the Syriac Versions frequently

---

[1] See *Light* 3996 a—e   On "drop," see Gesen 643 a.
[2] See Rashi on Prov. v 3.
[3] Jer. Targ. on Numb xxxv. 33   I follow Walton's Text ("*inundat* terram," and so Etheridge)   Others repeat *tânaph* in the place of *nâtaph*.

JESUS AND THE SABBATH

render "hypocrites," when applied to the Pharisees, "accepters of persons" (lit "accepters with persons, or faces")[1]. This may be explained as follows. In Greek literature, outside the LXX, during the first century, *hupocritai* (our *hypocrites*) meant "stage-players" and nothing else. The Syriac translators therefore interpreted "*hupocritai*" as "maskers" or "those that take masks" (since all stage-players wore masks). But "mask," in Greek as in Latin, was sometimes rendered by a word (*prosōpon*) that more usually meant "*person*[2]." Now to "*take, or accept, persons*" was Biblical Hebrew, and Biblical Greek, for "*favour persons*," meaning (for the most part) "judge unjustly[3]" Hence they inferred, as a correct rendering of "*hypocrites*," the phrase "*takers, or accepters, of persons*."

But in truth Jesus appears to have applied the term *chânêph* to the Pharisees, by no means in the sense of "*accepters of persons*," but in that much stronger sense in which Isaiah and Jeremiah spoke of the nation and the guides and teachers of the nation, the priests and prophets, as being "polluted" and "polluters"—being practically apostates to what Ezekiel called the "idols" in their own hearts[4]. It is strong language. But it is not stronger than that of Francis Bacon. "The great

---

[1] Palest , e g Mt vi 2, 5, renders it "false-dealers" (Gesen. 1055 b), Delitzsch has *chânêph*. SS has "accepters of (lit with) persons" in Mt vi 2, Gk ὑποκριταί, but *chânêph* in vi. 7 (see *Thes Syr* 1322 on *chânêph*), where Curet. has "accepters of persons," Gk ἐθνικοί On "accept with person," see *Thes Syr* 2393 "*accepit aliquem secundum faciem* vel *personam eius*," προσωπολημπτεῖν

[2] See Steph *Thes* on (1) προσωπεῖον "mask" and on (2) πρόσωπον "person"—used in Attic sometimes for προσωπεῖον. In Latin, "*persōna*" means primarily "mask," and derivatively "personage," "character," "person "

[3] Comp Lev xix 15 "Ye shall do no unrighteousness in judgment . thou shalt not *respect the person* (lit *take the person*, λήμψῃ πρόσωπον) of the poor . ." Hence Rom ii 11 προσωπολημψία "*favouritism*" and Acts x 34 προσωπολήμπτης

[4] Ezek xiv 3

atheists indeed are hypocrites, which are ever handling holy things, but without feeling, so as they must needs be cauterized in the end[1]."

§ 9. *The absence of technical terms in John*

The mention of Herodians or leaven of Herod by Mark, but not by the parallel Luke who seems to identify it with hypocrisy, must be considered, along with the non-mention of Herodians anywhere by John, as affording a specimen of the instances where we must *not* expect Johannine intervention. John does not favour Mark against Luke. But it should be added that he does not favour Luke against Mark by a mention of hypocrisy or hypocrites. Those terms are nowhere used by John. These Johannine omissions raise a question as to what, in the Fourth Gospel, corresponds to "hypocrisy" in the Three. The writer gives us no one term for it but warns us against it as a Protean evil. It is heart-callousness[2]. It is also the self-sufficient blindness of the blind who say "We see[3]." Again, it may be called the repletion of those who are filled to satiety with the waters of self-satisfaction so that they have "no room" for the Water of Life[4]. These are cosmopolitan thoughts—callousness, blindness, and satiety. But "hypocrisy"—in its Greek verbal form—and "leaven" and "Sadducee" and "Herodian," and other terms denoting local and transient expressions of cosmopolitan evil, are not cosmopolitan and therefore not Johannine. When the Fourth Gospel was at last published, the Herods were probably extinct or near extinction. "Herod the fox[5]" had long ago lost his tetrarchy in the attempt to become a king[6]. "Herod

---

[1] *Essays* xvi. 60.
[2] Jn xii. 40 (R V.) "hardened their heart."
[3] Jn ix. 41.
[4] Jn viii 37—8   [5] Lk xiii. 32
[6] Joseph. *Ant.* xviii 7 2

the king"—*i.e.* Herod Agrippa I—after killing James the brother of John, had been smitten by an angel of God and eaten by worms[1]. Herod Agrippa II—called by Paul "king Agrippa"—the last of the Herods, who sided with the Romans in the war that destroyed Jerusalem, died about the end of the first century[2].

Perhaps there was some confusion in late first-century traditions among Christians about the various Herods who rose up against Christ and Christ's Church, fulfilling the Psalmist's prophecy about "the kings of the earth[3]." Justin Martyr speaks of a Herod as "king of the Jews" at the time when the LXX was written[4]. He also calls Herod Antipas "king of the Jews," and refers to Hosea as making a prediction about him in the words "a present to the king[5]." Mark himself was responsible for some such confusion, having begun his narrative about Herod's oath with the words "Herod *the king*" where Matthew and Luke have "Herod *the tetrarch*[6]." And who could say whether the "Herodians" derived their name from Herod the Great or from Herod Antipas? It is not surprising that John decided to drop the Herods altogether—especially as Luke had introduced Herod Antipas, just before the Crucifixion, as playing an important part about which Mark and Matthew say nothing. In any case John's silence about them is consistent and complete. For an evangelist who deals so amply with the acts and words of John the

---

[1] Acts xii 1—23

[2] Schurer 1 1 92, quoting Photius, *Biblioth cod* 33

[3] Ps ii 2, Acts iv 25—6   Herod the Great, according to Matthew alone, rose up against the child Jesus   Herod Antipas, according to Luke alone in the Gospels, "set at naught" the man Jesus; or, according to Luke in the Acts, Pilate and Herod were "gathered together" against Christ. See *Son* 3183 *c—d*

[4] *Apol* §31   [5] *Tryph.* §103, comp Hos. x 6

[6] Mk vi 14, Mt xiv. 1, Lk ix 7   Later on Mt xiv. 9 (λυπηθεὶς ὁ βασιλεὺς) resembles Mk vi 26 (περίλυπος γενόμενος ὁ βασιλεὺς), in the story of the oath (which is wholly omitted by Luke).

JESUS AND THE SABBATH

Baptist we might have thought it impossible to suppress the name of the prince that put him to death. But he does suppress it. "John," he says, "was not yet cast into prison." But who imprisoned him, and when, and why, and with what result—about all this he tells us nothing[1].

---

[1] Jn iii. 24.

CHAPTER X*

THE CONCOURSE TO JESUS
[Mark iii. 7—12]

§ 1. *Jesus "withdrew"*

IN Mark, after "took counsel how they might destroy him," it is said "And Jesus with his disciples *withdrew to* (or, *toward*) the sea[1]." And then comes a description of the concourse of the multitudes to Him from many regions.

In attempting to ascertain the exact meaning of a withdrawal "*to*, or *toward*, the sea," the question arises "From what place did Jesus withdraw?" The last place mentioned in Mark is a "synagogue," but the text varies between "a synagogue"

---

* For titles of previous Parts of Diatessarica referred to by abbreviations in this Volume, see pp 545—6 For other abbreviations see pp. xxiii—xxvi.

[1] Ἀνεχώρησεν πρὸς τὴν θάλασσαν. Ἀναχωρέω, "withdraw," from which "anchorite" is derived, would generally (not always, as may be seen from its use in Hermas) signify a retirement of more duration than is implied by ὑποχωρέω, "step back" (which sometimes means "give ground") In N T the preposition with which it is used is nowhere else πρός, but only εἰς (Mt 11 12 etc and Jn vi. 15) of withdrawing *into* a district or *into* the privacy of (Jn vi 15) "the mountain" Some MSS read εἰς here (Mk iii 7) Prof Swete says (on Mk iii 7) " πρός gives the direction or locality of the retreat " In the following remarks, R V "*to*" will be mostly retained, though "*toward*," or "*to the neighbourhood of*," would be a more exact rendering

and "the synagogue" given (without alternative) by R.V. and W.H. severally —

Mk iii. 1	Mt. xii. 9	Lk vi. 6
And he entered again into *the synagogue* (W H. om. *the*)	And he departed thence and went into *their synagogue*	And it came to pass on another sabbath that he entered into *the synagogue*

Codex B and ℵ omit the article, but the rest of the Greek MSS insert it, and so does the Syro-Sinaitic Version discovered since the publication of W.H.'s text. Professor Swete urges that "we speak of going 'to church' or being 'in church' when no particular building is intended." But we do not speak of going "*into* church." In N.T. elsewhere, we find "went into *the synagogue*" or "into *their synagogue*" or "into *their synagogues*[1]" etc., but nowhere "went *into* synagogue." Moreover, even if Mark did here (uniquely) use "into synagogue" as we use "to church," it would still be probable that he meant "went into synagogue in Capernaum," as John writes "These things said he *in synagogue* as he taught *in Capernaum*[2]." For Mark's last mention of synagogue in the singular referred to the synagogue at Capernaum[3]. Now, therefore, if he says that Jesus "entered *again into synagogue*," a reasonable interpretation is "he entered *again into synagogue in Capernaum*." In the interval, Jesus had repeatedly entered into "synagogues" of Galilee[4], but Mark may now be intending to relate a second act of Jesus in the synagogue of Capernaum.

This has a bearing on the meaning of "withdrew to the sea."

---

[1] Mt xii 9, Mk i 21, 39, Lk iv. 16, 44, vi 6, Acts xiii. 14, xiv. 1, xvii. 10, xviii 19, xix 8 When Luke means "in a synagogue" he says (xiii 10) "in one of the synagogues," though ἐν συναγωγῇ might have been used to mean "in a synagogue" as in Jn vi 59, xviii. 20.

[2] Jn vi 59 ἐν συναγωγῇ, R V txt "in the synagogue," marg "in a synagogue." [3] Mk i 21—29.

[4] Mk i. 39 "went into *their synagogues* throughout all Galilee."

THE CONCOURSE TO JESUS

For the words could hardly mean "*withdrew* from the synagogue in Capernaum to the seaside in Capernaum," a distance of a few furlongs at most. The expression, in itself, would not be appropriate; and it is clear that these multitudes from many regions could not resort to Him immediately on the beach. The parallel Matthew has "And Jesus, perceiving [it], withdrew from thence," omitting "to the sea." But Luke has here—what Mark places a little later on as the preface to the appointment of the Twelve—"And it came to pass in these days that he went out into the mountain to pray[1]." That is to say, Luke, differing from Mark's order, places the appointment of the Twelve before, not after, the concourse of the people[2].

These disagreements indicate that Mark has placed here one of many traditions about the "withdrawing" of Jesus, which he alone has connected with (1) "the sea," and with (2) "a little boat" that is to "wait on" Jesus; and that the later Synoptists, besides omitting these two points of connection, differ as to the time and circumstances of the "withdrawing," or, as Luke calls it, the "going out into the mountain." All agree that at (or, near) this time, a great "number" or "multitude" or "multitudes," either "followed" Jesus, or

[1] Mk iii 7	Mt xii 15	Lk vi 12
And Jesus with his disciples withdrew to the sea	And Jesus, perceiving [it], withdrew from thence	And it came to pass in these days that he went out into the mountain to pray
		Lk vi 17 And he came down with them and stood on a level place.

[2] In Matthew, the concourse of the people is placed very early (Mt. iv. 24—5), the appointment of the Twelve, later (x 1—5); the healing on the sabbath, and Christ's consequent "withdrawing," later still (Mt. xii. 9—15). Matthew adds that when Christ "withdrew," (xii 15) "many followed him," but he does not enumerate the regions whence they came.

THE CONCOURSE TO JESUS

"came to hear him and be healed," or "hearing what great things he did, came to him." In the texts, as given below[1], it will be seen that Mark does not mention "multitude" except in his parenthesis about the "little boat," whereas he mentions

[1] Mk iii 7—12

(7) And Jesus with his disciples withdrew to (or, toward) the sea and a great number (πλῆ-θος) from Galilee followed
(8) And from Judaea, and from Jerusalem, and from Idumaea, and beyond Jordan, and about Tyre and Sidon, a great number (πλῆθος), hearing what great things he did, came unto him
(9) And he spake to his disciples, that a little boat should wait on him because of the multitude (ὄχλον), lest they should throng him
(10) For he had healed many, insomuch that as many as had plagues (lit scourges) pressed (lit fell) upon him that they might touch him
(11) And the unclean spirits, whensoever they beheld him, fell down before him, and cried, saying, Thou art the Son of God.
(12) And he charged them much that they should not make him known

Mt xii 15a, iv 24—5, xii 15b—17

(xii 15a) And Jesus, perceiving [it], withdrew from thence, and many followed him ...
(iv 24—5) And the report of him went forth into all Syria; and they brought unto him all that were sick, holden with divers diseases and torments, possessed with devils (or, demoniacs) and epileptic, and palsied, and he healed them
(25) And there followed him great multitudes (ὄχλοι) from Galilee and Decapolis and Jerusalem and Judaea and [from] beyond Jordan
(xii 15b foll) And he healed them all,
(16) And charged them that they should not make him known·
(17) That it might be fulfilled which was spoken by (or, through) Isaiah the prophet, saying ...

Lk vi. 12a, vi 17—19

(vi 12a) And it came to pass in these days that he went out into the mountain to pray....
[Here follows vi 13—16 the choosing of the Twelve]
(vi. 17—19) And he came down with them, and stood on a level place, and a great multitude (ὄχλος) of his disciples, and a great number (πλῆθος) of the people from all Judaea and Jerusalem, and the sea coast of Tyre and Sidon, which came to hear him, and to be healed of their diseases,
(18) And they that were troubled with unclean spirits were healed
(19) And all the multitude (ὄχλος) sought to touch him for power came forth from him, and healed [them] all

THE CONCOURSE TO JESUS

"great number" and then "number great[1]" as first "following," and then "coming to," Jesus, while Luke distinguishes the "great *multitude* of *his disciples*" from the "great *number* of *the people.*"

All this shews that Luke was dissatisfied, and not unreasonably, with Mark's tradition What the sense demands is, that Jesus, in order to escape from the combined attack of the Pharisees and the Herodians, passed *out of the tetrarchy of Herod Antipas across the sea* One journey of this kind is described by John It follows the persecution of Jesus by the Jews after He had performed an act of healing on the sabbath It is also the only occasion where John describes the "*multitude*" as "*following*" Jesus. It also mentions acts of healing, called "signs," as the reason for the "following." Like Luke, John here describes Jesus as ascending a "mountain," but not quite in the same terms. John writes as follows· "After these things Jesus departed beyond the sea of Galilee [that is, the sea] of Tiberias. And there followed him a great multitude because they were [continually] beholding the signs that he was doing on the sick. And Jesus went up into the mountain and there sat with his disciples[2]."

---

[1] Mk iii 7—8 πολὺ πλῆθος...πλῆθος πολύ is noteworthy (1) Mark never uses πλῆθος again (2) It conveys a notion of fulness, applicable (as Luke mostly applies it) to a whole nation, city, army, congregation, or even a number of sick folk crowded into one building (Jn v 3), or fish crowded into a net (*ib* xxi 6, comp Lk v 6) That is not appropriate here in Mark But it may be allusive to promises in Genesis concerning the seed of Abraham In LXX, the earliest uses of πλῆθος are connected with such promises, Gen xvi 10 (to Hagar) οὐκ ἀριθμήσεται ἀπὸ τοῦ πλήθους, xvii 4 (to Abraham) ἔσῃ πατὴρ πλήθους ἐθνῶν, comp *ib* xxxii 12, xlviii. 16, 19 Πλῆθος occurs only eight times in Genesis, so that the word would readily convey this Abrahamic allusion to readers of Mark who were also readers of LXX Taken in this way, πλῆθος coming at the beginning and the end of the Marcan list of seven districts that contributed to the Concourse to the Messiah, would mean "the great multitude of the seed of Abraham according to the Promise "

[2] Jn vi. 1—3 "*went up* (ἀνῆλθεν) into the mountain" differs

THE CONCOURSE TO JESUS

Almost all Mark's traditions about "boats" and "crossing" the lake, when compared with their Synoptic parallels, shew early differences and confusions[1]. John's parallel seems to shew how Mark may have gone wrong by mistaking "withdrew across the sea" for "withdrew to the sea[2]." Moreover this Johannine passage uses the Marcan word placed at the head of this section, "*withdrew,*" not indeed at the beginning but at the end of the narrative thus. "The men, therefore, seeing the signs (*or*, sign) that he had done, began to say, This is of a truth the prophet that is to come into the world. Jesus, therefore, perceiving that they purposed to come and snatch him away that they might make him a king, *withdrew* back-again into the mountain, [by] himself, alone[3]."

---

from Lk. vi. 12 "went out (ἐξελθεῖν) into the mountain." There is also a difference as to the moment at which Jesus began to be with His disciples. The parall Mk iii 13 says "And he goeth up into the mountain and calleth unto him whom he himself would." This suggests, but does not mention, an interval. But Lk vi 13 "and, *when it was day*, he called his disciples" indicates that Jesus was alone for a time. It is not so in John, Jesus is not "alone" till He ascends the mountain for the second time (Jn vi 15).

[1] *E g* Mk iii 9 ἵνα πλοιάριον προσκαρτερῇ αὐτῷ is, in SS "that they *should bring near* to him a boat," and in Lat MSS "ut navicula (*or*, in navicula) sibi *deserviret* (or, *deservirent*)." Now in Aramaic (Levy *Ch* 1 34 *a*) and in Syriac (*Thes Syr* 213, 216) there is a similarity, amounting almost to identity, between the words meaning "*boat*" and "*teaching*." Προσκαρτερεῖν διδαχῇ occurs in Acts ii 42. Among the Galilaean Apostles an ancient precept may have been in vogue, coming from Christ Himself, in which there was a play on the two words, "See that ye serve me in *the boat*," "See that ye serve me in *the teaching*" (or "Serve *the boat*," "Serve *the teaching*") The Boat, in early Christian poetry, would mean the Church.

[2] In Mk iii. 7 ἀνεχώρησεν πρὸς, some MSS have εἰς. But ἀναχωρεῖν εἰς (see p 372, n. 1) would naturally imply withdrawal *into* a region. The LXX exhibits a multitude of various corruptions of phrases with πέραν, and perhaps πρός, here, is one of them. Aquila in Exod xxviii 26 has πρὸς πέραν.

[3] Jn vi. 14—15. Ἀνεχώρησεν πάλιν might mean "*withdrew [back] again*," i e. "*withdrew a second time*." And possibly it is intended to suggest this. The first ascent of the mountain (vi. 3) might be of

THE CONCOURSE TO JESUS

There is some evidence tending to shew that Greek writers in the first and second centuries made careful distinctions between "withdrew" and synonymous or homonymous terms Philo expressly says "Moses does not *flee* from Pharoah, he *withdraws*[1]." Yet, curiously enough, in the passage last quoted from John, the Curetonian Syriac and Codex *a* read "*flee*" for "*withdraw*[2]." Matthew repeatedly describes Jesus as "*withdrawing*," whereas Luke never does, and Mark does so only here[3]. Luke however twice uses another word, which he perhaps deemed less strong than "*withdrew*" and better adapted to mean temporary retiring, as it were, for a breathing-space[4].

Probably John did not trouble himself so much about these verbal distinctions as about the moral effect likely to be produced on readers by Matthew's frequent statements that Jesus "withdrew," when jibed at by critics like Celsus[5] Celsus said that Jesus "used to run away" and "most ignominiously hide himself." John says elsewhere, in effect, "He did not hide Himself He was hidden by the Providence of God[6]" And here he says, in effect, "It is true that on one occasion Jesus did, in a remarkable way, *withdraw*. But why? Not to avoid

---

the nature of a *first* "*withdrawal*" from enemies of one kind (persecutors), and this might be a *second withdrawal* from enemies of another kind (misguided admirers) But the primary meaning appears to be "*back-again*," i e "He withdrew from His admirers to *the place where He had been before* "

[1] Philo i 90 Οὐ φεύγει Μωυσῆς ἀπὸ τοῦ Φαραώ ..ἀλλὰ ἀναχωρεῖ
[2] In Jn vi 15, א¹ also has φεύγει, and Blass has it in his text
[3] In Mt iv 12, xiv 13, xv 21, the parall Mark has not ἀναχωρέω. Marcus Antoninus iv § 3 condemns people that seek for themselves "*retirements* (ἀναχωρήσεις)," and "*rustic-retreats* (ἀγροικίας)" and "seaside-places (αἰγιαλοὺς)" and "mountains "
[4] Lk. v. 16, ix 10. Ὑποχωρέω in Justin Martyr *Tryph* § 9 means "stepping-aside [from noisy companions for a quiet talk] "
[5] See Origen *Celsus* ii 10 " ἐπονειδιστότατα κρυπτόμενος διεδίδρασκεν ὁ Ἰησοῦς "
[6] See *Joh. Gr* 2538—43, 2724 on Jn viii 59, xii 36 ἐκρύβη.

THE CONCOURSE TO JESUS

persecution, but to escape from those who wished to make Him a king."

§ 2. *"To[ward]*[1] *the sea," "Galilee," "beyond Jordan"*

We have above recognised, and tried to explain as a corruption, the use of "toward the sea" by Mark alone But there is also, if not a difficulty, at all events something like a superfluity, in "Galilee," which is used by Mark and Matthew. For apparently the intention is to emphasize a concourse of people to Jesus *from distant parts*; and He was in "Galilee" already Luke therefore seems justified in omitting it Luke also omits "beyond Jordan." This phrase he never uses, so that we cannot be surprised. But looking closely into his text we see that under the guise of *"by-the-brine*[2]*"*—in connection with "Tyre and Sidon"—he does insinuate something about the *"sea,"* only not Mark's *"sea"*—which Luke calls *"the lake"*—but the genuine salt sea, the Mediterranean. "By-the-brine," meaning "sea-coast," occurs nowhere else in N.T. But it occurs in Isaiah's well-known prophecy quoted above by Matthew concerning Christ's Advent. *"The way of the sea*, beyond Jordan, Galilee of the nations," where the LXX has "and the rest that [inhabit] *the [land] by-the-brine* and beyond Jordan, Galilee of the nations[3]." Noting that Matthew retains the Hebrew *"way of the sea,"* we ask whether it could be expressed in Greek by *"toward the sea,"* so as to agree with the Marcan phrase that caused us so much difficulty. And we find that in Ezekiel the Hebrew *"way of"* is represented by the Greek *"toward"* (the preposition used by Mark) nine times[4].

---

[1] On πρός, "to," or "toward," see above, p 372, n. 1, p 377, n. 2.
[2] Lk vi. 17 τῆς παραλίου Τύρου καὶ Σιδῶνος, parall to Mk iii. 8 περὶ Τύρον καὶ Σιδῶνα, which drops the thought of "sea."
[3] Mt iv. 15 quoting Is ix. 1.
[4] Ezek. xl 20—xlii. 15 (Trommius).

THE CONCOURSE TO JESUS

This clears up much that was obscure For now we see that, in choosing these particular districts, and even in using these particular expressions, the Evangelists may have been influenced by prophecy Matthew, who has quoted Isaiah, *interprets the whole consistently as referring to the sea of Galilee.* Luke *refers the whole consistently to the Mediterranean.* Mark "*conflates*" *the two*[1]. The first part of his list (including "toward the sea") refers to the sea of Galilee; the second part ("Tyre and Sidon") refers to the sea of the West, though not called "sea." Mark's first words therefore do not mean (or, at least, did not originally mean) that Jesus retired from His conflict with the Pharisees in the Capernaum synagogue and literally walked down "to the sea " They meant that when He thus retired from His enemies, His manifestation still proceeded, for His retiring was, as it was written by Isaiah, "by the way of the sea, Galilee of the Gentiles," so that "the people sitting in darkness saw a great light."

§ 3. "*From Idumaea* (i.e. *Edom*)"

This is the only mention of "Edom" in N.T. Why mention Edom, rather than Trachonitis, Ituraea, Abilene, mentioned by Luke[2]? The answer suggested by the last section is "From prophecy." But what prophecy? There are poetic mentions of Edom or Idumaea in the LXX of Isaiah and the Psalms. where the name may represent "the kingdom of blood," the enemy of Israel[3]; but there are none that would apply to a gathering such as is here described, a concourse of nations to the conquering Messiah.

There is, however, in the Hebrew text of Amos—but mistranslated in the LXX—one mention of Edom that would

---

[1] For "conflation," see *Clue* 20—155.

[2] Lk. iii. 1.

[3] See Jerome on Ps lx. 9 and Is lxiii. 1. "Edom," in Jewish tradition, regularly represents "Rome" (see Levy i. 29), *e g.* "Hadrian, king of Edom."

exactly apply: "In that day will I raise up the tabernacle of David...and I will raise up his ruins...that they may possess the remnant of *Edom* and all the nations that are called by my name[1]." This prophecy is actually quoted in the Acts, as being uttered by James, the President of the Council of Jerusalem, in favour of "Symeon," who (he says) "hath rehearsed how God did first visit the Gentiles." But James is made to quote it from the LXX, which substitutes "*Adam*" for "*Edom*[2]." Hence, in the Acts, James is made to say "that the residue of *men* may seek after the Lord, and all the Gentiles upon whom my name is called[3]" But it may be taken as certain that James did not quote the LXX. "The Hebrew words of Amos," as *Horae Hebraicae* says[4], "quoted by James do suit very well with his design and purpose" Parts of Mark's Gospel appear to have come, in substance, from Peter; and, if Peter heard James at the Council of Jerusalem using this prophecy about "Edom" in favour of the inclusion of the Gentiles, it seems probable that Peter would also use it (even if he had not used it before) in enumerating the various quarters from which came the concourse of people to Jesus at the time when He was forced to flee from the Pharisees and Herodians[5].

Besides explaining the Marcan "Idumaea," this hypothesis of an original Hebrew "Edom" enables us to explain why Matthew makes a mention of "Syria" here. "Syria" is *Aram*, and *Aram* is repeatedly confused with *Edom*, the two words

---

[1] Amos ix 11—12

[2] Acts xv 17 Comp Levy 1 29 *a*, which says that in *Lev. r* (s 22, 165 c) we must read אדום, "Edom," for אדם, "Adam" or "man"

[3] "Seek after," in LXX, indicates that they took ירש, "*possess*," for דרש, "*seek*."

[4] *Hor Heb.* on Acts xv. 17.

[5] Jerome on Amos ix 12 paraphrases "the remnant of Edom" as "quicquid reliquum fuerit de Regno sanguinario atque terreno" where "the kingdom of *blood* and *earth*" alludes to "Edom," *red*, and "Adam," *earth*. He adds another interpretation based on the LXX "hominum."

being almost identical[1]. Matthew appears to have read "Edom" as "Aram," and to have placed it first as indicating that the "hearing," or "report," of the Gospel went forth first to "the whole of Syria." After this, from the different parts of Syria came, as Mark and Luke say, "hearers[2]." Matthew's addition of "Decapolis," after "Galilee," strengthens the allusion—since Decapolis was a group of cities mainly Gentile—to Isaiah's "Galilee of the Gentiles"

§ 4. *The Johannine view of the concourse to Jesus*

The only passage in which the Fourth Gospel speaks of a "great multitude" as "following" Jesus is the one mentioned above, introducing the Feeding of the Five Thousand[3]. The description of the multitude there, as following Jesus because of His "signs," and the whole sequel of the miracle, indicate that this "following" of Jesus was only rudimentary and preparatory. Those who admire Him as the promised "prophet" seek to make Him a king, and He "withdraws" from them. His "sign" is not understood. Before this time Jesus must have chosen the Twelve. He refers to the choice as, in some sense, a failure, "Was it not I that chose you, the Twelve (SS you *all*), and one of you is a devil[4]?" It is also said that "many of his disciples went back and walked no more with him[5]" The whole narrative suggests disappointment.

---

[1] See *Clue* 6 shewing how "Syria," or "Aram" ארם, in 2 S. viii. 12 (also 13) is parall to 1 Chron xviii 11 "Edom," אדום (spelt ארם in Ezek xxv 14, Gesen 10 a) where LXX has Idumaea in both books See also 1 K xi 25, 2 K xvi 6

[2] Mk iii 8
...and from Idumaea...*hearing how many [great deeds]* he *was doing*, came unto him

Mt. iv 24
and there came (lit) *his hearing* (ἀκοή) into the whole of Syria

Lk vi. 17
...who came *to* hear him.

[3] Jn vi 2   See Addendum, p 386.   [4] Jn vi. 70
[5] Jn vi 66   That the "disciples" were numerous is not implied in the Fourth Gospel before Jn iv 1 "*more disciples* than John."

THE CONCOURSE TO JESUS

If we might accept, as true, what the Pharisees (according to John's account) were forced to confess about Jesus, "Lo, the world is gone after him," we might infer that John regarded Christ's riding into Jerusalem, amid the acclamations of multitudes preceding and following Him, as a real instance of "following." But on the contrary the Evangelist seems to

Jn ii. 2 "Jesus also was bidden, and *his disciples,*" *ib.* ii II "and *his disciples* believed on him," seem to refer merely to six previously mentioned or implied (including Nathanael) Jn ii. 12 "after this he went down to Capernaum, he...and *his disciples*" tells us nothing as to their number Nor does Jn ii 22 "*his disciples* remembered," for that refers to a period after the Resurrection But we learn something from Jn iii 22 "Jesus came, and *his disciples,* into the land of Judaea ..and there he tarried with them and baptized," when taken with iv 1—2 "Jesus was making and baptizing *more disciples* than John, although Jesus himself baptized not, but *his disciples*" For these passages imply that *some* disciples of Jesus had by this time begun to baptize with His sanction or appointment, and that the whole number of Christ's disciples was now large

In Mark, the first mention of "disciples" may imply that they were many, ii 15 "He was sitting at meat in his [Levi's] house, and many publicans and sinners sat down with Jesus and [with] his disciples, [making altogether a great multitude] for they [*i e* the disciples] were [by this time] many, and they habitually-followed him (ἠκολούθουν αὐτῷ)" But the text is doubtful D and the Latin codd have "there were many *who* (or, *who also*) followed him"— perhaps meaning this as an explanation of "disciples," namely, habitual followers, out of whom the Twelve were selected

Luke is the only Evangelist that expressly declares the Twelve to have been *selected out of* the disciples (vi 13 "He called (προσεφώνησεν) *his disciples and he chose from them twelve*") whereas Mark says (iii 13—14) "*calleth unto him* (προσκαλεῖται) *whom he himself would .and he appointed twelve*" Luke also mentions (vi 17) "a great multitude (ὄχλος πολὺς) of his disciples"—a very rare use of ὄχλος, a word often used in a depreciatory sense On Matthew's omission of "choosing," see p. 388 foll

The impression left on us by John is that he desires to exalt the true and spiritual "disciple"—as compared with "apostle" or "one of the Twelve"—and to suggest that the details of the choosing of the Twelve were unimportant At the same time he tells us what no other Evangelist does, that many of the disciples abandoned Jesus at an early period

THE CONCOURSE TO JESUS

suggest—and almost to take pleasure in suggesting—that these multitudes and these acclamations signified very little. It was Christ's "sign" (we are told), not Himself, that roused the multitude to enthusiasm. "For this cause also the multitude went and met him, for that they had heard that he had done this sign[1]." When a Johannine statement of this kind is made it may be taken as a warning that the faith of the "multitude" is rudimentary[2].

Is it an accident that immediately after this false alarm of the Pharisees (false, at least, in the letter) that "the world" had "gone after" Jesus, "certain Greeks" are introduced as petitioning to "see Jesus"? The language implies but a small number,—"certain Greeks among those that went up to worship at the feast[3]"—but the narrative of their introduction to Jesus through the two Greek-named Apostles Philip and Andrew, and the immediate exclamation of Jesus "the hour is come that the Son of man should be glorified," imply that the prediction of Isaiah is being fulfilled "Arise, shine, for thy light is come, and the glory of the Lord is risen upon thee... nations shall come to thy light, and kings to the brightness of thy rising[4]." The context in Isaiah mentions "the isles" more particularly among these arriving worshippers—a term that applies to the Mediterranean islands and coasts where Greek civilisation prevailed.

The term "isles," as used in Hebrew, might include the coasts of Italy, too, and so point to Rome. And this leads us to ask whether the Fourth Gospel, the only one that mentions "Greeks," has anywhere introduced a mention of "Romans,"

---

[1] Jn xii 18. Contrast Jn iv 42 "Now we believe, not because of thy speaking, for we have heard for ourselves, and know, that this is indeed the Saviour of the world"

[2] Concerning this "multitude" it is said (Jn xii 28—9) that, after there came a voice out of heaven, "The multitude, therefore, that stood by and heard it, said that it had thundered"

[3] Jn xii. 20   [4] Is lx 1—3

384 (Mark iii 7—12)

whom also no Synoptist mentions. John mentions them once, "The Romans will come and take away our [holy] place and our nation," so say "the chief priests and the Pharisees[1]" That is perhaps significant of the attitude of the Fourth Evangelist toward the Romans (compared with the Greeks) as regards the part they were to play in the Dispensation of the Gospel. Rome was the cosmopolitan sword of the Retribution of the Lord, striking down and levelling, so as to produce material peace and order. Greece was the cosmopolitan and reasonable language of the Lord—not His Logos, or Word, but His instrument for expressing the Word to the civilised seekers after truth and wisdom throughout the Roman Empire.

It is reasonable to suppose that the Evangelist was familiar with the prophecy of Amos, as interpreted by Luke in the Acts, that the Church was to "possess the remnant of Edom," where "Edom" was taken by Luke (as by the LXX) to mean "man." We have also abundant reason for supposing that John was familiar with the remarkably divergent Synoptic interpretations of "Edom," (1) in Mark, Idumaea, (2) in Matthew, Aram, *i.e.* Syria, (3) in Luke, perhaps (as in Acts) simply "men," not needing to be mentioned since the context implied it. How was John to deal with these variations, and with the spiritual underlying fact? He would keep himself clear from all these difficult and—for his readers—unedifying details. Yet the fact, the great fact of the Concourse of the Nations to the Messiah, needed to be expressed. But why should it be expressed so early? To many it must seem premature in the Synoptists. Moreover it was connected by Mark with acts of exorcism in the most materialistic form—a phenomenon that the Fourth Gospel never mentions.

As therefore John places his account of the Draught of Fishes at the close of the Gospel instead of the beginning, so he places his account of the manifestation of the Coming of the

---

[1] Jn xi 48.

THE CONCOURSE TO JESUS

Nations. He does not deny the truth of the Synoptic accounts, nor does he arbitrate between them. But he regards them all as expressions of rudimentary truth. The real glory of the Lord could not be revealed till the hour had come for the Son of man to be glorified. And then the representative of the influx of the nations was not Idumaea nor Syria, but "certain Greeks[1]."

---

[1] The other Johannine mention of "Greeks" is in Jn vii 35 "Will he go to the dispersion among (*lit* of) the Greeks and teach the Greeks?" on which see *Joh Gr.* **2046**, *Son* **3606** *a*.

Addendum

The Johannine Concourse to Jesus is placed by John where Mark places his account of a second Concourse, just before the Feeding of the Five Thousand. There Mark and Matthew insert, while Luke omits, the statement that Jesus (Mk vi 34, Mt xiv. 14) "came forth and *saw a great multitude*." John describes Jesus as (Jn vi 5) "*lifting up his eyes* and *seeing that a great multitude cometh unto him.*" This is a mystical restatement of Mark (*Joh Gr* **2616**). Luke has a previous mention, parallel to Mk-Mt, of "multitudes following", but he does not repeat it, as they do, in connection with "seeing."

When we discuss the Feeding of the Five Thousand, it will be shewn that Mark has several traditions about the "many" whom the Messiah will redeem, omitted by Luke and restated by John, and that Mark's view of the multitudes that flocked to the Messiah was influenced not only by Isaiah but also by Daniel and Amos.

CHAPTER XI*

THE APPOINTMENT OF THE TWELVE

[Mark iii. 13—19]

§ 1. *"Going up into the mountain"*

MATTHEW probably assumes—what Mark and Luke state—that Jesus went up into the mountain about the time of the appointment of the Twelve, described below[1]. The explanation

---

* For titles of previous Parts of Diatessarica referred to by abbreviations in this Volume, see pp 545—6. For other abbreviations see pp xxiii—xxvi

[1] Mk iii 13—19 (R V.)

(13) And he goeth up into the mountain, and calleth unto him whom he himself would and they went unto him
(14) And he appointed twelve, (*some anc. auth. add* whom also he named apostles) that they might be with him, and that he might send them forth to preach,
(15) And to have authority to cast out devils (*lit* demons)
(16) And Simon he surnamed Peter,
(17) And James the [son] of Zebedee,

Mt x 1—4 (R V)

(1) And he called unto him his twelve disciples, and gave them authority over unclean spirits, to cast them out, and to heal all manner of disease and all manner of sickness
(2) Now the names of the twelve apostles are these The first, Simon, who is called Peter, and Andrew his brother, James the [son] of Zebedee, and John his brother,
(3) Philip, and Bartholomew, Thomas, and Matthew the publican, James the [son] of Alphaeus, and Thaddaeus,

Lk. vi. 12—16 (R V.)

(12) And it came to pass in these days, that he went out into the mountain to pray, and he continued all night in prayer to God
(13) And when it was day, he called his disciples and he chose from them twelve, whom also he named apostles,
(14) Simon, whom he also named Peter, and Andrew his brother, and James and John, and Philip and Bartholomew,
(15) And Matthew and Thomas, and James [the son] of Alphaeus, and

THE APPOINTMENT OF THE TWELVE

of Matthew's omission is probably this, that Matthew does not follow Mark (as Luke does) in placing the appointment of the Twelve, and their names, a good deal before the sending forth of the Twelve. Matthew combines the appointment with the sending. Or rather, he does not describe the appointment at all, but later on, when he comes to describe Christ's sending of "his twelve disciples," he inserts the names (without inserting the appointment) previously given by Mark and Luke. Both the appointment of the Twelve, and the naming of some of them, were probably assumed by Matthew to have taken place just before the Sermon on the Mount[1].

Similarly, as we have seen above, the appointment of the Twelve is nowhere described by John, but is referred to by Jesus as past, soon after the single occasion on which He "went up into the mountain and there sat with his disciples[2]." By his silence John avoids raising difficult questions: "Why did Jesus appoint persons whom He called 'apostles,' i e 'sent,' and yet apparently not 'send' them at the time? When did

Mk iii 13—19 (R V) (contd)	Mt x 1—4 (R V) (contd)	Lk vi 12—16 (R V.) (contd)
and John the brother of James, and them he surnamed Boanerges, which is, Sons of thunder (18) And Andrew, and Philip, and Bartholomew, and Matthew, and Thomas, and James the [son] of Alphaeus, and Thaddaeus, and Simon the Cananaean (or, Zealot). (19) And Judas Iscariot, which also betrayed him	(4) Simon the Cananaean, (or, Zealot) and Judas Iscariot, who also betrayed him.	Simon which was called the Zealot, (16) And Judas [the son, or brother] of James, and Judas Iscariot, which was the traitor

[1] Mt v 1—2 "And seeing the multitudes he went up into the mountain, and when he had sat down, his disciples came unto him [*Here would come the appointment of the Twelve*] And he opened his mouth and taught them, saying...."

[2] Jn vi 70, vi. 3

THE APPOINTMENT OF THE TWELVE

Jesus send them, and to whom? And what was their task or their message? And how could they adequately discharge their task or give their message if they had not yet received the Holy Spirit?" These questions will come before us much later on in detail. But we shall have to touch on some of them in this Chapter when discussing phrases peculiar to Mark in the Appointment of the Twelve.

§ 2. *"Whom he himself would he calleth to himself*[1]*"*

The phrase "whom he himself would" seems chosen by Mark in order to express absolute and uncontrolled action. A parallel may be found in Theodotion's rendering of Daniel "*Whom he himself would* he slew; and *whom he himself would* he smote, and *whom he himself would* he raiseth up; and *whom he himself would* he put down[2]" But this is said concerning the despotic Nebuchadnezzar. It is not surprising that the later Synoptists object to it. When Matthew describes the sending (not the choosing) of the Apostles, he retains "*called to himself*" in the sense of "*called up*," "*called into his presence*," thus· "*having called to himself* his twelve disciples he gave them authority....*"[3] Luke expressly uses the word "choose-out," thus "He called his disciples [orally] to him, and, having *chosen-out* twelve from them...."[4] Thus he says, in effect, "Do not mistake Mark's 'calleth-to-himself' as meaning 'calleth to be apostles,' and as implying a technical *klēsis* or 'calling.' The Lord first *called orally into his presence a number of disciples. From these He chose out twelve*. That is what Mark means when he goes on to say 'And they went to Him and *He made* [*from their number*] *Twelve* whom also He named apostles....'"

The result is that neither Mark nor Matthew ever describes

---

[1] Mk iii 13 προσκαλεῖται, Mt x 1 προσκαλεσάμενος Lk. vi. 13 προσεφώνησεν more definitely suggests "called aloud to"

[2] Dan v 19 Theod rep οὓς ἠβούλετο αὐτός

[3] Mt. x. 1   [4] Lk vi. 13, comp. Mk iii. 13—14

THE APPOINTMENT OF THE TWELVE

the Twelve as "*chosen*" by Jesus. Both Mark and Matthew elsewhere use the adjective "chosen," or "elect," but not of the Twelve. Thereby a difficulty is avoided—namely the difficulty of supposing that one of the "elect" or "chosen," whom Jesus Himself "chose," could be a traitor. Both Mark and Matthew imply elsewhere—in their versions of Christ's Discourse on the Last Days—that "the elect" cannot go wrong[1] And Matthew expressly distinguishes them from those who are merely "called": "Many are *called*, but few are *chosen*[2]." Luke, however, faces the difficulty, though he softens it a little by dropping the words of Mark "whom he himself would."

John faces the difficulty, or rather he magnifies it and overrides it. He does not seek shelter under the Marcan phrase of "making Twelve" as if it applied to the mere appointment of a class, official rather than personal. On the contrary, he adopts Luke's "chose-out." But he goes further. He brings Jesus before us, in the midst of the Twelve, saying to them personally· "[*Was it not*] *I* [*that*] *chose-out you*, the twelve, and one of you is a devil[3]?"

§ 3 "*Apostles*"

The word "apostle," *apostolos*—which in literary Greek means almost always a naval expedition[4]—comes before us

---

[1] Mk xiii 20, 22, 27, Mt xxiv 22, 24, 31 They say "if it were possible," in language implying that it is not possible There is no parallel ἐκλεκτός in Luke. But there is Lk xviii 7 (pec) "will not God surely avenge his elect?"

[2] Mt xxii 14

[3] Jn vi 70 On this paradox, and on the Johannine treatment of it, see *Beginning* p. 201 John's use of ἐκλέγομαι in three passages—always in Christ's words—will be dealt with in detail in The Fourfold Gospel, Section iv

[4] See Steph. *Thes.*, quoting no exceptions in literary Greek except *Herodot* 1 21, v. 38, where it is used of a herald bringing proposals for a truce, or of someone coming on a political errand (not of a mere messenger).

THE APPOINTMENT OF THE TWELVE

here in all the Synoptists, raising several questions. (1) What did *apostolos* mean to the Synoptists, and to what Aramaic word and meaning did it correspond? (2) Was the name given to a chosen few of His disciples by Jesus Himself, or by the Church afterwards? (3) Assuming that they were "twelve," have we evidence to shew that Jesus chose them with a view to some relation between them and "the twelve tribes of Israel"? If so, to what relation? (4) What does *apostolos* mean in N T. outside the Synoptists?

(1) "Apostle," in LXX, occurs only once There it represents the Hebrew *"sent,"* but not in a literal or local sense The prophet Ahijah, sitting at home, says to the wife of Jeroboam, who has come to consult him, "I am *sent* unto thee with heavy tidings"—meaning that he is God's spiritual messenger or spokesman[1]. In modern Jewish congregations, the term *"sent,"* Sheliach, is applied to one of the congregation who "reads the service" for them on a week-day[2]. The title is frequent in the Talmud, where it is applied to the official who repeats prayers for the congregation, as being its "spokesman" or "representative" If he makes a mistake, says the Mishna, it is a bad sign for those whom he represents, for "The *apostle (lit one sent) of anyone is as he himself [by whom he is sent]*[3]" *Horae Hebraicae* says that Sheliach is connected by Maimonides with a word meaning "associates" or close cooperators[4]. A Targum on Jeremiah ("the love of thine espousals, how thou

---

[1] 1 K xiv 6 (A) "I am a hard *apostle* unto thee (ἀπόστολος πρὸς σὲ σκληρός) "

[2] See *The Religion and Worship of the Synagogue* (Oesterley and Box) p 314 on "*Sheliach Tsibbûr*, 1 e messenger of the congregation "

[3] See *J Berach* v 6 (5) (Schwab, transl) "If he be representative of a congregation, it is a bad sign for his constituents, *for a man's representative is like himself,*" (B *Berach* 34 b, Goldschmidt) "*denn der Bevollmachtigte des Menschen ist diesem gleichbedeutend*"

[4] *Hor Heb* (on Mt x 1) on *"apostles,"* שליהי, and *"companions"* or "*associates,*" שותפין, a term applied (Levy iv 619 a, quoting *Nid* 31 a) to God, and father, and mother, as being "associated in the birth of every human being "

391 (Mark iii. 13—19)

THE APPOINTMENT OF THE TWELVE

wentest after me in the wilderness") describes Moses and Aaron as the "two *sent-ones, apostles,* or *representatives*" of the Bridegroom, the Lord, in bringing about the "espousals[1]." In the Fourth Gospel, John the Baptist, who is introduced as "a man, *sent* from God," says later on, "I am *sent* before him," *i e.* before Jesus, and declares that "*the friend* [John] of the bridegroom [Jesus] rejoiceth greatly because of the bridegroom's voice[2]." These passages seem to identify "sheliach," in some contexts, with "friend." They also illustrate the variety of the meanings that might attach themselves to the term. "*Apostolos,*" or "representative," would naturally mean one thing when applied to a person representing a congregation, repeating a fixed form of prayer, and quite a different thing when applied to a person representing a prospective bridegroom. In any case, *apostolos* would be something quite different from "messenger[3]."

From Gentile sources we learn that the term *apostolos* was also applied by Jews, after the destruction of Jerusalem, to elders of the Jews or rulers of synagogues, appointed by the Patriarch to collect a tribute from those abroad[4]. Epiphanius

---

[1] Jerem ii 2 (Targ) "I remember ..the love of your fathers, who believed in my Word, and went after *my two Apostles,* Moses and Aaron in the wilderness " So the "Apostle" Paul says to the Corinthians (2 Cor xi 2) "I *espoused* you to one husband "

[2] Jn i 6, iii 28—29 These passages favour the view (*Joh Gr.* 2371, 2722 *b—c*) that Jn i 30 means "after me cometh [the] *husband* (ἀνήρ)" as distinguished from (*ib* i 6) "man (ἄνθρωπος) "

[3] Both in Hebrew and in Greek, "messenger" (or "angel"), ἄγγελος, would be a separate word, having no connection with "send" The Heb "*send*" is rendered by Gesen 1018 "*commission,*" when applied to God "*commissioning*" a leader or prophet, *e g* Moses in Exod iii 12 "Commissioning" is also perhaps implied in Gen xlv 5 "God did *send* me before you" (see context)

[4] See Lightf *Galat* p 93 quoting *Cod Theodos* xvi Tit viii 14 "archisynagogi sive presbyteri Judaeorum vel quos ipsi *apostolos* vocant, qui ad exigendum aurum atque argentum a patriarcha certo tempore diriguntur," and Julian *Epist* 25 τὴν λεγομένην παρ' ὑμῖν ἀποστολὴν κωλυθῆναι

392 (Mark iii 13—19)

THE APPOINTMENT OF THE TWELVE

speaks of a class of notables who were called "apostles" and constituted a Council under the Patriarch[1]   This is very late evidence, and is not alleged to be corroborated from the Talmud. But it accords with what we might expect, and with a phrase from the Acts concerning "letters from Judaea[2]"   If such a cabinet council of Jewish "notables," ready to act as "commissioners" for general purposes in foreign parts, became prominent after the destruction of Jerusalem, when tribute was no longer required for the temple service, and if the members were called *apostoloi* in Greek, it might influence the meaning conveyed by the term to Christians toward the end of the first century   The notion of "sending abroad" might hence become more prominent, overshadowing, especially for Greeks, the original and Hebrew notion of "appointing as representative[3]."

(2) In proof of the statement that Jesus called some of His disciples "apostles" we may certainly quote from Luke

---

[1] Epiph *Haeres* xxx p 128, τῶν παρ' αὐτοῖς ἀξιωματικῶν ἀνδρῶν ἐναρίθμιος ἦν   εἰσὶ δὲ οὗτοι μετὰ τὸν Πατριάρχην 'Απόστολοι καλούμενοι, προσεδρεύουσι δὲ τῷ Πατριάρχῃ...

[2] Acts xxviii 21 οὔτε γράμματα περὶ σοῦ ἐδεξάμεθα ἀπὸ τῆς 'Ιουδαίας. Comp Acts ix 2 ἐπιστολὰς εἰς Δαμασκὸν πρὸς τὰς συναγωγάς.

[3] In Justin *Tryph* § 75, Justin proves to the Jew Trypho, from Is vi 8 "send me," that prophets sent to bear a message from God are called "*both messengers and apostles of God*"   But Jews would know this already   It would be Greeks that would need such a proof

Mt xxiii 34 "I send unto you *prophets and wise-men and scribes*," and the parall Lk xi 49 "The Wisdom of God said 'I will send to them *prophets and apostles,*'" are probably both paraphrases of Prov ix 3 "She [*i e*. Wisdom] hath sent forth her *maidens*," LXX δούλους, Aq παιδίσκας, Theod νεάνιδας, Sym κοράσια   To this Origen is probably alluding in *Hom Jerem* xiv 5 "Who is it that beareth (γεννᾷ) *prophets*?   The Wisdom of God   ..And '*the children of Wisdom*' is a phrase (ἀναγέγραπται) also in the Gospel, (Lk vii 35, comp Mt xi 19) and [in Proverbs ix 3] '*Wisdom sendeth her children*' (ἀποστέλλει ἡ σοφία τὰ τέκνα αὐτῆς)"   In Prov ix 3, "*Maidens*" is interpreted as (1) Adam and Eve, (2) Moses and Aaron, (3) Ezekiel, (4) the Israelites (see Breithaupt's Rashi, and *Lev r.* Wu pp 70—71, *Numb r* Wu p 279)

393   (Mark iii. 13—19)

THE APPOINTMENT OF THE TWELVE

"*whom also he named apostles*" Possibly we may quote the same clause from Mark[1]. But even if it is genuine in Mark it may mean "whom, [later on], he named apostles." And the omission of the clause by Matthew, as well as by many MSS or versions of Mark, makes inferences from this part of the Threefold Gospel unsafe In the Synoptists, Jesus is nowhere represented as using the word "apostle[2]." But in the Fourth Gospel Jesus uses the term once, along with "servant," thus: "A *servant* is not greater than his lord, neither an *apostle* greater than he that sent him[3]" Something like this—something of the nature of a warning to Christ's followers against arrogance—occurs in Matthew's version of a passage in the Double Tradition· "A *disciple* is not above his master (*or*, teacher)," where Matthew (though not Luke) adds "nor a *servant* above his lord[4]." But John, in his version of this warning, inserts "apostle" where the earlier Gospels do not. What may we infer from this?

In the first place we may infer that John desires us to connect the word, as Greeks would naturally connect it, with the notion of "sending," or "sending [on an errand][5]," and, at the same time, to prevent the unintelligent and (so to speak) technical use of the term by some Christians who used it in such a way as to include what Paul calls "false apostles[6]" He seems to imply here, "There is nothing so very great in being *sent on an*

---

[1] Mk iii 14, Lk vi 13   W. H insert the clause in Mk, but, since the publication of their text, SS has been discovered, which omits it

[2] "Using," *i e* in Christ's own person   The above-quoted Lk xi. 49 "*The Wisdom of God said* 'I will send...*apostles*...'" is not uttered in Christ's own person

[3] Jn xiii 16 οὐδὲ ἀπόστολος μείζων τοῦ πέμψαντος αὐτόν

[4] Mt x 24 (and sim Lk vi 40)   Origen, on Jn xiii 16, says "By the side of this are similar words," and proceeds to quote Matthew and Luke separately and fully.

[5] "Send [on an errand]" πέμπω, on which see *Joh Voc* 1723 *f*, *g*, and *Son* 3623 *n*

[6] 2 Cor xi 13

THE APPOINTMENT OF THE TWELVE

errand, the question is how one discharges the errand." And, later on, some such thought is expressed when Jesus says, "No longer do I call you servants, for the servant knoweth not what his lord doeth; but I have called you friends[1]." This means, in effect, "No longer do I call you, as I called you above, mere servants and *mere apostles or messengers*. For the mere servant, or the mere messenger—bearing perhaps a closed letter—knows not the will and purpose beneath his Master's words and actions. But you are now my companions and associates in will and purpose " This brings us back to the Hebrew thought of the Sheliach, as being a man's "representative," or "*as he himself [by whom he is sent]*" If we ask for a definition of "what his lord doeth," it is given in the preceding sentences "This is my commandment, that ye love one another, even as I have loved you Greater love hath no man than this, that a man lay down his life for his *friends* Ye are my *friends*, if ye do the things that I command you."

It is an interesting suggestion, this—that Jesus called the disciples at one time by one title ("servants" or 'apostles"), and at another by another ("friends"). Probably we are not to take it as true in a definite and literal sense. But we may infer from it that John desires to warn us against attaching importance to a single title such as "apostle," even when uttered by Jesus, apart from His general attitude toward the inner circle of His disciples, and apart from the language that He used to them on other occasions

The facts reviewed above are against the supposition that on one special occasion, early in Christ's career, He selected from His disciples twelve whom He then named *apostoloi*, and that Luke alone (or perhaps Mark and Luke, but not Matthew) preserved the record of this fact. A passage in Mark points rather to the conclusion that Jesus would have called His representatives (among other appellations) His "little ones."

---

[1] Jn xv. 14—15

(Mark iii 13—19)

THE APPOINTMENT OF THE TWELVE

At all events, it is in connection with "receiving *little ones*"—illustrated by a scene in which Christ actually takes a child in His arms—that Mark introduces the doctrine of "receiving" the Son as the representative of the Father[1] Such a doctrine, when reproduced in Greek for Greeks and Gentiles, might well seem obscure until it was explained that the "little ones" were (or, at all events, included) Christ's "representatives," called in Aramaic His "*sent ones*," that is to say, in Greek, His *apostoloi* Then Matthew might (as he does) apply it to the Twelve, and Luke might (as he does) apply it to the Seventy

John seems to say to us, "An 'apostle of Christ' is not a real 'apostle' unless he is something more than a messenger reporting facts that he witnessed in Jerusalem or Galilee about Christ He must be a 'friend' of Christ, and in Christ's secret, so as to 'know what his lord doeth' That secret is 'love,' not our love, but Christ's love The type of the true 'apostle' is 'the disciple whom Jesus loved'"

(3) Passing to the title of "The Twelve," as uttered by Christ, we find it in the Synoptists only once, and there in Mark alone —

Mk xiv 20	Mt xxvi. 23	Lk. xxii. 21
[It is] *one of the twelve*[2], he that dippeth with me in the dish	He that dipped his hand with me in the dish, the same shall betray me	But behold, the hand of him that betrayeth me is with me on the table.

It occurs also once in the Fourth Gospel, "Was it not I

---

[1] Mark has this doctrine of "receiving" representatives nowhere except in connection (ix 37) with "little children," where it is parallel to Mt xviii 5, Lk ix 48 But Matthew repeats a version of it (x 40) in connection with the Sending of the Twelve, and Luke a version of it (x 16) in connection with the Sending of the Seventy

[2] There was no need to insert "one of the twelve" for clearness, since Mark has already said (xiv 17) "He cometh with the twelve" and has represented Jesus as saying (*ib* 18) "One of you shall betray me"

THE APPOINTMENT OF THE TWELVE

that chose *you, the Twelve,* and one of you is a devil[1]?" Before considering this as an apparent instance of Johannine Intervention, and as possibly having some relation to "the twelve tribes of Israel," let us turn to a passage in Matthew and Luke where Jesus is represented as promising to some of His disciples that they shall "sit on thrones (or, twelve thrones) judging *the twelve tribes of Israel.*" The contexts in Matthew and Luke are very different, and there is good reason for doubting whether either form of the utterance proceeded from Jesus[2]. At the same time we must not ignore the probability—we may almost say certainty—that pious Jews in the first century would think and speak of "the twelve tribes" as representing the whole of the spiritual Israel, to be redeemed

---

[1] Jn vi 70 There was no need to insert "*the twelve*" here, in view of the preceding words (*ib* 67) "Jesus said unto *the twelve*" Also, that "the twelve" gathered the fragments, after the Feeding of the Five Thousand, is suggested (though not necessitated, see Mk viii 19—20) by *ib* 12—13 "said unto *his disciples,* Gather they filled *twelve baskets*" Luke is the only Evangelist that mentions (ix 12) "*the twelve*" at the outset of the Feeding of the Five Thousand, parallel to (Mk vi 35, Mt xiv 15) "*his* (Mt *the*) *disciples*"

[2] Mt xix 28, Lk xxii 30 (see *Son* **3419***b*) In Lk, *Diatessaron* omits the words "*sit on thrones...Israel*" Mt xix 28 is an insertion in a passage parallel to Mk x 29—30 (in answer to Peter's question "What shall we have?") where Mark and Luke have nothing about "thrones" Luke places the utterance at the Lord's Supper, presumably after Judas has gone out, so that Judas is not included in the promise Matthew, whose narrative gives no grounds for excluding Judas, adds (xix 30) "many that are first shall be last," which might be regarded as pointing to the falling away of Judas This clause is also in the parallel Mark, but not in the parallel Luke (xviii 30 foll) Luke places "first. .last" earlier (xiii. 30) at the end of an answer to the question (*ib* 23) "Are they few that be saved?" Coming where it does, Mt xix 28 appears to supplement and explain the Marcan tradition about the "hundredfold" reward that would be the lot of Christ's faithful followers "The Lord did not mean literally that His disciples should receive the things of this world a hundredfold; He meant that His disciples should be with Him, sharing His glory, 'judging the twelve tribes of Israel'"

THE APPOINTMENT OF THE TWELVE

in accordance with God's promise. Paul was a fervent follower of Christ, yet he speaks with fervour of "our twelve tribes[1]" And this may have a bearing on the Johannine phrase "you the Twelve"

To "judge the twelve tribes of Israel" would not necessarily convey, to a Jew conversant with the Scriptures, the notion of condemning Israel[2]. Jacob, in obscure language, had prophesied, "*Dan* [i e. *judgment*] shall judge his people[3]." This was supposed to refer to Dan's descendant, Samson, defending Israel against the Philistines. But the Jerusalem Targums represent Jacob as looking further on and subordinating the judgments of Gideon and Samson to a higher judgment of redemption[4]. That such a judgment was to be brought about by the Messiah, and that His disciples were to be His chosen assistants in bringing it about, in connection with "the twelve tribes," could hardly fail to find a place in Christ's thought, though not perhaps often in His doctrine[5].

---

[1] Comp Acts xxvi 6 "And now I stand [here] to be judged for the hope of the promise made by God unto our fathers, unto which [promise] *our twelve tribes*, earnestly serving [God] night and day, hope to attain"

[2] See Gesen 192 *a* on דין, which does not always mean "condemn" It often means "vindicate." Comp *Test XII Patr Judah* xxiv 6 "A rod of righteousness shall spring up therefrom for the nations to *judge and save* all them that call on the Lord"

[3] Gen xlix 16 (literally) "Dan shall judge his people like one (*sic*) the tribes of Israel" This is taken by *Gen. r.* and *Sota* 10 *a* as a prediction that Dan shall judge his people "*like ONE*," namely God, or "*like one*," namely the *unique tribe*, Judah (but *not* "like one of the tribes")

[4] Targ Jer II (and sim Jer I) "Our father Jacob hath said, My soul hath not waited for the redemption of Gideon Bar-Joash, which is for an hour, nor for the redemption of Samson, which is a creature-redemption, but for the Redemption as to which thou hast said in thy Word that it shall come for thy people, the sons of Israel, for this, thy Redemption, my soul hath waited"

[5] Jerome explains Mt xix 28 thus, "Ye too shall sit in the thrones of those judging, *condemning the twelve tribes of Israel*, because,

THE APPOINTMENT OF THE TWELVE

"The twelve tribes" are mentioned by Ezekiel, the Prophet of the New Temple, immediately after the mystical description of the healing waters that were to issue from the Temple, and of the trees that were to bring forth fruit "*every month*"—which appear in Revelation as "the tree of life bearing *twelve [manner of] fruits, yielding its fruit every month*[1]." If a Messiah appointed certain of the disciples to be more especially "with" Himself[2], and to bear fruit for the Redemption of Israel, it would be natural that He should have Ezekiel's Temple and Ezekiel's trees in view. All the more bitter would be His disappointment when He found that one of His twelve "trees" was destined to bring forth no fruit. "Are there not twelve tribes in Israel?" would be almost as patent an axiom for a genuine Jewish prophet as "Are there not twelve hours in the day?" We have to weigh this thought in our Gentile minds before we can realise what might be meant in "Was it not I that chose *you, the Twelve, and one of you is a devil?*"

Returning to the words of Jesus, "[*It is*] *one of the Twelve*," recorded by Mark alone as uttered in answer to the questioning of the disciples as to which of them was to "betray" Him, we

---

whereas ye believed, they would not believe." But such an explanation is, at best, one-sided. The parallel Luke xxii 30 has, along with "*judging*," the words "*that ye may eat and drink at my table in my kingdom.*" It seems a poor promise to the Twelve to say that they shall feast, while they "*condemn*" *their countrymen.* No doubt a righteous "judgment" of Israel included a condemnation of that which was worst, as well as a purification of that which was best, but a Jewish prophet would not fix his thoughts, or those of his disciples, solely on the former. When Rachel says, at the birth of Dan ("judgment") (Gen xxx 6) "God hath *judged me*," she means "God hath pronounced sentence *in my favour*," and the LXX has "God hath judged *for me*."

[1] Ezek xlvii 1—12 ending with "new fruit every month. and the leaf thereof for healing," and followed by *ib* 13 "This shall be the border...according to *the twelve tribes of Israel*." Rev xxii 2 describes "the tree of life" as being "on this side of the river and on that."

[2] Mk iii 14 see below, p 404

find that they confirm the view taken above of the similar Johannine tradition *"you, the Twelve."* Both in Mark and in John, "the Twelve" conveys an allusion to the fulness of God's Promise. That "one of the Twelve" should prove a "traitor," indicated a mysterious falling short of the fulfilment of God's will. It was recognised as a paradox by Him who came to do God's will, and He leaves it a paradox—"I chose you" and "One of you is a devil." By Matthew and Luke the Marcan clause is omitted—perhaps as being superfluous John appears to emphasize its meaning.

(4) Passing to the Epistles and the Acts, we perceive two aspects of the term Apostle, not always kept distinct —first, the representative, secondly, the attesting missionary. When Paul says "Am I not *an apostle*? Have I not *seen Jesus* our Lord[1]?" he perhaps implies that to have "*seen Jesus*," after His resurrection, was a necessary condition for apostleship. But when he goes on to say, "Are not ye my work in the Lord? If to others I am not an apostle, yet at least I am to you, for the seal of mine apostleship are ye in the Lord," he certainly implies that something more is needed. A genuine apostle must not only have "*seen the Lord*" but must also, as His representative, transmit His Spirit to converts.

According to Paul, there were, beside other attesters to Christ's resurrection, "above five hundred brethren," of whom "the greater part" were still living when he wrote to the Corinthians[2]. It is not likely that all these lived up to the high standard of apostleship reached by Paul himself. It is conceivable that some of them relied too much on their personal remembrances of the Lord, and too little on His Spirit[3]. In one and the same context, we read that Jesus

---

[1] 1 Cor ix 1 A V places "am I not free?" after, instead of before, "am I not *an apostle*?" injuring the sense

[2] 1 Cor xv 6

[3] Comp Lk xiii 26 "We ate and drank in thy presence and thou didst teach in our streets," parall to Mt vii 22 "Did we not

THE APPOINTMENT OF THE TWELVE

"appeared to Cephas, then to *the Twelve*, then...to above five hundred brethren at once...then to *James*, then to *all the apostles*[1]" This is supposed to mean that James the Lord's brother was by this time included in "the apostles[2]," but it does not appear probable that "*all the apostles*" included the "*five hundred brethren*" The passage, as a whole, leaves a confusing impression

Lightfoot argues, from the Epistles, that Andronicus, Junias, and Silvanus were probably called apostles[3], and adds that "If some uncertainty hangs over all the instances hitherto given, the apostleship of Barnabas is beyond question," because Luke records the consecration of Barnabas and Paul together (by the Church at Antioch), and then names them as "apostles" together[4]. If this argument is sound, it seems to follow that when Luke called Paul an apostle, for the first time, long after his conversion, he gave him this title not because Paul had "*seen the Lord*," nor because Paul had been "*sent*" by the Lord's voice speaking near Damascus, to preach the Gospel to the Gentiles, but because he had been sent forth as a missionary, by the Church of Antioch influenced by the Holy Spirit[5]

---

prophesy in thy name and in thy name cast out devils, and in thy name do many mighty works?" Both of these classes are rejected (as, in effect, "false-apostles") because what they "work" is wrong "Eating and drinking" is mentioned by Peter in the Acts thus (x 40—41) "Him God raised up on the third day, and gave him to be made manifest, not to all the people but unto witnesses elected beforehand (προκεχειροτονημένοις) by God, unto us, *who did eat and drink with him* after he rose from the dead"

[1] I Cor xv 5—7
[2] See Lightfoot *Galat.* p 96.
[3] See Lightfoot *Galat.* p 96, on Rom xvi 7 and I Thess ii 6
[4] Lightf *Galat.* p 96 quoting Acts xiii 2—3, xiv 4, 14
[5] Acts xiii 4 "sent forth by the Holy Spirit" Paul is not described precisely as "*sent*" to the Gentiles in the earliest narrative of his conversion, but only in the later ones, Acts xxii. 21, xxvi 17. Barnabas seems to be at first distinguished from "*the apostles*" in Acts iv 36—7, where it is said that he "was surnamed Barnabas *by the apostles*"

THE APPOINTMENT OF THE TWELVE

There do not appear any grounds for thinking that this Lucan view was commonly held, namely, that any Church—the Church at Ephesus, for example, or Corinth, or Rome—could create an "apostle" in this way. Perhaps Luke was led to adopt this view by a desire to base Paul's claim to be an apostle on something more definite than a vision. It is certainly remarkable that he should in this unobtrusive way—so unobtrusive that a hostile critic might call it surreptitious—slip into the Acts his first mention of Paul as "apostle." And it is all the more remarkable because in that passage he places Barnabas first. Thus Luke is able to say, in effect, about both "They were *apostles*, because they were *sent* from the Church at Antioch at the instance of the Holy Spirit."

In the Acts, it is assumed, and especially in Petrine speeches, that the primary duty of an apostle is to be a witness of Christ's acts and especially of His resurrection[1]. The coopting of a twelfth Apostle, immediately after Christ's resurrection, is spoken of as "necessary[2]." But later on, when the Gospel had been widely proclaimed, no attempt is made to coopt a twelfth again in the place of the first apostolic martyr, James the brother of John[3]. "The Apostles" is used to mean the twelve Apostles in Jerusalem—without any mention of "the Twelve" except in one passage, where the Grecian Jews murmur against the Hebrews and "*The Twelve* called the multitude of the disciples unto them[4]." After Paul and

---

[1] Acts i. 22, and see "witness" and "witnesses" in i. 8, ii. 32, iii. 15, iv. 33, v. 32 etc.

[2] Acts i. 21 δεῖ

[3] Acts xii. 2. What are the "names" implied in Rev xxi. 14 "upon them *the twelve names of the twelve apostles of the Lamb*"? No answer is given in the context. That the writer would preserve the number "twelve" at any cost is indicated in the Sealing of Israel (Rev vii. 4 foll.) where "twelve thousand" are sealed out of "every tribe of the sons of Israel," making twelve times twelve thousand in all, Manasseh being inserted and Dan omitted.

[4] Acts vi. 2

402 (Mark iii 13—19)

THE APPOINTMENT OF THE TWELVE

Barnabas have been called "*apostles*[1]," the term is never used again without the addition of "*the elders*," the two together constituting the central authority in Jerusalem[2]

Reviewing the evidence as a whole, we have not only to contrast the frequent and suspicious mention of "apostles" in Luke's Gospel with the rarity of the term in the other three Gospels, but also to note the dexterity with which Luke uses the term in the Acts so as to avoid resting Paul's claim to be an apostle on Paul's claim to have "seen Jesus[3]." Yet it is scarcely credible that Paul did not say to others, beside the Corinthians, "Have I not seen the Lord?" but contented himself with throwing the burden of proof on the "witnesses to the people" who "came up with him from Galilee to Jerusalem" We are led to the conclusion, that although Luke did his best to attain, in his Gospel, a correct use of the title "apostle," he was probably misled (1) by the complexity of the meanings of the Aramaic term, (2) by his desire (natural but misleading) to adhere to one consistent view of the title as always implying a "witness," and perhaps (3) by some initial obscurity in the Hebrew or Aramaic from which Mark's tradition was initially derived[4]. The result was that Luke read

---

[1] Acts xiv 4, 14   [2] Acts xv. 2, 4, 6 etc , xvi 4

[3] Paul's first apostolic speech says concerning the risen Saviour Acts xiii 30—31) "God raised him from the dead, and he was seen for many days by *them that came up with him from Galilee to Jerusalem who are now his witnesses to the people*" It makes no mention of the fact that he himself has "seen Jesus"

[4] In Mk iii 14 "appointed. .that they might be *with him*," the Clementine Hebrew (1688) renders "*with him*" by עמו But this might mean "*his people*" In 1 K viii 62 "all Israel *with him*," LXX omits "*with him*," apparently taking it as "*people*" and superfluous, while the parall 2 Chr vii 4 Heb (followed by LXX) has "and all *the people*," apparently taking עם as "*people*," and "Israel" as superfluous Heb "*people*" is rendered by "*with*" in Dan ix 26, Ps xlvii. 9, cx 3, Heb "*with*" is rendered "*people*" in 1 Chr xii 18 See *Clue* **246** "*People*," in Heb (Gesen. 766) sometimes means "*followers*" in the sense of "*retainers*," and it is rendered by LXX

THE APPOINTMENT OF THE TWELVE

into the word "apostle," as a term used before Christ's resurrection, a meaning that it did not acquire till after Christ's resurrection, and used it in this anticipatory sense[1].

§ 4. *"That they might be with him, and that he might [from time to time] send them to preach*[2]*"*

(1) *"That they might be with him"* is omitted both by Matthew and Luke. (2) *"Preach"* is mentioned by Matthew ("Go ye and preach") in the Sending of the Apostles[3], and by

---

"servant" in Ps. lxxviii 71, lxxx 4. It could not have been used in Mark's original here. But if Luke found a tradition interpreting Mk iii 14 as "*his people*," he might think it worth while to explain that the term meant "followers of an intimate kind, called *apostles*." Comp. 2 K. iv 42 "Give unto *the people*," Rashi, "*the disciples* whom he [i.e. Elisha] was wont to support (sustentabat)"

[1] Similarly Luke appears to have read into the word "*deacon*," or, "*minister*," διάκονος, the sense that it acquired after Christ's resurrection—but with an opposite result. When Mark and Matthew use it, the parallel Luke alters it into the verb διακονέω. Comp. Mk ix 35, x 43, Mt xx 26, xxiii. 11, with Lk xxii 26. Luke shrinks from representing Jesus as saying, as in Mark, "He shall be last of all and *minister*, or *deacon*, of all." Even when Luke records (Acts vi 2—6) the appointment of seven disciples to "minister to tables"—presumably called διάκονοι—he himself does not call them by that name, and, in Acts viii 5, "Philip" is mentioned so abruptly—meaning, but not saying, "Philip the second in the list of the seven appointed above"—that Isidorus (see Cramer *ad loc.*) is at great pains to explain that Philip the Apostle is not meant.

On the other hand, John represents Jesus as saying (xii 26) "If any man is [of a mind] to *become-minister* (or, *deacon*) (διακονῇ) to me, let him follow me, and, where I am, there also shall be my *minister* (or, *deacon*)." Comp. Clem Alex 793 on the true Gnostic, "Such a one is, in reality, a presbyter of the Church, and a true *deacon* [i.e. *minister*] of the will-and-purpose (βουλήσεως) of God.. and he will sit in the four and twenty thrones judging the people (Rev iv 4)." It is interesting to note that, in the only passage where Clement of Rome mentions "*deacon*," he says (§ 42) that it goes back to ancient times, and he misquotes, in support of his assertion, Is. lx 17 Heb. "*overseers...exactors*," LXX ἄρχοντας... ἐπισκόπους, as ἐπισκόπους...διακόνους.

[2] Mk iii. 14.   [3] Mt. x 7.

THE APPOINTMENT OF THE TWELVE

Luke ("he sent them forth to preach") in the Sending[1], but not here "*That they might be with him*" seems from the Fourth Gospel to have been really the primary object of the appointment of the Twelve by Jesus. The simplicity of the phrase perhaps prevented Matthew and Luke from realising its latent force. It is an understatement, implying "That they might become imbued with Christ's Spirit and hence fitted to testify to Him, that is, to become His witnesses or martyrs." Isaiah represents God the Saviour as saying to Israel—whom He created and formed and redeemed—"thou art mine," "I will be with thee," "I am with thee," and then "Ye are my witnesses, and my servant whom I have chosen[2]." But whereas the Old Testament promises that God will be with men, the New adds the promise that, as a consequence, men will be with God. Jesus says, in the Fourth Gospel, "When the Comforter is come...he shall bear witness of me, and ye also bear witness, because ye *have been with me from the beginning*[3]." Both in the Prophecy and in the Gospel there is perhaps an assumption that "*from the beginning*" is not confined to mere literal time. It may imply sometimes an initial and spiritual predisposition to become "witnesses" for God, from birth onwards, or even—according to Pauline doctrine—before birth, as in the case of Jacob, a "beginning" that goes back to God's purpose as its origin.

The close of Christ's Prayer to the Father in the Fourth Gospel repeats a form of the Marcan phrase in a new aspect, as though Jesus said, first, "In the beginning I appointed the Apostles that, where I was, they also *might be with me* [*on earth*]," and, secondly, "And now I pray, O Father...that, *where I am, they also may be with me* [*in heaven*], that they may behold

---

[1] Lk ix. 2.

[2] Is xliii. 1—10, rep. *ib.* 12 and xliv. 8 "Fear ye not, neither be afraid. have I not declared unto thee of old and shewn it? and ye are my witnesses."

[3] Jn xv. 26—7.

THE APPOINTMENT OF THE TWELVE

my glory which thou hast given me, for thou lovedst me before the foundation of the world[1]." The disciples of Jesus could not preach Jesus till they "knew" Him. The Fourth Gospel implies that, until the Spirit of Jesus came to them, they all, to some extent, fell short in that "knowing"—like Philip. Jesus included all the disciples ("you")—not Philip alone ("thee")—when He said, "Have I been so long *with you* and dost thou not know me, Philip[2]?" Jesus had been "*with*" them, preparing them to be "*with*" *Him*; but the preparation was not yet complete[3].

On this first point, then, John may be said to intervene, giving to Mark's phrase a force, not contrary to probable fact and history, though perhaps not contemplated by Mark himself. But on the second point, the "preaching" of the Twelve, he neither does nor can intervene, since he never uses the word "preach" or "proclaim," and since the thought is alien from his Gospel[4] He prefers to speak of "bearing witness." But even as to "bearing witness," it is almost certain that John would not have said that Jesus appointed the Apostles *that they might at once "bear witness" concerning Himself.* It is not till the night before the Crucifixion that He says "It was not ye that chose me, but it was I that chose you, and appointed you, that ye may go and bear fruit, and that your fruit may remain[5]."

---

[1] Jn xvii 24 There is a connection, more easily felt than defined, between the foreordained unity of the disciples with the Saviour and "before the foundation of the world."

[2] Jn xiv 9

[3] See Ps cxxxix 18 "I am still *with thee*," and Rashi's comment "Behold I have come to the end of the generations which thou hast marked out, beginning from the first ages up to this day. Still is this generation of Israel *with thee and abideth in thy fear, nor have I departed from thee.*"

[4] See *Beginning* pp 45—6 John prefers to contemplate God as the Father represented by the Son, rather than as the King "proclaimed" by the Herald

[5] Jn xv 16

THE APPOINTMENT OF THE TWELVE

Here, however, we must do Mark the justice to note that his language ("that he might [from time to time] send" or "that he might be [hereafter] sending") does not denote a single and immediate sending[1]. It seems probable that the phrase was inserted here, out of place, to explain the preceding clause "whom also he named *apostles* (i e *persons-to-be-sent*)," and that Mark meant, in effect, "*not that He might send them at once but that He might have them ready to be sent hereafter.*"

John, in the Fourth Gospel, nowhere describes the Apostles as being absent from Jesus, except for very short intervals, first, during His dialogue with the woman of Samaria; and secondly, during the storm at night, after the Feeding of the Five Thousand. After the first absence, Jesus says to them, "Lift up your eyes", after the second, "Fear not[2]" There is nothing amounting to reproach in either case; but there is a suggestion that the disciples were not in a condition to be left to themselves by their Master. They might be able to "cast out devils" On that point the Fourth Evangelist is absolutely silent But he gives us the impression that they were not as yet able to "preach the Gospel"

This last sentence covers all that we need say about the verse in Mark that follows the one we have been discussing, namely, "and to have authority to cast out devils[3]." It appears to be out of place here, and Luke accordingly omits it. But even if it were in place, the Fourth Gospel could not be expected to insert it.

---

[1] In Mark, ἵνα, when followed by the present subjunctive, denotes (or may denote) continual or habitual action or state, e g iii 9, iv 12 (quotation), vi 8 (perhaps), vi 12 (μετανοῶσιν, see Swete), vi 41 (rep viii 6) παρατιθῶσιν (perhaps), xi 28 ("that thou shouldst continue doing these things"), xiii 34 Contrast Mk x 13 ἵνα ἅψηται with Lk xviii 15 ἵνα ἅπτηται

[2] Jn iv. 35, vi 20

[3] Mk iii. 15 καὶ ἔχειν ἐξουσίαν ἐκβάλλειν τὰ δαιμόνια The construction is not καὶ ἵνα .., as in the previous verse And there is no mention of "healing diseases"

THE APPOINTMENT OF THE TWELVE

5 *"James the [son] of Zebedee and John the brother of James¹"*

Luke does not think it necessary to define John as the brother of James, or to emphasize the fact that both are sons of Zebedee. It is true that, in his first mention of the two brothers, he describes them as "James and John, sons of Zebedee", but he adds "who were partners with Simon² " "Zebedee" he never mentions again either in the Gospel or in the Acts. "Partners with Simon" accords with the way in which he presents "John" to his readers in the Acts, where "Peter and John" come first in the Apostolic list³, and "Peter and John"—acting and speaking as one person—go up to the Temple together, heal a lame man together, and afterwards, as one, defend themselves from the charges brought against them before the Sanhedrin⁴. James the son of Zebedee is not mentioned in the Acts (apart from the Apostolic list above mentioned) except to record his death, and then he is described, not as the son of Zebedee but as "the brother of John⁵ " When Paul speaks about the "partnership" extended to him by "James and Cephas and John" the famous "pillars" of the Church in Jerusalem, he refers not to James the son of Zebedee but to "James the Lord's brother" who was not one of the Twelve; so that the passage implies, within a Triumvirate,

---

¹ Mk iii 17
And James the [son] of Zebedee and John the brother of James.

Mt x 2
James the [son] of Zebedee and John his brother.

Lk vi 14
And James and John.

² Lk. v. 10

³ Acts i 13 "both Peter and John and James and Andrew (ὅ τε Πέτρος καὶ Ἰωάνης καὶ Ἰ. καὶ Ἀ), Philip and Thomas, Bartholomew and Matthew, James [the son] of Alphaeus, and Simon the Zealot, and Judas [the son, *marg* brother] of James "

⁴ Acts iii 1—11, and note especially iv 13 τὴν τοῦ Πέτρου παρρησίαν καὶ Ἰωάνου (not τοῦ Ἰ), 19 ὁ δὲ Πέτρος καὶ Ἰωάνης (not ὁ Ἰ.) ἀποκριθέντες εἶπαν.

⁵ Acts xii. 2.

THE APPOINTMENT OF THE TWELVE

an inner Duumvirate of two members of the Twelve, Peter and John, working together as we find them working in the Acts[1].

In his Gospel, Luke adheres at first to the old Galilaean order, which placed the elder son of Zebedee before the younger, and he does this also here, in the List of the Apostles, and in another tradition peculiar to himself, in which he describes "the disciples James and John" as desiring to call down fire on a Samaritan village and receiving a rebuke[2]. But at the raising of Jairus' daughter, and at the Transfiguration, where Jesus selects three to accompany Him, Luke gives John the priority, describing them as "Peter and John and James[3]" There was only one John among the Apostles, so that "Peter and John" at the beginning of an Apostolic list could not be ambiguous, and "Peter and John and James" would naturally suggest the James that was John's brother; whereas, in some contexts, "Peter and *James*"—referring to Apostles—might mean "Peter and *James the son of Alphaeus.*"

The Fourth Gospel does not contain the name "James." Nor does the Evangelist mention "John" except when he means the Baptist (or Simon Peter's father). In the first chapter of his Gospel, John the son of Zebedee, unnamed, is implied as one of the first pair of disciples, and his brother is probably implied almost immediately afterwards along with Simon Peter; but we do not know this for certain till we look back to that first chapter from the close of the Gospel where he mentions, for the first and last time, "the sons of Zebedee[4]." It is one of many curious points of contrast between Luke and John that "the sons of Zebedee" occurs, in the former, only at the beginning, and, in the latter, only at the close.

---

[1] Gal 1. 19, ii. 9   [2] Lk. ix 54

[3] Lk viii. 51, but Mk v 37 "Peter and James and John the brother of James" (Mt om.), Lk ix 28, but Mk ix 2 "Peter and James and John," Mt xvii 1 "Peter and James and John his brother."

[4] Jn xxi 2.

THE APPOINTMENT OF THE TWELVE

§ 6   *"Sons of thunder" in Mark, "thunder" in John*

It has been supposed by many that "sons of thunder" meant "preaching the gospel with thunder of eloquence." In that case, it might be illustrated by what Aristophanes says about Pericles, that he "lightened and thundered and threw Greece into chaos[1]." But this interpretation, though natural for Greeks ignorant of Hebrew, does not accord with (1) the frequent Biblical use of one and the same word, *kôl*, for "thunder" and for "voice," (2) the Biblical use of *kôl* to mean the voice of Jehovah, (3) the Jewish use of the term *Bath kôl* to mean "a voice from heaven."

It is probable that Matthew and Luke omitted the appellation because of its obscure and apparently unedifying nature. We might therefore reasonably expect John to intervene about it, but for the fact that he never mentions, by name, either James or John to whom Mark gives this appellation. Once only does he mention them as a pair, "the sons of Zebedee," but never by their names. We cannot therefore demand that the Fourth Evangelist should say, directly, "John the son of Zebedee and James his brother were called 'sons of thunder,' but in a sense not commonly understood." All that we can expect is that in some indirect way he should convey to us some spiritual notion of what "thunder" might represent, leading us inferentially to some spiritual notion of what "sons of thunder" might mean when applied by Jesus to the sons of Zebedee. If he does not do this, the rule of Johannine Intervention is broken. But the rule has been shewn to hold in so many cases where at first sight it appeared to be broken, that we are bound to be cautious before saying "It is absolutely certain that 'thunder' in John has no connection at all with 'sons of thunder' in Mark."

In the ancient commentary on Mark attributed to Jerome,

---

[1] Aristoph. *Acharn.* 531

(Mark iii 13—19)

THE APPOINTMENT OF THE TWELVE

it is said about Peter, James, and John, "Jesus *named them Boanerges, that is, Sons of Thunder,* since the exalted desert of *these three* deserves to hear, on the Mountain, the thunder of the Father, thundering through the cloud, 'This is my beloved Son'"—referring to the Transfiguration[1]. Very similar is the explanation of Origen who says that the "Boanerges" were to send forth to men the utterances of the divine thunder, being, indeed, not thunders, but "Sons of Thunder," because they are "begotten from the mighty-voicedness of God, who thunders and shouts mightily from heaven to those who have ears and are wise[2]." The Voice of the Father from heaven, in the Synoptists, did not expressly reveal anything except the divine Sonship of Jesus ("This is my beloved (*or,* chosen) Son[3]") But it also implied that His Word was preeminent ("hear ye him") even above the teaching of Moses and Elijah, who were present conversing with Him on the mountain And Luke goes further still, and tells us that Moses and Elijah spoke with Jesus "concerning his departure which he was to

---

[1] See *Son* 3468 *b* quoting "Et imposuit Simoni nomen Petrus De obedientia ascendit ad agnitionem et Jacobum . et Joannem et imposuit eis nomina Boanerges, quod est filii tonitrui, *quorum trium sublime meritum in monte meretur audire tonitruum Patris* " The writer seems to be playing on the meaning of "Simon," "*hearing,*" when he says that he ascended from "*hearing and obeying* (*obedientia*)" to "*hearing and understanding* (*agnitio*)"

[2] *Introduction* p 171, quoting Origen *Comm Matth* xii 32 See also *Son* 3468 *a—b* quoting Pseudo-Jerome and Origen The former distinctly says that Peter, James, and John were all called Boanerges One of the quotations given from Origen (in *Comm Matth* xii 32) appears inconsistent with this But add Origen's *Pref to Rom* about changes of names "In Evangeliis quoque ex Simone Petrus et filii Zebedaei filii tonitrui nuncupati sunt," which seems to point to an original "[He that became] Peter from Simon (ὁ ἐκ Σίμωνος Πέτρος) and the sons of Zebedee, were [all] called Sons of thunder " The context makes the meaning doubtful But if Peter (as Pseudo-Jerome says) heard with "understanding (*agnitio*)" the divine message, was not he entitled (as well as his two companions) to be called "a son of thunder"?

[3] Mk ix 7, Mt xvii 5, Lk ix 35

accomplish in Jerusalem[1]." "Departure" points to the Sacrifice on the Cross And its "accomplishment" points to the fulfilment of the Law and the Prophets. "The Law instituted sacrifice as a type, Prophecy predicted its accomplishment, the Son *was* the accomplishment"—that appears to be the thought at the bottom of Luke's addition

All through the Synoptic narrative of the Transfiguration, though "thunder" is not mentioned it is implied. The texts speak of a "cloud" as well as a "voice from heaven," and it is easily conceivable that unbelievers present on that occasion would have said that "it thundered." This turns our minds to the only passage in N.T. (apart from Revelation) where "thunder" is mentioned. "There came therefore a voice out of heaven [saying] I have both glorified it and will glorify it again The multitude, therefore, that stood by and heard it, said that it had *thundered* Others said, An angel hath spoken to him[2]" The utterance of the Voice is quite different verbally from that in the Synoptists, but it is similar spiritually. For the Father is responding to the prayer of the Son, "Glorify thy name." And that again points back to a prediction "The hour is come that the Son of man should be glorified," and to a declaration that this "glorifying" will be a "dying" in order to "live," as "a grain of wheat" dies and, by dying, "beareth much fruit" In word, this is very different from Luke's mention of the Lord's "departure which he should accomplish in Jerusalem"; but in spirit it is very similar.

What does the Fourth Evangelist accomplish for his readers by this detail about "thunder"? Would it not have sufficed, after stating what the Voice said, to add "But the multitude understood it not"? Perhaps he wishes to shew that in such cases God might sometimes speak through what the common people would call (and rightly from their point of view)

---

[1] Lk. ix 31.
[2] Jn xii 28—9 βροντὴν γεγονέναι

THE APPOINTMENT OF THE TWELVE

"thunder." Others, a higher class, might call it "an angel." Others—such as the disciple, John the son of Zebedee, in whose name the Gospel was written—being "begotten of the thunder of God," might recognise the voice of God in the "thunder" to which they were akin, and they might receive in part (without fully comprehending) the revelation conveyed by it, namely, that the Father would be glorified by the Son in some kind of victory over death achieved by obedience to the Law of the Spiritual Harvest.

The Johannine narrative at this point is of such a dignity and depth, that it would seem in bad taste, as well as contrary to probability, to suppose that the writer would convey, under this unique mention of "thunder," any direct reference to a mere phrase like "the sons of thunder" as an appellation of the sons of Zebedee. If that had been the case, he would (one might suppose) have indicated that the Evangelist, presumably John the son of Zebedee, received some special insight. This he has done elsewhere, but not here. All that we can say then is this, that (1) throughout his Gospel he represents the author as being anything but "a son of thunder" in the western sense, but, on the contrary, as singularly retiring, (2) he represents the author as being, on at least three occasions, possessed of special insight[1]. Also (3) he leads his Gentile readers to regard "thunder" in an aspect new to them. It is perhaps Jewish rather than Hebraic, belonging to Jewish developments of Hebraistic thought which represent "thunder" as the type of God's deep secrets of Redemption.

§ 7. *"Thaddaeus" in Mark, "Judas of James" in Luke*[2]

"Thaddaeus," a form of the name Judas, is found in both the Talmuds[3]. It is also assigned in one treatise to one of

---

[1] See Jn xix. 35, xx. 8, xxi. 7.
[2] Mk iii 18, Lk. vi 16
[3] See Levy iv 627 *b*, and *Hor. Heb.* on Mt. x. 3.

THE APPOINTMENT OF THE TWELVE

five disciples of Jesus, all of whom are put to death by the Sanhedrin with grim jests playing on their several names and quoting Scripture. The name means an offering of thanks or of praise Thaddaeus, playing on this, says "Shall *Thaddaeus* be slain? It is written 'Psalm for *thank-offering*.'" They reply, with a counter-play, "Surely *Thaddaeus* shall be condemned, for it is written 'Whosoever offereth the sacrifice of *thank-offering* glorifieth me[1].'" This resembles the Johannine tradition. "The hour cometh that he that slayeth you shall think that he *offereth [religious] service* to God[2]"

The verb "praise" is assumed in Scripture to be the origin of the name "Judah" in accordance with the words of Leah ("I will praise the Lord") and Jacob's prediction ("thy brethren shall praise thee[3]"). When, therefore, in the Lucan parallel to "Thaddaeus," we find "Judas of James," we see no great difficulty in the inference that "Thaddaeus" may be a vernacular form of "Judas," and that one reason for its acceptance was a desire to distinguish this Judas from Judas Iscariot[4].

This being the case, when we find John introducing a disciple as "*Judas not Iscariot*[5]," we are justified in taking it as one of the very many instances where John intervenes to clear up an obscurity in Mark That Mark was obscure may be inferred not only from Luke's deviation, but also from the fact that in Matthew many authorities read "Lebbaeus" for "Thaddaeus," and Origen expressly accepts the reading "Lebbaeus" in Matthew's Apostolic list[6]. That John should

---

[1] See Levy iv 630 *a*, quoting *Sanhedr* 43 *a* (Ps. c. (title), and l. 23), and *Hor Heb* on Mt ix 9

[2] Jn xvi. 2 λατρείαν προσφέρειν τῷ θεῷ

[3] See Gesen 397 *a*, quoting Gen. xxix 35, xlix. 8, and other passages

[4] See *Hor Heb* on Mt. x. 3 "It is a warping of the name *Judas*, that this apostle might be the better distinguished from *Iscariot*"

[5] Jn xiv. 22

[6] See Origen's *Pref. Epist Rom.*

THE APPOINTMENT OF THE TWELVE

have been dissatisfied with Luke's correction "Judas of James," is not surprising. There were already, in the Apostolic lists, James the son of Zebedee, and James the son of Alphaeus; and, before the Gospels were committed to writing, there came into prominence in the Church a third James, James the Lord's brother, presiding over the Council of Jerusalem. To add a fourth (as the father of an apostle) might well seem inexpedient. We may accept this, then, as a case of Johannine Intervention.

But, instead of "Judas not Iscariot," the Syro-Sinaitic version has "*Thomas*," and the Curetonian Syriac "*Judas Thomas.*" In the only quotation by Origen of this passage, the Latin mentions simply "quidam discipulus[1]." Also John informs us—and he is the only Evangelist that does this—that "*Thomas*" was "called *Didymus.*" "Thomas" meant "twin" in Hebrew, and "Didymus" meant "twin" in Greek. Hence "Judas Thomas" would mean "Judas the twin." But the Syro-Sinaitic version assumes that he is identical with the Apostle commonly known as "Thomas." In that case Thaddaeus and Thomas in Mark would have to be regarded as two names for one person. This view would at all events enable us to understand the extraordinary assertion of Celsus that the apostles were "ten," or "some ten or eleven," in number[2].

We may naturally regret that John does not tell us something fuller and more positive about this Thaddaeus, or Lebbaeus, or Judas of James, as, for example, whether he was identical

---

[1] Origen *Cant* lib iii (Lomm xv 41), quoting Jn xiv 22
[2] See Origen *Cels* i 62, ii 46. The context shews that Celsus does not mean *ten* "tax-gatherers and sailors"—as though two others might have some other pursuit—but that, as Origen says (*ib* i 62) Celsus "*did not know even the number of the Apostles.*" Perhaps he identified (Mt ix. 9) Matthew the tax-gatherer (s above, p 284) with (Mk ii 14) "Levi the [son] of Alphaeus" (called by Luke simply (v 27) "a tax-gatherer named Levi") and hence with "James the son of Alphaeus," reading Mt x 3 as "Matthew the tax-gatherer [also called] James the [son] of Alphaeus"

THE APPOINTMENT OF THE TWELVE

with Levi the Publican, or, at all events, what *other* surname he had, if any, since Iscariot was not his surname. But he perhaps knew that the Apostle had more surnames than one and that there were various traditions about them. And he did not desire to follow Luke in adding to the names of the complex Apostolic list. John's intervention may well seem to us inadequate, but at all events he intervenes.

§ 8. *"The Cananaean" in Mark, "he that was called Zealot" in Luke*

It is commonly stated that "the Zealots" originated under the auspices of Judas of Galilee; and Josephus is quoted as authority for this statement[1]. But when Josephus describes the rise of what he calls "a fourth sect" of the Jews under Judas of Galilee, he makes no mention of "Zealots[2]." I have found no earlier authority for this assertion about "Zealots" than a passage in the Wars of Josephus describing the excesses of the freebooting followers of John of Gischala shortly before the siege of Jerusalem[3] There, his language implies that these freebooters and murderers were taking and perverting a name that had been in use before—as it is used in the Epistles

---

[1] On Gal 1 14 περισσοτέρως ζηλωτὴς ὑπάρχων τῶν πατρικῶν μου παραδόσεων, Lightfoot says "St Paul seems to have belonged to the extreme party of the Pharisees (Acts xxii 3, xxiii 7, xxvi 5, Phil iii 5, 6) whose pride it was to call themselves 'zealots of the law, zealots of God.' To this party also had belonged Simon, one of the Twelve, thence surnamed the zealot, ζηλωτὴς or καναναῖος, i e קנאן. A portion of these extreme partizans, forming into a separate sect under Judas of Galilee, took the name of 'zealots' *par excellence*, and distinguished themselves by their furious opposition to the Romans." This gives the impression, without exactly stating, that *"zealots" began to be used as a sectarian term under Judas of Galilee* Other writers have committed themselves to this statement

[2] Joseph *Ant* xviii 1. 6

[3] Josephus says that Jesus and Ananus (*Bell* iv 3. 9) "tried to stir up the people against 'the *zealots*'—*for this was what they called themselves, as though [they were zealots] for good pursuits*, and *not zealots for the worst possible crimes, and passing bounds [in evil-doing]*."

THE APPOINTMENT OF THE TWELVE

and the Acts—to denote those zealous for the observance of the Law, but not as yet of any particular class[1]. We have therefore to put aside the notion that "Simon the Cananaean" meant "Simon *who had once been one of the Zealots such as those who followed Judas of Galilee*[2]." If Luke, being greatly impressed by the events attending the fall of Jerusalem, believed Mark's tradition to mean that Simon had been, in old days, a political "Zealot" such as Josephus describes, it would seem that Luke was mistaken.

Then the question arises whether "Cananaean" meant simply "zealous" in a good sense, a laudatory epithet such as we find in "Justus." Such a laudation, applied to an apostle before he became an apostle, would be unique among the Twelve[3]. Again, did it refer to birthplace and mean "a man of Canana" or of some place similarly named? Against this, too, there is the same objection. No other Apostle in the list is supposed to be called by a birthplace name[4] except Judas Iscariot, and that supposition is very doubtful; probably there is a play on "Iscariot[5]." This brings us to a

---

[1] Paul's expression (Gal i 14) "*above measure zealous,*" together with the context ("I persecuted the church of God") indicates the direction in which the "zeal" would often be manifested (see Levy iv 332 *b* on the term applied to Phinehas (Numb xxv 11) as "*a zealot and the son of a zealot*") It is used in the Mishna concerning those who execute a sentence of death, *Sanhedr.* 81 *b*

[2] In Mk iii 18 and Mt x 4, several inferior authorities have (as A V) "Canaanite" Jerome on Mt x 2—4 says (1) "appellatur Chananaeus de vico Chana Galilaeae," and (2) "in alio Evangelista scribitur Zelotes Chana quippe Zelus interpretatur"

[3] It is found, in Acts i 23, about one (of two) put forth for possible election, but not elected, to be one of the Twelve, and also in Col iv 11.

[4] *Horae Hebr* on Mt x 3 suggests that Lebbaeus may be a place-name, but I believe that view is not generally accepted.

[5] "Iscariot" is popularly supposed to be "a man of *Cariot*," a place alleged to be mentioned in Josh xv 25 "Kerioth." But the full name there given is "Kerioth-Hezron" This is rendered by LXX and Syr "*cities* of Hezron," meaning the group of cities that make up Hezron or Hazor Origen (on Mt xxvi 14—16) regards

THE APPOINTMENT OF THE TWELVE

similar question about "Cananaean": "Are there any facts indicating that it might be connected *both with a place and with some moral meaning*?" In favour of this hypothesis we may allege such instances as there are in the *Aboth* where Rabbis are occasionally introduced with a birthplace name; in most of them there appears to be a play on the name[1].

If the Marcan "Cananaean" was originally a birthplace name, with a play on it, "Cana" is the name that suggests itself (as it did to Jerome). In that case the birthplace of this Simon would be also the birthplace of Nathanael But here we are met by the fact that the Syriac versions regularly call Nathanael's birthplace *Catné* In Josephus there are several places called "Cana," but the forms greatly vary. He mentions "the village *called Cana*," and "a village of Galilee *called-by-name Cana*," in such a way as to suggest that the word "Cana" might have some recognised meaning[2]. Various

---

"Judas Iscariot" as being distinguished from "Judas not Iscariot" by the addition of the "native-place," and says "I have heard it explained that the name of the native-place (*patria*) is, in Hebrew, *suffocated*" See Gesen 698 *b* on סכר = (1) "stop up," (2) "hire" From (1) comes (*Hor Heb* on Mt x 4) *Iscara*, strangling, "the roughest death" From (2) would come suggestions of Judas as the "*hireling*" Jerome (on Mt x 4) connects the name either with place of birth or with "*Issachar*," "hire" Note also the Greek word regularly used for the "*betrayal*" of Jesus, παραδίδωμι, uniquely represented in Is xix 4 by Heb סכר, i e *sâchar* The supposed play on "*suffocate*" accords with Jewish traditions about the painful nature of this death, and with the emphasis laid on it in the Gospels and the Acts Comp *Hen VI* (B) I 1 124 "For *Suffolk's* duke, may he be *suffocate*!"

[1] See *Beginning* p 311, n. 1, quoting e g. *Sabb*. 55 *b* "We always need *Modai* (knowledge), for Eleazar the [man] of *Modai*[*m*] (knowledge) said...."

[2] *Bell*. 1 17 5 τὴν καλουμένην Κανᾶ (*sic*) κώμην (Lat. *Canacome*), *Vit.* § 16 ἐν κώμῃ τῆς Γαλιλαίας ἣ προσαγορεύεται Κανά. For προσαγορεύεσθαι applied to a place-name that has a meaning, comp *Bell*. 11. 19. 4 τὴν τε Βεθεζὰν προσαγορευομένην καὶ τὴν [? τὴν καὶ] Καινόπολιν with *ib* v. 4. 2 ἐκλήθη δὲ ἐπιχωρίως Βεζεθὰ τὸ νεόκτιστον μέρος ὃ μεθερμηνευόμενον...καινὴ λέγοιτ' ἂν πόλις.

THE APPOINTMENT OF THE TWELVE

readings of Cana[1] are Αναν, Ισανας, and κανατα or καμαθα. In Hebrew, *ktn* means "little," and it might be used of a person, as in Ezra, "the *Little-one (katan)*," or of anything little, as "the finger[2]." Genesis says that the city of "Zoar" was so called because it was "a little one," and "Cana" might be another instance of a place called "Little-town[3]." In Aramaic, the name of "Cattin," "Little-one," was common, and Levy compares it with "Paul," *i.e* Paulus, "the little one[4]" One of the most famous of all the Rabbis, placed in the same category with Hillel, was called Samuel the Little (*Hakkatan*), and it was questioned whether he was so called because he "held himself to be little" or because he was only a little less than Samuel the Great[5].

If Simon the Cananaean was regarded as born at Catna or Cana, the birthplace of Nathanael, and if Judas was regarded as called Iscariot from the name of his birthplace, it would seem to be more than a mere coincidence that the two place-names come together at the end of the Apostolic list. A contrast would seem to be intended. What may be the precise meaning of "Iscariot" is very doubtful. But the connection between Nathanael and Cana in the Fourth Gospel suggests that there may have been a play on the place-name—Nathanael, the only one of the disciples praised by Jesus as "an Israelite indeed," being called "from Catna (or Cana)" because he counted himself "a little one," and remained one of Christ's little ones till the end. The name "Catanaean," when applied to Simon, might naturally be corrupted into the familiar "Canaanite," which some authorities have in Matthew and

---

[1] Josephus mentions more than one place of that name.
[2] Gesen 882 *a* quoting Ezr viii 12 (R V Hakkatan), 1 K. xii. 10, 2 Chr x 10
[3] Gen xix 20, 22.   [4] Levy iv 284 *b*
[5] Levy iv 283 *b*   In Eph iii 8 "I am less than the least...," Delitzsch uses the Heb. *zoar* above quoted from Genesis But the thought is the same as that about Samuel the *Katan* or *Kattin*. See Taylor on *Aboth* iv. 26.

THE APPOINTMENT OF THE TWELVE

Mark, or else, when this was seen to be absurd, into "Cananaean."

It is disappointing to be unable to arrive at any more definite conclusion about the precise nature of John's purpose in giving so early and prominent a place to "Cana," as the scene of two of Christ's "signs," and then in dropping it till near the conclusion of his Gospel, where he mentions it, without any apparent reason, for the third and last time. There seems an intention to suggest to the readers that there is a mystery about it, and that, as Origen says, "It is not for nothing that there are two visitations of Jesus in Cana[1]." Take the context of the first mention of the name—"Jesus answered and said unto *him* [i.e. *Nathanael*]....And he saith unto *him* [i.e. *Nathanael*] 'Verily...the Son of man.' And on the third day there was a marriage in *Cana of Galilee*...[2]"—followed by the miracle of the Water made Wine in the bridegroom's house. The second mention is connected with the healing of the "nobleman's" son[3]. And now take the third and last:—"Thomas called Didymus, and *Nathanael of Cana in Galilee*[4]" Why does the Evangelist, in the first of these passages, keep back from his readers what he suddenly springs upon them in the last, that the scene of the wedding there described was also the home of the disciple addressed in the preceding verse? No one can confidently say. But many will feel that the Evangelist in his final mention of Cana seems to desire to magnify both Cana and Nathanael, as though he said, "Note how this little village of Cana comes in again at the last. It was the scene of the first of the 'signs.' It was the scene of the first separately recorded act of healing. And now it is to be thought of as the

---

[1] Origen on Jn iv. 46 (Lomm ii 116) He regards the two visitations as typical of the Saviour's "two visitations to the world, the former that He may gladden those that feast with Him, the latter that He may raise up him that was near death"

[2] Jn i 50—ii 1   [3] Jn iv 46.

[4] Jn xxi 2

THE APPOINTMENT OF THE TWELVE

home of Nathanael, to whom the first promise was made, and who, though not reckoned in the earliest Gospels as one of the Twelve, was one of the Seven to whom the Lord gave the Bread and the Fish after the Resurrection."

Jerome connects Christ's praise of Nathanael with His praise of the "tax-gatherer" who, Luke's Gospel says, was "justified"; and certainly the story of Nathanael under the fig-tree might be so told as to resemble that other Lucan story of the tax-gatherer, Zacchaeus, who is described as being "*little*" in stature and as climbing up into a tree where he was seen by Jesus[1]. Also Clement of Alexandria says that "Zacchaeus, or, according to some, *Matthias* (sic), the chief of the tax-gatherers," uttered the promise of restitution which made the Saviour say that He had "found that which was lost[2]." "Matthias," though here perhaps identified with Matthew the tax-gatherer, is mentioned in the Acts as the name of the thirteenth Apostle, co-opted into the place of Judas Iscariot[3].

It is not unreasonable to suppose that the writer of the Fourth Gospel was deeply impressed by what may be called the comparative failure of the rank and file of the official "Twelve" as compared with Paul and many nameless missionaries—not belonging to the Twelve, yet true Apostles—who founded Churches, or prepared the way for founding them, in the West[4]. Nathanael may have seemed to him the type of

---

[1] See *Son of Man* 3375 *i* quoting Jerome (on Ps xxxii. 2 and Lk xviii 13)

[2] Clem Alex 579, quoting the words addressed to Zacchaeus (Lk xix. 10) "Matthias," "Matthew," and "Nathanael," all come from the Heb *nathan*, "give"

[3] Acts i 26

[4] Such as Priscilla and Aquila, but left unnamed See *Beginning* p. 339 Note Acts xxviii 13—14 "We came to Puteoli, *where we found brethren, and were intreated to tarry with them seven days*" Does not this make it probable that Paul's hosts were resident at Puteoli where they would constitute a little Christian community, entitled to be called the Congregation or Church of Puteoli?

THE APPOINTMENT OF THE TWELVE

them, and perhaps, at the close of his Gospel, in adding to his name "from Cana," John desired to suggest that this apostle began from, and ended in, the true home of the children of God, the House of God's little ones.

For the rest, John not only fails to satisfy our curiosity about some of the obscurer members of the Synoptic Twelve, such as Bartholomew, Thaddaeus (called by some Lebbaeus), Simon the Cananaean (called by Luke the Zealot), and James the son of Alphaeus (said to be James the Little), but he even adds to our difficulties by adding another Simon. For he tells us that Judas Iscariot was son of Simon. And if any Christians at the end of the first century had built up explanations of the name Iscariot as being predictive of treachery, he seems to dash to the ground such superstructures by telling them that *this Simon, the father of the traitor, was himself called Iscariot*, so that Judas was "[son] of *Simon Iscariot*." That is when the traitor's name is for the first time mentioned[1]. Later on, he calls the traitor "Judas the Iscariot," and then "Judas, the son of Simon, [namely, Judas] Iscariot[2]." But finally he returns to his first appellation, "Judas, the son of *Simon Iscariot*[3]." Perhaps the Evangelist's object was really to destroy these superstructures above mentioned. Or perhaps he found some saying that "Judas, the last in the Apostolic list, was son of Simon, the last but one," and maintaining that Cananaean or Zelōtes meant Iscariot[4]. In opposition to these he says, in effect, "True, the traitor *was* the son of a Simon, but not of that Simon. Nor was there anything in the traitor's appellation that marked him out for treachery, for the appellation belonged to the traitor's father also." In any case we

---

[1] Jn vi 71. [2] Jn xii 4, xiii 2
[3] Jn xiii 26.
[4] If it could be shewn that the Latin *sicarius*, "assassin," existed as a Hebraized word, there would be something to be said for this view. But Krauss gives no instance of it.

422 (Mark iii 13—19)

THE APPOINTMENT OF THE TWELVE

may be sure that the Fourth Evangelist had some purpose in these strange variations—which, at all events, have the result of making us reflect that other small statistical and historical discrepancies in the Synoptists might be explained without discredit to the writers if we knew all the facts

CHAPTER XII*

THE KINGDOM OF GOD, A FAMILY
[Mark iii. 20—35]

§ 1. *Jesus, in Mark, said by His "friends" to be "beside himself"[1]*

IN Mark, "he cometh into a house" might, as R.V. margin says, mean "he cometh home." In that case the house might be the one first mentioned in this Gospel, namely Peter's, in Capernaum[2] But the omission of the clause by Matthew

---

* For titles of previous Parts of Diatessarica referred to by abbreviations in this Volume, see pp 545—6. For other abbreviations see pp xxiii—xxvi

[1] Mk iii. 20—21
(20) And he cometh into a house (*or*, home) And the multitude cometh together again, so that they could not so much as eat bread.
(21) And when his friends (*or*, family) heard it, they went out to lay hold on him for they said, He is beside himself

Mt xii. 22—3
(22) Then was brought unto him one possessed with a devil, blind and dumb: and he healed him, insomuch that the dumb man spake and saw
(23) And all the multitudes were amazed, and said, Is this the son of David?

Lk xi 14
And he was casting out a devil [which was] dumb And it came to pass, when the devil was gone out, the dumb man spake, and the multitudes marvelled

[2] Οἶκος in Mk iii 20 must be distinguished from οἰκία. Mark's first mention of οἰκία is in i. 29 ἦλθαν εἰς τὴν οἰκίαν Σίμωνος καὶ Ἀνδρέου His first mention of οἶκος is in ii 1 ἠκούσθη ὅτι ἐν οἴκῳ (W H marg εἰς οἶκον) ἐστίν, where the meaning is "at home," in "*the house* of

THE KINGDOM OF GOD, A FAMILY

and Luke suggests that it seemed to them ambiguous or out of place.

This, however, is a trifling matter as compared with Mark's use of the word rendered by R.V. "is beside himself" in Mark, but "were amazed" in Matthew[1]. Matthew never uses it again, and his use of it here implies that he transferred it from "Jesus" to "all the multitudes" because he considered the latter application more seemly. Luke seems to have approved of the transference, but prefers the usual word to express "marvel" or "wonder[2]." The Mark-Matthew verb literally means "*stood outside* [of himself, *or*, of themselves]," and a very slight change would turn it into the literal phrase "stood outside" the door of a house[3] etc. A little later on, all the Synoptists, including Luke, say that the mother and the brethren of Jesus "*stood outside*" seeking Him[4]. This confirms the view that we are here in the region of Greek (not Hebrew or Aramaic) tradition, and that there was very early difference of opinion about a Greek phrase, literally meaning "stand outside," in a narrative that served as an introduction to some saying of Christ about His "mother" and His "brethren[5]"

Simon and Andrew" above mentioned Οἶκος in Mk ii 11, 26 τὸν οἶκόν σου, and τὸν οἶκον τοῦ θεοῦ, is defined In Mk iii 20, οἶκος being undefined, ἔρχεται εἰς οἶκον may mean "He cometh home [again]," i e to Peter's house above mentioned However, even if this is Mark's meaning, we cannot feel sure that he is right

[1] Mk iii. 21 ἔλεγον γὰρ ὅτι ἐξέστη, Mt xii 23 καὶ ἐξίσταντο πάντες οἱ ὄχλοι (where the pl. πάντες οἱ ὄχλοι is to be noted as being a very rare expression)

[2] Lk. xi 14 ἐθαύμασαν οἱ ὄχλοι

[3] That is to say, it would turn εξεστησαν into εξωεστησαν.

[4] Mk iii. 31—2 ἔξω στήκοντες .ἔξω ζητοῦσίν σε, Mt. xii 46 ἱστήκεισαν ἔξω ζητοῦντες..., [Mt. xii. 47 ἔξω ἑστήκασιν ζητοῦντες...], Lk. viii 20 ἑστήκασιν ἔξω ἰδεῖν θέλοντές σε. The contexts vary, but all have "stand outside."

[5] Codex D (in Mk iii 21) has "and when they heard about him, the scribes and *the rest* (so also *e* as well as *d*) went out to seize him, for they said that he is making them mad," και οτε ηκουσαν περι αυτου

THE KINGDOM OF GOD, A FAMILY

It would be interesting, verbally, to shew how, beside this particular Greek word, other causes—and particularly the use of "go forth"—may have contributed to the confusion of the Synoptic tradition[1]. But historically the chief interest of the parallel narratives lies in the fact that Mark's tradition gave the impression that Christ's own "friends," or "family[2]," said "He is beside himself." The deviations of Matthew and Luke from Mark, and the alterations of Mark itself in Codex D, confirm this view.

Yet the extraordinary freedom of Mark's text elsewhere in using the third person plural of a verb without a pronominal subject, to mean that *people* "said," or "did," this or that, leaves us free to believe that the meaning may be "And when his friends heard it they went out to lay hold on him; for

---

οι γραμματειν (sic) και οι λοιποι εξηλθον κρατησαισαι (sic) αυτον ελεγον γαρ οτι εξεστατι (sic) αυτους SS "and when *his brothers* heard" "The rest" might easily be confused with "brothers" owing to Hebrew corruption (s *Corrections* 348 a)

[1] The same Syr. verb occurs in Mk iii 21 "they had *gone out* to take hold of him," and *ib* "he hath *gone out of his mind*," and Lk. xi. 14 "when the devil had *gone out*" Some play on the double meaning of "go-out" may explain why Matthew and Luke here insert a tradition about a deaf-mute devil (Matthew adds "blind") that is caused (Luke says) to "*go out*" One of the earliest LXX uses of ἐξίστημι is Gen xlii 28 ἐξέστη ἡ καρδία αὐτῶν, Heb "their heart went out," Targums "the knowledge of their hearts went out" That Matthew (xii 22) should add "blindness" to "deafness" may perhaps be explained by the fact that he has just (*ib* 21) been quoting Isaiah, and in Isaiah's prophecy about the healing of the ransomed of Israel, (Is xxxv 5) "the eyes of the blind" precedes "the ears of the deaf" followed by "the lame" and "the dumb"

[2] See Field, *Otium Norvicense* p 18, on Mk iii 21 οἱ παρ' αὐτοῦ. And to his numerous instances add *Berlin Urkunde* 385 (2nd cent) "I salute my mother, and my brothers, and Sempronius, and *his family* (τοὺς παρ' αὐτοῦ)" In *ib* 998 (101 B C) as in *Oxy. Pap.* 246 ll 27, 31 (A D 66) ὁ παρὰ may denote an agent. And here, if the context permitted, it might mean Christ's messengers or agents But the context does not permit

THE KINGDOM OF GOD, A FAMILY

people were saying, He is beside himself[1]." Somewhat similarly Mark adds, at the end of the controversy of which we are here discussing the introduction: "[This he said] because [*people*] *were saying* (or, *beginning to say*), He hath an unclean spirit[2]." If that is the meaning, then the friends of Jesus may have gone forth to put a friendly restraint on Him, not because they themselves believed Him to be insane, but because the charge was beginning to be widely repeated in various forms by enemies whose object it was to represent Jesus as a dangerous or law-breaking lunatic, who ought to be put to death.

Before passing from this tradition about Jesus as being "beside himself," we must point out that Matthew, in an earlier chapter, has another form of the narrative of the healing of a dumb man possessed with a devil; and there he agrees with Luke in substituting "marvelled" for "beside themselves [with amazement]," and also in making no mention of blindness[3].

---

[1] See *Joh Gr* 2425 *b*, *Son* 3180 *b*, 3281 *a*. Note especially —

Mk vi 14	Mt xiv. 1—2	Lk ix 7
καὶ ἤκουσεν Ἡρῴδης, φανερὸν γὰρ ἐγένετο τὸ ὄνομα αὐτοῦ, καὶ ἔλεγον (marg ἔλεγεν)..	ἤκουσεν Ἡρῴδης. . καὶ εἶπεν .	ἤκουσεν δὲ Ἡρῴδης ...καὶ διηπόρει διὰ τὸ λέγεσθαι ὑπό τινων

Here Codex D and several Latin codd agree with B in reading (in Mark) ἔλεγον (or ἐλέγοσαν) in spite of the greater facility of the singular, which Matthew adopts

[2] Mk iii 30 ὅτι ἔλεγον, Πνεῦμα ἀκάθαρτον ἔχει

[3] Mt ix 32—3 (R V) "And as they [*i e* two blind men previously mentioned] went forth, behold there was brought to him a dumb man possessed with a devil. And when the devil was cast out, the dumb man spake, and the multitudes marvelled, saying, It was never so seen in Israel " This miracle takes place in a "house" (ix 28 "when he had come into *the house* the blind men came to him") where Jesus had healed two blind men who had appealed to Him as "son of David " Having just healed blindness, Jesus now heals dumbness In Rushbrooke's *Synopticon* p. 150 (containing the Double Tradition of Matthew and Luke) Mt. ix. 32—4 is immediately followed by Mt. xii 22—4, both being paralleled to the single narrative of Lk xi 14—15 This Double Tradition is almost entirely confined to words of Jesus Here it contains an act

THE KINGDOM OF GOD, A FAMILY

§ 2. *"He hath Beelzebub," in Mark*

It will be observed below that Matthew and Luke call Beelzebub "the prince of the devils," whereas Mark does not[1].

---

[1] Mk iii 22—6 (R V.)

(22) And the scribes which came down from Jerusalem said, He hath Beelzebub, and, By (*or*, in) the prince of the devils casteth he out the devils

(23) And he called them unto him, and said unto them in parables, How can Satan cast out Satan?

(24) And if a kingdom be divided against itself, that kingdom cannot stand

(25) And if a house be divided against itself, that house will not be able to stand

(26) And if Satan hath risen up against himself, and is divided, he cannot stand, but hath an end.

Mt xii 24—8 (R.V.)

(24) But when the Pharisees heard it, they said, This man doth not cast out devils but by (*or*, in) Beelzebub the prince of the devils

(25) And knowing their thoughts he said unto them, Every kingdom divided against itself is brought to desolation; and every city or house divided against itself shall not stand

(26) And if Satan casteth out Satan, he is divided against himself, how then shall his kingdom stand?

[(27) And if I by (*or*, in) Beelzebub cast out devils, by (*or*, in) whom do your sons cast them out? therefore shall they be your judges

(28) But if I by (*or*, in) the Spirit of God cast out devils, then is the kingdom of God come upon you. (Not in Mk, see p 446)]

Lk xi 15—20 (R V)

(15) But some of them said, By (*or*, in) Beelzebub the prince of the devils casteth he out devils.

(16) And others, tempting [him], sought of him a sign from heaven.

(17) But he, knowing their thoughts, said unto them, Every kingdom divided against itself is brought to desolation, and a house [divided] against a house falleth (*or*, and house falleth upon house)

(18) And if Satan also is divided against himself, how shall his kingdom stand? because ye say that I cast out devils by (*or*, in) Beelzebub

[(19) And if I by (*or*, in) Beelzebub cast out devils, by (*or*, in) whom do your sons cast them out? Therefore shall they be your judges.

(20) But if I by the finger of God cast out devils, then is the kingdom of God come upon you. (Not in Mk, see p 446.)]

Note that Matthew's earlier narrative omits the name Beelzebub, thus (ix 34) "But the Pharisees said, By the prince of the

THE KINGDOM OF GOD, A FAMILY

Mark's language is consistent with the view that Beelzebub means one of many inferior devils, under Satan the prince of the devils According to Mark, the scribes may have said that Jesus was possessed by this inferior devil, the agent of Satan, and that Satan gave to Jesus, through the possession of this inferior devil, power to cast out other devils.

Beelzebub appears to be nowhere mentioned in the Talmud, either as Beelzebub or as Beelzebul[1]. The names Asmodeus and Sammael are frequent, as well as Satan; but Beelzebub occurs only in the Bible. There, it is the name of a foreign god, to whose oracle the king of Samaria sends messengers to know whether he will recover from sickness. Elijah meets them and says that the king shall die as the penalty of his inquiry[2]. The name means "lord (*baal*) of flies." But "lord (*baal*)" is easily confused, or might be contemptuously interchanged, with *bala*, "swallow," as in Isaiah where "*lords* of the nations" is rendered "*swallowing* the nations" by the LXX[3]. Now Jesus accused the Pharisees of "straining at a gnat" while "swallowing a camel," meaning perhaps, *inter alia*, that they swallowed the adultery of Herod Antipas while they condemned, in poor folk, the slightest infraction of the Levitical laws of eating, drinking[4], etc. They, on the other hand, would certainly accuse Christ of blasphemy in forgiving sins, and especially sins of "women that were sinners." The *Onomastica Sacra* explains "Baalzebub," and even "Beelzebul,"

---

devils casteth he out devils " On the spelling of the name, "Beelzebub" or "Beelzebul," see below W H follow B in reading Βεεζεβούλ.

[1] See Levy's copious list of Hebrew words compounded of "Beel-," *i e* Baal, 1. 248—9

[2] See 2 K 1 2, 3, 6, 16. LXX ἐν τῷ (bis ἐν τῇ) Βάαλ μυῖαν, Aq ἐν Βααλζεβούβ, Sym. παρὰ τοῦ Βεελζεβούλ ("ὁ Ἑβραῖος," βαβαλ ζεβουβ)

[3] Is xvi 8 καταπίνοντες, comp Numb xxi 28 "*the lords of*," κατέπιεν

[4] Mt xxiii. 24, on which see Wetstein and Schottgen quoting *Gittin* 90 *a* on the different courses open to anyone into whose cup a fly falls when he is on the point of drinking It alludes to the relations between a husband and a wife.

THE KINGDOM OF GOD, A FAMILY

as "swallowing flies," and this may easily be explained as a reproach likening Jesus to one who drank wine full of flies, being possessed with an evil spirit, a "*Baal*zebub," or "*lord of* flies," who was also a "*Bala*zebub," or "*swallower of* flies[1]." This may help us to answer the question "How is it that elsewhere the enemies of Christ are described as saying about John the Baptist '*He hath a devil*,' but about Jesus 'Behold, a gluttonous man and a winebibber, a friend of tax-gatherers and sinners'—*as though Jesus had not 'a devil'*[2]?" The answer appears to be, partly, that these words represent the earlier (not the later) language of Christ's enemies, and partly that, even from the beginning, the spirit that provoked them in Jesus was one of so genial, bright, and festive a nature that they could not call it a "devil" in the sense in which they imputed "a devil" to the Baptist. Christ's spirit was intensely humane. It sympathized with flesh and blood, even with sinners. It did not rave, it did not brood. It seemed very different from the spirit of John the Baptist. The Pharisees had to take time to classify and label it[3].

Perhaps their habit of contrasting John the Baptist with Jesus led them to the name they selected. Men likened John to Elijah, and Christ's own followers would admit the likeness.

---

[1] See *Onomast.* p. 45 "*Baalzebub* (2 K. 1), devorans muscam," p 66 "*Beelzebub* (Lk. xi 15), habens muscas, aut vir muscarum In fine ergo nominis B litera legenda est, non L, musca enim zebub vocatur," *ib* 176 Βεελζεβούλ (Mk iii 22), καταπίνων μυίας, 182 Βεελζεβούλ, δαίμων βακηλώσεως, 188 Βεελζεβούλ, δαίμων καπηλεύς ἢ καταπίνων ἐν ἀναπαύσει στόματος (it adds that it is the name of an obscene Priapus)

[2] Mt xi 18—19, Lk vii 33—4

[3] Matthew mentions Beelzebub in Mt x 25 "If they have called the master of the house Beelzebub, how much more [shall they call] them of his household!" This is in the precepts to the Apostles which Mark places long after the Synoptic tradition about Beelzebub The Synoptists represent Jesus as being present at entertainments But John goes further and says that He was present at (ii 1—2) a γάμος where He made wine. In LXX (Gen xxix 22, Esth ii 18, ix 22) γάμος=Heb. (Gesen. 1059 *b*) משתה "[occasion for] drinking."

THE KINGDOM OF GOD, A FAMILY

Now Elijah spent his life in striving against the false god Baal, and almost the last act of it was to pronounce the penalty of death on the king of Samaria (as above described) for consulting the oracle of Baalzebub, "the god of flies." By a play on *Baal*, the word would mean "swallowing flies," that is, condoning impurities, in sinful men and women. By a play on *zebub*, "fly" would become "dung," *zebul*. This would express the Pharisaic loathing for the food that Jesus deigned to eat, along with tax-gatherers and sinners, and with unwashed hands.

There may have been, and probably there were, in the controversies about Baalzebub and exorcism, other allusions that cannot now be recovered. The same Hebrew that in Isaiah means *"Go-forth!"* addressed to an idol, is used by Delitzsch to render *"Go-forth!"* in Mark, addressed by Jesus to an evil spirit; but in Isaiah, the LXX has *"dung,"* and the three Translators have similar renderings[1]. In Aramaic there is the same possibility of a play on the meanings *"go-forth"* and *"excrement"*[2]. It is conceivable that some of the Pharisees, tired of hearing the *"Go-forth!"* successfully pronounced by Jesus the Exorcist, may have varied their abusive appellations by calling Him, at one time "the Lord of *flies,"* Baalzebub, at another "the Lord of *dung,"* Baalzebul.

§ 3. *The "brethren" of Jesus, in John*

John represents the brethren of Jesus as urging Him to go up to Jerusalem at the very time when the Jews were plotting

---

[1] For the frequency and (we may almost say) the systematic character of word-distortion in connection with objects of idolatrous worship, see *Hor Heb* (on Mt xii 24) which begins by quoting R Akiba on Is xxx 22 "Thou shalt cast away [the idol].. thou shalt say to it *Go-forth* (צא)" This should have been rendered by LXX ἔξελθε (as in Mk v 8 ἔξελθε, Del. צא), but LXX has "dung," κόπρον, and simil Aq See also Levy iv 176 *b* where *Pesikta* (Wu. p 144) similarly interprets *"go-forth"* as *"dung"*

[2] See Levy iii 424 *b*. The noun is also used of the unchaste and lewd, comp. Levy *Ch* ii. 122 *a*.

THE KINGDOM OF GOD, A FAMILY

to kill Him[1]. By this paradox he achieves two results. First, he indirectly denies that Christ's brethren—though they "did not believe on him[2]"—said that He was "beside himself." Secondly, he distinguishes the ignorant people in Galilee, who knew nothing about the plots of the rulers in Jerusalem, from an inner circle of the people of Jerusalem, who knew all about them. When Jesus said in Jerusalem, "Why seek ye to kill me?" the *"multitude"* (that is, of the pilgrims) answered, "Thou hast a devil; who seeketh to kill thee[3]?" But, soon afterwards, "some therefore of *them of Jerusalem* said, Is not this he whom they seek to kill?....Can it be that the rulers indeed know that this is the Christ[4]?"

Thus the Fourth Gospel helps us to perceive the force of the Marcan tradition, in the passage under discussion, "the scribes that came down from Jerusalem." It is omitted by Matthew and Luke[5]. But it explains the nature of the controversy and the shape given to it by Christ's enemies. The name "Baalzebub" was Biblical, and the plays on it were such as would come from scribes, not from "the people of the land."

§ 4. *"A devil,"* in John

The word "demon" or "devil[6]," in John, is never used except in three passages. In these, it is applied to Jesus Himself. One has been quoted above—"Thou hast a devil," uttered by "the multitude," who are ignorant of the plots against Jesus, and who resent the words "Why seek ye to kill me?" In the second, "the Jews" are the speakers, "Say we

---

[1] Jn vii 1—3 "The Jews sought to kill him...His brethren, therefore, said unto him, Depart hence and go into Judaea."
[2] Jn vii 5.   [3] Jn vii 19—20   [4] Jn vii 25—6
[5] Mk iii 22, Mt xii 24 "the Pharisees," Lk xi 15 "some of them," *i.e.* of the multitudes. So in Mk vii 1, Mt xv 1 (Lk om the whole) "scribes" coming "from Jerusalem" originate a controversy about "unwashen hands."
[6] "Demon" or "devil," *i.e.* δαιμόνιον (not διάβολος, which occurs in Jn vi 70 (without the article) and viii 44, xiii 2 (τοῦ διαβόλου)).

THE KINGDOM OF GOD, A FAMILY

not well that thou art a Samaritan and hast a devil?" and they repeat the charge in answer to His denial[1]. This, too, follows a saying of Jesus "Ye seek to kill me[2]" In the third, "there arose a division again among the Jews because of these words," *i e* because of His parable about the Good Shepherd ("I lay down my life for the sheep; and other sheep I have, which are not of this fold...and they shall become one flock, one shepherd"), "and many of them said, He hath a devil and is mad, why hear ye him? Others said, These are not the sayings of one possessed with a devil. Can a devil open the eyes of the blind[3]?"

In all three instances the charge of "having a devil" is preceded by some words of Jesus implying predictions either of His death, or of His laying down life. In these, the sacrifice of the Cross appears to be indicated in two aspects, first, as a murder ("seek to kill me," twice repeated), then, as an act of devotion in "the good shepherd" contending against "the wolf" ("I lay down my life"). The Gospel appears to reserve this charge of "having a devil" mostly for occasions where Jesus is regarded by the Jews as a lunatic or fanatic, with exaggerated apprehensions of danger or imaginations of self-conceit.

But something more seems to be intended in the second instance, "Say we not well that *thou art a Samaritan* and hast a devil[4]?" For here there is a suggestion of something very different from fanaticism—of anti-patriotic feeling of a special kind, not of being a Herodian, or a Greek, but of being "*a Samaritan.*" Possibly the Jews are regarded as inferring that, because Jesus made war against the method of conducting the

---

[1] Jn viii 48—52 [2] Jn viii 37, 40
[3] Jn x 15, 16, 19—21
[4] Jn viii. 48 ἀπεκρίθησαν οἱ Ἰουδαῖοι. Οὐ καλῶς λέγομεν ἡμεῖς, *i e* "Do we not well say among ourselves, we (emph) [Jews in Jerusalem]...?" Origen rightly observes, "It is likely...that they often used to say this to one another."

THE KINGDOM OF GOD, A FAMILY

sacrifices in the Temple on mount Moriah, He therefore favoured the worship in the Temple on mount Gerizim.

If that was the case, the Fourth Gospel meets it in the Dialogue with the woman of Samaria, where Jesus teaches that the time is at hand when neither on mount Moriah nor on mount Gerizim will God be worshipped as of old, but in every place where people worship "in spirit and in truth[1]." Neither here nor anywhere could this Gospel find room for an obscene name like Beelzebub or Beelzebul; but there is perhaps a distant allusion in the same Dialogue to the charges of (1) "gluttony" and (2) "wine-bibbing" and (3) friendship with "tax-gatherers and sinners." For, first, Jesus is offered food yet does not eat; secondly, He says "Give me to drink" but is recorded, not as drinking, but as proclaiming and proving His power to give "living water"; and thirdly, though the disciples "marvel" that He "speaks with a woman"—apparently because it was a little beneath their conceptions of the dignity of their Teacher—yet the implied result is that she feels convicted of sin ("he told me all that ever I did") and the expressed result is that "many of the Samaritans believed on him because of the word of the woman[2]."

The ancient commentary on Mark attributed to Jerome allegorizes the peculiar Marcan tradition—that Jesus "came to a house"—and says that His disciples "thought that He was being changed to madness (in furorem verteretur) because the scribes that had come from Jerusalem said, He hath Beelzebub." "The house," it says, "is the primitive Church. As the heavens are exalted above the earth, so are God's ways above our ways.... Hence our Lord is changed to madness [in the eyes of His disciples] when He says, Unless ye shall eat the flesh of the Son of man and drink His blood ye shall not have

---

[1] Jn iv 20 foll.

[2] Jn iv. 7—39   In iv 40 foll it is implied that this belief was rudimentary and that the Samaritans soon passed beyond it   But still it was a beginning

THE KINGDOM OF GOD, A FAMILY

life in yourselves[1]" The Fourth Gospel nowhere connects Christ's doctrine of the necessity of this "eating" and "drinking" with the charge of madness; but this commentary, connecting the two, may induce us to ask ourselves "Is it not probable that when the Fourth Evangelist wrote down these words about the mystical eating and drinking of Christ's body and blood, he had in view the accusation brought against Him of being a *'glutton'* and a *'winebibber'?*" If so, there is a vein of irony underlying the whole of the Johannine account of the Jewish reception of Christ's mystery, as though the Evangelist said to himself, "Just at the moment when the Lord Jesus rose to the highest point of the revelation of the Father through the pure sacrifice of the Son, who was to give His flesh for others to eat, and His blood for others to drink, the Jews saw nothing in the Son except a human being possessed with a demon of gluttony, intoxication, and impurity"

§ 5. *Mark's first mention of "parables"*

Mark's first mention of parables demands attention, apart from any importance here attached to the word, for the simple reason that Matthew and Luke agree in omitting it[2], so that it raises the question of Johannine intervention. We cannot of course expect that John would intervene as to the application of the word to exorcisms, for John never mentions exorcisms; but does he, directly or indirectly, intervene as to the general meaning of the word "parable" and as to the subject of Christ's teaching "in parables," a phrase common in Mark and Matthew later on and here used by Mark for the first time?

---

[1] Pseudo-Jerome on Mk iii 23 foll., quoting Jn vi 53.
[2]

Mk iii 23	Mt xii 25	Lk xi 17
καὶ προσκαλεσάμενος αὐτοὺς ἐν παραβολαῖς ἔλεγεν αὐτοῖς .	εἰδὼς δὲ τὰς ἐνθυμήσεις αὐτῶν εἶπεν αὐτοῖς....	αὐτὸς δὲ εἰδὼς αὐτῶν τὰ διανοήματα εἶπεν αὐτοῖς .

THE KINGDOM OF GOD, A FAMILY

It should be noted that Luke mentions "parable" at a very early stage in his Gospel, and in Christ's own words—His first words uttered publicly—"Doubtless, ye will say unto me *this parable*, 'Physician, heal thyself[1].'" There it means simply "*proverb*." Again, we have seen above that Luke separates the homely warning against "patching" from what precedes by inserting "He spake a *parable* also unto them[2]," where Mark and Matthew omit the insertion, and make the discourse continuous. Matthew's course is quite different. He introduces what may be called "a parable-epoch" in Christ's life, using the word no less than twelve times in one chapter, introducing it with the words "He spake many things to them in *parables*," and including a quotation from the Psalms "I will open my mouth in *parables*, I will utter things hidden from the foundation of the world[3]." In the Hebrew, "parable" is parallel to "dark-sayings," thus. "I will open my mouth in a *parable*, I will utter *dark-sayings* of old[4]"

Obviously "parable," when thus used, is different from "parable" meaning a mere proverb like "Physician, heal thyself." And the questions now before us are, "In what precise sense did Mark use the phrase 'in parables,' thus brought suddenly before us concerning the 'casting out' of Satan by Satan? And why do the parallel Matthew and Luke, instead of the Marcan clause, have 'knowing their thoughts (*or*, purposes)?'"

An answer to both questions is suggested by the parallelism in Scripture between "*parables*" and "*dark-sayings*." It is antecedently probable that Mark, who does not quote prophecy as Matthew quotes it[5], might nevertheless, in his first mention of Christ's parables or "dark-sayings," allude to the Psalmist's utterance (which Matthew quotes). In that case Mark might

---

[1] Lk iv 23
[2] See Mk ii. 21, and parallels, above, p 336, comp p 307.
[3] Mt xiii. 3, 35.   [4] Ps lxxviii. 2 (R V)
[5] See *Beginning* p 207.

have before him a tradition in which "dark-sayings" was substituted for "parable" Now the Hebrew for "dark-saying" (frequent in Aramaic also) is said perhaps to mean, in Daniel, "*double-dealing*[1]," and we have seen that Matthew paraphrases it, in the Psalms, as "*things hidden* (or *secret*)." It might therefore be wrongly taken by Matthew and Luke here as referring to the "*secret-thoughts*" *of the scribes*[2]. If that is so, Mark's text is verbally correct in recording that here for the first time the doctrine of Jesus was described by the old tradition as being "in dark-sayings"—a term erroneously taken by Matthew and Luke as referring to the thoughts of Christ's enemies

From the verbal question we pass to the historical or theological one, "In what sense were these and other 'parables' of Jesus 'dark-sayings'?" No answer appears to be satisfactory if it implies that all the parables of Christ were "dark-sayings" to their hearers merely because their hearers took them literally Some of them could not have been taken literally. The question is complicated by the fact that the Hebrew word meaning "parable" also means "proverb." And the existence of some complication is indicated by the fact that the Fourth Gospel never uses "parable" but does use "proverb." This Johannine use of "proverb" must receive our attention before we come to a conclusion about the Marcan use of "parable."

---

[1] See Gesen 295 *b* quoting Dan viii 23 "understanding *dark-sentences*" ("skilled in *double-dealing* (Bev)")

[2] As to the additional parallelism between Mk προσκαλεσάμενος and Mt -Lk εἰδώς, the explanation suggested in *Corrections* 365 is not satisfactory It is perhaps more probable that the simple preposition "in" ("*in* dark-sayings he said to them") was paraphrased as "seeing" because "dark-sayings" was taken as meaning "[their] dark-thoughts"

THE KINGDOM OF GOD, A FAMILY

§ 6. *John's mention of "proverbs"*

John mentions "*proverb*," the Greek *paroimiā*, in two passages of his Gospel, given below[1]. In the second, the context seems to require us to suppose that "proverb" denotes obscurity But if that, and nothing else, had been his meaning, he could have used "enigma," the word used by Paul when he says "For now we see by means of a mirror, in *enigma*, but then [we shall see] face to face[2]" Etymologically *paroimiā* is alleged to mean a "roadside-saying[3]." The brevity natural in the talk of those who meet one another on the road, would be increased when a specimen of the talk was caught up and passed from mouth to mouth. Frequent usage would rub down a proverb as it rubs down a coin. Aristotle, who calls proverbs "transferences from one form to another," shews how transference and brevity might combine to produce obscurity[4] Yet for the most part they are not obscure but clear to everybody, being the condensed wisdom (or reputed wisdom)[5] of antiquity handed down in a form commending itself to the Greek "man by the way," whom we now call "the man in the street" There

---

[1] Jn x 6 "This *proverb* (παροιμίαν) spake Jesus unto them," preceded by (*ib* 5) "they [*i e* the sheep] know not the voice of strangers", xvi 25 "These things have I spoken unto you in *proverbs* (παροιμίαις) the hour cometh when I shall no more speak unto you in *proverbs* but shall tell you plainly of the Father" To His following words the disciples reply (*ib* 29) "Now speakest thou plainly and speakest no *proverb*"

[2] 1 Cor xiii 12.

[3] See Steph *Thes* and Hesychius No other explanation is so probable

[4] Aristot *Rhet* iii 11 quoting a proverb about "Hares to Carpathus," very much like "Rabbits [imported] to Australia" But here it is the local colour rather than the brevity that obscures Very few of Aristotle's numerous proverbs are obscure They are almost all short, except where a verse is quoted whole

[5] See Aristot *Rhet* i 15 Among the cynical proverbs are "Kill the son if you kill the father" Contrast the proverb about fathers and sons in Ezek xviii 2 "*proverb*," LXX παραβολή, Aq. παροιμία

THE KINGDOM OF GOD, A FAMILY

is no alleged instance in Greek literature where "proverb," or *paroimiā*, is anything but a short saying—apart from LXX, which we must now consider.

The LXX does not use the word *paroimiā*—not even in such expressions as "it became a proverb" and "the proverb of the ancients[1]"—until the title and the first verse of Solomon's Proverbs. Even here the LXX is not consistent in its context. For whereas the Hebrew says "The *proverbs* of Solomon... understand a *proverb*," the LXX has "The *proverbs* of Solomon ...understand a *parable*[2]." An Appendix to Proverbs is introduced thus in Hebrew, "These also are *proverbs* of Solomon." Here LXX has "*instructions* of Solomon," but some MSS "*proverbs*" (and so apparently Symmachus) whereas Aquila and Theodotion have "*parables*[3]." These are the only instances of "proverb" in LXX except in Ben Sira[4]. We may say therefore, with hardly any exaggeration, that *paroimiā* in canonical LXX is confined to titular or technical mentions of the Proverbs of Solomon, which, being very short, might naturally be entitled, in Greek, proverbs rather than parables. So far as they go, these facts do not give any support to the view that the Fourth Evangelist would be induced by LXX to use the word *paroimiā* otherwise than in its regular sense, that is, "proverb." Nor is any such evidence forthcoming from the renderings of the other translators[5]

---

[1] 1 S x 12, xxiv 13
[2] Prov 1 1—6 παροιμίαι Σαλωμῶντος νοήσει τε παραβολήν. The title, in LXX, is "Proverbs" (not "Parables")
[3] Prov xxv 1 (on which see Field *ad loc* and *Auct* p 24)
[4] Sir vi 35, viii 8, xviii 29, xxxix 3, xlvii 17 *Oxf Conc* gives the Heb of two of these as *mâshâl*, "parable," and the Heb. of one as (see above, p 436) "dark-saying"
[5] In two or three instances παροιμία is used by Symmachus or Aquila to indicate a proverb of the ancients or to distinguish one class of sayings from another, e g Ezek xviii 2 LXX παραβολή, Aq. παροιμία ("the fathers have eaten sour grapes and the children's teeth are set on edge") Παροιμία does not occur in the Indices to

THE KINGDOM OF GOD, A FAMILY

Jerome calls attention to the difference between "parables" and "proverbs." He suggests that "parable," as a rule, implies obscurity, whereas "proverb" implies past use and present retention. But he also adds, less safely, that "proverbs" are "for the most part" so obscure that they might be called by the same name as "parables[1]." For this startling statement he alleges no proof except one of the two passages we are investigating, "These things have I spoken to you in *proverbs*." But we need a great deal of proof. It is true that here and there a proverb in the Old Testament may be found of a nature to be obscure to those who do not know its circumstances, such as "Is Saul also among the prophets?" But who can say that Jesus, in the Fourth Gospel or in the Three, dealt in such "proverbs" as these? They are non-existent in the Gospels. Many of Christ's Johannine *sayings* are obscure, as for example, about His being "lifted up" or "glorified," or about His "flesh" and "blood" as being "given" for men· but can these be called "*proverbs*"? It must be admitted, however, that Origen—though he does not go so far as to assert with Jerome that proverbs are "mostly" obscure—is led, by the combined influence of the title of Solomon's Proverbs and the Johannine saying about "speaking in *proverbs*," to infer that, in the latter, "*proverbs*" means "*enigmas*[2]"

Epictet and Marc Ant , nor in Goodspeed except Athenag xxxiv 1 and Melito (Euseb iv 26 14) quoting the title of Proverbs

[1] See Jerome on Prov 1 1 "Notandum autem quod in vulgata editione pro parabolis, quae Hebraice משלים vocantur, παροιμίαι, id est proverbia dicuntur Sed nec ipsum nomen abhorret a vero Quae enim parabolae recte nuncupantur, quia occulta sunt, possunt non incongrue etiam proverbia vocari quia talia sunt quae merito saepissime ore colloquentium versari ac memoria debeant retineri Nam et proverbia plerumque tam obscure dicuntur, ut merito eadem possint etiam parabolarum nomine notari, Domino attestante, qui ait Haec in proverbiis locutus sum vobis Venit hora cum jam non in proverbiis loquar vobis, sed palam de Patre annunciabo vobis "

[2] See *Cels* iv. 87 quoting Prov xxx 24—8 about the ants, the conies etc , on which Origen remarks "But I do not make use of

THE KINGDOM OF GOD, A FAMILY

At this stage of our investigation we may be tempted to stop and say, "It is useless to search further, for it is certain that in this last Johannine passage "proverb" implies doctrine misunderstood; and it is waste of time to hunt for reasons why John used *paroimiā* in this (admittedly) new sense, and rejected the Synoptic '*parable*' which he might have used in its (admittedly) old sense to express exactly the same thing." This temptation will be resisted by those who believe that the Evangelist was incapable of pedantry, and who are convinced that he was influenced, to a much greater extent than is commonly supposed, by mystical considerations, such as would connect themselves with all books attributed to Solomon and especially to his Proverbs and his Song

Looking at the matter thus, we shall perceive that there would be a mystical fitness in regarding Christ's sayings on earth as "proverbs." As the first son of David uttered "proverbs," so did the second, the ideal Son of David. It is of the essence of a proverb that it should be old Accordingly the first Johannine use of the word is in a passage where Jesus describes, at some length, the relation between the Shepherd and the Sheep, stating one of the oldest and most familiar

---

these sayings as if they were clear (ὡς σαφέσι, but Philoc om ὡς), but, in accordance with the title—for the book [containing them] is entitled *Proverbs*—I investigate these sayings as *enigmas* (αἰνίγματα) For it is the custom for these men (?) (τοῖς ἀνδράσι τούτοις,? *for the [men] learned [in these things]* ἴδρισι) to divide into many classes those expressions that indicate one meaning at first sight but convey another meaning on reflection—of which [classes they declare] one to be 'proverbs' (ὧν ἐν εἶναι τὰς παροιμίας, Philoc ins ἐν) Wherefore also in our Gospels the Saviour is recorded to have said, (Jn xvi. 25) 'These things have I spoken to you in *proverbs*..." Comp Origen *Prolog Cant* Lomm xiv. 309 where he again quotes Jn xvi 25 prefixing the remark "*Proverbia* attitulavit libellum suum, quod utique nomen significat aliud quidem palam dici, aliud vero intrinsecus indicari Hoc enim et *communis usus proverbiorum docet*, et Joannes (xvi 25). ." This does not say that proverbs are mostly "obscure" It says merely that their common meaning is *not literal*

THE KINGDOM OF GOD, A FAMILY

truths. We may sum it up as saying "The sheep follow only their shepherd." Yet after this it is added "This *proverb* spake Jesus unto them; but they understood not what things they were which he spake unto them[1]"

The meaning appears to be this Jesus said to His countrymen, in effect, "The sheep of Israel, the true flock, will follow none but the Shepherd of Israel " But the Jews did not know even the meaning of the terms They did not know the nature of the true "shepherd," they did not know the nature of the true "sheep." The words, to them, were nothing but a threadbare "proverb" that conveyed no appeal to their hearts Hence Jesus proceeds to explain and particularise the proverb by saying "*I* am the good shepherd" and "*I* lay down my life for the sheep" But with what result? They did not know Him. The "*I*," therefore, conveyed no new knowledge to their minds The "*proverb*" remained where it was—old, trite, and unprofitable as yet to most, waiting for the living Spirit, the Power from heaven that should personify the "proverb," or replace it by a Person speaking in their hearts[2].

Similarly, in the second Johannine passage, Jesus had just spoken a general truth or "proverb" about "a woman in travail having sorrow" as the necessary condition for "the joy that a human being is born into the world," and He refers to it and to similar sayings as proverbs thus· "These things have I spoken unto you in *proverbs*[3]" The disciples imply that, even if this

---

[1] Jn x. 6 οὐκ ἔγνωσαν τίνα ἦν ἃ ἐλάλει αὐτοῖς Comp 1 Tim 1 7 μὴ νοοῦντες μήτε ἃ λέγουσιν μήτε περὶ τίνων διαβεβαιοῦνται The subject was altogether out of their range of vision

[2] Rashi's commentary on the first verse of Proverbs (*lit* "likenesses" or "comparisons," *mishle* from *mâshal* "liken" or "compare") is "Omnia illius verba sunt similitudines et parabolae Lex Divina comparatur mulieri bonae (sive honestae), cultus autem idolatricus feminae meretrici" That seems to suggest that all the "proverbs" or "likenesses" are based on the likeness of the Law to Wisdom, the Good Woman, the Spirit of God, the Mother of man

[3] Jn xvi 21—5

had been once the case; it is not so now, "Lo, now speakest thou plainly and speakest no proverb." That is to say, "We understand it all. The 'travail' means that we are to go through a sore trial before we hail thee as Messiah on thy throne. We are prepared for such 'travail.' We shall be faithful to thee." They speak honestly, but in fact they know nothing about what they speak about. "Messiah," "throne," "travail," "human being born into the world"—all these things, in their spiritual significance, are out of their sight, up above as it were, in a region of a higher dimension. There they must remain, out of the view of the disciples, till the Spirit of their Lord, having gone up for them to the Father in heaven, shall come down again to take up its abode in their hearts, and to make them capable of seeing what Christ sees, because they can think what Christ thinks, being able to say, with Paul, "We have the mind of Christ[1]."

§ 7. "*Parable*" *implies comparison*

From what has been said in the last section we infer that John preferred to describe as proverbs, rather than as parables, Christ's teaching about the Kingdom of God, because the former term more distinctly implied old, rudimentary, and general truths, whereas the latter implied comparisons. Possibly John may have thought that, at the period when he was writing, enough and more than enough had been said about "comparisons." The comparisons implied in the old parables dealt with *things*, or with *persons regarded as mere agents*, whereas John preferred for the most part to write of *persons regarded as individuals*[2]. Isaiah represents God as saying to the idolatrous world "To whom will ye liken me...and *compare* me that we

---

[1] 1 Cor. ii. 16.
[2] The Johannine parable, or proverb, of the Good Shepherd, is an exception.

THE KINGDOM OF GOD, A FAMILY

may be like[1]?" John writes sometimes about human persons through whom he dramatically expressed divine truths, but sometimes about divine Persons, about the incomparable God, the Father, the Son, and the Holy Spirit.

In the Synoptic Gospels, the Kingdom of God is "compared" to the sowing of a corn-field, to a net, to leaven, to a mustard-seed, and to other things on earth corresponding to the things of the Kingdom in heaven. Mark has not hitherto even mentioned the Kingdom of God except in Christ's first public utterance "The kingdom of God hath drawn near[2]." Nor has this kingdom been defined by Mark except indirectly, by signs of healing and by forgiveness of sins. Here, therefore, when illustrating the kingdom that is invisible by comparing its conditions with those of visible kingdoms, the word "comparison," or "parable," comes appropriately. Perhaps Matthew thought it better not to introduce the word for the first time here, because Jesus seemed to him to be speaking mainly in a negative or hypothetical way, of a kingdom "divided against itself" or regarded as the kingdom of Satan There was no formal and positive comparison, such as we find in the Parable of the Sower, and in the other Parables, which Matthew groups together after his manner[3].

But if we are to do justice to Mark's mention of "parables" here, we must pay attention to his arrangement of Christ's utterances. For Mark—differing from Matthew and much more from Luke—places very soon after this discussion a definition

---

[1] Is xlvi 5 The only instance of מָשָׁל meaning "likeness" is (Gesen 605 b) Job xli 33 (25) "upon earth there is not *his likeness*," *i e* anything that is like God and can be compared with Him, and there Targ and Rashi have "his dominion" (meaning "any one that has dominion over him").

[2] Mk i 15

[3] The first instance of "parable" in Matthew is xiii 3 "He spake to them many things in *parables*," and one parable follows another up to *ib* 53 "And it came to pass when Jesus had finished these *parables* .."

THE KINGDOM OF GOD, A FAMILY

of the Family of God[1]. If Mark intends the discussion to lead up to the definition, then the phrase "in parables" is well adapted to indicate that Jesus is beginning to bring before His hearers the parallelism between the Kingdom of God in heaven and a Family of God on earth, in order to shew them, by "parables," what the Gospel implies.

§ 8. *"The strong [one]*[2]*"*

From "Satan" Mark passes to "the strong [one]," whom Irenaeus and Jerome regard as here representing Satan. In view of that early interpretation, "mighty [one]" may be regarded—at least temporarily and hypothetically—as likely to have been the original meaning. The distinction is important. Aquila uses "strong one," "*El*," to denote God, but "mighty [one]," "*gibbôr*," in a neutral sense, capable of being applied either to a hero or to a tyrant. In its first Biblical instance, the Hebrew "mighty one" means what LXX and the Syriac call "giants"; and, though the good sense is more frequent, it is applied in the Psalms to a man mighty for evil: "*Why boastest thou thyself in mischief, O mighty man*[3]*?*"

---

[1] Mk iii. 35 "Whosoever.. is my brother, and sister, and mother" follows, at a short interval, this discussion about the kingdom (iii 24—30) In Matthew, xii 50 "Whosoever. ." follows xii 25—32 (the discussion about the kingdom) at a longer interval Matthew xii 33 foll interposes discourses on "the tree and its fruits," "the sign of Jonah," and "the unclean spirit succeeded by seven unclean spirits." Luke places the definition of the family (viii. 21) *before* this discussion (xi. 17—22).

[2] The Greek word, ἰσχυρός, is twice rendered by A V "mighty" (Rev x 1, xviii 21) when applied to an angel "Strong" is a more accurate rendering. "Mighty" corresponds better to δυνατός. But the A V. rendering may usefully remind us that Mark's Hebrew or Aramaic original, if one existed, may have meant "mighty," not "strong"

[3] See Gesen 150 *a*, and Gen. vi. 4 "mighty [men]" LXX οἱ γίγαντες, Aq. οἱ δυνατοί, Sym. οἱ βίαιοι On Ps lii. 1, the Midrash represents David as expostulating with Doeg, "*the mighty man,*" and telling him what the true "*might*" is: "What sort of *might* is this

THE KINGDOM OF GOD, A FAMILY

Gibbôr is rendered by the LXX mostly "strong," but frequently "mighty" or "giant," and occasionally "combatant" or "warrior[1]."

It will be seen below that although the Synoptists agree in using the term "strong [one]," it is regarded in a more warlike aspect by Luke than by Mark and Matthew[2]. Luke also makes

---

when a man sees his neighbour at the edge of a pit and pushes him in?....Is it not a more real *might* to hold out your hand to your neighbour and prevent him from falling in?" The Aramaic and Syriac "giant" (Levy *Ch* i 148 *a*) is a form of the Heb. "mighty-man," *gibbôr* (strengthened by inserting *n*) In Ps lii 1, LXX has ὁ δυνατός, and Targ. "potens," but Syr. "gigas"

[1] Trommius gives *gibbôr* as γίγας (15), δυνατός (80), ἰσχυρός or ἰσχυρότερος (20), μαχητής (16), πολεμιστής (2).

Comp Is xlix 24 "Shall there be taken from the *mighty-one* (*gibbôr*) that-which-he-hath-taken, and shall the captivity [of the] righteous-one" [*i e* according to Rashi, Jacob] "be delivered?" Ibn Ezra apparently takes "the captivity [of the] righteous one" as an appositional genitive, "the captivity [consisting] of the righteous one," that is, "the righteous captive" The Targum (Walton, "Targum aliud") says "Is it possible that he should be delivered from the impious Esau?"—making Esau the *gibbôr*

The LXX μὴ λήμψεταί τις παρὰ γίγαντος σκῦλα.., renders *gibbôr* by γίγας, "Shall a man take from a giant spoils?" Sym renders *gibbôr* by δυνατός See Field on Is xlix 24—5 for other variations in the Greek translations The Hebrew suggests the thought of Israel, taken captive by one who is "mighty," and delivered by one who is Mightier But the Mightier is not mentioned by that title Luke (it will be seen) supplies the title Compare, or contrast, *Solomon's Psalms* v. 4 οὐ γὰρ λήψεται σκῦλα ἄνθρωπος παρὰ ἀνδρὸς δυνατοῦ, *i e* "A man will not [be able to] take spoils from *a mighty warrior* [*such as God is*], [but he must resort to prayer]"

[2]
Mk iii 27 (R.V)	Mt xii 27—30 (R V)	Lk. xi 19—23 (R V)
(27) But no one can enter into the house of the strong [man] and spoil (διαρπάσαι) his goods, except he first bind the strong [man], and then he will spoil (διαρπάσει) his house	(27) And if I by (*or*, in) Beelzebub cast out devils, by (*or*, in) whom do your sons cast them out? therefore shall they be your judges. (28) But if I by (*or*, in) the Spirit of God cast out devils,	(19) And if I by (*or*, in) Beelzebub cast out devils, by (*or*, in) whom do your sons cast them out? therefore shall they be your judges (20) But if I by the finger of God cast out devils, then

446 (Mark iii 20—35)

THE KINGDOM OF GOD, A FAMILY

two warriors instead of one He appears to be trying to meet a difficulty arising from Mark. For Mark leaves us in doubt as to who it is that "spoils" the goods of the mighty man The verb here rendered "spoil"—which must be distinguished from the Lucan noun "spoil"—is extremely rare in early Christian literature; but Ignatius uses it, and apparently with allusion to this Mark-Matthew tradition, when he writes to the Romans "The prince of this world desires to *spoil* me[1]" On the other hand, Irenaeus twice interprets the "*spoiler*" as being the Lord, and "the strong [one]" as being Satan[2] He recognises a difficulty implied in calling Satan "*the strong [one]*"— because "the" implies pre-eminence in strength, and, properly speaking, one should call God alone "*the strong [one]*"—and he

Mk iii 27 (R V) (*contd*)	Mt xii 27—30 (R V) (*contd*)	Lk xi 19—23 (R V) (*contd*)
	then is the kingdom of God come upon you	is the kingdom of God come upon you
	(29) Or how can one enter into the house of the strong [man], and spoil (ἁρπάσαι) his goods, except he first bind the strong [man] ? And then he will spoil (διαρπάσει) his house.	(21) When the strong [man] fully armed guardeth his own court, his goods are in peace,
		(22) But when a stronger than he shall come upon him and overcome him, he taketh from him his whole armour wherein he trusteth, and divideth his spoils (σκῦλα).
	(30) He that is not with me is against me, and he that gathereth not with me scattereth	(23) He that is not with me is against me, and he that gathereth not with me scattereth

[1] Ign *Rom* § 7 ὁ ἄρχων τοῦ αἰῶνος τούτου διαρπάσαι με βούλεται. The word διαρπάζω occurs but thrice in the early Christian writers, (1) here, (2) Euseb *H. E* iv 26 5 (quoting Melito) of "plunderers" (as distinct from extortioners), (3) Hermas, *Sim* ix 26 2 of those who "plunder" the livelihood of widows and orphans The Lucan noun "spoil," σκῦλον, occurs only here in N T
[2] Iren. iii 8. 2, v 21 2—3

THE KINGDOM OF GOD, A FAMILY

probably felt that the difficulty would be a very great one for Greeks, who knew that *El*, "God," meant "the strong one"; but he explains that Satan is here called "the strong one," not as being absolutely strong, but as being strong in comparison with men, whereas the Lord is the strong one "for all purposes and truly"—"the absolutely strong one" His explanation is good and sound, and it helps us to see how Luke, feeling that such an explanation was needed—and feeling that Mark implied "a stronger one" in the one who can bind "the strong one"—introduced "the absolutely strong [one]" as *a second "strong [one]," whom he called "stronger" than the first*

Moreover Irenaeus partially explains the Marcan character of "Spoiler" or "Despoiler" applied to the Lord, saying "We were *the vessels (vasa) and the house* of this [strong man]...for he put us to whatsoever use he pleased, and the unclean spirit dwelt within us" He adds that Satan was "strong against those human beings who were his utensils (adversus eos qui *in usu ejus* erant homines)." Thus he explains the Mark-Matthew "instruments" or "utensils," or "vessels," which our Version renders "goods," but which Luke paraphrases as "panoply." Paul is said to be a chosen "utensil" or "vessel," and Paul himself speaks of others as "utensils" or "vessels of wrath," or "vessels of mercy[1]," so that the explanation of the term given by Irenaeus is a justifiable one If Mark had written "utensils of war," a phrase twice occurring in O T where "utensils" (R.V. "weapons") is rendered by LXX "armour[2]," Luke's paraphrase would have been justified; but, as it is, "utensils" is a safer rendering And this is implied by Irenaeus in the words "vasa" and "in usu[3]."

Still there remains a difficulty in the peculiar Marcan verb here rendered "spoil," but more strictly meaning

---

[1] Acts ix 15, Rom ix 22, 23
[2] Jerem xxi. 4, Ezek. xxxii. 27, LXX ὅπλα
[3] Similarly Jerome (on Mt xii 29) "*vasa* ejus nos quondam fuimus"

THE KINGDOM OF GOD, A FAMILY

"pillage," in its usual modern (not its ancient) sense—the act of an army or a crowd, not of a single person.

The Greek word is a compound of "snatch" capable of meaning "snatch-apart," "snatch and separate[1]" The Thesaurus gives but few instances of it, the LXX Concordance a great number; but in neither is there any instance where it is used of the act of a single person[2] Mark twice describes the Assailant as "pillaging"; and as "pillaging," first the "utensils" and then the "house" Matthew describes him first as "snatching[3]" (without any notion of separation) applied to "the utensils," and then as "pillaging" applied to the "house." Luke drops the notion of "pillaging," but like Matthew (as distinct from Mark) he describes the Assailant (whom he calls "the stronger [one]") as doing two actions, namely, first, "taking away the panoply" of "the strong man," secondly, "distributing his spoils[4]." In "distributing," Luke retains a form of the tradition about "pillaging[5]."

Matthew's substitution of "snatch" for "pillage" in the first part of the sentence suggests an intention, not consistently carried out, to interpret thus "How can anyone go into the

---

[1] Διαρπάζω occurs in LXX about 38 times

[2] Plato 807 B describes animals *torn in pieces* "*by another animal*" This does not constitute an exception Aristotle uses the word twice, but the agents are plural (Bonitz)

[3] Ἁρπάζω, in N T is used of "snatching" for the purpose of rescuing in Acts xxiii 10 "from the midst of them," Jude 23 "from the fire"

[4]
Mk iii. 27	Mt xii 29	Lk xi 21—2
ἀλλ' οὐ δύναται οὐδεὶς εἰς τὴν οἰκίαν τοῦ ἰσχυροῦ εἰσελθὼν τὰ σκεύη αὐτοῦ διαρπάσαι ἐὰν μὴ πρῶτον τὸν ἰσχυρὸν δήσῃ, καὶ τότε τὴν οἰκίαν αὐτοῦ διαρπάσει	ἢ πῶς δύναταί τις εἰσελθεῖν εἰς τὴν οἰκίαν τοῦ ἰσχυροῦ καὶ τὰ σκεύη αὐτοῦ ἁρπάσαι, ἐὰν μὴ πρῶτον δήσῃ τὸν ἰσχυρόν, καὶ τότε τὴν οἰκίαν αὐτοῦ διαρπάσει	ὅταν ὁ ἰσχυρὸς καθωπλισμένος φυλάσσῃ τὴν ἑαυτοῦ αὐλήν, ἐν εἰρήνῃ ἐστὶν τὰ ὑπάρχοντα αὐτοῦ. ἐπὰν δὲ ἰσχυρότερος αὐτοῦ ἐπελθὼν νικήσῃ αὐτόν, τὴν πανοπλίαν αὐτοῦ αἴρει ἐφ' ᾗ ἐπεποίθει, καὶ τὰ σκῦλα αὐτοῦ διαδίδωσιν

[5] Comp Is liii. 12 (LXX) τῶν ἰσχυρῶν μεριεῖ σκῦλα (Aq. λάφυρα) on which see *Son* 3272 a.

THE KINGDOM OF GOD, A FAMILY

house of the mighty [one, the mighty robber and oppressor like Nimrod, the mighty hunter of the souls of men][1] and *snatch* [*out*] *his* [*own*] *property*, except first he bind the mighty [one]?" This would accord with a Jewish tradition that the spies sent by Joshua spoke impiously about Jehovah, saying "We are not able to go up against the people of Canaan, for '*they are stronger than He*'"—as if they said, "*Not even the Lord of the House* [i.e. *God*] *is able to bring forth His goods* (lit. *vessels*) *from thence*[2]." In opposition to this saying, Matthew may regard the Assailant as shewing His power to "bring out His goods from the house," and then as "pillaging" or "breaking up" the house itself, so that it may no more be used as a storehouse for stolen things, that is to say, as a prison-house of human souls stolen for a time from the service of their Creator to be the slaves of Satan.

The evidence, so far, points to the conclusion that Mark is right and Luke wrong in interpreting an original Hebrew "vessels." But "spoil" or "pillage" does not seem quite appropriate. We could see its appropriateness better if we could find some ancient Biblical tradition where "spoil" is used in a good sense,—and this, on some very epoch-making occasion where the metaphor of rescue from a prison is implied; so that the Tyrant of the prison, who has been "despoiling" others, is now himself "despoiled." Such an occasion would be the liberation of Israel from their prison-house, Egypt, under the bondage of "the strong [one]," Pharaoh. And here we find the word "spoil" used in two passages, quaint indeed but evidently intended to suggest the fulfilment of a

---

[1] See above, pp 58—9, and *Son* 3512 *a*

[2] See *Sota* 35 *a* and *Menach.* 53 *b* quoting Numb xiii 31 "They are stronger than *we*," where the Hebrew "we" is read as if it were "HE." See Wagenseil's *Sota* p 732, saying that some take *goods* as meaning *armour*, "Sed nobis placuit generaliori sensu exponere, et uti vetus interpres Hebraeus Matthaei Tilianus, per לבוז את כליו quod Capite xii 29 apud Evangelistam est, τὰ σκεύη αὐτοῦ διαρπάσαι, expressisse deprehenditur"

THE KINGDOM OF GOD, A FAMILY

law of retribution—"Ye shall *spoil* the Egyptians," says the Lord to Moses, and, later on, the saying is fulfilled, "they *spoiled* the Egyptians[1]." To Abraham the promise had been made that Israel should come forth from their prison-house "with substance," and this promise is now fulfilled[2].

Mark's brevity has left his text open to misunderstanding —if we may judge from the Ignatian saying "the prince of this world desires to pillage me"—as if he possibly meant "Be strong in the Lord. No evil spirit can pillage the house of your soul unless it first bind the strong [and good] power within you." Mark would have been clear if he had written, more fully, "No one, unhelped by God, can enter into and pillage the house of the strong [one]...but I have done so, acting with the power of God and casting out the spirit of evil." Matthew and Luke have both supplied additions to this effect[3]. Both of them suggest an allusion to the contrast in Exodus, where the power of God, acting through Moses, is contrasted with the power that was not of God, acting through the enchanters of Pharaoh. But Luke does this with special distinctness in his phrase *"the finger of God," a very rare expression, used by Pharaoh's enchanters to denote their recognition of a power beyond their own*[4].

---

[1] Exod. iii 22, xii 36. The LXX "vessels," σκεύη, occurs in the context of both these passages to describe the "spoil" The Heb word is the one above mentioned meaning "utensils" of any kind, but here "jewels," as also in Exod. xi 2

[2] Comp. Wisd x 17 "She [i e Wisdom]..rendered (ἀπέδωκεν) to the righteous the wage (μισθὸν) of their labours," where the margin rightly refers to Gen xv 14, Exod xii 35—6, and where the context shews that the "jewels" received in this act of "spoil" are regarded as the "wage" that their oppressors had kept back from them. Philo, on Gen. xv 14 "substance," says (i 512) that it consists of "all that belongs to discipline (παιδείας)," and he implies that it includes the "strong virtues of self-control and endurance"

[3] Mt. xii 28 foll., Lk xi. 20 foll, see p 446 foll.

[4] Exod. viii 19 "This is *the finger of God*" It occurs also in Exod. xxxi. 18, Deut ix 10, "written with *the finger of God*," but not elsewhere (in A V)

THE KINGDOM OF GOD, A FAMILY

§ 9. *The "spoiling" of the Egyptians*

The examination of the above-mentioned Synoptic variations leads us to believe that the original tradition about "spoiling" was based on some reference to the "spoiling of the Egyptians." The Hebrew word there rendered "*spoil*" means, in the active, "strip" or "plunder," but in the causative, "snatch away" or "deliver," and, in the passive, "deliver oneself" or "be delivered[1]." The form there used occurs in only one other Biblical passage in the sense "spoil[2]." But Ezekiel uses it of Noah, Daniel, and Job "*delivering* their [own] souls[3]." When the word occurs for the first time, in a command of God, some scribes of the LXX vary the reading[4]; and the variations should prepare us to find variations in metaphors in which the redemption of man from sin, or the rescue of the souls of men from Sheol, is likened to the rescue of Israel from its house of bondage in Egypt.

The Synoptic language may be illustrated by Paul's language about "putting off the body of the flesh" and "putting off the old man[5]." The "old man" is regarded partly as the man's own fetters, and partly as the fetters belonging to Satan. But further, in stripping them off, one may be regarded as stripping off Satan, gaining a victory over him, and carrying off spoils from him[6]. In the context, Paul describes Jesus Himself as

---

[1] Gesen 664 *b* נצל

[2] Gesen. 664 *b* gives the *piēl* of נצל as occurring in Exod iii 22, xii 36 ("spoil the Egyptians"), and 2 Chr xx 25 "precious jewels (σκεύη ἐπιθυμητά) which (Heb *and*, not *which*) they *stripped* for themselves (καὶ ἐσκύλευσεν (A -αν) ἐν αὐτοῖς (A ἑαυτοῖς))," comp Lk xi. 22 (SS) "his plunder also he divideth *for himself*" (D, αυτο for αυτου)

[3] Ezek xiv. 14, 20

[4] Exod. iii. 22 LXX σκυλεύσατε, v r συσκευάσεται, συσκευάσατε, Aq. σκυλεύσετε or συλήσατε

[5] Col ii 11 ἀπεκδύσει, iii. 9 ἀπεκδυσάμενοι.

[6] Philo i 512 describes the mind that descends from heaven as being, like Israel in Egypt, "fettered in (ἐνδεθῇ) the straits of the body," and as wrestling with the passions and "dashing them to

THE KINGDOM OF GOD, A FAMILY

"*having put off from himself* the principalities and powers"; and there, having regard to the memorable "spoiling of the Egyptians," we ought not perhaps to insist on limiting the Apostle to the strict Greek use of the middle form of the verb, but to admit that he may also include the notion of "*despoiling*[1]."

The uncertainty about the exact interpretation of the phrase "spoiling the Egyptians," and the difficulty of giving it an edifying or seemly meaning, may account for the fact that it is seldom referred to in the Talmuds. But it is frequently referred to in the Midrash. Rashi enters into a long discussion of the phrase when first used in Exodus, remarking that the Targums render it "empty out the Egyptians"; and a tradition in Midrash, commenting on an instance of the word in Deuteronomy ("to deliver thee") asks whether it means (1) "overshadow thee" or (2) "empty forth all the wealth of the Gentiles and give it to thee[2]." These and other passages, if fully quoted, would confirm the conclusion that the Synoptic variations as to "spoiling" go back to ancient Hebrew traditions about the Exodus

§ 10 *The "casting out" of "the ruler of this world"*

John nowhere represents Jesus as saying that He has *conquered "the ruler of this world"*—which is the Johannine

the ground ($\tau\rho\alpha\chi\eta\lambda\iota\zeta\omega\nu$)," whence it obtains as its prize "strong virtues" These are the "substance" promised (Gen xv 14) to Abraham's descendants after their bondage in Egypt (and granted in the "spoiling" of the Egyptians, to which, however, Philo does not refer)

[1] See *Light* 3837 *a* on Col ii 15 The Pauline metaphors are seldom mixed But of course different metaphors are suggested by (1) "Christ is in us," (2) "we are in Christ" We are to "*put on* the new man" But "the new man" is also "the *inner* man."

[2] See Rashi on Exod iii 22, and *Lev r.* on Lev xix. 2 (Wu. p. 164) quoting Deut xxiii 14 and Exod iii. 22 (on which the Midrash mostly deals with the "asking" for "jewels," e g. *Mechilt.* on Exod. xii 6, Wu p. 14)

453 (Mark iii 20—35)

THE KINGDOM OF GOD, A FAMILY

equivalent of *"the ruler of the devils."* But Jesus says "I have *conquered the world*," and yet also "I came...to *save the world*[1]." Again, Jesus exclaims triumphantly *"The ruler of this world hath been judged,"* and yet "I came not *to judge* the world[2]" Thus, although it would be difficult to find authority for the Greek "conquer," as meaning "win over" or "bring over to one's side," the Evangelist does yet make us feel that this—namely, "winning over," or "gaining to one's side"—is the sense in which the Messiah "conquers" The Messiah's conquest is for the good of all—including the good of the conquered. Using the word "conquer" thus, John is not able to apply it, as Luke does, to a combat between Christ and Satan in which Satan is "the strong" and Christ "the stronger," so that Satan is conquered by Christ. If Satan were "*conquered*" by Christ—in the Johannine sense—Satan would cease to be Satan, and would become, in reality and truth, an angel of light.

Why does John shrink from this, the Lucan notion—of a combat between "the strong" and "the stronger"? Partly, perhaps, because it implies a similarity between Satan's strength and Christ's, as though they were similar in nature and dissimilar only in degree But partly it is because John has a conception of his own (or rather has grasped a conception of Christ's) which suggests an entirely new notion of "strength," hardly to be discerned in O T., except through glimpses here and there in the Law and the Prophets. This "strength" is just the opposite of "seizing," "plundering" and "snatching." The wolf comes to "snatch" the sheep, but the Good Shepherd "layeth down his life" for them[3]. That is the Shepherd's strength—laying down His life. Using one metaphor, we might say (but John perhaps would not say) that by this

---

[1] Jn xvi. 33, xii 47.

[2] Jn xvi. 11 (*Joh Gr* **2477** b, a judgment "that *has just* been ratified"), xii 47.

[3] Jn x 11—12 "snatch," ἁρπάζειν

strength He conquers the wolf. Using another metaphor, we might say, with John, that by this strength He causes "the ruler of this world" to be "cast out"

In the midst of this tradition about "spoiling" or "spoils," the Double Tradition here inserts, and attributes to Christ, words that go to the bottom of the difference between the Conqueror on the one hand and the Snatcher or Robber or Pillager on the other "He that is not with me is against me, and he that gathereth not with me scattereth[1]." The English word "conquer" etymologically implies "gathering together" or "collecting" And in Latin, too, a "conquisitor" meant a "recruiting officer." But in Greek, "snatch," *harpazein*—which is latent with us in the familiar word "*harpy*"—is applied to creatures that "gather" nothing and "recruit" no one, but bring with them nothing but defilement and desolation The righteous Conqueror "gathers," the Snatcher "scatters"

These etymological distinctions might, in some circumstances, be put aside as pedantry, but not so here For the Greek "conquer" hardly occurs in LXX as the representative of a Hebrew word, and John has a hard task before him in attempting to illustrate, for East and for West, a new kind of conquest, the conquest of the incarnate Son of God. Self-conquest, the philosopher's conquest of his own passions, philosophers could understand Also the Book of Wisdom well says that "Virtue in the age to come walks crowned in God's procession, having *conquered* in the contest for the prize that brings no defilement[2]" But John desires to suggest to us a higher conquest than this—a conquest in which the Conqueror dies for His enemies, and, by His death, causes His Spirit to steal into their hearts and dominate their affections, so as to make them henceforth His citizens and His soldiers. We have

---

[1] Mt xii 30, Lk xi 23
[2] Wisd iv 2 ἐν τῷ αἰῶνι στεφανηφοροῦσα πομπεύει, τὸν τῶν ἀμιάντων ἄθλων ἀγῶνα νικήσασα

THE KINGDOM OF GOD, A FAMILY

seen that this thought is brought before us in connection with the Good Shepherd, but now we have to note how it is brought before us again in connection with the Johannine prediction that "the ruler of this world shall be cast out[1]."

That prediction is preceded—and we may also say (at least partly) caused—by the coming of "certain Greeks[2]." And if we go back step by step from the prediction to the cause, we shall find that we are in a new Exodus from Egypt "The ruler of this world" corresponds to Pharaoh, and is the worldly conception of God as a god of power, or rather as gods of powers, differing in will, and destitute of the unity that belongs to the God of Truth. As Israel after the flesh was delivered from the material bondage of Egypt, so the "Greeks" (representing the Gentile world that is to become Israel after the spirit) are to be delivered from bondage to the spiritual Egypt Jehovah, the God of Israel, was "glorified" at the Red Sea, and is not said to have been "glorified" before[3] So here, the Son, in prospect of the second Exodus, exclaims to the Father, "Father, glorify thy name," and receives the reply "I have both glorified it and will glorify it again[4]." That means, or that includes the meaning, "I have glorified it in Israel after the flesh, and I will glorify it in Israel after the spirit."

But at this point we go back to something deep and mysterious, and quite beyond the range of the Song of Moses. For the Son has been saying "Now is my soul troubled, and what shall I say? 'Father, save me from this hour'? Nay for this cause came I, unto this hour[5]." And, before that, He

---

[1] Jn xii 31 (R V) "Now is the (*marg* a) judgment of this world, now shall the prince of this world be cast out"

[2] Jn xii 20

[3] Δοξάζω does not occur in the Bible till the Song of Moses at the Red Sea, and then it occurs as follows (Exod xv 1—21) ἐνδόξως γὰρ δεδόξασται .οὗτός μου θεὸς καὶ δοξάσω αὐτόν ἡ δεξιά σου, κύριε, δεδόξασται ἐν ἰσχύι δεδοξασμένος ἐν ἁγίοις...ἐνδόξως γὰρ δεδόξασται

[4] Jn xii 27—8

[5] Jn xii 27, on which see *Joh Gr* **2057, 2512** *b—c*.

THE KINGDOM OF GOD, A FAMILY

has said "He that loveth his life loseth it," and again, before that, "Except a grain of wheat fall into the earth and die, it abideth by itself alone, but, if it die, it beareth much fruit," and lastly—to go back last to that which is first—"The hour is come that the Son of man should be glorified[1]." And all this is the sequel to nothing but the simple fact that Jesus has heard from Andrew that "certain Greeks" have come to Philip saying "Sir, we would see Jesus[2]."

Why does the Evangelist lead us on so slowly (some may be disposed even to say tediously) from the Greeks to Philip, and from Philip to Andrew, and from Andrew at last to Jesus—and all this about nothing but a simple petition to "see Jesus"—and then leave us as it were in a blind alley, with no answer to the petition, but with a new and startling exclamation about "glory" and "the grain of wheat" that must "die"? Is it not because the writer feels that he is leading us to the threshold of a profound mystery to be approached as it were by altar steps, one by one, and to be approached slowly lest we stumble?

If he has the Exodus of Israel in view, must he not also have the Passover of Israel in view? In that case, he has before him the thought of Jehovah as "a man of war," saying to Pharaoh, through Moses, "Israel is my son, my firstborn.... Let my son go, that he may serve me; and thou hast refused to let him go, behold, I *will slay thy son, thy firstborn*[3]." As contrasted with all this, how marvellous is the mystery of the second Exodus, wherein the Father sends His Firstborn, as Man, and as waging "war," but war of a new kind—not to "slay" men, but to die for them, that in dying He may sink like a seed, deep into the human heart, there to spring up and drive out all its noxious weeds, leaving no room in it for anything except Himself.

It will be observed that John does not deny the truth of the view that Jesus waged a war against evil, and that He used the words "the ruler of this world shall be *cast out*." But he

---

[1] Jn xii 25, 24, 23.   [2] Jn xii 21
[3] Exod iv 22—3

(Mark iii 20—35)

THE KINGDOM OF GOD, A FAMILY

supplements the Synoptic and negative doctrine of "casting out" by a Johannine and positive doctrine of *bringing in*. He cautions us against laying too much stress on Christian aggressiveness against evil, and too little on Christian receptiveness of good, and especially of that kind of "good" which comes to us through the presence of the sacrifice of Christ in our hearts, the dying "grain of wheat," which, even while it dies, and because it dies, quickens us with power to drive out evil by causing good to grow up in its place.

§ 11. *"All things shall be forgiven to the sons of men,"*
  in Mark

Matthew and Luke omit *"to the sons of men"* and insert a statement about *"the Son of man*[1]*."* In Hebrew, "*say concerning* a person" is sometimes expressed by "*say to*"—meaning "*say [with respect] to.*" But "forgive," meaning "remit," would also be followed by "*to,*" both in Hebrew and in Greek ("remit to them"). Mark's original may have been "All things shall be remitted whatsoever [men][2] shall say *to* (i.e. *against*)

---

[1] Mk iii 28—29 a

(28) Verily I say unto you, All their sins shall be forgiven unto the sons of men, and their blasphemies wherewith soever they shall blaspheme·

(29) But whosoever shall blaspheme against (εἰς) the Holy Spirit hath never forgiveness,...

Mt xii 31—32 a

(31) Therefore I say unto you, Every sin and blasphemy shall be forgiven unto men, but the blasphemy against (*lit* of) the Spirit shall not be forgiven.

(32) And whosoever shall speak a word against (κατὰ) the Son of man, it shall be forgiven him; but whosoever shall speak against (κατὰ) the Holy Spirit, it shall not be forgiven him,...

Lk. xii 10

And everyone who shall speak a word against (εἰς) the Son of man, it shall be forgiven him but unto him that blasphemeth against (εἰς) the Holy Spirit it shall not be forgiven

[2] For the non-pronominal subject "they," meaning "men," in Mark, see *Joh Gr.* 2424, 2425 *b*. On "say *to*," see *Son* 3371 *e*

the Son of man." If "*to*" was connected with "remitted" and taken as the "to" after "remitted," it would naturally be supposed that "remitted to *the Son of man*" must be an error for "remitted to *the sons of men*," and this would seem to agree with what preceded ("[men] shall say"), the meaning being "All things that they may say shall be forgiven to the sons of men[1]." The parallel texts contain some minor divergences that might be explained on the hypothesis of obscure Greek; but the hypothesis of the Hebrew "*to*" meaning "*concerning*" seems also necessary[2].

It was necessary to mention this deviation of Matthew and Luke from Mark, in conformity with the plan of this work, which aims at setting before the reader all such deviations in order that he may see whether John does, or does not, intervene; but it is obvious that this is not a case where we could expect Johannine intervention. For Matthew and Luke do not here *omit* anything of importance. They *insert* something of importance, but in omitting "to the sons of men" after "forgiven" they omit nothing but a sonorous phrase that can be omitted without the least detriment to the sense. For to whom can forgiveness of sins be granted except "to the sons of men"? We do not pledge ourselves to prove that John intervenes where Matthew and Luke *insert* something that is not in Mark. Nevertheless in the next section it will be shewn that John does intervene as to Mark's following words, and in such a way as to indicate that he attempts to throw fresh light on the distinction between sins that can, and sins that cannot, be forgiven.

---

[1] See *Son* 3177, where these Synoptic parallels are discussed. It is there suggested that Mark's original contained (1) "forgiven *to the sons of Adam*," as well as (2) "say *to [1]e against*] *the Son of Adam*," and that the similarity has caused "to the Son of Adam" to be dropped as a repetition

[2] Ὅς ἐάν, in Matthew, would be easily confused with ὅσα ἐάν, in Mark Πᾶς, in Luke, is applied to the offender, πᾶς ὅς ἐρεῖ, but in Mark (πάντα), and Matthew (πᾶσα ἁμαρτία), to the offence

THE KINGDOM OF GOD, A FAMILY

§ 12. (R.V) "*Guilty of an eternal sin,*" *in Mark*

Luke stops short after "shall not be forgiven"; Mark and Matthew add phrases expressing negatively the duration of the non-forgiveness; Mark also adds a phrase expressing positively, in a very unusual way, "liability" in respect of "an eternal sin[1]."

The Greek word rendered by R V. "guilty" means etymologically "held in," or "included in." Sometimes it means merely "involved in" some discreditable practice[2]; but it is more often used technically in a legal sense to mean "held in the grasp of a statute," "included in a legal charge," "liable to a penalty." In that sense, "liable" is not quite so strong as "condemned" or "found guilty", for the prosecution may be dropped so that the verdict may not be pronounced[3]. The word is not a good one to use in religious or theological doctrine, for it may imply legal guilt that is not moral guilt. Plutarch describes how the Lacedaemonians bade the Athenians "banish

---

[1] Mk iii 29—30 (R V)
..hath never forgiveness, but is guilty of an eternal sin Because they said, He hath an unclean spirit, οὐκ ἔχει ἄφεσιν εἰς τὸν αἰῶνα, ἀλλὰ ἔνοχός ἐστιν αἰωνίου ἁμαρτήματος ὅτι ἔλεγον Πνεῦμα ἀκάθαρτον ἔχει

Mt xii 32 (R V)
...it shall not be forgiven him, neither in this world (*or*, age) nor in that which is to come, οὐκ ἀφεθήσεται αὐτῷ οὔτε ἐν τούτῳ τῷ αἰῶνι οὔτε ἐν τῷ μέλλοντι

Lk. xii 10
..it shall not be forgiven, οὐκ ἀφεθήσεται

[2] Comp Plutarch i 1057 E—F *Galba* § 13 ἀργυρίου μὲν ἐσχάτως καὶ παρ' ὁντινοῦν ἥττων, ἔνοχος δὲ καὶ τοῖς περὶ γυναῖκας ἁμαρτήμασιν, i 607 A *Agesilaus* § 20 εἰδὼς οὖν ἔνοχον ὄντα τοῖς ἐρωτικοῖς τὸν Ἀγησίπολιν, and perhaps i 864 c *Cicero* § 7 ἀπελευθερικὸς ἄνθρωπος ἔνοχος τῷ ἰουδαΐζειν. See also Ast's Index to Plato, and Bonitz's Index to Aristotle

[3] Comp. Plutarch i. 767 B *Cato* § 17 οἱ δὲ τοῦτο παθόντες εὐθὺς ἦσαν ἔνοχοι φόνῳ, καὶ τρόπον τινὰ προηλωκότες ἀπήγοντο πρὸς τοὺς δικαστάς, where "liable" is explained by "and, so to speak, convicted beforehand"

THE KINGDOM OF GOD, A FAMILY

the pollution in which the whole race of Pericles, on the mother's side, was *involved* or *liable*[1]." That is to say, Pericles was entangled in the meshes of a Law that made him responsible for what was done by his mother's ancestors, treating him as though he had done what he had not done. Less unfairly, but still with some degree of exaggeration, Hermas says that, if you listen to slander, you will be "liable for the sin of the slanderer[2]."

Matthew uses it in the sense of "liability" to various tribunals or punishments, varying according to the offence; and the exact force of his words and the nature of his allusions are still obscure[3]. Paul says that those who partake unworthily of the Eucharist are "*liable [to the charge] of the body and the blood of the Lord*"; and the Epistle to the Hebrews says that Christ died to deliver "those who, through fear of death, were, throughout all their life, *liable [to the charge] of slavery*[4]." In the first of these passages our Versions have "guilty of"; in the second, "subject to." But the meaning in the second is explained by the precept of Epictetus to "*call any man a slave*" if he fears anyone or anything[5]. Perhaps therefore the Epistle to the Hebrews is better rendered by Tyndale and the Geneva

---

[1] Plutarch I 170 A *Pericl* § 33 τὸ ἄγος.. ᾧ τὸ μητρόθεν γένος τοῦ Περικλέους ἔνοχον ἦν. With the dative, ἔνοχος sometimes means "liable to [a charge of]," e g ἔνοχος ψευδομαρτυρίοις, but this can be expressed by a genitive, ἔνοχος φόνου for ἔνοχος [γραφῇ] φόνου, "liable to a charge of murder"

[2] Hermas *Mand* II 2 (*bis*) ἔνοχος τῆς ἁμαρτίας τοῦ καταλαλοῦντος. See also *ib* iv 1 5, where a husband, living with a wife whom he knows to be unfaithful and unrepentant, is said to be ἔνοχος τῆς ἁμαρτίας αὐτῆς. Ἔνοχος occurs nowhere else in the Early Fathers or Apologists, except Just Mart *Apol.* § 16 ἔνοχός ἐστιν εἰς τὸ πῦρ, freely quoting Mt v 22, and Aristid § 13 ἔνοχοι θανάτου.

[3] Mt v 21—2, on which see *Hor. Heb* Mt xxvi 66 ἔνοχος θανάτου, and Mk xiv 64 simil. are the only other instances of ἔνοχος in the Gospels, apart from the Marcan passage under discussion

[4] 1 Cor xi 27, Heb. ii. 15.

[5] See Epictet. iv. 1. 54—7.

THE KINGDOM OF GOD, A FAMILY

Version "they were *in danger of bondage*[1]," meaning that those spoken of might at any time be legally adjudged to be bondservants, because they had not in their hearts the Spirit of sonship—which alone could make them free, as Jesus said. "If therefore the Son shall make you free, ye shall be free indeed[2]." And the same explanation applies to the first passage. "Guilty" is somewhat too strong for the meaning, which appears to be "They have not crucified the Lord, but they act in such a way as to make themselves *liable to the charge of having done so.*"

Now, returning to Mark, in the light of this conclusion as to the meaning of "liable," we see that he intends us to understand the imminence, as it were, of some very great sin, or judgment for sin, which will fall on those who were saying about Jesus "He hath an unclean spirit." Instead of the usual word for "sin," Mark has one that means "act-of-sin." It is very seldom used except in the plural, but Aquila is recorded to have used the singular in a passage where Isaiah says to Israel that they shall cast away the "idols which your own hands have made for you—*a sin*[3]." Ibn Ezra explains this as meaning "*a sin κατ' ἐξοχήν, a sin that surpasses all others.*" Similarly the warning in Mark may mean that those who said "Jesus has an unclean spirit" were setting up an idol of darkness in their hearts, and bringing on themselves the judgment described in Ezekiel, "Thus saith the Lord God: Every man of the house of Israel that taketh his idols into his heart....I the

---

[1] Comp. *Merchant of Venice* IV 1 362 "You stand within his danger"

[2] Comp. Jn viii 36

[3] See Ibn Ezra on Is xxxi. 7 'Ἁμάρτημα, in sing, and without "every," does not occur elsewhere in N T. (1 Cor. vi 18 being no exception) In canonical LXX, ἁμαρτία (sing. or plur.) is about eighteen times as frequent as ἁμάρτημα, and the sing of ἁμάρτημα is rarer than the plural, especially in the prophets. In the Apologists, the sing is very rare, and in the Early Fathers the sing does not occur at all.

THE KINGDOM OF GOD, A FAMILY

Lord will answer him therein according to the multitude of his idols," followed by the threat, "I will cut him off from the midst of my people[1]."

§ 13. *"Guilty," in LXX*

The thought of "*an eternal sin*" in Mark appears to correspond to the thought of "*an abiding sin*" in John, implied where Jesus says "If ye were blind ye would have no sin, but now ye say 'We see.' *Your sin abideth*[2]." But the Marcan word "liable" appears to have nothing Johannine about it. Being technical, and legal, and alien from Johannine thought, it seems to stand as an obstacle in the way of supposing that John, in the same passage in which he may be alluding to the thought of "an eternal sin," may also be alluding to the Marcan thought of legal "guilt" or "liability."

But let us look into the LXX use of the word. It is too artificial to express any one Hebrew thought, so that it is very rare and hardly ever occurs except as a paraphrase to express some phrase mentioning "blood[3]." Putting aside the first instance, a paraphrase of "he shall surely die[4]," we come to an edict about house-breaking in Exodus (LXX) (*lit.*) "If in the house-breaking the thief (*kleptēs*) be found, and be smitten, and die, *there is no murder for him. But, if the sun be risen upon him,* [*he* i.e. *the man that smites*] *is liable, he shall die-in-return*[5]." The corresponding Hebrew is "*there is not for him blood* (pl.) *If the sun be risen upon him,* [*there is*] *blood* (pl.) *for him Restoring he shall restore* (i.e. *he shall make full restitution*)."

---

[1] Ezek. xiv. 4—8   [2] Jn ix. 41

[3] Ἔνοχος corresponds to Heb. fifteen times, and mostly represents "blood" or some phrase mentioning "blood"

[4] Gen xxvi 11 (Heb. lit.) "dying he shall die," θανάτου (v.r. θανάτῳ) νοχος ἔσται

[5] Exod. xxii 2—3   The Gk of the italicised words is οὐκ ἔστιν αὐτῷ φόνος   ἐὰν δὲ ἀνατείλῃ ὁ ἥλιος ἐπ' αὐτῷ, ἔνοχός ἐστιν, ἀνταποθανεῖται

THE KINGDOM OF GOD, A FAMILY

The clause about sunrise appears to have caused difficulty. It is very obscurely paraphrased by the Targums. Onkelos alters it thus· "There is not for him blood. *If the eyes of witnesses fall upon him*, there is blood for him. Restoring he shall restore" The Jerusalem Targum has, for the difficult clause and for what follows, (Etheridge) "*If the thing be as clear as the sun that he was not entering* to destroy life, and one hath killed him, the guilt of the shedding of innocent blood is upon him, and, if spared from his hand, restoring he shall restore."

We cannot be surprised if this Law about the *Kleptēs* or Housebreaker—so hard upon the innocent householder if interpreted exactly—was allegorized even by those Jewish authorities who are not prone to allegory. Rashi says that it "is a kind of similitude," and that the sun represents "peace"; and herein he is following the consensus of the Talmuds and of the ancient Midrash[1]. For the purpose of illustrating the Fourth Gospel Philo is more important than any of these, and he allegorizes in the same way, though in a style of his own He applies the "sunrise" to the internal and "shining" self-conceit of a mind within us (*i e* the householder) which fancies that it can "see through all things and arbitrate on all things." Such a mind, he says, kills the soul's vitalising truth. Hence "It is guilty. It shall die in return[2]."

---

[1] The sun would "rise" at one moment for a householder on a hill and perhaps many minutes afterwards for his neighbour in a valley In practice, therefore, the Law would turn, not on "sunrise" but on "daylight" See Breithaupt's note on Rashi (Exod xxii. 2—3) referring to *Mechilt* ad loc and to *b Sanhedr*. 72 *a—b*, and *j Sanhedr*. viii. 8

[2] Philo i 94 on Exod xxii 1 foll ἐὰν δὲ ἀνατείλῃ ὁ ἥλιος, τουτέστιν ὁ φαινόμενος λαμπρὸς νοῦς ἐν ἡμῖν, καὶ δόξῃ πάντα διορᾶν καὶ πάντα βραβεύειν, καὶ μηδὲ ἐκφεύγειν ἑαυτόν, ἔνοχός ἐστιν, ἀνταποθανεῖται τοῦ ἐμψύχου δόγματος ὃ ἀνεῖλε

Comp *Introduction* p 22, n. 2, "In the new-born proselyte, the old eye must be closed before the new one is opened, see Levy iv. 154 *b* quoting *Lev r*. (on Lev xii 2)."

THE KINGDOM OF GOD, A FAMILY

The Law about the Housebreaker, if interpreted according to common sense, seems clear enough. But we are not concerned with its common-sense interpretation. What we are concerned with is (1) the use of the Greek word for "liable" in the LXX version of the Law, (2) the subtle discussions and allusions that might rise out of attempts to make the Law workable and yet not to depart from the letter of Scripture, (3) the influence of all these things on Christian thought in the first century.

§ 14. *"Ye say, 'We see.' Your sin abideth*[1]*," in John*

Passing back to John from these Jewish traditions about the Law of the *Kleptēs* or Housebreaker, we have to remember that several Christian traditions lent themselves to a metaphor about the Day of the Lord as being in some sense "like a *Kleptēs, Thief,* or *Housebreaker,*" coming in the night. It is added by Matthew and Luke to a precept bidding the disciples "watch" for their Lord, as though these Evangelists meant "Watch for the coming of the Lord as men watch for the coming of a thief[2]." Outside the Fourth Gospel, the word "thief" in the

---

[1] Jn ix. 41.
[2] Mk xiii. 35—6

Mk xiii. 35—6	Mt xxiv 42—4	Lk. xii 37, 39—40
(35) Watch therefore. for ye know not when the lord of the house cometh, whether at even, or at midnight, or at cock-crowing, or in the morning; (36) Lest coming suddenly he find you sleeping.	(42) Watch therefore, for ye know not on what day your Lord cometh (43) But know this, that if the master of the house had known in what watch the thief was coming, he would have watched, and would not have suffered his house to be broken through (*lit* digged through) (44) Therefore be ye also ready. for	(37) Blessed are those servants whom the lord when he cometh shall find watching verily I say unto you that he shall gird himself and make them sit down to meat and shall come and serve them.... (39) But know this, that if the master of the house had known in what hour the thief was coming, he would

singular is used, with hardly any exceptions, concerning the Day of the Lord, or the Coming of the Lord, "as a thief (*Kleptēs*)" in the night[1]. Now even if "*Kleptēs*" occurred repeatedly in the LXX, as it very well might throughout the legal parts of the Pentateuch, it would still be highly probable that many of the Christian traditions about the Lord coming as a *Kleptēs* in the night would allude to the coming by night of the *Kleptēs* in Exodus. But the allusion is made almost a certainty when we find that, apart from one Deuteronomic mention of a kidnapper as "a thief of men," the word "*Kleptēs*" does not occur again in the Law. And there is not a single instance of it in the historical books[2].

Let us attempt to enter into the thought of a Christian Jew of the first century, applying his mind to the Marcan saying, attributed to Jesus, that those who said "He hath an unclean spirit" were "*liable* to an eternal sin," and endeavouring to penetrate to the truth at the bottom of this technical and legal word, which had been rejected by Matthew and Luke.

"The Greeks use 'liable,'" he might say, "concerning one who is involved or entangled in some fault or legal crime or in

Mk xiii 35—6 (*contd*)	Mt. xxiv 42—4 (*contd*)	Lk xii 37, 39—40 (*contd*)
	in an hour that ye think not the Son of man cometh	have watched, and not have left his house to be broken through (*lit* digged through) (40) Be ye also ready for in an hour that ye think not the Son of man cometh.

[1] The only exceptions are Lk xii. 33 "Where thief draweth not near" (Mt vi. 19—20 "thieves"), 1 Pet iv 15 "suffer as a murderer or a thief" "Thief" refers to the Coming of the Lord in Mt xxiv 43, Lk xii 39, 1 Thess. v. 2, 4 (W H marg R V. txt), 2 Pet iii. 10. Note especially Rev. iii. 3 "If therefore thou watch not *I will come as a thief*," *ib* xvi. 15 "Behold, *I come as a thief*"

[2] It occurs in Exod. xxii 2 (1), Deut. xxiv. 7, and not again till Job xxiv. 14.

THE KINGDOM OF GOD, A FAMILY

the meshes of some statute law. But in the Law of Moses it has a special meaning. It says, in effect, about those who strike a deadly blow at one whom the Law calls a thief, '*If they could not see, they shall not die, but if they could see, they must die, they are liable.*' The Messiah '*came as a thief*' to those whom Matthew describes as 'the Pharisees,' and Mark as 'the scribes that came down from Jerusalem.' He '*broke in*' on the house built up by their traditions[1]. He seemed likely to despoil them of the glory they received from men. He was, in fact, the Prince of Peace. His Coming was as the dawn, the rising of the Sun of Righteousness But they would not see, even while they declared 'We do see' What they saw, was—in the light of their own self-kindled conceits[2]—the Thief. What they did not see, was the Prince of Peace and Life, whom they smote, saying, 'We see.' Later on, they said 'His blood be on our heads.' So they became 'liable.' The 'blood' was exacted."

The language of John is very different (as it always is) from the corresponding language in Mark. But there appears to be a correspondence of thought between them, and especially if we give weight to the Marcan phrase, "the scribes that came down from Jerusalem" The "scribes" stood for the guardians of the Law, and in Jerusalem sat the Council that guarded the Law, as being the Light of God What class was in greater danger of saying—as the Pharisees say in the Johannine narrative—"We see," when really they did not see? And who more needed the warning against "liability" to an "abiding" or "eternal" sin?

---

[1] For the Pharisees, regarded as "builders," or, in hostile language, "daubers of the wall" see *Light* 3996 *a*, *d* (and comp. Mk xii 10, Mt. xxi. 42, Lk. xx. 17).

[2] Comp Is. 1 10—11 contrasting, in effect, the "light" of "the name of the Lord" with men's self-kindled flame ("walk ye in the flame of your fire...ye shall lie down in sorrow").

THE KINGDOM OF GOD, A FAMILY

§ 15. *"Because they said 'He hath an unclean spirit*[1]*'"*

It was pointed out above that the Marcan phrase "He hath Beelzebub," non-occurrent in Matthew and Luke, was replaced in John by phrases more intelligible to Greeks. Here Mark repeats the phrase in a new form, and it is again omitted by Matthew and Luke. They perhaps did not think that Mark clearly brought out the connection between "Whosoever shall blaspheme against *the Holy Spirit*" and "He hath *an unclean Spirit.*" A link was needed indicating that "*the Holy Spirit*" was "*the Spirit with which Jesus was casting out evil spirits*"; so that to call *this* spirit "unclean" was to call the Holy Spirit "unclean." Such a link Matthew and Luke have inserted previously[2]. Having inserted it, they perhaps regard Mark's inference as now superfluous, and they omit it.

John never mentions the word "unclean," and never uses the word "spirit" in a bad sense; so that he cannot be expected to intervene verbally here. But he conveys to us a sense of the moral degradation implied in those who brought such charges against Jesus when he represents Him as saying, concerning those who seek to kill Him, "Why do ye not understand my speech? [Even] because ye cannot hear my word. Ye are of [your] father the devil," and, later on—when they say "Thou art a Samaritan and hast a devil"—"I have not a devil, but I honour my Father, and ye dishonour me"—which implies that they indirectly "dishonour" the Father[3]. He also indicates that this "dishonouring" of one who seeks not his own glory, by those who seek nothing but their own glory, will be "judged." This, which implies, in Marcan language, a

---

[1] Mk iii 30

[2] Mt xii. 28 "But if I *by the Spirit of God* cast out devils, then is the kingdom of God come upon you," Lk xi. 20 "But if I *by the finger of God* cast out devils, then is the kingdom of God come upon you." Mark iii. 26—7 omits this.

[3] Jn viii 43—4, *ib.* 48—9.

sin for which they will be "liable," is implied by John in the words, "I seek not mine own glory, there is one that seeketh and *judgeth*[1] "

Here and elsewhere the Fourth Evangelist desires to lead his readers away from thoughts about exorcisms and the ways of evil "spirits"—thoughts that often encouraged the use of charms, and incantations, and magic remedies—to fundamental things, to kindness and love, and humanity. David was declared by Jewish tradition to have said to the murderer Doeg—"Why boastest thou thyself, O mighty man, in mischief? The kindness of God [is] all the day[2]." The same thing, in effect, Jesus was continually saying to the Pharisees: "The kindness of God is for all the day and for every day. It is never out of season." Those who loathed His acts of kindness—wrought by Him, the Son, in the power of the Spirit of the Father—simply because they happened to be wrought on the sabbath, appeared to Jesus to be loathing the kind Spirit of the Father Himself, and to be storing up for themselves an abiding sin.

It might seem that what follows should be reserved for a new Chapter, since nothing has directly or obviously pointed to the thought of Christ's family, which will now come before us. But in fact this thought has been by implication pointed to from the beginning of the present Chapter, where Christ's own kinsfolk were described as saying that He was "beside himself." Those who said this, though they were His "family" after the flesh, were not His "family" after the spirit. And it is to this subject that we shall now proceed—Christ's family "after the spirit," in other words, the Family of God, and Christ's definition of it.

---

[1] Jn viii. 50, comp *ib.* xii. 43 "They loved the glory of men more than the glory of God "

[2] Ps lii 1, s. above, p 445.

THE KINGDOM OF GOD, A FAMILY

§ 16. *"See! My mother, and my brethren"*

"See," in Mark, and "behold," in the parallel Matthew, as given below[1], are severally active and middle forms of the same verb. The middle, in Biblical Greek, is frequently used to introduce a new event, and is very rarely if ever used with an object. But the active is occasionally thus used, and in such instances it would mean "See thou[2]." Here it is not followed in Mark by an object. But we might perhaps supply

---

[1] Mk iii 31—5 (R V)

(31) And there come his mother and his brethren, and, standing without, they sent unto him, calling him.
(32) And a multitude was sitting about him; and they say unto him, Behold, thy mother and thy brethren without seek for thee
(33) And he answereth them, and saith, Who is my mother and my brethren?
(34) And looking round on them which sat round about him, he saith, See (R V. Behold) (ἴδε), my mother and my brethren (nom)!
(35) For whosoever shall do the will of God, the same is my brother, and sister, and mother

Mt xii 46—50 (R V)

(46) While he was yet speaking to the multitudes, behold, his mother and his brethren stood without, seeking to speak to him
[(47) And one said unto him, Behold, thy mother and thy brethren stand without, seeking to speak to thee]
(48) But he answered and said unto him that told him, Who is my mother? and who are my brethren?
(49) And he stretched forth his hand towards his disciples, and said, Behold (ἰδού), my mother and my brethren (nom)!
(50) For whosoever shall do the will of my Father which is in heaven, he is my brother, and sister, and mother

Lk viii 19—21 (R V)

(19) And there came to him his mother and brethren, and they could not come at (συντυχεῖν) him for the crowd
(20) And it was told him, Thy mother and thy brethren stand without, desiring to see thee
(21) But he answered and said unto them, My mother and my brethren are these which hear the word of God, and do it

Mt. xii. 47 is placed by W H. in margin. And R V. says that some ancient authorities omit it

[2] Gen. xxxi 12, Numb. xxvii. 12 (rep Deut xxxii. 49), Ps. ix 13, xxv. 18, 19 etc., Jn xx. 27, Rom. xi 22.

THE KINGDOM OF GOD, A FAMILY

one thus: "And looking round on those seated in a circle round him he said [to the messenger] *See thou* [these]! My mother and my brethren [are these]!" It is worth noting that although Matthew uses the ordinary "*behold*," instead of "*see thou*," he nevertheless inserts a clause ("said to *him* that told him") to shew that Jesus made His reply in the first instance to *a single person*, who had told Him that His friends were seeking Him[1]

There seems to be a kind of retorting repetition in the verb of seeing, first used *to* Jesus, and then used *by* Jesus But the point of the retort is blunted in Mark by the change of the form of the verb from "*Behold* (ἰδού), thy mother and thy brethren...seek thee," to "*See thou* (ἴδε), my mother and my brethren." The point is retained in Matthew, if we adopt the fuller reading of his text, which repeats "behold" thus, "*Behold* (ἰδού), thy mother and thy brethren stand without, seeking to speak to thee," followed (at a very slight interval) by "*Behold* [*I reply unto thee*] (ἰδού), my mother and my brethren [are here]" Also the discrepancy between the Marcan plural ("*they say*") and the Marcan singular ("*see thou*") is removed by Matthew, who inserts once (or perhaps twice[2]) an intimation that Jesus was talking to one person only Luke leaves it an open question whether the announcement was made by one person or more. He also drops "behold" and "see" altogether But the impression left on us by Mark and Matthew is that the earliest tradition laid some emphasis on the words.

Some of the variations are explicable from a Hebrew original of Mark stating that the mother and brethren of Jesus were "standing outside and *calling him*, or *calling to him*[3]."

---

[1] If Mt xii 47 is an interpolation, we may explain it as an attempt to justify the insertion in Mt xii 48

[2] Once, if Mt xii 47 "one said unto him" is rejected, twice if it is accepted Matthew adds a second, or third, ἰδού in xii 46 ἰδοὺ ἡ μήτηρ .

[3] Gesen 895 says that Heb "call," "summon," is usually

THE KINGDOM OF GOD, A FAMILY

Mark, assuming that they were standing outside the door of a house and that they *"called" him by sending a messenger*, inserts *"sent."* Matthew and Luke do not venture to insert this *"sending."* They prefer to paraphrase "calling." Matthew takes it to mean *"attempting to call."* Luke ("they could not *come at* him," lit. *"meet with* him") appears to have confused the Hebrew *"call"* with the Hebrew *"meet"*—the two being constantly confused in LXX[1]. This leads him to use a Greek word unique here in N T. and non-occurrent in canonical LXX[2]. It means "meet"; but the Grammarian Photius says expressly that it means "meet by accident, and is not to be used of meeting purposely for an interview[3]." Perhaps Luke may mean "they were not able to get so much as a casual word with him, *or even a glance at him*" And hence, perhaps, later on, he says "desiring to *see thee*" In any case, the use of this remarkable word indicates that Luke is taking special pains to shew that the tradition spoke of *"meeting"* and not of an unseemly attempt on the part of Christ's friends to *"call"* to Him over the heads of the surrounding crowd.

Passing to the Fourth Gospel, which does not narrate this incident, we cannot expect to find anything Johannine that

---

followed by "to," and Delitzsch inserts "to" in Mk iii 31, but Syr (Walton) has no "to" ("ut evocarent eum ad se ipsos")

[1] See *Corrections* 472 *c* referring to Prov xx 6 (R V txt) *"proclaim,"* marg *"meet,"* and xxvii. 16 (R V txt) "encountereth," (marg) *"bewrayeth itself"* (i e lit *"proclaimeth* itself"). But the statement "In Proverbs, whenever συναντᾶν ('befall') occurs, it = Heb 'call,'" should have been modified by adding "4 out of 6 times where *Oxf Conc* gives an undoubted Heb equivalent"

[2] Συντυχεῖν, only in 2 Macc viii. 14 "before they *met-together*" (marg "*engaged-in-battle*")

[3] See Steph. *Thes* on συντυγχάνω In Lk. viii 19, SS and Syr (Walton) have "speak with him," Curet "see him" (taken from Lk. viii. 20), Palest "draw near to him," *a* "colloqui ei," *b* "adire ad eum," *d* "contingere ei" No variation of the Greek MSS is alleged On confusions connected with Heb "meeting," see *Notes* 2999 (iii) *a—k*.

THE KINGDOM OF GOD, A FAMILY

bears on the trifling divergence of Matthew and Luke from Mark's "sending"; but we may ask whether John has anything corresponding to the thought expressed in Mark—and with special vividness in the Syriac—"See, my mother! And see, my brethren[1]!" The thought is, that the disciples of Jesus—the circle of those on whom, as Mark says, Jesus "looked round," or to whom, as Matthew says, He "stretched out his hand"—are His true family. This is expressed to some extent by John in the Last Discourse where Jesus says to the disciples "If a man love me, he will keep my word; and my Father will love him, and we will come unto him and make our abode with him," and afterwards, "Ye are my friends, if ye do the things that I command you[2]."

In this, the words "mother," and "brethren," and the vivid expression in Mark-Matthew (and especially in Mark) "see!" are wanting But something like them is given us in the scene where Jesus, with hands stretched out on the Cross, "seeing his mother, and the disciple standing by whom he loved, saith to his mother, Woman, *see*, thy son! Then he saith to the disciple, *See*, thy mother[3]!" For here the disciple whom Jesus loved appears to be regarded as the type of all the disciples whom Jesus loves, and whom, by His love, expressed in the death on the Cross, the Son embraces in the arms of His kindness and carries upward into the Family of the Father[4].

---

[1] Mk iii 34, SS and Syr (Walton) Schlatter (on Jn iii. 29) calls attention to the use of Heb "*see!*" to express a climax A messenger says to Israel "Thy sons are come," "Thy sons-in-law are come," and awakens some response, but not equal to that elicited by "*See*, thy husband!"

[2] Jn xiv. 23, xv 14

[3] Jn xix 26—7 Ἴδε, ὁ υἱός σου....Ἴδε, ἡ μήτηρ σου. A slight pause seems desirable between "See!" and the following nominative.

[4] Comp Origen *Comm Joann* 1 6 "We must therefore venture to say that whereas the firstfruits of all the Scriptures are the Gospels, the firstfruits of the Gospels are the Gospel according to John No one can receive its meaning (νοῦν) unless he has lain on the breast of

THE KINGDOM OF GOD, A FAMILY

§ 17. *"Whosoever shall do the will...," in Mark*[1]

Mark defines *"will"* by adding *"of God"*; Matthew, by adding *"of my Father in heaven."* This is explicable on the supposition of an original *"doeth the WILL,"* a use of the word *"almost universally misunderstood"* in a passage in the first Epistle to the Corinthians[2], and likely to be discarded by Luke

---

Jesus, and unless he has received Mary from Jesus, to become (γινομένην) his mother also." But is the Johannine narrative compatible with the tradition in Mk xv 40, Mt xxvii 55 about "women beholding afar off"? That must be considered in its order. Here we may note that Luke differs greatly from Mark and Matthew. Lk xxiii 48—9 mentions, 1st, sympathetic "multitudes" as "having beheld," 2nd, "his acquaintances (γνωστοὶ αὐτῷ)" described as "standing afar off," and 3rd, "women. seeing" these things but *not* necessarily included in those who are "afar off" (ἱστήκεισαν δὲ πάντες οἱ γνωστοὶ αὐτῷ ἀπὸ μακρόθεν, καὶ γυναῖκες αἱ συνακολουθοῦσαι αὐτῷ. ὁρῶσαι ταῦτα). Luke's language points to Ps xxxviii 11 "My lovers and my friends stand aloof from my plague, *and my kinsmen stand afar off"* (with perhaps a thought of Ps xxxi 11 "a fear unto mine acquaintance") On "kinsmen" Jerome says *ad loc* "Apostoli vel reliqui discipuli, de quibus ait Evangelista, 'Cum autem apprehendissent eum, stabant omnes noti ejus a longe'" Jerome's editor refers to Lk xxiii 49, but the words are not there, nor are they in Lk xxii 54 or in any Gospel.

The Psalmist's *"afar off"* suggests the possibility that the Synoptic "afar off" was derived from the Psalms and not from historical fact. If we could accept Luke's narrative, we might believe that the women at all events were, as John says (xix 25), "standing by the cross," and, if there were also present sympathetic "multitudes," it becomes easy to suppose that some of the Apostles had returned from their flight, and witnessed the crucifixion. There remain, however, very great difficulties, and especially the difficulty of explaining how the beautiful Johannine tradition could have been passed over by all the Synoptists when mentioning the presence of the women.

[1] Mk iii 35

[2] See 1 Cor xvi 12 "it was not the WILL," on which see *Paradosis* 1220 a, quoting Lightfoot on Ign. *Eph* § 20

THE KINGDOM OF GOD, A FAMILY

as obscure. But this does not suffice to explain Luke's avoidance of "will" in the following parallel —

Mt. vii 21	Lk vi 46—7
Not..."Lord, Lord", but he that doeth *the will of my Father that is in the heavens*	Why "Lord, Lord" and do not *the things that I say* heareth *my words* and doeth them

This seems to shew a Lucan dislike of the phrase "doing God's will" applied to ordinary believers. When Luke does connect man's "*doing*" with God's "*will*" he inserts "*according to*," as if to say, "The servant cannot do *the [whole] will* of the Master, he can only *do in accordance with it*[1]" These passages—and perhaps one in the Acts, where "will" is used in the plural[2], indicate that, although the Psalmist says to God "teach me to *do thy will*[3]," Luke does not accept the phrase—when it is in the singular, and refers to God's whole "will"—as suitable for the ordinary believer

It must be added that this noun (*thelēma*, "will") is very rare in literary Greek; and the single instance of it given in the Concordance to Aristotle connects "our [human] will" with "sensation" and "[passionate] desire" in such a way as to shew that a Greek might take "the will" to mean "fleshly desire[4]" Luke, at all events, whatever may be his motive, never speaks of "doing God's will," and on one occasion he seems to go out

---

[1] Lk xii 47 "That servant, who knew his lord's will, and made not ready, *nor did according to his will*"

[2] θέλημα, which occurs thrice in the Acts, is used once with ποιεῖν, in a quasi-quotation, but in the plural (xiii 22) ὃς ποιήσει πάντα τὰ θελήματά μου (not found in LXX)

[3] Ps cxliii 10 Its use in Ps xl 8, and the Christian application of it to the sacrifice of the Messiah (comp Heb x 5—7) might dispose Luke not to apply it to the ordinary believer, who profited by the sacrifice

[4] Steph *Thes* gives no instance of θέλημα in literary Greek But Bonitz gives it as occurring once in Aristotle *De Plantis* 1 1 21 καὶ τὸ τοῦ ἡμετέρου δὲ θελήματος τέλος πρὸς τὴν αἴσθησιν ἀποστρέφεται This is preceded by ἡ γὰρ ἐπιθυμία οὐκ ἔστιν εἰ μὴ ἐξ αἰσθήσεως

THE KINGDOM OF GOD, A FAMILY

of his way to use "will" in a bad sense[1]. Also, where Mark and Matthew represent Jesus as saying to the Father "Not what (*or*, as) I *will*," a very ordinary verb, Luke has "Not my *will*"— an expression that would not be used in literary Greek, but capable of meaning "not my will [after the flesh][2]."

Perhaps this attitude may be illustrated by Paul's ironical reproach to the hypocrite, "If thou...gloriest in God and knowest the WILL...thou therefore that teachest another, teachest thou not thyself[3]?" These pretended "knowers" of "the WILL" were sometimes impostors or fanatics. It might seem humbler, safer, and truer, to limit oneself to "*the word*," assuming that this expressed "*the will*." The spoken "word of God" was something definite, publicly proclaimed or "preached," in the Gospel, for all to do. Israel at the foot of Mount Sinai said "All that the Lord hath spoken we will do." The new Israel must follow that precedent. First they must "hear," then they must "do." Some such thought as this may have led Luke to deviate from the Marcan tradition "do the will of God" and to express it by "hear the word of God and do it."

John adopts an entirely different plan. Beginning from "word," he implies that "the WORD" is primarily not anything definite that can be expressed in written letters or vocal pulsations of the air. It is an unutterable Spirit of Life, Light, and Sonship, underlying the uttered "word" of the Gospel. Those who received it received "authority to become children

---

[1] Lk xxiii 25 "delivered Jesus over *to their will* (i.e. to the will of the Jews)." The parall. Mk xv 15, Mt xxvii 26 have "and delivered over Jesus, having scourged him, that he might be crucified."

[2] Mk xiv 36, Mt xxvi 39, Lk xxii 42. In the context, where Mk-Mt has $εἰ\ δυνατόν\ ἐστιν$, Lk has $εἰ\ βούλει$, "if thou dost so *will-and-purpose*."

[3] Rom ii 18—21. On $θέλημα$ see *Paradosis* **1220** *a*. Dalman p. 211 quotes 1 Macc. iii. 60 (Engl Vers.) "as the will of God is in heaven," where LXX has "as may be the WILL ($θέλημα$) in heaven."

THE KINGDOM OF GOD, A FAMILY

of God"; and the explanation of the birth of these "children" introduces the first mention of "will," when we are told that they were "begotten, not from blood (pl.), nor from the *will* of the flesh, nor from the *will* of man [*i.e.* the husband] but from God[1]." After this, Jesus is repeatedly represented as saying that He has come "to do the will," or that He "seeks [to do] the will," of the Father, and as declaring what "the will" of the Father is[2].

So far, Luke might go with John. For Luke himself would admit that all this was true about the Son, even though he thought the language too lofty to be applied to the Son's disciples. But now John proceeds to assert, not only that man can "do God's will," but also that by "doing God's will," or even by "willing to do" it, man arrives at a knowledge concerning the Gospel, as to "whether it be of God" or not[3].

John seems to mean that God's "will," revealed in Christ, is, primarily, kindness—what we call, in men, "humanity[4]" If a man is truly humane, he is a man such as God intended to make from the beginning. In the Fourth Gospel, this very simple thought, after Jesus has stamped it with His approval, is put into the mouth of one who has experienced His kindness and power, the man born blind "We know that God heareth not sinners; but if any man be a worshipper of God and *do his will*, him he heareth[5]." This is the last Johannine mention of the word "*will*."

---

[1] Jn 1 12—13 On ἀνδρός, "husband," see *Joh Gr* 2371 *a*, *Son* 3583 (x)

[2] Jn iv 34, v 30, vi 38, 39—40.

[3] Jn vii. 16—17 "My teaching is not mine, but his that sent me If any man willeth to do his will, he shall know of the teaching, whether it be of God, or [whether] I speak from myself "

[4] Comp. Jn 1 17 "*grace* (χάρις) and truth came through Jesus Christ" See *Son* 3495 *c*, and 3566 *a*, "John appears to substitute *charis* for *éleos*" To this add that the Hebrew *chesed*, "kindness," is rendered "*grace*" by Symmachus in Ps xxxi. 7, xl. 10, lxxxix. 24

[5] Jn ix. 31 Θέλημα occurs in 1 Jn ii 17 where "the will of God"

THE KINGDOM OF GOD, A FAMILY

§ 18   *The difference, as to "the will," between Luke and John*

In all this, there is more than a mere verbal difference between Luke and John[1]. There is a difference of method[2].

is contrasted with "the lust (ἐπιθυμία) [of the world]," and v 14 "if we ask anything according to his will "

[1] On the verbal question, note that the only instance recorded in which the Greek translators of O T use βούλημα is in Ps 1 2 (LXX) θέλημα, and see Clem Alex 114 (quoted in *Light* 3817 (1) *e*) distinguishing God's θέλημα, which is ἔργον and κόσμος, from His βούλημα, which is man's salvation, "and this is called Ecclesia "

[2] Does Luke *ever* write with latent allusion, as John repeatedly does ? I cannot recall an instance of it unless the following is one, Lk xxiv 21 "But we were hoping that he [and no other] is [indeed] (αὐτός ἐστιν) the destined redeemer of Israel. Yea, and besides all these things, *this is* [*now*] *the third day that he is passing* (or, *he is now passing his third day*) from the time when these things came to pass (τρίτην ταύτην ἡμέραν ἄγει ἀφ᾽ οὗ ταῦτα ἐγένετο) " Ἄγω, "spend," or "*pass* [*through*]," is used of stages of disease by Galen (whom Wetstein *ad loc.* quotes) on a patient "*Passing* [*through*] *the fourth day* [of his illness] (τετάρτην ἡμέραν ἄγων) he was absolutely without pain," and "We must see *what day of the disease the man is passing through* (πόσην ἄγει τοῦ νοσεῖν ἡμέραν)," i e what is the number of the day   The idiom ἄγω ἡμέραν had been made famous by Epicurus in a letter from his deathbed Diog Laert x 22 "We write these words to you while *passing* [*through*] *the blessed day and at the same time the final day of our life* (τὴν μακαρίαν ἄγοντες, καὶ ἅμα τελευταίαν, ἡμέραν τοῦ βίου, ἐγράφομεν ὑμῖν ταυτί) "   This saying was translated by Cicero, and by Seneca, and attacked (as inconsistent) by Epictetus (see notes on Epict ii 23. 21 ed Schweig). Luke could not fail to know it   If he is alluding to it, he means, "The disciples are unconsciously speaking the truth   They do not say 'Three days have now passed' or 'It is now the third day' or 'He is in the third-day-stage' (comp. Mk viii 2, Mt. xv 32 (with var read) and Jn xi 39), but 'He is now passing the third day'—as though He were still in being, although they know not where. And indeed He *was* in being and 'passing the third day,' that day of transition, not from one stage of death to another but from death to life   He was '*passing*,' as His '*third day*,' what Epicurus called (but how differently !) 'the blessed day and the final day ' "

Note what Alexander the Great says, in answer to the question "Where have the Macedonians buried you ? " (Lucian, *Dial Mort*

THE KINGDOM OF GOD, A FAMILY

John explains and adapts old tradition whereas Luke substitutes a new one. But further, there is a difference, not perhaps in theology but in spiritual feeling. Luke, as we may perceive from his Gospel and the Acts, rather likes to dwell on the "counsel" and "purpose" of God, the Homeric *boulé*, in preference to the LXX or Hebraic *theléma*, which would, in literary Greek, mean "pleasure" or "liking." The latter—if we might apply the term "instinct" to God metaphorically—might be called the divine instinct rather than the divine intellect[1]. There is something more passionate in John than the Lucan "foreordained counsel of God" when the Son touches on, and rejects, the thought that He should "lose" anything that the Father had "given" to Him. "I am come down from heaven, not to do mine own will, but the will of him that sent me. And this is the will of him that sent me, that of all that which he hath given me *I should lose nothing*, but should raise it up at the last day. For this is the will of my Father, that every one that beholdeth the Son and believeth on him, should have eternal life[2]" For such a passionateness the reader was prepared, not only by the phrase "begotten from God" in the

---

xiii 3) "*This is the third day* (τρίτην ταύτην ἡμέραν) *that I am still lying in Babylon*. But Ptolemy my armour-bearer promises that, if he can ever get a little leisure from his worries, he will take me to Egypt and bury me there, *that I might become one of the Egyptian Gods*" There seems to me a jibe at Christians, as also perhaps in Lucian's *Icaromenippus* § 22 "*On the third day* (τριταῖος) *I drew near to heaven*."

Ἄγει, in Luke, is not rendered correctly by the Syriac and most of the Latin versions. The instances of ἄγειν ἡμέραν collected by Steph *Thes.* and Wetstein clearly shew that it ought never to be rendered as if ἄγειν were εἶναι If there is an allusion here, the recognition of it is important because it bears, not only on this one passage but on others also, illustrating Luke's Hellenic way of looking at things

[1] Βουλή occurs in no Gospel but Luke (vii 30 τὴν βουλὴν τοῦ θεοῦ, xxiii 51) Acts ii 23, xiii 36, xx. 27 mention "the counsel of God," comp. Acts iv. 28.

[2] Jn vi 38—40

THE KINGDOM OF GOD, A FAMILY

Prologue, but also by what follows, in the first Discourse on Regeneration, concerning God's gift to men: "For God so loved the world that he gave his only begotten Son, that whosoever believeth on him might not be lost, but might have eternal life[1]."

A difference may be also perceived between the Lucan and the Johannine doctrines concerning "*hearing* the word." We have seen how Luke inserts "*hearing*," in the parallels under consideration, so that "*hearing* and doing" are connected by him and applied to the definite precepts of the Gospel. Previously Luke has introduced a mention of "hearing" in the Teaching of Jesus for the first time thus: "But I say unto you, [namely] *those hearing*, 'Love your enemies[2].'" The parallel Matthew omits "*those hearing*[3]." What does this insertion mean?

Does Luke intend to make a distinction between hearers and non-hearers, meaning a distinction between the "poor," who accept the Gospel, and the "rich," who reject it? At all events, in his Gospel, Christ's preceding words have been utterances to "the rich" concerning woe: "Woe unto you, the rich...woe unto you when all men praise you! For so did their fathers use to do to the false prophets[4]." Nothing of this is in Matthew. Are "the rich" addressed as present ("you") although absent? Or are they present and "rich" in their own estimation as well as rich in worldly wealth, like the Laodiceans in Revelation?

On the other hand, may not "*those hearing*" mean—without any intended contrast between rich and poor—"*those who hear me, not in name but in deed*," "*those who hear me with their hearts*"?

---

[1] See *Son* **3440** *d* "Comp Jn iii. 16 'might not be lost,' vi 39 'that I might not lose aught of that which he hath given me'. English cannot express the double meaning of ἀπολέσαι, 'lose' or 'destroy.'"

[2] Lk. vi 27 ἀλλὰ ὑμῖν λέγω τοῖς ἀκούουσιν, Ἀγαπᾶτε....

[3] Mt. v 44.

[4] Lk vi 24—6

THE KINGDOM OF GOD, A FAMILY

The answer is doubtful[1]. The conclusion of the discourse likens those that "hear" Christ's words without "doing" them to men building a house on the sand. This is compatible with either view, but perhaps rather favours the view that "those hearing" is to be taken as meaning "those who really hear me," that is to say, "those who are ready to make my words their deeds."

In the Fourth Gospel, Christ's first mention of "hearing"—apart from an incidental mention of "hearing" the "sound" of the wind[2]—is supplemented by a mention, not of "doing" but of "believing". "He that *heareth* my word and *believeth* him that sent me[3]." In the next verse, with a change of case, "hearing" may perhaps be rendered "hearkening," with advantage to the sense· "The hour cometh, and now is, when the dead shall *hearken to* the voice of the Son of God, and they that have *hearkened* shall live." A little later, it is implied that the "hearkening" must produce on all some kind of moral effect, on the evil, for judgment, as well as on the good, for reward: "All that are in the tombs shall *hearken to* his voice, and shall come forth; they that have done good, unto the resurrection of life; and they that have done evil, unto the resurrection of judgment[4]."

This is not the place to discuss the Johannine doctrine of "hearing" as a whole[5]. But it may be pointed out that John

---

[1] In Lk., Codex *e* has "sed vobis qui *nunc* auditis dico," *Diatess* has (Lk vi 26—7) 'Woe unto you when men praise you! for so did their fathers use to do to the false prophets Unto you do I say, [you] *that hear*, (Mt v 13) Ye are the salt of the earth..." Tertull *Adv Marc* comments on Lk vi 27 (ad loc) "'*Sed vobis dico*,' inquit, 'qui auditis,' ostendens hoc olim mandatum a Creatore, '*Loquere in aures audientium*'"—(which T and T Clark refer to 2 (5) Esdr xv. 1 "ecce loquere in aures plebis meae..," but it seems to point to some passage in O T, perhaps Exod xi 2 "speak in the ears of the people")

[2] Jn iii 8   [3] Jn v 24
[4] Jn v 28—9.
[5] For a discussion of it, see *Joh Voc* **1612—20**

differs remarkably from all the Synoptists when he quotes the well-known prophecy of Isaiah about those who, "seeing, do not see, and hearing, do not hear." The Prophet describes Israel as virtually dead—in "heart," "ears," and "eyes." The Synoptists, in their threefold tradition[1], make no mention of "heart," but only of "hearing" and "seeing." John, on the other hand, inserts "heart," and retains "see with their eyes," but omits "ears[2]." Why does he do this? Partly perhaps to shew that the "heart" is the source of all the mischief, but partly also to shew that "the ears"—in this spiritual sense—may be included in, or identified with, "the heart[3]." A man must have a human "heart" in order to "hear the voice" of Him who created man in His own image

All this is metaphor, whether we say "heart" or "ear"— and perhaps also, whether we say "do the *will* of God," or "do the *word* of God." For can we assert literally that God has a "*will*" like ours, any more than a "*word*" like ours? And in favour of the Lucan tradition "those that *hear the word of God and do it*," it may be urged that it contains a useful protest against a religion of mere words or visions. It pledges us to "*do*" the New Law as the Israelites, at the foot of Sinai, pledged themselves to the Old Law with a promise of "*doing*," or *works*: "All that the Lord hath spoken we will *do*[4]" Nevertheless the essential meaning of the older tradition of Mark is on a higher spiritual level, and we are indebted to John for drawing it out for us, and for helping us to rise up to it.

If we reflect on the position of Jesus at the time when His enemies began to plan His destruction, and a little before He began to reveal to His disciples that their hostility would have

---

[1] Mk iv 12, Mt. xiii 13—14, Lk viii 10. But Matthew, *in his single tradition*, (Mt xiii. 15) quotes Isaiah fully

[2] Jn xii 40

[3] John nowhere mentions the words "deaf" and "dumb," *Joh Voc* 1614—15

[4] Exod xix. 8, rep xxiv. 3, 7

THE KINGDOM OF GOD, A FAMILY

a temporary success, we shall perceive that it somewhat resembled the position of the Psalmist, who declares that he has "published righteousness in the great congregation[1]." When the righteous God bade Him heal on the sabbath, He had obeyed, and could say to God, with the same Psalmist, "I have not hid thy righteousness within my heart[2]." But the rulers of the people had turned against Him with such virulence that He was forced to add, and again from the same Psalm, "They seek after my soul to destroy it[3]." At such a crisis, it could hardly be other than necessary that there should rise to His thought, and perhaps to His lips, the well-known context (quoted also in the Epistle to the Hebrews) which says, in the first place, "Sacrifice and offering thou hast no delight in," and then, "Lo, I am come—in the roll of the book it is written of me—I delight to *do thy will*, O my God[4]."

If this was so, an allusion to that Psalm might be expected at this stage of Christ's career, as a preparation for the subsequent utterances of Gethsemane (found in all the Synoptists) which, in slightly varying forms, point to the doing of God's "will" by the Sacrifice on the Cross[5]. The Epistle to the Hebrews quotes the Psalmist's words in full, putting them into the mouth of Jesus as uttered by Him "when he cometh into the world[6]." But they would not be so appropriate at the moment when Jesus first came forward to proclaim the Gospel of Peace as they would be at the period which we have reached. For now Jesus had "published righteousness," that is to say, the New Righteousness, the altruistic doctrine, implying the Law of Sacrifice, contained in the Sermon on the Mount. Now,

---

[1] Ps xl 9   [2] *Ib.* 10.   [3] *Ib.* 14

[4] *Ib* 6—8, quoted in Heb x 5—7. Comp Mt xii. 7 "If ye had known what this meaneth, I desire mercy and not sacrifice (Hos. vi. 6)"

[5] Mk xiv 36, Mt xxvi. 39, Lk xxii. 42, where Mk and Mt. have forms of θέλειν but Lk. θέλημα (see above, p 476).

[6] Heb. x 5—7, quoting Ps. xl. 6—8.

THE KINGDOM OF GOD, A FAMILY

too, He had gathered round Him a band of disciples of whom He could say that although they were still greatly ignorant, they were greatly sincere, openhearted, and loyal. They did not know "the will" as Jesus knew it, but they could already say, with Him, so far as they knew it, "We delight to do it." For this cause, as the Epistle to the Hebrews says, He was "not ashamed to call them brethren[1]." They were the beginnings of His Family, the Family of the Children of God, more commonly known as the Kingdom of Heaven.

---

[1] Heb. ii. 11

INDICES

INDICES

TO "INTRODUCTION" AND "BEGINNING"

		PAGE
I.	Scriptural Passages	487
II.	English	502
III.	Greek	510

TO "PROCLAMATION"

I.	Scriptural Passages	512
II.	English	526
III.	Greek	542

INDICES TO "INTRODUCTION" AND "BEGINNING"

I SCRIPTURAL PASSAGES

GENESIS			GENESIS			GENESIS		
		PAGE			PAGE			PAGE
1	2	121, 123, 302	15	4	115	27	40	100*
	16–18	31		10	407	28	10 foll	134
	20	16		15	301		11	427
	26	135, 411	16	6	80		11–12	135
	31	115		7	182		13	160
2	2	100*		9	182		15	97*
	6	375		10	182	29	25	199
	8	447		11	182	32	10	449
	10	211	17	1	378		11	318, 327
3	6	337		22	100*	36	43	126
	8	41	18	1	182–3	37	14	260
	18	137		1 foll	146, 182		15	142*, 243
	21	342		16	182		34	298
	22	399		20	439	39	18	206
	24	148, 183		33	100*, 182	42	4	438
4	3–5	419	19	1	182	43	1	439
	10–12	410		1 foll	182	49	10	403, 428
	21	394		25	328		18	344
6	4	94	21	17	182		33	100*
	13	244		34	298	50	24	149
7	18	439	22	1	74*, 164–5			
8	1	122–3		2	31		EXODUS	
	7	70		10	31			
	11	115		12	31	1	13	88
	13	115		13	12, 115	2	2	89
9	2	159		16	31		11	94
	5	383	23	6	89		12	93*
11	7	411	24	27	23		13	94
	32	213	25	22	416		23	94
12	1	213, 229		25	69	3	2	444
14	18	301		27	378	4	18	260
15	1	74*, 97*, 18, 23	26	24	97*, 392	5	2	439
				31	260		9	439
	3	115	27	30	100*	7	5	439

The references to "Introduction" are distinguished by an asterisk.

INDICES TO "INTRODUCTION" AND "BEGINNING"

EXODUS			LEVITICUS			DEUTERONOMY		
		PAGE			PAGE			PAGE
7	17	439	1	1	89	25	9	79
8	10	439	7	20	402		10	79
9	14	261		21	402	30	20	18
	22–33	452	8	23, 24	60*	32	4	397
	33	452	9	23, 24	64*		6	387
12	1–2	183	10	9	126		8–9	7
	37	152	11	45	149		9–11	121
	44	49	12	2	22*		11	121, 153
13	2	182	15	25	94		16	387
14	2	437	16	6	402		20	19
	3	418, 437		15	402		21	387
	16	446	19	23	447		43	174, 177
	31	391, 447	20	2–5	387		45	100*
15	1	94, 391, 395, 416	23	11	130*	33	26	184
	3	139, 316		15–16	130*			
	8	395					JOSHUA	
	9	418, 437		NUMBERS				
	10	446				4	5–21	452
	11	184	2	31	184	8	22	407
	12	440, 448	6	2	126	9	11	206
	16–17	448	7	89	41	11	18	298
	25	164, 418	11	16	84	23	1	298
16	18	432	13	31	77	24	7	298
17	9	347	14	34	157		23	44
	15	444	15	32–6	101*			
19	1	226	17	8	448		JUDGES	
	2	444	20	10–12	195			
	3	226		15	298	6	34	69
	4	152, 418		24	67*	7	15	396
	9	226	22	37	199	11	4	89*
	10	226	23	19	134	13	7	313
	11	226	24	7	211	14	8	89*
	16	226		24	159	15	1	89*
20	20	164	35	5	407		4	407
21	2	80				16	17	313
	11	397		DEUTERONOMY				
	31	402					RUTH	
22	20 foll	384, 387	4	17	113			
	22	384		38	77	2	16	379
	26, 27	884	5	5	29			
24	10	xxii		31	137		1 SAMUEL	
29	20	60*	7	1	77			
	29	402, 405		15	261	1	1	126*
	42	41	8	2	166	10	5	394
31	14–15	101*		3	179	16	1	35
32	14	134		15	160, 166		6	345
33	12	149		15–16	167		7	315
	14	184	13	4	447		22	112*
	15	184	15	10	375	17	12	106, 315, 316
	21	427	17	6	107*		55–8	112*
34	28	157, 195	20	10 foll	301	24	6	345
35	2–3	101*	24	9	84			
39	1	402	25	4	375			
	39	402						

The references to "Introduction" are distinguished by an asterisk.

SCRIPTURAL PASSAGES

1 SAMUEL

		PAGE
24	11	336
25	6	300
28	15	439
29	3	370

2 SAMUEL

1	14	336
	16	381
4	6	361
5	6–8	158*
	14	18*
12	24	18*
	31	80*
13	1	80*
15	1	80*
	11	378
	30	274
21	18	80*
23	1 foll	74*
	8 foll	74*
24	1	164
	14	439
	16	61*
	25	61*, 63*

1 KINGS

1	33	402–3
2	37	381
	42	199
4	24	159
6	8	364
	24	152
8	10	64*
	11	64*
	37	119*
	47	56
	52–3	65*
	54–5	63*
19	3–8	155
	10–18	202
20	43	80*
21	1	80*
	19	381
22	18	199

2 KINGS

1	8	69
4	28	199
6	6	451

2 KINGS

		PAGE
6	11	403
9	13	206
10	11	363
16	13	403
18	4	69*
	13	75*
20	1–11	58*
23	13	33*
	21	68*
	22	68*

1 CHRONICLES

1	1	70*
2	13	316
3	2	55*
4	18	107
11	10 foll	74*
	41	55*
12	18	18, 69, 300
20	3–4	80*
21	1	164
	13	439
	15	61*
	26–7	63*
	27	61*
22	4	396
23	27	75*
29	9	378
	17	378–9

2 CHRONICLES

5	11–14	64*
6	41–2	65*
7	1–3	63*
18	17	199
20	20	391
21	12	55*
23	14	148
24	20	69
28	14	370
29	3–31	21 69*
30	1–27	69*
32	1	75*
	24	58*
35	18	68*
	20	76*
	22–5	77*
36	14	69*
	15	69*
	16	77*
	23	70*

EZRA

		PAGE
2	1	210
3	12	65*
6	3	65*
	16	65*

NEHEMIAH

5	10	231, 363
9	26	118

ESTHER

4	4	206

JOB

7	1	235
14	14	235
16	2	284
30	5	118
33	23–4	287
34	24	128
38	6	412
	26	430
41	22 (14)	416

PSALMS

1	3	450, 451
2	2	343
	9	128
	12	126–7
4	6	165
6	8	176
8	2	276
	4	135
16	5	18
	10	312
18	26	127
19	1	396
21	13	417
22	1	169
	20	31
	21–31	169
	29	386
25	1	111
29	5	31*
31	11	363
33	1–2	395
	2	394
	7	395

The references to "Introduction" are distinguished by an asterisk

INDICES TO "INTRODUCTION" AND "BEGINNING"

PSALMS		
		PAGE
33	17	395
34	8	338
35	17	81
36	8	386
39	1	376
40	8	92, 420
45	2–4	23, 25, 347
	4	347
	6	347
	7	25, 342, 347
46	7–11	272
55	6	120
	13	363, 371
	19	411
60	4	440
63	1	159–60, 169, 397
65	1	397
68	22	110
	26	417
69	9	197
	21	170
71	15	397
72	9	159
74	12	411
	15	439
76	1	363
77	19	446–7
78	2	410
	17	160
	58	387
79	4	197
	12	197
81	2	394–5
	5	395
85	9–11	135
86	4	111
88	8	362
	18	362
91	6	168
	11–12	161
	15	444
92	14–15	386
96	13	74
97	7	174
104	4	183, 446
	25	397
106	12–13	392
107	30	68*, 88*
116	3	436–7
	10	389
118	5	437
	10–12	437
	17	437
	18	437

PSALMS		
		PAGE
122	6–8	275, 300
	9	275
132	1 foll.	65*
	8–10	65*
143	8	111
	9	393
147	5	396
148	7–8	15
	8	14

PROVERBS

3	31	387
4	1	127
	3	127
8	1	46
	22	121
	29	412
	30	121
	31	121
9	2–3	231
	2–4	230
13	13	260
14	3	449
15	30	217, 386
18	10	393
20	7	127
23	26	172
24	5	79
28	13	263
31	2	126
	23	363

ECCLESIASTES

4	13–14	89
9	12	357
10	9	436

SONG OF SONGS

1	2	57
	4	78
	6	401, 403
2	12	121
3	7	403
4	1	121
7	3	126
8	12	401, 403

ISAIAH		
		PAGE
1	2	19
	16–18	57
	22–5	58
	25	124
4	2	328
5	26	440
6	1	133*
	8	41
7	9	391
	14	97*, 272
	16	272
	20	440
8	7	439, 440
	8–10	272
9	1	88*, 224
	1–2	109, 206
	6	272
10	33–4	106
	34	134
11	1	106, 134, 211, 314, 316, 318, 325–7, 331, 449
	1–2	315
	1–10	106
	2	34, 120
	4	448–9
	10	198, 316, 442, 449
	11	387
	12	316, 442
	15	441
	15–16	440
	16	442
14	13	325
	19	318, 325
19	5	440
	21	363
21	2	444
25	7	202
28	13	436
30	17	440
35	1 foll	238
	1–10	261
	3	261
40	1–3	40
	1–11	261
	2	235, 251
	3	33, 42, 235
	3–6	41, 44
	3–8	33
	5	385
	9	234
	11	151
	27–31	236

The references to "Introduction" are distinguished by an asterisk

SCRIPTURAL PASSAGES

ISAIAH			JEREMIAH			EZEKIEL		
		PAGE			PAGE			PAGE
41	16	126	20	15	132	36	26	57, 85, 84
	27	234	23	5	326		29	119*
42	1–3	206	24	1	187	37	1 foll	83
	13	211		2–5	337		1–14	91
43	2	454	25	12	235		10	118
52	7	80, 217, 234	29	10	235	38	2	333
	10–12	385	31	15	104*	39	11	375
53	1	34, 217		33	408		29	83
	2	88, 159	33	15	326	48	35	70*, 233
	4	259, 444	37	13	370			
	17	92	39	9	370			
54	1	106, 318	46	16	228			
	13	84	47	6	62*		DANIEL	
55	1	874	49	24	437			
	3	159*	50	5	393	1	7	328
56	3	393	51	25	33*		10	436
57	18–19	281				2	46	371
	19	300, 420				3	5	394
58	6	240, 242		LAMENTATIONS			5–15	395
	7	383					7	394
	8	385	1	3	437		10	394
	10	196		16	327		13–30	328
	11	385	2	4	83		15	394
59	16	93*	4	4	261	7	8	318, 327
	19	446		7	312	8	12	235
60	10	263					16	146, 185
	21	319				9	21	146, 185
61	1	59, 238, 242,		EZEKIEL			24	312
		247 336, 342				10	1	235
	1–2	23, 240, 242,	1	1	83		11	137, 274
		247		2	133*		19	274
	2	134–5*		5	135	11	7	327
62	4	18*		10	135	12	7	28*
63	9	442 foll		26	90, 135			
	11–12	446	2	1	137			
64	1	112		2	118		HOSEA	
	2	113	3	1	138			
66	17	362, 407		12	138	1	1–2	4
				12–14	148		9	275
				16–17	99	3	4	397
	JEREMIAH			24	118	6	2	43*
			4	6	157	10	11	177
2	6	159	8	3	151, 387	11	1	103*
	13–25	32*	11	19	65		1–3	418
	32	397	14	6	56–7		4	78
3	14	57	16	5–8	144	14	2	420
	22	57		22	381			
4	6	440	18	30	56–7			
	31	437–8	19	10	381			
5	21	397	21	30	62*		JOEL	
6	14	266	23	35	118			
8	11	266	27	7	440	2	28	83–4
11	19	93	28	16	152		28–9	84
13	16	28*	32	2	440		32	181
15	12	128	36	25 foll. 52, 57, 91				

The references to "Introduction" are distinguished by an asterisk.

INDICES TO "INTRODUCTION" AND "BEGINNING"

AMOS		
		PAGE
8	1 foll	187
	11	160

JONAH		
1	4	435–6

MICAH		
5	2	77, 211, 247
	5	247, 282

NAHUM		
1	15	234
2	7	150

HABAKKUK		
1	13–15	357
2	3	74

ZECHARIAH		
1	3	44, 57
2	11	393
	15 (11)	393
3	8	326, 328
4	6	77
	7	33*
6	12	326–8
9	9	133, 247
	10	247, 282
10	6	263
12	10	84–5, 171–2
	10–14	85
13	1	85, 172
	4	69

MALACHI		
1	6	19
2	17	37
3	1	33, 37, 257
	1–3	36
	2	71*
	7	57
	7–8	58
4	1	126

MATTHEW		
		PAGE
1	1	98*, 8, 343
	3	18*
	3–6	18*
	6	18*
	16	343
	17	104*
	18–21	343
	20	122*
	22	103*
	23	97*, 103*, 272
	24	122*
2	2–4	343
	6	211
	13	103*
	14	103*
	15	103*, 418
	22–3	104
	23	103*, 309, 314
3	1	4, 43, 45–9, 94
	2	42, 45–7 56 foll, 237
	3	34*, 34 foll, 40 foll
	4	68
	5	43, 67
	6	48–9, 64
	7	47, 72, 96
	7–10	65
	9	98*, 65
	11	11*, 50, 75, 79–82
	12	81–2, 94, 124, 126
	13	84*, 94, 96, 100, 102
	16	123*, 110–18
	17	116–17
4	1	148–9, 154
	2	157 foll
	3	157
	4	154, 179
	5	151–3
	6	161
	8	149–50
	11	173, 176 foll.
	12	204, 206–7
	12–17	102*, 216
	13 foll	109, 310
	14–16	206
	15	88*, 207
	16	88*
	17	88*, 141*, 6,

MATTHEW		
		PAGE
4	17	207, 216–17
		237
	18	207
	19	112*
	23	209, 237
5	1–12	121*
	3	246
	13	121*
	48	378
6	9	121*
	21	288
	22	378
	23	375
7	28	99*, 100*, 269
	29	151*, 269
8	6	231
	7	232
	14	212
	22	213
	25	114*
9	2	144*
	9	77*
	22	260
	23	111*
	24	111*
	25	111*
	27	158*
	28	222
	36	164
	38	148
10	2	144*
	10	80
	12	259
	19	286
	20	286
	21	264
	34	264
	37	50*
11	1	99*, 100*
	3	27, 74
	5	111*
	7	43
	9	36
	10	36
	11	38
	19	313
	23	220
	27	94*
12	15	206
	23	157*, 242
	29	78
	46 foll	221
13	14	263
	15	263

The references to "Introduction" are distinguished by an asterisk

SCRIPTURAL PASSAGES

MATTHEW		MATTHEW			MATTHEW		
	PAGE			PAGE			PAGE
13 35	410, 413	21	16	276	28	1	106–7*
53	100*		17	86*		2 foll	191
53–8	241		19	28*		5	310
55	221		20	29*		6	191
56	221		21	29*		9	123*, 173*
58	4*		33 foll	187		15	105*, 325
14 3–9	56*	22	16	329		18	270
6	407	23	35	410		19	129*, 273
16	196	24	1	86*, 366		20	99*, 107*,
27–32	59*, 66*		2	86*			174*, 271
32–3	45*		7	119*			
35	209		8	132*			
15 21	4*		10	264		MARK	
24	200		14	238			
32	196		49	360	1	1	1–31, 147
39	147*	25	11	174		1–4	33 foll.
16 1	145		13	236		2	34*, 33, 36
2	23*		34	413		2–6	32–71
8–9	45*	26	1	100*		3	42 foll , 235
13–16	147*		2	243		4	4, 43, 45–9,
16	147*, 342–3		8	366			59
18	71*, 98*		13	238		5	48–9, 64, 67,
21	148*		14	366			208
22	148*		21	366		6	68–71
23	148*		28	48		7	72–80
24	148*		30	85*		7–8	72–92
28	171*		31	103*, 164		8	11*, 50, 81
17 1	79*		38	154*		9	84*, 93–109
5	124		39	428		9–11	93–140
18 6	118*		51	60*		10	123*, 110–
7	31		52	60*			122, 447
10	135, 288		53	188, 190		11	116, 147
12	155		54	188		12	148 foll , 154,
17	71*, 98*		55	71*, 189			165
20	97*, 271		56	189, 370		12–13	141–203
19 1	100*		58	361		13	89*, 146,
13	20		61	69*			156–66, 173–
28	15		63	343			80
20	222		68	343		14	79*, 89*,
20	167*		69	310, 313, 360,			102*, 142*,
22	168*			364–5			6, 204–32,
25 foll.	270		71	314, 362			234, 278
28	270	27	17	343		14–38	90*
30	158*, 310		20	93*		15	141–2*, 5–6,
21 2	103*		22	343			233–303
3–7	102*		34	104*		16	102*, 207
4	103*		37	321		21	95*, 207, 269
7	103*		40–44	345		21–8	220
9	156*, 74, 275,		43	104*		22	151*, 269
	321		46	169		23 foll	151*
10	92–4*		48	170		24	150*, 310
11	92*, 94*,		54	170		27	268–9
	102–3, 321		56	107*		28	208
14	158*		57	104*, 102		29	212
15	275		61	107*		38	211

The references to "Introduction" are distinguished by an asterisk

INDICES TO "INTRODUCTION" AND "BEGINNING"

MARK			MARK			MARK		
		PAGE			PAGE			PAGE
1	39	209, 237	9	11–13	70	14	67	310, 313
	39–45	90*		19	163		68	362
	45	4*		33	95*		69	314
2	1	89*, 95*		41	55	15	11	93*
	5	144*		49	49*		26	321
	10	144*, 147		50	121*, 262		30	345
	12	224	10		222		31	345
	13–14	77*		13	20		32	343, 345
	14–22	230		17	143*, 264		34	125, 169
	23 foll	257		18, 21	263		35–6	70
3	3	407		23, 27	263		36	170
	5	93*		35	167*		39	170
	7	206		42 foll	198, 270		40	107*
	16	144*		45	270		43	102
	17	171*		47	310		44	26*
	21	242		52	264		47	107*
	27	78	11	7	102*	16	1	107*
	31 foll	221		9	275		5	191
	35	221		10	156*, 74, 321		6	191, 310, 325
4	36	25*		11	92–4*		9	106*, 194
	38	114*		15	94*		12	107*
5	34	260		19	86*		15	129*
	39	111*, 191		20	28*		17	107*, 109*, 161, 270
6	1–6	241		23	29*			
	3	221		27	94*		18	107*, 161, 270
	5–6	4*		32	382			
	9	80, 311	12	1 foll	187		19	110*
	17–26	56*		40	384		20	110*
	34	48*, 164	13	1	366			
	37	196		1–2	86*		LUKE	
	50–51	66*		3	120*			
	51–2	45*		4	177	1	1–4	108* foll
	55	209		8	119*, 132*		2	124*
7	4	49		11	286		5	124*, 126*, 133*, 210
	22	375		12	264			
	24	4*		33	236		8	126*
	34	23*	14	4	366		16	172*
8	2	196		10	366		17	8, 70, 323
	9	147*		18	366		19	146, 185
	11	145		24	48		21	126*
	12	23*		26	85*		26	146, 185
	14	48*		27	164		26–8	122*
	17	45–6*		34	154*		31–3	343
	18	45*		36	428		33	98*
	22–6	23*		43	115		36	124*, 125*
	27–9	147*		47	60*		39	94
	29	147*, 342		49	189		40	415
	31	148*		50	370		41	415
	32	148*		54	361		42	415
	33	148*		58	69*		43	97
	34	148*		60	407		44	418
	38	403		61	343, 349		47	344
9	1	171*		62	349		55	127*
	2	79*		66	360		69	344
	7	124		66–7	364			

The references to "Introduction" are distinguished by an asterisk

SCRIPTURAL PASSAGES

LUKE		LUKE		LUKE	
	PAGE		PAGE		PAGE
1 71	344	3 31	18*	6 8	407
75	127*	38	127*, 9	10	93*
76	124*	4 1	67, 108, 148,	14	144*
77	124*, 344		150, 154–7	20	246
78	273	2	94, 157, 177	20–23	121*
79	273	4	179	32–4	23
80	43	5	149–50, 152	42	403
2 1	133*, 94	9	151–3	7 2	231
2	126*	10	161	3	232
6	126*	11	161	11	109*
11	344	13	176 foll	13	111*
14	136, 274	14	141*, 6, 204,	17	209–10
22	149		207, 217	19	27, 74
23	132	15	141*, 6, 207,	22	111*
26	345		217, 223	24	48, 155
27	126*, 360	16	207, 310	26	36
29	274	16–30	241	27	36
30	274	18	59, 240, 342	28	38
40	23	18–21	6	34	313
42	257	19	134–5*, 243	36–50	40*
43	126*	21	6, 23	47	145*
44	362	22	23, 250	50	274
46	71*	23	151*, 207,	8 19 foll	221
49	94*, 257		220, 279	23	435–6
52	23, 95	24	4*	24	114*
3 1	124*, 126*,	26	7*	37	209
	133*, 24, 95,	29	228	45	114*
	220	30	229	48	260, 274
1–20	95	31	95*, 217, 220	52	191
2	124*, 133*,	31–2	269	52–5	111*
	135*, 5, 24,	31–7	220	9 3	80
	43, 46, 69,	33 foll	151*	11	48*
	95, 155	34	310, 320	13	196
2–4	40 foll.	34–5	150*	17	147*
3	43–6, 67, 95,	36	268–9	18 foll	147*
	108, 208	37	208	20	147*, 342
3–6	44	38	212	22	148*
4	42, 155	41	345	23	148*
4–6	33	43	210, 211, 238	26	403
7	65, 67, 72, 96	44	209, 210, 237	27	171*
8	98*, 65	5 1	112*, 114*,	28	79*
9	65		207	33	114*
15	345, 348	4 foll.	222	35	124
16	11*, 50, 75,	5	114*	37	109*
	79, 81, 345	6	113*	49	114*
17	81–2, 124,	7–10	277	54	113
	126	8	113*, 123*	60	213
18	81	9	123*	10 1	77*, 110*
19	216	10	112*	2	148
20	216	16	4*	4	80
21	84*, 110–12,	17	89*	5	259, 273–4
	117	20	144*	6	259, 273–4
22	123*, 117–	20–26	224	8	110*
	19, 274	27	77*	18	276
23	125*, 6, 250	39	230, 337	19	161

The references to "Introduction" are distinguished by an asterisk

495

INDICES TO "INTRODUCTION" AND "BEGINNING"

LUKE			LUKE			JOHN		
		PAGE			PAGE			PAGE
10	21	276	21	25	119*	1	1	14
	22	94*		26	119*		2	14
	41	263		37	86*		3	14
	42	263	22	3	366		4	14
11	1	121*, 217		25 foll	270		5	16
	2	121*		29	94*		6	5, 17, 37
	5–8	122*		32	172*		7	17, 222
	14–16	242		37	174*		8	17, 76
	16	145		38	61*		9 foll	17, 20, 76
	21	78, 274		39	85*		10	17
	22	78		42	428		11	25*, 17, 19
	34	375		43	177		12	44*, 141*,
	50	410, 414		50	60*, 61*			19–21, 222,
12	11	286		51	60*, 61*			229
	12	286		53	177, 189, 370		13	140*, 21, 38
	34	288		54	360, 361, 370		14	22, 25, 45,
	40	236		55	361			136
	45	360		56	310, 360,		15	24, 34 foll,
	51	264, 274			364			46, 65, 73, 76
13	1–3	279		57	360		16	24–5, 136
	7	28–9*		58	314		17	24–5, 58, 347
	27	176		66	69*		18	xxii, 25–31,
14	18	382	23	2	344–5			253, 347, 350
	21	360		5	93*		20	66, 348
	26	50*, 61*		6	279		21	70
	32	274		11	329		23	33, 42, 45
	34	121*		32	150		25	50, 348
	35	121*		34	173		26	13, 51, 101,
15	4	155		35–43	345			408
	8–10	200		36	170		27	13, 51, 76,
	17	118		38	321			79, 101
16	9	287		47	170		28	68, 101–2,
17	6	29*		49	362			109
	9	23		50–52	102		29	85, 88–92, 94,
	11–13	114*	24	3	110*			97–8, 101,
18		222		4	181, 191			109, 225
	15	20		5	310, 325		30	76, 78, 347
	37	310, 314		6	191		31	13, 45
19	9	344		10	107*		32	51, 98, 117–
	10	213		13 foll.	107*			18
	37	158*, 274–5		19	320		33	13, 87, 51,
	38 foll	92*, 94*,		22	123*			89, 99, 111,
		156*, 74, 275,		23	123*			117–19, 124
		321		26	346		34	37, 98, 117,
	41	160*		33	165*			124
	42	160*, 274		34	191		35 foll	39, 94, 98,
20	9 foll	187		36 foll	165*			225, 248
21	5	86*, 366		36–7	292		36	85, 88–92,
	6	86*		39–43	123*			248
	8	236		43	297		37	87, 248
	11	119*		45	115*		38	94*, 191, 248
	14	286		46	346		39	xxi, 248, 338
	15	123*, 286		47	7		40	130*
	16	264		49	94*, 128–9*		41	130*, 144*,
	19–26	119*		50	276			348, 402

The references to "Introduction" *are distinguished by an asterisk.*

SCRIPTURAL PASSAGES

JOHN		JOHN		JOHN	
	PAGE		PAGE		PAGE
1 42	143*, 249	4 7	158	6 64	201
43	98, 212, 225, 249	8	195–6	66	370
44	105, 212	20	33*	68	147*, 11, 223, 349, 355
45	102, 104, 250	21	33*	69	147*, 342, 355
46	338	22	33*, 216, 344	70	56*, 115*, 149*, 199, 201, 347, 355, 366
47	13	23	216		
49	132, 171	24	216		
50	114, 171, 348	25	75, 216, 348		
51	10, 114, 132, 171, 178, 186, 193, 222, 288, 447	26	216, 348	71	149*, 201, 355
		29	338, 348		
		31	195		
		32	158, 179, 195	7 1	198
2 1	220, 225	34	179, 195, 404	3–5	197
2	219	35	132*, 187	5	197, 219, 221, 242
4	159*	42	32*		
6 foll	58, 86	43	227	6	244
10	159*	44	227	7	244
11	16*, 159*, 222, 230	45	227–9, 279	8	244
		46	220, 227	26	348
12	94*, 151*, 220	47	232	27	348
		48	232	31	348
13	71*	49	232	39	52
16	32*, 94*, 257	5 2	180	41	323, 348
17	197, 275	3	180	42	323, 348
18	145	13	6*	52	322–3
19	72*	14	60	8 6–8	364
20	134*	14–16	76*	12	131*, 60
21	70*	19	5*	17	33
23 foll	151*, 228	35	40, 47	21	60
25	144*	6 5	145	23	364
3 2	228	6	145	32	60
3–5	xv, 245	9	132*	39	19, 65
8	57*	13	227	41	65
11	27	14	146*, 227	42	65, 211
12	27	15	146*, 133, 198	56	24
13	xvi	15–21	40*	57	133–4*
14	44, 165	19	227	59	229
16	201	20	59*, 66*	9 1–7	23*
17	201	21	26*, 45*, 59*, 66*, 88*	6	22*
19	202			7	22*
22 foll	54–6			16	56*
22–6	216	23	25*	24	56*
23	16*, 68, 300	26	197	25	56*
24	16*	27	197	31	56*
25–30	39	30	145	39	60
28	37, 348	31	44, 145	40	60
29	292	32–58	xvi	41	60
31	27, 87, 119, 300	39	201	10 11	128
		41	147*	22–3	131*
4 1	215	42	250	24	349
2	54–6	45	84	26	349, 401, 403
3	216	49	44	27	349
4	216	51	294	28	349
6	158, 168, 453	60	147*, 149*	35	33

The references to "Introduction" are distinguished by an asterisk

INDICES TO "INTRODUCTION" AND "BEGINNING"

JOHN			JOHN			JOHN		
		PAGE			PAGE			PAGE
10	39	229	13	33	20	18	11	60*
	41	238	14	1	303		13	135*, 351
11	3	155*		2–3	xvi		14	351
	5	155*		8	145		15	351 foll, 356–9
	24	15		9	xxi–ii, 253			
	25	15		16	119, 281–2, 284		16	351 foll, 356–9
	33	23*, 153*, 155*, 144		17	119, 281–2		17	351 foll, 356–9
	35	160*		18	281			
	36	24*, 155*		19	281		18	351
	37	24*		20	281		19	351
	38	23*		22	124*		20	351
	41	23*		23	200, 281		21	351
	49	135*		25	281		22	351
	51	135*		26	119, 281, 284		23	351
	54	44		27	136, 280–4, 300, 303, 374, 401–4		24	351
12	1	130*					25	351, 366
	1–8	40*					33–9	133
	4	366		28	136, 282–4		36	xv, 190, 245, 401, 404
	13	156*, 74, 133, 321		30	177, 198			
			15	3	xxii		39	133
	14	247		4	419	19	3–21	133
	15	133		5	419		5	87*
	17	156*		6	419		7	63
	18	156*		7	11		17	87*
	19	160*, 186–7		8	419		19	314
	20	160*		9	401, 404		28	174*, 158, 169, 171
	20 foll	187		11–16	24 292			
	21	145, 186–7, 247		16	347, 419		30	174*
				17	347		34	26*, 85
	22	186		18	347		35	26*, 85
	23	187		19	347		36	85
	24	132*, 187	16	8	142*, 286		37	85, 171
	25	61*		11	198, 286		38	76*
	27	154*, 160*, 144, 188		16	43*	20	2	325
				21	132*, 438		2 foll	359
	28	188		33	136, 280, 283, 286, 303, 347, 438		3	358
	29	171*, 180					10	192
	31	186, 198, 276					11	192
	32	78	17	3	350		12	180, 192
	38	217		8	11		13	191–2
	39–43	61		12	200		14	192
	40	263		13	292		15	192, 248
	47	294		17	404		17	173*
13	1	174*		24	411, 414		18	191
	1 foll	146*		26	xxi, 203		19	136, 282
	10	xxii, 63	18	1	87*		19 foll	165*, 136, 282, 292
	14	63		4	87*			
	18	347		5	314, 321		19–23	115*
	21	153*, 161*, 144		6	66*, 314, 370		20	292
							21	136, 282, 292
	27	303		7	314, 321		22	119, 292
	30	131*, 303		8	87*, 189		23	60, 292
	31	161*		9	189, 200		24	165*
	32	161*		10	60*		24–9	123*

The references to "Introduction" are distinguished by an asterisk.

SCRIPTURAL PASSAGES

JOHN		ACTS		ACTS	
	PAGE		PAGE		PAGE
20 26	79*, 136, 282, 298	7 45	360	27 13–18	118*
		9 2	330	18	109*
29	194	5	331	20	298
30	164*, 297, 347	8	360	24	295
		19	177	28 12	120*
31	164*, 33, 297, 347	29	108*	30	114*
		10 15	295	31	114*
21 1 foll	77*, 167*, 298	36	260, 278, 342		
		37	7, 238, 278	ROMANS	
1–14	165*, 299	38	102, 238, 342		
2	167*, 359	11 15	3, 7		
3	277	26	329	1 1	235
4	357	12 13	360	4	110*, 175
6–11	113*	13 25	3*, 76, 79	2 16	38*
7	113*	31	278, 298	8 15	19
9 foll	48*	34	159*	23	19
11	113*	16 6–10	286, 295	31	272
14	299	9	455	38–9	XVIII
18	169*, 452	12	118*	9 22	439
19	169*	16	360	28	177
23	169*	30	143*	10 7	149
		17 26	128*, 7	14 foll	80
		30	7	16	217
ACTS		18 2	339	11 2–4	156
		3	339	5	156
1 1–3	115* foll	8	339	29	374
3	123*, 166*, 296, 298	10	111*, 295	33	XIX
		25	47	12 1	389, 419
8	277	28	91*, 101*	8	377
11	278, 280	19 13	108*	11	110*
21–2	7	13–19	XVII	13 8	63, 263
2 1–21	320	20 12	128	15 1–3	197
2–4	277	22–3	150	12	198
7	278	23	150, 295	16	235
9	339	21 1	109*	33	271
17–18	84	10	298	16 3–7	339
22–7	346	27	177	10	39*
22–36	320	28–9	360	25	38*
33	346	36	332		
36	346	37	360	1 CORINTHIANS	
37	143*	22 2	332		
42–4	277	4	332		
3 6–15	320	8	314, 320, 331–2	1 10	1
13	128			12	38*
26	128	17–21	187	14–15	67
4 10	320	24	360	25–7	77
25	128	24 2	266	2 10	XIX
25 foll	129	5	320, 330	3 4	38*
26	342–3	26	266	22	38*
27	128, 342	25 14	298	4 14	20
30	128	17	109*	8 6	110*
5 35 foll	126*	26 9	320	10 2	450
37	279	11	332	4	25
6 14	320	15	331	27	110*
7 20	89	27 5	118*	11 23	110*, 294

The references to "Introduction" are distinguished by an asterisk

INDICES TO "INTRODUCTION" AND "BEGINNING"

1 CORINTHIANS

		PAGE
11	24–5	421–2
12	2	150
	3	346
14	2 foll	286
15	1–8	38*
	5–8	106*, 165*
	32	162
16	9	114

2 CORINTHIANS

1	8	162
	21	342
2	12	114
	14	294
4	8	438, 443, 445
	13	389
5	16	91*
	17	3
	20	278
6	8–10	445
8	2	377
	5	377
9	7	375
	11	377
	13	377
11	7	235
	26	453
12	2	111
	8	176
	9	295
	18	32*
13	11	271

GALATIANS

1	15–17	155
2	6	120*
	9	277
4	1–2	19
	19	132*, 20
	22 foll.	360
	24–6	156
5	22	292
6	1–2	63
	10	176*

EPHESIANS

1	4	411
2	14	247, 282
	17–18	281

EPHESIANS

		PAGE
2	19	377
3	17–19	XVIII
	18	XIX
	19	272–3
5	1–2	19
6	12	276

PHILIPPIANS

1	5	1
2	29	382
3	12	294
4	7	273
	9	271
	15	1, 3

COLOSSIANS

1	18	3
2	2	XXIII

1 THESSALONIANS

2	2	235
	8	235, 294
	9	235
3	5	157
5	12	390

2 THESSALONIANS

2	13	3

1 TIMOTHY

3	16	175
4	6	109*

2 TIMOTHY

2	8	38*
3	10	109*

PHILEMON

	17	382

HEBREWS

		PAGE
1	6	174, 360
	8	347
	9	25, 342, 347
2	5–18	147
	17–18	143
3	11–4	10 391
4	8	391
	15	143
6	2	49
	5	338
7	2	275
8	8	177
9	7	135*
10		49
	13–14	57
	25	135*
10	1	135*
	3	135*
	22	57
	34	143
	37	74
11	11	410–11
	17	31
	37	69
12	21	202
13	13	87*
	15	420
	20	149

JAMES

1	5	374, 377, 379
3	2	63

1 PETER

1	1	339
	10	87
	12	174
	20	12
2	1–3	338
	2	389
3	8	144
	19	175
4	12–14	366
	17	235

2 PETER

2	3	32*
	13	263

The references to "Introduction" are distinguished by an asterisk.

SCRIPTURAL PASSAGES

1 JOHN			3 JOHN			REVELATION		
		PAGE			PAGE			PAGE
1	1–2 1	289	13		175*	2	27	128
	5	137*				3	20	124*, 173*
	8	263				4	1–2	111
2	1–2	289		JUDE			5	171*
	20	290				5	9	87
	21	290	3		2	6	1	171*
	28	291				7	17	128
3	2	19				10	4	171*
	21	291				12	5	128, 131
4	17	291		REVELATION			7	276
	20	253, 350					15	440
5	4	283	1	1	433	13	8	12
	6–8	85		4	77	14	4	87
	14	291		5	198, 433		6	235
				7	85	19	10	184
				8	77		15	128
	2 JOHN			9	168–9*, 433	21	1	450
				20	433	22	1–2	376, 407
	12	175*	2	24	xix		8–9	184

The references to "Introduction" are distinguished by an asterisk

INDICES TO "INTRODUCTION" AND "BEGINNING"

II. ENGLISH

["c w" means "confused, or confusable, with"]

Aaron, the rod of **448**
Abba **121***
Abel, Philo on **419**
"Able, not," applied to Jesus **4-8***, **23***
Abraham, a rock **97***, the inheritor of divine things (Philo) **23**, the philanthropy of **65**; three men appearing to **182**, the Call of **213**; "the Hebrew" **445**
Acquire, c w make jealous **387**
Acta Pilati **26***, **105***, **371**
Acts of John, the **48***, **201**
Adam, son of **128***, **9**
After, sometimes a misleading word **79***, a these things **74*** foll., a this **75*** foll., a these words **77*** foll., a (or, behind), ambig **75**; s also Behind
Agathodaimon **86**
Akiba **57**, and Bar Cosiba **319**
Allusions, in Jn to Mk **20*** foll., in birthplace-names **311**
Alpha privative **396**
Ambassadors (LXX) = besiege (R V) **444**
Andrew **359**
Angel, the theophanic **182**
Angels, ascending and descending **134** foll., of the little ones **135**, Lucan and Johannine **136**, ministering to Jesus **173**, of God, ambig **174**, personal **181-6**, names of, brought from Babylon **181**, a and wild beasts **147** foll., a and men interchanged **191**
Anointed, the **347**
Antipas, Herod, Josephus on **47**
Aorist tense, diff from imperfect **173**

Aphesis, remission **59, 63**
Apollos **38-9***, **101***, **47**
Appointed-time, Jn on **243**, and feast **244**
Aquila and Priscilla **339**
Arabia, Paul's visit to **155**
"Archon," Hebraized **198**
Arrian **154***, **265**
Article, the, with infinitive **126***
As, omitted **153**
Ascend, and pray **110**
Ascension, the **173***
Ashes of the heifer, the **57**
Atonement, the Day of **66**
Augustine, St **153***
Authority, Christ's **268-73**

Babes, or lambs of God **88**, the mouth of **276**, unborn, praising God **417**
Baptism, the "cup" and **168***, baptism **46** foll., of John, the, continued by disciples of Jesus **53**, the Baptist's conditions for **64**, with blood **83**, of Jesus, the **93-140**
"Baptisms" for purification **49**
Baptist, John the, attitude of, to the Temple **95***, baptizing **32-71**, preaching or prophesying **72-92**, length of public life and preaching of **48**, **129**, teaching of, probably varied **52**, **130**, "two disciples" of **39**, clothing and food of **68**, Johannine non-intervention in matters affecting **71**, Essene views imputed to **92**, and Elijah **70**, and Ezekiel **83**, s also Intervention

The pages of "Introduction" are distinguished by an asterisk.

502

ENGLISH INDEX

Baptize 46 foll, and enlighten 98; "b into the Jordan" 100, "b in my name" 273
Bar (Heb and Aram), meaning of 124, in O T twice = son 126
Bar Cosiba, and Akiba 319
Barley, mentioned by Jn alone 132*, loaves of 167*
Barnabas (the writer) 3; doctrine of, on the Tree, *i e* Cross 450
Bashan 110
Batanea 110
Bath, carrying sandals to the 80
Bath Kol 181
Beasts, s Wild-beasts
Become 16, distinct from "be" 13
Beersheba 155
Beget, "the Father that begot the Universe" (Philo) 29
Begin, "began to say" 7
Beginning, the 135*, of the Gospel 124*, 1-31
Behind, or after 3*, "to go b. Satan" 150*, s also After
Behold, in Heb 114, parall. to "straightway" etc 115
Belief, or faith 222
Believing 21, the precept as to, Mark on 223
Besiege (R V) = ambassadors (LXX) 444
Bethabarah 109
Bethany, meaning of the name 109
Betharabah 109
Bethlehem, and Nazareth 104
Bethsaida 213
Betray, or deliver over 146*, the word, rare in Jn 150*
"Beyond Jordan" 44, 109
Birthplace-names 107, 311
Blind, healing of the 157*, comp 23*, the b and the lame 158*
Blood, baptism with 83
Boanerges 171*
Bread, to the Five Thousand, first given and then multiplied 196
Brethren, Christ's 220, 221
Bridegroom, the Psalm of the 25, 347, of Israel, the 226, s Man
Brother, s Brethren
Buddha, the 93*
Bythos xix

Cain 17, and Abel 420
Calendar, the Jewish 130*
Came-to-pass, s Come
Cana, and Sinai 225, the Gospel of 229

Capernaum 151*, 206 foll; three visits to 95*
Captives, the return of the 238
Cedars, two, on Mount Olivet 81*
Celsus 54*, 103*, 106*, 7, 101, 113, quoting the *Timaeus* 30
Chariot, the, in Ezekiel 137
Charioteer, the, Christ as 90
Child-adoption, the word, not in Gk 19
Children, including both sexes 20, "c of God," not in O T 19
Chrestus, as mentioned by Cicero 337, a name in Suetonius 340
"Christ" and "Christian" misunderstood 336
Christ's first words, in Mk and Mt 234, in Lk 238, in Jn 247
"Christian," the termination in 329, and Nazoraean 329, misunderstood 336
Chronicles, Books of, the 15*, omissions in 55* foll
Chronological "order" 108*
Chronology, Johannine 42*
Chrysostom, (?) quotes from Clem Alex 175, on Christ's brethren, misquotes 220, on Nazoraean 332, s also 134*, 192, 368
Cicero, on Thucydides 117*, on "the world only-begotten" 28
Clean water, in Ezekiel 57
Clement of Alexandria, on:—"the elders from the beginning" 17*, *paideia* 127, Philip 213, John pursuing a robber 294, envy 399, s also 31, 88, 151, 174, 193, 243, 287, 338
Clement of Rome 1-2
Clothe, connected with the Spirit 69
Come, "it came to pass," not distinctively Matthaean 100*, "he that cometh" 74, "may it come on me if" 75
Comforter, the, Menahem a name of 134
Confessing of sins 66
Conflation, in Mk 116
Conscience, in Philo 142*
Cornfields 89*
Cosmocrator 198
Cosmos, identified with heaven 29, this c (in Philo) 285
Create, and beget, in Philo 30
Cross, and rod 128, taking up the 450
Cup, and baptism 168*, "c or rather font" 86

The pages of "Introduction" are distinguished by an asterisk

Danger (Gk)=strait (Heb) 434 foll , "dangers from (*lit* of) rivers" 453
Darkness 16, 302
Dates, in Lk, defective 125*, in Scripture 133*
"Daubers of the wall " 98*
David, the son of 157*
Day, third d , three days etc , s. Third, Three, etc
Days, in those d 93, many d 298
Dead, the, are raised 111*
Declaring God 25
Dedication, the Feast of the 131*
Deliver over, and betray 146*
Deluge, the 121–3, Philo on 122; Josephus on 123
Demon, "the mid-day d " 168
Demosthenes, used by later writers 117*
Descent as a dove 119
Desire, of Jesus, the 214
Despot, the, and the king 78
Destroy, and lose 200
Details, picturesque, often a mark of late tradition 156*
Diatessaron, the 26*, 112*, 165*, 237
Dionysius of Halicarnassus 83*, on Thucydides 117*
Disarrangements in Jn 81*
Disciples, Christ's, when first mentioned in Jn 219
Dove, a 113, descending as a d 118, the d as a symbol 120
Doves, sold for pence of gold 258
Dragon of Egypt, the 440
Drawing, the strength of the king 78
"Drink this first," in Isaiah (LXX) 224
Drought, a land of 159

Eagle, in Deuteronomy 122, e = pediment of a temple 152
Ear, the, of the High Priest's servant 60*
Edessa 334
Edom (*i e* Rome) 160
Egypt, the Dragon of 440
"Elders from the beginning," Clem. Alex. on the 17*
Elect, c w son or purifier 124, the e of God 124
Elias, in Clem Rom 341, in Justin Martyr 341, s also Elijah
Elijah, "a lord of hair" 69, E and Elisha 53, and John the Baptist 70, s also Elias
Elisabeth, and Mary 99

Elisha, and Elijah 53
Elohim, =gods 174
End, the, of the Gospel 124*
Enlightened, and baptized 98
Ephesus xiii, xvii
Epictetus, the Manual of 154*, the gospel of 265, on peace 265, 293, on "storm" 267, on the Galilaeans 279, s also 78, 82
Epiphanius, on "Jessaeans" 317
Eschatological doctrine, given privately 296
Essenes, the 95–6*, 92, 317
Euphrates, the 440
Eusebius 120*, on the order of the Gospels 16*, on Nazara, Netzer, Nazir, etc 311
Evangelion, or good-message 10, 239
"Excellent, most" 116*
Exorcisms, omitted by Jn 150*
Eye, the old, to be closed before the new is opened 22*
Ezekiel, on —sprinkling 52, 83; water of purification 57, a new heart 66, his vision 137, his transportation 151, E and John the Baptist 83

Faith 145*, or belief 222
Fame (Gk)=hearing (Heb) 217
Fast (vb), not in the Pentateuch 157, fasting 178, 195
Father, of the Cosmos, the 30, 31
Feast, and appointed-time 244
Feasts, of the Jews, the three great 130*
Fifty, "not yet f years old " 133*
Fig-tree, the withered 28*, miracle and parable of 187
Fire, prayer answered by 63*; baptizing with 72, metaph 82
First (*or* Chief), "my f " 77
First words of Jesus, in Lk and Jn 94*, s also Christ
Firstborn, applied to Jesus 175
Five, books in the Psalms, Pentateuch etc 100*
Flesh, all 84
Follow, and tarry 170*, f the stronger 78
"Font full of Mind, the" 86, "cup, or rather f " 86
Footsteps of God, the 446
Forgiveness of sins, the 144*
Forty years, substituted by Chrysostom for fifty years 134*, forty days, the, after the Resurrection 295, 298

The pages of "Introduction" *are distinguished by an asterisk.*

ENGLISH INDEX

"From," may mean "a man from" 102 foll
Fruit, sought by Jesus 187
Fruits of Israel, the three, Philo on 244
Fulfilment of Scripture 102*, 189
"Furcifer," and "crucifer" 450
Furnace = "Ur" 157*

Gabriel 142*, 182, 185, 248
Galilaeans 279, Luke on 278
Galilee, Christ's journeying to 204–32, witnesses to Christ from 278
Gamaliel 126*
Gate-keeper, c w "in the midst" 362
Genealogies of Jesus, the two 18*, 8–9
Genealogy, the Johannine 138*
Genitive, Possessive, the 422, Heb circumlocution of 427
Glory, in Jn, three stages of 155*, meaning of 22
Gnostics xviii–xx
Going out, applied to Christ 86*
Good, i e Redemption 105
Good tidings, s Gospel
Gospel, beginning of the 1–31, Christ's, simple and homelike 305, the word, not mentioned by Lk and Jn 9–11, comp 239, g or good-tidings 259
Gospels, the order of the 9* foll
Gospel of the Hebrews, the 103*, 34
Grace, through Jesus Christ 22 foll, "g is poured out on thy lips" 25, "g and truth," the, of the Anointed Bridegroom 347
Great people, the, c w "the many" 64
Greek thought 12

Hardening of the heart, the, in Mk 45*
Harvest, beginning of the 89*, vision of the 187
Hearing (Heb) = report or preaching 217
Heaven, in Jn xvi, identified w Cosmos 29, not mentioned in 1 Jn 290
Heavens, the opening of the 41*, 83, 112, 252
Hebrew, translation from 112*, 121*, narrative 111
"Hebrew," first mention of 323, i e Crosser (of the Euphrates) 445

Hegesippus 152, on the Galilaeans 279
Heifer, the ashes of the 57
Hemerobaptist, a 62
Heracleon 168*
Herald, the Baptist a 45
Hermas, mentions "beginning" only once 3
Hermes, wandbearing 445, conductor of souls 449
Hermetic treatises 85
Herodians, explained as "soldiers of Herod" 329
Hezekiah 58–9*, 328, or the Messiah 261
"Him, to" (Heb) c w "not" 442
Histories, Hebrew, order in 73*
Horae Synopticae 4*, 21* foll
Hosea, on "the third day" 152*
Host, or appointed-time 235
Hour, the sixth 168
Husband 78, s also Bridegroom

I, in Jn xx, in Jn, = "the Love of God in me" 306
Ignatius 41
Image, and likeness 135
Imperfect tense, different from aorist 173
In, or into 118, 151, 154
Infinitive, with article 126*
"Ink and pen" 175*
Instruction (LXX), c w purity or son 125
Intervention, Johannine, 4–8*, 20–36*, 87*, 92–6*, 148*, xi foll, 76, 119, 166 foll, 178 foll, 242, and *passim*
Non-intervention in matters affecting John the Baptist 66, 68–71
Into, or in 118, 151, 154, = "in the body of" 118
Irenaeus, on Johannine chronology 133*, s also xviii, 4, 243
Irony, Johannine 250
Isaac, the binding of 156*
Israel, i e Seeing God (Philo) 127

Jacob, the dream of 134, the ladder of 179
James the Just, martyrdom of 152
Jealous, "make jealous" c w "acquire" 387
Jerome, on the Johannine Prologue 19*, quotes LXX "drink this first" 224, on the wine of Wisdom 231, on Nazoraean 314, explains Herodians 329, s also

The pages of "Introduction" are distinguished by an asterisk

505

INDICES TO "INTRODUCTION" AND "BEGINNING"

103*, 168*, 176*, 57, 151, 166, 287, 299, 368, 443
Jerusalem, meaning of the name 233, 275
Jessaeans 317
Jesse, the name 315
Jesse, the son of 106, legends about 316
Jesus, called "the Lord" 109*, beginning to preach 233–303, called son of Joseph 250, J and Joshua 347
"Jesus Christ," not in Lk's Gospel 346
"Jews, the," in Mt 105*
Johannine Epistle, the first, relation of to the Gospel 289, does not mention heaven 290, or peace 291
John, c w Jordan 101
John (the Apostle), pursuing a robber 294
John (the Baptist), s Baptist
John (the unknown author of the Fourth Gospel), allusions in 20* foll, order and arrangement in 130* foll, does not mention the word "gospel" 9–11, subordinates baptizing to bearing witness 50, preparatory events in 108, "king" in 133, s also Intervention
Jordan, the Circle of the 68, c w John 101, "beyond J" 44, 109
Josephus 126*, and Luke, resemblance 115*, the *Contra Apion* of 116–117*, on —the Baptist's death 47, baptism or immersion 62, the Essenes 92, the Deluge 123, Bethsaida 213, the Galilaeans 279
Joy, in Jn 292
Judaea 210, v r Galilee 209
Judas (Iscariot), contrasted with Peter 146*, chosen by Jesus 199
Judas the Galilaean 279
Justin Martyr, on —Galilaeans 279, "Sunday" 302, "Christian" 336, the term Christus 340 foll, the rod 451; s also 45, 113, 158, 330

Kindness, and mercy 136
King, the, and the Despot 78, when used in Jn 133
Kingdom, of God, the xv, Jn on 245
Kings, Books of, the 15*
"Kiss the Son" 125
Know, frequ in 1 Jn 290
Kôl, voice or thunder 181

Ladder, Jacob's 135
Lamb, the, foreknown 12, of God 85
Lambs of God 88
Last Days, the Discourse on the 120*, 297
Law, and grace 24
Lazarus, the Raising of 155*
"Leap in the womb" 415
Learn by experience 338
Life, in Jn 11, three kinds of, Philo on 13, connected with light 15
Lift up, in Jn, for "crucify" 165, in Sym, for "tempt" 165
Lifting up 111
Light, in Jn 15–18, connected with life 15
Lights, the Feast of 131*
Likeness, and image 135
Little Child, the 304
Little One, the typical 131
Locusts 70
Logoi, in Philo, = angels 179
Logos, the 12; a Mediator 29, aspects of 85
Look about, c w. take delight in 263
Lord, Jesus called the 109*
Love, why not in Jn's prologue 26
Loved, c. w pitied 263
Luke, order and arrangement in 108*, resemblance of, to Josephus 115*, does not mention the word "gospel" 9–11, chronology of 94, mentions an angel by name 185
Luther, on repentance 236

Mabog, or Magog 334
Magog, or Mabog 334
Mammon, Jerome on 287
Man, = husband 78
"Man of Soco, a" 107
Men, the three, that appeared to Abraham 182, and angels interchanged 191
Many, the, c w the great people 64, m days, meaning of 298
Marcan peculiarities, a collection of 20*
Marcion 220
Mark, order and arrangement in 82* foll, vague as to time and place 84*, conflation in 116, alone has "be-at-peace" 262, on Nazarene 310, s also Marcan
Marriage, deprecated by Epictetus for the Stoic 266

The pages of "Introduction" are distinguished by an asterisk

ENGLISH INDEX

Martha 15
Martyrdom 168*
Mary, and Elisabeth 96–9
Matter, "turned to flight by God" 302
Matthew, order and arrangement in 97*
Meek, or poor 247
Melchizedek 233
Menahem, the Comforter, a name of the Messiah 134, 284
Mercy, and kindness 136
Messiah (or Messias 348) as Son, Elect, Purifier 127, named Menahem 134, 284, named Peace 301, coming with a scourge 259, M. or Hezekiah 261, M or Zerubbabel 328, the wand or rod of 445
Michael 182, 184–5
Mid-day demon, the 168
Midst, in the, c w gate-keeper 362
Miracles omitted, in Chron and Jn 58*
Moment of time, in a 152
Monogenēs xviii, 21, in Plato 28
Moses, a lamb in a balance 88, named Tobiah 89, M and angels of wrath 202, the rod of 448
Mother, the, the Holy Spirit regarded as 120, Christ's 221
Mountain, and plane-tree 29*
Muratorian Tablet, the 19*
Mystery of God, the, i e Christ xxiii

Name, from birthplace 107, 311
NAME, the, how used 55, O NAME =O God 66
Narrative, inconsistent 112*
Nathan, the son of David 18*
Nathanael, Christ's Dialogue with 251
Nazarene 102 foll, and Nazoraean 309
Nazareth 102 foll, nowhere mentioned in Talmuds or Josephus 106, Nazarene, Nazoraean etc, rare in early Christian writings 332–3
Nazarite, and Nazirite 311
Nazerini, Pliny on 309, 332
Nazirite, and Nazarite 311
Nazoraean 102 foll, and Nazarene 309, and Christian 329
Negative, combined with positive 13
Netzer, the Branch or Rod of Jesse 106, and *Tsemach* 326, the name of a disciple of Jesus 318

New heart, a 66
New Year, the, among the Jews 57
Not, c w "to him" 442
Numbers, made symmetrical in Jewish tradition 104*

Omissions, historical 55* foll
Only begotten xviii, 26–31
Opening of the heavens, the 112
Order, in Hebrew histories 73*, historical, how defined 82*, order and arrangement in Mk 82* foll, Mt 97* foll, Lk 108* foll, Jn 130* foll
Origen, on —Christ's rod 128, "periit" and "perdidi" 200; Philip 213, Christ's brethren 220, babes 276, the name of Solomon 283, darkness 302, "dangers from rivers" 453, s also 4, 5, 21, 30, 85, 97, 101, 109, 113, 151, 166–8, 190, 225, 243, 273
Owe, in Jn 63

"Paper and ink" 175*
Papias 177*
Paraclete, the 280–97, Philo on 284–5
Paraleipomena, a title 15*, = "things omitted" 53*
Passover, the 68*, going up to 257
Paul, visit of, to Arabia 155, on "dangers from rivers" 454
Peace 304, in Jn 136, in Epictetus 265, 293, in the Four Gospels 267–303, Christ our 247, good tidings of 259, or health 260, prepared before war 283, a name of Messiah 301, the first 301, threefold 301, not mentioned in John's first Epistle 291
Pediment, in Gk, eagle 152
Perichōros, Hebraized 208
Peter, walking on the waves 59*, contrasted with Judas 146*
Philanthropy, of Abraham, the 65
Philip (Herod) 213
Philip the Apostle 213
Philo, on —three kinds of life 13, the inheritor of divine things 23, God "begetting the Universe" 29, the Deluge 122, *paideia* 127, Jacob's ladder 135, 179, the Brazen Serpent 161, the two serpents 167, the food of Moses 195, the three fruits of the

The pages of "Introduction" are distinguished by an asterisk

INDICES TO "INTRODUCTION" AND "BEGINNING"

spiritual Israel **244**, the convicting conscience **248**, the Paraclete **284**, this world **285**, peace **301**, darkness **302**, "Hebrew" **323**, Abel **419**, s also **275**, **316**
Pinnacle of the temple, the **152**
Pitied, c w loved **263**
Place, in Jn xvi
Plane-tree, and mountain **29***
Plato, on Monogenēs **28**
Pliny, on Nazerini **309**, **332**
Pluperfect, none in Hebrew **210**
Plutarch xvii, on Monogenēs **30**
Polycarp **2**
Polytheists, and Gnostics xvii
Poor, or meek **247**
Positive, combined with negative **13**
Possessive Genitive, the **422**
Pour out, in O T **83**
Pray, and ascend **110**
Prayer, answered by fire **63***
Prayers, short **122***
Preach, not in Jn **45**, p and bear witness **17**, **32**
Proarchē xix
Prologue, Johannine, the **13** foll
Proofs, in Luke **120***
Propator xix
Prophecy, evidence from **101***, Mk alludes to, but does not quote **102***
Prophets, the language of **87**
Proselyte, the old eye in, to be closed **22***
Purification, the water of **57**, with water **66**, how expressed **124**
Purifier, c w elect or son **124**
Purifying, the Jews' manner of **58**

Rabbīm, i e many, c w rabbi **64**
"Ram, a certain," Jewish tradition on **12**, comp **115**
Raphael **179**, **182**
Ravens, the, that supplied Elijah **70**
Reception, doctrine of xxi
Red sea, the **439**, **454**
Refrain, Matthew's use of **99***, **100***, "fourteen generations" **104***
Regeneration, expressed in different metaphors **18**
Remission, of sins **48**, **59**, r and washing **62**
Repentance **56**, a baptism of **49**, Luther on **236**
Reproach, a, in O T **197**
Resurrection, traditions of the **106***
"Retaining," of sin **60**
Return, meaning repent **56**
Return of the Captives, the **238**

Revelation, the, mentions no angel but Michael **184**
Rich ruler, the **264**
"River, the," i e Euphrates **440**
Rivers, mighty **439**, dangers from (*lit* of) **453**
Rod, the **451**, and the cross **128**, of the Messiah **445**, of Aaron **448**, of Moses **448**, of the "mouth" **448**, rod, shoot, or sceptre **449**
Rome, represented by Edom **160**
Ruler of this world, the **198**

Salem, meaning of **233**, **301**
Salvation **344**
Samaria, the woman of **30***, **32***
Samuel, Books of, the **15***
Sandals, shod with **80**
Satan, "go behind S" **150***
Saviour, in Lk **344**
Scourge, Messiah coming with a **259**
Sea, the, in Mk **87***, "on the s" or "by the s" **67***
"Seeing God" xxii
Self = (Syr) soul **111**
Self-troubling of Jesus, the **153***
Seraph **160**
Serpents, lit and metaph **161**, two, in Philo **167**
Services, of Jewish servants **80**
Seventy, the sending of the **110***
Shechinah, the **183**
Shel (Heb) **403**, **426–7**
Shepherd (vb), and break in pieces **128**
Sibylline Oracles, the **113**
Sign, or ensign **440**
Simile, with "as" omitted **153**
Sin, in Jn **60**, retaining s **60**
Sins, the forgiveness of **144***
Sinai, and Cana **225**
Six, a mystical number **225**, s days **130***
Sixth, the s hour **168**, the s day **226**
Solomon, meaning of the name **233**
Son, c w elect and purifier **124**
Son of God, a, meaning of **21**
Son of Man **132**, **133**, a title obscure for Gentiles xx
Soul, for self **110**
Spirit, the **111**, descent of, on Jesus **117** foll , Spirit and Holy Spirit **119**, Holy Spirit, the, regarded as the Mother in heaven **120**
Spitting, healing with **22***
Spread forth, and stretch forth **452**
Sprinkling **83**
Stand before God **137**

The pages of "Introduction" *are distinguished by an asterisk.*

ENGLISH INDEX

Stoic, the 266
Stones, raising up sons from 98*, metaph 65
Strabo, on Judaea 210
Straightway, parall to "behold" etc 114 foll
Stretch forth, and spread forth 452
Stronger, follow the 78
Suckling = pupil 88
Suetonius, on Nero's "praiseworthy punishment of Christians" 331

Tables of the Law, the, broken by Moses 202
Tabor 151
Talmuds, the, on Jesus 6*
Targums 156*
Tarry, and follow 170*
Temple, the 69*, Christ's visits to 92* foll
Tempt, in the Four Gospels 144 foll, God tempting Israel 164, c. w uplift 165
Temptation, implied in Jn 194
Temptation of Christ, the 141–203, place of, in Jn 98
Terah, father of Abraham 213
Tertullian 168*, 243, on Nazarene 312
Tetragrammaton, the 66
"Then," characteristic of Mt. 94
Theodotion 46, 88
Theomachy 126*
Third day, Hosea on the 152*
Thirst, metaph and lit, in Jn 166
"This man" = I 42
"This was he" 35
Three, years 28*, in t days, omitted by Lk, emphasized by Jn 43*
Threefold warning, a 95*, t. repetition 300, t peace 301
Thucydides, deficient in "order" 83*, "proofs" in 115*, used by later writers 117* foll
Thunder, and voice 171*
Time of service, or warfare 235
Tishbite, the 323
Tobiah, a name of Moses 89
Tongues, speaking with 286
Translation from Hebrew 112*, 121*
Transportation, spiritual not literal 151–3
Tree, "God taught Moses a t" 418
Tsemach, and *Netzer* 326

Unclean, not mentioned in Jn 268
"Unique [ones], these," i e. Abraham and Isaac 31
Unleavened bread, the feast of, before the harvest 89*
Up, "lead up" and "lead" 148 foll
Uplift, s Lift
Ur of the Chaldees 157*

Valentinians 243
Vine of David, the Holy 318
Vinegar, offered to Christ 170
Voice, and thunder 171*, diff from word 41, from heaven, the 123 foll

Wand of Hermes, the 449
War, in heaven 276, w and peace, the first 301
Warfare, or time of service 235
War-Psalm of the Jews, a 127
Washing, and remission 62
Water, of purification, the 57, and blood 84
Way = sect 330
Weeks, the Feast of 89*
Well-pleasing, men of 274
Wheat, to pray that it may be parched 82, i e the Law 126
Whispering over a wound 22*
Whole-burnt-offering 110
Wild-beasts, and angels 147, in Mk 158, lit. and metaph. 162
Wilderness, regarded metaphorically 43, of Judaea, the 43, of Sinai, the 44, "in or into the w." 154
Wine, mingled by Wisdom 230
"Winter, it was" 131*
Withdrawing, Christ's 206
Witness, bear w and preach 17, 32
Witnesses, two or three 107*
Women, testimony of 105*, 124*, witnesses of the Resurrection 298
Word, in Jn 11, diff from voice 41
World, this, the powers of, are wild beasts 167

Year, high priest for that y 135*, of the Lord, the acceptable 134*, 243

Z (Aram) interchanged with tz 324
Zebedee, the sons of 167*
Zerubbabel, called Nehemiah 327

The pages of "Introduction" are distinguished by an asterisk.

INDICES TO "INTRODUCTION" AND "BEGINNING"

III. GREEK

[c w. means "confused, or confusable, with"]

Ἀγαπάω ἠγάπησεν c w ἠπάτησεν 263
ἀγαπητός 31
ἄγω ἤγετο 150
ἀετός (*architect*) 154
αἷμα, not = "blood relation" 382
-αῖος, the termination, in Gk 331
ἀκοή 217
ἀλείφω ἠλειμμένος 337
αλλα, unaccented, may mean "others" or "but" 25*
ἁμαρτάς 62
ἁμάρτημα 63
ἀμνός and ἀρνίον 92
ἀνάβλεψις 238
ἀνάγκη 119*
ἀνάγω 149
ἀνασείω ἀνέσεισαν v r ἔπεισαν 93*
ἀνατολή, "branch" 328
ἀναφυή 328
ἀναχωρέω 206
ἀνήρ 79, 347
ἀνοίγω 112, ἀνεῳγότα 114, 447
ἄξιος 79
ἁπλότης 377
ἀπό and ἐκ 104-5, 212, and παρά 295
ἀπόλλυμι 200
ἀπορία 119*
ἀποψύχω 119*
ἅπτομαι and κρατέω 173*
ἀρνίον and ἀμνός 92

ἄρσεν (*neut*) with υἱόν 131
ἄρχω 198
ἀσκαρίζω 418
ἄφεσις 59, 62
ἀφθόνως 373-4, 398
ἀφίημι 176, ἀφέντες ambig 370
ἀφίστημι ἀπέστη 176

Βάθος and βυθός xix
βάπτισις 62
βαπτισμοί 49
βαστάζω 79
βρέφος 20
βυθός and βάθος xix

Γνώριμος 17*
γνωστός 363, c w δοῦλος 231, γ. τῷ and ὁ γ τοῦ 358
γνωτός 363
γράφω 104

Δαίμων · κρατήρ ἀγαθοῦ δαίμονος 86
δέχομαι and λαμβάνω 229
διαρρήγνυμι 112
διαφορότης 95*
δοκέω δοκοῦντες 120*
δόκιμος 120*
δοῦλος 230, and παῖς 231, c.w γνωστός 231

Ἐθήμων 357, 371
εἰρηνεύω 262, and ὑγιαίνω 260

εἰρήνη and σωτηρία 260
εἰς ἔρχομαι εἰς τινα 118
εἰς ἕν perh for "the one thing [needful]" 263
εἰσάγω 360
ἐκ and ἀπό 104-5, 212
ἐκβάλλω 148
ἐκλέγομαι 347, ἐκλελεγμένος 124
ἐκπύρωσις 15
ἐκτείνω χεῖρας 452
ἐλευθερία 59
ἐμβλέπω 263, 365
ἐμός 404
ἐνιαυτός 135*
ἐν τῷ with infinitive 112*, 121*, 126*, 111
ἐνισχύω 177
ἐξέρχομαι ἐξῆλθον ambig 168*, ἐξῆλθον, meanings of 211
ἐξηγέομαι 25-6
ἐξηγητής 26
ἑξῆς 109*, 115*
ἐξουσία 177
ἑορτή 244
ἐπαύριον 98
ἐπιστάτης ἐπιστάτα 114*
ἐπιστέλλω 1
ἐπιστρέφω · ἐπιστρέψας, preceding στήρισον 172*
ἐπιχειρέω 116*
ἐράω ἐρῶν τοῦ ἀποθανεῖν 167
ἔρημος, ἡ 155

The pages of "Introduction" are distinguished by an asterisk.

GREEK INDEX

ἔρχομαι with εἴς τινα 118, ἐρχόμενος, ὁ 74
ἔρως 167-8
ἐρωτάω 284
εὐαγγελίζομαι 234
εὐαγγέλιον 10, 11, 234
εὐθέως 114
εὐθύνω 44
εὐθύς 114

Ζωή 289

Ἡμέρα ἐπὶ πλείονας ἡμέρας 298

Θέλω ἠθέλησεν 212
θηρίον 159
θλῖψις 438
θυρωρός, ἡ 360

Ἱεράομαι ἱερώμενος 285
ἱκανός 79

Καθεξῆς 108*
καιρός 244
καταβολὴ κόσμου 408-14
κάτω 364
κιθάρα 394
κίνδυνος 434 foll
κινύρα 394
κοινός κοινά and κοινωνία 277
κοινωνία = two Heb words 277
κόσμος, two meanings of 30
κρατέω and ἅπτομαι 173*
κρατὴρ ἀγαθοῦ δαίμονος 86
κράτιστε 116*
κρείσσων 79
κύπτω 80

Λαμβάνω and δέχομαι 229
λιμός and λοιμός 119*
λόγος ὁ ἀρχάγγελος καὶ πρεσβύτατος λ 29,
diff from ῥῆμα 124*,
diff from φωνή 388
λοιμός and λιμός 119*
λύω 79

Μαρτυρέω in the Gospels 32
μαρτυρία in the Gospels 32
μαρτύριον, "death by martyrdom" 170*

μονογενής 28, 30, 31

Νάβλη 394
νεολαία 20
νέος 357
νικάω 283

Ὀπίσω 150*, 76, implies (1) revolt, (2) repulse 370
οὖν 227

Παιδεία 127
παιδίον 230
παιδίσκη 360
παῖς, applied to Jesus, 128, π and δοῦλος 231
παλιγγενεσία 15
παρά and ἀπό 295, π
πόδας = except as to the feet 63, π. τοῦ and π τῷ 101
παραγίνομαι 46
παράκλησις in Isaiah (LXX) 282
παράκλητος, not in LXX 284
παρακολουθέω 109*
παραλαμβάνω 25*, 149
παρατίθημι τὸ παρατιθέμενον 110*
παρρησία 291
πᾶς πᾶσιν (neut pl) 108*
πατρίς 228
πείθω ἔπεισαν v r for ἀνέσεισαν 93*
πειράζω πειράζων, ὁ 157
πέλαγος 118*
περιάπτω 361, 366
περιβλέπω 263, περιβλεψάμενος 93*
περιέχω περιεῖχε τὸν τρόπον, literary use of 16*
περιπατέω 90
περίχωρος 208
πίπτω (1) "fall," (2) "fall away," "desert" 370
πλήθω and πληρόω 235
πληρόω and πλήθω 235
ποιμαίνω 128
ποῦς παρὰ πόδας, "except as to the feet" 63
πρότερον and πρῶτον 114*

πρῶτον and πρότερον 114*
πτερόν (architect.) 154
πτερύγιον 152

Ῥαβδίον 449
ῥάβδος and ῥακτηρία 449, and σκῆπτρον 449
ῥήγνυμι 112
ῥηθείς, ὁ, only once applied to persons in the Gk Bible 34
ῥῆμα 124*

Σανδάλιον 80
σκῆπτρον and ῥάβδος 449
σκιρτάω 418
σος 425
στρατόπεδον 119*
συμπαθέω 143-4
συμπάσχω 143-4
συνήθης 371
συντελέω 177
σῶμα 118
σωτήρ 344
σωτηρία 344, and εἰρήνη 260

Ταράσσω ἐτάραξεν ἑαυτόν 153*
τεκμήριον 115*
τεκνίον 20
τεκνοθεσία, no instance of 19
τρόπος, literary use of 16*

Ὑγιαίνω and εἰς εἰρήνην 260
υἱοθεσία 19
ὑπάγω 150*
ὑπόδημα 80
ὑπολύω 79
ὑπομιμνήσκω 284
ὑποστρέφω 148, 150

Φήμη 217
φιλανθρωπία 65
φωνή λέγων 115, φ diff from λόγος 388
φωτισμός 97

Χρηστός and χριστός 336-8
χριστός meaning "lotion" 337, χ and χρηστός 336-8

Ψαλτήριον 394

The pages of "Introduction" are distinguished by an asterisk

INDICES TO "PROCLAMATION"

I. SCRIPTURAL PASSAGES

GENESIS			GENESIS			EXODUS		
		PAGE			PAGE			PAGE
1	2	345	18	21	184	3	7–8	184
	26	172, 342	19	20	419		12	392
	27	277, 342		22	419		22	451–3
2	9	78		27	236	4	22–3	457
	10	245	20	9	131	6	14	140
	22	317	21	2	215		25	140
3	6	78		14	236	8	19	451
	8	15, 16		15	196	11	2	451, 481
4	1	279	22	3	236	12	6	214–15, 453
	4	280	24	5	147		8–11	81
	6	257	25	24	192		12	11
	7	171, 275–6		27	58		13	11
5	21–4	98	26	11	463		17	312
6	3	42		13	106		19	295
	4	445	27	28	321, 337		23	11
7	13	312	29	22	430		35	451
10	8	58		35	414		36	451–2
	9	57–8	30	6	399		42	216
11	5	184		8–20	112	13	14	162–3
	7	184		18–20	112	15	1–21	456
	27–8	58		20	111, 123		9	33
	32	138	31	12	470		16–18	12
12	1	136, 138	32	12	376		25	182, 344
	18	131		28	134		26	157, 228
14	9	297	38	27	192	16	4	182
	14	168	42	28	426		12	214
15	2	142	43	30	253		15	161
	14	451, 453		31	253		15 foll	188
	15	273	45	5	392	19	6	63
16	7	345	48	16	376		8	482
	10	376		19	376	22	1 foll	464
	13	345–6	49	8	414		2	466
	14	345		9	275		2–3	463–4
17	4	376		14	147		31	302
	23	312		16	398	23	1	60
	26	312		17	275		15	60
18	4	236		22	345	24	3	482
	8	46		25	345		7	482

SCRIPTURAL PASSAGES

EXODUS			DEUTERONOMY			I SAMUEL		
		PAGE			PAGE			PAGE
28	26	377	9	10	451	6	5	292
	30	349	13	4	50		20	17
29	39	16	16	6	215	10	12	439
	41	16	20	20	78	16	7	290
30	8	214	22	11	335	20	27	128
31	13	353	23	11	214		30	128
	18	451		14	453	21	1	348
33	23	345	24	7	466	22	16–18	348
34	28	46		13	214	24	13	439
			25	2	121	26	16	121
				18	206			
LEVITICUS			27	26	289			
			28	22	196	2 SAMUEL		
6	20	16		60	166			
10	16	192		61	166, 213	8	7	63
12	2	464	30	3	228		12	382
13	15, 16	224		19	224		13	382
16	1	118	32	22	196		14	141
	17	136		29	162	12	5	121
	29–31	311		49	470	15	18	10
	30	331	33	13	345	19	24	209
19	2	453		18	112	24	1	211
	15	368		27	345		12	200
	19	335						
	23	78						
	31	156	JOSHUA			I KINGS		
23	27–9	311						
	28–30	312				8	62	403
25	9	312	3	16	17	10	11	140
	10	312	5	11	329		22	140
26	16	196		12	329	11	25	382
	33	38	7	19	292	12	10	419
			9	5	336	14	6	391
			15	25	417	17	18	5
NUMBERS			18	28	241		22	61
			24	2	138	18	29	16
11	6	188		13	206	19	12	109
13	31	450					19	10
19	2	155, 157					20	10
	9	156	JUDGES			21	7–13	366
21	28	429				22	35	215
23	6	192	3	28	148		36	17, 215
	18	127	4	6	113			
	19	127		10	113	2 KINGS		
25	11	417	5	14	112			
27	12	470		15	112	1	2	429
35	33	366–7	6	11	351		3	429
				14	134		6	429
				24	351		16	429
DEUTERONOMY			8	32	351	2	3	317
			14	19	105		5	317
1	16	288				4	27	299
	17	288, 290					42	404
	31	207	RUTH			6	19	49
2	14	224, 267					32	366
5	1	60	4	10	182	12	21	111
7	15	186, 213						

A. P.

INDICES TO "PROCLAMATION"

2 KINGS		
		PAGE
13	2	147
15	5	195
16	6	382
17	30	297
	31	297
19	4	195
20	13	170

1 CHRONICLES		
1	10	58
12	18	403
	32	112
16	28	140
18	11	382
	13	141
20	3	141
21	1	211
	10	200
22	17	141
25	8	21

2 CHRONICLES		
7	4	403
9	10	140
	21	140
10	10	419
18	34	215
20	25	452
24	26	111
25	12	62
26	20	195
31	3	16

EZRA		
2	63	349
8	12	419
	21	43

NEHEMIAH		
7	65	349
9	25	78

ESTHER		
2	18	430
	19	209
5	10	136
6	10	209

ESTHER		
		PAGE
6	12	136
8	2	136
9	22	430

JOB		
9	8	14
15	34	365
17	7	362
20	5	365
24	14	466
26	11	195
32	18	156
	19	156, 339
34	30	365
36	13	365
41	33	444

PSALMS		
1	2	478
2	2	370
9	13	470
16	8	38
17	7	191
19	5	315, 324
25	18	470
	19	470
31	7	477
	11	474
32	1–2	266
	2	421
33	9	167
34	12	224
37	24	202
38	8	254
	11	474
40	6–8	483
	8	475
	9	483
	10	477, 483
	14	483
41	9	121
42	1	339
	2	204
	5	256
	11	256
43	5	256
45	7	41
47	9	403
50	23	414
51	2	331
	9 foll	266
52	1	445–6, 469
60	9	380

PSALMS		
		PAGE
63	1	204
68	27	111
	31	39
69	20	360
73	7	364
	27	295
77	19	13
78	2	436
	71	404
80	4	404
89	2	353
	12	37
	24	477
91	12	356
92	title	354
100	title	414
104	20	356
	22	275
	23	356
106	9	160
107	3	37
	35	7
110	3	403
114	2	170
	8	7
119	69–71	363
	83	339
	116	202
129	8	10
136	8–9	170
137	1	43
139	18	406
143	10	475
145	14	202

PROVERBS		
1	1	440, 442
	1–6	439
3	8	228
4	22	228
5	3	367
6	26	58–9
9	3	393
	5	182
	8	195
10	16	61
	20	362
11	9	365
	19	61
13	14	346
14	27	346
19	6	209
20	6	472
25	1	439
27	16	472

SCRIPTURAL PASSAGES

PROVERBS		
		PAGE
29	26	209
30	24–8	440

ECCLESIASTES		
3	2	342

SONG OF SONGS		
1	8	323
	15	323
3	4	103
7	1	321
	4	7
	9	341
8	1 foll	323

ISAIAH		
1	15	99
2	4	195
	11	327
	17	327
3	22	336
4	5	315
6	8	393
	9	227
	10	227, 229, 271, (?) 362
9	1	111, 379
	1–2	9, 13
	1–6	143
	12	304
11	2	75
	3	271–2
14	1	295
16	8	429
17	13	255
19	4	418
	8	34
25	11	97–9
30	6	105
	22	431
	27	251
31	7	462
33	14	365
	21	97
35	5	426
38	21	224
39	2	170
	7	63
40	15	201

ISAIAH		
		PAGE
40	22	324
	28	207
41	4	134
	17	204
43	1	134
	1–10	405
	12	405
44	8	405
46	5	444
49	24	446
	24–5	446
50	10	467
	11	467
51	19	360
52	7	234–5
53	3	165–6
	4	163, 191, 194, 216, 235, 250
	6	227
	8	325
	12	227, 449
54	17	209
55	1	204, 337
58	1–6	312
	10	312
60	1–3	304, 384
	17	404
61	1	168, 324
	1 foll	324
	2	168, 337
	2–11	337
	10	324
	10 foll	324
62	5	324
63	1	380
	9	253
	15	253
65	8	337

JEREMIAH		
2	2	392
	13	346
3	6–8	295
4	19	256
13	16	292
16	16	57, 59
17	13	346
21	4	448
30	3	326–7
	7 foll.	326–7
	8	327
31	20	252–3
33	8	331
39	9	20
	10	20

LAMENTATIONS		
		PAGE
2	6	254
4	20	325

EZEKIEL		
1	1	43
4	6	39
14	3	156, 368
	4–8	463
	14	452
	20	452
16	3	302
	46	39
18	2	438–9
19	2	275
25	14	382
26	5	34
29	3	275
32	27	448
34	4–16	227
37	9 foll	75
40	20–42	15 379
47	1–2	38
	1–12	399
	2–5	97
	5	92, 97
	8	85
	9–10	80
	10	37
	12	78, 209, 399
	13	399

DANIEL		
2	12	257
4	17 foll	170
	19	103
5	19	389
7	10	209
	12 foll	170
8	7	159
	18	195
	21	304
	23	437
9	21	194
	26	403
10	4	43
	20	304
11	2	304
	30	251, 254
	32	366
12	2	61

INDICES TO "PROCLAMATION"

HOSEA

		PAGE
3	4	349
5	11	367
6	1	239
	1–3	237
	2–3	148
	3	237, 244
	6	353, 483
10	6	370
13	1	250
	14	250
	15	250
	16	250

JOEL

2	16	315, 324
3	6	304

AMOS

9	11	381
	12	381

OBADIAH

	3	141

JONAH

1	6	20

MICAH

4	2	239
5	2	244
	5	244

HABAKKUK

1	14	58
	15	58
	17	33

ZEPHANIAH

3	10	39

ZECHARIAH

2	4	243
3	2	160

ZECHARIAH

		PAGE
9	9	304
	10	304
	13	302, 304
12	10–14	155
13	1–2	155
14	21	302

MALACHI

4	2	230

MATTHEW

1	19	145
2	12	372
	22	37
3	8	78
	11	50
4	3	188
	6	356
	9	168
	12	222, 378
	12–13	158 foll
	13	154, 179
	13–15	110
	13–16	178
	15	379
	15–16	13
	17	3
	18	26–7, 32, 46, 126, 133
	18–22	1–153
	19	47, 57 foll
	20	135 foll, 142, 144 foll.
	21	34, 101, 106, 129
	21–2	108 foll., 124 foll.
	22	110 foll, 135 foll, 139 foll, 144 foll.
	23	165, 233 foll.
	23–4	181, 190
	23–5 1	163, 234
	24	167, 210, 213, 233, 382
	24–5	105, 374 foll.
5	1	181, 234
	1–2	388
	2–7	29 163
	3	234
	6	205, 306
	9	121

MATTHEW

		PAGE
5	11	249
	13	481
	14	351
	20	286
	21–2	461
	22	461
	44	480
	46	286–7
	47	287
6	2	368
	5	368
	7	368
	16–18	313
	19–20	466
7	21	475
	22	167, 233, 400
	27	355
	28–9	154 foll
8	1–4	190, 246–60
	1–15	163
	1–17	235
	2	203
	3	190
	5	179
	5–13	190
	6	197–8, 200
	8	202
	8–9	164
	10	191
	11–12	293
	14	27, 145, 192, 196–9
	14–15	190
	15	169, 193
	16	163–4, 213–17 foll.
	16–17	210, 217–31
	17	163, 191, 216 foll.
	18	327
	21–2	10, 52
	22	139
	26	160
9	1	185
	1–2	263
	1–8	261–83
	2	198–9
	8	264
	9	8, 13, 414–15
	9–13	284–306
	12	213
	13	129
	14	308
	15	309, 314 foll, 326
	16	336 foll.
	17	338 foll.

516

SCRIPTURAL PASSAGES

MATTHEW		MATTHEW		MATTHEW	
	PAGE		PAGE		PAGE
9 27	11, 12, 13	12 32	458, 460	19 29	136 foll.
27–30	220	33 foll	445	30	397
28	427	34	346	20 20	3, 113, 119
30	251, 255	39 foll	300	20–3	109
32–3	427	43	166	22–3	108
32–4	427	44–5	220	26	404
34	428	46	425, 471	28	257
35	240, 364	46–50	470 foll.	30	11–13
35–8	165	47	425, 470, 471	33	21
37	152	48	471	34	220, 251
10 1	165, 389, 391	50	445	21 1	41
1–4	387 foll	13 1–3	105	18	207
1–5	374	2	140	19	79
1–15	153	3	436, 444	23	19
2	27, 126, 408	13	482	31–2	287, 294 foll.
2–4	417	13–15	228	32	322
3	413–17	14	363, 482	38	48
4	417–18	15	228, 363, 482	42	467
5	298	35	436	22 4	48
7	404	47 foll.	72	14	130, 390
12	121, 276	53	444	16	365
13	121, 276	14 1–2	370, 427	18	268
15	276	9	370	37–40	286
16	396	13	378	42	349
24	24, 394	14	386	23 7–8	21
25	24–5, 430	15	240, 397	11	404
40	243, 396	16	188	24	429
11 18–19	430	25 foll	13	26	320
19	287, 393	31	100	34	393
23	183	33	364	37	242
28	48, 306	35	213	24 3	27
12 1–4	347–51	15 1	432	22	390
5–8	352–5	21	37, 299, 378	24	390
7	483	21–8	298 foll	31	390
9	373	22	302	42–4	465
9–14	356 foll	24	300	43	466
9–15	374	32	478	25 1–13	315
11	87	16 4	300	34	48
15	105, 268,	6	365	26 6–8	296
	374–5	8	268	10	268
16–17	375 foll	9	364	14–16	417
19	260	13	37, 241	17	234
21–2	426	17	128	18	234
22–3	424–7	18	126	23	396
22–4	427	25	67	25	21, 22
23	425	17 1	409	29	336
24	431–2	4	22	33	55
24–8	428 foll.	5	411	37	113
25	435	15	167, 200	37–8	257
25–32	445	22	309	38	255, 257
27	157	24–7	88	39	102 foll.,
27–30	446–52	18 5	396		476, 483
28	468	17	287	46	238
28 foll.	451	19 15	219	49	21–2
29	448–50	21	48	58	53
30	455	27	136 foll., 142	59	103
31	458	28	397–8	66	461

517

INDICES TO "PROCLAMATION"

MATTHEW			MARK			MARK	
		PAGE			PAGE			PAGE
26	71	103	1	30	192, 199	3	12	160
	73	103 foll		31	169, 193		13	377, 389
27	1	103		32	213–17		13–14	383, 389, 399
	16	309		32–4	217–31		13–19	387–423 *passim*
	17	309		34	164, 169, 210			
	18	280		35	237		14	394, 399, 403–4
	25	295		35–8	233			
	26	476		35–9	232–45 *passim*		15	407
	41	206					16	126, 133
	46	16		36	52, 148, 237		17	408
	48	206		38	137, 237, 240 foll		18	27, 413, 417
	49	299					20	424–5
	55	117, 474		39	181, 373		20–21	424–7
	56	3, 108, 113, 117 foll		40–44	190		20–35	424–84 *passim*
				40–45	246–60 *passim*			
28	1	328					21	425–6
	6	48		41	190, 251		22	430, 432
	9	26		43	251, 255		22–6	428 foll
	10	26	2	1	185, 424		23	435
	18	177		1–2	185		23 foll	435
	20	319		1–12	261–83 *passim*		24–30	445
							26–7	468
				2	263		27	446–53
	MARK			3	199		28–9	458 foll
				4	199		29–30	460
1	1–3	348		8	269		30	427, 468
	7	10, 50		11	425		31	425, 472
	14	180		12	229, 265		31–5	470–84
	15	3, 444		13–14	8–9		32	425
	16	5, 26, 32, 46		13–17	284–306 *passim*		34	361, 473
	16 foll	65					35	445, 474
	16–20	1–153 *passim*		14	415	4	1–2	105
	17	47, 57 foll, 309		15	199, 383		12	228, 363, 407, 482
	18	135 foll, 142, 144 foll		17	129, 306			
				18	308 foll		14	263
	19	34, 101, 106		18–22	307–46 *passim*		22	343
	19–20	108 foll					35	327
	20	110 foll, 124 foll, 129, 135 foll, 139 foll, 144 foll		19	309, 315		39	160
				19–20	314 foll	5	8	431
				20	326		18–20	233
				21	336 foll, 436		29	208
				22	338 foll		30–33	233
	21	137, 179, 373		23–6	347–51		35–7	233
	21 foll	65		25	277		37	409
	21–8	154–89 *passim*		26	425	6	2	364
				27–8	352–5		5	219
	22	169	3	1	357, 373		6	179, 240–41, 364
	23–8	233		1–6	356–71			
	27	154, 162, 168–9		4	359		7	165, 168
				5	360		8	407
	29	27, 137, 145, 373, 424		7	372–7		8–13	153
				7–9	105		12	407
	29 foll	65		7–12	372–86 *passim*		14	370, 427
	29–31	190					26	257, 370
	29–34	190–231 *passim*		8	376, 379–82		31	48
				9	377, 407		32	48
				10	181		34	8, 386

518

SCRIPTURAL PASSAGES

MARK		MARK			LUKE	
	PAGE			PAGE		PAGE
6 35	397	12 38	14		3 7	294
36	240	41–4	233		8	78
37	188	13 3	27		12	287, 294
41	407	20	390		13	287
48–9	13	22	390		14	294
52	363–4	27	390		16	50
56	240	34	407		4 3	188
7 1	432	35–6	465		6	157, 168
4	276	14 3	199		11	356
24	299	5	255		16	373
24–30	298 foll.	6	299		18	168
26	302	13	233		19	337
28	21	17	396		23	183, 330, 436
30	201	18	396		24	183
8 2	478	20	396		25–7	301
6	407	25	336		29	183
12	255	29	55		30	178–9, 183
15	365	33–4	257		31	178–9
17	268, 364	34	255, 257		31–7	154 foll
19–20	397	35	102 foll		32	169
23	219	36	476, 483		34	20, 183
23–7	241	42	238		35	183
35	67	45	21		36	154, 164, 168–9
9 2	409	54	53		38	27, 126, 145, 192, 199
5	21–2	55	103			
7	411	64	461		38–9	190 foll
25–7	207	69	103		38 foll	65
27	193	70	103 foll		39	160, 169, 193, 196
35	404	72	35			
37	243, 396	15 1	103		40	210, 213–17, 219
38	109, 218	10	280			
38–9	167	15	476		40–41	217–31
38–40	233	31	206		41	160, 164, 169, 218
10 5–6	277	34	16			
13	407	36	206, 299		42	52
21	48	40	108, 117 foll, 474		42–4	233 foll
23	361				43	240–43
28	136 foll, 142	41	117		44	233, 241, 373
29	136 foll	45	269		5 1–2	5 foll
29–30	139, 397	16 1	108, 328		1 foll	65
35	113, 119	5	38		1–3	1–153
35–40	109	6	48		2	83
43	404	8	281		3	101, 126
45	257	17–20	230		3 foll	1
46 foll	12				3–10	4
51	21	LUKE			4	37, 126
52	220, 251	1 7	106		5	20, 126
11 2	215	11	38		6	5, 376
12	207	18	106		7	93
13	79	62	94		7–10	41
21	21	2 20	229		8	5, 95, 126
27	17, 19	25	313		9	62
28	407	36	106, 111, 113		9–11	1–153
12 7	48	37	313		10	47, 59, 61 foll, 113, 126, 408
10	467	48	20			
13	365	3 1	179, 380			
35	349					

INDICES TO "PROCLAMATION"

LUKE

		PAGE
5	10–11	108 foll.
	11	135 foll,
		139 foll,
		144 foll
	11–12	137
	12–14	190
	12–16	246–60
	13	190
	16	237, 378
	17	185, 241, 263, 358
	17–26	261–83
	18	199
	24	198
	25	199, 229
	26	229, 265
	27	8, 415
	27–32	284 foll.
	30–33	310
	32	129
	33	308 foll.
	34	309
	34–5	314 foll.
	35	326
	36	323, 336 foll.
	37–8	338 foll
	39	340
6	1	348
	1–4	347–52
	5	339, 352
	6	373
	6–11	356 foll
	10	361
	12	235, 374–7
	12–16	387 foll
	13	377, 383, 389, 394
	14	27, 126, 408
	16	413
	17	235, 374, 379, 382–3
	17–19	105, 375 foll.
	20	234
	21	205
	22	249
	24–6	480
	26	481
	27	480–81
	32, 33	287
	40	25, 394
	45	346
	46–7	475
7	1–10	190
	2	197, 201, 203
	5	185
	7	202
	7–8	164

LUKE

		PAGE
7	9	191
	16	229
	29–30	287, 294 foll
	30	479
	31–5	296
	33–4	430
	34	287
	35	393
	36–50	296
	47–8	299
8	2	296
	4	105
	10	228, 363, 482
	19	472
	19–21	470 foll
	20	425, 472
	21	445
	22	327
	24	160
	51	409
9	1	168
	1–5	153
	2	405
	3 foll	276
	7	370, 427
	10	378
	11	269
	12	240, 397
	13	188
	18	241
	23	49
	24	67
	28	409
	31	412
	33	22
	35	411
	48	243, 396
	49	109, 218
	49–50	167
	50	49
	51	49
	51–2	241
	51–5	298
	54	109, 409
	56	241
	57	49
	59	49
	59–60	10, 52, 139
	61	49
10	1	41
	1–12	153
	2	152
	5–6	121, 276
	12	276
	15	183
	16	243, 396
	21	255

LUKE

		PAGE
10	42	296
11	14	424–6
	14–15	427
	15	430, 432
	15–20	428 foll
	17	435
	17–22	445
	19	157
	19–23	446 foll.
	20	468
	20 foll	451
	21–2	449
	22	452
	23	455
	24	166
	25–6	220
	29 foll	300
	41	320
	49	393–4
12	1	365
	10	458–60
	33	466
	37	465
	39	466
	39–40	465
	47	269, 475
	48	269
13	6	79
	10	373
	11–16	169
	13	229
	14–17	359
	22	240–41, 364
	23	397
	26	167, 233, 400
	28	293
	30	397
	32	366, 369
	32–3	148
	34	242
14	2	267
	5	87
	12–13	131
	26	68
	34 foll	351
15	4–32	300
	30	294
16	20	200
17	14–15	220
	33	67
18	7	390
	9	286
	10–14	287
	11–12	313
	12	314
	13	421
	15	407

520

SCRIPTURAL PASSAGES

LUKE			LUKE			JOHN		
		PAGE			PAGE			PAGE
18	22	48	24	42–4	83	2	19	208
	23	257		43	83		22	151, 383
	28	136 foll, 142		45–9	44		23–4	221, 238
	29	136 foll.		47	242	3	2	23, 244
	29–30	139					2–14	221
	30 foll	397		JOHN			3	74
	35 foll	12					5	75
	37	12	1	5	282		6	74
	41	21		6	244, 392		8	481
	42	220, 251		7	147		10	23
19	1–9	287		9	282		14 foll	76
	10	300, 421		11	12		15	274
	41	362		12	172, 175, 271		16	480
20	1	19		12–13	477		22	151–2, 383
	14	48		14	182		24	180, 371
	17	467		17	477		25–6	331
	20	365		18	123, 182		26	23, 311
	34	309		21	95, 226		28–9	392
	41	349		26	18		29	317, 333, 473
	46	14		29	16		30	152
21	6	326		30	392	4	1	382
	7	27		36	15, 16		1–2	152, 383
22	18	336		36–9	16		5–6	345
	21	396		37	70, 237		5 foll	76
	26	404		37–9	52		6 foll	206
	30	397, 399		37–40	70		7	152
	33	55		38	20, 23, 70, 117		7–39	434
	40 foll	257		38–9	123, 182, 221		13–18	205
	41	102 foll		39	15, 132		14	345
	42	476, 483		40	51, 114, 133		17–18	297
	43–4	257		41	27, 70, 114, 142		20 foll	434
	44	255					27	346
	46 foll	238		42	109, 126, 129, 132, 133		29	434
	53	356					31	23
	54	53, 474		43	132, 147		32	23, 207
	58	103		43–4	27, 52, 139		34	244, 477
	59	103 foll.		44	70		35	407
	66	103		45	142		35–8	152
23	1	103		47	70, 132		38	206
	25	476		48	132		40	221
	36	206		49	238		40 foll	298, 434
	44–6	16		49–50	23		41	298
	48–9	474		50–2	1 420		42	298, 384
	49	117, 474		51	74, 123		45	221
	51	479	2	1	317		46	222, 420
	55–6	328		1–2	151, 430		46–52	197
24	11	44		2	129, 383		46 foll	203
	12	54		3	123		47	201, 209
	21	141, 335, 478		3–4	124		48	185, 221
	23	44		6–8	344		52	203, 247
	27–31	44		8–9	318		54	203, 221–3
	30	84		10	341–2	5	1–21	76
	39	44		11	182, 383		3	199, 268, 376
	41	77		12	151, 178–80, 185, 221–2, 383		4	267
	41–2	77 foll					5	267
	42	77, 81, 84					6	199, 224–5, 268
	42–3	44		13	185, 222			

INDICES TO "PROCLAMATION"

	JOHN			JOHN			JOHN	
		PAGE			PAGE			PAGE
5	8	208, 263	6	70	130, 382, 388, 390, 397, 432	10	18	175
	9	263					19–21	433
	10	263		71	422		23	17
	11	263	7	1	17		27	52
	13	209		1–3	432	11	7	239
	14	220, 268		5	120, 432		7–11	355
	15	225, 269		14	178		8	23
	16	225, 269, 328		16–17	477		9–10	355–6
	17	328, 355		19–20	432		15	239
	18	225		22–3	355		16	45, 239
	19	225, 248, 268, 270		23–4	290		31	52
				25–6	432		33	174 254, 258
	19–20	351		28	178		33–5	362
	21	208, 271		35	303, 386		38	254
	24	244, 274, 481		37	205, 306		39	478
	25–8	130		38	76, 346		43	260
	26–7	176, 271		39	152		48	303, 385
	28–9	481		42	244		54	17
	30	225, 270–71, 290, 477		48–9	289	12	4	422
				51	51		7	299
	40	225		51–2	289		15	304
6	1	7	8	1–11	296		18	384
	1–3	376		2	295		19	280
	2	52, 226, 382		12	52		20	384, 456
	3	377, 388		20	178		20–21	303
	5	188, 386		25	309		20–24	29
	7–9	28		26	51, 271		21	71, 457
	9	86		31 foll	177		22	32
	11	86		36	462		23	457
	12–13	397		37	433		24	457
	14	377		37–8	369		24–32	177
	15	52, 226, 238, 269, 372, 377–8		38	51		25	68, 457
				40	51, 271, 433		25–6	52
				42	244, 309		26	404
	19	13		43–4	468		27	258, 456
	19–21	17		44	279, 432		27–8	456
	20	407		48	433		28–9	384, 412
	22	91		48–9	468		31	189, 456
	25–6	23		48–52	433		32	68, 76, 130, 208, 306
	32	309		50	469			
	33–58	185		59	11–12, 378		32–3	303
	35	205, 309	9	1	11–12		36	378
	38	477		2	23		36–7	303
	38–40	479		3–5	351		39–40	228
	39	480		4–5	355		40	271, 280, 362–3, 369, 482
	39–40	477		16–34	291			
	44	76		24	229, 292			
	45	51		31	477		43	228, 280, 469
	53	309, 435		39–41	293		47	176, 454
	59	178, 185, 364, 373		41	369, 463, 465	13	2	422, 432
			10	3	129, 130, 276		5	76
	63	76		4	52, 227		13	24
	66	382		5	52, 438		16	24, 394
	66–7	177		6	438, 442		18	121, 130
	67	397		11–12	454		18–26	177
	68	76, 148		15	433		21	174, 258
	69	186		16	483		23	121

522

SCRIPTURAL PASSAGES

JOHN			JOHN			ACTS		
		PAGE			PAGE			PAGE
13	24	94, 118	19	41	343	2	13	338
	25	118	20	4–6	54		23	479
	26	422		6	52		32	402
	30	356		8	413		38–41	88
	34	343		16	23, 26		41	104
	36	52–3		16–22	44		42	377
	37	52–3		17	23, 26	3	1–11	29, 408
14	9	71, 149, 406		18	26		2	267
	22	414–15		21	273		3	60
	23	123, 473		22	273		7	193
	26	25		23	271, 273–4		15	402
	27	273		27	45, 470	4	4	104
	31	208, 238	21	2	28, 113–16, 409, 420		13	408
15	9	334					13–19	29
	9 foll	25		3	91		19	408
	11	333		3–4	19		22	267, 269
	14	395, 473		4	96, 140		25–6	370
	15	25, 51, 395		5	84 foll, 95–6		28	479
	16	130, 406		6	35 foll, 86, 91, 376		33	402
	18 foll	249					36–7	401
	19	130		6 foll.	39	5	15	223
	22	282		7	54, 72, 91–2, 115, 117, 141 foll, 413		32	402
	26–7	405				6	2	402
16	2	414					2–6	404
	8–11	291		7–19	1	7	19	68
	11	454		8	86, 91, 98, 107, 140	8	5	30, 404
	19–24	335					12	30
	21–5	442		9	77, 83, 86–7		14	29
	22	319		10	86		14–25	40
	25	438, 441		11	42, 86, 89		17	219
	27	244		12	48		26–38	39
	28	244		13	69, 77, 86		27–8	39
	29	438		15	55	9	2	393
	30	244		15–17	109, 128		12	219
	33	281, 335, 454		15–22	45		15	448
17	2	176		18	97		17	219
	11	290		18–19	99		30	140
	13	335		19	52, 54, 229		32	40
	15	130		20	54, 72, 115		33	199
	24	406		20–24	115		34	229
	25	175, 290		21	55		41	193
18	5	309		22	52, 54, 133, 282	10	1	30
	15	52–3					6	43
	18	87		23	115		34	368
	20	178, 181, 185, 364, 373		24	116		38	168, 212, 216
				25	133			229
	38 foll	280					40	401
19	10	271			ACTS		41	401
	10–11	176				11	3	301
	25	118, 474	1	3 foll.	82, 84		10	87
	26	118		8	402		20	40
	26–7	473		13	408	12	1–23	370
	28 foll.	205		21	402		2	402, 408
	31	328		22	402	13	2	401
	34	76		23	417		3	219, 401
	34–7	206		26	421		4	401
	35	124, 413					14	373

523

INDICES TO "PROCLAMATION"

ACTS			ROMANS			GALATIANS		
		PAGE			PAGE			PAGE
13	22	475	11	7–25	363	2	9–11	40
	30–31	403		22	470		11	31
	36	479		25	227		15	286
	43	218		33	343	3	10	289
14	1	373	12	11	339			
	4	401, 403		15	362			
	14	401, 403	13	1	168	EPHESIANS		
15	2	403	15	19	242			
	4	403		20	30	2	13–14	124
	6	403		20–24	30	3	8	419
	17	381	16	7	401	4	18–19	364
16	4	403		18	156	5	1	147
	13	43					11	195
	23	276					18	321
	27	276	1 CORINTHIANS			6	16	203
17	10	373						
18	19	373	2	16	443			
	25	339	4	9	212	PHILIPPIANS		
19	1	39		16	147			
	3 foll	153	6	18	462	1	8	252
	6	219	7	14	74	3	5	416
	8	373		31	13		6	416
	13	233	8	10	199		12	62
20	27	479	9	1	400		17	147
21	8	30		5	144		19	156
	9	77	10	27	2	4	17	207
22	3	147, 416	11	1	147			
	21	401		21	321	COLOSSIANS		
23	6	269		27	461			
	7	416	12	1 foll	231	1	20	124
	10	449		9	230	2	11	452
26	5	416		28	230		15	453
	6	398		29	230	3	9	452
	12	170	13	12	438	4	11	417
	17	401	15	5–7	401		14	208
	18	168		6	400			
27	30	18		7	46			
28	8	199, 219, 229		55	250	1 THESSALONIANS		
	13	421	16	12	474			
	14	421				2	6	401
	21	393				5	2	466
	27	228–9	2 CORINTHIANS				4	466
			2	14	62			
ROMANS			3	14	364	1 TIMOTHY		
				15	364			
1	11–12	30	4	7	338	1	7	442
2	11	368	5	7	281	6	13	68
	18–21	476	11	2	392			
4	7–8	266		13	394			
	16–17	342				2 TIMOTHY		
8	17	250						
	21	150	GALATIANS			2	5	203
	26	260					19	45
9	22	448	1	14	416, 417		26	62
	23	448		19	409	3	6	211
10	5	291	2	9	41, 409			

SCRIPTURAL PASSAGES

TITUS		
		PAGE
3	3	211

HEBREWS		
1	9	41
2	11	484
	15	461
3	1	41
	14	41
4	2	45
5	7	260
6	4	41
	19	91
10	1	331
	2	331
	5–7	475, 483
12	3	229
	8	41
13	9	211

JAMES		
1	2	211
	18	145
4	4	295
5	16	229

1 PETER		
		PAGE
1	6–7	211
2	24	229
3	10	224
	19	328
4	10	211
	12	211
	15	466

2 PETER		
3	10	466

1 JOHN		
1	7	331
	9	291, 331
2	1	291
	2	281
	7–8	343
	8	11
	10	356
	17	11, 477
	18	277
	22	277
	29	291
3	7	291
	10	277, 291
	11	277

1 JOHN		
		PAGE
3	12	278, 291
	13–15	279
	17	312
4	3	277
5	14	478
	19	281

2 JOHN		
7		277

JUDE		
23		449

REVELATION		
1	6	63
2	1	16
3	3	466
4	4	404
5	10	63
7	4 foll.	402
10	1	445
16	15	466
18	21	445
21	14	402
22	2	78, 209, 399

INDICES TO "PROCLAMATION"

II. ENGLISH

[*" c w "* means *"confused, or confusable, with"*; *" conn. w."* means *"connected with."*]

Aaron, an apostle **392**
Abiathar, in Mk **347**, *i e* Urim and Thummim **349**, the name, meaning of **351**
Abide, with Jesus **182**, in Jn, conn w conversion **221**, "your sin abideth" **465**
Abraham, the three visitors to **46**, the Call of **136**, cast into a furnace **59**, rising early **236**, requited by God **236**, and Abram **134**
Abram, and Abraham **134**
Accepters of persons, and hypocrites **368**
Acquire (Heb) conn w the name of Cain **279**
Act-of-sin, and sin **462**
Acts of the Apostles, the, mentions only a few acts of few apostles **29**
Acts of John, the **49, 94, 122, 140, 145**, on the Call of the Fishermen **95**
Adam, A of old, *i e* the first man, sings of the sabbath **354**, the second A, doctrine of, not in Talmuds **354**, c. w. Edom **381**
Adonai **24**
Afar off, in Ps, and conn. w the Crucifixion **474**
Afflict your souls, *i e.* fast **311**, afflicting the soul, in a new way **312**
After, come a me **49**, with "go" and "come" **146**

Agapae, the Christian **321**
Agōmen, "let us go," Hebraized **238**
Akiba **272**
Alexander the Great **478**, questioning the wise men of the south **64**
Alive, taken **62**
All, leaving a things **136** foll , a things = "own" and "house" **136**, a sickness = every kind of sickness **166**
Allusion, Johannine, approaching intervention **434–5**, in Luke, latent **478**, in Mark **436**
Ambiguity, caused by separate Logia **329**
Anachronism **350**
Anaxagoras **66**
Anchor, a Christian emblem **90**, not mentioned in O T. **91**
Andreas, a fictitious name **32**
Andrew **26**, etymologically = "man" **16**
Anger, "was angered" and "had compassion" **251**
Anointing of Jesus, the, in Mk, Mt , and Jn **296**, the, in Lk **293, 296**
Antichrist, Cain an **277**
Antioch, the Church of **31**
Antiochus Epiphanes **366**
Antipas, Herod **366**, called "fox" **366**, perhaps referred to in a Zadokite work **367**, the adultery of **429**

ENGLISH INDEX

Antipatriotism, imputed to Jesus 433
Aorist tense, the 218
Aphès, "let alone," in Aram 299
Apostle, in LXX 391, diff from messenger 392, the term, applied to Aaron and Moses 392, a Jewish commissioner 393, an a of Christ must be a friend 396, Paul, why called an a 401, a twelfth, the coopting of 402
Apostles 390, mission of 2, minor, traditions about 65, the, in Jn, never absent from Jesus 151, disciples, as distinct from 383, "my two a " 392, the term not used by Jesus in Synoptists 394, in the Acts 402, supplemented by "elders" 403, order of the names of 408 foll, false a 401, s Appointment, Choose, Sending, Twelve
Apostolic Constitutions, the 325, on fasting 316, 319, s also 327
Apostolos, a naval expedition 390
Appearance, judging according to 290
Appointment of the Twelve, the 387–423
Aquila and Priscilla 31, 421
Aram, *i e* Syria 381, 382, c w Edom 381, 382
Aramaic, Gk words in 299, s also 37, 57, 104, 194, 196, 294, 377 etc
Arbitrariness, in Christ's actions, disclaimed 268
Aretas 366
Aristotle, on authority 171, on proverbs 438, s also 66, 360, 475
Armour 448, and utensils 448
Arrian 175
Artemis 88
"As it were a little" 103
Asmodeus 429
Atheists 369
Atonement, the Day of 311
Authority, meaning of 263, 271, in Mk 160, in Mk and Lk 157–60; in Lk 159, 167, in Mt 163–6, in Gk first-century writers 169 foll, in Jn 174 foll, 263, a and the spirit of sonship 174, to become children of God 175, to lay down life 175, to judge, subordinated 176, to forgive 263, over evil desire 171, 276, of Satan, contrasted w Christ's teaching 173, of the Man over the Beast 283, based on knowledge 171, Aristotle on

171, Epictetus on 171, a. and goodness, Philo on 170

Baal 431
Baal "lord," c w *bala* "swallow" 429
Baalzebub, a biblical name 432
Babel 184
Babylon, king of 58
Baptism, Constantine's 78, Jn on 74, of children, questions as to 74, by the Apostles before the Resurrection 153, conn w. Eucharist in the fishing at Tiberias 89, fasting before 332
Baptist, John the, (Mt) "believed" by "harlots" 294, contrasted with Jesus by Pharisees 430, disciples of 237, 307, prophecies of Isaiah underlying the utterances of 324
Baptize, s Baptism
Barabbas, "Jesus B " 309
Barak 113
Bar Cochba (*or* Cosiba) 272
Barley loaves, five 69
Barnabas (in the Acts) 401
Barnabas (the writer) 38, 172–3
Bartholomew, and Nathanael 133
Bartimaeus 12
Bath kôl, a voice from heaven 410
Bear witness, in Jn 406
Beast, the, *i e* the Serpent and all the power of the enemy 283, authority of the Man over 283
Beasts, the 356
Beckon, in Lk 93
Become, to, c w "to life" 57–60; and "live" 61
Beelzebub (*or* Beelzebul), called prince of the devils in Mt.-Lk but not in Mk 428, not mentioned in the Talmud 429, "He hath B ," in Mk 428
Before, "sit before" as a pupil 147
Begin, "began to," or "attempted to," expr by imperf 218
Beginning, from the 405
"Behold !," and "see !" 471
Beloved disciple, the 54, 71, 115, 133, 473
"Beside himself," said of Jesus, in Mk 424
Bethesda, the pool of 76
Bethsaida, House of Fishing 27, 70, B of Galilee 71
Betrayal of Jesus, the 418
"Beyond Jordan," not in Lk. 379

Birthplace-names 417, 419
Blind, the 12, the man b from birth 11, 227
Blindness, the healing of 11, ins by Mt, not in parall Lk 426
Boanerges 108 foll, 410–13
Boat, a, Lk omits phrases mentioning 105, distinguished from a "little boat" 91, b. and teaching 377
Boats, Mk's traditions about 377, two 35, 46
"Bone, of the day, the" 312
Bottle, a, in the smoke 339
Bowels, the sounding of the 252
Boy, son, and servant 197–8
Bread, "for the sake of my b,", i e because ye have received my statute 182
Breakfast, a military 82
Breath of life, in Genesis 273
Brethren, the, of Jesus, in Jn 431, my b 470
Bride, Israel the 324
Bride-chamber, the children of the 315
Bridegroom, the, in the Synoptists 314, the mystical 315; the children of 315, the friends of 317, the meaning of, if uttered by Jesus or if uttered by the Baptist 318, Hebrew and Jewish traditions about 323
Broiled, a b fish 77, 80, c w "visible" 82, conn w. the Passover 83, b with fire, a military order 81
Brotherhood, Joseph the type of 356
Brothers, c w "the rest" 426, s Brethren

Cain, conn w. the first mention of sin in the Bible 275, the man-killer, in 1 Jn 277, antichrist 277, meaning of the name 279
Call, i e invite 129, in Jn 129, different meanings of 131, and choose 129, 389, "he calleth whom he would" 389, c. w. meet 472, s also Calling
Called by name, and called to become 134
Calling, the divine 129, 134, to repentance 131, how expressed by Jn 127 foll., effective 132, to sinners 284–306, the, of the Fishermen 1–153, of Apostles 387–423; of Abraham 136; of sheep by the Shepherd 130 foll, of Israel 270
Callous, "make c" 362 foll
Callousness, the, of Gentiles 364, of Israel 364
Cana 123, 182, drawing water at 344, in Syr Catné 418, v r for in Josephus 419, conn w Nathanael 419–20; Origen on 420
Canaanite, the, regarded as defiling 302
Canaanitish, and Syrophoenician 302
Cananaean, in Mk 416
Canopy, the bridal, children of the 315, in Odes of Solomon 324
Capernaum, going down to 178, Marcion's Gospel began from 179, means "field of consolation" (Origen) 179; typical of Gentiles 183, in Jn 221 foll, Peter's house at 424, Christ's teaching in 185 foll, s also Synagogue
Captive, first mention of in O.T. 168, taken c 62
Captives, release to the 168
Captivity, c w repentance 228
Carrying the Child Israel 207
Cast, and spread 33, "casting" c w "draught of fishes" 104
Cast down, and lying down 198
Cast out, diff from conquer 454, casting out, the, of the ruler of this world 453
Catna or Catné, (?) = "Little town" 419
Celsus, declares exorcism an imposture 167, describes Jesus as "running away" 378, s also 285
Cephas, "stone" 104
Chaberim 41
Charcoal, a fire of 87
Charge, sternly (or strictly) 248, 253; i e. roar, bellow, murmur 251
Child, the Feast of the, at Circumcision 342
Children, baptism of, questions as to 74
Choose, and call 129, 389, the Twelve, chosen 390, the Twelve, not chosen in Mk and Mt 390
Choosing of the Twelve, the, 130, Mt's omission of 383, in Jn 390
Christ, called a "Fisher" 88, the call of, to sinners 284–306, the, expected by the people 332
Chronological divergences 1, c. order 190, Mt's arrangement, not c. 190

ENGLISH INDEX

Chrysostom, not a safe guide in Johannine interpretation 36, on the "breakfast" in Jn 77, on Christ's mourning 255, s also vii, 142, 222, 256, 264, 292, 356

Circumcision, the, and the Gentiles 41, the Feast of the Child at 342

Cities of three classes 240

City, Christ's own 185

Clement of Alexandria, on —honeycombs 80, "one fishing" 87, Zacchaeus or Matthias 421, s also 11, 33, 50, 51, 63, 66, 84, 88, 96, 287, 304, 404

Clement of Rome, on authority 172, on deacons 404

Come, s. After and Hither

Coming down, ascribed to God 184

Coming forth, the first mention of in O T 245, "came forth" and "was sent" 242-3

Commanding one, the 367

Commandment, old and new, a 343

Comparison, implied in parable 443

Compassion, having 252, "had c." and "was angered" 251

Concourse to Jesus, the 372-86, in Jn 382, 386

Conflation 326

Conquer, Gk, hardly mentioned in canon LXX 455, diff fr cast out 454

Conqueror, diff fr robber 455

Conquest, Christ's 455, diff fr selfconquest 455

Constantine, and baptism 73

Constrained, c w mingled 45

Constraint, not used by God to produce love 177

Coopting, the, of a twelfth Apostle 402

Cosmos, the, in Philo 210

Council of Jerusalem, the 381

Covering, of sin, the 265

Crates 336

Cross, the, following Jesus 90

Crossing the lake, Mk's traditions about 377

Crucifixion, symbolized 99

Cry, and peace 215

Cubits, in symbolic narrative 98

Cup, of martyrdom 116

Cure, s Heal and Therapeutic

Cynic, the, in Epictetus 172

Daily, take up the cross d. 49

Dan, $i\ e$ judgment 398

"Danger of bondage, in" 462

Dark-sayings 439, parall to parables 436, in what sense parables are 437

David, the first son of, $i\ e$ Solomon 441

Day, the third 148, in that d. or in those days 325, the same, lit "bone of the day" 312, of the Lord, the, as a thief 465, the fourth d of disease 478

Days, are coming 326, in those d 325

Deacon, $i\ e$ minister 404, avoided by Lk 404, Clem Alex and Clem Rom on 404

Decapolis 382

Delivered up to the sabbath, ye are not 353

Demon (*daimonion*), in Jn 432

Depart after, and follow 144, 150, d after, implies a missionary journey 146

Descending, God described as 184

Desire life 224

Destroy, or lose 480

Devil, $i\ e$ *daimonion*, in Jn 432, "hast a d", conn w. "art a Samaritan" 433, $i\ e$ *diabolos*, thrice in Jn 432

Diatessaron, the 65, 178, 185, 221-2, 397, 481

Didaché, the 173, on fasting 320

Didymus, $i\ e$ twin 415

Disciple, a 24, 383, 394, "the d whom Jesus loved," s Beloved

Disciples, in Jn 382, of Jesus, the number of 382, as distinct from Apostles 383

Discipline, Philo on 451

Disease, and sickness 165, every d, meaning of 166, how regarded by Mt and Lk 196; as punishment for sin 213, affecting the body through the will 213

Diseases, divers 210, names of, avoided by Jn 202

Dispersion, the, $i.e$ the scattered Jews 303

Disquieted, = Heb. sound, murmur, roar etc 257

Distortion of words, Jewish, about idols etc 431

Distribute, and pillage 449

Divers diseases 210

Doeg 445, 469

Dogs, might mean Gentiles 302, Gentiles are like d. (*Clem. Hom.*) 301

A P.   529   34

INDICES TO "PROCLAMATION"

Dominion 170, **444**
Dramatic method of Jn, the **68**, 130, 185, 280, 332, 361, **444**
Draught (Aram.), c w. part 37
Draw, water in Cana 344
Draw near to (Heb and Syr) = touch 194
"Draw out the soul" 312
Drinking, conn. w Beelzebub 430, wedding (Heb) = an occasion for d 430, s Eat(ing)
Dropsical, how expressed 267
Dropsy 267
Dung = Heb "go forth" 431

Earth, on the, c w "on the land" 141
Eat, "fit-to-eat" 77, "tree of eating," *i e* fruit-tree 78, eating with the uncircumcised 301, eating and drinking with Jesus 401
Eatable, the Gk word very rare 85
Edom, in Jewish tradition = Rome 380, Hadrian king of E 380, the remnant of 381, 385, c w Adam 381, c w Aram 382
Egypt, bondage in 452
Egyptians, forbade their priests to eat fish 66, the spoiling of the 451–2
El, God, *i e.* the strong one **448**, said to be "often applied to Christ" 73
Elder, and priest x
Elders, supplementing apostles 403
Elect, or Chosen, the, cannot go wrong 390, s Chosen, Choose
Election of Israel, the 226
Eliezer, symbol of the Help of God 168
Elijah 9–10, 317, and the widow's child 61, the Baptist regarded as 10, comp 430–31
Elisha 317, the calling of 9
"Empty the sword " 33
En (Heb) = eye or fountain 345
Envy, of Cain and the Jews 279
Ephod, or divine oracle 349, Israel without 349
Ephrem 41, 250–51
Epictetian doctrine, early circulation of 175
Epictetus, on —following 51, authority 171, freedom from trouble 174, 258, fever 203, moral healing 248, borrows Christian phrases 203, s also 48, 206, 238, 247
Epicurus, on spending his last day 478

Epistatēs 22
Esau 58, the *gibbôr* or mighty one 446
Essenes, the 38
Eternal sin 460
Ethiopia 39
Eucharist, and Baptism, connected, in the fishing at Tiberias 89
Eusebius 30, 212
Even, at, = between the two evenings 214
Evenings, between the two, and late 214
Every disease, meaning of 166
Evil desire, one of three stages of evil 156
Exceeding-sorrowful 257
Excommunication, real and unreal 293
Exodus, conn w Passover **457**; a second 161, comp **456**
Exorcism, Jewish 156, discussed in the 1st century 167, e and evil spirits, Jn silent about **469**
Eye, the good and the evil **346**, the old, in proselytes 464, c w fountain 345
Ezekiel, on —the fishermen 37, the River 38, 78, the Shepherd 227, the twelve tribes 399
Ezra-Apocalypse, the 38

Faith, the nature of 265
Faith-healing, Christian, became rare in the 1st century 230–31
Family, the Kingdom of God a 177, **424–83**, of God, a **445**
Fast (vb), parall to pray 320, fasting 311, the wrong kind of 312, for the nation 313, Maimonides on 314, conn w purification 331, before baptism 332, not mentioned in Jn 333, and sabbathizing 328, on the fourth and the sixth days 319, "on this one Sabbath" 327, spontaneous 335
Father, the, *i e* God 474 foll, regarded as the Giver 175, **479–80**, of the Cosmos (Philo) 210
Father's house, = home 139
"Fatten the heart" 363
Feast, master of a 317, of the Child, at Circumcision 342, or "joy" 124
Fever 192, rebuked by Christ 160, in O T 196, how explained by Rashi 196, = fire (Aram) 196, Jn's view of 202, metaph. 203

530

ENGLISH INDEX

Fields, in Mk 137
Fig-tree, the barren, conn. w. Christ's hunger 207
Finding 142
Finger of God, the 451
Fire (Aram)=fever 196; answer with f =have respect to 280
Firstborn, slaying the 457
Fish, the one 69, the, an emblem 72, fish-anagram, the 73, a broiled 77
Fishes, the miraculous draught of 1 foll, one hundred and fifty-three 42, Plato on men as 66, the breathing of 66, Philo on 66, and fish 69, proverbially dumb 88, the Egyptian priests forbidden to eat 66, s also *Ichthus* and *Opsarion*
Fish (vb), and hunt 57, 61, and draw upward 68
Fisher, Christ called a 88, fishers of men 61, how expressed by Jn 68
Fishermen, the Calling of the 1–153
Five, senses, the 297, the number 297
Flee, and withdraw 378
Flies, wine full of 430, swallowing f, i e condoning impurities 431
Flock, of Israel, the 227
Follow, and tarry 100; and depart after 144, 150, not used metaphorically in the Epistles 147, we must f God, not man 50, 148, f the mightier one 51
Following, in Jn 50, 70, in Stoical philosophy 146
Forgive, authority to 263, forgive sins =give life 271, forgive sins and retain sins 272, and heal 228
Forgiveness, of sins, the 261–83, the O T. vocabulary of 265, healing without 267
Forty years, perhaps symbolical 267
Forward, "went forward a little" 102
Founding of the Church in Antioch, Eusebius on the 30
Fountain, of the Holy Spirit, the 75, and well 344–5, in Jacob's Song 345, first mention of 345, =eye (Heb *En*) 345, God the most ancient of Fountains (Philo) 346
Four, passions, the 297
Friend of the Bridegroom, the 317
"Friends, ye are my" 395
From, "hearing from" 51
Fruit, due from Apostles 79
Furnace, Abraham cast into a 59

Galilee, the sea of 7, ="Galilee of the Gentiles" 71, in Ezekiel (LXX) 85, men or customs of, contrasted with those of Judaea or Jerusalem 317, 432, v r for Judaea 233
Garment, the patched 335
Gathering, a house of, =synagogue 267, a g of waters 267
Gehazi 299
Genesis, a second 273
Gennesaret, the lake of 7
Gentile (Heb), resembles bailiff (Heb) 287
Gentiles, the, and the Circumcision 41, parall to sinners 287, "like dogs," in Clem. Hom 301, "dogs" might mean G 302
Gerizim 297, 434
Gethsemane, the Agony in 255, the Tempter present in 257, and the narrative of Lazarus 260
Giant, a, 58, =mighty one 445
Gibbôr, or mighty one, Esau the 446
Give, "they gave" c w "he gave" 83
Giving, the Father regarded as 175, 177, 188, 479–80
Glorifying God, a refrain, om. by Jn 229
Glory 228, 280, 386, 469
Glutton and winebibber, alluded to in Jn 435
Go, "let us go," i e let us go forward 238
Go after =accompany 146, go after, in Bible and Talmud 147
Going down to Capernaum, not a mere geographical expression 184
Going forth, before dawn 234, of the Messiah 236, the Messianic, sure 244, "go forth," the utterance of an exorcist 431
Going out, var senses of 426
God, regarded as recovering His goods from a robber 450, the image or likeness of 342, the finger of 451, s Family, Father, Kingdom
Godless, and hypocrite 365
Goodness and authority, Philo on 170
Gospel, the net of the 38, the harvest of the 152, the new wine of the 340, g and mountain 284
Gospels, the firstfruits of the 478
Gospel of the Egyptians, the 119
Grace, and kindness 477

Greece, mentions of, in prophecy 304
Greek, a, in Mk 301
Greeks 384, in Jn 301–4, distinct fr Jews and Scythians 303, the Exodus of the 456
Greek thought, different from Hebrew 91
Greek words, in Heb or Aram. 25, 209, 238, 263, 299
Gregory of Nazianzus 348
Grief, sympathetic 361
Grieved, Jesus being, or "grieving in sympathy" 360
Groan, or be moved with indignation 254, groaning from within, forbidden by Epictetus 258
Guilty, in LXX 463, of an eternal sin 460

Hadrian, "king of Edom" 380
Hagar 345
Haggada, the, called new wine 337
Hand, by the h of = by the side of 267
Hands, stretching out or spreading out the, double meaning of 97–9
Harden, a paraphr of "make fat" 362
Hardening, *i e* callousness, diff from obstinacy 362, of the heart, in Mk 362
Harlots 293, mentioned by Mt. but not by parallel Lk 287, 294
Harpy, conn w "snatch" 455
Harvest, the, of the Gospel 152
"Hate," diff from "love not" 277
Healing 190–231, the first miracle of 190, the leaf for 209, Christ's, sometimes conditional or tentative 217, 220, (i) iatric, (ii) therapeutic 208, in Jn and Synoptists 227, national 228, through the Law 228, and forgiving 228, without forgiveness 267, on the sabbath 356, ambig 229, of a leper 246–60
Hear, *i e.* really hear 481, in Jn 481, and hearken 481
Hearing the word, Lk. and Jn on 480
Hearkening, must produce a moral effect 481
Heart, s Harden
Hebraized Greek words, s Agōmen, Krabattos, Paraclete, Therapeia, and Greek Words
Hebrew thought, different from Greek 91

Hellas, Philo on 302
Hellene, in canon LXX 304
Hellenes, in Jn 302
Hellenis, *i e* Greek woman 302
Heracleon 221, on Christ's going down to Capernaum 179
Hermas (the writer), 211, 362, 447, 461, on Michael 84, language of 106, on fasting 320–21
Herod Agrippa I 370
Herod Agrippa II 370
Herod Antipas 366, 429, s Antipas
Herods, various, confused 370, particularised by Mt and Lk, dropped altogether by Jn 370
Herodians, the, in Mk 365
Heterogeneous things, Philo on mixing 335
Hexaemeron, a 15
Hillel 21
Hire, s Issachar
Hired-servants, with the 110
"Hither!" 47 foll, a form of, in all the Gospels but Lk 48
Holy, and righteous 290
Holy one of God, only in two Biblical passages 186
Holy Spirit, the fountain of the 75, the sin against the 458
Home, the thought of, in Jn 123, or house 424
Honeycombs 81
Horae Hebraicae 157, 200, 240, 315, 317, 349, 381, 391, 414, 417, 431
Horeb, the rock in 75
Hosea, on "the third day" 148
Hour, the tenth 15; the ninth 16, the sixth, = noon 215; c w a while 103
House = "own" and "all things" 136, *i e* all that one has 137, h of thy father 136; h or home 139, 424, Peter'o, in Capernaum 424
Housebreaking, the Law on 463
Hunger, not attributed to Jesus by Jn 207, not attributed to Jesus by Mk in the Temptation 207, of Jesus, for fruit from the fig-tree 207, and thirst for goodness (Philo) 205
Hunt, and fish 57, metaph. 58
Hunters of men 61
Hyperbole 200, in Mk 218, 359
Hypocrisy, what corresponds to, in Jn 369
Hypocrite, and lawless 365
Hypocrites = accepters of persons 368; atheists are 369; callous or cauterized 369

ENGLISH INDEX

Iatric 208
Ichthus, or Fish, an emblem 72, Tertullian on the 72, *ichthus* and *opsarion* 86
Idumaea, *i e* Edom 380
Ignatius, on —the Resurrection 45, the strong one 447
Illusions, in the Book of the Universe xiv
Image of God, the 342
Imma, or Mother 118, *Imma* (or *Emma*) Salome 118
Imperfect tense, the 218
In, or against 255
Indignation, moved with 254
Infinitive, with Greek "in," a sign of transl from Heb 153
Infirmity, the man in 267, c w the paralytic 267
Insertions, to indicate who is speaking 324
Instinct, divine 479
Intervention, Johannine 12, 16, 17, 56, 100, 108, 186, 205, 208, 239, 244, 248, 254, 263, 288, 296, 305, 310, 340, 350, 351, 354, 362, 386, 397, 400, 405, 406, 410, 414, 415, 432, 435, often not direct 122, 434, occurs sometimes where the Synoptists agree 288, when not to be expected 459, comp 369
Irenaeus 111, 267, on "the strong one" 445, 447–8
Irony, Johannine 244, 289, 292, 344, 435
Isaiah 304, prophecies of, underlying the Baptist's utterances 324, "fattening the heart" in, an unintelligible metaphor for Greeks 363, variously quoted in the Gospels 482
Iscariot, the name, meaning of 417, Simon Iscariot 422
Isles, in Heb 384
Israel, the election of 226, the calling of 270, the lost sheep of the house of 300, in Egypt 452, the name, meaning of 134, 304
Israelites, the, God's stationarii, *i e* outposts 321
Issachar 111–12, conn w "hire" 418

Jacob, and Israel 134, the song of J 345
James the brother of the Lord 401, 415
James the son of Zebedee 408, the protomartyr of the Twelve 133

Javan, the sons of 302
Jerome, on —"Touch me not" 26, "a fish broiled on the coals" 77, fish and a honeycomb 89, the virginity of the beloved disciple 90, the defilement of marriage 90, Zebulon and Naphtali 111, Peter forsaking his wife 144, Jewish exorcism 157, Christ's "own city" 185, the children of the bridegroom 315, Abiathar in Mk 348, the "second-first sabbath" 348, Antiochus Epiphanes 366, the remnant of Edom 381, judging Israel 398, Simon Chananaeus 417, Nathanael and a "tax-gatherer" 421, "parable" and "proverb" 440, the strong [one] 445, Satan's "vessels" 448, Christ's kinsmen near the Cross 474, s also 242, 275
Pseudo-Jerome 434, on hired-servants 110, on Boanerges 411
Jerusalem 241, Paul preached "from," not "in" 242, Christ's visit or visits to 243, a new and enlarged 243, "a third," with the Saints and the Messiah 243, the Twelve Apostles in 402, the scribes that came down from 432, s also Galilee
Jesus, healing 190–231, "looking-round" 361, weeping, in Lk and Jn 362, and the sabbath 347–71, the concourse to 372–86, and the Pharisees, at the parting of the ways 359, contrasted with the Baptist by the Pharisees 430
Jewish thought, about thunder 413, different from Greek 91
Johannine Epistle, the first 277
John, the name, grace of God 128, and Jonah 127, s also 109
John (the Apostle), how a "martyr" 116, the brother of James 408
John (the Baptist), s Baptist
John (*i e* the Fourth Gospel), rarely in verbal agreement with Lk 67, homeliness of 123, calling, how expressed in 127, does not aim at completeness 151, its relation to Stoicism 259, selects details fit for symbolism 267, is of the nature of poetry 274, liable to be called gloomy 280, dramatizes 280 (and s Dramatic method), is cosmopolitan 369, explains and adapts the old where Lk substitutes something

new 479, is described by Origen as the firstfruits of the Gospels 473, alone mentions proverb not parable 437, alone mentions Greeks and Romans 301-3, 384-5, omits refrains about glorifying God 229, avoids mentioning — names of diseases 202, hunger on the part of Jesus 207, "sinners" (except in one passage) 291, fasting 333, Herod and Herodians 369, technical terms 369, 394

John, on —Christ's resurrection 44, following 70, baptism 74; authority and the spirit of sonship 174, 263, the great "exorcism" 177, fever 202, thirst 204, Messianic "raising" 207, healing (excludes conditional healing but not conditional permanence of recovery) 220, 227, collective faith-healing 230, forgiving sins and retaining sins 272, the terms "righteous" and "righteousness" 288, joy 333, the good wine 340, the old and the new 343, the disciples 382 foll , the choosing of the Twelve 390, thunder 413, the brethren of Jesus 431, "a devil" 432, proverbs 438, the will of the Father 477, hearing the word 480, s also Dramatic method, Intervention, Irony

Jonah, *i e* dove 128, and John 127, and Nineveh 299, the sign of 300

Joseph, typifies brotherhood 356

Josephus, on —prayer by the sea 43, Jewish exorcism 157, John the Baptist 366, zealots 416, Cana 418, s also 58, 240, 344

Joy, in Jn 333, not immunity from tribulation 335, ="feast" 124

Judaea, v r Galilee 233, contrasted with Galilee 317

Judah, the name, conn w praise 414

Judas of Galilee 416

Judas of James, in Lk , =Thaddaeus in Mk 413

Judas Thomas 415

Judge (vb), sometimes = vindicate, not condemn 398, Heb judge =LXX judge for 399, Dan shall judge 398

Judging, non-forgiveness expressed by judging 272, j according to appearance 290

Judgment, on a lower plane than redemption 176, conditions of 271

Justa 301

Justin Martyr, antedates a Herod 370, s. also 33, 48, 51, 95, 212, 393

Killing oneself in order to live 64

Kindness 353, the world built up with 353, "the k of God, all the day" 469, grace and 477

Kindnesses, the bestowal of 353

King, the attempt to make Jesus a 238

Kingdom of God, the 444, conn w. healing 166, a Family 177, 424-83

Kinsmen, Christ's, near the Cross 474

Know· the Lord "knew" His own 45

Kôl, "thunder" or "voice" 410

Krabattos, a Hebraized word 263

Lake, of Gennesaret 7

Lamb, the passover 214

Land, on the, c w "on the earth" 141

Late, and "between the two evenings" 214

Law, and authority, in Mt 163, of Moses, the, does not enjoin fasting 311, the giving of, regarded as a wedding 323

Lawless, and hypocrite 365

Lay out for burial 200

Lazarus, the narrative of, and Gethsemane 260

Leah 123

"Leaving all things" 136, in Lk 139, what was left, contrasted with what was found 142

Lebbaeus 414, 417

Left hand, the, =the north 39

Leper, the healing of a 190, 246-60, not healed instantaneously 220, a name of the Messiah 250

Leprosy, Christ angry with 250, smitten with l =touched 195

"Leprous," for "stricken," in Isaiah (Aq and Sym) 194, 250

Levi the Publican 416

Liability 460

Liable 460, 466

Lie, lying down and cast down 198

Life, the river of, in Ezek 78, the tree of, in Rev 78, giving life = forgiving sins 271

Light, the, w "I am" and "Ye are" 351

Lights and Perfections, = Urim and Thummim 351

534

ENGLISH INDEX

Likeness of God, the 342
Literal, the, mixed with the spiritual 52, 54
Literalism and metaphor 141
Little one, Paul the 419, Samuel the 419, "held himself to be little" 419
Little ones, s Receiving
Live, let live, and cause to live 62, and become 61
Logia, separate 329
'Looking round on," applied to Jesus 361, in Mk 361
"Lord!", only used once in Mk 21, lord (Heb) c w swallow 429
Lose, and destroy 480
Lost sheep of Israel, the 300
"Love not," diff fr "hate" 277
Lucae historiam, conj for lucem historiae 183
Luke, never describes Jesus as walking 14, does not mention the term Rabbi 20, subordinates the other Apostles to Peter 31, rarely in verbal agreement with Jn 67, and Greek metaphor 66, use of rare and unique expressions in 84, reduces poetry to prose 96, writes as a historian 103, as a stylist 48, 106, omits phrases mentioning a boat 105, is silent as to Zebedee 108, his view of Petrine tradition 106, favours tax-gatherers 287, omits the Anointing in Bethany 296, omits Christ's saying about fasting 313, differs from Mk's order 374, omits "beyond Jordan" 379, Mediterranean in, parall to sea of Galilee in Mt 380, is misled as to the term "apostle" 403, avoids the noun deacon or minister 404, his first mention of parable 436, dislikes the phrase "doing God's will" 475, substitutes a new tradition where Jn explains and adapts an old one 479, allusion rare in 478
Luke, on —the Resurrection 44, James and John 109, authority 157–9, 167, Christ rebuking diseases 169, disease 196, the good wine 340, the power of the Lord 358, apostles as chosen from disciples 383, Zealot 416, hearing 480

Macarius 7, 13, 33
Maimonides 59, on fasting 314
Man, the worker 356, "the old man" 452, son of, s Son

Manifold, applied to diseases 210, and many-folded 212
Man-killer, Cain the 277, the devil a, from the beginning 279
Man-killing = killing men as sacrifices 278
Manna, Philo on 161, named *Man*, i e *prepared* 161
Many, the Messiah will redeem 386
Marah, the water of 344
Marcion 183, 249–50, on Christ's going down to Capernaum 179
Mark, not a historian 56, free from artificiality 146, seldom quotes prophecy, but alludes to it 155, 216, 436, does not impute hunger to Jesus in the Temptation 207, prefers the *therapeutic* to the *iatric* vb 209, combines two Greek translations 214, uses "they" indefinitely 357, 426, hyperbole in 218, 359, errors in 348, first mention of parables in 435
Mark, on —teaching and authority 160, a "Greek woman" 301 foll, Abiathar 347, "looking round on" 361, the Herodians 365
Mark-Luke, contains not more than five narratives omitted by Mt 232
Martyr, i e witness 116
Martyrs, the Seven 212
Martyrdom, the cup of 116
Master (*epistata*) 20, of a feast 318
Matthew, disregards chronology 164, 190, omits the naming of the Twelve 127, omits five narratives of Mk-Lk 232, alone mentions the lost sheep of the House of Israel 300, perhaps misdates some precepts to the Twelve 306, Messianic refrain in 165, "Sea of Galilee" in, parall to Mediterranean in Lk 380, a parable-epoch in 436
Matthew, on —authority 163, disease 196, prophecy fulfilled 216, 436, poverty 234, the Samaritans 298
Matthias, or Zacchaeus 421
Mediterranean, in Lk, parall to sea of Galilee in Mt 380
Meet, c w call 472
Messiah, the, going forth 236, s Christ
Metaphor, Synoptic 64, 338, 346, Greek, and Luke 66, and literalism 141, of hunger, the 207, bondage to 344, "fattening the heart," a m obscure to Greeks 363

Metaphors **452**, **482**, varied **130**, of forgiveness **265**, Pauline **453**
Michael, in Hermas **84**
Midrash, copious where Talmud is silent **453**
Mighty [one], = giant **445**, mightier, the **446**
Mingled, c w constrained **45**
Missionaries, the Twelve as **150** foll.
Missionary journeying, s Sending
Mite, the widow's, why omitted by Mt **233**
Moses, the song of **345**, **456**, an apostle **392**
Mother, or *Imma* **118**, "my m and my brethren" **470**, the, (in Philo) is Wisdom **210**, comp **442**
Mountain, the, conn w gospel **234**
Mourn, "no good man mourns" (Epict) **258**
Multitude, the, concourse of to Jesus **372–86**

Naaman **300**
Name, birthplace names **417**, **419**
Nathanael of Cana **23**, **47**, **420**, and Bartholomew **133**, conn w. a "tax-gatherer" by Jerome **421**
Nature, following God according to **50**
Navy, and servants **140**
Nebuchadnezzar **58**, **170**, the fire of, less than the fire of fever **196**
Necromancers **156**
Net, the, of the Gospel **38**
Nets, washed, emptied etc **33**, spread the, ambig **34**
New, the, and the old **307–46**, Jn on **343**
Newness, natural and artificial **337**
"Next village-towns, the" **242**
Nicely, "getting on n ," in Jn and Epict **247**
Nicodemus, Christ's Dialogue with **75**
Nimrod **58**, **450**
Nineveh **299**
Ninth hour, the **16**
Non-forgiveness, expressed by judging **272**
Nonnus vii, **85**, **95**, **142**, **256**
Noon, = the sixth hour **215**
North, the, = the left hand **39**

Oath, of Herod Antipas, the **366**

Old, the, and the new **307–46**, Jn on **343**, "old man, the" **452**
One, *i e* the unique one **398**
Opsarion, and *ichthus* **86**
Oracle, the Son has no need of an **350**
Origen, on —Nimrod **58**, a portion of broiled fish **83–4**, Peter fishing **88**, unworthy exorcists **167**, lunacy **167**, Heracleon **179**, Capernaum, as typical of Gentiles **183**, healing by touch **191**, fever **203**, the man bearing a pitcher of water **234**, the Anointing in Bethany **296**, the lost sheep of Israel **300**, Jesus Barabbas **309**, the old wine-skins **338**, dashing the foot against a stone **356**, Boanerges **411**, Lebbaeus **414**, Cana **420**, proverbs and enigmas **440**, the Fourth Gospel as the firstfruits of the Gospels **473**, s also **121**, **169**, **222**, **242**, **275**, **285**, **304**, **393**, **415**, **417**
Own [property], one's = Heb one's house **136**

Pallet **263**
Papias, on Andrew **29**
Parable **330**, implies comparison **443**, (Heb) = dark saying **436**, in what sense a dark saying **437**, (Heb) also means proverb **437**, Mk's first mention of **435**, Lk 's first mention of **436**, not used by Jn **437**, a parable-epoch in Mt **436**
Paraclete, the **25**
Paralytic, the **261**, the healing of the **223**, c w the man in infirmity **267**, (?) error for pyretic **198**
Paranymphs **317**
Paroimia, not in LXX before Proverbs of Solomon **439**
Part (Aram), c w draught **37**
Parts, the, = regions **35–7**, of Galilee etc **37**
Pass by, applied to Jesus **8**, **11**, c w stand **17**
"Passer over," the **11**
Passion, in Chrysostom, imputed to Jesus **256**
Passions, the four **297**
Passover, the first **81**, **161**, p lamb, the **214**, conn w Exodus **457**
Patched garment, the **335**
Paul, why called an apostle **401**, "the little one" **419**
Peace, in Jn **121**, the redemptive

ENGLISH INDEX

stream of **124**, sons of **120**, and "cry" **215**, the first mentions of **273**, rejected **276**, s Salome
People, =followers **403**, c w "with" **403**, "they" meaning **357, 426**
Perātes, the **11**
Perfect (vb), and repair **34**
Perfections, "Lights and P" **349**
Person, c w mask **368**
Persuade, and urge **218**
Peter, the alarm of, at the draught of fishes **5**, following Jesus **53**, conn w a fire of charcoal **87**, swimming to Jesus **91**, the name, method of introducing **126, 133**, s Cephas
Petrine tradition **106, 216**
Pharaoh, the strong one **450**
Pharisees, the, regarded by Jesus as polluted and polluters **368**, the earlier and the later accusations of **430**
Philip the Apostle **52, 70, 406**, the call of, and that of Abraham **139**, following **148**
Philip the Evangelist **30, 39**
Philo, typical of the philosophic Jew **302**, on —the voice of God walking **16**, God as standing **18**, angelic eating **46**, following God **50**, fishes **66**, Abraham's threefold leaving **137**, manna **161**, goodness and authority **170**, powers and Logos **170**, hunger and thirst for goodness **205**, the Therapeutae **210**, the "seducer" **297**, Hellas **302**, mixing heterogeneous things **335**, God as the most ancient of fountains **346**, discipline **451**, Israel in Egypt **452**, sunrise (allegorized) **464**, s also **168, 212, 275, 304**
Phinehas, a zealot **417**
Phrynichus, the grammarian **263**
Picturesqueness, in Mk and Jn **32**
Pilate, boasting of authority **176, 271**
Pillage, and distribute **449**
Pitcher of water, allegorized by Origen **234**
Plato, on —following God **50**, men as fishes **66**, broiled meat as better than boiled **80**, s also **82, 149, 170, 209, 211, 290, 449**
Plutarch **66, 360, 460–61**, on a military breakfast **82**
Poetry, and prose **141**, in Jn and Lk **96**
Pollute by murder **365**
Pool, healing near a **223**

Pŏrōsis, hardening **362**
Possess, c w seek **381**
Post-resurrectional acts and words of Christ **1, 56–7, 151**, precepts to the Twelve **306**, appearances of Jesus **46**
Poverty, views of, in Mt and Lk **234**
Power of the Lord, the, in Lk. **358**
Pray, parall to fast **320**
Prayer, implied in standing **236**
Prayers by the sea **43**
"Preach," not in Jn **406**
Prejudice, only one of several causes of text corruption **309**
Prepared, s Manna
Preserve, and save **67**
"Priest," and "elder" x
Priests, not recognised in N.T. ix
Priscilla **31, 421**
Proof **44**
"Proofs" ix, **79**
Prophecy, often alluded to, but only once quoted, by Mk **436**
Propitiation for sins, the Temple as **353**
Prose, and poetry **141**
Proselyte, c w adulterer **294–5**, the old eye in, must be closed before the new eye is opened **464**
Proverb, =Heb parable **436–7**, Jn uses proverb, not parable **437** foll
Proverbs, not obscure **438**
Psychics **325**
Publican, s Tax-gatherer
Purification, conn w fasting **331**
Pursue, ambig **235, 237**, p to know the Lord **237**

Questioning **331**, at the Passover **162**

Rab, "great one" **20**
Rabbi **20** foll, not in Lk **20**, explained only by Jn **20–22**
Rabboni **23–4**
Rachel's children **252**
Raising the sick **193**, "raising," Messianic, Jn's view of **207–8**
Rashi, on Galilee in Ezekiel **85**, s also **39, 57, 97, 113, 196, 253, 302, 367, 406, 442, 453, 464**
Rebuke **160**, rebuking diseases, Lk on **169**, rebuking Satan **169**, and reprove **195**
Receiving little ones **396**
Refrain, Messianic, in Mt **165**,

INDICES TO "PROCLAMATION"

about glorifying God, om by Jn 229
Release to captives **168**
Reminding of Peter, the **4–5**, a fit name for a Lucan narrative **4**
Remission, s Forgive
Repair, and perfect **34**
Repentance, not in Jn **129**, c w captivity **228**
Reprove, and rebuke **195**, = touch **195**
Respect, "had respect to," and "answered with fire" **280**
Rest, the, c w "brothers" **426**
Restorer of the lifeless, God is the **208**
Resurrection, Christ's **44**, Ignatius on the **45**, attesters to the **400** foll , s Post-resurrectional
Retaining sins, not a Jewish phrase for excommunication **274**, in the Targums **275**, and forgiving sins **272**
Retention of sins, results from the rejection of peace **276**
Retribution, the law of **451**
Revelation, the Tree of Life in **78**
Revivification, in Jn **208**
Right side, on the **35**, **37**, right-hand parts, the, = the south **39**
"Righteous," technical sense of **285–6**, and righteousness, Jn's use of **288**
Righteousness, above holiness, in Jn **290**
Rising early, conn w Abraham **236**
River, visions by a **42–3**, of life, in Ezekiel **38**, **78**
Robber, diff fr conqueror **455**
Romans **384**, mentioned in no Gospel but the Fourth **303**
Rome, the church in **30**, represented by Edom **380**
Round, "those round Peter" **94**
Rubbing corn in the hands **348**
Ruler of this world, the casting out of the **453**

Sabbath, the, the attitude of Jesus to **347** foll , the Son of man is lord of **352**, ye are not delivered up to **353**, a song for **354**, healing on **356**, fasting "on this one s" **327**
Sabbath-breaking, the charge of **263**
Sabbathizing, a sabbath of **311**, and fasting **328**

Salom(e), in Mk **117**, in Talmuds **117**, taken as meaning Peace **118**
Samaria, the woman of, in Jn **296–7**
Samaritan, thou art a, conn w "hast a devil" **433**
Samaritans, variously viewed in the Gospels **298**, Matthew on **298**
Sammael **429**
Samuel the Little **419**
Satan **168**, **429**, binding the diseased **169**
Save, and preserve **67**
"Say concerning," expressed by "say to" **458**
Scent, i e discernment, attributed to the Messiah **272**
Scribes, coming down from Jerusalem (Mk) **432**, language of **432**
Scythians, Greeks distinct from **303**
Sea, on, or by the **16**, by the, how expressed by Lk **379**, the way of the **13**, **42**, **379**, of Galilee **7**, of Galilee, in Mt, parall to Mediterranean, in Lk **380**, prayers by the **43**
Seals, Christian **87**
Season (vb), or make new **339**
Second-first sabbath, the **348**
See, God's seeing the soul makes the soul see **346**
"See!" (Heb) expresses climax **473**, and "behold!" **471**
Seek, c w possess **381**
Self-conquest **455**
Send, two Gk words for **244**
Sending of the Twelve, the **394** foll , not mentioned in Jn **150**, of the Seventy, the **2**, **396**, s Apostles and *Shelıach*
Sent, was sent and came forth **242**, **243**
Septuagint, Josephus on the **32**, quoted by James in Acts **381**
Seraph, and serpent **205**
Serpent, the brazen **205**, and seraph **205**
Servant, son, or boy **197–8**
Servants, and navy **140**, s also Hired-servants
Seventy, the sending of the **2**, **396**, Seventy disciples, the **151**
"Seventy-two" disciples, the **41**
Shalôm, i e peace **120** foll , s Salome
Sheep, metaph **227**, **442**
Shelıach, the **395**, *Shelıach Tsıbbûr*, i e the messenger of the congregation **391**
Shepherd, the, in Ezekiel **227**, the "proverb" about in Jn **442**

ENGLISH INDEX

Shepherding 55
Shoshbenin 317
Sickness and disease 165, God's Kingdom and the removal of 166
Side, the right 37, on the right 35
Sidon, Tyre and, Christ's journey to 299
Sign, of Jonah, the 300
Signs, "make-signs" c w "swim" 92
Simon the Cananaean, not = one of the Zealots 417
Simon Iscariot, in Jn 422
Simon Peter, s Peter
Simonian sect, the 18
Sin, the first mention of, conn w Cain in O T and w retaining in the Targums 275, covered 265, eternal in Mk, abiding in Jn 460, 463, a s that surpasses all others (Ibn Ezra) 462, and "act-of-sin" 462
Sinner, only in one passage of Jn 291, the woman that was a, in Lk 293, 296-7
Sinners, technical sense of 286, parall to Gentiles and tax-gatherers 286-7, Christ's Call to 284 foll
Sins, the forgiveness of 261 foll, the retaining of 272, 274
Sit before 147
Sixth hour, the, *i e* noon 215
Smell, *i e* discernment, attributed to the Messiah 272
Snatch, and harpy 455
Solomon, supposed to have discovered method of exorcizing 157
Son, servant, or boy 197-8
Son of, sometimes depreciative 127, = "worthy of" 121
Son of man, the, *i e* the Person representing humanity, misinterpreted as the Person above humanity 353, is lord of the sabbath 352
Sons, of thunder 116, of peace 120
Sonship, the spirit of, in Jn 174
Soul, a, in fish 66, "O my soul" (Heb) = "my soul" (LXX) 256, draw out the 312
Sound (Heb) = murmur, growl, groan 252, = be disquieted 257
South, the = right-hand parts 39
Speaker, insertions to indicate who is the 324
Spend, *i e* pass through, of stage of disease 478
Spies, Joshua's 450

Spirit, in the, or against the 255, s also Holy Spirit
"Spirit, an unclean," in Mk 468, in Mk and Lk 157
"Spirit, the unclean," in Zechariah 154, only once in O T 155, 157
Spiritual, the, mixed with the literal 52, 54
"Spitting to the right" 38
Spoil, in good sense 450
Spoiling of the Egyptians, the 451-2
Spoils 452
Spread, and cast 33, spreading out (or stretching out) the hands, *i.e* swimming 97
Stand, c w. "pass by" 17, or "teach" 17, implying prayer 236
Standing, symbolical 16
Station, a 320-21
Stationarii, *i e* outposts 321, adopted into Hebrew 321, Israelites are God's 321
Stone, applied to persons, implying callousness 128
Stone's cast, a 102, 104, 107
Strength, of Satan 454, of the Shepherd 454, of Christ 454
Stretch, and lay out for burial 200, stretch out the hands 97, 99
Stricken = (Aq and Sym) leprous 194, 250
Strong one, the 445-6, = *El* 448, and mighty-one (*Gibbôr*) 445
"Substance," promised to Abraham's descendants 453
Sun, the, allegorized in the law about housebreaking 464
Swallow (vb), c w lord 429
Swim, c w "make-signs" 92, Peter swimming to Jesus 91, swimming and spreading out the hands 97
"Sword, empty the" 33, of the Spirit, the 304, Zion a 304
Sympathetic grief 361
Synagogue, teaching in 178, 364, in s at Capernaum 185 foll, a, and the 372-3
Syria, *i e* Aram 381-2
Syrophoenician woman, the 298, 305, S and Canaanitish 302

Talmud, silent, where Midrash is copious 453
Targum, s xxiv, xxv
Tax-gatherers, or publicans 286, parall to sinners 287, favourably regarded by Lk 287
Teach, and stand 17, "he taught

INDICES TO "PROCLAMATION"

them" parall to "his word" 159, Jesus only thrice described by Jn as teaching 178, teaching (Syr and Aram) c w boat 377
Teacher = (LXX) perfect 21
Teaching, Christ's, not "with authority" in Lk 159, Mk's view of 160, conversion by, not mentioned in Jn 181, in synagogue 178, 364, in synagogue at Capernaum 185 foll , contrasted w Satan's authority 173
Technical terms, in Synoptists 284, absent in Jn 369, 463, comp 394
Temple, the 78, as propitiation for sins 353, the building of, regarded as a wedding 323, a third 239
Temptation, the 207
Tempter, the, in Gethsemane 257
Tentative action, how expressed 217
Tenth hour, the 15
Terah, Abraham's father 138
Tertullian, on —the Ichthus 72, the going down to Capernaum 179, fasting 320, 322, s also 74, 183, 186, 249, 325–6, 481
Testaments of the Twelve Patriarchs, the, on fasting 320, s also 113, 398
Thaddaeus, in Mk, = Judas of James in Lk 413, in Talmuds 413, = thank-offering 414
Thelēma, s Will
Therapeia, healing, a Hebraized word 209, the leaf for 209
Therapeutae, the, Philo on 210
Therapeutic 208, meaning of the term, in (1) LXX and (2) Gospels 209, preferred by Mk 209
"They" undefined, (ambig) 357, comp 361, = people 426, 458
Thief, or housebreaker, the 465, in Pentateuch, v rare 466, the Messiah, or the Day of the Lord, coming as a 465–7
Third day, the 148, 239, "he is now passing his third day" 478, third temple, the building of a 239
Thirst, Jn's view of 204, 206, in O T and Philo 204–5, spiritual 339, Christ's, mystical 206
Thirty-eight years 224, perhaps symbolical 267
This, Heb fem., used mystically 161, "What is this ?" 161
Thomas the Apostle 44, the name, meaning "twin" 415

Thrones, sitting on, and judging Israel 397
Thunder, or voice 410, implied in the Transfiguration 412, in Jn 410, Jewish thought about 413, sons of 109, 116, 410
Tiberias 7, 85
Torments, manifold 212–13
Touch (Heb and Syr)=draw near to 194, and reprove 195, touched = smitten with leprosy 195; touching, in healing 194
Toward (Gk)=Heb way of 379
Transfiguration, the, thunder implied in 412
Tree of eating, i e fruit-tree, in Ezekiel 78, t of life, in Revelation 78
Tribes, the twelve, = spiritual Israel 397
Trouble, non-existent, for the Epictetian philosopher 174
Troubled, applied to Jesus in Jn 258, men are not t by facts (Epict) 258
Truth, uttered in jest or mockery 338, 342, s Irony
Twelve, a part of God's beneficent order 356, t manner of fruits 78, 399, t tribes, the 399, t tribes, our 398, t Apostles of the Lamb, the 402
Twelve (Apostles), the, as missionaries 151, the Appointment ot 374, 387–423, as "chosen" 390, not "chosen" in Mk and Mt. 390, "the Twelve," as uttered by Christ 396
Twin = (1) Didymus, (2) Thomas 415
Two, conn w probation 98, two hundred cubits 98
Tyre and Sidon, Christ's journey to 299

Unclean spirit, the, in O T only once 154–5, an, in Mk 158, 468, in Mk and Lk 157
Unclean spirits, and authority 154–89
Untroubledness, in Stoic philosophy, the 259
Upholding, in Ps 202
Ur, i e the Light, I am 351
Urge, and persuade 218
Urim and *Thummim*, the 349
Utensils, and armour 448

Vessels, or utensils 448, and armour

540

ENGLISH INDEX

448, *i e* spoils 451; interpreted rightly by Mk, wrongly by Lk 450, s. also Boats
Viaticum, the spiritual 69
Village-towns, the next 242
Virginity, Jerome on 90
Visible, c w broiled 82
Visions, by a river 42–3; influence of, on Jn 259
Vocative, Heb, dropped in LXX 256
Voice, or thunder 410, of the Lord God 15

Walk, Jesus described as walking 13, 15 foll, w after the Lord your God 50, w after, in O T. 147
Warrior, giant, strong [one], etc 446
Water, in Jn 76, of Marah, the 344, drawing w in Cana 344, metaph, of the Law and of the Gospel 344
Waters, a gathering of 267
Way of, the, (Heb) = Gk toward 379, way of the sea, the 42, 379
Wearied, applied to Israel and to Jesus 206
Wedding, the building of the temple a 323, Heb lit = " [occasion for] drinking" 430
Wedlock, mystical, the Pauline doctrine of 324
Weeping of Jesus, the, in Lk and Jn 362
Well, and fountain 344–5
"What is this ?" 161
"While, a," c w "an hour" 103
Whole or sound, = Heb living 224
Wife, leaving house and w, in Lk 137, of Peter, the 143, to lead about a 144
Will (n), *thelēma*, rare in literary Gk 475, the, of God 474, difference as to in Lk and Jn 478
Wine, metaph 337, the old, *i e* the Law 323, the new, *i e* the Haggada 337, this year's 336 foll,

the good, only once in O T 341, for the sake of my, *i e* because ye have received my ordinance 182
Winebibber, a, alluded to by Jn 435
Wine-skins, new 156
Wisdom, the Good Woman 442, Wisdom of God, the, regarded as speaking 242
With, c w people 403, "that they might be with him" 404
Withdraw, and flee 378
Witness, bearing, in Jn 406
Woman, the Good, Wisdom as 442
Word, the, as a person, yet with impersonal influence 245
"Word, his" parall to "he taught them" 159, "speak in word" 202
Word of God, the, in Lk, where Mk has "will" 474–6
Words, distortion of, Jewish, about idols 431
Worker, man the 356
World, the, diff. senses of 281, built up with kindness 353
Worthy of, expressed by "son of" 121

Years, thirty-eight 224, 267, thirty-eight and forty, perhaps symbolical 267
Yetzer, or tendency, the evil 275

Zacchaeus, and Nathanael 421, or Matthias 421
Zadokite work, fragments of a 367
Zarephath, the widow of 300
"Zealot" in Lk 416, at first = zealous for observance of the Law 417, acquired a new meaning just before the siege of Jerusalem 416
Zebedee 3, 4, 107, and Zebulon 111, the sons of 138, in Jn 113, in Lk and Jn 409
Zebulon 111–12, 123, 140
Zered, the brook 224

INDICES TO "PROCLAMATION'

III. GREEK

["c w" means "confused, or confusable, with"]

Ἄβυσσος 345
ἅγιος and δίκαιος 290
ἀγρός παρακλήσεως, ι e Capernaum 179
ἄγω and φέρω 215, ἄγωμεν 238–40, ἅ ἡμέραν, of disease 478
ἀθλέω: νομίμως ἁ., in Epict. 203
αἴνιγμα 441
αἴρω and βάλλω 200; and ἐπιβάλλω 200
ἀλλότριος 30
ἁμάρτημα and ἁμαρτία 462
ἁμαρτία and ἁμάρτημα 462
ἁμαρτωλός and ἐθνικός 287
ἀμφιβάλλω 35, 142
ἀμφίβλημα 142
ἀμφιβολεύς 34
ἀνακεράννυμι: ἀνακραθείς 45
ἀνανεύω 97, ἀνανεύσατε "lift up your heads" 97; c w ἀνανέω, quod vid
ἀνανέω: ἀνανεῦσαι "swim up" 97
ἀνασπάω 87
ἀναφωνέω 84
ἀναχωρέω 372, 377; and φεύγω 378
ἀναχώρησις 378
ἀνήρ 16, "husband" 392, 477, ἀνδράσι, perhaps c. w ἴδρισι 441
νθρακιά 87

ἀνθρωποκτονέω 278
ἀντίχριστος 277
ἄνωθεν 74
ἀπαίρω: ἀπαίρομαι and ἀποδημέω 316
ἀπέρχομαι: ἀπῆλθε v. r. ἐπῆλθε 10
ἀποδημέω and ἀπαίρομαι 316
ἀπόλλυμι, lose or destroy 480
ἀποσπάω 102
ἀποστέλλω 244
ἀπόστολος 390 foll
ἅπτομαι and ἐλέγχω 195; and προσεγγίζω 194, ἀφημένον = ἐν ἀφῇ 194
ἀριστάω 48
ἁρπάζω 449, 454–5
ἀρρωστία 165
ἀρχιτρίκλινος 318
ἁφή 191, ἐν ἀφῇ = ἀφημένον 194
ἀφίημι 135, and ἰάομαι 228, ἄφες 299

Βάλλω 34, and αἴρω 200; and ἐπιβάλλω 200; βεβλημένην = κατέκειτο 199; βέβληται "laid out for burial" 200
βάσανος: βάσανοι 213
βίαιος and γίγας 445–6
βολή "casting," c w βόλος 104, λίθου βολήν 102
βόλος, three meanings of 104, c w βολή 104

βουλή, in no Gospel but Lk 479
βούλημα 145, and θέλημα 478
βούλησις 404
βούλομαι 145
βρώσιμος 77–8

Γαλιλαία 85
γάμος 430
γίγας and βίαιος 445–6
γίνομαι γενέσθαι 57, 60, ἐγένετο, for ἔζησεν 61
γινώσκω ἔγνω "took cognisance of", 45, γνούς 268–9
γλεῦκος 338
γνωστός 474
γυνή 144

Δαιμόνιον, in Jn 432
δελεάζω 88
δεξιός εἰς τὰ δεξιὰ μέρη 35, ἐκ δεξιῶν 36
δεῦρο 48
δεῦτε 47 foll, poetic 48
δευτερόπρωτος 348
διάβολος, in Jn 432
διάκονος 404
διανεύω c w διανύω 97
διανύω c w διανεύω 97
διαρπάζω, rare in early Christian writers 447, in LXX 449
διέρχομαι 17
δίκαιος and ἅγιος 290, and δικαιοσύνη 291, δικαιότατος, applied to God in Plato 290

GREEK INDEX

δικαιοσύνη 291
δοξάζω, not in O T before the Song of Moses 456, δ τὸν θεόν 229
δυνατός and ἰσχυρός 445–6, and μαχητής 446, and πολεμιστής 446
δυσμή δυσμαί and δύω 214–15
δύω (δύνω) and δυσμαί 214–15

Ἐγγαστρίμυθος 156
ἐγείρω 208, and ἴστημι 195
ἐδράζω 18, 140
ἐθνικός 368, and ἁμαρτωλός 287
εἰρήνη 215
εἰς and πρός 372, 377
ἐκεῖθεν 102, 105
ἐκλέγομαι 390
ἐκλεκτός 390
ἐκνεύω (and ἐκνέω) 92–5, ἐκνεύσαντες, variously rendered 95
ἐκτείνω χεῖρας 99
ἐλέγχω and ἅπτομαι 195
ἔλεος 353
ἑλκύω 76
ἐμβριμάομαι 251, ἐ τῷ πνεύματι 254
ἐμπεριπατέω 16
ἐμπυρίζω 280
ἐμφωνέω 84
ἐν τῷ, with temporal infinitive 153
ἐνεργέω 172
ἐννεύω, only once in N T 94
ἔνοχος 463, with dat or genit 461
ἐξέρχομαι 8, 218, with ἀπό, ἐκ, and παρά 244, ἔξελθε 431
ἐξίσταμαι 425, ἐξέστη ἡ καρδία 426, ἐξέστησαν and ἔξω ἔστησαν 425
ἐξουσία 170 foll, defined as ἐπιτροπὴ νόμου 170, (?) = ἐξ οὗ ἐὰν 173
ἔξω ἔστησαν, c w ἐξέστησαν 425
ἐπάρατος 289
ἐπέρχομαι· ἐπῆλθε v r ἀπῆλθε 10
ἐπί 135

ἐπιβάλλω ἐπιβαλών 35, and αἴρω 200, and βάλλω 200
ἐπιδίδωμι 80, 84
ἐπιζητέω 52
ἐπικατάρατος and ἐπάρατος 289
ἐπιρράπτω 336
ἐπίσκοπος 404
ἐπιστάτης 22, ἐπιστάτα 20 foll
ἐπιστρέφω 228
ἐπιτίθημι ἐπιθείς and ἐπιτιθείς 219
ἐπιτιμάω 160
ἐπιτροπὴ νόμου, s ἐξουσία
ἕπομαι 50
ἑσπέρα 215
ἔχω 85, ἔχεις (or ἔχετε) τι, 77, 85, ἐχόμενος 241, κακῶς ἔχω 203, 213, κομψῶς ἔχω, in Epict 203, κομψότερον ἔχω, in Jn 247

Ζάω ἐγένετο for ἔζησεν 61
ζέω 339
ζηλωτής 416 foll
ζήτησις 331
ζωγρέω 62
ζωογονέω 67–8, and περιποιοῦμαι 67
ζωοποιέω 67, 76

Ἡγέομαι ἡγούμενος = Syr rab, vulg rector 318
ἡμέρα τετάρτην ἡμέραν ἄγω 478

Θέλημα 145, 476, 483, rare in literary Gk 475, with ποιεῖν 475, and βούλημα 478
θελητής 156
θέλω 224
θεραπεύω and ἰάομαι 209 foll, 219, θ preferred by Mk 209
θριαμβεύω 62

Ἰάομαι and θεραπεύω 209 foll, 219, ἰ most frequent in Lk 208, 229, ἰώμενος 228–9, ἰ and ἀφίημι 228
ἰατρός, applied to Lk 208
ἴδε 473, and ἰδού 471

ἴδιος εἰς τὰ ἴδια 136
ἰδιώτης 258
ἰδού and ἴδε 471
ἴδρις ἴδρισι conj. for ἀνδράσι 441
Ἰησοῦς, contracted 809
ἴκτερος 196
ἴστημι ἑστώς 18, ἱ and ἐγείρω 195
ἰσχυρός and δυνατός 445–6
ἰχθύς and ὀψάριον 86

Καινός and νέος 336–7
κακῶς ἔχω 213, κ. πάσχω 200
καλέω 129, 131
Καναναῖος 416
κατάγω 140 141
καταδιώκω 148, parall to ἐπιζητέω 52
κατάκειμαι κατέκειτο = βεβλημένην 199
καταλαμβάνω 62
κατανεύω, κατανέω, and κατανύω 92, 93, 97
κατατίνω 429–30
καταρτίζω 34
κεράννυμι κραθέντες c w κρατηθέντες 45
κηρίον 81
κλέπτης 463 foll
κοινωνός 41
κομψῶς (or κομψότερον) ἔχω 203 247
κοπιάω 206
κόσμος ὁ κ ὅλος 281–2
κράβαττος 263
κρατέω κρατηθέντες c w κραθέντες 45, κρατεῖν ἁμαρτίας 274
κραυγάζω 260
κραυγή 260
κύκλος κύκλῳ 240
κυνηγός 58
κωλύω ἐκωλύομεν or ἐκωλύσαμεν 218
κώμη 240–41
κωμόπολις 240–41

Λέγω ἔλεγον v r. ἔλεγεν 427
λίθος λίθου βολήν 102
λόγος and ῥῆμα 161

Μαλακία 165
μαχητής and δυνατός 446, and πολεμιστής 446
μελίσσιον 81

543

INDICES TO "PROCLAMATION"

μέρος 37 εἰς τὰ δεξιὰ μέρη 35, τὰ μέρη τῆς Γαλιλαίας etc. 37
μέροψ 88
μέτοχος 41
μισθωτός 110
μοιχαλίς 295

Νέος and καινός 336–7
νεῦσις, meanings of 92
νευστέον 92
νεύω 92
νέω, compounds of 92
νῆσος νήσους and Ἰησοῦς 309
νηστεύω and ταπεινόω 311
νικάω, rare in LXX 455
νομίμως, in Epict 203
νόσος 165
νυμφίος, insertion of 323

Ξυνέπομαι 50

"Οδε=(Heb)"behold!" 192
οἰκία 424
οἶκος and οἰκία 424
ὀπίσω 49
ὀπτάνω 82
ὀπτός 80, two meanings of 82
ὄχλος πολύς 383, πάντες οἱ ὄχλοι 425
ὀψάριον and ἰχθύς 86
ὀψία, in LXX only in Judith 214
ὄψον 84

Πάθος and πένθος 256
παιδίον παιδία and παῖδας 96
παῖς ambig 198, π. and παιδίον 96, παισίν v r πᾶσιν 141
πάλιν 377
παντοῖος, and πᾶν γένος 166
παρά. with verbs of hearing 51, οἱ παρ' αὐτοῦ 426
παραβολή 438–41
παράγω 8 foll , 11
παραδίδωμι 353, 418
παράλιος 379
παραλυτικός, not earlier than Mk 198
παράλυτος 198
παραλύω παραλελυμένος 198

πάρετος and πυρεκτικός 198
παροιμία 438–41
πᾶς πάντα=Heb. "the house of" 136, πᾶν γένος, for παντοῖος 166, πάντες οἱ ὄχλοι 425, παισίν v r πᾶσιν 141
πατριά 140
πέμπω 244, 394
πένθος and πάθος 256
πέραν 377
περὶ οἱ περὶ Πέτρον 94
περιβλέπομαι 361
περίλυπος 257
περιπατέω 13–14 foll.
περιποιοῦμαι and ζωογονέω 67
πηγή and φρέαρ 345
πηρόω and πωρόω 362–3
πλῆθος 253, in Mk and Lk 376, earliest uses of in LXX 376
πλήρης θεός, ὁ 210
πλοῖον and πλοιάριον 91
ποιέω θέλημα 475
ποικιλία 212
ποικίλος 210–11
πολεμιστής and δυνατός 446
πόλις 240–41
πολύπλοκος 212
προαιρετικός 156
προβαίνω προβάς 101–2, 106
προέρχομαι προελθών and προσελθών 102
πρός 379, and εἰς 372, 377
προσαγορεύομαι 418
προσβαίνω προσβάς 101
προσεγγίζω and ἄπτομαι 194
προσέρχομαι προσελθών and προελθών 102
προσήλυτος 294
προσκαλοῦμαι 383, 389
προσκαρτερέω 377
προσκόπτω 355–6
προσφάγιον 85
προσφωνέω 383, 389
προσωπεῖον and πρόσωπον 388
πρόσωπον and προσωπεῖον 388, πρόσωπον λαμβάνειν 368
πρωΐ and πρῶτον 114
πρῶτος (or πρῶτον) and πρωΐ 114

πυρεκτικός and πάρετος 198
πυρετός 196
πυρόω c. w πωρόω 362
πωρόω 362 foll ; c w. πηρόω and πυρόω 362

Ῥῆμα and λόγος 161
ῥίπτω and σπαράσσω 158
ῥώξ 337

Σεληνιαζόμενος 167
σκεῦος σκεύη 451–2
σκυλεύω, v r συσκευάζω and συλάω 452
σκῦλον σκῦλα 446–7
σπαράσσω and ῥίπτω 158
σπλαγχνίζομαι 251–2
στατίων 321
συγκεράννυμι συνκεκερασμένους 45
συγχέω συγχεῖται 256
συλάω· συλήσατε v r. for σκυλεύσατε 452
συλλυπέω 360
συμμισούμενος, ὁ 249
συναγωγή ἐν σ. 178, 185, 373
συναντάω 472
σύνθεσις κατὰ σύνθεσιν 42
συνταλαίπωρος 249
συντυγχάνω 472
συσκευάζω, v r. for σκυλάω 452

Ταλαιπωρέω (trans) 249
ταπεινόω and νηστεύω 311
ταράσσω ἐτάραξεν ἑαυτόν 254
τέλειος 21
τρικλίνιον 318

Ὑποκρίνομαι, -κρισις, -κριτής 365–8
ὑποχωρέω 372, 378

Φέρω and ἄγω 215
φεύγω and ἀναχωρέω 878
φθορεύς 297
φονοκτονέω 366
φρέαρ and πηγή 345
φυλάσσω 68
φωνέω 129, 130

Χρῄζω 49

www.ingramcontent.com/pod-product-compliance
Lightning Source LLC
Chambersburg PA
CBHW052110010526
44111CB00036B/1602